T0329095

CAMBRIDGE LIBRARY COLLECTION

Books of enduring scholarly value

Technology

The focus of this series is engineering, broadly construed. It covers technological innovation from a range of periods and cultures, but centres on the technological achievements of the industrial era in the West, particularly in the nineteenth century, as understood by their contemporaries. Infrastructure is one major focus, covering the building of railways and canals, bridges and tunnels, land drainage, the laying of submarine cables, and the construction of docks and lighthouses. Other key topics include developments in industrial and manufacturing fields such as mining technology, the production of iron and steel, the use of steam power, and chemical processes such as photography and textile dyes.

History of the Manufacture of Iron in all Ages

James Moore Swank (1832–1914) was a US expert on iron and steel, and wrote widely about the industry. In 1873 he became secretary of the American Iron and Steel Association. This second edition (1892) of his influential book on iron manufacture was significantly expanded compared to the 1884 original, with 132 more pages, 15 extra chapters, and revisions throughout the text. Swank aimed to move away from the highly technical approach and European focus that had dominated previous works. Instead, he would emphasise names, dates, facts and results, and give special attention to the growth of the industry in the United States while providing an international context. He includes every country and US state that produced iron. The book is organised chronologically, and provides a fascinating account of the manufacture of iron from the ancient Egyptian period through early modern Britain to late nineteenth-century America.

Cambridge University Press has long been a pioneer in the reissuing of out-of-print titles from its own backlist, producing digital reprints of books that are still sought after by scholars and students but could not be reprinted economically using traditional technology. The Cambridge Library Collection extends this activity to a wider range of books which are still of importance to researchers and professionals, either for the source material they contain, or as landmarks in the history of their academic discipline.

Drawing from the world-renowned collections in the Cambridge University Library, and guided by the advice of experts in each subject area, Cambridge University Press is using state-of-the-art scanning machines in its own Printing House to capture the content of each book selected for inclusion. The files are processed to give a consistently clear, crisp image, and the books finished to the high quality standard for which the Press is recognised around the world. The latest print-on-demand technology ensures that the books will remain available indefinitely, and that orders for single or multiple copies can quickly be supplied.

The Cambridge Library Collection will bring back to life books of enduring scholarly value (including out-of-copyright works originally issued by other publishers) across a wide range of disciplines in the humanities and social sciences and in science and technology.

History of the Manufacture of Iron in all Ages

And Particularly in the United States from Colonial Times to 1891

James Moore Swank

CAMBRIDGE UNIVERSITY PRESS

Cambridge, New York, Melbourne, Madrid, Cape Town, Singapore,
São Paolo, Delhi, Dubai, Tokyo, Mexico City

Published in the United States of America by Cambridge University Press, New York

www.cambridge.org
Information on this title: www.cambridge.org/9781108026840

© in this compilation Cambridge University Press 2011

This edition first published 1892
This digitally printed version 2011

ISBN 978-1-108-02684-0 Paperback

HISTORY

OF

THE MANUFACTURE OF IRON

IN ALL AGES,

AND PARTICULARLY IN THE UNITED STATES FROM COLONIAL TIMES TO 1891.

ALSO A SHORT HISTORY OF

EARLY COAL MINING IN THE UNITED STATES

AND A FULL ACCOUNT OF THE

INFLUENCES WHICH LONG DELAYED THE DEVELOPMENT OF ALL AMERICAN MANUFACTURING INDUSTRIES

BY

JAMES M. SWANK,

SECRETARY AND GENERAL MANAGER OF THE AMERICAN IRON AND STEEL
ASSOCIATION FOR TWENTY YEARS, FROM 1872 TO 1892.

SECOND EDITION, THOROUGHLY REVISED AND GREATLY ENLARGED.

PHILADELPHIA:
THE AMERICAN IRON AND STEEL ASSOCIATION,
NO. 261 SOUTH FOURTH STREET.
1892.

Printed by
ALLEN, LANE & SCOTT,
Nos. 229-231 South Fifth Street,
Philadelphia.

PREFACE TO THE SECOND EDITION.

In presenting to iron and steel manufacturers and to others a second edition of the History of the Manufacture of Iron in All Ages I copy from the preface to the first edition, which appeared in 1884, the following sentences explanatory of the considerations which led to its publication.

"No historical record of the iron industry of the scope of that which is here presented has been undertaken by any of the authoritative writers upon iron and steel. Such standard works as those of Alexander, Overman, Percy, and Bauerman are more technical than historical, while the excellent history of Mr. Scrivenor was published more than forty years ago, and relates almost entirely to the iron industry of Great Britain. None of the works mentioned devote much attention to the growth of the American iron industry. Most of them, indeed, were written before our iron industry became especially noticeable for either enterprise or productiveness. The history of that industry, written from a sympathetic standpoint and with a full knowledge of details, and particularly with a knowledge of its marvelous growth in the last few decades, had yet to be written, and this service I have endeavored to perform in the present volume in connection with the history of the manufacture of iron in other countries. I have aimed especially to preserve in chronological order a record of the beginning of the iron industry in every country and in every section of our own country, and to follow this record with a circumstantial account of the introduction into our country of all modern methods of manufacturing iron and steel. Names of persons and places, exact dates, authentic statistics, and accomplished results have been preferred to technical details, although these have not been neglected.

"In the collection of the materials for this volume I have been exceedingly fortunate in possessing a personal acquaint-

ance with most of the leading actors in the wonderful development of our American iron industry during the present century, and in learning from their own lips and from
their own letters many of the incidents of that development.
It is the exact truth to say that, if the preparation of this
history had been delayed for a few years, it could not have
been written, for many of these pioneers are now dead."

The reasons for the appearance of the first edition having been given above I now add that this second and last
edition has been prepared because much new information
relating to the early iron history of our own country and of
other countries has come into my possession since 1884, and
because seven succeeding years of great activity in the development of the world's iron and steel industries have been
productive of important statistical and other results which
are eminently worthy of preservation in a condensed and
permanent form. The second edition contains 132 pages of
historical details more than the first edition. In the first
edition there were 48 chapters. Nearly every chapter in that
edition has been in part rewritten. In the present edition
there are 63 chapters. Among the entirely new chapters of
the second edition is one relating to the early discoveries of
coal in the United States, and another detailing the connection of the Washington and Lincoln families with the manufacture of iron in colonial times. All accessible statistical information relating to the world's production of iron, steel,
coal, and iron ore has been brought down to the latest possible periods.

Due credit is given in the text to the printed authorities which have been consulted. My thanks are due to the
friends who have assisted me in many ways in the collection
and verification of the fresh historical and statistical materials which are now presented. I also express my obliga-
tions to my proof-readers, Mr. William M. Benney and Mr.
William G. Gray, who have with great pains assisted me to
guard against all errors of a serious character.

PHILADELPHIA, January 1, 1892.

CONTENTS.

CHAPTER I.
THE EARLIEST USE OF IRON.

Iron first made in Asia and in Northern Africa—Evidences of the early use of iron by the Egyptians, the Chaldeans, the Babylonians, and the Assyrians—Iron and steel frequently referred to in the Old Testament—Known to the Medes and Persians and to the people of India, China, Japan, and Corea—Decay of the iron and steel industries of Asia and Africa, ... Pages 1-10

CHAPTER II.
THE EARLY USE OF IRON IN EUROPE.

Grecian fables concerning iron and steel—Both metals frequently mentioned in the writings of Homer, Hesiod, Herodotus, and other early Grecian writers—Evidences of the early manufacture and use of iron and steel by the Greeks—Made by the Etruscans and the Romans; also in Scythia, Noricum, Moravia, and Hungary—The early iron and steel industries of Spain and the Basque provinces—Of France, Belgium, Germany, Holland, Switzerland, Austria, Sweden and Norway, Russia, and Finland—The Krupps of Essen—The Russian iron industry in the eighteenth century, ... Pages 11-32

CHAPTER III.
BEGINNING OF THE BRITISH IRON INDUSTRY.

Iron known to the Britons before Cæsar's invasion but not much used—Made by the Romans in many parts of Britain—Remains of Roman iron works still to be seen—Iron made in Britain by the Anglo-Saxons and the Danes—The British iron industry extended by the Normans—Greatly promoted in the reign of Edward III.—Characteristics of the British iron industry in the 13th and 14th centuries—The smith in English history—The first use of cannon in England, ... Pages 33-44

CHAPTER IV.
THE BRITISH IRON INDUSTRY FROM THE FIFTEENTH TO THE NINETEENTH CENTURY.

The manufacture of iron in England greatly extended about the beginning of the 15th century—Introduction of blast furnaces into England—"Many great guns" cast in Sussex—Wire first drawn by a mill in England in 1568—Invention of the slitting mill—Birmingham in the time of Henry VIII.—The art of tinning iron introduced into England from the Continent in 1670—Growing scarcity of wood for charcoal in England in the 16th and 17th centuries—Only 59 furnaces left in England and Wales in 1740—England a large importer of iron from Sweden in the 17th and 18th centuries and from America and Russia in the 18th century—First use of coal in the British iron industry—Henry Cort's invention of the puddling furnace and grooved rolls—Other innovations—Beginning of the British steel industry—Sheffield in 1615—Biographical notices of some distinguished men connected with the British iron trade, Pages 45-55

CHAPTER V.
THE IRON INDUSTRY OF WALES, IRELAND, AND SCOTLAND.

Iron made in Wales under the Romans—Extension of the iron industry of Wales in the 16th century—Merthyr Tydvil an iron centre—Iron made in Ireland in the reigns of

Elizabeth and James I., and afterwards—The iron industry of Ireland extinct in 1840—
Iron scarce in Scotland in the middle ages—Remains of ancient iron works in Scot-
land described by W. Ivison Macadam—Beginning of the modern iron industry of
Scotland—Carron Furnace—The Devon Iron Works, ... Pages 56–61

CHAPTER VI.

THE BRITISH IRON INDUSTRY BUILT UP BY BRITISH INVENTIVE GENIUS.

The 18th century begins a new era in the British iron industry—Great Britain becomes
the first iron manufacturing country—The inventions of Payne and Hanbury, of
Darby, Huntsman, Smeaton, Cort, Watt, Stephenson, Neilson, Crane, and Nasmyth—
Also at a later day of Bessemer, Mushet, and Charles William and Frederick Siemens, ... Pages 62–64

CHAPTER VII.

EARLY PROCESSES IN THE MANUFACTURE OF IRON AND STEEL.

Description of the rude direct processes of manufacturing iron which were used by the
ancients—They are still used—Goatskin bellows—The present method of making steel
in India—Methods of making iron in China, Cambodia, Corea, and Japan—Japanese
and Corean bellows described—Iron made in Belgium and England in the days of the
Romans without an artificial blast—A refinery forge described by Virgil—Diodorus
and Pliny describe the early furnaces of Southern Europe—The Catalan forge of
Spain—The first mention of coal—Used in Anglo-Saxon times—Were the Greeks and
Romans familiar with cast iron ? . . . .   Pages 65–79

CHAPTER VIII.

MEDIÆVAL AND EARLY MODERN PROCESSES IN THE MANUFACTURE OF IRON AND STEEL.

Revival of the iron industry in Europe in the 8th century—The wolf furnace, or stückofen, first mentioned—The osmund furnace—The blauofen and flussofen—The hochofen—
The blast furnace in use about the beginning of the 14th century—The Catalan forge
and the German bloomary in general use—Description by Dr. Parsons of an English
blast furnace and refinery forge of the 17th century—Also by Walter Burrell—Puddling
furnaces and coke blast furnaces not used on the Continent until the 19th century—
Leather and wooden bellows for blowing blast furnaces—The trompe, or water-blast—
Origin of the rolling mill—Slitting and rolling mills as "late improvements"—John
Houghton describes a slitting mill—Mechanical features of the English iron industry
at the beginning of the 18th century—Professor Åkerman's account of the origin of
the slitting mill and rolling mill—Various ancient and modern methods of making
steel—Agricola describes the early German method—Thomas Turner's description of
cemented steel—Percy, Grüner, and other authorities on steel quoted—Dud Dudley's
account of the foot-blast—Ancient and modern methods of producing steel compared
—The bauernofen, ... Pages 80–99

CHAPTER IX.

FIRST ATTEMPT BY EUROPEANS TO MANUFACTURE IRON IN THE UNITED STATES.

Iron made in northern latitudes only—Not known to the aboriginal inhabitants of America except when of meteoric origin—First discovery of iron ore in the Atlantic colonies made in North Carolina in 1585—Iron ore sent from Virginia to England in 1608—
An iron enterprise on Falling Creek, Virginia, undertaken in 1619—Destroyed by the
Indians in 1622 before it had made any iron—No further attempts to make iron in
Virginia for nearly a hundred years—The site of the Falling Creek enterprise described by R. A. Brock, of Richmond, ... Pages 100–107

CHAPTER X.

BEGINNING OF THE MANUFACTURE OF IRON IN THE NEW ENGLAND COLONIES.

The first successful iron enterprise in America established by Thomas Dexter, Robert Bridges, and others at Lynn, Massachusetts, in 1645, when a blast furnace was put in operation, followed in 1648 by a forge at the same place—Full description of these pioneer iron works—The site of these early iron works described—The first iron article made in America still preserved—Joseph Jenks—Henry and James Leonard— "Where you can find iron works there you will find a Leonard"—A furnace and forge built at Braintree, in Massachusetts—The next iron enterprise in New England established near Taunton—James Leonard and his sons go to Taunton—George Hall—Other members of the Leonard family—King Philip—"John Ruck and others of Salem"— Iron made at Concord, Rowley Village, Topsfield, and Boxford, all in Massachusetts— The Whittington Iron Works—The Chartley Iron Works—King's Furnace—The Hopewell Iron Works—Iron works at New Haven established by Captain Thomas Clarke, John Winthrop, Jr., and others in 1658—Iron made in Rhode Island as early as 1675, when a forge at Pawtucket was destroyed by the Indians, ... Pages 108-119

CHAPTER XI.

EXTENSION OF THE MANUFACTURE OF IRON IN NEW ENGLAND.

The first furnace in Plymouth county, Massachusetts—Lambert Despard and the Barkers— The Bound Brook and Drinkwater iron works—The various enterprises of Hugh Orr— The first cast-iron tea-kettle—The first slitting-mill in the colonies—Douglass's description of the iron industry of New England in 1750—Extension of the iron industry into Western Massachusetts about 1750—Rapidly extended in Eastern Massachusetts—Description of Federal Furnace in 1804—The bog and pond ores of Massachusetts—The first steel works in Massachusetts—Eliphalet and Jonathan Leonard—Iron enterprises in Rhode Island before the Revolution—Stephen Hopkins, the signer of the Declaration, and General Nathanael Greene made iron—Hope Furnace—Cranston and Cumberland Hill—The Salisbury iron district in Connecticut—Early iron enterprises at Lime Rock and Lakeville—Colonel Ethan Allen an iron manufacturer at Lakeville—Early iron enterprises on Mount Riga—Prominence of the Salisbury district—Milo Barnum and William H. Barnum—The Holleys—Other early iron enterprises in Connecticut— Connecticut the first of the colonies to make steel—Early iron enterprises in Maine, New Hampshire, and Vermont—The early nail and tack industry of New England— Nails made in chimney corners—The first nail-cutting machine, ... Pages 120-135

CHAPTER XII.

EARLY IRON ENTERPRISES IN NEW YORK.

The early Dutch settlers of New York did not make iron—Philip Livingston establishes the first iron works in New York on Ancram creek before 1740—Lawrence Scrawley's plating forge at Wawayanda, in Orange county, built about 1745—Other early enterprises in Orange county—The Townsends—The great iron chain across the Hudson in 1778 which prevented British vessels from passing West Point—The Sterling Iron Works of the Townsends described—Early iron works in Dutchess, Westchester, Putnam, and Suffolk counties—Development of the Champlain district about 1800—Early iron enterprises in other parts of New York—John Brinkerhoff—Erastus Corning—The Piersons at Ramapo—Henry Burden and his inventions, ... Pages 136-145

CHAPTER XIII.

EARLY IRON ENTERPRISES IN NEW JERSEY.

The first iron works in New Jersey established at Tinton Falls, in Monmouth county, about 1674—The Leonards of Massachusetts—Development of the magnetic ores of Northern New Jersey about 1710 at Whippany—Early iron works at Morristown—The

Dickerson mine—Many early iron works in Northern New Jersey described by Dr. Joseph F. Tuttle and Hon. Edmund D. Halsey—Peter Hasenclever and the Ringwood Company—Robert Erskine—Lord Stirling, John Jacob Faesch, and others—The Hibernia and Mount Hope furnaces—The Fords—Early iron works in Andover township in Sussex county—Whitehead Humphreys—Durham boats—The Union Iron Works, and Oxford, Sterling, Ogden's, and Mount Holly furnaces—William Allen and Joseph Turner—Early iron works in Southern New Jersey—Batsto and Atsion furnaces—Charles Read—William, Jesse, and Samuel Richards—Mark Richards, or Reichert—Old Boonton slitting mill in the Revolution—Benjamin and David Reeves—The first rolling mill in New Jersey—Peter Cooper, Abram S. Hewitt, and Frederick J. Slade—Dr. Morse's description of the iron industry of New Jersey in 1795, ... Pages 146–162

CHAPTER XIV.

BEGINNING OF THE MANUFACTURE OF IRON IN PENNSYLVANIA.

Iron not made in Pennsylvania until after the arrival of William Penn in 1682—Penn encouraged the opening of iron and other mines—First iron made in Pennsylvania experimentally before 1692, but at what place is not known—The first historic iron works in Pennsylvania established by Thomas Rutter, an English Quaker, on the Manatawny, in Berks county, in 1716—Rutter's enterprise was a bloomary, probably called Manatawny Forge—Coventry Forge, on French creek, in Chester county, built by Samuel Nutt, also an English Quaker, in 1717 or 1718, the second iron enterprise in Pennsylvania—Colebrookdale Furnace, in Berks county, built by a company, of which Thomas Rutter was a member, about 1720, the third iron enterprise—Thomas Potts, Jr.—Pool Forge—"A person named Kurtz"—Durham Furnace built in 1727—Other early iron enterprises in Eastern Pennsylvania established between 1725 and 1750—In 1728 there were "four furnaces in blast in the colony"—Reading Furnace on French creek—William Branson—Samuel Nutt, Jr.—Benjamin Franklin invents the Franklin stove in 1742—Warwick Furnace—The Vincent Steel Works—The Windsor Forges—John, David, and Robert Jenkins—Mrs. Martha J. Nevin—Valley Forge and its history—The iron enterprises of William and Mark Bird—Charming Forge—George Ege—Oley Furnace—A forge on Crum creek, in Delaware county, built about 1742, by John Crosby and Peter Dicks, which "ruined Crosby's family"—Sarum Iron Works built as early as 1742—John Taylor—"A plating forge to work with a tilt-hammer" in Byberry township, Philadelphia county, in 1750—Two steel furnaces in Philadelphia in 1750, and others built before the Revolution, ... Pages 163–178

CHAPTER XV.

THE MANUFACTURE OF IRON IN PENNSYLVANIA EXTENDED TO THE SUSQUEHANNA.

Elizabeth Furnace, built in 1750 by John Huber, a German, the first iron enterprise in the present county of Lancaster—Baron Stiegel one of its early owners—Robert Coleman a later owner—Pool Forge built by James Old about 1765—His other iron enterprises—Biographical sketches of James Old and Robert Coleman—Cyrus Jacobs—Peter Grubb builds Cornwall Furnace in 1742—His other iron enterprises—His sons, Curtis and Peter—Martic Furnace and Forge—Hopewell and Speedwell forges—The iron industry crosses the Susquehanna as early as 1756, ... Pages 179–185

CHAPTER XVI.

CHARACTERISTICS OF THE EARLY IRON INDUSTRY OF PENNSYLVANIA.

In 1750 Pennsylvania was the most advanced of all the colonies in the manufacture of iron—Cornwall, Warwick, and Reading furnaces were large structures for their day—Description of these furnaces—Also of the workmen employed at the early furnaces and forges of Pennsylvania—The patriarchal character of early Pennsylvania ironmasters—"Good old colony times," . . . . Pages 186–190

CHAPTER XVII.

THE MANUFACTURE OF IRON IN PENNSYLVANIA AFTER THE REVOLUTION.

First iron enterprises in the Lehigh Valley undertaken after 1800—William Henry's bloomary forge near Nazareth—Hampton Furnace near Shimersville—The Heimbachs—Samuel Helfrick and the Balliets—A rolling mill built at South Easton by John Stewart and others in 1836—Bloomaries in Carbon county—The Cheltenham Rolling Mill built in 1790—Benjamin Longstreth establishes the first iron enterprise at Phœnixville in 1790—Clemens Rentgen and his novel iron enterprises—Early iron enterprises in Schuylkill county—Federal Slitting Mill built by Isaac Pennock in 1795—Brandywine Rolling Mill and its successor, the Lukens Rolling Mill—Dr. Charles Lukens—Mrs. Rebecca W. Lukens—Mount Hope Furnace and other iron enterprises in Lancaster, Lebanon, and York counties—The Reynolds family—Early iron enterprises in Adams, Franklin, and Cumberland counties—Thaddeus Stevens—The Chambers brothers—The Haldeman family—Michael Ege—Early iron enterprises in Dauphin county and in the Upper Susquehanna Valley—The Scrantons—The enterprises of Karthaus & Geissenhainer in Clearfield county—Other early iron enterprises in the Susquehanna Valley—The pack-horse days, ... Pages 191-203

CHAPTER XVIII.

THE MANUFACTURE OF CHARCOAL IRON IN THE JUNIATA VALLEY.

The Juniata Iron Company organized in 1767, but it did not make iron—Joseph and Benjamin Jacobs—Bedford Furnace, at Orbisonia, in Huntingdon county, built in 1788, the first iron enterprise in the Juniata Valley—Followed by Bedford Forge at the same place in 1791—Centre Furnace, in Centre county, the second in the Juniata Valley, built in 1791 by Col. John Patton and Col. Samuel Miles, both Revolutionary officers—Other early iron enterprises in Centre county—Roland Curtin—Hardman Philips erects a forge and screw factory at Philipsburg, in Centre county, in 1817—Bernard Lauth—Barree Forge, on the Juniata, and Huntingdon Furnace, on Warrior's Mark run, built in 1794 and 1796—The Shoenbergers, Judge Gloninger, George Anshutz, and other early ironmasters in Huntingdon county and in the present county of Blair—The Royers, Elias Baker, and Roland Diller—Martin Bell—Early iron enterprises in Bedford and Fulton counties—Also in Mifflin and Juniata counties—Freedom Forge, in Mifflin county, built before 1795—Hope Furnace, in the same county, built by General William Lewis in 1798, who also built Mount Vernon Forge, in Perry county, in 1804—Other early iron works in Perry county—Cemented steel made at Caledonia, near Bedford, before 1800 by William McDermett, whose daughter Josephine married David R. Porter, an ironmaster on Spruce creek, Huntingdon county, who afterwards became Governor of Pennsylvania—Henry S. Spang, John Lyon, Anthony Shorb, Andrew Gregg, George Schmucker, and General James Irvin early Juniata ironmasters—Juniata iron in high repute, ... Pages 204-212

CHAPTER XIX.

THE EARLY MANUFACTURE OF IRON IN WESTERN PENNSYLVANIA.

First mention in 1780 of iron ore in Western Pennsylvania—John Hayden—The Alliance Iron Works, on Jacob's creek, in Fayette county, built by William Turnbull, Peter Marmie, and Col. John Holker in 1789 and 1790, and consisting of a furnace and a forge, the first iron enterprise west of the Alleghenies—The Alliance Furnace, which was put in blast on November 1, 1790, followed closely by Union Furnace, on Dunbar creek, in Fayette county, built by Isaac Meason in 1790, and put in blast in March, 1791—Other early iron enterprises in Fayette county—Jeremiah Pears—The enterprises of John Hayden—The Oliphants—John Gibson—The Brownsville Steel Factory, owned by Truman & Co., built before 1811—Jacob Bowman's Nail Factory, at Brownsville, built about 1795—The Plumsock Rolling Mill, in Fayette county, the first in the United States to roll bar iron and use puddling furnaces—Isaac Meason and his son, Col. Isaac Meason—An early iron enterprise in Greene county—Early iron enterprises in Westmoreland county—General Arthur St. Clair and Bishop John Henry Hopkins—Early iron enterprises in Somerset, Cambria, and Indiana counties—George S. King—The Cambria Iron Works commenced in 1853—Early iron enterprises in Beaver, Mercer, and Lawrence counties—The Crawfords—Early iron enterprises in other western and northwestern counties—The Great Western Iron Works, ...   Pages 213-224

CHAPTER XX.

EARLY IRON ENTERPRISES IN ALLEGHENY COUNTY, PENNSYLVANIA.

Beginning of the iron industry at Pittsburgh about 1792, when George Anshutz built a small blast furnace at Shady Side—Proofs of the erection of this furnace, which was abandoned in 1794—The first iron foundry at Pittsburgh built by Joseph McClurg about 1805—The first nail factories in Pittsburgh, Porter's, Sturgeon's, and Stewart's, in operation in 1807, their united capacity being "about 40 tons of nails yearly"—In 1810 "the manufacture of ironmongery" at Pittsburgh had "increased beyond all calculation"—The first rolling mill at Pittsburgh built by Christopher Cowan in 1811—Followed in 1819 by the Union Rolling Mill, on the Monongahela, which had four puddling furnaces, the first in Pittsburgh—Other early rolling mills in Pittsburgh—The first rolling mill in Allegheny City—Clinton Furnace, in Pittsburgh, built by Graff, Bennett & Co. in 1859, the first successful furnace in Allegheny county—Statistics of the iron and steel industries of Pennsylvania, ... Pages 225-232

CHAPTER XXI.

THE EARLY MANUFACTURE OF IRON IN DELAWARE.

The Swedes and the Dutch on the Delaware did not make iron—Iron Hill, in Pencader hundred, New Castle county, Delaware, discovered and so named as early as 1661—The Colonial Records of Pennsylvania mention its existence in 1684—An account by Emanuel Swedenborg of early iron enterprises in New Castle county operated by Sir William Keith and others—Abbington Furnace—John Ball's bloomary forge—Early iron enterprises in Sussex county—Millsborough Furnace probably the last furnace operated in the State—Rolling mills at Wilmington and in its vicinity, . Pages 233-239

CHAPTER XXII.

EARLY IRON ENTERPRISES IN MARYLAND.

The first iron enterprise in Maryland was a bloomary forge, erected at the head of Chesapeake Bay, in Cecil county, a short time before 1716—The iron enterprises of Stephen Onion & Co. and Joseph Farmer at North East and its vicinity—Merged in the Principio Company, an English corporation—This company built Principio Furnace, the first furnace in Maryland, in 1723 and 1724, and a forge at Principio in the same years—Both probably at work in 1725—John England superintended their erection and their operations for many years—The Principio Company, through Mr. England, builds a furnace on the lands of Captain Augustine Washington, in Virginia, in 1725 and 1726—Further history of the Principio Company, which was for many years the leading iron company in America, and was active until the Revolution—"A certain Mr. Washington"—George P. Whitaker—The Ridgely family—The Dorseys—The Snowdens—Early iron enterprises in Queen Anne, Frederick, and Washington counties—The Johnsons—The iron industry of Maryland greatly extended before the Revolution and also afterwards—The Avalon Iron Works "built by the Dorseys" about 1795—Development of the manufacture of coke pig iron in Western Maryland in 1837 and immediately succeeding years—The first heavy iron rails in the United States made at Mount Savage, in Western Maryland, in 1844—A bog-ore furnace on the Eastern Shore of Maryland in 1830—A furnace at Georgetown, D. C., built in 1849—Government iron works at Washington, ... Pages 240-257

CHAPTER XXIII.

THE IRON INDUSTRY ESTABLISHED IN VIRGINIA.

Revival of the iron industry in Virginia about 1715 by Governor Spotswood and a colony of Palatinates—The first furnace in Virginia built at Fredericksville, in Spottsylvania county, near the North Anna river—The next furnace in Virginia built in Orange county, on the south side of the Rapidan—An air furnace at Massaponax, five miles below Fredericksburg, on the Rappahannock—Accokeek Furnace—All these enterprises described by Col. William Byrd, the second, in 1732—Mr. W. H. Adams fixes the exact location of the first three of these enterprises—The connection of the Washington family with the iron industry of Virginia and Maryland—Extension of the iron industry of Virginia into the Valley of Virginia—Zane's Furnace and Forge, on Cedar creek, in Frederick county, were "built before any iron works in this region"—Followed by Pine Forge, in Shenandoah county—Henry Miller's furnace on Mossy creek, Augusta county, built about 1775—Other early iron works in the Valley of Virginia and in Southwestern Virginia—Jefferson's account of the iron industry of Virginia in 1781 and 1782—Ross's celebrated iron works—Household industries in Virginia about 1790— Great expansion of the charcoal iron industry of Virginia—Many furnaces and forges enumerated by Lesley in 1856—The first rolling mill in Virginia built on Cheat river about 1812 by Jackson & Updegraff—Wheeling a prominent iron centre before the civil war—Its first rolling mill built by Dr. Peter Shoenberger and David Agnew in 1832—The Tredegar Iron Company at Richmond—Statistics of the iron and steel industries of Virginia and West Virginia, ... Pages 258–271

CHAPTER XXIV.

THE MANUFACTURE OF IRON IN NORTH CAROLINA.

Iron made in "Carolina" as early as 1728 and exported to England—Virginia and Carolina hoes sold in New York before the Revolution—Iron enterprises on tributaries of the Cape Fear, Yadkin, and Dan rivers before the Revolution—That event stimulated the establishment of other iron enterprises in Guilford, Cleveland, and other counties—Before 1800 there were many iron enterprises in Lincoln, Stokes, and Surry counties—After 1800 the iron industry was still further extended in Lincoln county, which had in 1810 six bloomaries, two rolling and slitting mills, and two naileries— It also became a prominent industry in Burke and Surry counties—Extended into many counties before the civil war—Bloomaries and the water-blast in general use— The iron industry of North Carolina now almost extinct, ... Pages 272–275

CHAPTER XXV.

THE MANUFACTURE OF IRON IN SOUTH CAROLINA.

The first iron enterprise in South Carolina established in 1773 by Mr. Buffington in the northwestern part of the State—Followed by other iron enterprises after the Revolution—The Era and Etna furnaces and forges in York county—The water-blast in use in this State—Nine bloomaries and other iron enterprises in South Carolina in 1810— A rolling mill for making sheet iron in this State about 1815—In 1840 there were four furnaces and a number of bloomaries, rolling mills, and other iron enterprises—In 1891 there was no iron or steel enterprise in South Carolina, ... Pages 276–278

CHAPTER XXVI.

THE EARLY MANUFACTURE OF IRON IN GEORGIA.

Georgia has no colonial iron history—The first iron enterprises in this State established probably after 1790, and near the Atlantic Coast—In 1810 there was a bloomary in Warren county, a forge in Elbert county, and a nailery in Chatham county—Hodge's and Sequee bloomaries, in Habersham county, built as early as 1830 and probably at an earlier day—Other bloomaries established after 1830 in Bartow, Union, Murray, Walker, and Dade counties, and abandoned before 1856, but other bloomaries were then in operation—Sequee Furnace, in Habersham county, built before 1832, probably the first furnace in the State—Etowah Furnace, in Bartow county; Allatoona, Union, Lewis, and Cartersville furnaces in Cass county; and Clear Creek Furnace, in Walker county —Later charcoal furnaces—Only six furnaces in 1891, two of which used coke—The first rolling mill in Georgia was probably Etowah, in Cass county, built about 1849— In 1891 there was only one rolling mill in the State—Rising Fawn Furnace the first furnace in the United States to use the Whitwell hot-blast stove—Description of the various Etowah iron enterprises as they existed about 1859—The iron industry of Georgia not now prominent, ... Pages 279-281

CHAPTER XXVII.

THE EARLY MANUFACTURE OF IRON IN KENTUCKY.

Bourbon Furnace, often called Slate Furnace, the first iron enterprise in Kentucky whose history has been preserved, built in 1791, on Slate creek, in Bath county—Complete history of this furnace by V. B. Young, Esq., of Owingsville, Kentucky—Sketch of its projectors and builders—In 1810 there were four furnaces and three forges in Kentucky—First furnaces in the Hanging Rock region of Kentucky built about 1817 and 1818—Names of the Hanging Rock pioneers—Extension of the iron industry in the Hanging Rock region—The first rolling mill in Kentucky appears to have been built at Covington in 1829—Present condition of the Kentucky iron industry—Many new iron and steel enterprises, ... Pages 282-287

CHAPTER XXVIII.

THE EARLY MANUFACTURE OF IRON IN TENNESSEE.

A bloomary at Embreeville, in Washington county, built in 1790, the first iron enterprise in Tennessee—Other early enterprises in the eastern part of Tennessee—Ross's Iron Works, on the Holston river, in Sullivan county, built before 1800—Other early iron enterprises in Tennessee built before and soon after 1800—Cumberland Furnace, in Dickson county, built by James Robinson in 1792—Yellow Creek Furnace, in Montgomery county, built in 1802—The iron industry of Tennessee greatly extended—Description of the iron industry of this State in 1856 by Lesley—Chattanooga the present iron centre of Tennessee—Account of its early iron enterprises—Bluff Furnace— James Henderson—The two Rockwood furnaces—The Roane Iron Company—Lewis Scofield—S. B. Lowe—The iron industries of Knoxville—Present condition of the Tennessee iron industry, ... Pages 288-292

CHAPTER XXIX.

THE MANUFACTURE OF IRON IN ALABAMA.

The first furnace in Alabama probably built about 1818 west of Russellville, in Franklin county—Abandoned in 1827—Early furnaces in Calhoun, Cherokee, and Shelby counties—Horace Ware—Early bloomaries in Shelby, Bibb, Talladega, and Calhoun counties—Many of them blown with the *trompe*, or water-blast—Iron enterprises in Alabama during the civil war—Furnaces and rolling mills built at Brierfield and Shelby— Discovery of coal in Alabama—The first iron enterprises at Birmingham and its vicinity—Later iron and steel enterprises in Alabama—Statistics of the production of pig iron in Alabama and other Southern States from 1880 to 1890—Wonderful progress in ten years, ... Pages 293-296

CHAPTER XXX.

PRIMITIVE CHARACTERISTICS OF THE SOUTHERN IRON INDUSTRY.

The wonderful development of the iron industry of Western North Carolina and East Tennessee many years ago an interesting fact—Furnaces blown with one tuyere and wooden tubs—"Thundergust forges"—The *trompe* in general use—Bar iron used as a medium of exchange—Never many bloomaries in Virginia—Old methods of making iron have passed away in the South, ... Pages 297-300

CHAPTER XXXI.

THE EARLY MANUFACTURE OF IRON IN OHIO.

Hopewell Furnace, in Mahoning county, the first iron enterprise in Ohio, commenced in 1803 and finished in 1804 by Daniel Eaton—Montgomery Furnace, built in 1806, also in Mahoning county, by Robert Montgomery and John Struthers, the second iron enterprise in the State—The first hammered bars in Ohio made at a forge at Niles-town, Trumbull county, in 1809, by James Heaton, who also built a furnace at Niles-town on Mosquito creek about 1812—The iron industry of Ohio extended to the shore of Lake Erie about 1825—Rebecca Furnace, at New Lisbon, Columbiana county, built in 1807 or 1808 by Gideon Hughes—Licking Furnace and Forge, near Zanesville, built by Moses Dillon about 1808—Early iron enterprises in Licking and Tuscarawas counties—The Zoar Community—Early iron enterprises in Adams county—Beginning of the manufacture of iron in the Hanging Rock region of Ohio—The Hanging Rock pioneers, John Campbell, Thomas W. Means, and others—Description by Mr. John Birkinbine of Olive Furnace, a curious structure—The good quality of Hanging Rock charcoal pig iron—The old charcoal furnace of the Hecla Iron and Mining Company—Early forges on the Ohio river—The first rolling mill at Cincinnati—Crucible steel works at Cincinnati built in 1832—Introduction of raw bituminous coal in the blast furnaces of the Mahoning Valley, first at Lowell, in 1846, by Wilkeson, Wilkes & Co.—Introduction of Lake Superior ores in Ohio blast furnaces—First shipments of Brier Hill coal to Cleveland made by David Tod in 1840—Mill Creek Furnace, the first iron enterprise at Youngstown, built about 1835—Beginning of the iron industry at Cleveland—Henry Chisholm, ... Pages 301–313

CHAPTER XXXII.

EARLY IRON ENTERPRISES IN INDIANA.

A "nailery" in Indiana Territory as early as 1810—In 1840 the census mentions a furnace in Jefferson county, one in Parke, one in Vigo, one in Vermillion, and three in Wayne county—A bloomary forge in Fulton county also mentioned—An early furnace in Monroe county—An early forge in Marshall county built about 1845 by Charles Crocker and a partner—Mishawaka Forge, in St. Joseph county—Other charcoal iron enterprises in Indiana—Development of the block-coal district of Indiana and the erection of furnaces to use this coal—The first rolling mill in Indiana built by R. A. Douglas, at Indianapolis, in 1857—Present condition of the iron and steel industries of Indiana, ... Pages 314–316

CHAPTER XXXIII.

EARLY IRON ENTERPRISES IN ILLINOIS.

Illinois Furnace, at Elizabethtown, in Hardin county, built in 1839, the first iron enterprise in Illinois for the manufacture of iron of any kind—No furnaces in operation in Illinois from 1860 to 1868—Development of the Big Muddy coal fields and the erection of furnaces at Grand Tower and elsewhere in Southwestern Illinois—Beginning of the iron industry at Chicago in 1857, when Captain E. B. Ward and others built the Chicago Rolling Mill—The first furnaces in Chicago built in 1868—Present condition of the iron and steel industries of Illinois, ... Pages 317–319

CHAPTER XXXIV.

EARLY IRON ENTERPRISES IN MICHIGAN.

Charcoal furnaces in Michigan before 1840—From 1840 to 1850 the iron industry of Michigan made no progress and possibly declined—From 1850 to 1860 three bog-ore furnaces were built in the southern part of the State—The development of the Lake Superior iron-ore region commenced with the first discovery by white men of the iron ore of this region in 1844, near the eastern end of Teal Lake, by William A. Burt—In 1845 the Jackson Mining Company was organized at Jackson, Michigan, and in 1847 it commenced the erection of a forge on Carp river which was finished in 1848,

and in that year the first iron made in the Lake Superior region was manufactured by
Ariel N. Barney—History of subsequent iron manufacturing enterprises in the Lake
Superior region and of the development of the iron ores of Lake Superior—The first
use of Lake Superior iron ore in a blast furnace occurred in Mercer county, Pennsylvania, in 1853—History of the Sharon Iron Company which used this ore—Statistics of
the production of Lake Superior iron ore—Captain E. B. Ward, ... Pages 320–328

CHAPTER XXXV.

THE EARLY MANUFACTURE OF IRON IN WISCONSIN.

Prior to 1859 there were three charcoal furnaces in Wisconsin—No others were built
until 1865, when a charcoal furnace at Iron Ridge, in Dodge county, was built by
the Wisconsin Iron Company, which was soon followed by several other furnaces—
Wisconsin had no rolling mill until 1868, when its first mill was built at Milwaukee
by the Milwaukee Iron Company—Present condition of the iron and steel industries
of Wisconsin, ... Pages 329–331

CHAPTER XXXVI.

EARLY IRON ENTERPRISES IN MISSOURI.

Ashebran's Furnace, on Stout's creek, about two miles east of Ironton, in Iron county,
built about 1815, probably the first iron enterprise in Missouri—Followed in 1819 or
1820 by a bloomary forge on Thicketty creek, in Crawford county, built by William
Harrison and Josiah Reeves—Blooms hammered at this forge under a spring-pole
hammer—Springfield Furnace, in Washington county, built in 1823 or 1824 by Eversol, Perry & Ruggles, the next iron enterprise in Missouri—Maramec Furnace, in
Phelps county, finished in 1829—Development of the iron-ore deposits of Iron
Mountain and Pilot Knob in 1836 and subsequent years—Furnaces built in this region—Commencement of the iron industry of St. Louis in 1850—Further history and
present condition of the iron and steel industries of Missouri, ... Pages 332–337

CHAPTER XXXVII.

THE MANUFACTURE OF IRON IN TEXAS.

Texas had one blast furnace before the civil war, located in Cass county—Erection of
other furnaces and of several bloomaries in Texas during the war—Charcoal furnaces
built in Texas after the war and in recent years—The first rolling mills in this State
built at Houston and at Fort Worth—A promising iron future for Texas, Pages 338–340

CHAPTER XXXVIII.

THE MANUFACTURE OF IRON IN VARIOUS WESTERN STATES.

The first blast furnace in Minnesota commenced in 1872 but not finished until 1880—
Later iron enterprises in this State—A bloomary built and in operation in Lawrence
county, Arkansas, as early as 1857—Iron once made in Carroll county, Arkansas, in
the hollow stumps of trees—The undeveloped iron resources of Arkansas—Early iron
enterprises in Kansas, Iowa, and Nebraska—The first iron enterprise in Colorado was
a small charcoal furnace at Langford, in Boulder county, which was finished and
put in blast in 1864—The first rolling mill in Colorado was removed in 1877 by William Faux from Danville, Pennsylvania, to Pueblo, and put in operation in 1878, the
product being re-rolled rails—Later iron and steel enterprises in Colorado—A forge in
Utah Territory, east of Salt Lake City, built as early as 1859, but the Mormons had
made iron many years before—Later but abortive iron enterprises, . . . Pages 341–345

CHAPTER XXXIX.

THE IRON INDUSTRY ON THE PACIFIC COAST.

First furnace and rolling mill in California—The iron and steel enterprises of California
fully described—The iron enterprises of Oregon and Washington, . . . Pages 346–347

CHAPTER XL.

THE FIRST IRON WORKS IN CANADA.

Description of the pioneer iron works in Canada, located near Three Rivers, in Quebec, and known as the Forges of St. Maurice—Commenced in 1737, when a blast furnace was built which was in operation as late as 1883, ... Pages 348-351

CHAPTER XLI.

THE MANUFACTURE OF IRON WITH ANTHRACITE COAL.

The distinctive charcoal era of the American iron industry ended about 1840, when both anthracite and bituminous coal began to be used successfully in blast furnaces— More charcoal iron made in the United States to-day, however, than in 1840 or any preceding year—Anthracite coal used experimentally in many American blast furnaces between 1815 and 1840, generally in connection with charcoal—Dr. Frederick W. Geissenhainer's experiments—Granted a patent in 1833 for the use of anthracite coal in the blast furnace—Builds Valley Furnace in 1836, and makes a few tons of pig iron exclusively with anthracite coal in the fall of that year—George Crane's experiments with anthracite coal in the blast furnace in South Wales in the same year—He successfully uses it in 1837—Visited in that year by Solomon W. Roberts, of Philadelphia, upon whose advice the Lehigh Crane Iron Company was organized— Mr. Crane's patents—Details of various attempts in the United States to make pig iron with anthracite coal between 1836 and 1839—Pioneer Furnace, at Pottsville— William Lyman—Anthracite furnaces in 1840—First anthracite furnace in the Lehigh Valley built in 1839 and 1840 by David Thomas for the Lehigh Crane Iron Company— Successfully blown in on July 3, 1840, and first cast made on July 4th—Biographical sketch of Mr. Thomas—Rapid growth after 1840 of the anthracite pig-iron industry— The first use of anthracite coal in connection with the manufacture of finished iron in the United States dates from 1812—First used under boilers in 1825 and in puddling in 1827, at Phœnixville, by Jonah and George Thompson, ... Pages 352-365

CHAPTER XLII.

THE MANUFACTURE OF IRON WITH BITUMINOUS COAL.

Remarkable that the use of bituminous coal in American blast furnaces should have been so long delayed—Experiments in the use of coke in blast furnaces in this country all unsuccessful until 1835, when William Firmstone was successful in substituting coke for charcoal at Mary Ann Furnace, in Huntingdon county, Pennsylvania—Sketch of his life—F. H. Oliphant successful in making coke pig iron at Fairchance Furnace, in Fayette county, Pennsylvania, in 1837—Various unsuccessful experiments to use coke in blast furnaces in Pennsylvania—Some successful experiments—Henry C. Carey—First notable success in this country in making pig iron with coke accomplished at Lonaconing Furnace, in Western Maryland, in 1839, followed in 1840 by equal success at two furnaces of the Mount Savage Iron Company in the same part of Maryland—Slow progress after 1840 in the use of coke in the blast furnace—Its use increased after 1850, and very rapidly after 1865—First coke furnaces south of the Potomac—The use of raw bituminous coal in the blast furnace successfully inaugurated in 1845 at Clay Furnace, in Mercer county, Pennsylvania, by Himrod & Vincent—This was a charcoal furnace—Mahoning Furnace, at Lowell, in Mahoning county, Ohio, the first furnace built expressly to use raw coal—Successfully blown in in 1846 for its owners, Wilkeson, Wilkes & Co., by John Crowther—Sketch of his life—Water power in general use in blowing furnaces down to 1840, . . Pages 366-375

CHAPTER XLIII.

STATISTICS OF PIG IRON PRODUCTION IN THE UNITED STATES.

The production of anthracite pig iron in the United States passes that of charcoal pig iron in 1855—Bituminous passes charcoal in 1869—Bituminous passes anthracite in 1875—The production of pig iron in the United States in 1890 exceeded that of Great Britain in 1882, her year of greatest production, ... Pages 376-377

CHAPTER XLIV.

THE MANUFACTURE OF BLISTER AND CRUCIBLE STEEL IN THE UNITED STATES.

Steel manufactured in a small way in several of the colonies both by the cementation process and "in the German manner"—The first steel in the colonies probably made in Connecticut in 1728 by Samuel Higley and Joseph Dewey—Steel made by Aaron Eliot, of Connecticut, in 1761, from bar iron which had been made from magnetic sand—In 1750 Massachusetts had one steel furnace—First steel made in New York in 1776 by Peter Townsend—New Jersey had one steel furnace in 1750—Pennsylvania had three steel furnaces in that year—Condition of the American steel industry in 1791, just one hundred years ago—Slow growth of the steel industry of the United States—Report on the state of the industry in 1831 by John R. Coates, of Philadelphia—Cast steel not then made in the United States—From 1831 to 1860 the steel industry of this country still continued to make slow progress—Full details of the establishment at Cincinnati in 1832, by William and John H. Garrard, of the first successful crucible steel works in the United States—Analysis of the crucible steel made at these works—Statistics of the steel industry of Pennsylvania in 1850, with the names of all the manufacturers—Pioneers in the manufacture of blister and crucible steel at Pittsburgh—Hussey, Wells & Co., in 1860, and Park, Brother & Co., in 1862, the first persons in the United States to meet with complete financial as well as mechanical success in the manufacture of crucible steel of the best quality—Full history of the Adirondack Steel Works—James R. Thompson—McKelvy & Blair—Statistics of the production of crucible steel in the United States, ... Pages 878–394

CHAPTER XLV.

THE INVENTION OF THE BESSEMER PROCESS.

Brief description of the Bessemer process—Beginning of Sir Henry Bessemer's experiments—Patents granted to him in England in 1855 and 1856—Robert F. Mushet's invaluable assistance in perfecting the Bessemer process—Bessemer's patents in the United States granted in 1856—William Kelly's claim of priority in 1857 conceded by the Commissioner of Patents—Mr. Kelly's own account of his invention of the pneumatic process—His experiments with a converting vessel at Johnstown in 1857 and 1858—Full account of Mr. Mushet's application of spiegeleisen to the Bessemer process—The first Bessemer steel rail ever laid down was made by Mr. Mushet—Sir Henry Bessemer's letter to Sir James Kitson in 1890—Sir Henry's immense profits from his invention—Mr. Mushet's pathetic complaint—Mr. Göran Fredrik Göransson's account of his part in perfecting the Bessemer·process—Invention of the basic process by Sidney Gilchrist Thomas, Percy C. Gilchrist, and George J. Snelus—Also by Jacob Reese—Experiments in the elimination of phosphorus by James Henderson and Colonel J. B. Kunkel—The Clapp-Griffiths and Robert-Bessemer processes—Joseph Gilbert Martien's experiments—Hon. Abram S. Hewitt's report on Bessemer steel at the Paris Exposition of 1867—Biographical sketches of Robert F. Mushet and Sidney G. Thomas, ... Pages 395–408

CHAPTER XLVI.

THE BESSEMER PROCESS IN THE UNITED STATES.

The Kelly patents controlled by a company—Experimental Bessemer steel works built for this company at Wyandotte, Michigan, in 1863 and 1864, by William F. Durfee—First Bessemer steel made in the United States by Mr. Durfee, in September, 1864—Bessemer steel next made by A. L. Holley, in February, 1865, at experimental works built at Troy in 1864 by Winslow, Griswold & Holley—Consolidation of the interests of the owners of the American patents of Bessemer, Mushet, and Kelly—List of the Bessemer steel works built in the United States down to 1876—First Bessemer steel rails made in the United States were rolled at the Chicago Rolling Mill in May, 1865—Statistics of the American and British Bessemer steel industries down to 1890—Biographical sketches of deceased American Bessemer steel pioneers, . . Pages 409–417

CHAPTER XLVII.

THE MANUFACTURE OF OPEN-HEARTH STEEL.

The open-hearth process briefly described—Its advantages—Invention of the Siemens regenerative gas furnace—First patent granted to Frederick Siemens in 1856—Experiments by Dr. Charles William Siemens in 1861 in the manufacture of cast steel with regenerative gas in an open-hearth—Experiments by Emile and Pierre Martin in France in 1864—Their principal patent granted in France in 1865—Subsequent operations of Dr. Siemens and the Martins—Their different methods described—Introduction of the regenerative furnace into the United States—Names of the pioneers who first experimented in its use—First open-hearth furnace in the United States built for Cooper, Hewitt & Co., at Trenton, New Jersey, in 1868, by Frederick J. Slade—First use of the regenerative furnace in the United States in the puddling of iron—Various direct processes—The production of basic steel in the United States—Statistics of its production—Also of the production of open-hearth steel in the United States and in Great Britain to the close of 1890—Biographical sketch of Dr. Siemens, ... Pages 418–425

CHAPTER XLVIII.

THE EARLY HISTORY OF IRON RAILS IN THE UNITED STATES.

First railroads built in the United States—The Quincy and Mauch Chunk railroads—The Baltimore and Ohio Railroad, commenced in 1828, the first in the United States that was built for the conveyance of passengers—Put in operation from Baltimore to Ellicott's Mills in 1830—Other early passenger railroads in the United States—Description of the track of the Baltimore and Ohio Railroad—Also of the rails first used on early American railroads—Strap rails—The Birkinshaw rail—The Clarence rail—The use of strap rails continued for many years—Cast-iron rails once made in the United States—Heavy iron rails not made in the United States until 1844—First American T rails made at Mount Savage, Maryland, in that year—The T rail an American invention—Robert L. Stevens the inventor—Full particulars of the invention—The first 30-foot, 60-foot, and 120-foot rails rolled in the United States—The first American locomotives—First street and elevated railroads in the United States—Statistics of iron and steel rails in the United States—Henry Thomas Weld, ... Pages 426–441

CHAPTER XLIX.

IRON SHIPBUILDING IN THE UNITED STATES.

Henry Hall's account of the first iron steamboats and steamships in the United States—Captain John Ericsson's iron vessels—Other iron vessels—Notable Transatlantic iron steamships built in the United States—W. Cramp & Sons—John Roach & Son—Full and correct account of the construction and career of the iron-turreted *Monitor*—Winslow & Griswold, iron manufacturers, took all the risks if it should prove to be a failure—Theodore R. Timby—Statistics of iron and steel shipbuilding in the United States down to 1891—Biographical sketch of John Ericsson, ... Pages 442–447

CHAPTER L.

THE HISTORY OF CUT AND WIRE NAILS.

Cut nails first made in the United States—Shubal Wilder's account of early cut-nail machines—Wire nails first made in the United States at New York in 1851 or 1852 by William Hassall—The American Wire Nail Company, at Covington, Kentucky, the pioneer in this country in the manufacture of the standard wire nail—Statistics of the production of cut nails and wire nails in the United States, ... Pages 448–451

CHAPTER LI.

IMPROVEMENTS IN AMERICAN BLAST FURNACE PRACTICE.

Interesting information concerning English and colonial pig iron in 1730—First application of the hot-blast in the United States made by William Henry in 1834 at Oxford

Furnace, New Jersey—Improvements in the hot-blast by Samuel Thomas and John Player—First fire-brick hot-blast stoves in the United States—Utilization of blast-furnace gases—David Thomas introduces powerful blowing engines—Good work by one of the Cooper furnaces at Phillipsburg, New Jersey, in 1850—Also by one of the Isabella furnaces near Pittsburgh—Also by Furnace F of the Edgar Thomson works near Pittsburgh—Also by Hinkle (charcoal) Furnace at Ashland, Wisconsin—First coke furnace " banked up " in the United States—Biographical sketches of Achilles Christian Wilhelm von Faber du Faur and Christian Edward Detmold, . . . Pages 452–458

CHAPTER LII.

THE MANUFACTURE OF TINPLATES IN THE UNITED STATES.

First tinplates made in the United States—Statistics of importations of tinplates into the United States from 1871 to 1890, ... Page 459

CHAPTER LIII.

MISCELLANEOUS FACTS RELATING TO THE AMERICAN IRON AND STEEL INDUSTRIES.

Natural gas first used in the manufacture of iron in 1874—First bar iron rolled in New England—The Phœnix wrought-iron column—John Griffen's valuable contribution to rolling-mill economy in 1846—Good work by the Reading Steam Forge in 1856—Description of Park, Brother & Co.'s steam hammer, built in 1881—Description of the steam hammer of the Bethlehem Iron Company, completed in 1891—Slitting mills in the United States in 1884—The first wire suspension bridge in the United States—First wire fence in the United States—Biographical sketches, ... Pages 460–466

CHAPTER LIV.

EARLY DISCOVERIES OF COAL IN THE UNITED STATES.

First mention of coal in the United States by Father Hennepin, who found it on the Illinois river in 1679—Discovered in Virginia in 1701—Discovered in Western Pennsylvania—Mines opened at Pittsburgh—In Clearfield county, Pennsylvania—Virginia mines the first worked in America—First shipments of Cumberland coal—Discovered west of the Mississippi by Lewis and Clarke in 1804—Anthracite coal discovered in the Wyoming Valley in 1766—Discovered at Carbondale and other places in Eastern Pennsylvania—Early experiments in its use—Incorporation of the Lehigh Coal and Navigation Company—First use of anthracite coal in smiths' forges and in dwelling houses —Coal in Alabama first noticed in 1834—Beginning of the manufacture of Connellsville coke—Statistics of the production of coal in the United States, . . Pages 467–478

CHAPTER LV.

BRITISH EFFORTS TO PREVENT THE DEVELOPMENT OF THE AMERICAN IRON INDUSTRY.

Full extracts from various English and American writers and from British statutes to show that it was long the settled policy of the British Government to prevent the development of any manufacturing industries in the American colonies except those which produced raw materials suitable for further manufacture in Great Britain—The colonial iron industry an especial object of unfriendly legislation, . . . Pages 479–493

CHAPTER LVI.

THE AMERICAN IRON INDUSTRY LONG DEPRESSED BY FOREIGN COMPETITION.

Depression in the American iron industry after the Revolution caused partly by low duties on competing foreign products—Pennsylvania opposed to protecting her iron industry in 1785—Dr. Schoepf's account of the American iron industry in 1788—Tariff legislation did not help the American iron industry until 1812, . . Pages 494–497

CHAPTER LVII.

IMPEDIMENTS TO THE CHEAP PRODUCTION OF IRON AND STEEL IN THE UNITED STATES.

Wages in the iron and steel industries of the United States higher than in Europe and the cost of transportation of raw materials greater because the distances they must be transported are longer—English testimony on these subjects, ... Pages 498–501

CHAPTER LVIII.

WASHINGTON AND LINCOLN THE DESCENDANTS OF COLONIAL IRONMASTERS.

The father of George Washington a manufacturer of pig iron at Accokeek Furnace, in Virginia—The two half-brothers of George Washington and other relatives were also pig-iron manufacturers—Abraham Lincoln descended from Mordecai Lincoln, a native of Hingham, Plymouth county, Massachusetts, who was one of the founders of the Bound Brook Iron Works, in Plymouth county, in 1703—Genealogy of the Lincoln family from Mordecai Lincoln to Abraham Lincoln, ... Pages 502–508

CHAPTER LIX.

PRODUCTION AND PRICES OF IRON AND STEEL IN THE UNITED STATES.

Statistics of the production of iron and steel in the United States from 1810 to 1890—Tables of prices of iron and steel in the United States from 1794 to 1890—Production of iron ore in the United States in 1880 and 1889, ... Pages 509–516

CHAPTER LX.

IMPORTS AND EXPORTS OF IRON AND STEEL BY THE UNITED STATES.

Colonial exports of pig iron and bar iron from 1717 to 1776—Values of the imports and exports of iron and steel by the United States from 1871 to 1890, ... Pages 517–518

CHAPTER LXI.

MISCELLANEOUS STATISTICS OF IRON, STEEL, IRON ORE, AND COAL.

Production of pig iron and coal by Great Britain and Germany for a long series of years down to the close of 1890—The world's production of basic steel to the close of 1890—The world's production of pig iron, steel, iron ore, and coal by countries in 1890 and other recent years—Percentage of production by the United States, . . . Pages 519–524

CHAPTER LXII.

IMPORTANT USES OF IRON AND STEEL IN THE UNITED STATES.

The people of the United States are the largest *per capita* consumers of iron and steel in the world—Details of the more important uses of iron and steel, . . . Pages 525–531

CHAPTER LXIII.

CONCLUSION.

General review of the progress of the world's iron and steel industries in the last hundred years—Also of the great progress in these industries made by the United States in the last thirty years—Comparison of the present development of these industries in the United States with their condition at various periods during the last hundred years, ... Pages 532–540

PERSONAL INDEX.

Names of the iron and steel pioneers and other iron and steel manufacturers, Pages 541–554

THE smith also sitting by the anvil, and considering the iron work, the vapour of the fire wasteth his flesh, and he fighteth with the heat of the furnace: the noise of the hammer and the anvil is ever in his ears, and his eyes look still upon the pattern of the thing that he maketh; he setteth his mind to finish his work, and watcheth to polish it perfectly.—Ecclesiasticus, 38, 28.

THE MANUFACTURE OF IRON IN ALL AGES.

CHAPTER I.

THE EARLIEST USE OF IRON.

THE use of iron can be traced to the earliest ages of antiquity. Copper and bronze, or brass, may have been used at as early a period as iron, and for many centuries after their use began they undoubtedly superseded iron to a large extent, but the common theory that there was a copper or a bronze age before iron was either known or used is discredited by Old Testament history, by the earlier as well as the later literature of the ancient Greeks, and by the discoveries of modern antiquarians.

In his inaugural address as President of the Iron and Steel Institute, delivered in May, 1885, Dr. John Percy, the eminent English metallurgist, briefly considered the question whether iron was or was not used before bronze. He said : "It has always appeared to me reasonable to infer from metallurgical considerations that the age of iron would have preceded the age of bronze. The primitive method, not yet wholly extinct, of extracting iron from its ores is a much simpler process than that of producing bronze, and indicates a much less advanced state of the metallurgic arts. In the case of iron all that is necessary is to heat the ore strongly in contact with charcoal; whereas, in the case of bronze, which is an alloy of copper and tin, both copper and tin have to be obtained by smelting their respective ores separately, to be subsequently melted together in due proportions, and the resulting alloy to be cast in moulds, requiring considerable skill in their preparation."

Iron was doubtless first used in Western Asia, the birthplace of the human race, and in the northern parts of Africa which are near to Asia. Tubal-cain, who was born in the seventh generation from Adam, is described in King James's version of the 4th chapter of Genesis as "an instructor of every artificer in brass and iron." In the revised version, which appeared in 1885, he is described as "the forger of every cutting instrument of brass and iron." The Egyptians, whose existence as a nation dates from the second generation after Noah, and whose civilization is the most ancient of which we have any exact knowledge, were at an early period familiar with both the use and the manufacture of iron, although very little iron ore has ever been found within the boundaries of Egypt itself. Iron tools are mentioned by Herodotus as having been used in the construction of the pyramids. In the sepulchres at Thebes and Memphis, cities of such great antiquity that their origin is lost in obscurity, butchers are represented as using tools the colors of which lead antiquarians to conclude that they were made of iron or steel. Iron sickles are also pictured in the tombs at Memphis. At Thebes numerous articles of iron have been found which are preserved by the New York Historical Society and are about three thousand years old. They include an iron helmet, with a neck-guard in chain armor ; a fragment of a breastplate, made of pieces of iron in the form of scales, one of which takes the shape of a cartouche and has stamped thereon the name of the Egyptian king, Shishak, who invaded Jerusalem 971 years before Christ ; and an iron arrow-head. A war-club, studded with iron spikes, and an iron instrument with a wooden handle, both found at Sakkarah, in Egypt, are in the same collection, which was made by Dr. Henry Abbott, an English surgeon, during a residence of twenty years in Cairo, where he died on March 30, 1859.

Thothmes the First, who is supposed to have reigned about seventeen centuries before Christ, is said, in a long inscription at Karnak, to have received from the chiefs, tributary kings, or allied sovereigns of Lower Egypt presents of silver and gold, "bars of wrought metal, and vessels of copper, and of bronze, and of iron." From the region of Memphis he received wine, iron, lead, wrought metal, animals, and other products. An expedition which the same king sent against Chadasha brought back among the spoil which it had taken "iron of the mountains, 40 cubes."

Belzoni found under the feet of one of the sphinxes at Karnak an iron sickle which is supposed to have been placed there at least six hundred years before Christ. In 1837 a piece of iron was taken from an inner joint of the great pyramid at Gizeh under circumstances which justify the theory that it is as old as the pyramid itself. Both of these relics are preserved in the British Museum. The reference to iron in Deuteronomy, iv. 20, apparently indicates that in the time of Moses the Egyptians were engaged in its manufacture, and that the Israelites were at least as familiar with the art as their taskmasters. "But the Lord hath taken you, and brought you forth out of the iron furnace, even out of Egypt." This expression is repeated in 1st Kings, viii. 51. A small piece of very pure iron was found under the obelisk which was removed from Alexandria to New York in 1880 by Commander H. H. Gorringe, of the United States Navy. This obelisk was erected by Thothmes the Third at Heliopolis about 1600 years before Christ, and removed to Alexandria twenty-two years before the Christian era. The iron found under it was therefore at least 1900 years old. Commander Gorringe died in New York city on July 7, 1885.

As iron ore of remarkable richness is now found in Algeria, in the northern part of Africa, occupying the territory of ancient Carthage, it is entirely reasonable to suppose that the Carthaginians, nearly a thousand years before Christ, and the Libyans and other native inhabitants whom the Carthaginians succeeded, would not be behind their Egyptian cotemporaries in a knowledge of the use and manufacture of iron. The Libyans were a highly civilized people. It is certain that the iron mines of Algeria were worked by the Romans before the Christian era. The native tribes in the interior of Africa have long made iron by the most primitive methods.

The development in modern times of the rich iron ores of Algeria is a most interesting historical fact, as the Algerian mines are the only mines of iron ore in either Asia or Africa which are now operated on an extensive scale, and the only mines worthy of mention on either continent from which the iron and steel works of Europe and America draw a part of

their supplies of ore. The present extensive development of
the Algerian iron-ore mines dates from about 1844. All the
iron ore that is mined is exported. In 1872 the shipments
from these mines to European countries, especially to France,
had greatly increased. In that year the total production of
the mines was nearly 400,000 tons. The total production in
1886 was 492,936 tons.

Iron ore is supposed to have been mined in Morocco long
before the beginning of the Carthaginian rule in Northern
Africa, and it is said that old Mauritanian iron-ore mines can
yet be traced at the foot of the Djebel Hadyd, a few miles
from Mogadore, on the Atlantic coast.

The use of iron and the art of manufacturing it were introduced into the southern and western portions of Arabia
at an early day, and this may have been done by the Egyptians; it is at least fully established that some of their own
works were located east of the Red sea. The ruins of extensive iron works of great antiquity and of undoubted Egyptian origin were discovered by Mr. Hartland near the Wells
of Moses, in the Sinaitic peninsula, about 1873. They are
fully described by St. John V. Day, in his *Prehistoric Use
of Iron and Steel*. Large heaps of iron cinder, very rich in
iron, are found near the works. The "iron furnace" from
which the Israelites were brought forth may have embraced these works. The countries which lie south of Egypt are
supposed by some antiquarian writers to have made iron in
large quantities in prehistoric times.

Iron was known to the Chaldeans, the Babylonians, and
the Assyrians, who were cotemporaries of the early Egyptians. Some writers suppose that the Egyptians derived their
supply of iron principally from these Asiatic neighbors and
from the Arabians. Ornaments of iron have been found in
Chaldean ruins, and Chaldean inscriptions show that iron was
known to the most ancient inhabitants of Mesopotamia. In
the ruins of Nineveh the English antiquarian, Layard, found
many articles of iron and various inscriptions referring to its
use. Among the articles discovered by him were iron scales
of armor, from two to three inches in length. "Two or three
baskets were filled with these relics." He also found "a perfect helmet of iron, inlaid with copper bands." In the Brit-

ish Museum several tools of iron are preserved which were found at Nineveh by Layard, including a saw and a pick. The art of casting bronze over iron, which has only recently been introduced into modern metallurgy, was known to the Assyrians. At Babylon iron was used in the fortifications of the city just previous to its capture by Cyrus, in the sixth century before Christ. In a celebrated inscription Nebuchadnezzar declares : "With pillars and beams plated with copper and strengthened with iron I built up its gates." The huge stones of the bridge built by his daughter Nitocris were held together by bands of iron fixed in place by molten lead.

The Book of Job, which relates to a patriarchal period between Abraham and Moses, contains many references to iron, even to "bars of iron," "barbed irons," "the iron weapon," and the "bow of steel." In the 19th chapter and 24th verse the "iron pen," which could be used to engrave upon a rock, is mentioned. In the 20th chapter and 24th verse iron and steel are both mentioned, showing that in the time of Job the two metals were both in use. "He shall flee from the iron weapon, and the bow of steel shall strike him through." In the 28th chapter and 2d verse it is declared that "iron is taken out of the earth." Job is supposed to have lived in the northern part of Arabia, in the land of Uz, which was separated by the Euphrates from Ur of the Chaldees, where Abraham was born. Iron ore of remarkable richness is said to be still found between the Euphrates and the Tigris.

Moses led the children of Israel out of Egypt fifteen or sixteen hundred years before the Christian era. In the story of their wanderings iron is frequently mentioned. When the Israelites spoiled the Midianites they took from them iron and other metals. "An instrument of iron" is mentioned in Numbers, xxxv. 16. Canaan, the land of promise, is described by Moses in Deuteronomy, viii. 9, as "a land whose stones are iron." Iron is said to be still made in small quantities in the Lebanon mountains. In Deuteronomy, xxvii. 5, 6, and in Joshua, viii. 31, the use of iron tools in building an altar of "whole stones" to the Lord is prohibited, which shows that the Israelites in the days of Moses not only possessed a knowledge of iron tools which would cut stone, but that the Egyptians, from whom they had recently separated, must have possessed the same knowledge. In Deuteronomy, xxviii. 48, a "yoke of iron" is mentioned.

After the Israelites came into possession of Canaan iron is frequently mentioned in their history, some of the earliest references being to chariots of iron, which the Canaanites used in their wars with them, and to various agricultural implements and other tools of iron and to iron weapons of war. The references to chariots of iron in Joshua, xvii. 16, and in Judges, i. 19, and iv. 3, show that the Canaanites were far advanced in the military art. In the elaborate description of the armor of Goliath it is said that "his spear's head weighed six hundred shekels of iron." Axes and saws and harrows of iron are mentioned in the reign of David, and axes and hammers and tools of iron are mentioned in the reign of Solomon. In Proverbs, xxvii. 17, Solomon speaks of one use of iron which shows that knives must have been made of it in his day. "Iron sharpeneth iron ; so a man sharpeneth the countenance of his friend." We read also in Ecclesiastes, x. 10 : "If the iron be blunt, and he do not whet the edge, then must he put to more strength." When David, about a thousand years before the Christian era, made preparations for the building of the temple he "prepared iron in abundance for the nails for the doors of the gates and for the joinings ;" and in his instructions to Solomon concerning it he said that he had prepared "brass and iron without weight," and that "of the gold, the silver, and the brass, and the iron, there is no number." When Solomon came to build the temple he sent to Hiram, king of Tyre, for "a man cunning to work in gold, and in silver, and in brass, and in iron." The Phœnicians were celebrated as workers in all the metals, and Tyre was their great city. Isaiah speaks of harrows of iron, and in the 34th verse of the 10th chapter iron axes are clearly referred to. "And he shall cut down the thickets of the forests with iron." Jeremiah speaks of "an iron pillar." In Amos we read of "threshing instruments of iron."

The great strength of iron is frequently referred to in the Old Testament. In Psalms, ii. 9, we read : "Thou shalt break them with a rod of iron ;" in cvii. 10, we read of those who sit in darkness as "being bound in affliction and iron ;" in cxlix. 8, we read also of binding "kings with chains, and their nobles with fetters of iron." Daniel says that "iron breaketh in pieces and subdueth all things."

Some writers have contended that the word which is translated iron in the Old Testament frequently means some other metal. It is a sufficient answer to this criticism to say that the translators of King James's version and of the revised version of 1885 agree in nearly every instance in their use of the word iron; but to this agreement of learned men three hundred years apart the yet more significant fact may be added that iron is frequently mentioned in the Old Testament in connection with other metals. In addition to the quotations already given sustaining this statement the reader is referred to Deuteronomy, xxviii. 23; 1st Chronicles, xxix. 2 and 7; Isaiah, xlv. 2, and lx. 17; Ezekiel, xxii. 20, and xxvii. 12. It may also be added that in Martin Luther's translation of the Old Testament into German he always uses the word *eisen* wherever the word iron appears in English translations.

In Jeremiah, xv. 12, the question is asked by the prophet: "Shall iron break the northern iron and the steel?" The northern iron and steel here referred to were probably products of Chalybia, a small district of Armenia, lying on the southeastern shore of the Black sea, the inhabitants of which, called Chalibees or Chalybians, were famous in the days of Asiatic pre-eminence for the fine quality of their iron and steel. Herodotus, in the fifth century before Christ, speaks of "the Chalybians, a people of ironworkers." They are said to have invented the art of converting iron into steel, but it is probable that, as they used magnetic sand, which is very free from impurities and is easily smelted in small quantities, they made steel mainly. Latin and Greek names for steel were derived from the name of this people. From the same source we obtain the words now in common use, chalybean and chalybeate.

Other eastern nations doubtless made steel at as early a day as the Chalybians. In Ezekiel, xxvii. 12, the merchants of Tarshish are said to supply Tyre with iron and other metals, and in the 19th verse of the same chapter the merchants of Dan and Javan are said to supply its market with bright iron. Tarshish is supposed to have been a city in the south of Spain, and Dan and Javan were possibly cities in the south

of Arabia. The name Tarshish may, however, have referred
generally to the countries lying on the western shore of the
Mediterranean and beyond the Pillars of Hercules. Dan and
Javan may have supplied iron made in the southern part of
Arabia, or they may have traded in the bright iron, or steel,
of India. The period embraced in the references quoted from
Ezekiel was about six hundred years before Christ. Both
Tyre and Sidon traded in all the products of the east and
the west for centuries before and for some time after Ezekiel,
and iron was one of the products which they supplied to their
neighbors, the Israelites.

The Persians and their northern neighbors, the Medes,
made iron and steel long before the Christian era, and so did
the Parthians and other Scythian tribes. The Parthian ar-
row was first tipped with bronze, but afterwards with steel.
The Parthian kings are said to have engaged with pride in
the forging and sharpening of arrow-heads. Herodotus says
that an "antique iron sword" was planted on the top of the
mount of worship used by the Scythians. Iron is still made
in Persia by primitive methods, and so also is steel, but both
in small quantities.

India appears to have been acquainted with the manufacture of iron and steel from a very early period. Day says
that in the British Museum are iron and steel tools, probably
three thousand years old, which were found in recent Indian
excavations. Ktesias, a Greek, who lived 400 years before
Christ, mentions Indian iron. When Alexander defeated Porus, one of the Punjaub kings, in the fourth century before
the Christian era, Porus gave him thirty pounds of Indian
steel, or wootz. This steel, which is still made in India and
Persia, was a true steel, of a quality unsurpassed even in our
day. It was and still is manufactured by a process of great
simplicity, similar to that by which crucible steel is now
made. Ages ago the city of Damascus manufactured its famous swords from Indian and Persian steel. Swords are still
made at Damascus, but of inferior quality. The cutlers of
India, however, now make the best of swords from native
steel. George Thompson told Wendell Phillips that he saw
a man in Calcutta throw a handful of floss silk into the air
which a Hindoo cut into pieces with his sabre.

The people of India further appear to have become familiar at an early period in their history with processes for the manufacture of iron on a large scale which have since been lost. A cylindrical wrought-iron pillar, which weighs many tons, is now standing at the principal gate of the ancient mosque of the Kutub, near Delhi, in India. A highly ornamented capital forms the upper part of the pillar. An inscription in Sanscrit is usually supposed to assign the erection of the pillar to the fourth century of the Christian era. In the ruins of Indian temples of great antiquity there have been found wrought-iron beams similar in size and appearance to those used in the construction of buildings at the present time. These iron beams are fully described by Day.

Two American scientists have visited in recent years the iron pillar at Delhi, and have favored us with their impressions concerning it—Mr. John C. F. Randolph, of New York city, visiting it in 1874, and Dr. Frank Cowan, of Greensburg, Pennsylvania, in 1884. Mr. Randolph says : " I sought to obtain a few grains of the metal for analysis, but it completely dulled two cold chisels worked by my servant, without producing any marks on the base of the pillar." Dr. Cowan circumstantially describes the pillar as follows : " The iron pillar is a polished and inscribed, cylindrical and tapering, shaft of metal, surmounted with a capital which consists of a series of beveled rims one above the other ; and, as it has been found to be by measurement, it has a total height of 23 feet and 8 inches, about 22 feet and 6 inches of which are above the ground and 14 inches below, and a diameter below of 16.4 inches and above of 12.05 inches. The capital is about 3½ feet long."

The period at which China first made iron is uncertain, but great antiquity is claimed for its manufacture in that mysterious country. Iron is mentioned in a Chinese record which is said to have been written two thousand years before Christ, and in other ancient Chinese writings iron and steel are both mentioned. Pliny the Elder, writing in the first century of the Christian era, thus speaks of the iron of the Seres, which is the Latin name for the people of China : " Howbeit, as many kinds of iron as there be, none shall match in goodness the steel that cometh from the Seres, for

this commodity also, as hard ware as it is, they send and
sell with their soft silks and fine furs. In a second degree
of goodness may be placed the Parthian iron." This early
reference to Chinese steel is historically very valuable.

Iron is supposed to have been made in small quantities
in Japan and Corea in ancient times. It is now made by
primitive methods in both these countries and in China, although modern methods have been attempted in both China
and Japan. The remarkable skill and taste of the Japanese
metal-workers in modern times, including their production
of swords of the finest temper and keenest edge and other articles of iron and steel, is well known and is a constant mar-
vel to the people of other countries. The Chinese and the
Coreans are also noted for their skill as armorers and in the
manufacture of various domestic utensils of iron and steel.

. Further inquiry in these pages into the evidences of the
use of iron by the oldest nations of antiquity is unnecessary.
It may be assumed as susceptible of abundant proof that
the knowledge of the use of iron was common to the people
of Asia and of Northern Africa long prior to the Christian
era. The Egyptians and their immediate neighbors in Asia,
and the Libyans and others in Africa, probably made iron
long before the days of Moses. The Phœnicians would carry
the art of making iron to their own great colony, Carthage,
which was founded as early at least as the ninth century
before Christ, and to all the colonies and nations inhabiting
the northern and southern and western shores of the Mediterranean. Phœnician and Carthaginian merchants obtained
iron from such western countries as Morocco and Spain, and
possibly even from India and China in the east, as well as
from nearer sources. But in time the merchants of Tyre
and the ships of Tarshish deserted the places that long had
known them ; empire after empire fell in ruins ; and with the
fading away of Asiatic and African civilization and mag-
nificence the manufacture and the use of iron in Asia and
Africa ceased to advance. Egypt has certainly not made
iron for about two thousand years, and probably no more
iron is made in all Asia to-day than was made in its borders
twenty-five centuries ago, when Babylon was "the glory of
kingdoms, the beauty of the Chaldees' excellency."

CHAPTER II.

THE EARLY USE OF IRON IN EUROPE.

THE authentic history of the use of iron in Europe does not begin until about the period of the first Olympiad, corresponding to the year 776 before the Christian era, although Grecian poetry and the fables of the Grecian heroic age have transmitted to us many references to iron long prior to that period. Authentic Grecian history itself does not begin until the first Olympiad.

One of the earliest of Grecian fables tells of the hurling of Hephæstus, or Vulcan, the Greek god of fire, from Olympus by Jupiter, and of his falling upon the island of Lemnos, where he established iron forges, afterwards forging the armor of Achilles and the weapons of Hercules. About the time of Moses, fifteen or sixteen centuries before Christ, the Phœnicians are said to have introduced into Greece the art of working in iron and other metals. Minos, king of Crete, is said to have been indebted to them for the tools which enabled him to build his powerful fleet. In the fifteenth century before Christ the burning of the forests on Mount Ida, in Crete, is said to have accidentally communicated to the inhabitants the art of obtaining iron from native ores. This discovery enabled the Idæi Dactyli, who were priests of Cybele, to introduce the manufacture of iron and steel into Phrygia, a Greek colony in Asia Minor.

So read some of the stories which have come down to us from the heroic age of Greece, all of which may be wholly fabulous, but there is nothing improbable in the conclusion· which may be derived from them, that they point to a very early use of iron by the Greeks. From Phœnicia certainly, and probably also from Egypt, they would be likely to derive some knowledge of its use in the mechanic arts about a thousand years before Christ. It is worthy of notice that the mythologies of both Greece and Egypt attributed the invention of the art of manufacturing iron to the gods, a fact which of itself may be regarded as affording sufficient proof of the great antiquity of the art in both of these countries.

The poems of Homer, who is supposed to have lived about 850 years before the Christian era, and therefore before the period of authentic Grecian history, make frequent mention of iron. The art of hardening and tempering steel is fully described in the reference to the plunging of the firebrand of Ulysses into the eye of Polyphemus, an act which is likened to that of the smith who "plunges the loud-hissing axe into cold water to temper it, for hence is the strength of iron." It would appear, however, from the offer by Achilles of a "mass of iron, shapeless from the forge," as a prize at the funeral games of Patroclus, that iron was not abundant in Greece at the time of the Trojan war, nor in the days of Homer himself. Troy fell in the year 1184 before the Christian era. Dr. Schliemann has found no traces of iron in its ruins. The address of Achilles to the Greeks when offering the prize indicates how valuable iron was to them in the heroic age.

> Stand forth, whoever will contend for this;
> And if broad fields and rich be his this mass
> Will last him many years. The man who tends
> His flocks, or guides his plow, need not be sent
> To town for iron: he will have it here.

When Pisander and Hippolochus begged Agamemnon to save their lives they offered him as ransom the "treasures" in the houses of Antimachus, their father, "brass, gold, and well-wrought iron." Homer mentions steel axes as valuable prizes to be contended for in the Grecian games, and he also mentions steel weapons of war, although rarely. He speaks again of some iron as being bright and white, the inference being that steel is referred to. The Right Honorable William E. Gladstone, in his *Homeric Synchronisms*, says: "Iron is in Homer extremely rare and precious. He mentions nothing massive that is made of this material." Mr. Gladstone cites a number of references in Homer to iron and steel—the arrowhead of Pandaros, the dagger of Achilles, "the cutting tool of the chariot-maker for such fine work as shaping the felloe of the wheel," a knife for slaying oxen, and axes and adzes of steel.

Hesiod, who is supposed to have been cotemporary with Homer, mentions iron and some of its important qualities.

He uses the phrases, bright iron and black iron. Lycurgus, who is supposed to have lived about the time of Homer and Hesiod, is said to have required the Spartans to use iron as money; he "allowed nothing but bars of iron to pass in exchange for every commodity." These bars, for which iron rings or quoits were afterwards substituted, may have been made from the iron ores which were found in abundance in Laconia, or they may have been obtained abroad.

We come next to that period of Grecian history which introduces us to historical personages and historical events. The iron ores of Elba were worked by the Greeks as early as the year 700 before Christ. They called the island Æthalia, "from the blazes of the iron works." The working of the ores of this island is mentioned by Herodotus, who lived in the fifth century before Christ; by Diodorus, a Sicilian historian of the first century before Christ; and by Strabo, a Greek traveler and geographer, who lived at the beginning of the Christian era. The Phœnicians made iron on the island of Eubœa at a very early day, and the Greeks afterwards followed the same pursuit on the same island. Strabo speaks of the mines of Eubœa as being partially exhausted in his day. In Bœotia, on the mainland of Greece, iron was also made in very early times, and probably in other parts of the Grecian mainland and on the Grecian islands where iron ore is now found. On the island of Seriphos the ore is so rich that many cargoes of it have been exported to the United States and Great Britain in recent years.

Herodotus speaks of iron heads to lances and arrows in his day. He also mentions a silver bowl inlaid with iron, the work of Glaucus the Chian, which Alyattes dedicated at Delphi about the middle of the sixth century before Christ. Chalybian steel was imported into Greece in the time of Herodotus; and in the time of Aristotle, who lived a century later, the Greeks were themselves familiar with the manufacture of steel. Sophocles, who died in the year 406 before Christ, speaks of the tempering of iron in water. The manufacture of swords of steel about this time received much attention in Greece, as it did elsewhere. The father of Demosthenes was a manufacturer of arms, and probably of steel swords, in the fourth century before Christ. Iron and steel

weapons began to displace those of bronze in most Mediterranean countries soon after the battle of Marathon, which was
fought in the year 490 before Christ. When Xerxes invaded
Greece, ten years after the battle of Marathon, the Assyrians
in his army carried wooden clubs " knotted with iron." The
use of iron scythes as well as iron sickles was common among
the Greeks about this time. Dr. Schliemann says that iron
was known to the Myceneans, whose capital city, Mycenæ,
was destroyed in the year 468 before Christ. In the fourth
century before Christ Alexander is said by Pliny to have
strengthened a bridge over the Euphrates, at Zeugma, with
a chain made of links of iron.

Daimachus, a writer who was cotemporary with Alexander, enumerates four different kinds of steel and their uses,
the Chalybdic, Synopic, Lydian, and Lacedæmonian. Each
kind of steel was adapted to the manufacture of particular
tools. From the Chalybdic and Synopic were made ordinary tools; from the Lacedæmonian were made files, augers,
chisels, and stone-cutting implements; and from the Lydian
were made swords, razors, and surgical instruments. The accounts left by this writer. and by other writers indicate great
proficiency in the use of steel by the Greeks, and the possession by them of much skill in its manufacture.

A few years ago some peasants, digging near the banks
of the Danube, on the Hungarian side, opposite to Belgrade,
turned up a very beautiful and finely preserved iron or steel
helmet, which is believed to be a specimen of antique Greek
work, dating from probably three or four centuries before
the Christian era. It was found in the midst of wind-blown
hillocks, or dunes, of dry, shifting sand; hence probably its
excellent state of preservation. The helmet is light and thin,
but by no means flimsy or unsubstantial. At the country
house of Mr. G. P. Morosini, at Riverdale, on the Hudson
river, in New York, is a costly collection of arms and armor
from the wars of long ago, which includes a Greek helmet
dating back hundreds of years before Christ. It has rusted
through in two places, and looks now like old sheet iron.

A description of one of the naval monsters constructed by
Archimedes for Hiero, king of Syracuse, about the middle of
the third century before the Christian era, shows the great

extent to which the use of iron had then been carried by the
Greeks. "To each of the three masts was attached a couple
of engines which darted iron bars and masses of lead against
the enemy. The sides of the ship bristled with iron spikes,
designed to protect it against boarding; and on all sides were
likewise grapples which could be flung by machines into the
galleys of the foe. The ship was supplied with twelve anchors, of which four were of wood and eight of iron."

According to accepted chronology Rome was built in the
year 753 before the Christian era. It reached the culmination of its power about the end of the first century of that era.
The period from its foundation to the beginning of its decline embraced about nine hundred years. During the first
part of this period Rome was favored with the experience of
older nations in the use and manufacture of iron, and during
the last part of it she greatly contributed by her energy and
progressive spirit to extend its use and increase its production. The Greeks were the great teachers of the Romans in
all the arts, including metallurgy; but the Etruscans, who
were neighbors of the Romans, and by whom they were in
time supplanted, also contributed greatly to their knowledge
of the arts of ancient civilization. The Etruscans, however,
owed their civilization in large part to the Tyrrhenian Greeks,
with whom they coalesced centuries before Rome was founded. Etruria was largely devoted to commerce, and among the
countries with which it traded were Phœnicia and Carthage,
as well as Greece and its colonies. From all these countries
Etruscan civilization was invigorated and diversified, and
Rome in its early days enjoyed the benefit of this invigor-
ation and diversification. That it early acquired from the
Etruscans a knowledge of the use and manufacture of iron
can easily be imagined, and subsequent direct contact with
Grecian colonies and with Greece itself would extend this
knowledge.

The island of Elba lay off the Etruscan coast, and, as has
already been stated, its iron ores were extensively used by the
Greeks about the time when Rome was founded. Its mines
were also worked by the Etruscans, and its ores were smelted
both on the island and on the mainland. They were also
taken to other countries to be converted into iron. After a

lapse of twenty-five centuries the iron ores of this celebrated island are still exported, many cargoes annually finding their way to the United States. The Romans would also obtain iron from the islands of Corsica and Sardinia, but chiefly from Corsica. This island was occupied by the Ligurians and the Etruscans about the time of the founding of Rome, and by the Etruscans for centuries afterwards. The Carthaginians succeeded the Etruscans, and the Romans the Carthaginians. Iron has been made in Corsica from the earliest times, and is still made in small quantities. The island has given its name to the Corsican forge, which is yet in use. A few years ago ten of these forges were in operation in Corsica, and they were probably identical in character with those which were used on the island when Rome was founded.

Iron is frequently mentioned in the early history of Rome. A war between the Romans and the Etruscans, the latter being led by their king, Porsenna, occurred in the year 507 before Christ, and among the conditions of peace exacted by the victorious Etruscan king was one which prohibited the Romans from using iron except for agricultural purposes. This incident confirms the theory that iron was in common use by the Greeks at the period mentioned. In the year 390 before Christ, when Rome was about to be ransomed from the Gauls, under Brennus, by a large payment of gold, Camillus, the Roman dictator, indignantly demurred, and declared that Rome should be ransomed with iron and not with gold, and that his sword alone should purchase peace. Another notable mention of iron in the early history of Rome occurs in the account of the defeat of the Carthaginian fleet in the first Punic war, in the third century before the Christian era. The consul, Duilius, took command of the hastily-constructed Roman fleet, and upon encountering the Carthaginian fleet he connected his ships with those of the enemy by means of grappling-irons, through which, and the superior prowess of the Romans, he secured for Rome, in the year 260 before Christ, its first naval triumph. The Etruscan town of Pupluna is said to have furnished Scipio with iron in the second Punic war, and it is stated that many thousand tons of scoria are now lying on the beach close to its site.

Some of the swords and javelins of the Romans were

certainly made of iron, or more likely of steel, as early as
the fourth century before the Christian era, but their agricultural implements, as has been explained in the reference
to Etruria, were made of iron at an earlier period. The Roman battering-ram, which was borrowed from the Greeks, had
a head of iron, and iron rings were placed around its beam.
The Romans used this engine of war at the siege of Syracuse
in the year 212 before Christ. Prior to this time iron and
steel tools were in common use among the shipwrights, carpenters, masons, and other tradesmen of Rome. At the beginning of the Christian era iron was in general use throughout the Roman empire, the supply being derived from many
countries which were subject to its sway. In the Acts of the
Apostles, xii. 10, is a statement which indicates that iron was
used at this period for architectural purposes and in public
works. "When they were past the first and the second ward
they came unto the iron gate that leadeth unto the city."
Iron was, however, used at this time especially for tools, agricultural implements, and weapons of offense and defense.

Pliny says that "iron ores are to be found almost everywhere." He describes in detail the various uses to which
iron was applied in his day, and places it at the head of all
the metals. Vestiges of iron used by the Romans in the first
century after Christ have been found in the ruins of the
Coliseum, which was built by the emperor Vespasian. This
iron was used as clamps to bind together the stones of that
remarkable structure. Iron has also been found in the ruins
of Pompeii, which was destroyed about the time the Coliseum
was built; also steel surgical instruments.

In the northern part of Italy, just south of the Alps, corresponding to Piedmont and Lombardy of the present day,
iron was made by the Romans in the first and second centuries before the Christian era. This part of Italy has continued to make small quantities of iron ever since the days of
Pliny, the business being mainly confined to small forges
and blast furnaces. Pliny speaks of the excellence of the
water at Comum, now Como, for tempering iron, although
he says that iron ores were not found there. Italy was very
prominent in the middle ages in the manufacture of ornamental smithwork of iron, and for the manufacture of arms

and armor its great city of Milan was widely celebrated from the end of the fourteenth to the end of the sixteenth century.

Among the provinces which contributed largely to the Roman supply of iron was Noricum, corresponding to the present Styria and Carinthia in Austria. Both Pliny and Ovid, who lived at the beginning of the Christian era, speak of Norican iron as being of superior quality, and it is certain that *ferrum noricum* was celebrated throughout·Italy before their day. The best of swords were made from it in the reign of Augustus and were favorably mentioned by Horace. The spathic ores of Styria and Carinthia are still held in high favor; and the supply of ore, especially from the famous iron mountains of Erzberg and Hüttenberg, shows no signs of exhaustion at the end of twenty centuries of almost constant use. Iron is still made in these provinces of Austria in small forges which are almost as primitive in character as those used by their ancient Celtic inhabitants. Celtic and Roman implements and medals, including a coin of the emperor Nerva, who lived in the first century of the Christian era, have been found in mounds of slag in the vicinity of Carinthian iron mines.

Cotemporaneously with the working by the Celts of the Norican iron mines, the Quadi, who inhabited the province of Moravia, lying north of Noricum, also made iron. The geographer, Ptolemy, who lived in the second century of the Christian era, makes mention of the Quadi as ironworkers. Iron was also made in Hungary at the beginning of the Christian era. A late writer, Anton Kerpely, of Buda-Pesth, says: " Even in the time of the Romans, and in the first century of our era, the excellent iron ores of Hungary were mined not far from the famous Trajan road and the Roman colonies lying near thereto." Great antiquity is also claimed for the iron industry of that vast country which was known to the Romans as Sarmatia, but is now known as Russia in Europe. The nomadic Scythians would doubtless carry the art of ironmaking to the Ural mountains, where iron ore was and still is abundant. One of the Greek poets calls Scythia " the mother of iron," Scythia comprising the countries lying north, east, and south of the Caspian sea.

The Phœnicians founded colonies in France and Spain

prior to the sixth century before Christ. They had settlements on the Garonne and Rhone in Southern Gaul. The ancient city of Massilia, now Marseilles, is supposed to occupy the site of a Phœnician trading-post which fell into the possession of the Phocæan Greeks about the period above mentioned, who gave to it great commercial and manufacturing importance. The Greeks planted other colonies in Southern France. The city of Tartessus, or Tarshish, is supposed to have been one of the Phœnician settlements in the south of Spain; the city of Gades, or Cadiz, was another. Tartessus stood between the two arms of the Guadalquivir; but in the time of Strabo, who died about the year 25 of the Christian era, it had ceased to exist. Gades was its near neighbor and still exists. The Phœnicians may have introduced the manufacture of iron among the native inhabitants of France and Spain; the Celtiberians of the latter country were certainly active in the mining and working of metals several hundred years before the Christian era, and maintained an extensive trade in metals with Tyre and Carthage.

Under Grecian influence, which succeeded that of the Phœnicians in Spain, the Celtiberians, who inhabited the central and northeastern parts of the country, continued to make iron, and to this was joined the manufacture of steel. The famous forges of Aragon and Catalonia were active during the Grecian occupation of Spain. The Carthaginians for a brief time succeeded the Greeks in Spain, and about two centuries before the Christian era the Romans succeeded the Carthaginians. The Romans greatly extended the arts of their advanced civilization among the native inhabitants of Spain. They gave special encouragement to the manufacture of iron and steel, although in justice to the Celtiberians it must be said that their metallurgical skill was at least equal to that of the Romans. Polybius, a Greek historian who flourished in the second century before Christ, says that the helmet and armor of the Roman soldier were of bronze, but that the sword was a cut-and-thrust blade of Spanish steel. At the battle of Cannæ, in the year 216 before Christ, the Romans had learned from the Carthaginians at very great cost the value of the Spanish sword.

Livy has recorded the fines which were imposed by Cato

the Censor on the Celtiberian iron works in the year 194 before Christ, after the Roman war with Spain. About the time these fines were imposed the town of Bilbilis, near the present Moorish-built town of Calatayud, in Aragon, and the little river Salo were celebrated as the centre of the iron district of Celtiberia. The water of the Salo was supposed to possess special qualities for tempering steel. The same excellence was attributed to some other streams in Spain and other ironmaking countries. Diodorus speaks of the excellent two-edged swords, "exactly tempered with steel," and of other arms which the Celtiberians in Aragon manufactured from rods of iron which had been rusted in the ground "to eat out all the weaker particles of the metal, and leave only the strongest and purest." He says that the swords which were manufactured from these rods "are so keen that there is no helmet or shield which can not be cut through by them." Plutarch, who died about the year 140 of the Christian era, gives the same account of the Celtiberian method of purifying iron. Pliny speaks of the excellent iron of Bilbilis and Turiasso, the latter a town in Tarragona, and of an extensive mountain of iron upon the coast of Biscay, probably Somorrostro. Iron ore from the coast of Biscay and other parts of Spain is now exported in large quantities to Great Britain, Germany, the United States, and other countries.

Toledo has been famous since the Roman occupation of Spain for its manufacture of steel swords, but this industry existed at Toledo before the appearance of the Romans. The town was captured by them in the year 192 before Christ. The Roman army from that time forward was provided with steel swords from Toledo and other places in Spain. The manufacture of Toledo blades probably attained its greatest development in the fifteenth and sixteenth centuries. A certain degree of mystery has always surrounded the manufacture of these swords, and the same may be said of the manufacture in ancient times of the equally celebrated Damascus blades.

The manufacture of swords at Toledo still continues in a restricted way. A recent traveler, describing the ruined condition of the ancient city, refers as follows to the building in which the famous blades were once forged in such great numbers : "A few artisans still work there for the Spanish army, but they do very little beyond turning out a few weapons for show."

The iron industry of Spain was the first in the world for hundreds of years after the Romans obtained a foothold in the country, surviving the downfall of the Roman power in the Peninsula in the fifth century after Christ and flourishing under the subsequent rule of the Visigoths. This distinction was strengthened when the Moors became masters of the greater part of Spain in the beginning of the eighth century of the Christian era. They stimulated the further development of the iron manufacture in the districts subject to their sway. At the same time the native inhabitants who had successfully resisted the Moorish arms continued to push their small Catalan forges still farther into the Pyrenees and along the coast of Biscay, lighting up the forests in every direction. So prominent did the iron industry of Spain become that its ironworkers were sought for by other countries, and on the French side of the Pyrenees, and in the mountains of Germany, and along the Rhine they set up many of their small forges. The Catalan forge, which received its name from Catalonia, has been introduced into every civilized country of modern times which produces iron, and it still exists in almost its original simplicity in the mountains of both Spain and France and in the Southern States of our·own country. Spain continued to make large quantities of iron and steel of the best qualities down to the closing years of the eighteenth century, when its iron and steel industries began to decline in consequence of the greater enterprise of other countries and their adoption of modern methods of manufacture. Germany and England had previously surpassed Spain in the quantity but not in the quality of the iron and steel they respectively produced.

The Basque provinces, in the northeastern part of Spain and in the extreme southwestern part of France, on the coast of Biscay, possessed an extensive iron industry from the days of the Romans until the period mentioned at the close of the last paragraph. In the fourteenth century Bilbao (pronounced Bilbo) became a centre of this industry, which included the making of swords of unsurpassed quality, like those of Toledo. Shakespeare frequently refers to the "bilbo," a Spanish sword, which derived its name from Bilbao. In the *Merry Wives of Windsor*, act 1, scene 1, Pistol says to Falstaff : "Sir John and master mine, I combat challenge of this latten bilbo." In act 3, scene 5, Falstaff says to Ford : "I suffered the pangs of three several deaths : . . . . to be compassed, like a good bilbo, in the circumference of a peck, hilt to point, heel to head," a comparison which shows the great flexibility of the Spanish sword. In *Hamlet*, act 5, scene 2, iron fetters called "bilboes" are mentioned by Hamlet in addressing Horatio, although their mention in *Hamlet* may be an anachronism. Sir Walter Scott also refers to the swords of Bilbao. In *The Lay of the Last Minstrel* we read as follows :

> His Bilboa blade, by Marchmen felt,
> Hung in a broad and studded belt ;
> Hence, in rude phrase, the Borderers still
> Called noble Howard "Belted Will."

A French writer, M. Alexandre Pourcel, has recently prepared with great care a most interesting and valuable account of the iron industry of the Basque provinces. He quotes first the statement by Pliny : "On the coast of Cantabria washed by the ocean a high mountain rises precipitously, which, incredible as it may appear, is nothing but an immense block of iron ore," which, he says, evidently refers to the mountain of Triano, (or Somorrostro,) in the Spanish province of Biscay, and then adds :

Oral tradition remained almost the sole depository of the history of the Basque country up to a comparatively recent period ; and the archives do not go back beyond the early years of the sixteenth century. The historians who wrote in the sixteenth and seventeenth centuries relate that from the tenth century the incomparable *vena dulce* was shipped on the river of Bilbao, the Nerba or Nervion, and transported to the different ports of the province of Guipuzcoa, to San Sebastian, Pasajes, and even to Saint-Jean-de-Luz, Cape Breton, or Bayonne. At the same period the Biscayans exported to France, the Netherlands, and England their iron, which had already become celebrated, and which they extracted from the *vena dulce*.

M. Pourcel next refers to a description of the Catalan process, written by Don Pedro de Medine in 1595, and says :

According to this author there were at that period in Biscay and Guipuzcoa, where the Somorrostro ore was sent, 300 *ferrerias*, each of which produced about 1,000 cwt. of iron and steel per annum, a total of about 300,000 cwt., (quintals,) or rather less than 15,000 tons, of which a third was immediately disposed of in these two provinces for naval construction; another third was turned into fire-arms, tools of every description, nails, and agricultural implements; while the remainder was exported in the form of bars. According to Father Gabriel de Henao, at the beginning of the sixteenth century there were more than 80 reducing hearths in Biscay, and in the middle of the following century, in 1658, he counted himself as many as 107 fires, producing iron in large lumps, and 70 working at finishing processes. The finished products of every description exceeded 100,000 cwt., (quintals,) about 4,900 tons. It was during the eighteenth century that the iron industry of the Basque country reached its apogee with a production in certain years of more than 12,000 tons in Biscay alone. At that time this province had 245 hearths in operation. The one description of ore which was smelted in the *ferrerias* of the Basque country and the neighboring provinces was the *vena dulce*, a red hematite, almost free from gangue, soft and sticky to the touch, and easily cut with a tool.

The works celebrated for forgings were situated, in Guipuzcoa. Don Jeronimo Ustariz, Royal Secretary for the Indies, in a memoir drawn up by order of Philip V., in 1724, with reference to the state of commerce and naval affairs, mentions the forges of Placencia, in Guipuzcoa, distant three leagues from the sea, as being capable of furnishing all the arms that the fleet might require, and all the iron work for shipping purposes, such as anchors, etc. In 1748, in a report on the artillery, presented to Ferdinand VI., the Marquis de la Ensenada, a celebrated statesman, expresses himself in the following terms: "Whereas the iron of Cantabria is the very best obtainable, it follows naturally that arms, such as muskets, pistols, carbines, etc., made with this iron, must be of the best quality. It is therefore of importance that the manufactories of Guipuzcoa, which make a specialty of this class of work, should be called into requisition for supplying Spain and America with this material." Towards the end of the century, in 1785, Guipuzcoa possessed eighteen manufactories of ships' anchors. These works supplied not only the state arsenals but exported their manufactures to France and England. Just about the same time we find from the official reports furnished to the seigniory of Biscay that there were 154 *ferrerias* in full work in this province, producing 7,300 tons of iron annually. From that time the ancient iron industry of Biscay has been constantly declining.

We have quoted liberally from M. Pourcel's account because of its great historic value. We are pleased to be able to supplement these details with the general statement that during recent years the iron industry of Spain is being revived through the introduction at Bilbao and elsewhere of modern processes of manufacture, to which its rich ores are so admirably adapted.

France did not at an early period in its history make the

same progress in the manufacture of iron that has been recorded of Spain, partly because it did not receive the same outside attention which made Spain a centre successively of Phœnician, Grecian, Carthaginian, Roman, Gothic, and Moorish civilization, but partly also because it did not possess as rich iron ores as those of Spain. It may be said, however, that iron weapons were well known to the Gauls who confronted the Romans hundreds of years before the Christian era and to their successors who opposed the armies of Julius Cæsar, who frequently refers to their use of iron. In speaking of the Veneti, who inhabited the southern part of Brittany, which forms the northwestern part of France, he makes the remarkable statement that the anchors for their ships were fastened to them with iron chains instead of cables. He also says that the benches of the ships were fastened with iron spikes of the thickness of a man's thumb. This circumstantial account denotes great familiarity with the use of iron by the Veneti. In describing the siege of Avaricum, the modern Bourges, a fortified town of the Bituriges, Cæsar says that "there are in their territories extensive iron mines, and consequently every description of mining operations is known and practiced by them." We have already referred to the existence of an early iron industry in the French part of the Basque provinces.

For hundreds of years after Cæsar's time only faint glimpses are furnished us of an iron industry in France. During this period it was doubtless wholly confined to Catalan forges. In the remains of a celebrated bridge erected by Charlemagne over the Rhine, at Mayence, in the latter part of the eighth century, and which have but recently been removed, iron in a good state of preservation, "being covered by only a thin layer of rust," has been found riveted to the wood-work. *Stücköfen*, or high bloomaries, were in use in Alsatia and Burgundy in the tenth century. When William the Norman invaded England in 1066 he was accompanied by many smiths who were armorers and horse-shoers, and were therefore skilled workers in iron. The modern blast furnace is supposed to have originated in the Rhine provinces about the beginning of the fourteenth century, but whether in France, Germany, or Belgium is not clear. A hundred years later, in 1409, there was a blast furnace in the valley of Massevaux in France, and it is claimed by Landrin that there were many blast furnaces in France about 1450.

Iron was made by the Belgæ as early as the time of Julius Cæsar, and possibly at an earlier date. Heaps of iron cinder, which antiquarians decide to be as old at least as the Roman occupation of Gallia Belgica, have recently been found on the tops of iron-ore hillocks in the provinces of Brabant and Antwerp, and in these cinder heaps have been discovered flint arrow-heads and fragments of coarse pottery, characteristic of the earliest dawn of civilization. During the Roman occupation iron was produced in many places, a fact which is attested by heaps of cinder or slag which yet exist and are found in association with Roman relics. It has been supposed that the iron which was made in Belgium at this period was produced in low bloomaries without an artificial blast. It is, perhaps, a more reasonable supposition that the Romans found this primitive method in use among the Belgians, and that they introduced an artificial blast by means of a leather bellows.

We do not again hear of the Belgian iron industry until the tenth century, when high bloomaries, or wolf furnaces, likewise known as *stücköfen*, were in operation in the valley of the Meuse. We are informed by M. Julien Déby, in a paper on the iron and steel industries of Belgium, that "iron was made to perfection in the Netherlands" in the twelfth century. In the fourteenth century high furnaces, or *flussöfen*, were in existence in Belgium. In 1340 a furnace of this kind was built at Marche les Dames, near Namur, to which special privileges were granted in 1345 by William, count of Namur. Franquoy refers to documentary evidence that there were *hauts fourneaux*, or blast furnaces, at Vennes and Grivegnée, near Liége, in Belgium, before 1400. All these furnaces, except the wolf furnaces, were true blast furnaces, producing cast iron. In 1560 there were in operation in the province of Namur, according to Karsten, 35 blast furnaces and 85 forges. In 1613 permission was granted to two armorers of Maestricht to convert iron into steel, probably cemented steel. The celebrated works of the John Cockerill Company, at Seraing, near Liége, were not established until 1817.

Near Saarbrücken, in Prussia, where the first battle between the French and the Germans occurred in the war of 1870, iron is said to have been made in the days of Roman ascendency, but the Germans do not appear during this period to have been as familiar with its manufacture as some of their neighbors. Tacitus informs us that "iron does not abound in Germany, if we may judge from the weapons in general use. Swords and large lances are seldom seen. The soldier grasps his javelin, or, as it is called in their language, his *fram*, an instrument tipped with a short and narrow piece of iron, sharply pointed, and so commodious that, as occasion requires, he can manage it in close engagement or in distant combat." He further says that the use of iron was unknown to the Æstyans, who inhabited the northern part of Germany lying upon the Baltic; "their general weapon was the club." The Gothinians are described by Tacitus as a people who "submit to the drudgery of digging iron in mines" for the Quadi, who were their neighbors. Ernest, the German editor of Tacitus, says that the Gothinians had iron of their own, and did not make use of it to assert their liberty. Tacitus wrote his *Treatise on Germany* near the close of the first century of the Christian era. Polybius states that the Teutons and the Cimbri, from Northwestern Germany, who invaded Italy and Gaul near the close of the second century before the Christian era, "were already familiar with iron, and possessed weapons of that metal."

From this time forward the condition of the German iron industry is enveloped in obscurity until the eighth century, when we hear of iron works, probably wolf furnaces, or *stücköfen*, in the district of the river Lahn, in Nassau, where iron of great celebrity was made by a guild of "forest smiths" in 780. We are informed by Maw and Dredge, in their very full report on the iron exhibits at the Vienna Exhibition of 1873, that "they had their special privileges, kept an iron mart at Wetzlar, and sent their products regularly to the great annual fairs at Frankfort-on-the-Main. This iron industry was especially flourishing during the thirteenth, fourteenth, and fifteenth centuries." During the eighth century we hear also of the iron industry of the principality of Siegen. There was a steel forge at the town of Siegen in 1288 which had been in existence before the eleventh century. The iron industry of this principality was very active during the middle ages.

About the middle of the thirteenth century *stücköfen* were in use in Siegen. Percy, in his *Metallurgy of Iron and Steel*, says that at the beginning of the fifteenth century pig iron was made in Siegen in *blauöfen*. Iron was made in Saxony as early as the eighth century. Alexander, in his *Report on the Manufacture of Iron*, made to the Governor of Maryland in 1840, informs us that the *flussofen* was introduced into Saxony in 1550, and that the wooden bellows was invented about this time by Hans Lobsinger, an organist of Nuremberg.

Iron was made in the Hartz mountains in the eighth century. Wolf furnaces and ore bloomaries were in existence in the Thuringian mountains in the tenth century, and blast furnaces in the fourteenth century. Alexander states that in the latter half of the sixteenth century there was a furnace in these mountains which was 24 feet high and 6 feet wide at the boshes, built by Hanssien, a Voigtlander.

Solingen, in Rhenish Prussia, was celebrated as early as the twelfth century for its swords and other cutting instruments. Swords of superior quality are still made in large quantities at the same place. In 1377 cast-iron guns were made near Erfurt, in Thuringia. In the fifteenth century pots, plates, cannon-balls, and other articles of iron, many of them of great artistic excellence, were cast at the celebrated Ilsenberg foundry in Germany, which is still in existence. Stoves are said to have been cast in Alsace in 1490. As early as 1509 they were cast at Ilsenberg.

The celebrated steel works of Fried. Krupp, at Essen, in Germany, were founded in 1815 by Friedrich Nicolai and Friedrich Krupp, under the firm name of Nicolai & Krupp, for the purpose of making cast steel. The partnership was soon dissolved, and the business was afterwards successfully conducted by Herr Krupp, who died on October 8, 1826, aged about 39 years. After his death the works were at first operated by his wife, Therese Krupp, and his oldest son, Alfred Krupp, the son subsequently assuming entire control. Alfred Krupp died on July 14, 1887, at the age of 75 years. He was born on April 12, 1812. The works are now in the hands of his son, Friedrich Alfred Krupp, grandson of the founder.

Holland does not appear to have ever had an iron industry, and the same remark may be made of Denmark, neither country producing iron ore. Iron and steel made elsewhere have, however, been manufactured in small quantities into various minor products in both countries. David Mushet quotes M. Verlit as authority for the statement that cast iron was known in Holland in the thirteenth century, and that stoves were cast from it at Elass in the year 1400.

Switzerland has undoubtedly made iron in small quantities from remote ages. It now has a few small blast furnaces and rolling mills, and in the manufacture of cutlery and machinery it is very active. The lake dwellers of Switzerland, who lived before the Christian era, possessed wrought-iron swords of wonderful workmanship; also other iron weapons and implements. See *Harper's Magazine* for February, 1890, for a brief account of the lake dwellers.

Recurring to the iron industry of Austria, Alexander says that the mines of Styria were "opened again" in 712. It appears probable that wolf furnaces were in use in Styria, Carinthia, and Carniola as early as the eighth century, which seems to be the epoch of their introduction in most European countries. These provinces became very prominent in subsequent centuries in the manufacture of iron and steel in Catalan forges. The first blast furnace in the Alps provinces was, however, introduced very much later than in Belgium or on the Rhine, the first in Carinthia being built in 1567, at Urtl; the first in Styria in 1760, at Eisenerz; and the first in Carniola in the early part of the present century. Iron was made in Bohemia and Silesia at an early period. "The Bohemian chronicler, Hajek, of Liboschan, mentions that iron works existed in 677, near Schasslau." Heaps of cinder and remains of wolf furnaces and ore bloomaries are numerous in Bohemia. In 1365 bloomaries were in use in Upper Silesia. Kerpely says that written descriptions are extant of the working of iron mines in Upper Hungary in 1326 and 1408. Iron slag has been discovered in Hungary at a depth of about one foot below the surface of the ground and in the midst of beautiful vineyards. It is probable that iron had been continuously made in Hungary and in various Austrian provinces in the period intervening between the dates above mentioned and the early operations in Noricum, Moravia, and Hungary which have already been referred to.

The iron industry of Sweden had an existence as early at least as the thirteenth century. A Swedish historian says that the oldest iron mine in Sweden is probably Norberg, in Westmanland, on the southern borders of Dalecarlia. There are documents still in existence, dated July 29, 1303, signed by Thorkel Knutson, the royal marshal, in which Norberg is mentioned as an iron mine. Exclusive privileges were granted to the miners of Norberg by King Magnus Ericsson in 1354. It is probable, however, that the manufacture of iron in both Sweden and Norway antedates the time of the vikings in the eighth and ninth centuries of the Christian era, as the remains of their vessels which have been discovered have been found to contain iron. It may also be said that, as iron was made in other European countries before this period, there is no good reason to doubt that it was also made in Sweden and Norway. At Taplow, on the Thames, in England, not far from Windsor Castle, the tomb of a Norse viking of undoubted identity was opened in 1883, and in it were found, among other articles, a rusted iron sword which fell into pieces when removed, an iron knife, the iron socket of a spear, an iron ring strengthening the inside of a bronze shield, and another iron ring strengthening the bottom of a bronze bucket. Still more recently there has been discovered at Gloppen, on the coast of Norway, a burial chamber 12 feet in length, formed of stone slabs, containing the remains of a man, two lance-heads of iron 12 inches long, an iron shield, some Roman gold coins perforated and worn as ornaments, some iron arrow-heads, and many bronze, glass, and other articles, all denoting a very early origin. In the valley of Valders, in South Norway, a sword, a spear, and an armlet have recently been found, the sword and spear being of iron and the armlet of bronze. On a farm in Tromsö sound, close to the North cape, the skeleton of a tall man was recently plowed up, and by its side lay an iron sword, a short and a long iron spear, three iron arrow-heads, the blade of a scythe, a small iron rod, and other articles. In East Gothia, in Sweden, an oval-shaped stone grave has been discovered, containing a skeleton, beside which were a sword, two spear-heads, and the remains of a shield and a helmet, all of iron. All these Swedish and Norwegian relics are of undoubted prehistoric origin.

In 1889 Paul B. Du Chaillu published in two volumes *The Viking Age*, in which he incorporates many evidences of the existence of an advanced iron industry among the Norsemen in the early centuries of the Christian era. His circumstantial statements are very interesting and very valuable.

In 1488 the celebrated mines of Dannemora, in Sweden, were opened. The celebrated cannon factory at Finspong "received its first privileges" in 1587, and the Åkers cannon factory, now abolished, dates from 1584. In 1614 Gustavus Adolphus promoted the immigration of German furnacemen into Sweden. The Walloon refining process, which takes its name from the Walloons, of Flanders, was introduced into Sweden from Flanders in the time of Charles the Twelfth, who reigned from 1697 to 1718. Percy states that the osmund furnace, which was a modification of the *stückofen*, was formerly very common in Sweden. Overman, in his *Manufacture of Iron*, says that this furnace was introduced into Sweden from Germany. We have proof of its existence in Finland as late in the present century as 1873. A *stückofen* was in operation in the province of Jemtland, in Sweden, as late as 1830. We have a record of the exportation of 2,200 tons of malleable iron from Sweden in 1559.

The iron industry of Russia dates historically from 1569, in which year, as recorded by Scrivenor, in his *History of the Iron Trade*, published in 1841, the English "obtained the privilege of seeking for and smelting iron ore, on condition that they should teach the Russians the art of working this metal." The first historical iron works in Russia, however, were established long afterwards, according to the same author, in the reign of the czar Alexy Michaelovitch, (1645 to 1676,) about sixty miles from Moscow, and were by Scrivenor said to be the only works in Russia prior to the reign of Peter the Great, who is reported to have worked in them before he set out, in 1697, on his first journey into foreign countries.

It is not known when the celebrated Russia sheet iron was first made. It is not mentioned in a circumstantial enumeration of the iron manufactures of Russia about 1798, to be found in Scrivenor. It is produced to-day on both sides of the Ural mountains, but chiefly on the Siberian side.

There is reason to believe that the Russians were skilled ironworkers and metallurgists long before the period which is mentioned by Scrivenor. The bells of Moscow (not made of iron, however,) have been famous for hundreds of years. Scrivenor himself refers to "the old ruinous iron works" at Olonetz, which he says were "restored" by Henning, a foreigner in the service of Peter the Great, about the year 1700. Herr Pechar, of Teplitz, in Bohemia, wrote in 1878: "Mining operations have been carried on in the Caucasus, Ural, Altai, and the Kirghise desert in the most remote ages. This is proved by the number of abandoned workings discovered by the Russians when they took possession of these districts. These conquerors, however, did not commence their working before the fifteenth century, from which time there was again a lapse of three hundred years before order and progress were firmly established by new mining legislation issued by Peter the Great, in 1719."

We have before us an account of a *Journey from St. Petersburg to Pekin*, undertaken in 1719 and completed in 1722, in which account there is a reference to the iron industry of Siberia which points to its origin as early at least as the preceding century. We quote as follows:

I can not leave Solikamsky without mentioning the rich iron mines in the country adjacent, at Kathenaburg, and other places of that district, which produce iron equal perhaps in quality to the best in the world. These works have of late been brought to great perfection by the skill and indefatigable industry of Mr. Demidof, a native of Russia, enabled and encouraged to carry them on by a beneficial grant from his majesty, who is always ready to assist and protect those who, by their ingenuity, form projects to the advantage of his country. These works, I am informed, are still capable of great improvement. The ore is very good, and rises in many places to the very surface of the earth, and may be dug at a small expense. As for wood to smelt it, no place in the world can have greater advantage. Besides, all the machines may be driven by water, and there is an easy communication by the rivers to St. Petersburg for exportation, and to many other parts of Russia for inland consumption. In these mines are often found magnets of various sizes. I have seen some of them very large and of high virtue. There are several other iron works in Russia; for instance, at Tula, Olonitz, and other places; but the metal is of an inferior quality to that of Siberia.

The narrative from which the above extract is taken was

written by Dr. John Bell, a Scotch physician, who accompanied Peter the Great's embassy to Persia in 1715, 1716, 1717, and 1718, and subsequently accompanied Peter's embassy to China in 1719, 1720, and 1721. For a biographical sketch of Dr. Bell see *Appleton's American Cyclopædia.*

In an English pamphlet on the British iron trade, printed between 1725 and 1731, and to be found in the *Journal of the Iron and Steel Institute* for 1885, the competition of Russian and especially of Siberian iron in British markets is freely commented upon. Bar iron only is referred to. It is scarcely possible that Siberian bar iron could have been made of such good quality that it would compete with other iron in British markets at the beginning of the eighteenth century if its manufacture in that remote region had been undertaken so recently as the preceding century. It is, we think, a far more reasonable theory that the knowledge of the manufacture of iron was carried by the ironmaking Parthians and Scythians into the Ural mountains before the Christian era, and that it was never lost by their successors, although new life was infused into the industry by Peter the Great.

Tacitus mentions the Finns (Fenni) in his *Treatise on Germany.* He says of them: "The Finns are extremely wild, and live in abject poverty. They have no arms, no horses, no dwellings; they live on herbs, they clothe themselves in skins, and they sleep on the ground. Their only resources are their arrows, which for the lack of iron are tipped with bone." A circumstantial enumeration of the iron industries of Finland in 1873 mentions 22 blast furnaces and 69 miscellaneous wrought-iron works, including "10 bloomaries or ancient furnaces, of a construction somewhat similar to the Catalan furnace, in which the iron ore is reduced directly to a mass of wrought iron, which is taken out of the bottom and front of the furnace and worked under hammers." These were osmund furnaces. Lake ores are chiefly used in the Finnish iron industry.

CHAPTER III.

BEGINNING OF THE BRITISH IRON INDUSTRY.

THE use of iron in a very limited way was known to the Britons before the invasion of England by Julius Cæsar in the year 55 before Christ. The Phœnicians, who traded with the Britons probably as early as the seventh century before Christ, may be supposed to have introduced among this barbarous people the use of iron, but we have no proof that they instructed them in its manufacture. The Phœnicians visited the Cassiterides (the Scilly Islands and Cornwall) to obtain tin. Herodotus speaks of obtaining tin from the Cassiterides in his day, the fifth century before the Christian era. The Greeks and Carthaginians succeeded the Phœnicians in trading with the Britons, but there is no proof that they taught them the art of making iron. They, as well as the Phœnicians, probably took iron into Britain in exchange for tin and other native products. Cæsar, in his *Commentaries*, says of the Britons who opposed his occupation of the island that " they use either brass or iron rings, determined at a certain weight, as their money. Tin is produced in the midland regions; in the maritime, iron; but the quantity of it is small: they employ brass, which is imported." This quotation appears to establish the fact that iron was a precious metal in Britain at the time of the invasion; it would at least seem to show that it was not in common use and could not have been used as an article of export. Cæsar nowhere mentions the use of iron weapons of war by the Britons. The Belgæ had passed over into Britain before Cæsar's time and made settlements upon its coast, and whatever arts they possessed they would of course take with them. It can not be proved that the Belgæ made iron in their own country before Cæsar's invasion of it; if it could be shown that they did it might safely be assumed that they would introduce their methods of manufacture into Britain. Cæsar says that a small quantity of iron was made in the maritime regions of the island, and this the Belgæ may have made.

If the manufacture of iron by the Britons prior to the Roman invasion is enveloped in obscurity and even in doubt, there can be no doubt that iron was made in considerable quantities during the Roman occupation of Britain, which nominally extended from about the middle of the first century of the Christian era to the year 411. The Romans, it may here be remarked, knowing the value of iron, encouraged its manufacture wherever their arms were borne and the necessary conditions existed. The remains of iron works which were in existence and were operated during their stay in Britain are still pointed out. Dismissing all speculation concerning the origin of the first iron works in Britain, the remains of some of these works may well receive attention. They relate to a most interesting period in the history of the British iron trade.

Large heaps of iron scoria, or cinder, as old as the Roman era, have been discovered in the wealds of Kent and Sussex, in the hills of Somerset, and in the Forest of Dean in Gloucester; also at Bierley, a few miles from Bradford in Yorkshire, and in the neighborhood of Leeds in the same county. On the moors in the parishes of Lanchester and Chester-le-Street in the county of Durham vast heaps of iron scoria of presumed Roman origin have been found; also in the valleys of the Reed and the Tyne in the county of Northumberland. There is also evidence that iron was made under the Romans in the counties of Surrey, Glamorgan, Monmouth, Hereford, and Worcester. Mr. Robert Hunt, in his history of *British Mining*, says: "We may trace the Romans from the wild country of the Forest of Dean, and the beautiful Wye scenery in the south, through the hills of Shropshire and Montgomeryshire, Cheshire, and the counties of Flint and Denbigh, and through the ancient country of the Cangi, or Kiangi, up to the shores of the Irish Channel." He also says that iron was made by the Romans in Derbyshire, Yorkshire, Cumberland, and other counties.

Many of the places and counties named above as having produced iron lie in the southeastern or southwestern parts of England, or within the ancient boundaries of South Wales, "the country of the Silures." Next to Cornwall, where tin was obtained by the Phœnicians and their successors, these southern portions of the country would be most likely to be visited and influenced by foreigners before the Roman invasion, and to receive the most attention after it. Cæsar describes the island of Britain as being shaped like a triangle, with one of its sides looking toward Gaul. "One angle of this side is in Kent, whither almost all ships from Gaul are directed."

The cinder above mentioned has almost invariably been found in connection with Roman coins, pottery, and altars. A coin of Antoninus Pius, who lived in the second century after Christ, was found in the Forest of Dean in 1762, together with a piece of fine pottery. Coins of other Roman emperors have been found in the cinder heaps of the Forest of Dean. In the cinder beds of Beauport, between Hastings and Battle, in Sussex, a bronze coin of Trajan has been found, and one of Adrian. These emperors lived in the first and second centuries after Christ. Coins found in the cinder heaps of Maresfield, not far from Uckfield, have dates ranging from Nero to Diocletian, or from the year 54 to the year 286 after Christ. In the cinder mounds of Sussex many specimens of Roman pottery have been discovered. Altars erected to Jupiter Dolichenus, the protector of Roman iron works, have been discovered in various places in England in association with the remains of prehistoric iron works.

In M. A. Lower's *Contributions to Literature* will be found an interesting account of the discovery of Roman relics in 1844, by Rev. Edward Turner, in the cinder beds of the parish of Maresfield in Sussex. This is followed by Lower with other proofs of the manufacture of iron in Sussex by the Romans. Recent researches by James Rock, of Hastings, in Sussex, throw additional light on the Roman and early British methods of manufacturing iron. Cinder beds, or cinder heaps, were once very numerous in East Sussex, and many of them still exist. The neighborhood of Hastings appears to have been a great centre of the iron industry "from the earliest times." The cinder heaps yet remaining are large enough to be quarried, and contain thousands of tons of scoria, some of the heaps having large oak trees growing upon their summits.

Much of the cinder has been found on the tops of hills

or mounds, a circumstance which justifies the belief that bellows were not employed in producing a blast, but that the
wind was relied upon to produce a draft sufficient to smelt
the ore in crude bloomaries, some of which were mere excavations, with covered channels leading to the hillside in the
direction of the prevailing winds. This primitive method
of making iron is that which appears to have prevailed in
Belgica at the same time. Bloomaries of similar form and
adaptation were in use in Derbyshire for smelting lead as late
as the seventeenth century. Scrivenor mentions that similar
furnaces were used by the Peruvians to smelt the silver ore
of their country before the arrival of the Spaniards. Other
bloomaries in Britain are supposed by Fairbairn and other
writers to have been simple conical structures, with small
openings below for the admission of air, and erected on high
ground that the wind might assist combustion. A still simpler method is supposed to have consisted in placing ore and
wood or charcoal in alternate layers in elevated positions, or
even in the lowlands. All these were wasteful methods. The
cinder found in England and Wales was very rich in iron; in
the Forest of Dean it was so rich and so abundant that in
the sixteenth century about twenty small blast furnaces were
engaged in smelting it.

It was stated in 1681 by Andrew Yarranton, in the second
part of *England's Improvements by Sea and Land*, that "within 100 yards of the walls of the city of Worcester there was
dug up one of the hearths of the Roman foot-blasts, it being
then firm and in order, and was 7 foot deep in the earth."
The foot-blast here referred to must have been a leather bellows, with which the Romans and their Mediterranean neighbors were certainly acquainted. There is nothing improbable
in the conclusion that the Romans while in Britain used both
the wind-bloomaries and the foot-blasts.

The emperor Adrian landed in Britain in the year 120,
and in the following year there was established at Bath, in
Wiltshire, a Roman military forge, or *fabrica*, for the manufacture of iron arms. This forge was close to the bloomaries
in Somerset and the Forest of Dean, from which it was supplied with iron. That the manufacture of iron in Britain at
this time and for some time subsequently was almost wholly

confined to the southern parts of England seems probable from a passage in Herodian, quoted by Smiles in his *Industrial Biography*, who says of the British pursued by the emperor Severus, in the year 208, through the fens and marshes of the east coast, that "they wore iron hoops round their middles and their necks, esteeming them as ornaments and tokens of riches, in like manner as other barbarous people then esteemed ornaments of silver and gold."

Percy quotes from the London *Times* an account of the opening of some prehistoric remains in the Cheviot hills, in the north of England, in 1861 and 1862, which revealed various evidences of the rude civilization of the early Celtic, or British, inhabitants, including pieces of iron slag. These remains are assigned by the *Times* to the Roman period of British history, but they may belong to a later period.

Strabo mentions the exportation of iron from Britain in his day, the beginning of the Christian era. This was before the Romans had subdued the Britons, but after the influence of Roman civilization had been felt in the island. During the Roman occupation of Britain iron was one of the products of the country which were regularly exported.

The Anglo-Saxons, who succeeded the Romans in Britain in the early part of the fifth century, used tools and weapons of iron, and it is a reasonable supposition that they produced all the iron that was required for their manufacture ; but their enterprise as iron manufacturers probably extended no further, although Bede, who is the earliest English historian, speaks of the importance of the iron industry in his day, the beginning of the eighth century. The Anglo-Saxon monks frequently engaged in the manufacture of iron. St. Dunstan, who lived in the tenth century, is said to have had a forge in his bedroom, and to have been a skilled blacksmith and metallurgist. One of the last of the Anglo-Saxon kings was Edmund Ironside.

During the ascendency of the Danes, and afterwards down to the accession of William the Conqueror in 1066, iron was made in the Forest of Dean and elsewhere, but in limited quantities. In *Doomsday-Book* mention is made of iron works in the counties of Somerset, Hereford, Gloucester, Cheshire, and Lincoln, but no mention is made of iron works in Kent,

Surrey, or Sussex. In the eleventh century the Anglo-Saxon plow consisted of a wooden wedge covered with iron straps, to which the Normans added the coulter. The shipbuilders of Edward the Confessor, the last of the Anglo-Saxon kings prior to Harold who lost the battle of Hastings, obtained supplies of bolts and bars of iron from the city of Gloucester. The antiquarian Camden says that "in and before the reign of William the Conqueror the chief trade of the city of Gloucester was the forging of iron; and it is mentioned in *Doomsday-Book* that there was scarcely any other tribute required from that city by the king than certain *dicars* of iron and iron bars for the use of the royal navy. The quantity required was thirty-six *dicars* of iron, a *dicar* containing ten bars and one hundred iron rods for nails or bolts." Giraldis Cambrensis, who lived in the twelfth century, speaks of "the noble Forest of Dean, by which Gloucester was amply supplied with iron and venison." Nicholls, in *The Forest of Dean*, says that in the time of Edward the First, in the latter part of the thirteenth century, the Free Miners of the Forest "applied for and obtained their 'customes and franchises,' which were granted, as the record of them declares, 'time out of minde.'" In 1282, according to Nicholls, there were "upwards of seventy-two" *forgeæ errantes*, or movable forges, in the Forest, each of which paid a license of seven shillings a year to the crown.

Scrivenor says that during the period from the Conquest to the death of John, in 1216, iron and steel were imported into Britain from Germany and other countries, the domestic supply being insufficient. The Normans, however, contributed much to the development of English iron and other resources. Green, in his *History of the English People*, says that one immediate result of the Conquest was a great immigration into England from the Continent. "A peaceful invasion of the industrial and trading classes of Normandy followed quick on the conquest of the Norman soldiery." In 1266 and subsequently we hear of iron works in Sussex which were not mentioned in *Doomsday-Book*. In the year 1300 the ironmongers of London complained to the Lord Mayor that the smiths of the weald of Sussex brought iron for wheels that was not what it ought to have been, "to the loss of the whole trade." In 1321 three thousand horseshoes and twenty-nine thousand nails were provided by Peter de Waltham, sheriff of Surrey and Sussex, for the expedition against Bruce in which Edward the Second attempted to retrieve the defeat at Bannockburn.

Still the English iron industry made very slow progress. Professor James E. Thorold Rogers, in his *Work and Wages*, informs us that during the reign of Edward the First (1274 to 1307) the most valuable articles in use by the English peasants were copper and brass pots and a few common iron utensils, all metals being exceedingly dear, and iron, relatively speaking, being the dearest of all. The iron utensils of this period were all made of hammered iron. It is mentioned by Scrivenor that there were but few iron mines in the north of England in the thirteenth and fourteenth centuries, and that, in the tenth year of the reign of Edward the Second, in 1317, iron was so scarce in that section and in Scotland that the Scots, "in a predatory expedition which they made in that year, met with no iron worth their notice until they came to Furness, in Lancashire, where they seized all the manufactured iron they could find, and carried it off with the greatest joy, though so heavy of carriage, and preferred it to all other plunder." The Scots at this time were in great need of iron, which they did not produce in large quantities in their small forges, and for which they were largely dependent on the Continent and on the favor or ill-fortune of England. Alexander says that there were iron works at Kimberworth, in Yorkshire, in 1160, and Smiles gives an extract from a contract for supplying wood and ore for iron "blomes" at Kirskill, near Otley, in Yorkshire, in 1352. A recent writer, Mr. H. A. Fletcher, says that "the earliest record which has been found of iron-ore mining in Cumberland seems to be the grant of the forge at Winefel to the monks of Holm Cultram Abbey, in the twelfth century, which also included a mine at Egremont, by inference of iron, being in connection with a forge; and Thomas de Multon confirms a gift to the same abbey *de quartuor duodenis minæ ferri in Coupland*." The Ulverston district in Lancashire appears to have been a seat of the English iron industry as early as the twelfth century.

Scrivenor mentions one art related to the manufacture of

iron which flourished in England from William to John if
the manufacture itself did not. The art of making defensive
armor was brought to such perfection during the period mentioned that "a knight completely armed was almost invulner-
able." The history of the crusades shows that the English
were then very proficient in the manufacture of both arms
and armor, as were the Turks and other Asiatic tribes who
resisted them. Smiles says that it was the knowledge of the
art of forging iron which laid the foundation of the Turk-
ish empire. By means of this art the Turks made the arms
which first secured their own freedom and then enabled them
to extend their power. The quality of the swords used by
the English and by their Infidel opponents is illustrated by
an incident related by Sir Walter Scott in the *Tales of the
Crusaders*. He describes a meeting between Richard Cœur
de Lion and Saladin, at which Saladin asks Richard to show
him the strength for which he is famous, and the Norman
monarch responds by severing a bar of iron which lies on
the floor of his tent. Saladin says, "I can not do that," but
he takes a down pillow from the sofa, and drawing his keen
blade across it it falls in two pieces. Richard says, "This is
the black art; it is magic; it is the devil; you can not cut
that which has no resistance." Saladin, to show him that
such is not the case, takes from his shoulders a scarf which
is so light that it almost floats in the air, and tossing it up
severs it before it can descend. Much of the iron which the
English used at this time in the manufacture of arms and
armor came from Spain.

Edward the Third, who reigned from 1327 to 1377, did
much to advance the manufacturing industries of England.
He protected domestic manufactures by legislation which restricted the importation of foreign goods, and he encouraged
the immigration into England of skilled workmen from the
Continent. The use of iron was greatly extended in his reign,
and its manufacture was active in Kent and Sussex and in
the Forest of Dean. Nevertheless the domestic supply did
not meet the wants of the people. Scrivenor says: "By an
act passed in the twenty-eighth year of Edward the Third no
iron manufactured in England, and also no iron imported and
sold, could be carried out of the country, under the penalty

of forfeiting double the quantity to the king; and the magistrates were empowered to regulate the selling price and to punish those who sold at too dear a rate, according to the extent of the transaction." This act appears to have remained in force long after Edward's death. Smiles quotes from Parker's *English Home* the statement that in the reign of this king the pots, spits, and frying-pan of the royal kitchen were classed among the king's jewels.

The methods of manufacturing iron which were followed in England in the thirteenth and fourteenth centuries were all of a slow and restricted character, although very greatly advanced beyond those which existed in the days of the Romans. Cast iron in all forms appears to have been still unknown; all iron was forged. The English were yet mainly devoted to agriculture, but were not even good farmers, their implements of husbandry and their methods of cultivating the soil being equally rude. Wool was their great staple, and this was largely exported to the Continent, where it was manufactured into finer fabrics than the English were capable of producing. Iron was often scarce and dear, because the domestic supply was insufficient. The iron industry on the Continent was at this period in a much more advanced stage of development than in England, and most of the Continental iron was also of a better quality than the English iron.

Professor Rogers, in his *History of Agriculture and Prices in England* and in his *Work and Wages*, gives many interesting details concerning the iron industry of England in the thirteenth and fourteenth centuries. Iron was made at this time at Tendale in Cumberland, and at or near the city of Gloucester; also in Kent and Sussex. It was doubtless made in many other places. Steel is frequently mentioned, the first reference to it being in 1267. It is not quite clear that all the steel used in England during the period under consideration was imported, but most of it certainly was. Much of the iron used was imported, frequent mention being made of Spanish and also of osemond iron. Osemond steel is also frequently mentioned. In 1281 Norman iron, of a superior quality, was bought for the Newgate jail. Spain appears to have been the principal source of the supply of imported iron. It is probable that the osemond iron and steel were chiefly obtained in Sweden, Norway, and Germany, the osmund furnace having been in use in these countries about this time. Iron and steel were generally bought at fairs and markets. The Spaniard attended the Stourbridge fair with his stock of iron, and iron from the Sussex forges was sold at the same place. The prices of iron and steel were usually lower near the sea and at the great towns in the south of England than elsewhere. Among the farmers it was customary for the bailiff to buy the iron that might be needed on the farm, and to employ a smith to make the horseshoes and nails and to iron the implements. Rogers says that " no direct information about the seasons, scanty as it is, is so frequent as that found in the notices which the bailiff gives of the great cost of iron." Iron for the tires of wagons and carts was so dear that many wheels were not ironed. Steel appears to have been but little used by the farmers.

Iron was sold in various forms. The iron made at the works at Tendale was sold in the form of blooms in 1333 and subsequently. Blooms were sold as early as 1318, but the place of their manufacture is not given. Slabs and bars of iron are also mentioned, but the commonest form in which iron was sold was the "piece," twenty-five pieces making a hundred-weight. " The small fagot of iron, each bar of which weighed a little over four pounds, was kept by the bailiff, and served as occasion required for the various uses of the farm." The Tendale bloom weighed about one hundred pounds, and having to be reworked was sold at a much lower price than other forms of iron. Steel was usually sold by the garb, or sheaf, each sheaf containing thirty small pieces, the weight of which is not stated. Rogers supposes that the pieces of iron and steel were of about the same weight, and that the price of steel was about four times the price of iron. Occasional mention is made of steel which was sold by the cake; it was "a little higher in value and much greater in weight than the garb." Steel made in the forges of Styria and other Austrian provinces is still produced in the form of a large cake.

Plow-shoes, which appear to have been iron points to wooden shares, are of frequent occurrence in the accounts quoted by Rogers, and so are lath and board nails, clouts and clout nails, and horseshoes and horseshoe nails. Horseshoes were not purchased from the smiths until about the close of the fourteenth century; down to that time the smiths were supplied by the bailiffs with the iron for their manufacture. "Hinges, staples, and bolts were occasionally manufactured by the village smith from iron supplied him by the bailiff, but were more frequently bought at the market-town or fair." Iron mattocks and hoes were used in the fourteenth century, as were iron sickles, scythes, and hay and other forks. Iron teeth for harrows were unknown, and it may be added that they were not much used in England until the seventeenth century. Domestic utensils of iron were not in general use; pots and similar articles used in the kitchen were usually of brass. A brass jug and pan are mentioned in 1272, a brass jug and basin in 1360, and two brass pots in 1383. Such iron utensils as were in use appear to have been made of wrought iron. Tinware was certainly unknown. Hammers, axes, pickaxes, and other tools were made of iron. Iron hoops were used for buckets and grain measures in the fourteenth century; "the iron-bound bucket that hung in the well" had an existence as early at least as 1331.

Other authorities mention that arrow-heads were manufactured at Sheffield in the thirteenth century, and that knives were manufactured at the same place in the fourteenth century, as they are to-day. Chaucer, who wrote his *Canterbury Tales* near the close of the latter century, in describing the miller of Trompington says that "a Schefeld thwytel bar he in his hose." Birmingham was then, as it is now, a centre of the manufacture of swords, tools, and nails.

Smiles pays a deserved compliment to the English smith, to whom England owes so much of its greatness. In Anglo-Saxon times his person was protected by a double penalty, and he was treated as an officer of the highest rank. The forging of swords was then his great specialty. William the Conqueror did much to exalt the art of the smith, to whom he was greatly indebted for his victory at Hastings, his soldiers being better armed than those of the Saxon Harold. At the close of the fourteenth century the smith had fairly entered upon the brilliant career which has since contributed so. much to the industrial pre-eminence of England. Mr. Picton, in a recent address, says: "Iron work at this period was of the most elaborate description. The locks and keys, the hinges and bolts, the smith's work in gates and screens, exceed in beauty anything of the kind which has since been produced." In a lecture before the Society of Arts in 1883 Mr. George H. Birch gives a pleasing description of the useful and ornamental treatment of iron by English and Continental smiths from the twelfth to the seventeenth century, dwelling especially upon the elaborate and beautiful hinges, railings, screens, and locks that are still preserved in ecclesiastical and other structures of mediæval and later origin.

In the fourteenth century cannon were used in England and on the Continent, although Appleton's *Cyclopœdia* gives us dates of their earlier use. The year-book of the town of Ghent, in Holland, dated 1313, says : " In this year was introduced the use of guns in Germany by a monk." This monk's name was Berthold Schwartz. A statue to his memory was erected at Freiburg in 1853. France, according to Scrivenor, appears to have used cannon as early as 1338, in which year it is stated that the government had an account with Henry de Faumichan "for gunpowder and other things necessary for the cannon at the siege of Puii Guillaume." Scrivenor says that " in the year 1327 we hear of cannon, which are then supposed to have been first used in England by Edward the Third in his invasion of Scotland." An English writer, Mr. C. D. Archibald, is said by Lower to have presented strong reasons for the belief that cannon were used by Edward in his expedition against the Scots in the year mentioned. England made prominent use of cannon in field warfare at the battle of Cressy and the siege of Calais in the year 1346, when the bowmen of Edward the Third were drawn up "in the form of a harrow," with small bombards between them, "which, with fire, threw little iron balls to frighten the horses." These bombards were made of "iron bars joined together longitudinally, and strengthened by exterior hoops of iron." But the archers of the English army continued to be the main reliance of the English kings for many years after Edward's first use of the bombards, and on the Continent gunpowder did not come into general use until the sixteenth century. At the battle of Pavia, in 1525, the matchlock was first used effectively, and it was then fired from a rest.

CHAPTER IV.

THE BRITISH IRON INDUSTRY FROM THE FIFTEENTH TO THE NINETEENTH CENTURY.

DURING the fifteenth and sixteenth centuries the manufacture of iron in England was greatly extended. The encouragement which Edward the Third and his immediate successors had given to the immigration of foreign workmen into England had resulted in the settlement in the country of many Flemish and French ironworkers, whose skill was eagerly sought by many landed proprietors who entered with zeal into the manufacture of iron. Sussex became the principal seat of this industry; it possessed iron ores and forests of timber, the latter supplying the necessary charcoal for fuel, and small streams furnished the requisite power to drive the "iron mills." As one marked result of the extension of the iron manufacture in England at this time the dependence of the country upon foreign sources of supply was greatly lessened, so much so that in 1483 an act was passed prohibiting the importation of gridirons, grates, iron wire, knives, hinges, scissors, and many other manufactured articles of iron or steel which competed with like articles of domestic production. Landrin, however, states that fine tools were still imported into England from Bilbao, in Spain, as late as 1548.

As early as the beginning of the fifteenth century blast furnaces were introduced into England from the Continent, and this event gave a fresh impetus to the iron industry of Sussex, Kent, Surrey, and other sections. Prior to the introduction of blast furnaces all iron that was made in England was produced in Catalan forges or high bloomaries directly from the ore, and was, therefore, when finished, wrought, or bar, iron. The bloomaries were doubtless modeled after the Continental *stücköfen*; indeed the English high bloomary was probably the exact counterpart of the *stückofen*. The first blast furnaces introduced into England were also probably the same in all respects as the *flussofen*, or *blauofen*, or the *haut fourneau*, of the Continent.

The exact date of the erection of the first blast furnace in England is unknown. Lower, in his account of the iron industry of Sussex, mentions an iron casting which was made in the fourteenth century. Mushet supposes that iron was cast in the Forest of Dean in 1540, and he says that the oldest piece of cast iron he ever saw bore the initials " E. R." and the date " 1555." Lower quotes some cast-iron inscriptions in Sussex which are dated 1581, 1582, and 1591. But even the earliest of these years is clearly not sufficiently early to be accepted as marking the period when blast furnaces were introduced into England. Camden, who lived between 1551 and 1623, says of Sussex : " Full of iron mines it is in sundry places, where, for the making and founding thereof, there be furnaces on every side, and a huge deal of wood is yearly burnt." He also says that the heavy forge-hammers, which were mostly worked by water-power, stored in hammer-ponds, beating upon the iron, "fill the neighborhood round about, day and night, with continual noise." In 1607 John Norden stated in a printed document that "there are or lately were in Sussex neere 140 hammers and furnaces for iron." In 1612 Simon Sturtevant said that there were then in England, Scotland, Ireland, and Wales " 800 furnaces, forges, or iron mills" making iron with charcoal, of which Dud Dudley, a few years later, estimated that about 300 were furnaces, the weekly product of which was about 15 tons each. The furnaces would be partly employed in making pots, kettles, mill machinery, and other castings direct from the ore. In the sixteenth century, as has already been stated, several furnaces were built in the Forest of Dean to rework the cinder which was found there in large quantities. The first furnaces built in the Forest were 15 feet high and 6 feet wide at the boshes. The furnaces at work in the Forest in 1677 were blown with bellows 20 feet long, driven by " a great wheel," turned by water.

Lower says that about 1557 " several Sussex families, enriched by the iron manufacture, assumed the rank of gentry." Smiles says that "the iron manufacture of Sussex reached its height toward the close of the reign of Elizabeth, when the trade became so prosperous that, instead of importing iron, England began to export it in considerable quantities in the shape of iron ordnance." This ordnance was cast, and the time referred to was the latter part of the sixteenth century. Bronze cannon had succeeded the bombards about the beginning of that century, and as early as 1543 cast-iron cannon were made in Sussex, at a place called Bucksteed, by Ralph Hogge, who employed a Frenchman named Peter Baude as his assistant. "Many great guns" were subsequently cast in Sussex, John Johnson and his son, Thomas Johnson, the former a servant of Peter Baude, being prominent in their manufacture. John Johnson is said to have "succeeded and exceeded his master in this his art of casting ordnance, making them cleaner and to better perfection." About 1595 the weight of some of the cannon cast in Sussex amounted to three tons each. At a later period, in 1648, Bishop Wilkins says in his *Mathematicall Magick* that "a whole cannon weighed commonly 8,000 pounds, a half cannon 5,000, a culverin 4,500, a demi-culverin 3,000. A whole cannon required for every charge 40 pounds of powder and a bullet of 64 pounds."

But a still greater honor is claimed for Peter Baude than that with which his name is above associated. Stow, in his *Chronicle*, quoted by Froude and Smiles, says that two foreign workmen, whom Henry the Eighth tempted into his service, first invented shells. "One Peter Baude, a Frenchman-born, and another alien called Peter Van Cullen, a gunsmith, both the king's feed men, conferring together, devised and caused to be made certain mortar pieces, being at the mouth from 11 inches unto 19 inches wide, for the use whereof they caused to be made certain hollow shot of cast iron, to be stuffed with fire-work or wild-fire, whereof the bigger sort for the same had screws of iron to receive a match to carry fire kindled, that the fire-work might be set on fire for to break in pieces the same hollow shot, whereof the smallest piece hitting any man would kill or spoil him." Lower gives the name of the "alien" above referred to as "Peter Van Collet, a Flemish gunsmith."

There is deposited in the library of the Historical Society of Pennsylvania, at Philadelphia, a stone cannon-ball, one of twenty-three which are said to have been fired at the boat in which Queen Mary and Douglass made their escape from Loch Leven in 1568. It is about nine inches in diameter, is round, but not smooth, and weighs probably fifteen pounds.

The exportation of cast-iron cannon became so extensive that complaint was made that Spain armed her ships with them to 'fight the ships of England, and the trade was for a time prohibited. But their manufacture continued on a large scale. Hume says that "shipbuilding and the founding of iron cannon were the sole manufactures in which the English excelled in James the First's reign," from 1603 to 1625. In 1629 the crown ordered 600 cannon to be cast for the States of Holland. England, however, continued to import from the Continent, but particularly from Sweden, Germany, and Spain, some of the finer qualities of iron and considerable quantities of steel.

Before 1568 all iron wire that was made in England was "drawn by main strength alone," according to Camden. The Germans, says this author, then introduced into the Forest of Dean and elsewhere the art of drawing it by a mill. Previous to the year mentioned the larger part of the iron wire and ready-made wool-cards used in England was imported. Scrivenor quotes Williams's *History of Monmouthshire* as authority for the statement that the iron and wire works near Tintern Abbey were erected by Germans. There can be no doubt that the iron industry of England in the fourteenth, fifteenth, and sixteenth centuries was greatly indebted to the inventive genius and mechanical skill of German, Flemish, French, and other emigrants from Continental countries.

Near the close of the sixteenth century there was introduced into England an invention for slitting flattened bars of iron into strips called nail-rods. This invention was the slitting mill. Scrivenor, upon the authority of Gough's *Camden*, states that Godfrey Bochs, of Liége, Belgium, set up at Dartford, in 1590, "the first iron mill for slitting bars." Dartford is a market town in Kent. Another story associates the name of "the founder of the Foley family, who was a fiddler living near Stourbridge," with the honor of introducing the first slitting mill into England, a knowledge of which he surreptitiously gained by visiting Swedish iron works and fiddling for the workmen. Percy states that Richard Foley, the founder of the Foley family at Stourbridge, who was first a seller of nails and afterwards a forgemaster, died in 1657 at the age of 80 years. In 1606 and 1618 patents were granted in England to Sir Davis Bulmer and Clement Dawbeny, respectively, for cutting iron into nail-rods by water-power.

The slitting mill, by whomsoever invented and perfected, greatly benefited the nail trade of England. Birmingham became the centre of this industry, and it was here, probably, that scantily-clad and poorly-paid women and girls were first regularly employed in England in the manufacture of nails. Hutton, who is quoted by Young in his *Labor in Europe and America*, says that in 1741 they were thus employed in the numerous blacksmith shops of Birmingham, " wielding the hammer with all the grace of their sex." They were called " nailers." Women and children are still employed at Birmingham and its vicinity in making nails and chains, and their condition is usually wretched and pitiable. Machinery was not applied to the manufacture of nails in any country until near the close of the eighteenth century. Nail-cutting machinery is an American invention.

Leland, a writer in the time of Henry the Eighth, (1509 to 1547,) refers to Birmingham as follows: " There be many smithes in the towne that use to make knives and all manner of cutting tooles, and many lorimers (saddlers) that make bittes, and a great many naylors ; so that a great part of the towne is maintained by smithes, whoe have their iron and sea-cole out of Staffordshire." He also says: " The beauty of Birmingham, a good market towne in the extreame parts of Warwickshire, is one street going up alonge almost from the left ripe of the brooke, up a meane hill by the length of a quarter of a mile. I saw but one paroch church in the towne." Camden, who wrote half a century later, describes Birmingham as "swarming with inhabitants and echoing with the noise of anvils."

The art of tinning iron was first practiced in Bohemia, and in 1620 it was introduced into Saxony. These countries for some time supplied all Europe with tin plates. The discovery of tin in Bohemia is said by Flower, in his *History of the Trade in Tin*, to date from 1240. In 1681 Andrew Yarranton asserted that tin plates were then made in England through his means, he having learned the art of making them in Saxony in 1665. The exact date of the introduction of the manufacture of tin plates into England by Yarranton is said to have been 1670. The first attempt to establish the new industry in England was made at Pontypool, in Monmouthshire, in that year, but it was not successfully established there until 1720. Scrivenor states that in 1740 the art "was brought to considerable perfection in England."

But, notwithstanding the progress which had been made in the development of the English iron trade, especially in the reigns of Henry the Eighth, Elizabeth, and James the First, an influence was at work which was destined to weigh heavily for a hundred and fifty years upon all further development. This was the growing scarcity of wood for the use of the forges and furnaces, mineral fuel, or pit-coal, not yet having come into use as a substitute for wood in these works. The forests of England in the ironmaking districts had been largely consumed by the "voragious" iron works, and there were loud complaints that the whole community would be unable to obtain fuel for domestic purposes if this denudation were persisted in. In response to these complaints an act was passed in 1558, the first year of the reign of Elizabeth, which prohibited the cutting of timber in certain parts of the country for conversion into coal or fuel "for the making of iron," special exception being made of the 'weald of Kent, the county of Sussex, and certain parishes "high in the weald of the county of Surrey." In 1563 a royal decree was issued abolishing the "bloomeries," or "iron smithies," in Furness in Lancashire, in compliance with a petition of the inhabitants, "because they consumed all the loppings and croppings, the sole winter food for their cattle." In 1581 an act to prevent the destruction of timber was passed, which set forth the increasing scarcity of timber for fuel in consequence of "the late erection of sundry iron mills in divers places not far distant from the city of London and the suburbs of the same, or from the downs and sea-coast of Sussex," and provided that "no new iron works should be erected within twenty-two miles of London, nor within fourteen miles of the river Thames," nor in certain parts of Sussex near the sea; nor should any wood within the limits described, with certain exceptions, be converted "to coal or other fewel, for the making of iron-metal in any iron-mill, furnace, or hammer." A more sweeping act was passed in

1584, which prohibited the erection of any new iron works in Surrey, Kent, and Sussex, and ordered that no timber one foot square at the stub should be used as fuel "at any iron work." It is said that these restrictions were not very rigidly enforced, but they served to narrow the limits within which the manufacture of iron could be conducted, although they did not abridge the manufacture itself. Lower says that, in the early part of the reign of Charles the First, who was beheaded in 1649, "the number of mills and furnaces had increased yearly, in spite of the statutes limiting their extension, and the waste of timber was again brought before the notice of government." This increase, however, was probably in districts of the country which had not previously been largely devoted to the manufacture of iron. Dudley, in his *Mettallum Martis*, says that about 1620 there were nearly 20,-000 smiths of all sorts within ten miles of Dudley Castle, in Staffordshire, and that there were also "many iron works at that time within that circle decayed for want of wood (yet formerly a mighty woodland country)."

About the middle of the seventeenth century the British iron industry experienced a serious check through the civil commotion known as the Cromwellian Rebellion which then prevailed. Many of the forges and furnaces in Sussex and in the south of Wales were destroyed, and they were not again rebuilt. Soon after the Restoration all the royal iron works in the Forest of Dean were destroyed, owing to the scarcity of timber. There was then much apprehension felt lest the Forest of Dean should fail to supply timber for the royal navy. Owing to the scarcity of timber many of the iron works in Kent, Sussex, and Surrey, and in the north of England were "laid down" in 1676, and England's supply of iron was largely derived from "Sweadland, Flanders, and Spain."

Notwithstanding these severe checks the iron industry of England bravely refused to be utterly destroyed, and as late as 1720 it was still second in importance to the manufacture of woolen goods. In 1724 it was the chief industry of Sussex. In 1740, however, only 59 furnaces were left in all England and Wales, and their total production was but 17,-350 tons of pig iron, or about 294 tons for each furnace. All these furnaces may not have been in blast, as it has been stated that, ten years later, in 1750, each of the charcoal furnaces of Monmouthshire produced 24 tons of iron in a week. Ten of the furnaces existing in 1740 were in Sussex, but in 1788 only two of these were left, and in 1796 only one is mentioned. In 1740 there were 10 charcoal furnaces in the Forest of Dean. Pig iron is still made in this district, but with coke as fuel. The iron industry of Kent, Sussex, and Surrey is now extinct. The last furnace in the weald of Sussex, at Ashburnham, was blown out in 1829.

During the seventeenth and eighteenth centuries England imported iron largely from Sweden, and in the latter century both Russia and the American colonies contributed to her supply. The scarcity of timber for fuel for blast furnaces in England continuing, a proposition was made in the British Parliament in 1737 to bring all pig iron from the British colonies in America; and in 1750, to facilitate the importation of pig iron from these colonies, the duty which had previously been imposed for the protection of British pig-iron manufacturers was repealed. At this time the business of manufacturing pig iron in some parts of Great Britain was still conducted upon such primitive principles that both charcoal and iron ore were carried to the furnaces of Monmouthshire on the backs of horses.

About the middle of the eighteenth century mineral fuel in the form of coke came into general use in the manufacture of pig iron in England, and the iron trade of that country and Wales at once revived, while that of Scotland may be said to have been created by the new fuel. As early as the beginning of the preceding century the celebrated and unfortunate Dud Dudley and others had experimented in England in the manufacture of iron with coke, but the first continuous and completely successful use of mineral fuel in the blast furnace was by Abraham Darby, of Shropshire, at his furnace at Coalbrookdale, in 1735, or possibly a year or two earlier. This coal was coked. The new fuel was at once introduced at other furnaces in England. Raw coal had previously been used in refineries. In 1740 a coke furnace was built at Pontypool, in Monmouthshire. In 1796 charcoal furnaces had been almost entirely abandoned in Great Britain.

Mr. Robert Hunt thus describes the early attempts that were made in England to manufacture iron with mineral fuel.

In the time of King James several patents for the manufacture of iron with pit-coal were granted, but with little success, till Dud Dudley, in 1619, succeeded in making coke pig iron at the rate of three tons per week. Previously, in 1612, Simon Sturtevant, and, in 1613, Ravenzon, made experiments in the same direction, but without success. During the Commonwealth patents were also granted, in one of which Oliver Cromwell was a partner. Again, in 1663, Dud Dudley secured his last patent, setting forth that at one time he was capable of producing seven tons of coke pig iron each week, the furnace being twenty-seven feet square, the blast impelled by bellows, which one man could work for an hour without being much tired. It was not, however, till the beginning of the 18th century that the successful application of coal, previously coked, was solved by Abraham Darby, of the Coalbrookdale iron works, Shropshire, giving a new and greater impetus to the iron industries of the kingdom.

The manufacture of pig iron with mineral fuel was greatly facilitated by the invention of a cylindrical cast-iron bellows by John Smeaton in 1760, to take the place of wooden or leather bellows, and by the improvements made in the steam engine by James Watt about 1769, both these valuable accessions to blast-furnace machinery being used for the first time, through the influence of Dr. Roebuck, at the Carron iron works in Scotland. The effect of their introduction was to greatly increase the blast and consequently to increase the production of iron. The blast, however, continued to be cold at all furnaces, both coke and charcoal, and so remained until 1828, when James Beaumont Neilson, of Scotland, invented the hot-blast, which is now in general use in Great Britain and other ironmaking countries.

These and other changes in the manufacture of pig iron were accompanied by equally important improvements in the manufacture of wrought, or finished, iron. In 1783 Henry Cort, of Gosport, England, obtained a patent for rolling iron into bars with grooved iron rolls, and in the following year he obtained a patent for converting pig iron into malleable iron by means of a puddling furnace. These patents did not relate to entirely new inventions in the manufacture of iron but to important improvements on existing methods, which had not, however, been generally employed. John Payne and Major Hanbury rolled sheet iron as early as 1728 at Pontypool, and patents were granted for grooved rolls to other

Englishmen before Cort's day. From Cort's time forward bituminous coal was used in the puddling furnace as well as in the blast furnace, but in its raw state. To the important improvements introduced by Cort the iron trade of Great Britain is greatly indebted. The refining of pig iron in forges and its subsequent conversion into bars and plates under a hammer formed the only general method of producing finished iron down to Cort's day, both in Great Britain and on the Continent, and it was wholly inadequate to the production of large quantities of iron of this character. With mineral fuel, powerful blowing engines, the puddling furnace, and grooved rolls Great Britain rapidly passed to the front of all ironmaking nations. But the foundation of this progress was the possession of mineral fuel, or pit-coal, of superior quality and in large and apparently inexhaustible quantities. On the Continent at this time the pit-coal which had been developed was supposed to be unsuited to the manufacture of iron. Owing to this belief and to the demoralization of all industries caused by the Napoleonic wars coke pig iron was not made on the Continent until 1826, when John Cockerill successfully introduced the use of coke at a blast furnace at Seraing.

Steel was largely made in England as early as 1609, and most probably in cementation furnaces, the product being known as blister steel and shear steel. The manufacture of steel by cementation did not, however, originate in England, but on the Continent. In the year mentioned John Hawes held the site of the Abbey of Robertsbridge in Sussex, upon which were eight steel "furnaces." The invention of crucible cast steel originated with Benjamin Huntsman, an English clockmaker, at Sheffield, in 1740, and not only Sheffield, the principal seat of its manufacture and of the manufacture of all kinds of cutlery, but all England as well has greatly profited by his discovery. The manufacture of cemented steel also became a leading industry of Sheffield in the eighteenth century.

At the beginning of the seventeenth century Sheffield contained 2,207 persons; at the census of 1881 it had 284,-508. As late as 1736 the population of Sheffield was only 10,121. A curious document sets forth that, "by a survaie of the towne of Sheffild, made the second daie of Januarie, 1615, by twenty-four of the most sufficient inhabitants there, it appeareth that there are in the towne of Sheffild 2,207 people; of which there are 725 which are not able to live without the charity of their neighbours; these are all begging poore. One hundred householders which relieve others. These (though the best sorte) are but poor artificers; among them there is not one that can keep a teame on his own land, and not above tenn that have ground of their own that can keep a cow. One hundred and sixty householders not able to relieve others. These are such (although they beg not) as are not able to abide the storme of one fortnight's sickness, but would be thereby driven to beggary. One thousand two hundred and twenty-two children and servants of the said householders, the greatest part of which are such as live of small wages, and are constrained to work sore to provide them necessaries."

Benjamin Huntsman was born in Lincolnshire, England, in 1704, of German parents, and died at Attercliffe, near Sheffield, on June 20, 1776. He was a member of the Society of Friends.

Robert Hunt was born at Devonport, England, on September 1, 1807, and died at Chelsea, England, on October 17, 1887.

Dr. John Percy was born at Nottingham, England, on March 23, 1817, and died at Paddington, England, on June 19, 1889.

Professor James E. Thorold Rogers was born at West Meon, in Hampshire, England, in 1823, and died at Oxford, England, on October 13, 1890.

CHAPTER V.

THE EARLY IRON INDUSTRY OF WALES, IRELAND, AND SCOTLAND.

In preceding chapters relating to the British iron industry our attention has been wholly occupied with the details of its development in England. We will now turn to the early iron industry of Wales, Ireland, and Scotland.

It has already been stated that iron was made in Wales during the Roman occupation of Britain. As the Welsh were a somewhat exclusive and practically an independent people down to a comparatively recent period it may be assumed that they have never since ceased to make iron, although we have found no details of its manufacture by them prior to the sixteenth century. At Crickhowell, in Brecknockshire, there were to be found a few years ago large quantities of scoria of supposed Roman origin. In the sixteenth century, owing to the scarcity of timber in England, some of the ironmasters of Sussex emigrated to Glamorganshire, in South Wales, where they founded the iron works of Aberdare and other iron works. Remains of the works in the Aberdare valley still exist. At Pontypool, on the Welsh border, a blast furnace was built by Capel Hanbury in 1565, to smelt the Roman cinder which was found there, and about 1620 "the Hanburys" are said to have built iron works at Llanelly. The development of the extensive iron industry of Merthyr Tydvil appears to date from about 1755, when the Dowlais iron works were established, although iron is said to have been made at Merthyr as long ago as 1660. In 1770 the first coke furnace in South Wales was built at Cyfarthfa. In 1788 there were six coke furnaces in South Wales. Cort's inventions were promptly appropriated by Welsh ironmasters. The first successful manufacture of pig iron with anthracite coal was accomplished by George Crane, an Englishman, at Yniscedwin, in Wales, in 1837.

Merthyr, at one time called the iron metropolis of Wales, is said to owe its name to Tydvil, the daughter of Brychan, the king of the district and a very devout old man, who was murdered in 420 by a party of marauding Saxons, or, as stated by others, Irish Picts, together with her father and brother. A church was erected on the spot to her memory and named after her, Merthyr Tydvil, or Tydvil the Martyr. Tydvil is not an uncommon feminine name in Wales to-day.

According to Scrivenor, iron-ore mines were opened in Ireland by the English who settled in the country during the reign of Elizabeth, and iron itself was extensively manufactured in Ireland by the English during the reign of James the First and afterwards. The most extensive works were in the provinces of Munster, Connaught, and Ulster, and in the counties of Queens, Kings, and Thomond. In some instances iron ore was taken from England to the sea-coast of Ulster and Munster in Ireland, the latter country then abounding in forests, but generally Ireland supplied both the ore and fuel. Most of the iron produced was in bars from forges, but ordnance, pots, and other articles were also cast in foundries or furnaces. The Rebellion of 1641 put an end to many of the English iron works in Ireland, some valuable works in the county of Mayo escaping. In 1660 Sir William Petty established extensive iron works in the county of Kerry, which continued in operation until the middle of the eighteenth century, when they were stopped in consequence of the scarcity of timber. In 1672 Sir William stated that one thousand tons of iron were then made in Ireland. Near the close of the seventeenth century an act of the British Parliament remitted the duties on bar iron and on iron slit and hammered into bars imported from Ireland, the manufacturing industries of Ireland being then greatly depressed. The iron industry of Ireland survived until the reign of George the Second, in the early part of the eighteenth century, when it came to an end in consequence of the scarcity of timber, the competition of English iron, and the unsettled condition of the country. An effort was made to revive it at the close of the century, but it met with slight success.

In 1840 there were no iron works in Ireland "going on," and in 1857 there was only one furnace standing in Ireland. There are now no iron works in the country. Irish ores were exported to the United States in 1879 and 1880, and in more recent years. In 1888 County Antrim in Ireland produced 129,235 tons of iron ore, and a small quantity was also produced in County Roscommon. In 1889 County Antrim produced 164,686 tons, but no ore was produced in County Roscommon. In all Ireland there were mined 91,904 tons of coal in 1888 and 103,201 tons in 1889.

It has already been incidentally stated that iron was very scarce in Scotland in the closing centuries of the middle ages, the Scotch people obtaining nearly all their supplies of iron at that time from other countries. The Scotch, however, were noted during the period mentioned for the excellence of their swords and armor, the former vying in temper with those of Toledo, Bilbao, and Milan. In Sir Walter Scott's story of *The Fair Maid of Perth*, the incidents of which are supposed to have occurred during the last years of the fourteenth century, the hero, Henry Gow, is an armorer, a forger of swords and bucklers and coats-of-mail. In 1547 an English chronicler wrote that "the Scots came with swords all broad and thin, of exceeding good temper, and universally so made to slice that I never saw none so good, so I think it hard to devise a better."

In a paper read in 1886 before the Society of Antiquaries of Scotland Mr. Ivison Macadam fully described the ancient iron industry of Scotland. The discovery of several mounds of iron slag in Argyleshire and elsewhere in 1881 had led him to investigate their origin. A list of many old bloomaries had been obtained at the time his paper was written. The ore used in most cases was bog ore, but occasionally red iron ore was used, and even clayband ore. The two last named may have been imported from England. The fuel was wood or peat charcoal, large supplies of which could be obtained in the neighborhood of most of the sites of these old iron works. Mr. Macadam exhibited specimens of the slag, charcoal, iron ores, and iron found in the ruins of the bloomaries. His valuable discoveries completely establish the fact that the inhabitants of Scotland in early times were familiar with the manufacture of iron in bloomaries, probably as early as the eleventh or twelfth century. We have already mentioned that pieces of iron slag have been discovered in the ruins of Celtic fortified towns in the Cheviot hills, on the boundary between England and Scotland, which may relate to a still earlier period.

Mr. Macadam gives a circumstantial account of a blast furnace which was erected in 1607 at Letterewe, in Ross-shire, Scotland, and which was successfully operated for many years. The foundations and other remains of this first of historic furnaces in Scotland are still to be seen. The furnace was situated on the north bank of Furnace Burn, which flows into Loch Maree about one mile to the south of Letterewe House. Sir George Hay, a native of Perthshire, was the owner of the furnace. An old manuscript refers to "the woods of Letterewe, where the said George Hay kept a colony and manufactory of Englishmen making iron and casting great guns, untill the woods of it was spent and the lease of it expired." Pennant, in his *Tour in Scotland*, (1769,) mentions "the remains of a very ancient iron furnace," and adds that "Mr. Dounie has seen the back of a grate marked S. G. Hay, or Sir George Hay, who was head of a company here in the time of the Queen Regent." Some of the ore used was found in the neighborhood, but a part seems to have been brought by sea from England. Mr. Macadam also describes the remains of two other iron works on Loch Maree that are probably as old at least as the Letterewe furnace, one of which, Fasagh, may have been a bloomary, working on bog ores, while the other, Red Smiddy, embraced a furnace, for the production of guns, grates, and other castings, and a forge for making wrought iron, the ores used being red hematite and clayband.

Of the earliest of modern blast furnaces in Scotland Mr. Macadam also gives a circumstantial account. There was a furnace at Invergarry about 1730, which was operated by a Liverpool company which used imported ore, at least in part. Some pigs of iron, inscribed "1732," have been found doing service as headstones in a disused graveyard at Gairlochy locks, on the Caledonian canal. A furnace was built at Bunawe, in Argyleshire, in 1730, by an Irish company. This furnace ceased to be operated in 1866. In 1878 its machinery was removed to England. The ore used was imported from Ulverston, in Lancashire. A furnace was built in the neighborhood of Abernethy, in Strathspey, in 1730, and there were also attached "four furnaces for making bar iron." At this furnace "Glengarry" and "Strathdown" pigs were produced. Brown hematite iron ore for the use of this furnace was brought from Tomintoul, in Banffshire, a distance of nearly twenty miles, "on pony back." A furnace called Craleckan, or Goatfield, at Inverleckan, or Furnace, on Loch Fyne, about eight miles distant from Inveraray, was built in 1754 by a Lancashire company, which brought its ore from England. Charcoal was taken to the furnace on the backs of a "string of from 30 to 40 ponies." This furnace also had a forge attached to it. The works ceased operations in 1813. The first blast furnace of the celebrated Carron iron works, about a mile from Falkirk, was built in 1759 and first put in operation on January 1, 1760. These works are still active.

Carron furnace was at first operated with charcoal, but coke was afterwards substituted. This furnace was the first in Scotland to use the new fuel. The manufacture of carronades was long a specialty of the Carron iron works, from which they took their name. In 1788 there were six coke furnaces in Scotland and the two charcoal furnaces of Bunawe and Goatfield.

There are now no charcoal furnaces in Scotland, none in Ireland or Wales, and but two in all England. These two furnaces were in blast in 1889. For several years they have produced but little iron. They are known as Newlands and Backbarrow, and are situated near Ulverston, in Lancashire. Backbarrow was built not later than 1711. Newlands was built in 1747.

About 1782 two blast furnaces, known as the Devon iron works, were erected in Clackmannanshire, Scotland. Mr. Richard Meade, in his *Coal and Iron Industries of the United Kingdom*, quotes Sir John Sinclair's description of these curious furnaces, written in 1792, which we reproduce below.

A steep bank rises more than 90 feet from the level of the river, and is composed of a rock, or very thick stratum of limestone, very dry and uniform in its texture, and almost free from cracks and fissures. Instead of the usual method of building with stone and lime, the several parts of the works have been formed in this bank by excavations made in the rock. Two furnaces, which are each 40 feet high and 14 feet in diameter, and also the spacious arches which give access to the workmen at the bottom of the furnace, to draw off the liquid metal and slag, are cut out of the rock. The roof which covers the casting house, a room 70 feet long, 50 feet wide, and 23 feet high, is supported by the sides of the quarry and the solid pillars of the rock that were left for the purpose in making the excavation. In like manner is formed the engine house and its apparatus, which is intended to supply the two furnaces with wind, by throwing at each vibration of the engine a sufficient quantity of air out of a large cylinder into a long gallery or close mine formed in the rock. This magazine of wind will contain 10,000 cubic feet of air, much condensed by the power of the engine, as the gallery is very closely shut up and made air-tight, having only two apertures, one to receive the supply of air from the air-pump and the other to admit a pipe that conducts the condensed air to blow the two furnaces.

Mr. Meade says that these works continued in operation for many years, but were stopped about the year 1858, and were soon afterwards dismantled.

At the close of 1889 there were 769 blast furnaces in Great Britain, of which only 444 were in blast during the year. Of the whole number there were 635 in England and Wales and 134 in Scotland. Of the furnaces out of blast many were of antiquated construction and will probably never again be active.

CHAPTER VI.

THE BRITISH IRON INDUSTRY BUILT UP BY BRITISH INVENTIVE GENIUS.

THE eighteenth century marked a new era in all those branches of manufacturing industry in which the British people have become prominent. It was the era of machinery, which then began to receive general attention as a substitute for hand labor. This era gave to the people of Great Britain the manufacture of India cotton goods, and it largely increased their woolen industry and also wonderfully developed their iron industry. It was in the eighteenth century that Great Britain, in consequence of her quick appreciation of the value of labor-saving machinery, became the first manufacturing nation in the world; in the preceding century four-fifths of all British workingmen were still farmers or farm laborers.

During the latter part of the eighteenth century and the whole of the nineteenth century down to the present time no other country has occupied so conspicuous a position in the manufacture of iron and steel as Great Britain. Spain and Germany had both been more prominent in the production of these essentials of modern civilization, but Great Britain spurned all opposition when she began to make pig iron with the aid of mineral fuel and powerful blowing engines. She had iron ores and mineral fuel in abundance, and her people had applied to the utilization of these products their invincible energy and their newly-developed inventive genius. Thenceforward the lack of timber for charcoal, which had previously almost destroyed her once flourishing iron industry, was no longer lamented and was but little felt. She was afterwards the first nation to refine pig iron in puddling furnaces and to make bar iron in rolling mills. France, Germany, and other Continental countries might have substituted mineral fuel for charcoal, invented the puddling furnace, or perfected the rolling mill and the steam engine, but none of them did.

The whole world is indebted to England and Scotland

for the inventions which gave a fresh impetus to the manufacture of iron in the eighteenth century. Payne and Hanbury, who first succeeded in rolling sheet iron; Darby, who
first successfully and continuously used coke in the blast furnace ; Huntsman, who invented the process of making steel in
crucibles ; Smeaton, who invented cast-iron blowing cylinders;
and Cort, who invented grooved rolls and the puddling furnace, were Englishmen ; while Watt, who perfected the steam
engine, was a Scotchman. It is also indebted to the same
countries for most of the inventions of the present century
which have further developed the manufacture of iron and
increased the demand for it, and which have almost created
the manufacture of steel. Stephenson, the Englishman, improved the locomotive in 1815, and in 1825 the first passenger railroad in the world was opened in England, his locomotive hauling the trains. The railroad is the greatest of
all the consumers of iron and steel. Neilson, the Scotchman,
invented the hot-blast in 1828; Crane, the Englishman, applied it to the manufacture of pig iron with anthracite coal in
1837 ; Nasmyth, the Scotchman, invented the steam hammer
in 1838 and the pile-driver in 1843; and Bessemer, the Englishman, invented in 1855 the process which bears his name
and is the flower of all metallurgical achievements—a share
in the honor of this invention, however, being fairly due to
the co-operating genius of Robert F. Mushet, also an Englishman, but born of Scotch parentage. The Siemens regenerative gas furnace, which has been so extensively used in the
manufacture of iron and steel, is also an English invention,
although the inventors, Sir William and Frederick Siemens,
while citizens of England, were natives of Hanover in Germany.

It is only just to add that Sir Henry Bessemer, although
born in England, is the son of a French refugee who settled
in England during the French Revolution of 1789, and that
Benjamin Huntsman, the inventor of the process for manufacturing cast steel in crucibles, was the son of German parents, although himself born in England. Mr. Göran F. Göransson, of Sandviken, Sweden, also assisted in perfecting the
Bessemer process. It was, however, enterprising and sturdy
England which nursed the genius of the great inventors we

have mentioned who were of Continental birth or extraction, and it was in England that the ripe fruits of their inventions were first abundantly gathered.

That Great Britain at the beginning of her manufacturing activity did not seek to extend the influence of her new light and life to other countries, but by various acts of Parliament sought to prevent the introduction of her inventions and the emigration of her skilled artisans into those countries, is not here a subject of comment; nor is the strict adherence of Great Britain to a policy of protection to home industries by customs duties during five centuries and down to almost the middle of the present century a subject of present comment. Both measures undoubtedly fostered the growth of British manufacturing industries, and in the end the world was benefited by British inventions, which found their way across the English channel and the Atlantic ocean, and by the example of British energy and British enterprise in the utilization of native manufacturing resources.

The United States is to-day a recognized and formidable rival of Great Britain in the manufacture of all forms of iron and steel, partly because we have abundant native resources for their production, and partly because we are of the same blood as the British people and their German ancestors, but chiefly because we have adopted and in many instances have improved upon her invaluable engineering and metallurgical inventions, the most important of which have been briefly summarized in this chapter.

CHAPTER VII.

EARLY PROCESSES IN THE MANUFACTURE OF IRON AND STEEL.

EXCEPT incidentally the various processes for the manufacture of iron which were in use in the early ages of the world's history, as well as in more recent times, have not been referred to in the preceding pages. Further notice of some of the processes that were successively in use before the beginning of the present century seems, however, to be desirable, if for no other reason than to show how rude and unproductive those processes were in comparison with the improved methods which are now in use.

The methods of manufacturing iron which were in use in Asia and Africa in the earliest ages were few in number and of extreme simplicity. They all produced wrought iron with the aid of wood or charcoal as fuel, although steel was also produced by some of them. One of these processes, still existing in Burmah, did not require an artificial blast. A perpendicular circular excavation, ten or twelve feet deep and open at the top, was made in the side of a bank or hillock, in which ore and fuel were placed in alternate layers, and to which the necessary draft for combustion was applied through one or more openings near the bottom. The product was a lump, or bloom, of iron. Another process applied an artificial blast to a small excavation in the ground, or to a low furnace built of clay or stone and standing alone, the product being also a lump of iron. This artificial blast was supplied by a bellows which was usually made of goat skins, having a nozzle, or tuyere, of bamboo and burnt clay, and worked by the feet or hands. It is an interesting scientific fact that the bellows and its tuyere, or nozzle, both of which in some form are in general use to-day wherever iron is made, are not only of prehistoric origin but are still used in all their primitive simplicity in the manufacture of iron. Goat-skin bellows are in use in India and in the interior of Africa to-day in connection with small furnaces. In some parts of

India, and in China, Japan, Borneo, and Madagascar, blowing cylinders of wood or bamboo, having valves and pistons, and worked like a pump by manual labor, are now used, and were probably used in remote ages. The bloom of iron, whether produced by natural or artificial blast, was reheated and freed from impurities and adhering charcoal by repeated hammering, in the course of which refining operation it was divided into suitable parts for practical use. The fire of the smith who gave to the iron its final shape was supplied with a goat-skin or bamboo blast. The ore which was smelted by these primitive processes was broken into small pieces and otherwise carefully prepared. In some parts of India and in several other Asiatic countries the ore was magnetic and well adapted by its purity to the manufacture of steel.

The manner in which the air was expelled from the goat-skin bellows of antiquity doubtless varied in different countries, but the pressure of the feet of one workman on two such bellows, each attached to a nozzle, or tuyere, was probably the method in most general use. This method is still used in Africa. Wilkinson, in his *Manners and Customs of the Ancient Egyptians*, quoted by Day, mentions his discovery at Thebes, on the walls of a tomb built in the reign of Thothmes the Third, about fifteen centuries before the Christian era, of the picture of an Egyptian furnace and bellows, with two workmen engaged in expelling with their feet the air from as many pairs of bellows, "consisting of flexible bags formed of the skins of animals, and each provided with a cord which the operator holds in his hands. From each of these flexible bags a tube proceeds into the heap of fuel and ore, and the blast is produced by the operator transferring the weight of his body alternately from one foot to the other. The bags are inflated by pulling up the upper part by the cord, this upper part having a hole or valve therein for allowing the air to enter, and which is closed by the heel of the operator on his again transferring his weight to it."

At a later period, in the days of Ezekiel, about six centuries before Christ, the use of a more powerful bellows than that above described is clearly implied. In the 22d chapter and 20th verse of the book of the prophet referred to we read as follows: "As they gather silver, and brass, and iron, and lead, and tin into the midst of the furnace, to blow the fire upon it, to melt it, so will I gather you in mine anger and in my fury, and I will leave you there and melt you."

The celebrated Indian steel, or wootz, which is chiefly used in the manufacture of sword blades, is obtained at the present time by remelting pieces of native iron in small crucibles which are only a few inches high, containing finely-chopped wood, the crucibles being placed in a furnace heated with a blast supplied by bellows usually made of goat skins or bamboo cylinders. More than two thousand years ago the process was substantially the same that it is now. It is described by Aristotle, who lived in the fourth century before Christ.

The method of manufacturing Indian steel in the Trichinopoly district in India in our day is fully described by the *East Indian Engineer* in the following words, which plainly suggest the crucible process perfected by Huntsman.

The process employed is very simple. Small quantities of iron are enclosed in a small earthen crucible with a few pieces of the wood of the avaram plant and two or three green leaves. A top is luted on, and, when dry, the whole is exposed to the heat of a small charcoal furnace till the iron is melted, a fact which the operator ascertains by picking up the crucibles in a long pincer and shaking them. The vessels are allowed to cool, and are then broken open, when a knob of steel is found at the bottom. Two sizes of ingots are made, weighing about 8 ounces and 10⅔ ounces respectively. The crucibles consist of a mixture of red earth and charcoal, made of paddy husks, kneaded together. The lid is of the same material and put on wet. It appears hardly to contract at all in drying, and a fairly air-tight vessel is consequently produced. The clay is not nearly refractory enough for the heat it is exposed to, as the crucibles are completely vitrified and spoilt at the end of a single operation.

The iron used is brought from the Namakal Taluk, of Salem, and appears to be a rough description of wrought iron. For the smaller size of ingot it is cut into pieces weighing as nearly as possible 10 ounces, (a small piece is added to make up the weight, if necessary,) and this quantity is placed in each crucible with ¾ of an ounce of pieces of the dry wood of the avaram plant. Two or three green leaves (the kind is a matter of no consequence) are placed on the top, and the charge is closed up with a lump of clay carefully plastered all round. Great care is taken in putting in the correct proportions of iron and avaram wood, and the operators assert that, if less is used, the iron is not melted, and, if more, it will not stand being worked afterwards. The green leaves probably serve in some way toward retarding the drying of the lid and preventing it from cracking.

The furnace consists of an inverted cone of earthwork about two feet in diameter and the same in depth, the apex opening into an ash-pit below. At one side, and protected from the heat by a mud wall, is a small shed in which two bellowsmen sit and work a couple of skin bellows most vigorously. The air is admitted into the furnace through a hole near the bottom. In preparing a furnace some straw is first placed at the bottom below the air-hole and charcoal is then thrown in to a suitable height. On this twenty-five of these conical crucibles are placed with the point downward, and, when all are in position they appear to form a sort of circle, and to be independent of the layer of charcoal below. More charcoal is placed above, and the furnace is then lighted through the air-hole. Fresh fuel is thrown on above from time to time, and one or two of the crucibles are occasionally lifted with long-handled pincers to allow the burning charcoal to fall through and replenish the supply below. The straw remains untouched by the fire throughout the process. The crucibles are given a sharp shake on these occasions, which is said to assist the process, and towards its conclusion allows of the operators ascertaining whether the iron is melted or not.

As the mouth of the furnace is open, the waste of fuel is enormous. After about an hour or an hour and a half the feel of a crucible, when lifted, shows its contents to be liquid. The process is then considered to be completed, and the crucibles are allowed to cool, after which they are broken open, a knob of steel being found at the bottom of each. The ingots are reheated and hammered into oblong pieces, in which shape they are sold. All the crucibles do not remain absolutely air-tight during the process, the lids becoming cracked without affecting the result.

The methods by which the iron pillar of Delhi and the heavy iron beams of Indian temples were forged will probably always remain a mystery. Metallurgists of the present day are certainly unable to understand how these large masses of iron could have been forged by a people who do not appear to have possessed any of the mechanical appliances for their manufacture which are now necessary in the production of similar articles. They could not have been forged by hand.

China is said by Day to have made steel long before the Christian era by the method revived in modern times of immersing wrought iron in a bath of cast iron, which modern method has been perfected in the open-hearth process.

In the interesting account by Dr. Bell of a *Journey from St. Petersburg to Pekin* from 1719 to 1721, from which we have already quoted, we find an allusion to cast iron in China at that period which is worthy of preservation, as it seems to indicate that the Chinese did not borrow the art of casting iron from the Europeans. Dr. Bell says : " My landlord being in his shop I paid him a visit, where I found six kettles placed in a row on furnaces, having a separate opening under each of them for receiving the fuel, which consisted of a few small sticks and straw. On his pulling a thong he blew a pair of bellows, which made all his kettles boil in a very short time. They are indeed very thin, and made of cast iron, being extremely smooth both within and without." The same writer refers as follows to the cannon then in use in the Chinese wall: "While we stopped at one of the gates to refresh ourselves I took the opportunity to walk into one of these towers, where I saw some hundreds of old iron cannon thrown together as useless. On examination I found them to be composed of three or four pieces of hammered iron, joined, and fastened together with hoops of the same metal. The Chinese have, however, now learned to cast as fine brass cannon as are anywhere to be found." The old cannon were bombards.

In the years 1881 to 1883 a French scientific commission, inquiring into the mineral resources of Indo-China, visited the important deposit of iron ore at Ph'nom Deck, in the province of Compong-Thom, in Cambodia. The manner in which this ore is converted into iron is very suggestive of the ancient methods which have been briefly described.

The native Khouys manufacture a small quantity of extremely pure iron, for which there is a great demand; it is exported to considerable distances, and serves as money over an immense area. A mixture of the ores is used, the chief being a brown hematite, containing under 40 per cent. of metallic iron, with over 2 per cent. of manganese, and associated with the surrounding tuff. The metallurgy is divided into two parts: first, the fabrication of an iron-sponge; and, second, the elaboration of the sponge and its transformation into small hammered bars. The sponge is made in a rectangular furnace, 8 feet by 3 feet, and 16 inches deep, which is constructed on a mass of earth nearly 3 feet above the ground. The walls and base of the furnace consist of refractory earth, mixed with very fine white sand. The charge is about 4 cwts. of mineral, with about 15 bushels of charcoal, in thin alternate layers.

The operation continues slowly for eight hours, the blast being distributed from a great number of bamboo tuyeres, the bellows, of curious construction, being made of buffalo and deer-skins; afterwards for two to four hours the blast is much stronger. During the operation the slag is frequently removed. The resulting sponge is sold to the native forges to be made into bars, which is accomplished by a laborious and primitive process. The bars are far from being homogeneous, some parts being of a steely character alternating with portions of soft iron. The bars weigh about 1 pound, and sell through Cambodia and Siam at prices attaining the rate of £60 per ton.

A recent traveler in Corea, C. Illing, describes as follows a Corean furnace and blowing apparatus of the present day, by means of which "good cast-iron household utensils are made" and "steel is produced on a small scale."

The author was unfortunately unable to inspect a Corean ironworks in operation. An old abandoned furnace he found, on measuring, to be 8 feet high. At top it had an elliptical section 4½ feet long and 2½ feet wide, whilst at bottom the section was more circular and measured 15 inches across. The blowing engine was formed of a pit, 8 feet long and 15 inches wide, semi-circular at the bottom. Its walls and floor were rendered air-tight by means of bricks and clay, carefully smoothed. In its centre perpendicular to its longitudinal axis there was a parting wall, and on this was the axis of ro-tation of a horizontal board fitting closely to the walls. This board was moved up and down like a see-saw by two workmen with their feet, where-by the air was alternately compressed in the two air-tight quadrants of the pit, and a continuous current was produced, which passed through two valves opening outwards into the pipe leading to the furnace. The iron ore was smelted with charcoal as fuel, and with lime as flux, and the white pig iron obtained was cast in clay moulds. Lumps of pig iron, 8 inches in diameter, were converted into malleable iron in small smithy fires, worked with a blast similar to that described, and from this iron knives, nails, scythes, etc., were made in the same forge.

In the official catalogue of the Japanese section of the Centennial Exhibition held at Philadelphia in 1876 the "old method" of smelting iron in Japan, which still exists side by side with modern methods, is described in detail as follows:

The smelting of iron by the old method is effected in small furnaces of rectangular section, built on the principle of the *stückofen*, 12 to 15 feet high. The building materials are fire-clay, and for the hearth a mixture of fire clay and charcoal powder. The blast is produced either by means of a pair of wooden box-bellows, moved by hand, or else by means of a sort of balance-bellows of peculiar construction. The magnetic ore is first calcined in large lumps and afterwards broken into smaller pieces with hand-ham-mers, then smelted with or without flux.

The furnaces for smelting the iron-sand are of a peculiar construction. The ground is dug out so as to form a pit 12 feet by 15, and 10 feet deep, and this is filled up to a depth of 9 feet with hard powdered charcoal; then comes a layer of clay and sand, which is dried and hardened by covering it with charcoal fire. The ashes being taken away, the pit is filled up with charcoal-powder, and the surface coated with a fire-proof mixture. Upon this foundation the furnace is built, 9 feet by 4 feet at the basis, and 4 feet high. The interior resembles to a great extent the well-known Rachette furnace, forming a wedge-like hollow space, with a horizontal section of 6 in length, and having a line of tweers (5 with the above dimension) on each of the long sides. When the smelting begins the furnace is en-tirely filled up with charcoal, the box-bellows are put to work, and 12 hours later, as the whole mass sinks down, iron-sand and charcoal are filled in. The smelting lasts two days and three nights. Generally 3,750 kilos of iron-sand are smelted with an equal weight of charcoal, and yield 45 per cent. of pig iron and 1 per cent. of steel in loops or blooms. When the above-named quantity has been smelted the liquid iron is run off, and as soon as the furnace is cool enough, the steel loops hanging against the walls are broken off. The whole process lasts about 8 days, viz., 2 days for building the furnace, 3 days for smelting, and 3 days for coating, for removing the steel, etc., and for cleaning the place in order to be able to build a new furnace.

The " balance-bellows of peculiar construction " above referred to aie very similar to the Corean bellows already described. The following minute description of the Japanese balance-bellows, taken from the same official source that has already been mentioned, will possess value for mechanical engineers who may have been interested in the Corean bellows.

Suppose a horizontal cylinder cut by two planes passing through the axis, and forming between them an angle of about 30°; two opposite sectors will be cut out. A rectangular plane, equal to the axial section, and balancing upon the axis of the primary cylinder, would fit the sides of the box in each position, and, when made to balance alternately from one side to the other, would act like the piston of a common box-bellows. According to this geometrical principle, the box of the bellows is composed of two cylindrical sectors, and the balancing plane is made of wooden boards, resting by its middle line upon a beam, which forms the central edge of the two sectors (or the axis of the aforesaid imaginary cylinder). The compressed air from each side is discharged into a short channel cut at an incline of 45 degrees into this beam, in the centre of which they unite into a main outward passage for the blast. At the place where these two oblique channels meet to form the main pipe, a flap-valve is placed, which, being put into motion by the compressed air, closes alternately, either of the two short channels whenever the opposite half of the balance-piston moves down. Two flap-valves, fitted each to one side of the piston, allow the outer air to enter one or the other half of the bellows. The balancing motion of the piston is produced by treading, two or three men standing on each end of this blasting machinery.

Mr. David Forbes, F. R. S., wrote in the *Journal* of the British Iron and Steel Institute in 1872 : " From information derived from Sir John Swinburne it appears that the negro tribes in the interior of Africa, some 800 miles from Natal, are extremely expert in the manufacture of wrought iron, which they smelt in little clay furnaces from the native ores. They sell the iron thus made, which is said to be extremely good in quality, at so low a price that it is cheaper than that which is imported by the settlers at the gold mines, who consequently employ it for their implements."

The primitive processes for manufacturing iron, or modifications of them, were adopted in Europe when that continent commenced to make iron. The manufacture of iron in Belgium and England without the aid of an artificial blast, about the time of the Christian era, has already been referred to. It is not known whether other European countries ever made iron in the same way. At Lustin, in Belgium, between Namur and Dinant, two ancient furnaces or bloomaries were discovered in 1870 on the top of a hill, with iron yet remaining in them. They consisted of simple oval excavations with rounded bottoms in a bed of clay, each 12 feet long and 9 feet wide, with a depth in the middle of 3 feet, the top being level with the surface of the surrounding soil. A channel excavated in the clay, but covered over with stones, conducted the wind into the lower portion of each furnace. The opening of this channel was turned in the direction of the prevailing wind, so that iron could only have been made on windy days. These bloomaries contained lumps of crude wrought iron.

The English antiquarian, Thomas Wright, in *The Celt, the Roman, and the Saxon,* quotes from Mr. Bruce's account of the Roman wall a statement concerning the discovery not many years ago of the character of the blast used in " the furnaces of the extensive Roman iron works " in the neighborhood of Epiacum, (Lanchester,) in England. Mr. Bruce says: " Two tunnels had been formed in the side of a hill; they were wide at one extremity, but tapered off to a narrow bore at the other, where they met in a point. The mouths of the channels opened toward the west, from which quarter a prevalent wind blows in this valley, and sometimes with great violence. The blast received by them would, when the wind was high, be poured with considerable force and effect upon the smelting furnaces at the extremity of the tunnels." In a foot-note Mr. Wright adds the following, which is curiously suggestive of the hot-blast: " We are told by the early Spanish writers that the Peruvians built their furnaces for smelting silver on eminences where the air was freest; they were perforated on all sides with holes, through which the air was driven when the wind blew, which was the only time when the work could be carried on, and under each hole was made a projection of the stonework, on which was laid burning coals to heat the air before it entered the furnace."

As no evidence exists that iron was ever made by the Romans in the south of Europe without the aid of an artificial blast, it may be fairly assumed that the Belgian furnaces above described and the methods of manufacture in England which are described by Mr. Bruce and others are of native origin. The Romans may for a time have continued the native practice, especially as the manufacture of iron in both Belgium and Britain would be mainly confined to the native inhabitants, but long before their withdrawal from these countries in the fifth century the superior practice of Southern Europe would be generally introduced.

In the south of Europe the bellows was certainly used to produce a blast long before the Roman invasion of Britain. Homer, quoted by Fairbairn, "represents Hephæstus as throwing the materials from which the shield of Achilles was to be forged into a furnace urged by twenty pairs of bellows." The bellows first used by the Greeks were probably made of goat skins, but subsequently, as early probably as the time of Homer, and certainly as early as the third century before Christ, larger and more powerful bellows were made of the hides of cattle, and larger furnaces or bloomaries were erected. These larger bellows were the same in principle as the common blacksmith's bellows of our day, and they would be used by the Greeks and Romans in smelting the ore as well as in refining and shaping the iron. Of their furnaces and forges we know but little. Virgil, who lived in the first century before Christ, gives us in the Fourth Georgic a view of a refinery forge as it doubtless existed among the Romans in his day.

> As when the Cyclops, at th' almighty nod,
> New thunder hasten for their angry god,
> Subdued in fire the stubborn metal lies:
> One brawny smith the puffing bellows plies,
> And draws and blows reciprocating air:
> Others to quench the hissing mass prepare:
> With lifted arms they order every blow,
> And chime their sounding hammers in a row:
> With labored anvils Etna groans below.
> Strongly they strike; huge flakes of flames expire:
> With tongs they turn the steel and vex it in the fire.

Diodorus of Sicily, quoted by Scrivenor, mentions the iron ores of Elba, "which the natives dig and cut out of the ground to melt, in order for the making of iron, much of which metal is in this sort of stone. The workmen employed first cut the stone in pieces, and then melt them in furnaces built and prepared for the purpose. In these furnaces the stones, by the violent heat of the fire, are melted into several pieces in form like great sponges, which the merchants buy by truck and exchange of other wares, and export them to Dicæarchea and other mart towns. Some of these merchants that buy of these wares cause them to be wrought by the coppersmiths, who beat and fashion them into all sorts of tools, instruments, and other shapes and fancies; some they neatly beat into the shape of birds, others into spades, hooks, and other sorts of utensils, all which are transported and carried about into several parts of the world by the merchants." This account was written in the first century before the Christian era.

Pliny describes the various kinds of iron and steel which were in use in his day, the first century after Christ, but gives us little insight into the methods by which they were produced. In the following vague description he seems to have intended to show that both iron and steel were made in the same furnace. He says: " There is a great difference, too, in the smelting; some kinds producing knurrs of metal, which are especially adapted for hardening into steel, or else, prepared in another manner, for making thick anvils or heads of hammers. But the main difference results from the quality of the water into which the red-hot metal is plunged from time to time. The water, which is in some places better for this purpose than in others, has quite ennobled some localities for the excellence of their iron, Bilbilis, for example, and Turiasso, in Spain, and Comum, in Italy, and this although there are no iron mines in these spots. It is a remarkable fact that when the ore is fused the metal becomes liquefied like water, and afterwards acquires a spongy, brittle texture. It is the practice to quench the smaller articles made of iron with oil, lest by being hardened in water they should be rendered brittle. Iron which has been acted upon by fire is spoiled unless it is forged with the hammer. It is not in a fit state for being hammered when it is red hot, nor, indeed, until it has begun to assume a white heat." The foregoing is a condensation of Pliny's full text, to be found in Scrivenor.

The reference in Diodorus to iron made in the form of "great sponges," and later in Pliny to iron of "a spongy, brittle texture," suggests the Catalan, or the direct, process of manufacture. In describing the Biscayan *ferrerias*, which were nothing but Catalan forges, M. Pourcel, from whom we have already quoted, says: "It is quite evident that iron obtained in the form of spongy masses from an ore almost chemically pure, with a fuel free from sulphur, is, by its molecular constitution as much as by its chemical composition, an essentially malleable metal, and capable of being kneaded, if the expression may be used, when hot."

In Spain, as we have seen, iron and steel were made many centuries before Pliny's time, the Catalan forge, or a modification of it, being used, and the product being either wrought iron or steel. The Catalan forge differed in no essential particular from the ordinary fire of a blacksmith, except that it had a sunken hearth, or crucible. The Corsican forge, which also existed before the Christian era, was a modification of the Catalan forge. The blast for these forges is presumed to have been primarily furnished by bellows made of goat skins or the skins of other small animals, but larger Grecian and Roman bellows were afterwards substituted. Bauerman, in his *Treatise on the Metallurgy of Iron*, cites Franquoy as authority for the statement that bellows with valves, "single acting and made of leather," were introduced by the Romans into Gaul in the fourth century of the Christian era.

Percy copies the following description of an old Catalan forge in Spain: "In 1823, at Bielsa, in Aragon, in the Spanish Pyrenees, some charcoal burners discovered in a forest of silver firs a small circular iron furnace only 2 feet and 1.59 inches high. The lower part or hearth was cylindrical up to the height of about 11.81 inches and then terminated in an inverted truncated cone; its diameter was 14.25 inches at the lower and 1.69 inches at the upper part; it had two tuyere beds at 11.81 inches from the bottom. Near the furnace were found two crude lumps of iron in the state in which they appeared to have been taken out, and which weighed from 30.9 pounds to 35.3 pounds. According to tradition the blast in these furnaces was produced with bellows of skin worked by hand. Accumulations of ancient slags are met with at high elevations in the Pyrenees, far from any water-course, and which doubtless were urged by a blast produced by manual labor." Scrivenor mentions portable forges in ancient France, and we have already referred to the movable forges of the Forest of Dean. These references suggest the portable blacksmith's forge of the present day.

M. Pourcel makes the following reference to the direct process in. use in Biscay: "The ore was treated in hearths, sometimes hollowed out alongside of the mine itself, but more frequently establishèd in the middle of the forests which supplied the charcoal and on the banks of streams. The traces of the old *ferrerias*, which are still met with in considerable numbers, situated in the mountains, near the mines, from which the timber has disappeared, on the banks of small torrents, and amongst heaps of slag, remain the witnesses of the old iron industry of Biscay. The work was carried on almost entirely by manual labor, and without doubt pretty nearly in the same fashion as among the Kabyles of the present day."

Much light is thrown upon the methods of manufacturing iron which prevailed in the south of Europe at the beginning of the Christian era by the discovery in 1870 of two ancient bloomaries or melting hearths in the vicinity of Hüttenberg, in Carinthia, on the Hüttenberg Railway. The place where these hearths were found is embraced within the limits of the ancient province of Noricum. Maw and Dredge describe the hearths as follows:

In the year 1870 a most interesting discovery was made during the construction of the Hüttenberg Railway. In a cutting a set of iron melting-hearths of Roman and Celtic times was found 6 feet below the present surface of the ground. These hearths consist of two holes or ditches, the upper one being supposed to have served as a calcining kiln, whilst the lower one represents the smelting furnace proper. These hearths were found near the mines of spathic ore in the neighborhood of Hüttenberg.

The calcining hearth is fitted with a layer of charcoal 1½ inches thick, upon which a 10-inch layer of clay forms the inside lining of the hearth. This lining was found burnt by the action of the calcining fire to a depth of 4 inches. The depth of the hearth is 2 feet, and its diameter 5 feet. The second or smelting hearth is placed at a distance of 16 feet from the former, and is 3 feet deep and 4 feet wide. The lining consists of a layer of 6-inch clay, upon which a fire-brick mass, consisting of clay and quartz, is uniformly spread to a thickness of 12 inches. This lining is burnt and glazed to a depth of 3 inches at the inner side, thus recording the higher temperature in this hearth during the smelting operation.

Both hearths are filled with *débris* of burnt clay and slag crumbled down from the walls of the hearths, which seem to have been raised one foot above the surface of the ground. The space between the two hearths is paved with stones. The slag contains many unburnt pieces of charcoal. The analysis of the slag has proved that the yield of the spathic ore in use, containing from 50 to 60 per cent. of iron, was only 15 to 20 per cent. The blast seems to have been furnished by bellows from the top of the furnaces. A Roman cornice has been found near the smelting hearth.

These discoveries point out a very primitive process as compared with our present means of iron smelting; but centuries vanished before any real improvements were introduced. Nevertheless we find that the preparatory calcination of the ore previous to its being introduced in the smelting furnace is a very ancient mode of economizing labor and fuel.

An analysis of the piece of iron found under the Egyptian obelisk which was removed in 1880 to New York shows that it must have been made by the direct process, and probably in a Catalan forge. The analysis, which was made for Mr. A. L. Holley by Dr. August Wendel, of Troy, is here preserved.

Iron	98.738	Copper	0.102
Carbon	0.521	Calcium	0.218
Sulphur	0.009	Magnesium	0.028
Silicon	0.017	Aluminum	0.070
Phosphorus	0.048	Slag	0.150
Manganese	0.116		
Nickel and cobalt	0.079	Total	100.096

Mr. Holley says that a clean fracture of the iron was similar to that of puddled steel, and mentions the further fact that the small amount of slag, as well as the fine fracture, indicates frequent reworking.

It is not definitely known whether any of the nations of remote antiquity were familiar with the use of coal, but there is some evidence to show that it was known in the days of the Greeks and Romans. Rev. Joseph Hurst, of Wadhurst, England, in an address read at the meeting of the Royal Archæological Institute of Great Britain and Ireland at Newcastle, in August, 1884, says: "That the ancient Greeks were acquainted with stone coal is evident from the words of Theophrastus, an author who lived three hundred years before Christ (*de Lapidibus*, N. 16): 'The coal commonly so-called, which is dug out of the earth for man's use, is of an earthy (or stoney) nature; it is kindled and burnt like coal (charcoal). Of this (stone) coal workers in iron make use.' Solinus has also been quoted for the use of stone-coal amongst the Greeks, and if the red-hot stones which, according to Pliny, were used by the Gauls for smelting copper were nothing more than stone-coal their efficacy would perhaps be rendered more intelligible to modern men of science." The quotation from Theophrastus does not inform us in what country coal was found in his day.

The compiler of the paper on iron in *Johnson's Cyclopædia* says of the Chalibees, who inhabited a part of the country south of the Black sea, that they "first used coal." He fortifies this statement in the following words: "Their iron was made, according to Aristotle, (322 B. C.,) from sand ore dug from river banks, washed, and put into the furnace along with the stone *pyrimachus,* (*fire-maker,*) that is, coal." There is coal on the southern shores of the Black sea, between the ports of Heraclea and Bardin, which is now mined in considerable quantities, but it is not probable that, if the above inference from the statement of Aristotle be correct, the Chalibees obtained their supply from this source. Nor would they have been likely to smelt magnetic sand with bituminous coal.

The use of bituminous coal, or pit-coal, by the Romans during their occupation of Britain, which terminated in the year 411, is claimed, but this use must have been very limited. Mr. Meade notes the use of coal in England in Anglo-Saxon times. He says: "As early as the year 852 there is a record of the abbey of Peterboro' receiving twelve cart-loads of fossil or pit coal." Mr. Macadam says that "coal was early known in Scotland," and he refers to a charter granted in 1291 to the abbot and convent of Dunfermline, giving them the privilege of digging coal. In the thirteenth century coal was sent to London from Newcastle by sea; hence the name which is still in use, sea-coal. The Sorbs and Wends, native inhabitants of the district of Zwickau, in Saxony, are said by Herr Pechar to have been familiar with the use of coal probably as early as the tenth century. Dr. Wedding states that "an insignificant consumption of coal in Germany for domestic purposes and brick and glass works can be traced with certainty as far back as the beginning of the fourteenth century." The beginning of coal mining in Belgium is said by Pechar to date as far back as the twelfth century.

With the exception of the Indian and Chinese methods of making steel the ancient processes which have been referred to were all direct processes, the iron or steel being obtained directly from the ore. The furnaces, whether large or small, were all bloomaries, because the product derived from the heated ore was obtained in the form of a lump or bloom of malleable iron or steel. If cast iron was sometimes obtained by the Mediterranean nations, or by Asiatic and African ironworkers, little evidence exists that it was run into moulds for the production of useful or ornamental castings. The weakness of the blast furnished by goat skins, bamboo, or the early leather bellows renders it highly improbable that cast iron was obtained by any of the more ancient processes. As we approach the Christian era the evidence of its existence increases.

Aristotle, who lived in the fourth century before Christ, has left an account of the manner in which the Greeks of his day converted wrought iron into steel, which furnishes some evidence that they were also familiar with cast iron. He is quoted by Day as follows: "Wrought iron itself may be cast so as to be made liquid and to harden again; and thus it is they are wont to make steel; for the scoria of iron subsides and is purged off by the bottom; and when it is often defecated and made clean this is steel. But this they do not often because of the great waste and because it loses much weight in refining; but iron is so much the more excellent the less recrement it has." The quotation from Pliny on a preceding page contains the most direct evidence we have of the making of cast iron by the Romans. It has been suggested that the battering-ram could only have been made of cast iron, but if so made could it have withstood the severe shocks to which it was subjected?

But, if the Mediterranean nations, and particularly the Greeks and Romans, knew how to make and utilize cast iron, this knowledge virtually became one of the lost arts, for there is no authentic mention of cast iron having been made in the northern and western parts of Europe until about six centuries ago, and if the Chinese, the Japanese, and the people of India ever possessed the art they kept it to themselves and made but little use of it.

CHAPTER VIII.

MEDIÆVAL AND EARLY MODERN PROCESSES IN THE MANUFACTURE OF IRON AND STEEL.

FROM the first to the eighth century of the Christian era the history of the manufacture of iron in all European countries is greatly obscured, and the processes which were in operation can not be described. In Asia and Africa the art had previously received less and less attention through the gradual transfer of political power and of civilization to the northern shores of the Mediterranean. But Greece, which had acquired much of this power and had absorbed most of this civilization, had in turn surrendered her leadership to Rome, and in the fifth century after Christ Rome herself fell before the northern barbarians. Except in Spain, where the Visigoths established a powerful empire in the fifth century, under which the arts of ancient civilization were encouraged, the iron industry is nowhere throughout Europe known to have flourished from the time when Rome commenced her final struggle with the northern invaders down to about the beginning of the eighth century. At this time we begin to hear of the iron industry taking a fresh start in many European countries, experiencing what in modern phrase we term a revival. And with this revival we hear authentically for the first time of the wolf furnace, or *stückofen*, in Austria, Bohemia, Germany, Belgium, and other Continental countries. In an address delivered at Liége, Belgium, in 1883, M. Ed. de Laveleye, of that city, said that, " in the eighth century, under Charlemagne, appeared the furnace called the *fourneau à masse*, or *stückofen*, which was higher than the old furnaces, and thus allowed a greater concentration of heat."

The wolf furnace, or *stückofen*, was a high bloomary, and was simply an enlargement of the primitive low bloomaries or forges. Percy says that the *stückofen* "is only a Catalan furnace extended upwards in the form of a quadrangular or circular shaft. The Germans call it *stück* or *wolf's ofen* because the large metallic mass which is extracted from the

bottom is termed *stück* or *wolf*." The word bloom fully expresses the English equivalent of both words. The word *loup*,
or *loop*, which is applied to a lump of imperfectly worked
iron, is identical with the terms *stück* and *wolf*, being derived
from the French word *loup*, signifying wolf. Overman says
that wolf furnaces, or bloomaries, of which there yet remain a
few in Hungary and Spain, are generally from 10 to 16 feet
high, 2 feet wide at the top and bottom, and about 5 feet wide
at the widest part. The early wolf furnaces were not more
than 10 feet high. An opening in the front, about 2 feet
square, called the breast, was kept open until the furnace was
heated, when, coincidently with the closing of the breast with
brick, the ore and charcoal were thrown into the furnace and
the blast was applied from "at least two bellows and nozzles,
both on the same side." The product was a mass, or salamander, of mixed iron and steel, which was taken out of the
breast and reduced under the tilt-hammer to blooms, and under smaller hammers to bars and other forms. The salamander, which usually weighed from 400 to 700 pounds, was first
cut into two nearly equal parts, which were called *stücke*. At
Eisenerz, in Austria, as stated by Jars, quoted by Percy, "the
lump was first cut half through in the centre with hatchets
by two men, each having one. It was afterwards completely
divided by means of wedges and large hammers." The annual production of a wolf furnace was from 100 to 150 tons.
Overman further says : " By this method good iron as well as
steel is always furnished ; in fact the salamander consists of
a mixture of iron and steel ; of the latter skillful workmen
may save a considerable amount. The blooms are a mixture
of fibrous iron, steel, and cast iron. The latter flows into the
bottom of the forge fire, in which the blooms are reheated,
and is then converted into bar iron by the same method
adopted to convert common pig iron. If the steel is not
sufficiently separated it is worked along with the iron." At
Solling, in Carinthia, a wolf furnace was built in 1775 which
was provided with two common bellows worked by water-
wheels, each bellows being 8 feet long and 3¾ feet broad.

While there can be no doubt that the earliest wolf furnaces were blown with leather bellows it is not known when
water-power was first used in producing the blast and in oper-

ating the hammers. Water-power for grinding grain is said by Knight, in his *Mechanical Dictionary*, to have been used about the beginning of the Christian era. In Agricola's *De Re Metallica*, printed at Basle in 1556, are numerous engravings which show that large tilt-hammers and leather bellows, operated by water-power, were used in the manufacture of iron and steel in Saxony at that time. In Flower's *History of the Trade in Tin* will be found two very interesting illustrations of the manner in which the bellows and tilt-hammer were operated by water-power in France in 1714. Prior to the introduction of water-power bellows were doubtless wholly operated by the feet or hands.

The osmund furnace, which is said by Percy to have been intermediate between the Catalan forge and the *stückofen*, but which had a much wider mouth than the *stückofen*, was formerly in use in Northern Europe, principally for smelting bog or lake ore, and was lately in use in Finland. It is said by Karsten, in his *Grundriss der Metallurgie*, printed at Breslau in 1818, to have been in use in Norway and Sweden at that date, but its use in these countries has now been abandoned. It derived its name from the Swedish word *osmund*, "which was applied to the bloom produced in this kind of furnace." Percy reproduces from Swedish sources two drawings of an osmund furnace, from which it would appear that it was about 7 feet high, rectangular in shape, with an opening or breast near the bottom similar to that of the *stückofen*, and was blown through one tuyere with two ordinary blacksmith's bellows, worked with treadles by a woman's feet. The ore used in Sweden was first calcined before being placed in the furnace, wood being used for calcining and charcoal for smelting. The product was good malleable iron, which was taken out of the breast in a lump, or *osmund*. Not more than 1½ tons of iron could be produced in this furnace in a week.

Percy says: "The transition from the old bloomary to the modern blast furnace was very gradual, and the *stückofen* is the final development of the furnaces in which iron in the malleable state was produced direct from the ore. By increasing the dimensions of the *stückofen*, especially its height, the conditions favorable to the formation of cast iron are obtained; and, indeed, in the *stückofen* cast iron was generally, if not always, produced in greater or less degree, to the annoyance of the smelter."

Percy further says that the *stückofen* was gradually superseded by the blast furnace, the first furnace which replaced the *stückofen* being the *blauofen*, or blue oven. He says that "originally there was no essential difference between them, these names being applied according to the nature of the metal which they yielded, and not in consequence of difference of construction," malleable iron being obtained with much less charcoal than was used when cast iron was desired. "When the *blauofen* was used as a *stückofen* it was only necessary to make an opening in the fore part of the hearth large enough for the extraction of the lump. One essential condition in working the furnace as a *stückofen* was to allow the slag free escape during the process, so that the lump of iron accumulating in the hearth might never be covered with slag, and so be protected from the action of the blast." The *blauofen*, which is not entirely extinct on the Continent, dates from about the beginning of the fourteenth century. The *flussofen* was substantially the same furnace as the *blauofen*. Blast furnace may properly be substituted for either term, although the phrase blast furnace means, strictly speaking, the fully developed *blauofen* or *flussofen*. *Hochofen* was another German name which was applied to the blast furnace, and it is still retained. Karsten says that in 1818 the *stückofen* was no longer used in Germany, except at Schmalkalden, which is a town in Prussia. He says, however, that many *stücköfen* were then in use in Hungary.

It has been stated in a preceding chapter that the blast furnace originated in the Rhine provinces about the beginning of the fourteenth century. We are unable to trace its existence to an earlier date than 1340, when the furnace at Marche les Dames in Belgium was built. It was many years, however, before the blast furnace was generally introduced on the Continent or in England. It was probably not introduced into Saxony until 1550. Agricola, who was a native of Saxony, does not describe it in his valuable work, which was first printed in 1530, but he describes the *stückofen* and the forges for refining iron and producing steel. Percy says that Agricola "appears to have been acquainted with cast iron," but this, as has already been shown, could have been produced by the *stückofen*.

The Continental nations of Europe are entitled to the credit of having fully developed the blast furnace from the primitive method of producing iron in the bloomary or Catalan forge. The virtual perfection of the blast furnace by the Germans, the Belgians, and the French in the fifteenth and sixteenth centuries marked a great advance in the art of manufacturing iron, and greatly enlarged the uses to which iron could be applied. The nations which have been mentioned were also the first among modern nations to cast iron in moulds, the Germans and French being especially noted at an early day for the artistic excellence of their iron castings.

The Catalan forge, with its modifications, continued to be used during the period covered by the development of the blast furnace, and, as has already been said, it is still in use in many countries, being especially adapted to the conversion of pure ores into malleable iron of superior quality. A modification of the Catalan forge, called the German bloomary, consisting more, however, in the treatment of the ore than in the construction of the hearth and its connections, was long very popular in Germany and the United States, but it has now been almost entirely abandoned in both these countries. After the commencement of the manufacture of cast or pig iron forges suited to the conversion of this product into wrought iron became necessary, but they did not differ in any essential details of construction or application from the Catalan forge and the refinery forges which had previously been found necessary in connection with the *stückofen*. Refinery forges have sometimes been called bloomaries, because pig iron is by them first reduced to a bloom before it is still further refined; but properly speaking a bloomary is a forge that converts iron ore into wrought iron by the direct process. The word bloomary is of Anglo-Saxon origin, the Anglo-Saxon word *bloma*, from which it is derived, meaning a mass, or lump. In *Doomsday-Book* the expression, *bloma ferri*, occurs several times.

In *The Forest of Dean* Nicholls quotes a· most interesting description of the blast furnaces and refinery forges of England in the latter part of the seventeenth century. It has already been mentioned that the blast furnace was introduced into England from the Continent about the beginning of the fifteenth century. The author, after recording events which occurred on April 27, 1680, a little more than two hundred years ago, says: "The mode then in use of operating upon the iron ore as described in manuscript by Dr. Parsons will be found in Appendix No. 5." This description is as follows:

After they have provided their ore their first work is to calcine it, which is done in kilns, much after the fashion of our ordinary lime kilns; these they fill up to the top with coal and ore until it be full, and so, putting fire to the bottom, they let it burn till the coal be wasted, and then renew the kilns with fresh ore and coal. This is done without any infusion of mettal, and serves to consume the more drossy part of the ore, and to make it fryable, supplying the beating and washing, which are to no other mettals; from hence they carry it to their furnaces, which are built of brick and stone, about 24 foot square on the outside, and near 30 foot in height within, and not over 8 or 10 foot over where it is the widest, which is about the middle, the top and bottom having a narrow compass, much like the form of an egg. Behind the furnace are placed two high pair of bellows, whose noses meet at a little hole near the bottom; these are compressed together by certain buttons placed on the axis of a very large wheel, which is turned round by water, in the manner of an overshot mill. As soon as these buttons are slid off, the bellows are raised again by a counterpoise of weights, whereby they are made to play alternately, the one giving its blast while the other is rising.

At first they fill these furnaces with ore and cinder intermixt with fuel, which in these works is always charcoal, laying them hollow, at the bottom, that they may the more easily take fire; but after they are once kindled the materials run together into an hard cake or lump, which is sustained by the furnace, and through this the mettal as it runs trickles down the receivers, which are placed at the bottom, where there is a passage open, by which they take away the scum and dross, and let out their mettal as they see occasion. Before the mouth of the furnace lyeth a great bed of sand, where they make furrows of the fashion they desire to cast their iron. Into these, when the receivers are full, they let in their mettal, which is made so very fluid by the violence of the fire that it not only runs to a considerable distance, but stands afterwards boiling a great while. After these furnaces are once at work they keep them constantly employed for many months together, never suffering the fire to slacken night or day, but still supplying the waste of fuel and other materials with fresh, poured in at the top.

Several attempts have been made to bring in the use of the sea coal in these workes instead of charcoal; the former being to be had at an easy rate, the latter not without a great expence, but hitherto they have proved ineffectual, the workmen finding by experience that a sea-coal fire, how vehement soever, will not penetrate the most fixed parts of the ore, by which means they leave much of the mettal behind them unmelted.

From these furnaces they bring the sows and piggs of iron, as they call them, to their forges; these are two sorts, though they stood together under the same roof; one they call their finery, and the other chafers; both of them are upon hearths, upon which they place great heaps of sea coal, and behind them bellows like those of the furnaces, but nothing near so large. In such finerys they first put their piggs of iron, placing three or four of them together behind the fire, with a little of one end thrust into it, where softening by degrees they stir and work them with long barrs of iron till the mettal runs together in a round masse or lump, which they call an half bloome: this they take out, and, giving it a few strokes with their sledges, they carry it to a great weighty hammer, raised likewise by the motion of a water-wheel, where, applying it dexterously to the blows, they presently beat it into a thick short square; this they put into the finery again, and, heating it red hot, they work it under the same hammer till it comes to the shape of a bar in the middle, with two square knobs in the ends; last of all they give it other heatings in the chaffers, [chafery,] and more workings under the hammer, till they have brought their iron into barrs of several shapes, in which fashion they expose them to sale.

All their principal iron undergoes the aforementioned preparations, yet for several other purposes, as for backs of chimneys, hearths of ovens, and the like, they have a sort of cast iron, which they take out of the receivers of the furnace, so soon as it is melted, in great ladles, and pour it into the moulds of fine sand in like manner as they do cast brass and softer mettals; but this sort of iron is so very brittle that, being heated, with one blow of the hammer it breaks all to pieces.

John Ray, the naturalist, writing a little earlier, in 1672, has also fully described, in two papers appended to his *Collection of English Words*, the blast furnaces and forges which existed in England in his day. "This account of the whole process of the iron work," he says, "I had from one of the chief ironmasters of Sussex, my honored friend, Walter Burrell, Esq., of Cuckfield, deceased." We give below a literal copy of this description.

THE MANNER OF THE IRON WORK AT THE FURNACE.

The iron mine lies sometimes deeper, sometimes shallower, in the earth, from four to forty [feet] and upward. There are several sorts of mine, some hard, some gentle, some rich, some coarser. The ironmasters always mix different sorts of mine together, otherwise they will not melt to advantage. When the mine is brought in they take small-coal [charcoal] and lay a row of it, and upon that a row of mine, and so alternately S.S.S., one above another, and, setting the coals on fire, therewith burn the mine. The use of this burning is to modify it, that so it may be broke in small pieces; otherwise if it should be put into the furnace as it comes out of the earth it would not melt, but come away whole. Care also must be taken that it be not too much burned, for then it will *loop*, i. e., melt and run together in a mass. After it is burnt they beat it into small pieces with an iron sledge, and then put it into the furnace, (which is before charged with coals,) casting it upon the top of the coals, where it melts and falls into the hearth, in the space of about twelve hours, more or less, and then it runs into a *sow*.

The hearth, or bottom of the furnace, is made of sandstone, and the sides round, to the height of a yard, or thereabout; the rest of the furnace is lined up to the top with brick. When they begin upon a new furnace they put fire for a day or two before they begin to blow. Then they blow gently and encrease by degrees 'till they come to the height in ten weeks or more. Every six days they call a *founday*, in which space they make eight tun of iron, if you divide the whole sum of iron made by the foundays: for at first they make less in a founday, at last more. The hearth by the force of the fire, continually blown, grows wider and wider, so that at first it contains so much as will make a sow of six or seven hundred pound weight; at last it will contain so much as will make a sow of two thousand pound. The lesser pieces, of one thousand pound, or under, they call pigs.

Of twenty-four loads of coals they expect eight tun of sows: to every load of coals, which consists of eleven quarters, they put a load of mine, which contains eighteen bushels. A hearth ordinarily, if made of good stone, will last forty foundays, that is, forty weeks, during which time the fire is never let go out. They never blow twice upon one hearth, though they go upon it not above five or six foundays. The cinder, like scum, swims upon the melted metal in the hearth, and is let out once or twice before a sow is cast.

THE MANNER OF WORKING THE IRON AT THE FORGE OR HAMMER.

In every forge or *hammer* there are two fires at least; the one they call the *finery*, the other the *chafery*. At the finery, by the working of the hammer, they bring it into *blooms* and *anconies*, thus:

The sow they, at first, roll into the fire, and melt off a piece of about three-fourths of a hundred-weight, which, so soon as it is broken off, is called a *loop*. This *loop* they take out with their shingling-tongs, and beat it with iron sledges upon an iron plate near the fire, that so it may not fall in pieces, but be in a capacity to be carried under the hammer. Under which they, then removing it, and drawing a little water, beat it with the hammer very gently, which forces cinder and dross out of the matter; afterwards, by degrees, drawing more water, they beat it thicker and stronger 'till they bring it to a *bloom*, which is a four-square mass of about two feet long. This operation they call *shingling the loop*. This done, they immediately return it to the finery again, and, after two or three heats and workings, they bring it to an *ancony*, the figure whereof is, in the middle, a bar about three feet long, of that shape they intend the whole bar to be made of it; at both ends a square piece left rough to be wrought at the chafery.

Note. At the finery three load of the biggest coals go to make one tun of iron. At the chafery they only draw out the two ends suitable to what was drawn out at the finery in the middle, and so finish the bar.

Note 1. One load of the smaller coals will draw out one tun of iron at the chafery. 2. They expect that one man and a boy at the finery should make two tuns of iron in a week: two men at the chafery should take up, *i. e.*, make or work, five or six tun in a week. 3. If into the hearth where they work the iron sows (whether in the chafery or the finery) you cast upon the iron a piece of brass it will hinder the metal from working, causing it to spatter about, so that it can not be brought into a solid piece.

John Houghton, in his *Husbandry and Trade Improved*, printed in 1697, calls the square first made a half bloom and the bar with the two knobs a bloom, the greater end being called the mocket head and the smaller the ancony end. At the third heat, there being five heats in all, the ancony end was reduced to a bar, and at the fourth and fifth heats the mocket head was also reduced.

The English blast furnaces and refinery forges which have been described were counterparts of Continental furnaces and forges of the same period. On the Continent, as well as in England, as described by Dr. Parsons, various castings were made direct from the furnace, which for this reason was often called a foundry. These castings, in addition to the articles mentioned by Dr. Parsons, embraced such domestic utensils as pots, kettles, skillets, gridirons, sad irons, andirons, clock weights, cog-wheels for mill machinery, grates, stoves, etc.

After coke came into general use in the blast furnaces of Great Britain the method of refining iron which is above described was somewhat changed in that country in details but not in principle. On the Continent, however, where charcoal continued to be the only fuel used, there was no change in the method of refining iron until the puddling furnace was introduced, after the beginning of the present century, in company with the rolling mill for rolling bar iron. The puddling furnace was introduced into Sweden, at Skebo, and into France, at Fourchambault, about 1820; into Belgium, at Grivegnée, by Michael Orban, in 1821; into Moravia, at Witkowitz, in 1829; into Rhenish Prussia about 1830; into Westphalia and Upper Silesia about 1835; and into Siegen and the Hartz mountains about 1840.

The erection of the first coke blast furnace on the Continent of Europe was commenced in 1823 at Seraing, in Belgium, by John Cockerill, an Englishman by birth but a Belgian citizen, and completed in 1826, when it was successfully blown in. Other coke furnaces in Belgium and elsewhere on the Continent soon followed. M. Ed. de Laveleye, of Liége, says that in 1769 an attempt to smelt iron ores by means of coke was made at Juslenville, near Spa, in Belgium, but without success. One of the coke furnaces of the Hoerde iron works in Germany is said to have been continuously in blast from July 3, 1855, to May 29, 1874, or almost nineteen years.

Wooden bellows, or tubs, as a substitute for leather bellows in connection with blast furnaces and forges, do not appear to have been used in England in the seventeenth century, although said to have been invented by Hans Lobsinger, of Nuremberg, in Germany, about 1550. They were certainly used in Germany eighty years later, in 1630, and in various parts of Great Britain in the eighteenth century. In 1750 leather bellows were used to blow the charcoal furnaces in Monmouthshire. As late as 1809 leather bellows 22 feet long and having oak planks two inches thick were still used in blowing some Scotch furnaces. Both leather and wooden bellows have been used in blowing the furnaces and forges of the United States, and the use of wooden bellows had not been wholly abandoned in this country as late as 1884.

The *trompe*, or water-blast, is said to have been invented in Italy. Its use has been mainly confined to some of the charcoal furnaces and Catalan forges of Germany, France, Spain, and Italy. We can not learn that it was ever used in any part of Great Britain. Although it is now generally abandoned it may yet be found supplying the blast for a few forges on the Continent, and as late as 1890 it had not entirely disappeared in the southern part of the United States. Professor Lesley described in 1858, in the *Iron Manufacturer's Guide*, the water-blast which was then in use in the Southern States in connection with Catalan forges. He said:

The use of the water-blast is all but universal. It consists of a box, say 5 by 2½ by 1½ feet deep, nearly immersed in the stream, directly underneath the forebay or flume. The water rushes down into its upper end from the forebay through a wooden pipe, say 8 inches square, separated in two by a space of an inch or two, as if the two joints of a stove-pipe had parted that much. Into this slit air is sucked by the falling water and driven out through another 3-inch tube at the lower end. Inside the box, and parallel with its lid, a plank called the "spatter-board" is set a few inches below the first tube. The water escapes from a hole under the water-level at the lower end of the box. This apparatus gives a cold, damp blast, with a great waste of water, but one that is very uniform.

The origin of the rolling mill for rolling iron into bars

or plates is not free from doubt. Scrivenor, quoting from
Coxe's *Tour in Monmouthshire*, says that "in the early part of
the eighteenth century John Hanbury invented the method
of rolling iron plates by means of cylinders." Flower, alluding to the manufacture of tin plates at Pontypool, says that
"the discovery of sheet-iron rolling followed in 1728, an invention claimed alike by John Payne and Major Hanbury,
and it was in a great measure owing to this improvement
that we were enabled to turn the tables upon Germany. The
tin-men were greatly delighted with the English plates; the
color was better, and the rolled plates were found to be more
pliable than the foreign ones, which were hammered." The
following is taken from Ure's *Dictionary of the Arts:* "In
1728 John Payne invented a process for rolling iron. This
seems to have at once led to the use of the flat or sheet rolls
for the manufacture of iron for tin plates; but it is very remarkable that no further progress was made in this discovery of rolling iron until 1783, when Henry Cort introduced the
grooved rolls." Percy says: "With respect to the invention
of grooved rolls it has been maintained that Cort's claim is
invalidated by the old patent granted to John Payne in 1728."
It is certain, however, that even plain rolls did not come into
general use until the rolling mill had been perfected by Cort,
the refinery fire, the leather and wooden bellows, the tilting-
hammer, and the water-wheel still holding their place in the
manufacture of finished iron on the Continent and in Great
Britain.

Dr. Johnson, in the diary of his tour in Wales and Monmouthshire in 1774, says that at an iron works he saw "round
bars formed by a notched hammer and anvil," and that at a
copper works he saw "a plate of copper put hot between steel
rollers and spread thin." The whole passage is as follows:

Wednesday, August 3 [1774]. * * * We went in the coach to Holy-
well. * * * We there saw a brass work, where the *lapis calaminaris* is
gathered, broken, washed from the earth and the lead, though how the
lead was separated I did not see; then calcined, afterwards ground fine,
and then mixed by fire with copper. We saw several strong fires with
melting pots, but the construction of the fire-places I did not learn. At a
copper work, which receives its pigs of copper, I think, from Warrington,
we saw a plate of copper put hot between steel rollers and spread thin. I
know not whether the upper roller was set to a certain distance, as I sup-

pose, or acted only by its weight. At an iron works I saw round bars formed by a notched hammer and anvil. There I saw a bar of about half an inch or more square cut with shears worked by water, and then beaten hot into a thinner bar. The hammers, all worked as they were by water, acting upon small bodies, moved very quickly, as quick as by the hand. I then saw wire drawn and gave a shilling.

We find by an examination of English patents that, on November 21, 1728, John Payne, an Englishman, obtained a patent for various improvements in the manufacture of iron, which consisted in part in the application of certain ashes, salt, etc., to pig or sow iron while in the refinery fire, "which will render the same into a state of malleability, as to bear the stroke of the hammer, to draw it into barrs or other forms att the pleasure of the workman, and those or other barrs being heated in the said melted ingredients in a long hott arch or cavern, as hereafter is described; and those or other barrs are to pass between two large mettall rowlers, (which have proper notches or furrows upon their surfass,) by the force of my engine hereafter described, or other power, into such shapes and forms as shall be required." Plain rolls for rolling sheet iron for tin plates are not referred to. Other patents were subsequently granted in England for the invention of rolls of various forms for rolling bar iron. In 1759 a patent was granted to Thomas Blockley for rolls which "are to be turned and formed of the requisite shape so as to shape the article as intended." In 1779 a patent was granted to William Bell for rolls which "have designs sunk in their surfaces."

In John Houghton's *Husbandry and Trade Improved*, printed in 1697, he speaks of slitting and rolling mills as "late improvements." This is the earliest reference we have found to a rolling mill in connection with a slitting mill. Such use of a rolling mill would probably precede its use for any other purpose in connection with the manufacture of iron. In Flower's *History of the Trade in Tin* the manufacture of tin plates at Mansvaux, in Alsace, in 1714, is fully described, and it is noticeable that the sheet iron then used was hammered. This description, which is illustrated, sustains the claim that either John Payne or Major Hanbury was fourteen years later, in 1728, the first person to roll sheet iron, an innovation which presumptively grew out of the use of the rolling mill in the manufacture of nail plates as early as 1697, as recorded

by John Houghton, and which innovation probably followed
Payne's invention of grooved rolls, patented in 1728.

We quote below John Houghton's statement concerning
the rolling mill just as we find it under the date of Friday,
October 22, 1697, in Bradley's edition of *Husbandry and Trade
Improved,* printed at London in 1727. After describing " how
the sows and pigs of iron are prepared for bars and drawn
into such " in the refinery forges, " which are of two sorts,"
the "finery" and the "chafery," he tells us in the following
words how the bars are converted into nail rods.

Whereof those they intend to be cut into rods are carried to the *slitting mills,* where they first break, or cut them cold, with the force of one of
the wheels, into short lengths; then they are put into a furnace to be heated red-hot to a good height, and then brought singly to the rollers, by
which they are drawn even, and to a greater length; after this another
workman takes them whilst hot, and puts them through the *cutters,* which
are of divers sizes, and may be put on or off according to pleasure. Then
another lays them straight also whilst hot, and when cold binds them also
into faggots, and then they are fit for sale.

And thus I have given an account of the *iron works* of *Staffordshire* from
the oar to the slitting mills, as they are now exercised in their perfection,
the improvement whereof we shall find very great if we look back upon
the methods of our ancestors that made iron in *foot-blasts* or *bloomeries,* by
means of treading the *bellows,* by which way they could make but one little
lump or *bloom* of iron in a day, not a hundred weight, leaving as much iron
in the *slag* as they got out. Whereas now they will make two or three tons
of cast iron in twenty-four hours; leaving the slag so poor that the founders can not melt them again to profit, not to mention again the vast advantage they have from the new invention of *slitting mills* for cutting their bars
into rods, above what they had antiently.

Houghton's whole account, from which the above extract
is taken, is entitled by him "a note of late improvements."

In the English pamphlet on the British iron trade, printed
between 1725 and 1731, and already referred to, there is conclusive proof that down to that time all bar iron was hammered. We quote literally from this pamphlet as follows:

Pig-iron is brought from the *furnace* to the *forge;* and there by being
melted and digested in the fire becomes a fixt and malleable substance ; and
by repeated heats in the fire, and repeated impressions of the hammer, is
beaten out into long bars or palasades, and upon that account is termed
bar-iron. *Furnaces* and *forges* are comprehended under one common name
of *iron works.* *Bar-iron* is of several sorts, distinguished by particular names
according to its dimensions and uses. The two most general are *merchant-
bar* and *mill bar:* The one being such shaped iron as is usually imported

by the merchant, about inch and half or two inches broad and one-third thick, and squares of different sizes. The other such as is proper for the *slitting* or *rowling-mill*, of double dimensions to the former. The *slitting* and *rowling-mills* are water-engines, whose use is to reduce bar-iron into small rods or thin plates, in order to save the expence of charcoal and human labour.

A letter of inquiry to Professor Richard Akerman, of the School of Mines, Stockholm, Sweden, requesting such information as might be in his possession concerning the origin of the slitting mill and the rolling mill, was answered as follows:

That slitting mills were in use before rolling mills is most probable and nearly certain. At the beginning of this century there could still be found slitting mills in which hammered but not rolled iron was slit. But all slitting mills were not made on the principle of rolling mills; many of them more resembled scissors.

The first publication about rolling mills in this country which I have seen or know about is *De Ferro*, by Emanuel Swedenborg, which was printed in 1734. Swedenborg speaks both about slitting machines on the principle of scissors, cutting three rods at a time, and about slitting mills in connection with rolling mills. He describes slitting mills in Sweden, in the Liége district of Belgium, in Germany, and in England; but he does not say a single word about where he thinks they originated. *Swedenborg does not say anything about grooved rolls.* In fact he only describes rolling mills in connection with slitting mills. On page 253 he speaks about Swedish rolling mills at Wedewåg, Avesta, and Stjernsund.

On the contrary, Christopher Polhem, in his *Patriotiska Testamente*, which was printed in 1761, ten years after his death when he was 90 years old, speaks about rolling mills as such, both for plates and bar iron. He says, in chapter 14, "much time and labor can be saved by good rolling mills, because a rolling mill can produce 10 to 20 and still more bars at the same time which is wanted to tilt only one bar with the hammer. Thus very thin bar iron can be made which is useful for hoops and mountings of several kinds. Steel also can be rolled out for knife blades, etc., which easily can be finished by the blacksmith. The rolls can be so made that the knife-steel becomes broad and thin on both sides, or gets the same shape as blades of common swords, and these can be cut lengthwise in two parts, thus giving suitable material for knives, etc. Rolls also can be made for producing quadrangular, round, and half-round bars, not only for iron but also for steel, as for all kinds of files which easily can be finished by the blacksmith."

In the next chapter Polhem describes the manner of making wrought-iron rolls covered with steel. Further on in the same chapter he speaks of rolls for rolling sheets: "As such rolls commonly have a length of three quarters, it follows that their diameter must be rather large; but, as thick rolls in comparison with slender ones have only a small effect in stretching, broad sheets can not be rolled. If not, two slender wrought-iron rolls are put between the two thick cast-iron rolls, which prevent the slender rolls from yielding. Such rolls I have put up at Stjernsund after having tried their effect by experiments on a small scale." After mentioning economical difficulties, in consequence of which he was obliged to leave unused both this and other expensive machines, he concludes with the following words: "Yet I willingly grant to others, who perhaps will live during more happy times, what I have not got opportunity to use for myself."

Polhem says nothing about the time when he put up the said rolling mill, but, if you remember that he was born 1661 and died 1751, it seems probable that it must have been during the first decades of the eighteenth century. Christopher Polhem was the greatest mechanical genius Sweden has ever produced, but whether he was the very first inventor of rolling mills it is impossible for me to say. At any rate he ought to be mentioned among the inventors of rolling mills. In fact, Polhem must be said to be the real inventor of what you call the Lauth rolling mill. The only difference is that Polhem used four rolls above each other, two small between two large ones.

Gabriel Polhem, a son of Christopher Polhem, in the *Transactions of the Royal Swedish Academy of Sciences* for 1740, gives a description of a rolling mill, "the invention of my father," which he (Gabriel Polhem) put up at the mint in Cassel, Germany. He says that the officers of the mint did not believe that a rolling mill could be of any use for the mint, but he was in 1733 ordered by King Frederick to put it up, and it proved most useful for getting more uniform thickness and weight of the coins. From this and other expressions in the description it is quite clear that the said rolling mill was the very first put up at any mint, but not long afterwards a rolling mill also was put up at the Swedish mint.

This communication from Professor Akerman is a very important one, especially in its reference to the use of the rolling mill for rolling plate and bar iron before 1751, the year of the death of Christopher Polhem. It proves that plate and bar iron were rolled before Cort's day, but probably not until after the rolling mill had been used as early as 1697 in connection with the slitting mill, as recorded by Houghton, nor until after the invention of sheet-iron rolling in 1728, with which the names of Payne and Hanbury are associated. The germ of the great invention by which iron and steel are rolled into so many and into such infinitely small and wonderfully large shapes in our day most likely originated with the man who added the rolling mill to the slitting mill, and after a laborious investigation we regret that we can not give his name nor definitely fix the date of his invention. Cort, however, is entitled to the credit of so improving upon all previous suggestions that the rolling mill in his hands became a successful invention for the numerous and important purposes to which it is now applied.

The methods of producing steel which were in use before Huntsman succeeded in making crucible steel at Sheffield, in 1740, to which event we have referred in the chapters relating to Great Britain, were substantially only three in number. The first method was either closely allied to or was wholly identical with the direct or Catalan process for producing iron, the product being variously known as natural steel, raw steel, or German steel. The second method was the Indian process for converting small pieces of bar iron into steel in crucibles, the product being wootz, or Indian steel. The third method was the cementation process, in which bars of the best iron were carbonized by being heated in contact with charcoal, the result being blister steel and shear steel. Steel produced by the cementation process is also known as German steel, because much attention was long given to its production by Germany. All these methods are yet in use. A Chinese method heretofore mentioned we pass over.

The first method, which requires the use of a forge, and which was originally applied to iron ore but afterwards to pig iron, is most observed in Germany and Austria. In Styria the finest tool steel is still produced by the old Frischen process, which consists in refining the excellent Styrian pig iron in small charcoal open hearths. The process is essentially primitive. Professor Tunner has given a complete account of the older open-hearth methods, which has been quoted by Dr. Percy. The small works for the production of Styrian open-hearth steel are distributed along the banks of rivers in the Styrian Alps, each of the works being located at a fall of the river capable of developing about 50 horse-power.

Allied to the above-mentioned process of making steel in open hearths which is still practiced in Germany and Austria is the following ancient German method, described by Agricola in his *De Re Metallica*, printed about the middle of the sixteenth century. We use Day's translation.

Make choice of iron which is apt to melt, and yet hard, and may easily be wrought with the hammer; for although iron, which is made of vitriolic ore, may melt, yet it is soft, or brittle, or eager. Heat a parcel of such iron red-hot, and cut it into small pieces, and then mix it with a sort of stone which easily melts; then set in the smith's forge, or hearth, a crucible, or dish of crucible metal, a foot and a-half broad, and a foot deep; fill the dish with good charcoal, and compass the dish about with loose stones, to keep in the mixture of stone and pieces of iron. As soon as the coal is thoroughly kindled, and the dish red-hot, give the blast, and let the workman put on by little and little all the mixture of iron and stone he designs. When it is melted, let him thrust into the middle of it three or four or more pieces of iron, and boil them therein five or six hours with a brisk fire; and, putting in his rod, let him often stir the melted iron, that the pieces may imbibe the smaller particles of the melted iron, which particles consume and thin the grosser ones of the iron pieces, acting like a ferment to them, and making them tender. Let the workman now take one of the pieces out of the fire and put it under the great hammer, to be drawn out into bars and wrought; and then, hot as it is, plunge it into cold water. Thus tempered, let him again work it on the anvil, and break it; and viewing the fragments, let him consider whether it looks like iron in any part of it, or be wholly condensed and turned into steel. Then let the pieces be all wrought into bars; which done, give a fresh blast to the mixture, adding a little fresh matter to it, instead of that which had been drunk up by the pieces of iron, which will refresh and strengthen the remainder, and make still purer the pieces of iron again put into the dish; every which piece let him, as soon as it is red-hot, beat into a bar on the anvil, and cast it, hot as it is, into cold water. And thus iron is made into steel, which is much harder and whiter than iron.

Mr. Thomas Turner defined cemented steel as follows in a lecture delivered at Birmingham, England, in 1889:

For the preparation of best steel for cutlery, tools, and similar purposes, it is still customary to adopt the cementation process, though the amount of steel so produced is relatively growing less and less each year. This process has been used for several centuries at least, and the origin of the method is unknown. Selected bars of Swedish or other best-quality iron are placed in closed chests and heated in contact with charcoal for about a week or ten days, depending on the temper which is desired. By this means the wrought iron, which was originally almost entirely free from carbon, takes up sufficient of that element to give the metal its characteristic properties. Usually some 15 tons of iron are converted in one operation, and 12 tons of good coal are consumed. The metal so obtained is covered on its surface with small blisters, formed by the reducing action of carbon on the small quantities of intermingled slag in the iron, and hence is called blister-steel. It is brittle in this state and crystalline in fracture. Blister-steel is broken up, piled, re-heated, and hammered, and so forms shear-steel, which was originally used for making wool-shears, but is now used for many other purposes. The milder varieties of blister-steel are used in producing shear-steel, while those which are a little richer in carbon are re-heated and hammered in the same way; but the operation is repeated a second time, and double shear-steel is produced. Shear-steel, though admirably suited for many purposes, is not quite uniform in character, and this uniformity can only be ensured by melting the metal, so as to allow it to mix thoroughly together, and to eliminate the slag and other intermingled impurities. Melted steel was unknown before the days of Huntsman. [This is disproved by Réaumur. See page 97.—J. M. S.]

Percy says of the cementation process, by which until in late years most of the steel of Europe and America was produced : " This is an old process, but little is known of its history. According to Beckmann there is no allusion to it in the writings of the ancients. It was well described by Réaumur in 1722, in his admirable treatise on the art of converting bar iron into steel." Landrin says : " Germany is also the first country where it was proposed to cement iron. Thence this art came to France, and was introduced at Newcastle-on-Tyne long before it was known at Sheffield, the present centre of that fabrication." The word cementation is derived from the former use with charcoal of chemical compositions called cements, which were, however, not needed.

Professor Grüner, of Paris, mentions that Réaumur, in his celebrated treatise, *The Art of Converting Iron into Steel*, published in 1722, says, on page 250, that " iron is transformed` into steel by immersing it for a short time in melted cast iron," and adds that " this process of steel manufacture is in use in some countries, and has already been described by Vanaccio in his *Pyrotechnie*, book I., chapter 7." Réaumur says in addition, on page 256, that steel may be obtained " by fusing iron scrap in cast iron," and that he has obtained " forge " steel by thus mixing with cast iron sometimes one-fourth and sometimes one-third of wrought iron. The immersion of wrought iron in a bath of cast iron is only a form of cementation, the absorption of carbon being the main object sought. The most common form of cementation, however, has been described on a preceding page by Mr. Turner.

In Dud Dudley's *Mettallum Martis*, published in 1665, and to be found reprinted *verbatim* in the *Journal* of the Iron and Steel Institute for 1872, the author gives the following description of the early English foot-blasts and of the later English high bloomaries, or *stücköfen*, which ʼlatter he says were still in existence in England at the time his account was written. With this extract from Dud Dudley's valuable treatise we close our citations from the old writers on the mediæval and early modern processes of making iron and steel.

Let us but look back unto the making of iron, by our ancestors, in foot blasts, or bloomeries, that was by men treading of the bellows, by which way they could make but one little lump or bloom of iron in a day, not 100 weight, and that not fusible, nor fined, or malliable, untill it were long burned and wrought under hammers, and whose first slag, sinder or scorius, doth contain in it as much, or more, iron then in that day the workman or bloomer got out, which slag, scorius, or sinder is by our founders at furnaces wrought again, and found to contain much yron and easier of fusion than any yron stone or mine of yron whatsoever, of which slag and sinders there is in many countryes millions of tuns and oaks growing upon them, very old and rotten.

The next invention was to set up the bloomeries that went by water, for the ease of the men treading the bellows, which being bigger, and the water-wheel causing a greater blast, did not onely make a greater quantity of iron, but also extracted more iron out of the slag or sinder, and left them more poorer of iron then the foot-blasts, so that the founders cannot melt them again, as they do the foot blast sinders to profit: yet these bloomeries by water (not altogether out of use) do make in one day but two hundred pound weight of iron, or there abouts, neither is it fusible, or malliable, but is unfined untill it be much burned, and wrought a second time in fire.

With the exception of the blast furnace, which was slowly developed from the high bloomary, and of the cementation process for producing steel, which doubtless originated during the period when the blast furnace was developed, no important improvement in the manufacture of iron and steel occurred from the revival of the iron industry in Europe about the beginning of the eighth century until we reach the series of improvements and inventions in the eighteenth century which have already been fully noticed in the chapters relating to the British iron industry, a period of a thousand years. It is about one hundred years since Henry Cort prominently brought the rolling mill and the puddling furnace to the attention of the ironmaking world, and scarcely a hundred and fifty years since coke was first successfully used in the blast furnace and steel was first made in England in crucibles. It is not two hundred and fifty years since the high bloomary, or *stückofen*, was in use in England for the production of wrought iron direct from the ore.

Since Huntsman's invention, which still gives us our best steel, there have been many other improvements in the manufacture of steel, and more recently there has been a very great relative increase in its production and use as compared with iron, until it has become a hackneyed expression that this is the age of steel. While this is true in the sense that steel is replacing iron, it is well to remember that the ancients made steel of excellent quality, and that the art of manufac-

turing it was never lost and has never been neglected. The
swords of Damascus and the blades of Toledo bear witness
to the skill in the manufacture of steel which existed at an
early day in both Asia and Europe. German steel was widely
celebrated for its excellence during the middle ages, and steel
of the same name and made by the same processes still occupies an honorable place among metallurgical products. Even
Huntsman's invention of the art of making the finest quality
of steel in crucibles, while meritorious in itself, was but the
reproduction and amplification in a modern age of a process
for manufacturing steel of equal quality which was known to
the people of India thousands of years ago.

The ancient and the early European processes for the
manufacture of both iron and steel do not compare unfavora-
bly with those of modern times in the quality of the products
they yielded. Modern processes excel those which they have
replaced more in the uniformity and quantity of their products than in their quality. The Germans once had a furnace
for making small quantities of iron by toilsome manual labor, one name for which, *bauernofen*, indicates that it was used
by farmers when they were not engaged in cultivating or
securing their crops. This was the *blaseofen*, or osmund furnace. In the present age mechanical skill of the highest order unites with the subtle operations of the chemist to produce
iron and steel in such quantities and with such uniformity
of product as to amaze not only the modern farmer, who
does not make a pound of iron, but also the student of history, the political economist, the practical statesman, and the
man of all wisdom.

CHAPTER IX.

FIRST ATTEMPT BY EUROPEANS TO MANUFACTURE IRON IN THE UNITED STATES.

HAVING traced in preceding pages, as briefly as the importance of the subject would permit, the early history of the manufacture of iron in the older countries of the world, especially in Great Britain, our mother country in this great industry as well as in national life, we now cross the Atlantic to the shores of that part of the New World which comprises the United States. In no other part of the American continent has the manufacture of iron ever risen to the dignity of a great national industry, and only in Canada of all the political divisions of North or South America outside of the United States has a serious effort ever been made to develop native iron resources. Indeed it is only in northern latitudes in both hemispheres that iron is made in large or even in noticeable quantities. This fact is only in part due to geological reasons. Climate and race tendencies have had much to do with the development of the metallurgical and all other productive industries in the belt of the earth's surface above alluded to, and which may well be called the ironmaking belt. It is here that we find

> That vigor of the northern brain
> Which nerves the world outworn.

This vigor is largely due to stimulating climatic conditions. The same gentle poet from whom we have just quoted tells us that

> There's iron in our northern winds;
> Our pines are trees of healing.

It would not be profitable to inquire minutely whether the mound-builders or any other aboriginal inhabitants of the United States, or the aboriginal inhabitants of any other part of the American continent, possessed a knowledge of the use and consequently of the manufacture of iron. It may be said with positiveness that it has not been proved that they possessed this knowledge even in the slightest degree, if we except the very rare use of meteoric iron. Antiquarians have not neglected a subject of so much importance, but their researches have produced only negative results. Rude hatchets and other small implements of iron have been found in situations which give color to the theory that they may have been of aboriginal origin and may have been made from iron ore, but the weight of much concurrent testimony is wholly against this supposition. Foster, in his *Prehistoric Races of the United States of America*, says that "no implement of iron has been found in connection with the ancient civilizations of America." He fully establishes the fact that the mound-builders manufactured copper into various domestic and war-like implements, but adds that the Indians of North America did not use copper in any form, although those of Central and South America did. Prescott, the historian of the conquest of Mexico and Peru, says that the native inhabitants of these countries, who were at the time of the conquest the most advanced in all the arts of civilization of the immediate predecessors of the white race in North and South America, were unacquainted with the use of iron, copper serving them as a substitute. Our North American Indians were certainly unacquainted with the use of iron when the Spaniards, the English, the Dutch, and other Europeans first landed on the Atlantic coast. Cotton Mather, in his *Life of Eliot*, says that among the Indians of New England "stone was used, instead of metal, for their tools," and other writers bear like testimony concerning all our Indians. The Rev. Dr. Joseph Doddridge, in his *Notes on the. Settlement and Indian Wars of the Western Parts of Virginia and Pennsylvania*, published in 1824, expresses the following opinions : "At the discovery of America the Indians knew nothing of the use of iron. Any people who have ever been in the habit of using iron will be sure to leave some indelible traces of its use behind them ; but the aborigines of this country have left none."

With regard to the use of meteoric iron by the aboriginal inhabitants of the American continent Professor F. W. Putnam, of Harvard University, the archæologist, writes us as follows : "I have found in the ancient mounds of Ohio masses of meteoric iron and various implements and ornaments made by hammering pieces of meteoric iron. This native iron the ancient people of Ohio used the same as they did native copper, native silver, and native gold, simply as a malleable metal. None of our peoples, I am confident, understood smelting iron or in any way manufacturing it from iron ore. The Greenland Eskimos made knives and other weapons from the native iron found in Greenland, but always by hammering, not by melting and casting. After contact with Europeans the Indian tribes obtained iron in various forms, and in due time learned to heat it and shape it as a blacksmith would do."

In the absence of any positive information confirming the use of any other than meteoric iron by any of the aboriginal inhabitants of America the interesting fact may be stated that iron has recently been made in Cherokee county in the western part of North Carolina by some members of the remnant of a band of Cherokee Indians. They used the primitive Catalan forge, which was introduced into North Carolina by the early white settlers, and from the iron so produced they made various tools and implements. The Cherokees when discovered by Europeans were among the most advanced of all the North American Indians in the arts which pertain to a civilized mode of life.

North Carolina first gave to Europeans the information that iron ore existed within the limits of the United States. The discovery was made in 1585 by the expedition fitted out by Sir Walter Raleigh and commanded by Ralph Lane, which made on Roanoke Island in that year the first attempt to plant an English settlement on the Atlantic coast. In his *History of American Manufactures* Bishop states that "Lane and his men explored the country along the Roanoke and on both sides from Elizabeth river to the Neuse." Thomas Hariot, the historian of the colony and the servant of Sir Walter, says that "in two places of the countrey specially, one about foure score and the other sixe score miles from the fort or place where wee dwelt, wee founde neere the water side the ground to be rockie, which, by the triall of a minerall man, was founde to hold iron richly. It is founde in manie places of the countrey else. I know nothing to the contrarie but that it maie bee allowed for a good marchantable commoditie, considering there the small charge for the labour and

feeding of men ; the infinite store of wood ; the want of wood
and deerenesse thereof in England; and the necessity of ballasting of shippes." But no attempt was made to utilize this
discovery, as the colonists were in search of gold and not
iron. In 1586 they quarreled with the Indians and returned
to England. A permanent settlement in North Carolina was
not effected until many years afterwards. Iron ore was not
mined in North Carolina nor was iron made within its
boundaries until after many of the other colonies had commenced to make iron.

In 1607 the first permanent English colony in the New
World was founded at Jamestown in Virginia by the Virginia
Company of London, and on the 10th of April in the following year, 1608, the company's ship, commanded by Captain
Christopher Newport, sailed from Jamestown loaded with iron
ore, sassafras, cedar posts, and walnut boards, and on the 20th
of May it arrived in England. From Neill's history of the
company we learn that the iron ore was smelted, and "seventeen tons of metal were sold at £4 per ton to the East India
Company." This was undoubtedly the first iron made by
Europeans from American ore. In 1610 Sir Thomas Gates,
who had spent some time in Virginia, testified before the
council of the company, at London, that there were divers
minerals, especially "iron oare," in Virginia, lying upon the
surface of the ground, some of which ore, having been sent
home, had been found to yield as good iron as any in Europe.
The iron here referred to was that which had been sold to
the East India Company.

In 1619 the Virginia Company sent to Virginia a number of persons who were skilled in the manufacture of iron,
to "set up three iron works" in the colony. The enterprise
was undertaken in that year and located on Falling creek, a
tributary of the James river, which it enters on its right or
southern bank in Chesterfield county, about seven miles below Richmond and about sixty-six miles above Jamestown.
In 1620, as stated by Beverley in his *History of Virginia*, "an
iron work at Falling creek in James river" was set up, "where
they made proof of good iron oar and brought the whole work
so near a perfection that they writ word to the company in
London that they did not doubt but to finish the work and

have plentiful provision of iron for them by the next Easter," in the spring of 1621. But neither plentiful provision nor any other provision of iron was made on Falling creek in 1621, owing to the death of three of the master workmen who had the enterprise in charge. In July of that year the company sent over John Berkley, "formerly of Beverstone Castle, Gloucester, a gentleman of an honorable family," to take charge of the work. He was accompanied by his son Maurice and twenty experienced workmen. In a letter from the company to the colonial authorities, dated July 25, 1621, it was stated that "the advancement of the iron works we esteeme to be most necessarie, by perfecting whereof we esteeme the plantation is gainer. We therefore require all possible assistance be given to Mr. Berkley now sent, and all furtherance to his ship, especially good entertainment at their landinge." On the 12th of August of the same year the company, in a communication to the authorities, wrote respecting the iron works and the saw mills which had been projected: "We pray your assistance in the perfectinge of these two workes; the profitt will redound to the whole collony, and therefore it is necessary that you extend your authoritie to the utmost lymitts to enforce such as shall refuse the help to a business so much tending to the generall good." On the 5th of December, 1621, the company again wrote, enjoining "all possible dilligence and industrious care, to further and accomplish those great and many designes of salte, sawinge mills, and iron." In January, 1622, the authorities wrote to the company that "the care we have taken of the iron workes we reserve to be reported by Mr. Thresurer and Mr. Barkley himself." On June 10th the company wrote of "the good enterance wch we have understood you have made in the iron works and other staple comodities," and added, "let us have at least by the next returnes some good quantitie of iron and wyne."

But before this last letter was written the colony had been visited by the Indian massacre of the 22d of March, 1622, in which John Berkley and all his workmen were slain and the works were destroyed. These works were not rebuilt. Beverley, writing in 1705, says that the project of iron works on Falling creek "has never been set on foot since, till of late;

but it has not had its full trial." In 1624 the charter of the Virginia Company was revoked. And thus disastrously ended the first attempt by Europeans to make iron in America.

The " good enterance " mentioned in the company's letter of June 10th doubtless referred to satisfactory progress in the construction of the works, but there is no positive evidence that iron was ever made on Falling creek. Letters from Mr. John Berkley had promised that " the company might relye upon good quantities of iron made by him " by Whitsuntide of 1622, but the massacre occurred before that time. Beverley, however, in referring to the Falling creek enterprise, says that " the iron proved reasonably good; but before they got into the body of the mine the people were cut off in that fatal massacre." The ore on Falling creek is described as having been brown in color. It was bog ore. Mr. Berkley declared that " a more fit place for iron workes than in Virginia, both for woods, water, mynes, and stone," was not to be found; and Mr. George Sandys wrote to the company on the 3d of March, 1622, that Falling creek was fitted for making iron " as if nature had applyed herselfe to the wish and dictation of the workeman; where also were great stones, hardly seene elsewhere in Virginia, lying on the place, as though they had beene brought thither to advance the erection of those workes."

We have failed to discover whether the works on Falling creek embraced a blast furnace and refinery or a bloomary only, but the frequent references to building stone in connection with the works, and the length of time and the number of workmen occupied in their erection, lead to the inference that a furnace formed part of the enterprise. It also seems reasonable to suppose that the phrase, " three iron works," already quoted in connection with the plans of the Virginia Company, meant a blast furnace, a finery, and a chafery, these works being used together in England at that day.

No further attempt to make iron in Virginia appears to have been made for many years after the failure on Falling creek. In a pamphlet entitled *A Perfect Description of Virginia*, published at London in 1649, it is stated that " an iron work erected would be as much as a silver mine." In 1650 another pamphlet, quoted by Bishop, says of iron ore in Virginia: "Neither does Virginia yield to any other province whatsoever in excellency and plenty of this oare." In 1687, and again in 1696, Col. William Byrd, the first of the name in Virginia, set on foot the project of reviving the works on Falling creek, but it was not carried into execution. This is the project referred to by Beverley in 1705 as not having had "its full trial."

To encourage manufactures in Virginia the exportation from the colony of hides, wool, and iron was forbidden by an act of the assembly in 1662, upon penalty of one thousand pounds of tobacco for every hide exported, fifty pounds of tobacco for every pound of wool exported, and ten pounds of tobacco for every pound of iron exported. The iron here referred to was doubtless crude, or cast, iron. This restriction was removed in 1671, "no successe answering the conceived hopes and apparent losses accruing to all inhabitants by the refusall of those concerned to buy the commodityes aforesaid," but it was reimposed in 1682. We can not learn that during the time covered by these enactments, and down to the beginning of the eighteenth century, there was a single pound of iron manufactured in Virginia. Notwithstanding the encouragement given by the Virginia Company and by some succeeding colonial authorities to the establishment of domestic manufactures the settlers of Virginia for a hundred years after the settlement at Jamestown devoted themselves almost entirely to the raising of tobacco and other agricultural products.

Mr. R. A. Brock, of Richmond, a gentleman who has devoted much time to historical research concerning Virginia, and who is at present corresponding secretary and librarian of the Virginia Historical Society, has recently published an account of some of the iron enterprises in the colony in the eighteenth century, from which the following interesting reference to the site of the iron works on Falling creek is taken.

The Falling creek tract fell to the possession of Col. Archibald Cary some time prior to the Revolutionary war. Upon it he erected his well-known seat, the name of which became in the records of the period a part and parcel of his personal designation as Archibald Cary of Ampthill. He erected a new iron works on Falling creek. "He purchased pigs of iron from Rappahannock, Patowmack, and Maryland. Of these he made bar iron. The profits, however, were so small that he abandoned his forge and converted his pond to the use of a grist mill about 1760. Nobody then knew of any iron mine convenient to Falling creek."

Falling creek is about a mile below Ampthill. Its waters still furnish motive power to a grist mill owned by Mr. H. Carrington Watkins, and known as the Ampthill mill. The creek is but an insignificant rivulet above the mill, but some twenty yards below it widens into a handsome little lake, and some quarter of a mile thence empties into James river.

About sixty yards from the mill, on the western bank of the creek and nearing the river, the writer picked up several small pieces of furnace cinder, presumptive relics of the iron works of 1622. The bluff adjacent and incumbent has, it is evident, from repeated washings of the soil, nearly covered the exact original site.

On the opposite side of the creek, and to the east of the mill, is clearly indicated the site of the forge of Archibald Cary. Here we found numerous pieces of slag or cinder, some of them fully a hundred pounds in weight, and an irregular area, an acre or more in extent, covered with finely-broken or comminuted charcoal to the depth of fully two feet; a memorial of the fuel used.

We were informed that about half a mile below Falling creek, near James river, there is a low piece of ground known to this day as Iron Bottom, where may be found plentifully what is known as bog iron on the surface. It will be recollected that the iron ore already cited as being mentioned by Sir Thomas Gates was described as "lying on the surface of the ground." We have also learned since our visit to Falling creek that at a point upon its banks, distant inward about two miles from the site of the iron works, there are numerous pits some five or six feet in depth, which it is evident, from the mineral character of their surroundings, furnished the crude ore for the original and ill-starred works.

In the eighteenth century Virginia became very prominent in the manufacture of iron, fulfilling in an eminent degree, although at a late day, the expectations which had been entertained of its iron-producing capabilities by the enterprising but unfortunate Virginia Company of London.

CHAPTER X.

BEGINNING OF THE MANUFACTURE OF IRON IN THE NEW ENGLAND COLONIES.

ALTHOUGH iron ore in this country was first discovered in North Carolina, and the manufacture of iron was first undertaken in Virginia, the first successful iron works were established in the province of Massachusetts Bay. In 1632 mention is made by Morton of the existence of "iron stone" in New England, and in November, 1637, the general court of Massachusetts granted to Abraham Shaw one-half of the benefit of any "coles or yron stone wch shal be found in any comon ground wch is in the countryes disposeing." Iron ore had been discovered in the flat meadows on the upper parts of the Saugus river, near Lynn, soon after its settlement in 1629, and in 1642 specimens were taken to London by Robert Bridges in the hope that a company might be formed for the manufacture of iron. This hope was soon realized in the formation of " The Company of Undertakers for the Iron Works," consisting of eleven English gentlemen, who advanced £1,000 to establish the works. John Winthrop, Jr., had previously gone to England, and he appears to have assisted Mr. Bridges in securing the organization of the company, becoming a member of the company, as did others among the colonists. Mr. Endicott, of Salem, in a letter to Governor Winthrop, dated December 1, 1642, says: "I want much to hear from your son's iron and steel." Thomas Dexter and Robert Bridges, both of Lynn, were among the original promoters of the enterprise. In his *History of Lynn* (1844) Alonzo Lewis says that in 1643 " Mr. John Winthrop, Jr., came from England with workmen and stock to the amount of one thousand pounds for commencing the work. A foundry was erected on the western bank of Saugus river. The village at the foundry was called Hammersmith by some of the principal workmen, who came from a place of that name in England." In Newhall's revision of Lewis's history, published in 1865, the iron works are said to have been located near the

site of the present woolen factories in Saugus Centre, not far
from Lynn, where large heaps of scoria are still to be seen.
" This iron foundry at Lynn," says Lewis, " was the first
which was established in America." Iron is not now manufactured at or near Lynn, except in its secondary forms.
There are here large iron foundries, and also wire works,
nail works, and various other iron enterprises of a reproductive character.

In 1644 and subsequently, as stated by Lewis, the general
court granted many special privileges to the company. On
March 7, 1644, it was granted three miles square of land at
each of six places it might occupy in the prosecution of its
business. On November 13, 1644, it was allowed three years
" for ye perfecting of their worke and furnishing of ye country
with all sorts of barr iron." The citizens were granted liberty to take stock in the enterprise " if they would complete
the finery and forge, as well as the furnace, which is already
set up." On May 14, 1645, the general court passed an order declaring that " ye iron worke is very successful (both in
ye richness of ye ore and ye goodness of ye iron)," and that
between £1,200 and £1,500 had already been disbursed, " with
which ye furnace is built, with that which belongeth to it, . .
and some tuns of sowe iron cast in readines for ye forge. . .
There will be neede of some £1,500 to finish ye forge." On
October 14th of the same year the company was granted
still further privileges by the general court, on the condition " that the inhabitants of this jurisdiction be furnished
with barr iron of all sorts for their use, not exceeding twentye
pounds per tunn," and that the grants of land already made
should be used " for the building and seting up of six forges, or furnaces, and not bloomaries onely." The grant was
confirmed to the company of the free use of all materials
" for making or moulding any manner of gunnes, potts, and
all other cast-iron ware." On May 6, 1646, Richard Leader,
the general agent of the company, who is described as being
a man of superior ability, purchased " some of the country's
gunnes to melt over at the foundery." On August 4, 1648,
Governor Winthrop wrote from Boston to his son, who had
removed to Pequod, Connecticut, that " the iron work goeth
on with more hope. It yields now about 7 tons per week."

On September 30th he writes again: "The furnace runs 8 tons per week, and their bar iron is as good as Spanish."

Newhall quotes from a Lynn account book for 1651 the following entry: "James Leonnarde, 15 days worke about finnerey chimneye and other worke in ye forge, 1 : 13 : 0. To ditto Leonard for dressing his bellows 3 times, 1 : 10 : 0." Edward Johnson, of Woburn, in describing Lynn in 1652, in his *Wonder Working Providence*, printed in 1654, says that "there is also an iron mill in constant use;" and Mr. Lewis states that, prior to 1671, "the iron works for several years were carried on with vigor, and furnished most of the iron used in the colony." After 1671 they were fitfully operated, and about 1688 they appear to have been finally abandoned. Their owners were harassed after 1651 with frequent lawsuits, arising from the overflow of the water in the dam. The fear that the works would create a scarcity of timber also appears to have added to their unpopularity. Rev. William Hubbard, in his *Present State of New England*, printed in 1677, says that "a work was set up at Lynn upon a very commodious stream, which was very much promoted and strenuously carried on for some time, but at length, instead of drawing out bars of iron for the country's use, there was hammered out nothing but contentions and lawsuits."

From the foregoing details it is plainly established that the enterprise at Lynn embraced a blast furnace, or "foundery," and a refinery forge. The term foundery was long a synonym for furnace, castings being made directly from the furnace, as has been previously stated. This usage continued in this country down to about the middle of the present century, and it is still followed in some European countries. That the furnace was in operation in May, 1645, is certain, and that the forge was in operation in September, 1648, is equally certain. These dates may be accepted as definitely determining, respectively, the first successful attempts in this country to make "sowe iron" and other castings in a blast furnace and to make "barr iron" in a refinery forge from "sowe iron."

Mr. Nathan M. Hawkes, of Lynn, furnished to the *Magazine of American History* for November, 1889, the following description of the exact site of the Lynn iron works.

Midway between Salem and Boston, the first and second capitals of
Massachusetts, there flows a serpentine little stream called the Saugus by
the Indians and their English successors. Tide-water meets the down-flow-
ing fresh water two miles from the bay between Round Hill on the west
and the dark forest on the east. Just where the currents lap each other on
the bank of the stream is a long sloping mound like a sea-serpent's back,
which to the passer-by seems but a freak of nature. The hand of man,
however, wrought that earth-work. At this point was the upper ferry crossed in the early days by Endicott and Winthrop and all the Puritan wor-
thies in the infancy of New England. The mound which lies at this point
upon the river-bank, and is known to the natives as "the cinder banks," is
the heaped-up scoria—the refuse, the remainder, the sweepings of an iron
foundry which was in full blast before the red man had cast his last linger-
ing look upon his beloved river and upon the blue waters of the Atlantic
beyond. The fleecy snows have mantled it, the sun has scorched it for two
centuries, and only an occasional curious observer has disturbed its scanty
covering of vegetation for some relic of the first manufacturing industry of
the continent.

The bog ore was largely taken from the meadows of the farms of Mr.
Adam Hawkes, two miles north of the works. Mr. Hawkes furnished the
ore, and he was also the persistent plaintiff in many suits against the company for flowing his lands. It is an interesting fact that, while the Puritans
abandoned all the mother country restrictions concerning the conveyance of
land, these fields that became the property of Adam Hawkes, and the site
where he built his first house, about 1630, have never been alienated from
his family, but are still occupied by his lineal descendants and are yet in the
same name. This tenacity of holding is an English trait, but it is rare even
in New England to witness a land tenure so long unbroken.

Joseph Jenks was a machinist at the Lynn works who
had come from Hammersmith in England and was a man of
much skill and inventive genius. He prepared the moulds
for the first castings that were made at Lynn. "A small iron
pot, capable of containing about one quart," was the first article cast at the furnace. In 1844 it was in the possession of
Mr. Lewis's mother, who was a lineal descendant of Thomas
Hudson, the first owner of the lands on Saugus river on which
the iron works were built, and who obtained possession of the
pot immediately after it was cast, "which he preserved as a
curiosity." "It has been handed down in the family ever
since," wrote Mr. Lewis in 1844. Mr. C. M. Tracy, of Lynn,
writes us in 1890 that by some carelessness years ago one leg
of the pot was broken off, when a leaden one was made and
clumsily substituted, but the remainder of the pot " is perfect to-day." " It is of the old dinner-pot pattern," adds Mr.
Tracy, " and, although holding only about a quart, is heavy

enough to make three in the hands of a modern founder." This first iron utensil cast in this country is now in the possession of two sons of Alonzo Lewis, residing at Etna Place, Lynn. Their names are Llewellyn and Arthur Lewis.

Joseph Jenks, who became the founder of a noted New England family, purchased from Richard Leader on January 20, 1647, the privilege of building a forge at the Lynn iron works for the manufacture of scythes and other edge tools. This enterprise was successful. In 1652 he made at these iron works, for the mint which was that year established at Boston, the dies for the first silver pieces coined in New England. On one side of these coins was the impression of a pine tree; hence the name by which they have since been known, "pine-tree shillings." In 1654 he made for the city of Boston the first fire engine made in America. In 1655 the general court granted him a patent for an improved scythe. His name is also associated with other inventions. He died in 1683. Mr. Hawkes says of the scythe which he invented : " This improvement consisted in lengthening the blade, making it thinner, and welding a square bar on the back to strengthen it, as in the scythe of to-day. Before this the old English blade was short and thick like a bush scythe. This invention lightened the labor and cheered the hearts of merry mowers till the mowing machine of our day superseded the old emblem of the husbandman."

Henry and James Leonard were also skilled workmen at Lynn. They and their descendants were afterwards identified with many colonial iron enterprises. The family name is the most noted in the annals of the New England iron industry. Rev. Dr. Fobes, in referring to the Leonard family in his *Topographical Description of Raynham, with its History*, written in 1793, says that " the circumstance of a family attachment to the iron manufacture is so well known as to render it a common observation in this part of the country, ' Where you can find iron works there you will find a Leonard.' " Henry and James Leonard are said to have learned their trade at Pontypool, in Monmouthshire. They were forgemen.

The second iron enterprise that was undertaken in New England embraced a furnace and forge at Braintree, in Norfolk county, about ten miles south of Boston. The works at

Lynn and Braintree belonged to the same company. Bishop says that on the 19th of November, 1643, a grant of 3,000 acres of the common land at Braintree was made to Mr. Winthrop and his partners, the Lynn company, "for the encouragement of an iron work to be set up about Monotcot river." The true spelling of the name of this river is Monontocot. But this grant, according to Lewis, was not surveyed until January 11, 1648. On the 29th of September, 1645, as stated by Lewis, the first purchase of land, consisting of twenty acres "for a forge at Braintree," was made from George Ruggles by Richard Leader, who was the general agent for the company of undertakers. The furnace was probably built in 1646. Robert Child, writing from Boston on the 15th of March, 1647, to John Winthrop, Jr., "at Pequot river," says of the Lynn and Braintree enterprises : "We have cast this winter some tuns of pots, likewise mortars, stoves, skillets. Our potter is moulding more at Brayntree as yet, which place after another blowing we shall quit, not finding mine there." We find, however, that iron ore was mined at Braintree in the early part of 1652, and that on the 28th of September of that year it was proposed at London on behalf of the undertakers to employ William Osborne at "Brantry furnas & fordges." Operations at the works were suspended in 1653, owing to the scarcity of ore. Henry Leonard is said to have superintended the erection of the Braintree works, although James Leonard was certainly connected with them, residing at Braintree in 1653, when he removed to Taunton. John Gifford was the manager of the Braintree works, according to Newhall. In 1651 he succeeded Richard Leader as the agent for the works at Lynn. John Adams and his son, John Quincy Adams, were both natives of Braintree.

The next iron enterprise in New England was located in the town, or township, of Taunton, (now Raynham,) in Bristol county, two miles from the city of Taunton. This enterprise was undertaken in 1652 by a company composed of citizens of Taunton, who employed Henry and James Leonard and Ralph Russell as practical ironworkers. At a town meeting at Taunton, held October 21, 1652, "it was agreed and granted by the town to the said Henry Leonard and James Leonard, his brother, and Ralph Russell free consent to come hither and join with certain of our inhabitants to set up a bloomery work on the Two-mile river." The works thus projected were put in operation in 1656. These works, which must be called the Taunton forge, are referred to by Lewis as "Leonards' celebrated iron works." But the Leonards contributed nothing toward their erection except their skill as ironworkers, James Leonard owning but half a share in the stock of the company and his brother not being a stockholder at all. George Hall was the first clerk and manager, which position he held almost continuously until his death in 1669. His successors were John Hall and others until 1683, when Captain Thomas Leonard became the manager, and so continued until his death in 1713. The forge long continued in a prosperous condition. Bar iron was made directly from the ore. As Henry Leonard was again at Lynn in 1655, and as James Leonard does not appear to have been there after 1652, it is certain that the latter and his sons and descendants were the only Leonards who became completely identified with the active operations of the Taunton forge. The Leonards long continued their connection with the Taunton works as master workmen. Ralph Russell did not remain at Taunton, and is said to have established a forge at Russell's Mills, "which place received its name from him."

There seems to have existed a strong bond of friendship between James Leonard and King Philip, the sachem of the Wampanoags. Elisha Clarke Leonard, in an address in 1886 before the Old Colony Historical Society, at Taunton, fully proves that in 1665 Philip gave to James Leonard the deed for a neck of land embracing about 150 acres, "lying by Mr. Brinton's land at Matapoyset, being bounded on each side by a brook," it being the intention of Mr. Leonard to "set up a mill or iron work if occasion were." But the deed was not confirmed by the colonial authorities, and Mr. Leonard was deprived of the Indian's gift.

In an address read before the Old Colony Historical Society, at Taunton, in July, 1884, Captain J. W. D. Hall said that the hammers and other heavy iron machinery for the Taunton "bloomerie" came from abroad; also that, on the division of Taunton in 1731, the iron works were included in the new town of Raynham. He also said that "the works

made from 20 to 30 tons annually, which brought from £400
to £675, averaging about $100 a ton of our currency. About
a year ago the old buildings were demolished, and the privilege, dam, and foundation walls alone remain of the ancient
Taunton iron works of 224 years—the oldest successful iron
manufactory in New England."

The Taunton forge, says Fobes in 1793, was situated on
"the great road, and, having been repaired from generation
to generation, it is to this day still in employ." In William
Read Deane's *Genealogical Record of the Leonard Family*, published in 1851, it is stated that "the old forge, though it has
been several times remodeled, has been in constant use for
nearly two hundred years, and is now in the full tide of successful operation. It is owned by Theodore Dean, Esq., who
is descended from the Leonards." The forge was at that time
employed in the manufacture of anchors. In 1865 it was
still so employed, with four forge fires, two hammers, and two
water-wheels, but about that time it ceased to be active and
has since been abandoned and dismantled.

In 1657 the general court of Massachusetts, owing to the
failure of the undertakers at Lynn and Braintree to furnish
the colony with a constant supply of iron, "whereby unsuf-
ferable damage may accrew," granted to the inhabitants of
Concord and Lancaster, and such as they should associate
with them, "liberty to erect one or more iron workes within
the limitts of theire oune toune bounds, or in any common
place neere thereunto." That this grant resulted in the establishment of iron works at Concord appears probable from
the grant by the court in 1660, to "yᵉ company in partnership in the iron worke at Concord," of "free liberty to digg
mine without molestation in any lands now in the court's
possession."

About 1668 Henry Leonard went to Rowley village, 25
miles northeast of Lynn, as stated by Newhall, "and there
established iron works." Lewis says that in 1674 Henry
Leonard's sons, Nathaniel, Samuel, and Thomas, contracted to
carry on these works for the owners, whose names are given
by Bishop as "John Ruck and others of Salem." The works
did not prove to be profitable. After establishing the Rowley
works Henry Leonard went to New Jersey, "and there again

engaged in the iron manufacture." At some time previous to his removal to New Jersey he appears to have been connected with the establishment of iron works at Canton, about four-teen miles south of Boston.

Other iron enterprises in Massachusetts speedily followed those that have been mentioned. In 1677 one of these works, the name of which has not come down to us, was destroyed by the Indians. About the same year iron was made at Tops-field, near Ipswich, and in 1680 its manufacture was com-menced at Boxford. Hubbard, writing about 1677, says that at that time there were in the colonies "many convenient places, where very good iron, not much inferior to that of Bilbao, may be produced, as at this day is seen in a village near Topsfield, seven or eight miles west from Ipswich." Mr. Tracy, however, informs us that there is a tradition that the Topsfield works were never very productive.

From the address of Captain Hall we glean the following additional information concerning early Taunton iron works.

Whittington iron works, on Mill river, were built by James Leonard, senior, "forgeman," in 1670. These works embraced a "bloomerie with one hearth." Mr. Leonard's three sons, Joseph, Benjamin, and Uriah, having served in the Taunton iron works at the "refining and bloomerie" trade, worked the forge. They also had a grist mill at the same place. Cap-tain Hall says that "this was the location of James Leonard's iron works." James Leonard died in 1691. The Whittington bloomary was continued by his sons and by their succes-sors for more than a hundred years. During the first fifty years it was supplied with bog ore mined in the vicinity of "Scadding's moire" and pond, and "along up Mill river to Winneconnet pond."

In the years 1696 and 1697 the Chartley iron works were built on Stony brook, within the limits of Taunton North Purchase. "The iron work and tools required were made at the Taunton iron works." These works were built by Thom-as and James Leonard, and embraced only a bloomary for the manufacture of bar iron. They went into operation in 1698. In 1713 George Leonard became the sole owner of these works and greatly enlarged them. The above enterprise was the origin of the noted Leonard iron works of Norton, and one of the chief causes of the organization and incorporation of that town in 1711. Native bog ore was always used.

A small forge, or " bloomerie," to use bog ore, was built about 1695 " at Taunton line, on Three-mile river, near the present site of North Dighton furnace," by Richard Stephens, "in connection with his son and others." In 1739 these works were enlarged. They appear to have been kept in operation until near the close of the eighteenth century.

" The first hollow-ware manufactory" in the Old Colony of New Plymouth was King's furnace, built on Littleworth brook, in the eastern part of Taunton, in 1724 and 1725, by a stock company of which John King was the principal member; hence the name, King's furnace. In 1725 the casting of hollow-ware was commenced, from the size of a pint kettle to a ten-pail cauldron. The ore first used was bog ore found in the neighborhood. This furnace was a successful enterprise. It was rebuilt in 1816, when it "employed about 30 moulders and men, doing a large business." Its wares were even transported to New York " by sloops at Weir village, which on their return brought pig iron and ore from New Jersey." The furnace was in operation for several years after 1839.

The Hopewell iron works, embracing a bloomary only, were built on Mill river, in Taunton, in 1739 and 1740, by Captain Zephaniah Leonard, to make bar iron from bog ore. The bloomary was succeeded by a rolling and slitting mill, erected by John Adam in 1776 and 1777. In 1782 the property passed into the hands of Samuel Leonard and others, of Taunton. Captain Hall says that " Russia and Swede iron, imported in bars, were rolled and converted into rods for the best of hammered nails, furnishing partial employment for many farmer nailers within an area of a dozen miles. Finally, the business proving unprofitable, the works were abandoned." We pass over other early Taunton iron works.

For a hundred years after its settlement in 1620 Massachusetts was the chief seat of the iron manufacture on this continent. Most of its iron enterprises during this hundred years were ore bloomaries, but there were blast furnaces also, although the latter as a rule produced only hollow-ware and other castings and not pig iron. During the period mentioned the iron industry of Massachusetts was confined to the eastern counties of the colony, where bog and pond ores formed the only kinds of ore that were obtainable. Charcoal was the only fuel used, and water-power was the only power employed.

The English settlement at New Haven closely followed Massachusetts in the manufacture of iron. John Winthrop, Jr., who removed from Lynn to Pequod, (New London,) Connecticut, in 1645, had obtained from the general court in the preceding year permission to set up an iron work, and in 1651 he obtained a grant of certain privileges to enable him to "adventure" in the manufacture of iron; but he does not seem to have embarked in the iron business until some time subsequently. On May 30, 1655, as we learn from Bishop, it was ordered by the assembly of New Haven "that if an iron worke goe on within any part of this jurisdiction the persons and estates constantly and onely imployed in that worke shall be free from paying rates." In 1658 Captain Thomas Clarke, in company with John Winthrop and others, put in operation an "iron worke" at New Haven, and in 1669 he seems to have been still engaged in the same enterprise, for in that year the general court of Connecticut continued the exemption already noted for another seven years, "for encouragement of the said worke in supplying the country with good iron and well wrought according to art." This enterprise embraced a blast furnace and a refinery forge. On the 22d of June, 1663, John Davenporte wrote from New Haven to John Winthrop, Jr., as follows: "The freshest newes here, & that which is *e re vestra*, is that they have bene blowing at the iron worke, and have runne, from the last 6th day to this 2d day, 5 sowes of iron, which are commended for very good; & this night it's thought they will run another, & begin to-morrow to make pots. The worke is hopeful, but the workemen are thought to be very chargeable and froward." This frowardness was due apparently to the influence of an old enemy of iron works and ironworkers, John Barleycorn. Bishop records "a proposition made in May, 1662, 'in yᵉ behalfe of Capt. Clarke, that wine and liquors drawn at the iron workes might be custome free,' which was allowed to the extent of one butt of wine and one barrell of liquors, and no more."

Rhode Island made iron soon after its settlement in 1636, certainly at Pawtucket and elsewhere as early as 1675, when a forge at Pawtucket, erected by Joseph Jenks, Jr., son of Joseph Jenks, the machinist at Lynn, was destroyed by the Indians in the Wampanoag war, as well as other iron works and infant enterprises. A third Joseph Jenks was Governor of Rhode Island from 1727 to 1732. The few iron enterprises that were established in this colony in the seventeenth century used bog or pond ore, but in the succeeding century rock ore was also used. There is a deposit of magnetic iron ore in Cumberland township, known as Cumberland hill. This hill, or mountain, is described as forming "a homogeneous mass of iron ore, about 500 feet long by 150 feet wide and 104 feet high, or, in bulk, equal to about 1,000,000 tons above water level, while, as the deposit shows an indefinite extension in depth, the quantity of this ore may be said to be practically inexhaustible." Hematite ore was found at Cranston.

Iron does not appear to have been made within the limits of Maine, New Hampshire, or Vermont until the eighteenth century.

We now give an engraving of the Lynn pot, the first iron article made from native ore in America, cast at Lynn, Massachusetts, in 1645, and still preserved. This engraving is from a photograph obtained in 1890 for this work by Mr. C. M. Tracy, of Lynn. The pot weighs 2 pounds, 13 ounces; its capacity is 1 quart less 1 gill; its inside measurement is 4.5 inches wide by 4.5 inches deep.

CHAPTER XI.

EXTENSION OF THE MANUFACTURE OF IRON IN NEW ENGLAND.

In his valuable essay on the iron ores and iron enterprises of Plymouth county, Massachusetts, printed in 1804, Dr. James Thacher says: "The first furnace for smelting iron ore known in the county of Plymouth was erected in the year 1702 by Lambert Despard (a founder) and the family of Barkers, his associates, at the mouth of Mattakeeset pond in the town of Pembroke, but the wood in the vicinity being exhausted the works were long since abandoned." In James Torrey's *History of Scituate*, in Plymouth county, written in 1815, mention is made of an iron enterprise in the township of Scituate, as follows: "In 1648 Mr. Timothy Hatherly, the principal founder and father of the town of Scituate, requested liberty of the colony to erect an iron mill. It was granted in 1650, conditional to be erected within three years, or the privilege, certain woodlands about Mattakeeset pond, (now Pembroke,) to revert to the colony. It did not, however, take place at that period, but 'a smelting furnace was erected on the precise grant by Mark Despard and the family of Barker about 1702.'" The enterprise of Despard and the Barkers was speedily followed by the erection of a bloomary forge on Bound brook, near Hingham, in 1703, by a company in which two brothers, Daniel and Mordecai Lincoln, were partners. In Torrey's *History of Scituate* mention is made of the erection of the Drinkwater iron works, near Abington, about 1710, by a person named Mighill, probably Rev. Thomas Mighill. Hingham and Abington are both in Plymouth county.

About 1722 a bloomary forge was built at Bridgewater, which was active in 1750. In 1738 Hugh Orr, a Scotchman, established at this place a gun factory, and about 1748 he made five hundred muskets for the province of Massachusetts Bay, which are claimed to have been the first muskets manufactured in this country. Subsequently he established a cast-iron cannon foundry at Bridgewater, and was instrumental in promoting various other manufacturing enterprises. In 1730 iron works were erected at Plympton, now Carver, which appear to have embraced a blast furnace, as mention is made of "the first cast-iron tea-kettle" having been cast at Plympton between 1760 and 1765. Bishop says: "That important utensil had been previously made of wrought iron, and was imported from England. A copper tea-kettle was first used at Plymouth, whence Carver was chiefly settled, in 1702."

The first slitting mill in the colonies for slitting nail rods is said by tradition to have been erected at Milton, in Norfolk county, as early as 1710. Bishop accords this honor to Middleborough, in Plymouth county, at a later day, but he does not give the date of its erection, except to indicate by the context that it was built before 1750. We have in our possession a very excellent draft of a slitting mill at Middleborough which is said to have been built by Judge Peter Oliver in 1751 and which was abandoned in 1830. This draft is by William H. Harrison, of Braintree, Massachusetts. It may be found reproduced in the *Transactions* of the American Society of Mechanical Engineers for 1881.

Mr. Tracy writes to us that in the old records of Essex county, Massachusetts, is this surprising undated entry, inserted between two other entries dated May 20th and June 17th, 1650: "A caveat is recorded of ye sale of ye slitting mill in Lyn by Richd Ledder for tenn powndes to Capt. Willm Hathorne."

In 1731 there were officially reported to be in Massachusetts "several forges for making bar iron, and some furnaces for cast iron or hollow-ware, and one slitting mill, and a manufacture for nails." The slitting mill referred to was located at either Milton or Middleborough. At the same time there were in all New England "six furnaces, meaning hollow-ware furnaces, and nineteen forges, meaning bloomaries, not refineries." "At that time," says Douglass, in his *British Settlements*, "we had no pig furnaces nor refineries of pigs" in New England. Refineries were in use about twenty years later.

There were officially reported to be four slitting mills in Massachusetts in 1750—two at Middleborough, one at Hanover, and one at Milton; also a plating-forge with a tilt-hammer, and one steel furnace. In 1750 Douglass thus described the iron industry of New England :

Iron is a considerable article in our manufacture; it consists of these general branches: (1) Smelting furnaces reducing the ore into pigs; having coal enough and appearances of rock ore. In Attleborough were erected at a great charge three furnaces, but the ore proving bad and scarce this projection miscarried as to pigs. They were of use in casting of small cannon for ships of letters of marque, and in casting cannon-balls and bombs toward the reduction of Louisbourg. (2) Refineries which manufacture pigs, imported from New York, Pennsylvania, and Maryland furnaces, into bar iron. (3) Bloomaries, which, from bog or swamp ore, without any furnace, only by a forge hearth, reduce it into a bloom or semi-liquidated lump to be beat into bars, but much inferior to those from the pigs or refineries. (4) Swamp ore furnaces; from that ore smelted they cast hollow-ware which we can afford cheaper than from England or Holland.

Bog or swamp ore lies from half a foot to two feet deep. In about 20 years from digging it grows or gathers fit for another digging; if it lies longer it turns rusty and does not yield well. Three tons of swamp ore yield about one ton of hollow-ware. One hundred and twenty bushels of charcoal are sufficient to smelt rock ore into one ton of pigs. The complement of men for a furnace is eight or nine, besides cutters of wood, coalers, carters, and other common laborers.

In New England we have two slitting mills for nail rods: one in Milton, eight miles from Boston, and another in Middleborough, about thirty miles from Boston, which are more than we have occasion for. Our nailors can afford spikes and large nails cheaper than from England, but small nails not so cheap.

In New England they do not forge bar iron sufficient for their home consumption by bloomaries and refineries; they import from England, New York, Jersies, Pennsylvania, and Maryland.

The development of the rich brown hematite iron ores of Western Massachusetts commenced about 1750. It is said, however, that as early as 1731 iron ore was taken on horseback in leather bags to Ousatonic, now Great Barrington, in Berkshire county, from Old Hill mine, in Litchfield county, Connecticut, a distance of sixteen miles, and worked in bloomary forges. A furnace was built at Lenox, in Berkshire county, in 1765, and it made pig iron in the following year. It had an exceptionally high stack for that day—28 feet high, and was blown with one tuyere. This furnace was torn down in 1881. Previous to 1773 a furnace was built at Furnace village, in Worcester county, and a few years after that date there were several bloomaries and one refinery forge in the same county. In 1793 the county contained several manufactories of edge tools, hardware, machinery, etc. In the township of Sutton there were at this time one axe, one hoe, and five scythe manufactories, and several naileries. In the whole county there were seventeen trip-hammers. At Springfield, in Hampden county, as stated by Bishop, some cannon were cast and some forging was done during the Revolution, but small arms were not made here until after the peace. The Government armory at Springfield was established in 1794.

While the iron industry of Massachusetts was being extended westward it made rapid progress in the eastern counties. Charlotte furnace at Middleborough was built in 1758, and was in operation for many years. During our two wars with the mother country it was employed in casting shot and shells. The shot which the *Constitution* carried in her conflict with the *Guerrière* were cast at this furnace. In 1784 there were seventy-six iron works in Massachusetts, "many of them small." At Amesbury, in Essex county, a furnace was erected about 1790, and at Boxborough, in Middlesex county, a bloomary forge was built about the same time. In 1795 Dr. Morse reported eleven slitting mills in Bristol, Norfolk, and Plymouth counties, which rolled and cut in that year 1,732 tons of iron into hoops and nail rods. Bishop says that "the two counties of Plymouth and Bristol had in operation in 1798 fourteen blast and six air furnaces, twenty forges, and seven rolling and slitting mills, in addition to a number of trip-hammers and a great number of nail and smith shops. Cut and hammered nails, spades and shovels, card teeth, saws, scythes, metal buttons, cannon balls, bells, fire arms, sheet iron for tin ware, wire, etc., were made in large quantities." In 1804 there were ten blast furnaces in Plymouth county, all producing castings exclusively. In 1830 only three of these were left—Charlotte, Federal, and Pope's Point, all in Carver township, and all in operation. There were also in 1804 ten forges in the same county, which were principally employed in working "old iron scraps," broken pots, kettles, etc., and produced in all about 200 tons of bar iron per annum.

Dr. James Thacher, who was a part owner of Federal furnace, wrote in 1804 a description of this furnace, which was built in 1794, and is said by him to have been the most valuable furnace with which he was acquainted, the manufacture of castings being "there prosecuted to great extent and advantage." The furnace was built of stone, as were all other Plymouth furnaces. It was 20 feet high and 24 feet square, its walls being 7 feet thick and its interior 10 feet in diameter. Charcoal was the only fuel used, and marine shells formed the only fluxing material. The furnace was lined with "fire stone" composed of "soft slate." A brick funnel at the top of the stack served "to convey off the blaze and smoke." The Doctor continues his description as follows :

At the bottom of an arch in the front of the furnace is an aperture, from which the workmen remove the scoria and dip out the metal. And in another arch on one side there is a small aperture for the insertion of the pipes of two large bellows 22 feet long and 4 feet wide, which being kept in constant alternate motion by the agency of a water-wheel 25 feet diameter, a powerful current of air is excited ; and being impelled upon the surface of the fuel the fusion of the metal is greatly accelerated. The whole of this machinery is included in a large wooden building, affording accommodation to the workmen with their apparatus for moulding and casting.

The specific articles manufactured at the Federal furnace are, besides hollow-ware of every description, Seymour's patent rolls for slitting mills, of a superior quality, cast in iron cylinders, potash kettles, stoves, fire-backs and jambs, plates, gudgeons, anvils, large hammers, cannon shot of every kind, with a vast variety of machinery for mills, etc.

The ores used in the furnaces and bloomaries of Eastern Massachusetts in the eighteenth century were chiefly native bog and pond ores. Dr. Thacher says, however, that in 1804 " a very considerable proportion of ore smelted in our furnaces is procured from the very productive mines at Egg Harbor in the State of New Jersey, of a reddish brown color, producing from 30 to 40 per cent. of excellent iron. The usual price is $6.50 per ton." He also says that "reddish brown" ore in large lumps was obtained from a mine on Martha's Vineyard, "affording about 25 per cent. and worth $6 per ton." The pond ores contained from 20 to 30 per cent. of iron, and the average price was about $6 per ton at the furnace. Bog ore, found in swamps and other low places, was of a "rusty brown color, yielding about 18 per cent. and worth $4 per ton at the furnace." The following letter from the Rev. Isaac Backus, of Middleborough, dated July 25, 1794, gives a description of the manner in which pond ores were obtained at that time.

Vast quantities of iron, both cast and wrought, have been made in this part of the country for more than a hundred years past ; but it was chiefly out of bog ore, until that kind was much exhausted in these parts, and then a rich treasure was opened in Middleborough, which had been long hid from the inhabitants. About the year 1747 it was discovered that there was iron mine in the bottom of our great pond at Assowamset; and after some years it became the main ore that was used in the town, both at furnaces and forges, and much of it has been carried into the neighboring places for the same purpose. Men go out with boats, and make use of instruments much like those with which oysters are taken, to get up the ore from the bottom of the pond. I am told that, for a number of years, a man would take up and bring to shore two tons of it in a day; but now it is so much exhausted that half a ton is reckoned a good day's work for one man. But in an adjacent pond is now plenty, where the water is twenty feet deep, and much is taken up from that depth, as well as from shoaler water. It has also been plenty in a pond in the town of Carver, where they have a furnace upon the stream which runs from it. Much of the iron which is made from this ore is better than they could make out of bog ore, and some of it is as good as almost any refined iron. The quantity of this treasure, which hath been taken out of the bottom of clear ponds, is said to have been sometimes as much as five hundred tons in a year.

Before proceeding further we may here refer to the first steel works in Massachusetts. In 1750 it was officially reported that there was then in Massachusetts " one furnace for making steel," but its location is not given. The first steel works in Massachusetts of which we can obtain circumstantial information were established at Easton, in Bristol county, in 1775 or 1776, by Eliphalet Leonard. In the early part of 1826 there appeared in the Boston *Patriot* a letter written by Jonathan Leonard, of Canton, in Norfolk county, which we find reprinted in the *New England Historical and Genealogical Register* for October, 1857, and from which we take the following extracts.

As to the making of steel, the first attempt made in this country so far as my knowledge goes was by my father, Eliphalet Leonard, at Easton, about the year 1775 or '76. He was led to that attempt by the extreme scarcity of steel and the difficulty of procuring it for his manufactory of fire-arms, then in great demand for the defense of the country. He constructed several furnaces, and so far succeeded as to supply himself and some of the most urgent wants of his neighbors.

In 1787 I obtained further insight into the business, and erected at Easton a furnace capable of making three tons at a batch. This was continued until 1808, when, in consequence of the commercial restrictions, I erected another at the same place capable of making ten tons at a batch, and afterwards from twenty to thirty tons a year. In 1813 I erected another furnace at Canton, where I now live, where I made at times about one hundred tons of steel a year.

Towards the close of the Revolution Samuel Downing, of Trenton, New Jersey, made considerable blistered steel. During the progress of the Revolution a certain German at Cumberland, in Rhode Island, made steel from the pig after the mode of his country. During the same time some was made at Amenia, in the State of New York. In 1809 a steel furnace was put in operation at Middleborough and another at Canton by Adam Kinsley, and another at Plymouth. About the year 1799 steel was made at Canton by Leonard & Kinsley after the German manner, and afterwards by Dunbar & Leonard. The manufacture of blistered steel is carried on extensively in New York and Philadelphia.

Cast steel has got much into use within a few years. Some was made here during the late war, but it was then difficult to obtain clay that would endure a heat sufficient to melt and take it out of the fire.

There was one Daniel Pettybone who pretended that he invented the welding of cast steel with borax and got a patent for his invention about the year 1802. He put the blacksmiths under contribution, and after his patent had run out he petitioned Congress to renew it. I told them that it was an art considerably well known among blacksmiths, and I procured several depositions from aged blacksmiths to prove that they had done it in this country as early as the year 1772, and occasionally from that time to 1819. Cast steel had been welded to iron in Canton in 1792, six years before Pettybone dated his invention. This was done by the use of borax. It has likewise been done by the help of bog iron ore powdered fine and sprinkled on the steel when at a white heat, and formed at that temperature a kind of gluey (glassy) substance which would stick the bars together.

The steel referred to by the writer of the foregoing letter as having been made by his father and himself was cemented steel, otherwise known as blister steel. The statement which he makes concerning the manufacture of steel "from the pig," "after the German manner," is very important, as it shows that this method of making steel was in use in this country in the last century side by side with the manufacture of blister steel—a fact not generally known in our day.

In the same letter Mr. Leonard gives the following information concerning the blast furnaces of Eastern Massachusetts in 1826: "There are if I mistake not ten or twelve blast furnaces at this time in the counties of Plymouth and Bristol, and one in Norfolk. General Leach seems to have taken the lead of late years in the furnace business. The iron made from bog ore at his furnaces in Easton and Foxborough is thought to be softer and better than in other places for machinery." Bog ore was therefore used in blast furnaces in Massachusetts as late as 1826. More than thirty years ago Professor J. P. Lesley wrote of the old bog-ore furnaces of Massachusetts as follows: "The old blast furnaces of Plymouth county, making a poor iron, in very small quantities, from an ochreous ore dug from the diluvium of the pond bottoms, are almost forgotten. Traditions of them remain only as jests at the primitive ways they were set to work in. One is described as situated on the bank of a stream and lashed to a large tree to protect it from the freshets; when an order came for a few tons of iron the neighboring farmers assembled and blew it in. Small furnaces and poor ore they served their day and are forgotten; obliterated by the over-rush of two commercial iron deluges, one from the English importers and the other from the anthracite manufacturers."

In 1721 Samuel Bissell, a blacksmith of Newport, Rhode Island, received a loan of two hundred pounds from the colonial treasury to enable him to carry on the manufacture of nails. In 1735 Samuel Waldo erected a furnace and foundry on the Pawtuxet river, in Rhode Island, which were afterwards known as Hope furnace. These are said to have been the most important iron works in the State during the eighteenth century. Cannon and other castings were made here. During the Revolution they were active in producing cannon, cannon balls, and other munitions of war. Hope furnace was located on the north branch of the Pawtuxet. In 1765 Stephen Hopkins, a signer of the Declaration of Independence, "began to work a bed of iron ore in the southeastern part of Scituate," as we learn from his biography written by William E. Foster, and in 1769, as we are informed by the same authority, he began the manufacture of iron at Hope furnace in company with Nicholas and Moses Brown and Israel Wilkinson. About the year 1735 three furnaces were erected in Cumberland township, in the northeastern part of the State, but they seem to have been abandoned before the Revolution. They made "cannon, bombs, and bullets" during the French war of 1755. In 1741 iron works were in operation on the south branch of the Pawtuxet river, in the town of Warwick, "for the refining of iron." They were owned by the sons of Jabez Greene. One of these sons was Nathanael Greene, the father of Major General Nathanael Greene of the Revolution, who was himself trained to work on the farm and at the forge. In 1770 he was in charge of a forge at Coventry, in Rhode Island, which was known as Greene's forge. In 1789 a rolling and slitting mill was established near Providence, on one of the branches of Providence river, and before 1800 a rolling and slitting mill had been established at Pawtucket Falls and other iron-manufacturing enterprises in various parts of the State. Bishop says that "manufactures of iron, including bar and sheet iron, steel, nail rods and nails, farming implements, stoves, pots, and other castings and household utensils, iron works for shipbuilders, anchors, and bells formed the largest branch of productive industry in the State toward the close of the eighteenth century."

The iron made in Rhode Island in the eighteenth century was obtained from native bog ore in large part, but native hematite and magnetic ore were also used, the latter coming from Cumberland hill, which has been referred to in the preceding chapter. We give below some extracts from a letter to the New York *Tribune*, written in October, 1873, and dated at Providence, Rhode Island, which contained a historical account of Cumberland hill, or Cumberland iron mountain.

During the French war, as early as 1755, the inhabitants of this colony made from the ore from this very mine, mixed with a hematite ore from Cranston, Rhode Island, cannon which were used in the service against the French and Indians, and thus it has aided in carrying out the far-reaching policy of the great Pitt. In 1800, also, cannon were again cast from these ores at Hope, a small village on the Pawtuxet river, in this State, for John Brown of Providence, who had a contract with the Government at this date to furnish it guns; and, what is singular, the guns were cast hollow, a supposed modern invention. At the foot of the mine is a meeting-house, with the date "A. D. 1700" over the door, the beams and joists of which would to-day be too unwieldy even for ship timber. Though Rhode Island people have not appeared to recognize the importance of this possession, still many places, such as Easton, in Massachusetts, which early entered into the production of iron, have regularly carted from this mine their supply.

Litchfield county, in Northwestern Connecticut, contains hematite iron-ore mines of great value, from which the ore for the celebrated Salisbury iron has been taken for over a hundred and fifty years. As early as 1734 a bloomary forge was erected at Lime Rock, in Litchfield county, by Thomas Lamb, which produced from 500 to 700 pounds of iron per day. A blast furnace was afterwards added to this forge at Lime Rock, and it is still active in 1890. About 1748 a forge was erected at the village of Lakeville, then called Furnace village, in the same county, and in 1762 John Haseltine, Samuel Forbes, and Ethan Allen purchased the property and built a blast furnace at Lakeville, but soon afterwards sold it to Charles and George Caldwell, of Hartford. It made two and a half tons of iron in twenty-four hours, and three tons of ore and 250 bushels of charcoal were used per ton of iron. Its blowing apparatus consisted of a pair of leather bellows driven by a water-wheel. In 1768 the furnace was sold to Richard Smith, of Hartford. Smith was a royalist and fled to England during the Revolution, but his furnace was used to produce large quantities of cannon, cannon balls, shells, etc., for the Continental army. After the Revolution it made cannon for the navy, potash kettles weighing nearly half a ton each, and pig iron for forges and foundries. This furnace was abandoned in 1830 or 1831, as we are informed by Samuel S. Robbins, president of the Lime Rock Iron Company, now in his 87th year. Colonel Ethan Allen, one of the original owners of Lakeville furnace, was one of the conspicuous figures of the Revolution. He was born in Litchfield county, but removed to Vermont while still a young man.

A bloomary forge on Mount Riga, in Litchfield county, was built about 1781 by Abner or Peter Woodin. It was afterwards owned by Daniel Ball, and was called Ball's forge. About 1806 Seth King and John Kelsey commenced to build a furnace on Mount Riga, but they were not able to finish it, and in 1810 it fell into the hands of Holley & Coffing, who completed it in that year and operated it for many years. The forge and furnace have long been abandoned. The latter was in operation as late as 1856.

About thirty furnaces have been built and operated within a radius of thirty miles of Lakeville, a few of which were in New York and Massachusetts, but the majority were in Connecticut. At the close of the eighteenth century Litchfield county contained many bloomaries, which made iron directly from the ore, and three slitting mills. At the same time this county was so prominent in the manufacture of nails that only Plymouth and Bristol counties in Massachusetts, of all the nail-making districts in the country, exceeded its production. The iron of Litchfield county is now used entirely for foundry purposes, and most of it is used in the manufacture of car wheels. The first foundry for melting pig iron in the Salisbury district was built at Lime Rock about 1830 and soon afterwards was purchased by Milo Bar-num, the founder of the present Barnum Richardson Com-pany, and the father of Hon. William H. Barnum. Charcoal is the only fuel used in the blast furnaces of this district.

The annual meeting of the United States Association of Charcoal Iron Workers in October, 1885, took place at New York, but an excursion was made to the Salisbury region in Connecticut. While at Lakeville the local committee had arranged for an address of welcome from ex-Governor A. H. Holley, a resident of the town, who had all his life been an iron worker, and whose son was the late A. L. Holley. Ill-ness prevented Governor Holley from attending, but he sent a letter of welcome, from which the following is an extract.

You are in the immediate vicinity of one of the oldest iron mines in this country, if not the oldest, it having been wrought more or less for about one hundred and fifty years. The iron produced from it has been proved, by various tests at the armories, arsenals, and navy-yards of the na-tion, to have greater tensile strength and resisting power than any other ever produced. This may seem like an arrogant boast, but the Government, some years since, ordered and received samples of the most noted irons, foreign and domestic, for the *purpose* of testing their strength, and the Sal-isbury iron endured strains that no other did or could.

You are also within a thousand feet of the site of the oldest char-coal furnace in all the region about us, erected between the years 1760 and 1770. The first cannon cast in the United States for service in the Revo-lution were made therein. A portion of them were used to arm the ship *Constitution*, the old *iron-sides* of the American navy. Every one of them bore the test required by the inspectors, and none were ever broken either by our own powder and balls or by those of the enemy. Since the opening and continued use of the old mine above referred to others of great value have been developed, within a circuit of fifty miles, which produce iron of an exceptionally good quality.

Oldmixon, in his *British Empire in America*, mentions " a small iron mill " as existing at Branford, in New Haven county, in 1741, on a small stream running into Long Island sound, and he adds that on many of the small streams and branches of the rivers which fall into the sound " bloomaries and small works for a variety of manufactures in iron were established, some of them quite early." The bloomaries were in part supplied with bog ore, " dug near them," and in part with better ores obtained elsewhere. Bishop says that in 1794 a slitting mill and other iron works had been erected in East Hartford, a forge at Glastonbury, and two furnaces at

Stafford "which made sufficient hollow and cast iron wares for the whole State." Lesley says that there were at one time, about the beginning of the present century, three furnaces on a branch of the Willimantic river, in Stafford, in Eastern Connecticut, near the Massachusetts line, a mile or two apart. Three forges near them converted their pig iron into bar iron. Hebron furnace was south of the above-mentioned furnaces, and Enfield forge stood a few miles east of Windsor Locks. All of these furnaces and forges were stopped about 1837, when Scotch pig iron began to come into the country as a substitute for foundry pig iron of domestic manufacture.

Connecticut was probably the first of the colonies to make steel. In 1728 Samuel Higley, of Simsbury, and Joseph Dewey, of Hebron, in Hartford county, represented to the legislature that the first-named had, "with great pains and cost, found out and obtained a curious art, by which to convert, change, or transmute common iron into good steel, sufficient for any use, and was the very first that ever performed such an operation in America." The certificates of several smiths, who had made a trial of the steel and pronounced it good, were produced. He and Joseph Dewey were granted the exclusive right for ten years " of practicing the business or trade of steel-making." A " steel furnace " was owned by Aaron Eliot, of Killingworth, in Middlesex county, previous to 1750, and in 1761 the Rev. Jared Eliot, of the same place, father of the above-mentioned Aaron Eliot, and grandson of John Eliot, the apostle to the Indians, succeeded in producing in a common bloomary forge, from 83 pounds of black magnetic sand, a bar of excellent iron, weighing 50 pounds, and in his son's furnace a part of the bar was converted into good steel. For producing this iron he was awarded a gold medal in 1762 by the London Society of Arts, which is now in the possession of Charles G. Elliott, of Goshen, New York. It is inscribed : " To the Rev. Jared Eliot, M. A., of N. England. MDCCLXII. For producing malleable iron from the American black sand." The medal was sent to Mr. Eliot from London in 1764 "by Thos. Fisher, to the care of our friend, Ben. Franklin." This sand, which is found in the southern parts of Connecticut, as well as in some other States, never received much further attention for conversion into iron or steel.

Aaron Eliot's "steel furnace" was doubtless a cementation furnace. In 1750 it was officially reported that there was then only one "furnace for making steel" in Connecticut, and this was probably Eliot's furnace.

Iron ore was discovered near Portsmouth, in New Hampshire, as early as 1634, some of which was sent to England, but we find no evidence that its discovery led to the establishment of any iron works in that colony. The manufacture of iron in this State probably dates from about 1750, when several bog-ore bloomaries were in existence on Lamper Eel river, but were soon discontinued. About the time of the Revolution there were a few bloomaries in operation in New Hampshire. In 1791 mention is made of iron works at Exeter. At Furnace village the magnetic iron ore of Winchester was first smelted in 1795 by a Rhode Island company. Franconia furnace, at Franconia, was built in 1811 by a company which was organized in 1805. This furnace was abandoned in 1865, and there is now no blast furnace in the State, nor any other enterprise for the manufacture of iron or steel except the steel works of the Nashua Iron and Steel Company, at Nashua.

Maine had a few bloomary forges in York county during the Revolution and for some years afterwards, but she has had but few blast furnaces. A small furnace, capable of yielding a ton and a half of iron daily, was erected at Shapleigh, in York county, about 1838. It was used to produce castings from bog ore, and cost only $13,000. A larger furnace, called Katahdin, was built in 1845 in Piscataquis county, and was lately active. This is the only furnace now in the State. Among its projectors and first owners was the Hon. John L. Hayes, a native of Maine, who afterwards became distinguished as a writer on economic subjects and as the secretary of the National Association of Wool Manufacturers, and who died at his home in Cambridge, Massachusetts, on April 18, 1887, aged 75 years. He was born at South Berwick, Maine, on April 13, 1812. A forge was erected near Katahdin furnace soon after 1845. In 1853 it made 700 tons of blooms. It was burned down about 1855. There were in 1884 two rolling mills in Maine, one at Portland and one at Pembroke, but the Pembroke mill has since been abandoned.

The manufacture of iron was commenced in Vermont

about 1775. Large deposits of iron ores similar to those of
Western Massachusetts and Western Connecticut had been
found in the southern and western parts of the State. In
Rutland county ore was mined before 1785. In 1794 there
were fourteen forges, three furnaces, and a slitting mill in this
county. In other counties there were seven forges in 1794—
one in Bennington, four in Addison, and two in Chittenden.
Before 1800 other forges and a slitting mill were added in this
State ; possibly a few furnaces. The township of Randolph,
in Orange county, had two forges and a slitting mill at this
period. About the beginning of the present century there
were twenty bloomaries in the neighborhood of Vergennes,
in Addison county, all built with Boston capital. The prominence of Vermont in the manufacture of iron has now been
lost. In 1890 the East Middlebury forge, its only remaining
iron enterprise, was finally abandoned.

The manufacture of nails was one of the household industries of New England during the eighteenth century. In
a speech in Congress in 1789 Fisher Ames said: "It has become common for the country people in Massachusetts to erect
small forges in their chimney corners; and in winter, and in
evenings, when little other work can be done, great quantities
of nails are made, even by children. These people take the
rod iron of the merchant and return him the nails, and in
consequence of this easy mode of barter the manufacture is
prodigiously great." In a description of the town of Middleborough, in Plymouth county, Massachusetts, written in 1793
by Nehemiah Bennet, it is mentioned that "the most common
and general employment of the inhabitants of said town is
agriculture, which seems to be increasing; though there are a
number of mechanicks. Nailing, or the business of making
nails, is carried on largely in the winters by the farmers and
young men, who have but little other business at that season
of the year." When Jacob Perkins, of Newburyport, Massachusetts, invented about 1790 his nail-cutting machine, which
was patented in 1795 and speedily followed by other inventions for the same purpose, the occupation of making nails in
the chimney corner met with a serious check. And with this
check to the making of nails in chimney corners the work
of the slitting mills in New England rapidly declined.

The manufacture of hand-made tacks was also a New England household industry during the last century, and down to about fifty years ago. A writer in the *Furniture Trade Journal* thus describes this long extinct industry : " In the queer-shaped, homely farm-houses, or the little, contracted shops of certain New England villages, the industrious and frugal descendants of the Pilgrims toiled providently through the long winter months at beating into shape the little nails which play so useful a part in modern industry. A small anvil served to beat the wire or strip of iron into shape and point it ; a vice, worked by the foot, clutched it between jaws furnished with a gauge to regulate the length, leaving a certain portion projecting, which, when beaten flat by a hammer, formed the head. By this process a man might make, toilsomely, perhaps 2,000 tacks per day." New England is now prominent in the manufacture of tacks in this country by machinery. More than two-thirds of our tack industry is controlled by Massachusetts and fully three-fourths by all of New England. Taunton is the centre of the New England tack industry.

The earliest notice we have seen of a machine for cutting nails occurs in Arnold's *History of the State of Rhode Island*. The author says : " It is said that the first cold cut nail in the world was made in 1777 by Jeremiah Wilkinson, of Cumberland, Rhode Island, who died in 1832, at the advanced age of 90 years." Bishop gives a description of Wilkinson's very crude attempts to make cut nails and tacks. Speaking of Wilkinson's tacks he says : " They were first cut by a pair of shears (still preserved) from an old chest lock, and afterwards headed in a smith's vice. Sheet-iron was afterwards used and the process extended to small nails, which he appears to have been one of the first to attempt. They were cut from old Spanish hoops, and headed in a clamp or vice by hand. Pins and needles were made by the same person during the Revolution, from wire drawn by himself."

All the bloomaries and refinery forges and old-style furnaces of New England have now disappeared, and in their stead have grown up reproductive iron industries of almost endless variety and vast extent, which employ large numbers of skilled mechanics and add greatly to the material wealth of the country. The machine shops, nail and tack factories, hardware establishments, foundries, locomotive works, bridge works, cutlery works, file and screw factories, agricultural implement works, axe and shovel factories, wire works, etc., together with a few steel works, modern blast furnaces, and rolling mills, form to-day a striking contrast to the bog-ore bloomaries, not much larger than a blacksmith's fire, and the small charcoal furnaces and chimney-corner nail factories of the last century. "All that," says Lesley, "has given way and disappeared before the inventive spirit of New England, sustained and incited by the wealth of its commercial cities." It may also with great propriety be added that it has "given way" partly because of the exhaustion of bog ores, partly because of the exhaustion of timber for charcoal, and partly because many of the streams which formerly furnished an abundance of water power are now either dried up or furnish a very small volume of water. All the primitive conditions have greatly changed and now belong to ancient history. There is a new era in New England.

Hon. William H. Barnum, for many years a member of Congress, and a United States Senator from 1876 to 1879, was born at Boston Corners, Columbia county, New York, on September 17, 1818, and died at Lime Rock, Connecticut, on April 30, 1889. He was one of the most prominent iron manufacturers of New England.

CHAPTER XII.

EARLY IRON ENTERPRISES IN NEW YORK.

DURING the rule of the Dutch in New York, from their first settlement on Manhattan Island in 1614 to their surrender to the English in 1664, iron ore was found in various places, but no effort to manufacture iron is known to have been made. Nor does it appear that the English established any iron works in the province until some time after the beginning of the succeeding century. A Parliamentary report, quoted by Pitkin in his *Statistical View of the Commerce of the United States of America*, printed in 1816, states that there were no manufactures in New York as late as 1731 "that deserve mentioning." Bishop quotes Governor Cosby as reporting in 1734 that "as yet no iron work is set up in this province." The Dutch were never noted as ironworkers in their old home in Holland.

The first iron works in New York of which we have authentic information were "set up," according to Bishop, a short time prior to 1740, on Ancram creek, in Columbia county, about fourteen miles east of the Hudson river, by Philip Livingston, the owner of the Livingston manor, and the father of Philip the signer of the Declaration. These works at first embraced only a bloomary, but as early as 1750 they appear to have embraced a blast furnace and a refinery forge. The supply of ore was obtained mainly from the "ore hill" in Salisbury township, Litchfield county, Connecticut, of which Mr. Livingston was a principal owner, and which had been developed a few years previously. The ore mines were about twelve miles distant from the Ancram works. Other sources of ore supply were found in the eastern part of the manor, near the Massachusetts and Connecticut lines. Notwithstanding the inconvenient location of the works, at a considerable distance from the mines and also from the nearest point of shipment on the Hudson river for the manufactured iron, they were prosperous until after the Revolution. In 1756 they are said to have been the only iron works in the province that were then in operation, although others had been undertaken. Of these silent or unfortunate enterprises Bishop mentions two furnaces in the manor of Cortland, and " several bloomaries which had not been worked for several years." At Marysburg, in the Livingston manor, were some bloomary forges which were operated about the time of the Revolution.

Peter Kalm, the Swedish traveler, writing in 1748, says of the commerce of New York : " Of late years they have shipped a quantity of iron to England." Some of this iron was doubtless made in Connecticut and New Jersey. Douglass, in his *British Settlements*, written in 1750, speaking of New York, says : " The article of iron in pigs and bars is a growing affair."

Bishop says that iron works were established in Orange county prior to 1750, but by whom he does not state. In 1750 Governor Clinton reported that, at a place called Wawayanda, in Orange county, about twenty-six miles from the Hudson, there was a plating-forge with a tilt-hammer, which had been built four or five years before, but was not then in use. It was the property of Lawrence Scrawley, a blacksmith. " It was the only mill of that kind in the province. There was no rolling or slitting mill or steel furnace at that time in the province."

In 1750 a vein of magnetic ore was discovered on Sterling mountain, in Orange county, and in 1751 Ward & Colton built a furnace at the outlet of Sterling pond. In Eager's *History of Orange County* it is stated that " at the early establishment of this furnace the charcoal used was transported several miles on the backs of horses from the mountains where it was burned, there being no roads at the time." Bishop says that in 1752 " Abel Noble, from Bucks county, Pennsylvania, erected a forge in Monroe, near the furnace, at which anchors are said to have been made." Eager says that the first anchor made in New York was made at this forge in 1753. In 1765 William Hawkhurst published an advertisement stating that he had lately erected " a finery and great hammer for refining the Sterling pig iron into bars," but the location of this enterprise is not mentioned.

The furnace of Ward & Colton and the forge of Abel Noble fell into the hands of Peter Townsend before the Revolution. They had been named the Sterling iron works, presumably after Lord Stirling, the owner of the land, who became a general in the Continental army, and who was engaged in the manufacture of iron in New Jersey before the Revolution. He may have been a part owner of the Orange county enterprises. (The Sterling works have always been spelled as here given, but Lord Stirling's name was differently spelled.) In 1773 Mr. Townsend made anchors at Sterling. We are informed by A. W. Humphreys that the anchors of the United States frigate *Constitution* were made here, and also the anchors for the first ships of war that carried the stars and stripes. In 1777 " the Townsends" had two forges with eight fires. In 1776 Mr. Townsend, according to Bishop, "produced the first steel in the province, at first from pig and afterwards from bar iron, in the German manner." Bishop says that " the first blister steel made in the State was made by Peter Townsend, Jr., in 1810, from ore of the Long mine on the Sterling estate," but the steel made by the elder Townsend in 1776 from bar iron was doubtless blister steel. The Long mine was discovered in 1761 by David Jones. Other valuable mines than those mentioned were discovered and opened on the Sterling estate in the last century. In 1777 a second Sterling furnace was built by "the Townsends," and in 1806 Southfield furnace was built by them about six miles distant from the Sterling mines, and it is still standing. The two early Sterling furnaces have been replaced by one modern furnace.

Other mines of iron ore were discovered in Orange county during the last century, and many furnaces and forges were built in connection with them which have long been abandoned. In 1756 there was a Forest of Dean furnace five miles west of Fort Montgomery, which was supplied with ore from the Forest of Dean mine, near which it stood. The furnace was abandoned twenty-one years later. Eager says that "Captain Solomon Townsend, a cousin of Peter Townsend, and who married his daughter Anne in 1783, purchased the mountain estate adjoining that of his father-in-law, which he named Augusta, and established the iron works, anchory, forges, etc., at the place." These works were on the Ramapo, three miles above the Orange county line, in Orange county. There was a forge and anchory on Murderer's creek during the Revolution, owned by Samuel Brewster; after the war they passed into the hands of his son-in-law, Jonas Williams. Queensborough furnace, which went out of blast about 1800, and which was built to make pig iron and not castings, was located about two and a half miles southwest of Fort Montgomery. A furnace was in operation at Craigsville during the Revolution. On the stream issuing from Hazzard's pond there was a furnace named Woodbury about the beginning of this century. Greenwood furnace, in Orange county, was erected in 1811 by the Messrs. Cunningham. In 1871 it was the only charcoal furnace in blast in Southern New York; since that year it also has been silent. During the last century Orange county was the chief seat of the iron manufacture in New York.

The following account of the great iron chain which was suspended across the Hudson river in 1778, to prevent the passage of the British vessels, is compiled from Benson J. Lossing's *Field Book of the Revolution.*

At the close of 1779 West Point was the strongest military post in America. In addition to the batteries that stood menacingly upon the hill tops, the river was obstructed by an enormous iron chain. The iron of which this chain was constructed was wrought from ore of equal parts from the Sterling and Long mines, in Orange county. The chain was manufactured by Peter Townsend, of Chester, at the Sterling iron works, in the same county, which were situated about twenty-five miles back of West Point. The general superintendent of the work, as engineer, was Captain Thomas Machin, who afterwards assisted in the engineering operations at Yorktown, when Cornwallis was captured. The chain was completed about the middle of April, 1778, and on the 1st of May it was stretched across the river and secured.

Colonel Timothy Pickering, accompanied by Captain Machin, arrived at the house of Mr. Townsend late on a Saturday night in March of that year, to engage him to make the chain. Townsend readily agreed to construct it, and in a violent snow-storm, amid the darkness of the night, the parties set out for the Sterling iron works. At daylight on Sunday morning the forges were in operation. New England teamsters carried the links, as fast as they were finished, to West Point, and in the space of six weeks the whole chain was completed. It weighed 180 tons.

The chain was stretched across the river at the narrowest point between the rocks just below the steamboat landing and Constitution Island opposite. It was fixed to huge blocks on each shore, and under the cover of batteries on both sides of the river. The remains of these are still visible.

"It is buoyed up," says Dr. Thacher, writing in 1780, "by very large logs of about sixteen feet long, pointed at the ends to lessen their opposition to the force of the current at flood and ebb tide. The logs are placed at short distances from each other, the chain carried over them, and made fast to each by staples. There are also a number of anchors dropped at proper distances, with cables made fast to the chain, to give it greater stability."

Mr. Lossing describes a visit which he made in October, 1848, to West Point, where he saw a portion of the famous chain. He says: "There are twelve links, two clevises, and a portion of a link of the great chain remaining. The links are made of iron bars, two and a half inches square, average in length a little over two feet, and weigh about one hundred pounds each. The British vessels did not pass West Point. The manufacture of this chain was a great achievement. The Sterling forges, at which the chain was made, are no longer in operation, but the Sterling works as a whole are now the oldest active iron works in New York. Two other iron chains were stretched across the Hudson during the war to obstruct its passage. One of these was at the mouth of Murderer's creek, the iron for which was made at the forge of Jonas Williams. The other chain was at Fort Montgomery. This chain was broken by the British in 1777.

The following description of the Sterling works, which were the most extensive in New York until after the beginning of the present century, is translated from a book published at Paris in 1801, and lately discovered in that city by Mr. O. H. Marshall, of Buffalo, New York, a gentleman of antiquarian tastes. It was written by the Marquis de Creve-Cœur, who was in the French service in the French and Indian war, and afterwards traveled extensively in this country.

Hardly had we put our horses in the stable than Mr. Townsend, the proprietor, came to meet us with the politeness of a man of the world. Having learned that the object of our journey was to examine attentively his different works, he offered to show us all the details, and at once led us to his large furnace where the ore was melted and converted into pigs of 60 to 100 pounds' weight. The blast was supplied by two immense wooden blowers, neither iron nor leather being used in their construction. This furnace, he said, produced from 2,000 to 2,400 tons annually, three-fourths of which are converted into bars, the rest melted into cannon and cannon balls, &c. From there we went to see the forge. Six large hammers were occupied in forging bar iron and anchors and various pieces used on vessels.

Lower down the stream (which afforded power to the works) was the foundry, with its reverberatory furnace (air furnace). Here he called our attention to several ingenious machines destined for different uses. The models had been sent him, and the machines he had cast from iron of a recently discovered ore, which after two fusions acquired great fineness. With it he could do the lightest and most delicate work. "What a pity," he said, "that you did not come ten days sooner. I would have shown you, first, three new styles of plows, of which I have cast the largest pieces, and which, however, are no heavier than the old-fashioned. Each one of them is provided with a kind of steel yard, so graduated that one can tell the power of the team and the resistance of the soil. Second, I would have shown you a portable mill for separating the grain from the chaff, followed by another machine by which all the ears in the field can be easily gathered without being obliged to cut the stalk at the foot, according to the old method."

From the foundry, we went to see the furnaces where the iron is converted into steel. "It is not yet as good as the Swedes," said Mr. T., "but we approach it—a few years more of experience and we will arrive at perfection. The iron which comes from under my hammers has had for a long time a high reputation and sells for £28 to £30 per ton." After having passed·two days in examining these divers works and admiring the skill with which they were supplied with water, as well as the arrangements for furnishing the charcoal for the different furnaces, we parted from Mr. Townsend.

Peter Townsend, an iron merchant, died on September 27, 1885, at his residence in East Twenty-third street, New York city. He was born at Chester, in Orange county, New York, in 1803, and was the third Peter Townsend in direct descent who has been identified with the iron industry of the State of New York. He was the grandson of the pioneer iron manufacturer referred to in this chapter, who died in 1783.

As early as 1765 there were iron works in Dutchess county, some of which were either then or at a later day supplied with iron ore from the Salisbury mines in Connecticut. The Maltby mine, at Millerton, was opened in 1750. A furnace and foundry at Amenia in this county were in operation during the Revolution, " at which steel and castings were made for the use of the army." James F. Lewis, of Amenia, says that the Amenia mine was opened about 1760, and that the ore was used during the Revolution for making guns, " being worked in a forge at what is now known as the ' old steel works.' "

In the manor of Philipsburg, in Westchester county, iron ore was mined and furnaces were erected before the close of the last century. About the time of the Revolution a furnace named Haverstraw and several bloomaries were in existence in Rockland county, on the western side of the Tappan Zee. Iron ore was mined in Putnam county in the latter part of the last century, some of which was taken to iron works on Long Island sound. A bloomary was in operation about the period of the Revolution at Patchogue, in Brookhaven township, Suffolk county, Long Island. At Riverhead, in Suffolk county, Captain Solomon Townsend established " a manufactory of bar iron" before the close of the last century.

About the year 1800 the celebrated Champlain iron district was developed. In 1801 probably the first iron works in the district were built at Willsborough Falls, on the Boquet river, in Essex county, to manufacture anchors. George Throop, Levi Highly, and Charles Kane were the proprietors. Among other early iron enterprises in this district were the New Russia, Jay, and Elba forges in Essex county, and the Eagle rolling mill at Keeseville in Clinton county. This district has been for a long time the most important iron district in the State, containing rolling mills, blast furnaces, and forges, but it is not so prominent now as it was formerly. The Champlain forges are all true bloomaries, manufacturing blooms directly from the rich magnetic and specular ores of the neighborhood. The district comprises the counties of Essex, Clinton, and Franklin. A forge was built at West Fort Ann, in Washington county, south of Lake George, about 1802, which used ore of precisely the same character as that obtained in the Champlain district.

It has already been stated that the Catalan forge, for the manufacture of iron directly from the ore, is still in use in the United States. In some of the Southern States it is used in the simple and inexpensive form in which it appears to have been introduced into this country, and which among metallurgists is known as the German bloomary. But in the Champlain district of New York the old Catalan forge, or German bloomary, has been greatly improved, so much so that the bloomary in use in this district, with its expensive machinery and uniform product, may be styled the American bloomary. It is fully described by Professor Thomas Egleston in a paper in the *Transactions* of the American Institute of Mining Engineers, volume VIII. The blast is heated, which was never done with the old Catalan forge, but most of the power is still supplied by a water-wheel. Charcoal is the only fuel used, and great care is taken in its manufacture, as well as in calcining the ore, which is of a very pure quality. The bloom produced in this forge usually weighs from 300 to 400 pounds. From the blooms are obtained billets of refined iron, which are used in the manufacture of crucible and open-hearth steel, plate and sheet iron, etc. About one ton of billets is produced at each forge in twenty-four hours. The blooms and billets are hammered into shape by a trip-hammer.

In 1883 there were in the Champlain district no fewer than 27 large forges, or bloomaries, for the manufacture of blooms. They embraced 171 forge fires. In the census year 1880 there were only 22 forges, with 141 fires, and they produced 31,580 net tons of blooms in that year. The production of Champlain blooms increased from 23,666 net tons in 1875 to 43,911 tons in the calendar year 1882. In 1890 the number of forges had been reduced to 14, with 102 fires, and their production in 1889 was only 12,397 net tons of blooms.

The Champlain district is a large producer of iron ore, much of which is annually shipped to other districts in New York and to other States. In 1889 the total quantity of iron ore shipped from the mines of this district, chiefly from Essex and Clinton counties, aggregated 642,092 gross tons.

West of the Champlain district, in the counties of Saint Lawrence, Jefferson, Lewis, Oswego, and Oneida, many charcoal furnaces were built about the beginning of the present century, among the earliest of which were Rossie furnace in Saint Lawrence county, Taberg furnace in Oneida county, and Constantia furnace in Oswego county. In the extreme western and southwestern parts of the State the few iron and steel enterprises that have had an existence during the present century have all been of yet more modern origin.

Nails were extensively manufactured by hand at Albany in 1787. Twenty years later, in 1807, John Brinkerhoff, of Albany, lighted the fires in his newly-erected rolling mill on the Wynantskill. The Troy *Daily Times* says that " the operations of the little wooden rolling mill built by him were confined to converting Russian and Swedish bar iron into plates, which were slit into narrow strips, and these cut to the required length and made into nails by hand." In 1826 the nail factory of John Brinkerhoff was sold at auction and purchased for $5,280 by Erastus Corning, who was then engaged at Albany in the hardware business. It now forms part of the works of the Troy Steel and Iron Company, the most extensive and important iron and steel works in the State, embracing a large rolling mill and large blast furnaces and a large Bessemer steel plant at Troy.

Between 1790 and 1800 there are said to have been twenty-three patents granted in the United States for nail-making machinery, and down to 1825 the whole number granted is said to have been one hundred and twenty. Among these patents was one issued to Josiah G. Pierson, of New York, on the 23d of March, 1795, and the machine covered by this patent is said to have been the first nail-cutting machine that produced satisfactory results and was generally used. The inventor was at the time a member of the firm of J. G. Pierson & Brothers, which in the same year established works at the village of Ramapo, in Rockland county, New York, for the manufacture of iron and nails, and which had previously, in 1787 or 1788, been engaged in the manufacture of cut nails, with an imperfect machine, in Whitehall street, in the city of New York. While the works were in New York the strips for the nails were rolled and slit at a mill near Wilmington, in Delaware, to which Swedish and Russian iron was sent, no other mill being available at the time. This inconvenience was avoided after the establishment of the works at Ramapo, which included a rolling and slitting mill. The manufacture of nails by Mr. Pierson's machine was here actively prosecuted until about 1830, when the same firm, which had been making blister steel at Hoboken for twenty years, removed its steel furnaces to Ramapo, and substituted the manufacture of spring steel for that of nails. The works of the Messrs. Pierson at Ramapo have been succeeded by those of the celebrated Ramapo Wheel and Foundry Company.

In *Hunt's Merchants' Magazine* for 1844 horseshoes made by machinery were cited as an illustration of the achievements of American inventive genius down to that time. We quote from the *Magazine* as follows: "Horseshoes furnish a similar proof of the bearing of the progress of inventions. An improved kind of horseshoes, made at Troy, New York, for some time past, is now sold at the price of only five cents per pound, ready prepared, to be used in shoeing the animal. At a factory recently erected fifty tons of these are now turned out per day; and, it is believed, they can be made and sent to Europe at as good a profit as is derived from American clocks, which have handsomely remunerated the exporter." These horseshoes were made at the Burden iron works, formerly the Troy iron and nail factory, which are still employed in their production.

It is not generally known that machine-made horseshoes were produced at so early a day in this country as 1844. The machine-made horseshoe was patented by Henry Burden in 1835. Other horseshoe patents were issued to him in 1843, 1857, and 1862. Mr. Burden was also the inventor of the hook-headed spike and of the Burden rotary squeezer—the latter in 1840. He was born at Dumblane, Scotland, on April 20, 1791, and died at Troy on January 19, 1871.

The iron industry of New York was not so prominent during the eighteenth century as that of some other States, but soon after the beginning of the present century the development of the Champlain district gave to it more prominence, which was still further increased after 1840, when anthracite coal was applied to the manufacture of pig iron. In 1870, and again in 1880, New York ranked third in the list of iron and steel producing States, Pennsylvania being first in the aggregate tonnage of iron and steel and Ohio second in the list in both years. But in 1890 New York was fifth among the States in the production of pig iron, Pennsylvania, Ohio, Alabama, and Illinois ranking above her in the order mentioned. In the production of steel of all kinds she was also the fifth in the list, being preceded by Pennsylvania, Illinois, Ohio, and West Virginia.

CHAPTER XIII.

EARLY IRON ENTERPRISES IN NEW JERSEY.

IN Mr. William Reed Deane's *Genealogical Memoirs of the Leonard Family,* already noticed, it is said that Henry Leonard left Rowley village, Massachusetts, early in 1674, "and at that time, or soon after, went to New Jersey, establishing the iron manufacture in that State." His sons Samuel, Nathaniel, and Thomas probably left Rowley village soon after their father's departure and followed him to New Jersey. Bishop says that Shrewsbury, a township lying northwest of Long Branch, in Monmouth county, was settled by Connecticut people soon after New Jersey was surrendered to the English by the Dutch in 1664, and that it was "to this part of Jersey" that Henry Leonard removed. About the time of the Connecticut settlement James Grover, who had resided on Long Island, also settled in Shrewsbury, and is said to have established iron works in that township, which he afterwards sold to Colonel Lewis Morris, then a merchant of Barbadoes, but born in England. On October 26, 1676, a grant of land was made to Colonel Morris, with full liberty to him and his heirs "to dig, delve, and carry away all such mines for iron as they shall find or see fit to dig and carry away to the iron work," which grant establishes the fact that the iron works in Shrewsbury were built prior to 1676, and that they were then owned by Colonel Morris. They were probably undertaken about 1674, the year in which Henry Leonard is said to have emigrated from Massachusetts to New Jersey. They were the first iron works in New Jersey.

In an account of the province of East Jersey, published by the proprietors in 1682, it is stated that "there is already a smelting furnace and forge set up in this colony, where is made good iron, which is of great benefit to the country." In his *History of New Jersey* Smith says that in 1682 "Shrewsbury, near Sandy Hook, adjoining the river or creek of that name, was already a township, consisting of several thousand acres, with large plantations contiguous; the inhabitants were computed to be about 400. Lewis Morris, of Barbadoes, had iron works and other considerable improvements here." In 1685 it was stated in *The Model of the Government of East New Jersey* that "there is an iron work already set up, where there is good iron made." In the same year Thomas Budd, in his *Good Order in Pennsylvania and New Jersey*, wrote that there was but one iron work in New Jersey, and that this was located in Monmouth county. All of these statements refer to the Shrewsbury works, which do not seem to have had a long life. According to Oldmixon they were located between the towns of Shrewsbury and Middletown, but other writers more definitely locate them at Tinton Falls. The original name was probably Tintern Falls, so called after Tintern Abbey in Monmouthshire. Bog ore was used. Many years ago a furnace named Bergen was built in Monmouth county, which has long been abandoned.

The rich deposits of magnetic iron ore in Northern New Jersey were discovered at an early day, and about 1710, as we are informed by the Rev. Dr. Joseph F. Tuttle, in his *Early History of Morris County*, written in 1869, settlements were made on the Whippany river, in Hanover township, in Morris county, and at a place now called Whippany, four miles northeast of Morristown, a forge was erected, but by whom is not now known. Bishop says that the first settlers of Hanover located there "for the purpose of smelting the iron ores in the neighborhood." They "early erected several forges and engaged extensively in the iron manufacture." Whippany is about fifteen miles east of the celebrated Succasunna iron-ore mine, in the present township of Randolph, and it was here that the settlers obtained their supply of iron ore. It was carried to the works in leather bags on pack-horses, and the bar iron was carried on horseback over the Orange mountains to Newark. Bishop mentions that "forges at Morristown, and some in Essex county, were long supplied in the same way from the rich ore of the mine. The ore was for some time free to all." This celebrated iron-ore deposit has long been known as the "Dickerson mine," so called after the Hon. Mahlon Dickerson, who was Governor of New Jersey in the early part of this century, and was subsequently and for many years a United States Senator from the same State.

Hon. Edmund D. Halsey, in the *History of Morris County*, says that "the tract embracing the Dickerson mine was taken up on account of its minerals" by John Reading in 1713 or 1714, who sold it to Joseph Kirkbride in 1716.

Dr. Tuttle says that in 1722 Joseph Latham sold a tract of land in the present township of Randolph, in Morris county, to "one John Jackson, who built a forge on the little stream which puts into the Rockaway near the residence of Mr. Jacob Hurd. The forge was nearly in front of Mr. Hurd's house," a mile west of Dover. Wood for charcoal was abundant, and the mine on the hill was not far distant. For some reason Jackson did not succeed in his iron enterprise, and was sold out by the sheriff in 1753. After his failure he is supposed to have removed to the western part of Virginia. "Jackson's iron works on Cheat river," in that State, mentioned by early writers, may have been established by him or his sons. Dr. Tuttle says that Rockaway was settled about 1725, or possibly as late as 1730, "at which time a small iron forge was built near where the upper forge now stands in Rockaway." This was the first forge at Rockaway. Mr. Halsey says that it was probably built by Job Allen; it was known as "Job Allen's iron works" in 1748. Dr. Tuttle adds that "forges were built on different streams, at Rockaway, Denmark, Middle Forge, Ninkee, Shaungum, Franklin, and other places, from the year 1725 to 1770." At Troy, in Morris county, as we learn from another source, a forge was built in 1743, which was in operation as late as 1860. In 1737, as we are informed by William Nelson, of Paterson, there is a reference to "the Busseton forge by Ringwood cold spring" in Passaic county. All these forges were bloomaries, manufacturing bar iron directly from the ore. In 1751 many of them did not individually produce more than five or six tons of iron in a year.

At the end of the seventeenth century and for some years after the beginning of the eighteenth century New Jersey was the only colony outside of New England that was engaged in the manufacture of iron, and this manufacture was almost wholly confined to its bloomaries. The rich magnetic ores, the well-wooded hillsides, and the restless mountain streams of Northern New Jersey afforded every facility for the manufacture of iron of a superior quality by this simple method, while the nearness of good markets furnished a sufficient inducement to engage in the business. The bloomaries of New Jersey were Catalan forges of the German type. Many of them were blown by the *trompe*, or water-blast.

Not much progress was made, however, in the establishment of the iron industry in New Jersey until the middle of the eighteenth century. From about 1740 down to the Revolution many blast furnaces and other iron works were built. The iron industry of New Jersey during the greater part of this period was exceedingly active, although hampered by restrictions imposed by the mother country. To the iron enterprises which were then built up within its borders the patriotic cause was afterwards greatly indebted for much of the iron and steel that was needed to secure its success.

Peter Hasenclever, a Prussian gentleman of prominence, who is usually referred to as Baron Hasenclever, emigrated to New Jersey about 1764 as the head of an iron company which he had organized in London, and brought with him a large number of German miners and ironworkers. His career in this country is very fully described by Dr. Tuttle in his history and by Mr. Halsey in a letter which we have received from him. Dr. Tuttle first gives an account of the Ringwood Company, which was organized in 1740 and was principally composed of several persons named Ogden, from Newark. In that year the company purchased from Cornelius Board sixteen acres of land at Ringwood, near Greenwood lake, in Bergen (now Passaic) county, where they built a furnace, afterwards buying from Board other property. In 1764 Joseph Board conveyed to the Ringwood Company a tract of land at Ringwood "near the old forge and dwelling house of Walter Erwin." On July 5, 1764, the Ringwood Company sold to "Peter Hasenclever, late of London, merchant," for £5,000, all of its lands and its improvements at Ringwood. The deed states that on the property there are "erected and standing a furnace, two forges, and several dwelling houses." It speaks of "Timothy Ward's forge;" also of the "old forge at Ringwood." In 1764 Hasenclever also bought from various persons other tracts of land at Ringwood and in its vicinity, and in 1765 he bought several tracts from Lord Stirling. These purchases were located at Ringwood, Pompton,

Long Pond, and Charlottenburg, all in what was then Bergen county. Hasenclever probably also purchased an interest in the iron-ore mines at Hibernia. Dr. Tuttle says that "Hasenclever at once began to enlarge the old works and build others at each of the places just named," that is, Ringwood, Pompton, Long Pond, and Charlottenburg. It is probable that he built a furnace and one or more forges at each place; three furnaces and six forges he certainly built. The furnaces were erected, respectively, as follows: Charlottenburg, on the west branch of the Pequannock; Ringwood, on the Ringwood branch of the Pequannock; and Long Pond, on the Winockie, about two miles from Greenwood lake. Charlottenburg was built in 1767, and was capable of producing from 20 to 25 tons of pig iron weekly. Long Pond was in blast in 1768. Hon. Abram S. Hewitt writes us that at Ringwood he has a pig of iron with "Ringwood 1770" marked on it by the founder, and Mr. William Nelson, of Paterson, writes us that he has seen at Charlottenburg a small pig of iron upon which was cast in raised letters "Charlottenburg 1770."

Hasenclever certainly succeeded in making good iron, some of which was shipped to England. He also made steel of good quality "directly from the ore." In 1768 he became financially embarrassed, and in 1770 was formally declared a bankrupt. He returned to Germany and became a successful linen manufacturer in Silesia. He was succeeded in the management of the company's estate by John Jacob Faesch, who had come to New Jersey with him, or soon after him, under an engagement as manager of the iron works for seven years. Faesch is said to have looked after his own interests more than those of the company. In 1771 or 1772 he was succeeded by Robert Erskine, a Scotchman, who appears to have met with success until 1776, when all the works were stopped by the opening of hostilities and Charlottenburg furnace was burned, but whether accidentally or by the opponents of the patriotic cause is not now known.

Robert Erskine was thoroughly loyal to the Revolutionary cause. He died at Ringwood in 1780, "and his grave occupies a retired spot about a quarter of a mile from the ruins of the old Ringwood furnace, near the road leading from Ringwood to West Milford." The inscription upon his tombstone reads: "In memory of Robert Erskine, F. R. S.; geographer and surveyor general to the army of the United States; son of Rev. Ralph Erskine, late minister at Dumferline, in Scotland. Born September 7, 1735. Died October 2, 1780, aged 45 years and 25 days." For some time he held a commission as captain in the New Jersey militia. New Jersey may well honor the memory of this early ironmaster.

The Adventure furnace at Hibernia in Morris county was a famous furnace during the Revolution, casting ordnance and other supplies.for the army. It was built in 1765. Mr. Halsey says that a tract of land was located on November 23, 1765, "about three-quarters of a mile above the new furnace called the Adventure." The name usually given to this furnace is Hibernia. Dr. Tuttle says that "the names of Lord Stirling, Benjamin Cooper, and Samuel Ford are connected with the original building and ownership of the Hibernia works." He also says that "Benjamin Cooper & Co." held "pew No. 6" in the old Rockaway meeting-house in 1768. A grant of certain privileges to encourage the enterprise was made by the legislature in 1769. In 1765 Ford sold his interest in the furnace to Anderson and Cooper, after which sale he was actively engaged for a number of years in the business of counterfeiting "Jersey bills of credit," which he afterwards pleasantly referred to as "a piece of engenuity." In 1768 he participated in the robbery of the treasury of the province at Amboy, his former partner, Cooper, being one of his associates. Ford was arrested in 1773, but escaped to Virginia; Cooper and others were also arrested and convicted, but all except one escaped punishment, and he was hanged. Previous to the time of his arrest, in 1773, Cooper appears to have sold his interest in Hibernia furnace to Lord Stirling, who became its sole owner about this time, Mr. Halsey thinks in 1771.

Mount Hope furnace, about four miles northwest of Rockaway, was built in 1772 by John Jacob Faesch, after he had severed his connection with the London Company. It was active until about 1825. It also was a noted furnace during the Revolution, casting shot and shells and cannon for the Continental army. In September, 1776, Joseph Hoff, who was then the manager of Hibernia furnace, wrote to Lord Stirling that Faesch had requested him "to inform you that he wanted 200 tons of pig metal, and wanted to know your price and terms of payment. Iron will undoubtedly be in great demand, as few works on the continent are doing anything this season." This letter indicates that at the time it was written Faesch owned or controlled a forge for converting pig iron into bar iron. Mr. Halsey says that he became the owner of Middle and Rockaway forges and the lessee of Mount Pleasant forge and the Boonton slitting mill. On the 14th of November, 1776, Hoff wrote to General Knox that there were 35 tons of shot at Hibernia furnace, and on the 21st of November he wrote that it was the only furnace in New Jersey which he knew to be then in blast. The Hibernia and the Mount Hope furnaces were both in blast in 1777. Mr. Halsey informs us that among the laws of New Jersey for 1777 is an act, passed October 7th, exempting from military service men to be employed at Mount Hope and Hibernia furnaces, and reciting the necessity of providing the army and navy of the United States with cannon, cannon shot, etc., and that the works "have been for some time past employed" in providing such articles, and "are now under contract for a large quantity." Faesch is said by Dr. Tuttle to have become the lessee of Hibernia furnace at some time during the war. He says "this must have been subsequent to July 10, 1778, at which date I find a letter to Lord Stirling from Charles Hoff, his manager at Hibernia, reporting to him what he was doing."

Faesch died at Old Boonton on May 29, 1799, and was buried at Morristown. Mr. Halsey says that he was born in the canton of Basle in Switzerland in 1729. Dr. Tuttle says that "in his day John Jacob Faesch was one of the great men of Morris county, regarded as its greatest ironmaster, one of its richest men, and one of its most loyal citizens." General Washington and his staff once visited him at Mount Hope.

Lord Stirling, whose proper name was William Alexander, was born in the city of New York in 1726 and died at Albany in 1783. As has been shown in the chapter relating to New York, his name has been given to one of the oldest and most successful iron enterprises in the country. His wife was a daughter of Philip Livingston, and a sister of Philip Livingston the signer of the Declaration.

Colonel Jacob Ford, Sr., was a large landholder in Morris county about the middle of the last century. In 1750 he built two forges, probably a finery and chafery, at Mount Pleasant, three miles west of Rockaway. There was a forge at this place in 1856, but in ruins. In 1764 John Harriman owned a forge called Burnt Meadow forge, at Denmark, about five miles north of Rockaway, of which Colonel Jacob Ford, Jr., afterwards became the owner. It was probably built by Colonel Jacob Ford, Sr., in 1750. About 1764 Colonel Ford, Jr., became the owner of the forge above Mount Pleasant and below Denmark, called ever since Middle forge, which was built by Jonathan Osborn in 1749. The United States now owns the site of the forge last mentioned. John Johnston had "iron works" at Horse Pound, now Beach Glen, a mile and a half below Hibernia, from 1753 to 1765, as appears from references in the title papers of adjoining lands.

In Andover township, in Sussex county, a furnace and a forge were built by a strong company before the Revolution, probably about 1760, and the works were operated on an extensive scale. About the beginning of hostilities the works were closed, the company being principally composed of royalists. The excellent quality of the iron made from the ore of the Andover mine led, however, to such legislation by Congress in January, 1778, as resulted in putting them in operation. Whitehead Humphreys, of Philadelphia, was directed by Congress to make steel for the use of the army from Andover iron, as the iron made at the Andover works was the only iron which would "with certainty answer the purpose of making steel." This action of Congress is given in detail by the Hon. Jacob W. Miller, in an address before the New Jersey Historical Society in 1854, who also records the interesting fact that William Penn was an early owner of the Andover mine. He says that "on the 10th of March, 1714, by a warrant from the council of proprietors, he acquired title to a large tract of land situated among the mountains then of Hunterton, now of Sussex, county, and William Penn became the owner of one of the richest mines of iron ore in New Jersey. This mine, since called Andover, was opened and worked to a considerable extent as early as 1760. Tradition reveals to us that the products of these works were carried upon pack-horses and carts down the valley of the Musconetcong to a place on the Delaware called Durham, and were thence transported to Philadelphia in boats, which were remarkable for their beauty and model, and are known as Durham boats to this day."

Franklin furnace, near Hamburg, in Sussex county, which was built in 1770 and abandoned about 1860, has been succeeded by one of the largest furnaces in the country. There were several forges at and near Hamburg in the last century.

Israel Acrelius, the historian of New Sweden, who resided in this country from 1750 to 1756, mentions five iron enterprises as then existing in New Jersey—the Union iron works, and Oxford, Sterling, Ogden's, and Mount Holly furnaces.

Oxford furnace, at Oxford, in Warren county, on a branch of the Pequest river, was built by Jonathan Robeson in 1742. Tradition says that it was first blown by a water-blast. Cannon balls were cast at this furnace in the French war of 1755 and for the Continental army. The furnace was in operation in 1880, using anthracite coal, but in 1882 it went out of blast and is now abandoned. We are informed by Mr. Edmund T. Lukens, secretary and general manager of the Oxford Iron and Nail Company, that "the original masonry, built in 1742, is still standing, encased in strengthening walls, which were added from time to time as the binding timbers of the old work burned or rotted off. The old stack was built in 6-foot rises, (after the first rise of 12 feet for working arch,) with 18 inches for each set-off, and these rises were bound with heavy timbers, keyed together at the corners." Through the courtesy of Mr. Lukens we now have in our possession a set of eight fine photographs, seven of which show from different points of view the stack and connected buildings of the famous old blast furnace of his company, while the eighth photograph represents the furnace mansion-house, in which Hon. George M. Robeson, ex-Secretary of the Navy, a descendant of Jonathan Robeson, was born. In 1880 Oxford furnace divided with Cornwall furnace in Pennsylvania the honor of being the oldest furnace in the United States that was then in operation.

The Sterling furnace referred to was Sterling furnace in New York, but this furnace, some particulars of which have already been given, was then probably embraced within the boundaries of New Jersey. Ogden's furnace was probably the Ringwood furnace built by the Ogdens about 1740, as stated on a preceding page. After the sale of that furnace to the London Company the Ogdens probably built a furnace about 1765 at Bloomingdale, in Passaic county. Mr. Halsey writes us that there was an old stack in good preservation at Bloomingdale (near Butler) in 1800, which was known as "Ogden's furnace." Mount Holly furnace was situated at the town of that name, in Burlington county. We are informed by Mr. Austin N. Hungerford that it was built in 1730 by Isaac Pierson, Mahlon Stacy, and John Burr. A forge was connected with the furnace. The works stood where the saw-mill at the south end of Pine street, on Rancocas creek, now stands. In 1775 sheet iron was manufactured by Thomas Mayberry at the forge at Mount Holly, some of which was used to make camp-kettles for the Continental army, and in 1776 shot and shells were made at the furnace. The British being informed that munitions of war were being made at the furnace they destroyed the works, which were not rebuilt.

The Union iron works were situated near Clinton, in Hunterton county, and embraced at the time of Acrelius's visit two furnaces and two forges, "each with two stacks;" also a trip-hammer and a "flatting-hammer." These works were then owned by William Allen and Joseph Turner, both of Philadelphia. William Allen was the chief justice of Pennsylvania from 1751 to 1774. Allentown, in Pennsylvania, was named after him. He was largely interested in the manufacture of iron in Pennsylvania and New Jersey, and with him was usually associated Joseph Turner. In October, 1775, Allen gave his "half of a quantity of cannon shot belonging to him and to Turner for the use of the Board of the Council of Safety;" but he remained loyal to the British crown, nevertheless, dying in London in 1780. The Union iron works appear to have been entirely abandoned in 1778. Judge Allen informed Acrelius that at these works, and also at Durham, a Pennsylvania furnace, one and a half tons of iron ore yielded one ton of pig iron, and that a good furnace yielded from twenty to twenty-five tons of pig iron every week.

Mr. Charles P. Keith's *Provincial Councillors of Pennsylvania* gives us the following details: "For about fifty years Turner was in partnership with William Allen in commercial business, the house of Allen & Turner [in Philadelphia] for a long time prior to the Revolutionary war being the most important in the colony. They also engaged in the manufacture of iron, and owned several mines in Pennsylvania and New Jersey. The Union iron works, in Hunterton county, New Jersey, were the most celebrated, the property at the date of Turner's will amounting to 11,000 acres." He died in 1783.

Except Mount Holly all of the furnaces named used magnetic ore; Mount Holly, according to Acrelius, used "brittle bog ore in gravel," which was "only serviceable for castings." But the existence of the forge and the further fact that pig iron has been found in the ruins of the works show that the ore was used for something else than castings. Acrelius mentions, but does not name, four bloomaries in New Jersey, all "in full blast" during his visit. His list of iron enterprises in New Jersey in his day is incomplete.

Several blast furnaces were built in the southern and southwestern parts of New Jersey at an early day to use the bog ore of that section. Of these the furnace at Mount Holly, already mentioned, was doubtless the oldest. Batsto furnace, also in Burlington county, was built about 1766 by Charles Read, who held many offices under the provincial government. It cast shot and shells for the Continental army. There was a forge connected with this furnace as early as 1786, when Batsto bars brought £30 per ton at New York in New York currency. A neighboring furnace, Atsion, was also built about 1766. A few bloomaries were also built in this section in the last century, to work bog ore. The "Jersey pines" furnished the fuel for the furnaces and bloomaries, and oyster shells supplied the fluxing material for the furnaces. It was stated in the chapter relating to New England iron enterprises in the last century that ore was taken from Egg Harbor, in New Jersey, to supply some Massachusetts furnaces. This was bog ore. Batsto furnace was situated on a branch of Little Egg Harbor river, and ran until 1846, when it was abandoned.

Mrs. Augustus H. Richards, of Philadelphia, has in her possession an iron plate cast at Batsto furnace, bearing the date 1766, which doubtless fixes the exact date of its erection. Of the early iron works in Southern and Southwestern New Jersey additional to the Mount Holly, Batsto, and Atsion enterprises, which have been specifically named, mention may be made of a few of the most prominent, nearly all built near the close of the last century or the beginning of the present century. Mr. Austin N. Hungerford, an expert in the preparation of various local histories relating to Pennsylvania and New Jersey, furnishes us with the following information.

In 1722 the erection of a bloomary forge was undertaken by Isaac Horner, Daniel Farnsworth, and Joseph Borden on the west side of Black's creek, which rises near Georgetown, in Burlington county, and runs a northeasterly course between Mansfield and Chesterfield townships and empties into the Delaware at Bordentown. On February 1, 1725, the partly-erected forge with the property connected with it was conveyed by the three proprietors to Thomas Potts, a son-in-law of Joseph Borden. On the same day he conveyed one undivided half of the property to Colonel Daniel Coxe, (of whom mention is made that he had been interested in the manufacture of iron for several years,) and one-fourth to John Allen, retaining one-fourth interest for himself. The forge was completed in the summer of 1725, and was probably operated for a few years, but no account of it has been obtained. The property afterwards passed into the possession of a Mr. Lewis, of Philadelphia. Thomas Potts had emigrated to this country in the ship *Shields*, which brought so many emigrants to West Jersey.

The most noted ironmaster in West Jersey prior to the Revolution was the Hon. Charles Read. In the year 1766 he built Batsto furnace on Batsto creek, a branch of Little Egg Harbor river, about six miles northeast from the present village of Elwood, on the Camden and Atlantic Railroad. An act of the legislature, passed June 20, 1765, enabled him to erect a dam across Batsto creek, and the same act enabled John Estell to erect a dam across Atsion river, at Atsion, where Charles Read soon afterwards erected Atsion furnace. Taunton furnace, erected by Mr. Read, was built in 1766 in Evesham township, on Rancocas creek. It was conducted by him until the assignment of his property on June 2, 1773. All these enterprises were in Burlington county.

About 1800 Hampton furnace and forge were erected on the Batsto branch of the Mullica river, about three and a half miles from Atsion. They became permanently idle about 1840. Speedwell furnace, situated on the north branch of Wading river, in Burlington county, was erected before the Revolution, but by whom is not ascertained. Gloucester furnace, situated on the south side of Little Egg Harbor river, in Mullica township, Atlantic county, was erected about the beginning of the present century. It was operated until about 1850, when it was abandoned. Martha furnace was situated on the Oswego branch of Wading river, about four miles from the head of navigation. It was built by one of the Potts family, of Potts-town, Pennsylvania, and blown in in 1793. In 1834 it produced 750 tons of castings. Weymouth furnace and forge were situated on Great Egg Harbor river, about six miles from May's Landing. They were erected in 1802 by Charles Shoemaker, George Ashbridge, Morris Robinson, John Paul, and Joseph M. Paul. The fires of the furnace have long since gone out. In 1834 the product of the furnace was 900 tons of castings, and of the forge, with its four fires and two hammers, 200 tons of bar iron. Monroe forge, near Weymouth furnace, was situated on South river, about three miles south-west from May's Landing. It was owned in 1820 by Lewis M. Walker and was abandoned about 1835. Cumberland furnace was situated at the head of the Manamuskin, in Cumberland county. The property on which it was lo-cated was purchased by Eli Budd in 1785, and he afterwards put up a forge for manufacturing iron and operated it for several years. In 1810 his son, Wesley Budd, erected a blast furnace. The furnace was operated until 1840, when it was abandoned, its last owner being Edward Smith, of Philadelphia.

Mr. Benjamin Snyder, of Lakewood, Ocean county, gives us the following additional information concerning several of the southern and southwestern iron enterprises in New Jersey.

Etna furnace was situated on a tributary of the south branch of the Rancocas creek, two and a half miles from Medford, and about four miles from Taunton, in Burlington county. It was built by Charles Read before the Revolution. Samuel G. Wright for many years owned Federal furnace, first known as Dover furnace, where now stands the village of Manchester, on the New Jersey Southern Railway, eight miles from Lakewood. In 1814 Jesse Richards purchased the water power of the Three Partners saw mill and erected the Washington furnace. The place has since been known by various titles, and is now called Lakewood. The enterprise was a failure, and after two years the furnace was abandoned. The stack, one of the best of its kind, was left standing, and in 1832 Joseph W. Brick came here from Burlington county, purchased the property, and put the furnace in blast in 1833. It continued in operation until the close of 1854, being the last of the South Jersey iron furnaces to "go out as a finality." The Monmouth furnace, afterwards called Howell works, eight miles east of Lake-wood, was built by William Griffith, of Burlington, was afterwards owned by Shippen & McMurtrie, of Philadelphia, and subsequently by James P. Allaire, of New York city. It was continued as a furnace with intervals of rest until about the year 1846. There was a furnace at Millville, in Cum-berland county, and a furnace called Hanover, in Burlington county, both the furnaces going out of blast about 1850. There was also a forge, known as Mary Ann forge, two or three miles below Hanover furnace.

Mr. Snyder mentions Etna furnace as having been built by Charles Read, but it is not mentioned by Mr. Hungerford. Tuckahoe furnace, on Tuckahoe river, in Cape May county, was built in the last century and has long been abandoned. It appears to have been sometimes called New Etna. There was certainly an Etna furnace on Tuckahoe river many years ago, probably in the last century.

It will be seen that the southern and southwestern parts of New Jersey produced iron at one time in large quantities from bog ores. Iron is not now produced from these ores in New Jersey in any form, nor is there a blast furnace in either the southern or southwestern parts of the State.

The Batsto iron works were well managed. On July 1, 1784, they passed into the hands of William Richards, who owned and operated them until 1809, when he was succeeded in their ownership and management by his son Jesse, who operated them until their final suspension in 1846. Another son, Samuel, was also prominently identified with the manufacture of iron in Southern New Jersey in the first half of the present century, as was also Mark Richards; who was not, however, a relative of the other persons of the same name who have been mentioned. Mark Richards was of Wurtemburger ancestry, the name being a corruption of Reichert, as we are informed by Louis Richards, Esq., of Reading, Pennsylvania; whereas the family of William Richards was of Welsh origin.

Mark Richards was born in Montgomery county, Pennsylvania. William Richards was born in Berks county, Pennsylvania, on September 12, 1738, and died at Mount Holly, New Jersey, on August 31, 1823. In early life he was employed at Coventry forge and Warwick furnace, in Chester county, Pennsylvania, and about 1768 he was employed at Batsto as founder. He was a soldier during the Revolution. In January, 1781, he became the manager of Batsto iron works. Mr. Richards was one of the great men among the pioneers of the American iron industry.

On November 10, 1750, Governor Belcher certified that there were in New Jersey "one mill or engine for slitting and rolling of iron, situate in the township of Bethlehem, in the county of Hunterton, on the south branch of the river Raritan, the property of Messrs. William Allen and Joseph Turner, of Philadelphia, which is not now in use; one plating-forge, which works with a tilt-hammer, situate on a small brook at the west end of Trenton, the property of Benjamin Yard, of Hunterton, which is now used; one furnace for the making of steel, situate in Trenton, the property of Benjamin Yard, which is not now used." Steel was, however, made at Trenton during the Revolution. A rolling and slitting mill was built at Old Boonton, in Morris county, before the Revolution, probably about 1770, by a member of the Ogden family. A more successful enterprise of the same kind was established at Dover, in the same county, about 1792, by Israel Canfield and Jacob Losey, who also added a factory for cutting nails, which were headed by hand in dies. In 1800 there were in this county three rolling and slitting mills, two furnaces, " and about forty forges with two to four fires each."

Mr. Halsey furnishes us with the following episode in the history of the Old Boonton slitting mill: "A slitting mill was erected at Old Boonton, on the Rockaway river, about a mile below the present town of Boonton, in defiance of the law, by Samuel Ogden, of Newark, with the aid of his father. The entrance was from the hillside, and in the upper room first entered there were stones for grinding grain, the slitting mill being below and out of sight. It is said that Governor William Franklin visited the place suddenly, having heard a rumor of its existence, but was so hospitably entertained by Mr. Ogden, and the iron works were so effectually concealed, that the Governor came away saying he was glad to find that it was a groundless report, as he had always supposed."

A nail factory was in full operation at Burlington in 1797. In 1814 or 1815 Benjamin and David Reeves, brothers, established the Cumberland nail and iron works at Bridgeton, in Cumberland county, and for many years successfully manufactured nails, with which they largely supplied the eastern markets. These works are still in operation. In 1812 a rolling and slitting mill was built at Paterson by Nicholas Delaplaine, Samuel Colt, and John Colt, which Mr. Nelson informs us made shovels and spades, also camp utensils, frying pans, etc., for the use of the army. In 1814 the manufacture of nails was commenced. At first the nails were headed by hand, but subsequently they were cut and headed by one operation. In 1820 the works were leased by Colonel Joseph Jackson, of Rockaway, and his brother William, and they rolled round and square iron. It is important to note the year in which the Jackson brothers rolled this iron, as the rolling of iron, except in connection with slitting mills, had but recently been introduced into this country. In 1822 they built the first rolling mill at Rockaway.

Peter Cooper engaged in the manufacture of iron at Trenton, New Jersey, in 1845, where, as is stated by the *American Cyclopædia*, "he erected the largest rolling mill at that time in the United States for the manufacture of railroad iron, and at which subsequently he was the first to roll wrought-iron beams for fire-proof buildings." He had previously, however, been prominently engaged in the manufacture of iron at Baltimore and in New York city. In connection with members of his family he also embarked in many other important iron enterprises in New Jersey. His name has been the most prominent and the most honored in the iron history of the State during the present century. He was born in New York city on February 12, 1791, and died at the residence of his son-in-law, Hon. Abram S. Hewitt, in the same city, on April 4, 1883, aged 92 years, 1 month, and 23 days.

A letter which we have received from Mr. Frederick J. Slade, treasurer of the New Jersey Steel and Iron Company, at Trenton, gives us the following information. "The first rolled beams made at these works were rolled in the spring of 1854. These were 7 inches deep, weighed about 81 pounds per yard, and were of the form known as deck beams. They were used in Harper Brothers' and the Cooper Union buildings, New York, and also on the Camden and Amboy Railroad as rails. They were rolled on a mill having three vertical rolls, as if a three-high train were turned on end, which were patented by William Burrows. 'I' beams were afterwards rolled in the same mill, which was, however, after a few years replaced by a three-high train having horizontal rolls, as in the present usual construction. The name of the works at that time was the Trenton iron works, owned by the Trenton Iron Company."

In 1784 New Jersey had eight furnaces and seventy-nine forges and bloomaries, but principally bloomaries.

In Jedidiah Morse's geography, printed in 1795, there is the following record of iron enterprises which were in existence in New Jersey a year or two earlier.

The iron manufactories are, of all others, the greatest source of wealth to the State. Iron works are erected in Gloucester, Burlington, Morris, and other counties. The mountains in the county of Morris give rise to a number of streams necessary and convenient for these works, and, at the same time, furnish a copious supply of wood and ore of a superior quality. In this county alone are no less than seven rich iron mines, from which might be taken ore sufficient to supply the United States; and, to work it into iron, are two furnaces, two rolling and slitting mills, and about thirty forges, containing from two to four fires each. These works produce annually about 540 tons of bar iron, 800 tons of pigs, besides large quantities of hollow ware, sheet iron, and nail rods. In the whole State it is supposed there is yearly made about 1,200 tons of bar iron, 1,200 ditto of pigs, 80 ditto of nail rods, exclusive of hollow ware and various other castings, of which vast quantities are made. Steel was manufactured at Trenton in time of the war, but not considerably since.

In 1802 there were in New Jersey, according to a memorial to Congress adopted in that year, 150 forges, "which, at a moderate calculation, would produce twenty tons of bar iron each annually, amounting to 3,000 tons." At the same time there were in the State seven blast furnaces in operation and six that were out of blast; also four rolling and slitting mills, "which rolled and slit on an average 200 tons, one-half of which were manufactured into nails." Of the forges mentioned about 120 were in Morris, Sussex, and Bergen counties.

Of the numerous charcoal furnaces which once dotted New Jersey not one now remains which uses charcoal, the introduction of anthracite coal in the smelting of iron ore, which took place about 1840, rendering the further production of charcoal pig iron in New Jersey unprofitable. The last charcoal furnace erected in the State was built at Split Rock, in Morris county, by the late Andrew B. Cobb, about 1862, but it was soon abandoned. Not one of the old bloomaries of New Jersey now remains. There were in the State in 1890, however, several forges for the manufacture of blooms from pig and scrap iron, and also a large number of rolling mills, steel works, wire works, pipe works, and anthracite furnaces.

In 1870 New Jersey was fourth in rank among the iron-producing States in the aggregate production of iron and steel, but in 1880 it had fallen to the fifth place. In 1890 it was tenth in the production of pig iron and seventh in the production of steel.

CHAPTER XIV.

BEGINNING OF THE MANUFACTURE OF IRON IN PENNSYLVANIA.

THE settlers on the Delaware, under the successive administrations of the Swedes and Dutch and the Duke of York down to 1682, appear to have made no effort to manufacture iron in any form. In the *Journal of a Voyage to New York* in 1679 and 1680 by Jasper Dankers and Peter Sluyter, who then visited the Swedish and other settlements on the Delaware, it is expressly stated that iron ore had not been seen by them on Tinicum Island or elsewhere in the neighborhood. Jasper Dankers says : " As to there being a mine of iron ore upon it, I have not seen any upon that island, or elsewhere ; and if it were so it is of no great importance, for such mines are so common in this country that little account is made of them."

Under the more active rule of William Penn, who sailed up the Delaware in the ship *Welcome* in 1682, the manufacture of iron in Pennsylvania had its beginning. In a letter written by Penn to Lord Keeper North in July, 1683, he mentions the existence of " mineral of copper and iron in divers places " in Pennsylvania. In his *Further Account of the Province of Pennsylvania*, written in 1685, speaking of " things that we have in prospect for staples of trade," he says : " I might add iron, (perhaps copper, too,) for there is much mine, and it will be granted us that we want no wood." In a letter to James Logan, the secretary of the province, dated London, April 21, 1702, he says, under the heading of " Iron Works : " " Call on those people for an answer to the heads I gave them from Ambrose Crawley. Divers would engage here in it as soon as they receive an account, which in a time of war would serve the country. Things as to America will come under another regulation after a while." To this letter Logan replied from Philadelphia, under date of October 1, 1702, as follows : " I have spoke to the chief of those concerned in the iron mines, but they seem careless, having never had a meeting since thy departure; their answer is that they have not yet found any considerable vein." Smiles, in his *Industrial Biography*, says: "William Penn, the courtier Quaker, had iron furnaces at Hawkhurst and other places in Sussex." It was, therefore, but natural that he should encourage the manufacture of iron in his province, and it was certainly through no indifference or neglect of his that this industry was not established at an early day. We have referred in the preceding chapter to his ownership in 1714 of the celebrated Andover iron-ore mine in New Jersey.

In 1692 we find the first mention of iron having been made in Pennsylvania. It is contained in a metrical composition entitled *A Short Description of Pennsylvania*, by Richard Frame, which was printed and sold by William Bradford, in Philadelphia, in 1692. Frame says that at "a certain place about some forty pound" of iron had then been made. The entire reference is as follows:

> A certain place here is, where some begun
> To try some Mettle, and have made it run,
> Wherein was Iron absolutely found,
> At once was known about some Forty Pound.

It is to be regretted that Frame was not more explicit in describing the place where this iron was made. It was possibly made in a bloomary fire; probably in a blacksmith's fire.

In 1698 Gabriel Thomas printed at London *An Historical and Geographical Account of the Province and Country of Pennsylvania and of West New Jersey in America*, in which mention is made of the mineral productions of these colonies. Alluding to Pennsylvania, he says: "There is likewise ironstone or ore, lately found, which far exceeds that in England, being richer and less drossy. Some preparations have been made to carry on an iron work." But neither these preparations nor the operations alluded to by Richard Frame appear to have led to practical results—certainly not to the erection of permanent works.

Mrs. James, in her *Memorial of Thomas Potts, Junior*, gives an account of the first successful attempt that was made to establish iron works in Pennsylvania. This event, which occurred in 1716, is briefly described in one of Jonathan Dickinson's letters, written in 1717, which we have seen: "This last summer one Thomas Rutter, a smith, who lives not far from Germantown, hath removed further up in the country, and of his own strength hath set upon making iron. Such it proves to be, as is highly set by by all the smiths here, who say that the best of Sweed's iron doth not exceed it; and we have accounts of others that are going on with iron works." Rutter's enterprise was a bloomary forge, located on Manatawny creek, in Berks county, about three miles above Pottstown. Mrs. James says that the name of this forge was Pool forge. There was certainly a Pool forge on the Manatawny as early as 1728, in which year it is mentioned in Thomas Rutter's will. The name of Rutter's pioneer enterprise may, however, have been Manatawny. In the Philadelphia *Weekly Mercury* for November 1, 1720, Thomas Fare, a Welshman, is said to have run away from "the forge at Manatawny." Bishop says: "A forge is mentioned in March, 1719-20, at Manatawny, then in Philadelphia, but now in Berks or Montgomery, county. It was attacked by the Indians in 1728, but they were repulsed with great loss by the workmen."

Hon. Samuel W. Pennypacker, of Philadelphia, a gentleman of antiquarian tastes, sends us the following letter concerning Pool forge.

I very cheerfully respond to your inquiry for information as to the date of the erection and the ownership of Pool forge. In 1725 James Lewis, Francis Rawle, George Mifflin, and John Leacock presented a petition to the Court of Quarter Sessions of Philadelphia asking for a road, in which they say: "Whereas, your petitioners having lately built a new fforge on Manatawny creek, and wanting a road from Colebrook ffurnace to the said new fforge and from thence to the great road that leads to Philadelphia, for ye more convenient carrying on ye business of ye said fforge and ffurnace," etc. The court thereupon appointed a jury, of which my forefather, Henry Pannebecker, was foreman, and consisting of himself and Barnabas Rhodes, Thomas Potts, and Anthony Lee, to lay out the road. They reported on March 2, 1726, saying: "Pursuant to an order of court hereunto annexed, we the subscribers have laid out a road from Colebrookdale ffurnace to Pool fforge, and from thence to the great road leading to Philadelphia."

The old document quoted in the above letter refers to Pool forge as "a new forge," which strengthens the theory that the name of the pioneer forge was Manatawny.

Mrs. James says that Rutter was an English Quaker, who was a resident of Philadelphia in 1685 and who removed in 1714 from Germantown "forty miles up the Schuylkill, in order to work the iron mines of the Manatawny region." She gives a *verbatim* copy of the original patent of William Penn to Thomas Rutter for 300 acres of land "on Manatawny creek," dated February 12, 1714–15.

The following obituary notice in the *Pennsylvania Gazette*, published at Philadelphia, dated March 5 to March 13, 1729––30, ought to be conclusive proof of the priority of Thomas Rutter's enterprise: "Philadelphia, March 13. On Sunday night last died here Thomas Rutter, Senior, of a short illness. *He was the first that erected an iron work in Pennsylvania.*" In his will, which we have examined, he is styled a blacksmith. Many of his descendants have been prominent Pennsylvania ironmasters. Mrs. James says that Dr. Benjamin Rush, a signer of the Declaration of Independence, was a great-grandson of Thomas Rutter. We have verified in the *Pennsylvania Gazette* the obituary notice above quoted.

The next iron enterprise in Pennsylvania was Coventry forge, on French creek, in the northern part of Chester county, which was built by Samuel Nutt, also an English Quaker. Egle's *History of Pennsylvania* says that Nutt arrived in the province in 1714, and that " he took up land on French creek in 1717, and about that time built a forge there. A letter written by him in 1720 mentions an intention of erecting another forge that fall." We have seen this letter. It is dated July 2, 1720, and is written in Friends' language. Nutt proposed to build the new forge on French creek. Mrs. James states that Nutt purchased 800 acres of land at Coventry in October, 1718. This was in addition to his earlier purchases. He probably made iron at Coventry in that year. Bishop refers to a letter written by Dickinson in July, 1718, stating that "the expectations from the iron works forty miles up the Schuylkill are very great." In April, 1719, Dickinson again wrote: "Our iron promises well. What hath been sent over to England hath been greatly approved. Our smiths work up all they make, and it is as good as the best Swedish iron." Dickinson probably referred to Nutt's forge as well as to Rutter's. The former, as well as the latter, at first made bar iron directly from the ore.

Coventry forge was in operation in 1756. In 1770 it is noted on William Scull's map of Pennsylvania. It was in active operation after the Revolution, and in 1849 and 1856 we again find it active, making blooms from pig iron. It made its last iron in 1870. The foundations and other parts of the old forge may still be seen. It is the oldest iron work in the State that is not wholly gnawed away by the tooth of time. It has been owned by the Chrisman family for over eighty years.

The next iron enterprise in Pennsylvania was undoubtedly Colebrookdale furnace, which was built about 1720 by a company of which Thomas Rutter was the principal member. It was located on Ironstone creek, in Colebrookdale township, in Berks county, about eight miles north of Pottstown, three-fourths of a mile west of Boyertown, and about two hundred yards from the Colebrookdale Railroad. Plenty of cinder now marks the exact site. A large flour and saw mill stands about one hundred feet distant. This furnace supplied Pool forge with pig iron, and in course of time other forges, one of which was Pine forge, to be referred to hereafter. The Colebrookdale company appears to have been composed of Thomas Rutter, James Lewis, Anthony Morris, and others, Rutter owning at one time a two-thirds' interest, as is shown by his will, on file in the office of the register of wills in Philadelphia, which we have examined.

In 1731, according to Mrs. James, Colebrookdale furnace and Pool forge were both owned by companies. In the list of owners of both establishments appears the name of Thomas Potts, the founder of a family of the same name which has ever since been prominent in the manufacture of iron in Pennsylvania and in other States. He died at Colebrookdale in January, 1752. He was in his day the most successful iron manufacturer in Pennsylvania. In his will, dated 1747, he leaves his " two-thirds of Colebrookdale furnace and iron mines " to his son Thomas, and his " one-third of Pine forge " to his son John. He was of either English or Welsh lineage. In 1733 the furnace was torn down and rebuilt by the company, Thomas Potts being the manager. Mrs. James writes to us: " I have a large calf-bound folio ledger of nearly 200 folios of Colebrookdale furnace, marked ' B.' The first date is August, 1728, but there are several pages referring to the first ledger, one of them in 1726. Mention is constantly made of sending 'piggs' to Pool forge, proving that this forge was then in full blast. 'A' would seem to be a large volume from reference to the folios," and therefore to have covered the operations of a number of years. Mrs. James thinks that it is lost. She adds that on the title-page of ledger B the name of Thomas Potts is written in connection with the year 1728, probably as the manager or lessee of the furnace. He was a resident of Manatawny as early as 1725.

On Nicholas Scull's map of Pennsylvania, published in 1759, Colebrookdale furnace is noted, and in a list of iron works existing in Pennsylvania about 1793, and published by Mrs. James, it is again mentioned, although it was not then active. We have not found it mentioned at any later period. A stove-plate cast at this furnace in 1763 was exhibited at the Philadelphia Exhibition of 1876. In 1731 pig iron sold at Colebrookdale furnace "in large quantities" at £5 10s. per ton, Pennsylvania currency, a pound being equal to $2.66⅔. It would seem that friendly Indians were employed at Colebrookdale, as "Indian John" and "Margalitha" are found in the list of workmen about 1728. The furnace was located in the heart of one of the richest deposits of magnetic iron ore in the United States. After being long neglected this deposit was mined a few years ago, but it is again neglected.

Redmond Conyngham, quoted in Day's *Historical Collections of Pennsylvania*, printed in 1843, says that iron works are supposed to have been established in Lancaster county in 1726 by a person named Kurtz, who is said by another authority to have been an Amish Mennonite. In Egle's *History of Pennsylvania* it is stated that Kurtz's works were on Octorara creek, and that it is possible they were in Maryland and not in Lancaster county. Conyngham also says that the enterprising family of Grubbs "commenced operations in 1728," also in Lancaster county. Both history and tradition are silent concerning the nature of these alleged "operations" at that time. We will refer to the Grubb family again.

Durham furnace, on Durham creek, about one and a half miles above its entrance into the Delaware river in the extreme northern part of Bucks county, was built in 1727 by a company of fourteen persons, of which Anthony Morris, William Allen, Joseph Turner, and James Logan (Penn's secretary) were members. Its first blast took place in the fall of 1727, and in November of 1728 James Logan shipped three tons of Durham pig iron to England. At the Philadelphia Exhibition of 1876 the keystone of Durham furnace, bearing the date 1727, was an object of interest. It is now in the office of Cooper & Hewitt, at Durham. The furnace was between 35 and 40 feet square and about 30 feet high. From the first this furnace made pig iron to be converted into bar iron, although subsequently, as early as 1741, stoves were cast at the furnace in large quantities. From a very interesting pamphlet account of Durham township by Herbert C. Bell, assisted by Charles Laubach and B. F. Fackenthal, Jr., printed in 1887, we learn that there were three forges on Durham creek, all below the furnace, and that many other forges in the neighborhood, on both sides of the Delaware, were supplied with pig iron from this furnace.

On Nicholas Scull's map of Pennsylvania (1759) an old and a new furnace and a forge at Durham are plainly noted. In 1770 two furnaces and two forges are marked in William Scull's map. But there was probably only one furnace. As late as 1780 negro slaves were employed at Durham, five of whom in that year escaped to the British lines. Much of the iron made at Durham was taken to Philadelphia in boats fashioned somewhat like an Indian canoe, and first built at Durham ; hence the term afterwards in common use, Durham boats. Large quantities of shot and shells for the Continental army were made at Durham furnace. The furnace was in active operation until 1791, with occasional intervals of suspension from various causes, when it blew out finally. In 1829 it was torn down to make way for a grist mill. In 1848 and 1851 two new furnaces were built at Durham, to use anthracite coal. In 1874 a new and very large furnace was built to take the place of the two furnaces just mentioned, which were torn down.

At least two distinguished Americans of the Revolutionary period were identified with Durham furnace. General Daniel Morgan, son of James Morgan, " ironmaster," and one of the owners of the furnace before 1773, was born in Durham township in 1736. In early life, before entering upon his adventurous career, he assisted his father at the furnace. Tradition says that he was also a charcoal burner at Durham. George Taylor, a signer of the Declaration of Independence, was at one time employed as a "filler" at Durham furnace, and subsequently he was the sole lessee of the furnace. He was born in Ireland, and came to Pennsylvania when a young man as a "redemptioner." The Morgan family was of Welsh origin. While George Taylor was the lessee of Durham furnace he cast stoves bearing the inscription, "Durham Furnace, 1774." A plate of one of these stoves, bearing this inscription, is fastened against the walls of the post-office at Easton.

In 1728 James Logan wrote that "there are four furnaces in blast in the colony." Colebrookdale and Durham were two of these, but the names of the others are in doubt.

The iron industry of Pennsylvania may be said to have been fairly established on a firm foundation at this time. In 1728–29 the colony exported 274 tons of pig iron to the mother country. The production of a Pennsylvania furnace at this period was about two tons of iron in twenty-four hours.

The manufacture of nails in Pennsylvania commenced at an early day. In 1731 George Megee, nailer, at the corner of Front and Arch streets, Philadelphia, advertised for sale, at wholesale and retail, all sorts of nails of his own manufacture.

The erection of other forges and furnaces proceeded with great rapidity in the Schuylkill valley and in other eastern portions of Pennsylvania after Rutter and other pioneers had shown the way. McCall's forge, afterwards called Glasgow forge, on Manatawny creek, in Montgomery county, a short distance above Pottstown and below Pool forge, was built by George McCall about 1725. Spring forge, on the Manatawny, in Berks county, west of Colebrookdale furnace and about five miles north of Douglassville, was built in 1729, probably by Anthony Morris. These forges, as well as Pool forge, were supplied with iron from Colebrookdale furnace. Green Lane forge, on Perkiomen creek, in Montgomery county, twenty miles above Norristown, was built in 1733 by Thomas Mayburry. The workmen once employed here were chiefly negro slaves. This forge was supplied with pig iron from Durham furnace before 1747. Mount Pleasant furnace, on Perkiomen creek, in Berks county, thirteen miles above Pottstown, was built by Thomas Potts, Jr., in 1738. A forge of the same name was built before 1743. Pine forge, on the Manatawny, in Berks county, about five miles above Pottstown, was built about 1740 by Thomas Potts, Jr. Oley forge, on the Manatawny, in Berks county, was built in 1744 by John Ross, John Yoder, and John Lesher, as we learn from Morton L. Montgomery, of Reading. It was finally abandoned about 1870. Spring, Glasgow, Mount Pleasant, and Green Lane forges were in operation down to the middle of the present century. Pine forge was converted into Pine rolling mill in 1845, and upon the site of Glasgow forge there was erected in 1874 a rolling mill which is now known as the Glasgow iron works.

Samuel Nutt built a furnace called Reading, on French creek, soon after he built Coventry forge. In this enterprise William Branson may have been a partner. Mrs. James says that two furnaces of that name were erected about a mile from each other, the second after the first was abandoned. The second furnace of this name was built on French creek, about 1736, by Samuel Nutt and William Branson. In the inventory of the estate of Samuel Nutt, which Gilbert Cope, of West Chester, has kindly placed in our hands, mention is made of "a ring round the shaft at the old furnace," and of "one tonn of sow mettle at new furnace." Acrelius, in speaking of the iron ore on French creek, says : " Its discoverer is Mr. Nutt, who afterwards took Mr. Branz into partnership." The reference is to William Branson. This event occurred as early as March 29, 1728, as their names then appear in the Philadelphia *Weekly Mercury* as partners. Acrelius further says : " They both went to England, brought workmen back with them, and continued together." Mrs. James says : " The 15th day of March, 1736, Samuel Nutt and William Branson entered into an agreement with John Potts to carry on their furnace called Redding, recently built near Coventry, and of which they are styled 'joint owners.'" At a meeting of the Provincial Council on January 25, 1737, "a petition of sundry inhabitants of the county of Lancaster was presented to the board and read, setting forth the want of a road from the town of Lancaster to Coventry iron works on French creek, in Chester county, and praying that proper persons of each of the counties may be appointed for laying out the same from

Lancaster town to the said iron works, one branch of which road to goe to the new furnace, called Redding's furnace, now erecting on the said creek." On October 7th of the same year commissioners were appointed to lay out the road.

Samuel Nutt died in 1737. In his will, dated September 25, 1737, he gave one-half of his "right" to Reading furnace and Coventry forge to his wife and the other half to Samuel Nutt, Jr., and his wife. He also made provision for the erection by his wife of a new furnace. This furnace was commenced in the same year, and was built on the south branch of French creek. It was probably finished in 1738. In 1740 its management fell into the hands of Robert Grace, a friend of Benjamin Franklin, who had recently married the widow of Samuel Nutt, Jr. This lady was the granddaughter of Thomas Rutter. The new furnace was called Warwick. The celebrated Franklin stove was invented by Benjamin Franklin in 1742, and in his autobiography he says: "I made a present of the model to Mr. Robert Grace, one of my early friends, who, having an iron furnace, found the casting of the plates for these stoves a profitable thing, as they were growing in demand." Mrs. James has seen one of these stoves, with the words "Warwick Furnace" cast on the front in letters two inches long. Warwick furnace continued in active operation during a part of almost every year from its erection in 1738 down to 1867, when its last blast came to an end and the famous furnace was abandoned. During the Revolution it was very active in casting cannon for the Continental army, some of which were buried upon the approach of the British in 1777, and have only recently been recovered, having lain undisturbed for a hundred years. The lower part of the stack of Warwick furnace still remains.

There is now among the relics in Independence Hall, Philadelphia, a cast-iron bell which was cast at Warwick furnace in 1757 and used at Valley Forge in 1777. It was presented to the authorities of Independence Hall in 1875 by Colonel J. M. Fegar. It bears the inscription in raised letters, " P. R. 1757." Mr. J. Wesley Pullman, of Philadelphia, has in his possession a highly ornamented stove plate which was cast at Warwick furnace in 1764 and bears that inscription. The name of John Potts also appears on the plate.

After Samuel Nutt's death Reading furnace became the property of his partner, William Branson. It is noted on Nicholas Scull's map of 1759. Coventry forge finally fell to Samuel Nutt's heirs.

At an uncertain period about 1750 William Branson and others established on French creek the Vincent steel works. They are thus described by Acrelius: "At French creek, or Branz's works, there is a steel furnace, built with a draught hole, and called an 'air oven.' In this iron bars are set at the distance of an inch apart. Between them are scattered horn, coal-dust, ashes, etc. The iron bars are thus covered with blisters, and this is called 'blister steel.' It serves as the best steel to put upon edge tools. These steel works are now said to be out of operation." Vincent forge, with four fires and two hammers, was connected with Vincent steel furnace, but the date of its erection is uncertain. It is noted on William Scull's map of 1770. The furnace and forge were located about six miles from the mouth of French creek and about five miles distant from Coventry forge, which was farther up the stream. Before February 15, 1797, a rolling and slitting mill had been added to the forge. We do not hear of the steel furnace after 1780, nor of the forge after 1800.

In 1742 William Branson, then owner of Reading furnace, bought from John Jenkins a tract of 400 acres of land on Conestoga creek, near Churchtown, in Caernarvon township, Lancaster county, on which he soon afterwards erected two forges, called Windsor. In a short time, as we are informed by James McCaa, " Branson sold out to the English company, who were Lynford Lardner, Samuel Flower, and Richard Hockley, Esqs., who held it [Windsor] for thirty years, when, in 1773, David Jenkins, son of the original proprietor, bought the half interest of the company for the sum of £2,500, and in two years afterwards bought the other half for the sum of £2,400, including the negroes and stock used on the premises." Robert Jenkins inherited the Windsor forges from his father David, and managed them with great success for fifty years, dying in 1848. They have since been abandoned.

David Jenkins was a member of the Pennsylvania legislature in 1784. Robert Jenkins was a member of the legislature in 1804 and 1805, and from 1807 to 1811 he was a member of Congress. Mrs. Martha J. Nevin, of Lancaster, who died at her home near that city on January 13, 1890, at the age of 85 years, was a daughter of Robert Jenkins.

Acrelius, narrating events which occurred between 1750 and 1756, mentions the enterprises of Nutt and Branson as follows: "Each has his own furnace—Branz at Reading, Nutt at Warwick. Each also has his own forges—Branz in Windsor. Nutt supplies four forges besides his own in Chester county." Nutt was not living at the time this was written, but Acrelius's confounding of ownership is easily understood. Nor is it probable that Branson operated Windsor forges in 1750. In that year he is reported as having then owned a furnace for making steel in Philadelphia, and about 1743 it is known that he sold Windsor forges to the English company, which was composed of his sons-in-law. William Branson was himself an Englishman, who emigrated to Pennsylvania about 1708 and became a Philadelphia merchant. He died in 1760.

Continuing up the Schuylkill valley we find in 1751 a forge called Mount Joy, at the mouth of East Valley creek, on the Chester county side of the creek, one-third of which was advertised for sale on the 4th of April of that year by Daniel Walker, and the remaining two-thirds on the 26th of September of the same year by Stephen Evans and Joseph Williams. In Daniel Walker's advertisement it was stated that the forge was "not so far distant from three furnaces." Pennypacker, in his *Annals of Phœnixville and its Vicinity*, says that the ancestor of the Walker family had come from England with William Penn, and "at a very early date had erected the small forge on the Valley creek." It is clear, however, that in 1751 Daniel Walker owned only one-third of the forge, Evans and Williams owning the remainder. In 1757, as we learn from Mrs. James, the forge was sold to John Potts by the executors of Stephen Evans. In 1773 it was owned by Joseph Potts, at which time it continued to be legally designated as Mount Joy forge, although for some time previously it had been popularly known as Valley forge. In that year Joseph Potts sold one-half of the forge to Colonel William Dewees. The pig iron used at Valley forge was supplied by Warwick furnace. In September, 1777, the forge was burned by the British, and in December of the same year the Continental army under Washington was intrenched on the Montgomery county side of Valley creek, opposite to Valley forge. General Washington's headquarters were established at the substantial stone house of Isaac Potts, also on the Montgomery county side of Valley creek. This house is still standing. Isaac Potts was not, however, at this time an owner of Valley forge.

After the Revolutionary war was ended Isaac and David Potts, brothers, erected another forge, on the Montgomery county side of Valley creek, and about three-eighths of a mile below the old Mount Joy forge. A new dam was built, which raised the water partly over the site of the old forge. About the same time, and as early as 1786, a slitting mill was built on the Chester county side of the stream by the same persons. The new forge was called Valley forge. It was in ruins in 1816. Other iron enterprises, of a reproductive character, were established at the town of Valley Forge early in the present century, and about 1818 cast steel to be used in the manufacture of saws was made here for a short time. About 1824 all the iron works at Valley Forge were discontinued.

William Bird was an enterprising Englishman who established several iron enterprises in Berks county before the Revolution. A person of this name was a witness of Thomas Rutter's will on November 27, 1728, when he appears to have been a resident of Amity township, Berks county. In 1740 or 1741 William Bird built a forge on Hay creek, near its entrance into the Schuylkill, where Birdsboro now stands. Hopewell furnace, on French creek, in Union township, which was in operation in 1883 but is now abandoned, is said by tradition to have been built by William Bird in 1759, but it may have been built by his son, Mark Bird, about 1765. As early as 1760 William Bird built Roxborough furnace, in Heidelberg township, the name of which furnace was subsequently changed to Berkshire. Dying in 1762 his estate was divided between his widow and his six children. Berkshire furnace fell to his son, Mark Bird, who sold it in 1764 to John Patton and his wife Bridget, who had been the wife of William Bird.

In 1789 Bridget Patton, again a widow, sold the furnace to George Ege, who abandoned it about 1792, in which year he built Reading furnace, on Spring creek, in Heidelberg township. On the site of Reading furnace two Robesonia furnaces were afterwards built, only one of which is now standing. Berkshire furnace manufactured shot and shells for the Continental army. Mark Bird built a rolling and slitting mill and a nail factory at Birdsboro about the time of the Revolution. At Trenton, New Jersey, he manufactured wire. He failed in business about 1788.

Charming forge, on Tulpehocken creek, in Berks county, was built in 1749 by John George Nikoll, a hammersmith, and Michael Miller. It was at first styled *Tulpehocken Eisen Hammer*. Mr. Montgomery says that it was owned in 1763 by Henry William Stiegel, and that in 1774 it was purchased by George Ege. About 1777 Mr. Ege purchased from Congress the services of thirty-four Hessian prisoners, for the purpose of cutting a channel through a bed of rock to supply with water-power a slitting mill which he had previously erected. W. & B. F. Taylor, the last owners of the forge, inform us that the mill-race here referred to was about 100 yards long, from 12 to 20 feet deep, and about 20 feet wide, and that it was cut through a mass of solid slate rock as smoothly as if done with a broad-axe. It was used until 1887, when the forge was abandoned. In 1889 the forge dam was washed away by a freshet.

George Ege was for almost fifty years one of the most prominent ironmasters in Pennsylvania. His possessions in Berks county were at one time princely. He died in December, 1830. He was a native of Holland.

On William Scull's map of 1770 Moselem forge, on Maiden creek, Berks county, and Gulf forge, on Gulf creek, in Upper Merion township, Montgomery county, are noted. Helmstead, Union, and Pottsgrove were the names of other forges existing as early as 1759 in the Schuylkill valley.

Oley furnace, on Furnace creek, a branch of Manatawny creek, about eleven miles northeast of Reading, was built about 1765, probably by Dietrich Welcker, as we learn from Mr. Montgomery. It was last in operation in 1886, but was abandoned in 1887 and dismantled in 1888.

There was a forge on Crum creek, about two miles above the town of Chester, in Delaware county, which was built by John Crosby and Peter Dicks about 1742. Peter Kalm, the Swede, in his *Travels into North America*, written in 1748 and 1749, thus describes it : "About two English miles behind Chester I passed by an iron forge, which was to the right hand by the road side. It belonged to two brothers, as I was told. The ore, however, is not dug here, but thirty or forty miles from hence, where it is first melted in the oven, and then carried to this place. The bellows were made of leather, and both they and the hammers and even the hearth [were] but small in proportion to ours. All the machines were worked by water. The iron was wrought into bars." The oven here referred to was a blast furnace, which was probably located in the Schuylkill valley, the pigs for the forge being boated down the Schuylkill and the Delaware and up Crum creek. Acrelius says that the forge was owned at the time of his visit by Peter Dicks, and that it had two stacks, was worked sluggishly, and had "ruined Crosby's family."

As early as 1742 John Taylor built a forge on Chester creek, in Thornbury township, Delaware county, where Glen Mills now stand, which he called Sarum iron works. In 1746 he added a rolling and slitting mill. These works are said to have been carried on with energy by Mr. Taylor until his death in 1756. Acrelius, writing about the time of Mr. Taylor's death, says : "Sarum belongs to Taylor's heirs, has three stacks, and is in full blast." Peter Kalm states that at Chichester (Marcus Hook) "they build here every year a number of small ships for sale, and from an iron work which lies higher up in the country they carry iron bars to this place and ship them." This iron work was probably Sarum. Taylor's rolling and slitting mill was the first in Pennsylvania.

John Taylor was descended from a family of the same name in Wiltshire, England, and was a nephew of Jacob Taylor, who was surveyor-general of Pennsylvania from 1707 to 1733. His business operations were upon an extensive and varied scale, and included the manufacture of nails as well as nail rods. The tradition is preserved by his descendants that soon after the erection of the slitting mill his storekeeper, in making one of his periodical visits to England to replenish his stock, surprised the Liverpool merchants by telling them that he could buy nails at Taylor's mill at lower prices than they quoted, a revelation which added weight to the clamor then prevailing in England for the suppression of slitting mills and similar iron establishments in America, and which agitation resulted in the passage in 1750 of an act of Parliament which prohibited the further erection of such works. But, as this act did not prohibit the carrying on of works that had already been erected, Taylor's slitting mill was kept in operation after his death, first by his son John and afterwards by the latter's son-in-law, Colonel Persifor Frazer. During the Revolution the superintendence of the estate, including the management of the iron works, devolved upon Mrs. Frazer. The works were abandoned soon after the war, owing in part to the industrial depression which then prevailed.

In 1750 there was a "plating forge to work with a tilt-hammer" in Byberry township, in the northeastern part of Philadelphia county, the only one in the province, owned by John Hall, but not then in use. In the same year there were two steel furnaces in Philadelphia, one of which, Stephen Paschall's, was built in 1747 and stood on a lot on the northwest corner of Eighth and Walnut streets; the other furnace was owned by William Branson, and was located near where Thomas Penn "first lived, at the upper end of Chestnut street." These furnaces were for the production of blister steel. There appear to have been no other steel furnaces in the province in 1750. Whitehead Humphreys was in 1770 the proprietor of a steel furnace on Seventh street, between Market and Chestnut streets, in Philadelphia, where he also made edge tools. In February, 1775, Uriah Woolman and B. Shoemaker, "in Market street, Philadelphia," advertised in Dunlap's *Pennsylvania Packet* "Pennsylvania steel, manufactured by W. Humphreys, of an excellent quality, and warranted equal to English, to be sold in blister, faggot, or flat bar, suitable for carriage springs." In Watson's *Annals* it is stated that about the year 1790 John Nancarro, a Scotchman, "had a furnace underground for converting iron into steel," located at the northwest corner of Ninth and Walnut streets, Philadelphia. We have already referred to the Vincent steel works in Chester county.

CHAPTER XV.

THE MANUFACTURE OF IRON IN PENNSYLVANIA EXTENDED TO THE SUSQUEHANNA.

ELIZABETH FURNACE, near Brickersville, on Middle creek, a tributary of Conestoga creek, in Lancaster county, was built about 1750 by John Huber, a German. It was a small furnace, and did not prove to be profitable. In 1757 Huber sold it to Henry William Stiegel and his partners, who built a new and larger furnace, which was operated until 1775, when, through Stiegel's embarrassments, it passed into the hands of Daniel Benezet, who leased it to Robert Coleman, who subsequently bought it and eventually became the most prominent ironmaster in Pennsylvania at the close of the last century and far into the present century. Bishop says that "some of the first stoves cast in this country were made by Baron Stiegel, relics of which still remain in the old families of Lancaster and Lebanon counties." Rev. Joseph Henry Dubbs, of Lancaster, says that Stiegel's stoves bore the inscription :

Baron Stiegel ist der Mann
Der die Ofen machen kann.

That is, " Baron Stiegel is the man who knows how to make stoves." On the furnace erected by Huber the following legend was inscribed :

Johann Huber, der erste Deutsche Mann
Der das Eisenwerk vollführen kann.

Freely translated this inscription reads : "John Huber is the first German who knows how to make iron."

In 1885 a cast-iron plate, about two and a half feet square, was found doing duty as the hearth of an old-fashioned fireplace in Lancaster. It bore on the under side an inscription which was not altogether legible, but the words " Stiegle " and " Elizabeth," and the date " 1758 " were plainly legible. The spelling of the Baron's name on this iron plate differs from the usual spelling, but this may have been an error of the pattern maker.

Stiegel's ownership of Charming forge in 1763 has heretofore been mentioned. In that year he sold a half interest to Charles and Alexander Stedman, of Philadelphia, and in 1773 the sheriff sold his remaining interest. Soon after 1760 he established a glass factory at Manheim, in Lancaster county, called the American flint-glass factory, which was in operation as late as 1774. He was a native of Germany, arriving in this country on August 31, 1750, (old style,) in the ship *Nancy*, from Rotterdam. He is buried in the Lutheran graveyard near Womelsdorf, in Heidelberg township, Berks county. In his last days he taught school in this township.

After Elizabeth furnace came into the possession of Robert Coleman he cast shot and shells and cannon for the Continental army, and some of the transactions which occurred between him and the Government in settlement of his accounts for these supplies are very interesting. On November 16, 1782, appears the following entry : "By cash, being the value of 42 German prisoners of war, at £30 each, £1,260;" and on June 14, 1783, the following : "By cash, being the value of 28 German prisoners of war, at £30 each, £840." In a foot-note to these credits Robert Coleman certifies "on honour" that the above 70 prisoners were all that were ever secured by him, one of whom being returned is to be deducted when he produces the proper voucher. Rupp, in his history of Lancaster county, mentions that in 1843 he visited one of the Hessian mercenaries who was disposed of in this manner at the close of the war for the sum of £80, for the term of three years, to Captain Jacob Zimmerman of that county.

Elizabeth furnace continued in operation until 1856, when it was abandoned by its owner, Hon. G. Dawson Coleman, the grandson of Robert Coleman, for want of wood.

Among the persons who were employed at Windsor forges under the English company was James Old, a forgeman. About 1765 he built Pool forge, on Conestoga creek, about a mile below Windsor forges. Early records mention his ownership of Quitapahilla forge, near Lebanon, and other forges in Chester, Lancaster, and Berks counties. In 1773 he was a lessee of Reading furnace, on French creek. In 1795 he conveyed Pool forge and about 700 acres of land attached to it to his son, Davies Old.

James Old was born in Wales in 1730. He emigrated to Pennsylvania previous to September 7, 1754, when his name for the first time appears in the register of Bangor church, at Churchtown, Lancaster county, as the contributor of £5 toward the erection of the church building. Soon after his settlement at Windsor he married Margaretta Davies, a daughter of Gabriel Davies, of Lancaster county. Gabriel Davies is supposed to have been the owner of the site on which Pool forge was built. James Old died on May 1, 1809, in his 79th year, and is buried in the graveyard of Bàngor church. He was one of the most enterprising and successful of early Pennsylvania ironmasters. He had a brother William, also a forgeman, who had been employed at Windsor forges, and who is said to have embarked in the manufacture of bar iron on his own account. James Old was a member of the Pennsylvania legislature in 1791, 1792, and 1793.

William Old, a son of James Old, married Elizabeth Stiegel, the daughter of Baron Stiegel. She is buried in the same rural graveyard which holds the remains of her father. The late Mrs. Henry Morris, of Philadelphia, was her granddaughter.

Robert Coleman was in his younger days in the service of James Old, and while with him at Reading furnace in 1773 he married his daughter Ann. Soon afterwards he rented Salford forge, above Norristown, in Montgomery county, and remained there three years. While at this forge he manufactured chain bars, which were used to span the Delaware river for the defense of Philadelphia against the approach of the British fleet. From Salford forge he went to Elizabeth furnace. He was born near Castle Fin, in Donegal county, and not far from the city of Londonderry, in Ireland, on the 4th of November, 1748. In 1764, when 16 years old, he left Ireland for America. He died at Lancaster in 1825, at which place he is buried. He was an officer in the Pennsylvania militia during the Revolution, a member of the State convention which framed the Constitution of 1790, a member of the legislature, raised and commanded a troop of cavalry during the whisky insurrection, was a Presidential elector-at-large in 1792 and a Presidential elector for his Congressional district in 1796, and for nearly twenty years was an associate judge of Lancaster county.

Cyrus Jacobs married Margaretta, another daughter of James Old, about 1782. At that time Mr. Jacobs was living at Churchtown, in the employment of James Old as a clerk at Pool forge. He was at Gibraltar forge in Berks county in 1787 and at Hopewell forge in Lancaster county from 1789 to 1792. In 1793 he built Spring Grove forge, on Conestoga creek, about three miles west of Pool forge, and in 1799 he purchased Pool forge from Davies Old. Pool forge was active until 1861 or 1862, and Spring Grove forge until 1866, after which years they were respectively abandoned. Cyrus Jacobs was born in 1761, and died in 1830 at Whitehall, near Churchtown. He is buried in the graveyard of Bangor church.

Cornwall furnace, located within the limits of the now celebrated Cornwall ore hills, on Furnace creek, in Lebanon county, a few miles south of Lebanon, was built in 1742 by Peter Grubb, whose descendants to this day have been prominent Pennsylvania ironmasters. He was the son of John Grubb, a native of Cornwall, in England, who emigrated to this country in the preceding century, landing at Grubb's Landing, on the Delaware, near Wilmington, at which latter place he is buried. There is evidence that Peter Grubb was already an ironmaster before he built Cornwall furnace, and a tradition in his family says that in 1735 he built a furnace or bloomary, most likely the latter, about five-eighths of a mile from the site of Cornwall furnace. He died intestate about 1754, and his estate, including the Cornwall ore hills, descended to his two sons, Curtis and Peter Grubb, who were afterwards colonels during the Revolution.

A few years after the death of Peter Grubb Acrelius wrote of Cornwall furnace as follows: " Cornwall, or Grubb's iron works, in Lancaster county. The mine is rich and abundant, forty feet deep, commencing two feet under the earth's surface. The ore is somewhat mixed with sulphur and copper. Peter Grubb was its discoverer. Here there is a furnace which makes twenty-four tons of iron a week and keeps six forges regularly at work—two of his own, two belonging to Germans in the neighborhood, and two in Maryland. The pig iron is carried to the Susquehanna river, thence to Maryland, and finally to England. The bar iron is sold mostly in the country and in the interior towns ; the remainder in Philadelphia. It belongs to the heirs of the Grubb estate, but is now rented to Gurrit & Co." This firm was doubtless Garret & Co.

During the Revolution Cornwall furnace cast cannon and shot and shells for the Continental army. It was in operation as late as 1882, and is still in good condition. It is the oldest charcoal furnace in the United States that is yet standing in its entirety. It has always used charcoal.

In 1785 Robert Coleman purchased a one-sixth interest in Cornwall furnace and the ore hills. After that year, through successive purchases from the Grubbs, he obtained four additional sixths of the Cornwall property. His total purchases of this valuable property remain in the hands of his descendants at this day.

Martic forge, on Pequea creek, near the present village of Colemanville, in Lancaster county, was built in 1755, and was last in operation in 1883. Early in this century cemented, or blister, steel was made here. Robert S. Potts, one of the last owners of Martic forge, wrote us a few years ago as follows: " There used to be a small rolling mill near the forge that stopped running some fifty years ago. There was also a charcoal furnace called Martic six miles east of the forge, but I have been unable to ascertain its history beyond the fact that it was owned and operated by the Martic Forge Company; when that was, however, or how long it was in blast, I can not learn. The old cinder bank is still visible. During the Revolution round iron was drawn under the hammer at the forge and bored out for musket barrels at a boring mill, in a very retired spot, on a small stream far off from any public road, doubtless with a view to prevent discovery by the enemy. The site is still visible." In 1769 Martic furnace and forge were advertised for sale by the sheriff, together with 3,400 acres of land and other property, " all late the property of Thomas Smith, James Wallace, and James Fulton." The furnace was in existence about 1793, but was not then active.

Robert S. Potts, surviving partner of the firm of Davies & Potts, which owned Martic forge for many years, died in June, 1886. Negro slaves were employed from the beginning in hammering iron at this forge, and it is a curious fact that negroes continued to be the principal workmen down to the abandonment of active operations in 1883. The forge was finally abandoned in 1886. A long row of stone houses was occupied by the negro workmen.

Hopewell forge, on Hammer creek, in Lancaster county, about ten miles south of Lebanon, was built by Peter Grubb soon after he built Cornwall furnace. Speedwell forge on the same stream, near Brickersville, in Lancaster county, was built about 1750, also by Peter Grubb.

The iron industry of Pennsylvania crossed the Susquehanna at a very early period. Acrelius says that there was a bloomary in York county in 1756, owned by Peter Dicks, who had but recently discovered "the mine." In Gibson's *History of York County* George R. Prowell, of York, locates this bloomary in Jackson township, on a branch of Codorus creek, where a forge known as Spring forge was built in 1770 to take the place of the bloomary. This forge was in operation as late as 1850, but was abandoned in that year. Spring forge was a famous enterprise in its day, pig iron being supplied to it from neighboring furnaces.

The researches of Mr. Prowell establish the fact that the first blast furnace west of the Susquehanna was built in 1763 on Furnace creek, in West Manheim township, in the extreme southwestern part of York county, by George Ross, a lawyer of Lancaster, and Mark Bird, of Philadelphia. It was called Mary Ann furnace. The building of the furnace was commenced in 1762. In 1763 the owners petitioned the court of York county to open a public road from their furnace "lately built at a great expense" to the road from the Conewago settlement to Baltimore, and in 1766 they petitioned the court to open a road from their furnace to the Monocacy road at Frederick Eichelberger's tavern. The name of the firm which owned the furnace was George Ross & Co. A great many stoves were cast at this furnace, and during the Revolution it cast many shot and shells. It finally went out of blast about 1800. George Ross was one of the signers of the Declaration of Independence.

In 1765 a forge was erected by William Bennett on the south side of Codorus creek, near its junction with the Susquehanna, in Hellam township, York county. In 1810 the property, which had previously been known as Hellam forge, was bought by Henry Grubb, and after that date the works

were known as Codorus forge. In 1836 Mr. Grubb added a
charcoal furnace, which made pig iron for the forge. Previous to this time the forge was supplied with pig iron from
Cornwall and other neighboring furnaces. Bar iron was shipped down the Susquehanna to tidewater and thence to Baltimore and Philadelphia. James Smith, a signer of the Declaration, owned these works during the Revolution, and they
were the cause of his financial ruin. The furnace ceased operations in 1850. The forge had previously been abandoned.

Soon after 1762 a furnace and forge were built at Boiling
Springs, in Cumberland county, forming the nucleus of the
Carlisle iron works, which afterwards embraced a blast furnace, a rolling and slitting mill, and a steel furnace. The
furnace and forge were built by a company composed of Joseph Morris, John Morris, Samuel Morris, Amos Stuttle, and
John Armstrong, all of Philadelphia. The site of these enterprises, with some contiguous territory, was purchased from
John Rigby and Nathan Giles. Michael Ege owned them
after 1782. On a tax list at Carlisle Robert Thornburg & Co.
appear as the owners of a forge in 1767 to which 1,200 acres
of land were attached. We can not locate this forge. Pine
Grove furnace, in the same county, was built about 1770 by
Thornburg & Arthur. In 1782 Michael Ege became a part
owner of the furnace and subsequently sole owner. A forge
called Laurel, built in 1830, was attached to this furnace.
Both the furnace and forge are still in operation. Holly furnace and forge, at Mount Holly Springs, in the same county,
are said to have been built about 1770 by a Mr. Stevenson.
The sites of both enterprises are still visible. The forge was
in existence as late as 1848. The furnace was torn down in
1855 to give place to a paper mill. It was once owned by
Michael Ege.

No other iron works west of the Susquehanna are known
to have been established previous to the Revolution.

CHAPTER XVI.

CHARACTERISTICS OF THE EARLY IRON INDUSTRY OF PENNSYLVANIA.

ALTHOUGH all the iron enterprises that were established in Pennsylvania prior to the Revolution have not been mentioned in the preceding pages, those which have been mentioned indicate remarkable activity in the development of the iron resources of the province. Pennsylvania was almost the last of the thirteen colonies to be occupied by permanent English settlements, and even after these settlements were made a long time elapsed, very strangely, before the erection of iron works was successfully undertaken. The manufacture of iron was not fairly commenced in Pennsylvania until 1716, but after this time it grew rapidly, and in the sixty years which intervened before the commencement of hostilities with the mother country probably sixty blast furnaces and forges and several slitting mills and steel works were built, a rate of progress which was not attained by any other colony in the same period.

In his *History of New Sweden* Acrelius says : "Pennsylvania, in regard to its iron works, is the most advanced of all the American colonies." Many of these enterprises were upon a scale that would have done credit to a much later period of the American iron industry. Cornwall and Warwick furnaces were each 32 feet high, 21½ feet square at the base, and 11 feet square at the top. Warwick was at first 9 feet wide at the boshes, but was afterwards reduced to 7½ feet. The forges were usually those in which pig iron was refined into bar iron "in the Walloon style," as stated by Acrelius. There were few ore bloomaries, and nearly all of these were built at an early day. Acrelius mentions only one of this class—Peter Dicks' bloomary, in York county. The smaller furnaces yielded only from 1½ to 2 tons of pig iron daily, but the larger ones yielded from 3 to 4 tons. Reading, Warwick, and Cornwall furnaces each made from 25 to 30 tons of iron per week. The furnaces were required to produce both pig iron and castings, the latter consisting of stoves, pots, kettles, andirons, and similar articles. Of the product of the forges Acrelius says that "one forge, with three hearths in good condition and well attended to, is expected to give 2 tons a week." The same writer says that "for four months in summer, when the heat is most oppressive, all labor is suspended at the furnaces and forges." The scarcity of water at this season would also have much to do with this suspension, all of the works being operated by water-power.

The German traveler, Schoepf, writing in 1783 of some Pennsylvania furnaces and forges, makes the following mention of Warwick and Reading furnaces: "Warwick furnace, 19 miles from Reading, near Pottsgrove, makes the most iron, often 40 tons a week; the iron ore lies 10 feet under the surface. Reading furnace, not far from the former, is at present fallen into decay. Here the smelting would formerly often continue from 12 to 18 months at a stretch."

At first large leather bellows were used exclusively to blow both the forges and the furnaces, but afterwards, about the time of the Revolution, wooden cylinders, or "tubs," were also used. It was not until after the beginning of the present century that steam-power was experimentally used to produce the blast at either furnaces or forges in Pennsylvania, or in any other State. Warwick and Cornwall furnaces, two of the best furnaces of the last century, retained their long leather bellows until the present century. Bishop says that Warwick furnace "was blown by long wooden bellows propelled by water wheels, and when in blast made 25 or 30 tons of iron per week." Reading furnace, a rival of both Warwick and Cornwall, was also blown with leather bellows. The Cornwall bellows was 20 feet 7 inches long, 5 feet 10 inches wide across the breech, and 14 inches wide at the insertion of the nozzle. Only one tuyere was used. The fuel used was exclusively charcoal, and the blast was always cold. Schoepf says that about 400 bushels of charcoal were required to produce from the ore a ton of hammered bar iron. He also says that mahogany was used to make the moulds for the castings at the furnaces, "because it warps and cracks the least."

The following notice of the workmen employed in making iron in Pennsylvania twenty years prior to the Revolution, and of the prices of iron at the same period, is taken from Acrelius, whose valuable history was printed in 1759, but covers the period of his visit from 1750 to 1756.

The workmen are partly English and partly Irish, with some few Germans, though the work is carried on after the English method. The pig-iron is smelted into "geese," ("gœsar,") and is cast from five to six feet long and a half foot broad, for convenience of forging, which is in the Walloon style. The pigs are first operated upon by the finers, (smelters.) Then the chiffery, or hammer-men, take it back again into their hands, and beat out the long bars. The finers are paid 30s. a ton and the hammer-men 23s. 9d. per ton; that is to say, both together, £2 13s. 9d. The laborers are generally composed partly of negroes, (slaves,) partly of servants from Germany or Ireland bought for a term of years. A good negro is bought for from £30 to £40 sterling, which is equal to 1,500 or 2,000 of our dollars, koppar mynt. Their clothing may amount to 75 dollars, koppar mynt, their food, 325 ditto —very little, indeed, for the year. The negroes are better treated in Pennsylvania than anywhere else in America. A white servant costs 350 dollars, koppar mynt, and his food is estimated at 325 dollars more, of the same coinage. For four months, in summer, when the heat is most oppressive, all labor is suspended at the furnaces and forges. Pig-iron is sold at the furnaces for from £3 6s. 8d. to £3 10s. per ton. Bar-iron at the forge brings £20 per ton, or 20s. per 100 pounds. It is sold dear, for six months credit is given. Pig-iron is sold in Philadelphia at £5 per ton; bar-iron, in large quantities, at from £14 to £16 per ton. It certainly seems remarkable that the price is diminished after the long transportation to the city; but in this people find their profit.

The iron-works of Pennsylvania lie mostly within forty miles of Philadelphia. The carriage for such a distance does not exceed twenty shillings sterling per ton. As a set-off to this is reckoned the return freight upon goods serviceable for the storehouse of the works.

The sheriff's advertisement for the sale of Martic furnace and forge, in 1769, already referred to, and which we give below, indicates very correctly the extent and character of a representative Pennsylvania iron enterprise before the Revolution.

By virtue of a writ to me directed, will be exposed to sale, by public vendue, on the 30th day of January inst., at 10 o'clock in the morning, at Martick Furnace, in Lancaster county, the said furnace and forge, together with upwards of 3,400 acres of land, thereunto belonging. The improvements at both furnace and forge are very good, viz.: At the furnace, a good dwelling-house, stores, and compting-house, a large coal-house, with eight dwelling-houses for the labourers, a good grist-mill, Smith's and Carpenter's shops, 6 good log stables, with 4 bays for hay, a number of pot patterns, and some flasks for ditto, stove moulds, &c., &c.; a good mine bank, abounding with plenty of ore, so convenient that one team can haul three loads a day; about 15 acres of good watered meadow, and as much adjoining may be

made: The Forge is about 4 miles distant, now in good order, with four
fires, two hammers, and very good wooden bellows, a dwelling-house, store,
and compting-house, with six dwelling-houses for the labourers, two very
good coal-houses, large enough to contain six months' stock, three stables,
Smith's and Carpenter's shops, two acres of meadow made, and about 1,500
cords of wood, cut in the woods at both places; there is plenty of water at
said works in the driest season, and they are situated in a plentiful part of
the country, where they can be supplied with necessaries on the lowest
terms: And to be sold the same day, a very good plantation, containing 200
acres of patent land, clear of quitrent, adjoining the lands of Benjamin
Ashleman, the Widow Haiman, and others, in Conestogo township. Also
two slaves, one a Mulattoe man, a good forge man, the other a Negro man,
and three teams of horses, with waggons and gears, &c. All late the property of Thomas Smith, James Wallace, and James Fulton; seized and taken
in execution, and to be sold by   JAMES WEBB, *Sheriff.*

Although the early furnaces and forges of Pennsylvania
were subject to vicissitudes which sometimes brought them
under the sheriff's hammer it is nevertheless true that their
owners were almost feudal lords, to whom their workmen and
their workmen's families looked for counsel and guidance in
all the affairs of life as well as for employment; whose word
was law; who often literally owned their black laborers, and
to whom white "redemptioners" were frequently bound for
a term of years to pay the cost of their passage across the
ocean; who cultivated farms as well as made iron; who
controlled the politics and largely maintained the churches
and schools of their several neighborhoods; who were cap-
tains and colonels of military organizations; whose wives and
daughters were grand ladies in the eyes of the simple people around them; whose dwellings were usually substantial
structures, which were well furnished for that day and ordered in a style of liberality and hospitality. The authority exercised by these old Pennsylvania ironmasters was indeed ba-
ronial, but it was also patriarchal. These pioneers were not
usually hard taskmasters; if they paid only low wages they
frequently made only small profits themselves; a tie of common interest, stronger than exists to-day under similar relations, bound master and workmen together. Whether the
workmen were their own masters or not they were virtually
fixtures of the furnace or the forge. The ladies of the "big
house" disdained not their poorer sisters, but were often their
teachers, often their nurses and physicians, and always knew

them by name and would recognize and greet them with politeness. If daily toil was the common heritage of the workmen and their families it may be said that their wants were few and their aspirations were humble. If there were bare floors in the little log houses there was food and there was warmth within their walls. The state of society here briefly described was not free from the dark spots which vice, selfishness, and ignorance give to society everywhere, but in the main it was kindly, satisfying, and uneventful. The years glided on with little change, and there was content on every hand. Those "good old colony times," when Pennsylvania was still a British province, and when George the Second or George the Third was king, are gone, and their mediæval flavor, their picturesqueness, and their placidity are also gone. The great State makes iron now in a different way.

CHAPTER XVII.

THE MANUFACTURE OF IRON IN PENNSYLVANIA AFTER THE REVOLUTION.

AFTER the Revolution the business of manufacturing iron received a fresh impulse in the eastern part of Pennsylvania and was further extended into the interior. Chester, Lancaster, and Berks counties shared conspicuously in the development at this period of the leading manufacturing industry of the State. Many blast furnaces and forges and a few rolling and slitting mills were built in these counties before 1800, and after the beginning of the present century this activity continued. A few of the earliest iron enterprises which were established after the Revolution in these and in other eastern and central counties will be mentioned, beginning with the extreme eastern parts of the State.

The first iron enterprises in the Lehigh valley, which is now one of the leading iron districts of the country, do not appear to have been undertaken until after the beginning of the present century. A bloomary at or near Jacobsburg, in Northampton county, is said to have been built in 1805. It was in operation as late as 1849. In 1808 William Henry, of Nazareth, built a bloomary in Bushkill township, Northampton county, about three miles north of Nazareth, which was started in 1809, making its first bar of iron on the 9th of March in that year. In 1824 Matthew S. Henry, a son of William Henry, built a furnace called Catharine, in Bushkill township, about half a mile from his father's bloomary. It made its first ton of pig iron on the 10th of May, 1825.

Hampton furnace, near Shimersville, in Lehigh county, was built in 1809 by David Heimbach and two partners named Wisselman and Cobelly. Mr. Heimbach soon purchased the interest of his partners and continued to operate the furnace until 1830, after which year it was owned and operated by various persons. It was in blast as late as 1857. In 1820 David Heimbach and his son David built Clarissa forge, on Aquashicola creek, in Carbon county. In 1827

David Heimbach the younger built Clarissa furnace at the same place, which he operated until his death in 1834. In 1837 the furnace and forge were both purchased by Joseph J. Albright, Samuel P. Templeton, and Jacob Rice, by whom their name was changed to the Ashland iron works. In 1841 the furnace and forge were both swept away by a freshet. The furnace was not rebuilt, but the forge was rebuilt, burned down, again rebuilt, and finally abandoned about 1860. On April 14, 1826, David Heimbach the elder purchased 129 acres of land on Pocopoco creek, near Weissport, in Carbon county, and on this tract he built in 1827 a furnace and forge, which he called New Hampton. The name of this furnace and forge was changed to Maria in 1836 by William Miller, who purchased them in that year. The furnace was finally blown out in 1859. All these were charcoal enterprises.

In 1826 Stephen Balliet and Samuel Helfrick built Lehigh furnace, on Trout creek, at the foot of the Kittatinny mountains, in Heidelberg (now Washington) township, in Lehigh county. It was a small furnace, 30 feet high and 7 feet wide at the boshes. The furnace was operated by this firm until the death of Mr. Helfrick in 1830. In 1832 Mr. Balliet became its sole owner. He continued to operate the furnace until his death in 1854. It has since been abandoned. In 1828 Mr. Balliet and Mr. Helfrick built Penn forge, in East Penn township, Carbon county, which was also jointly operated by them until the death of Mr. Helfrick, and subsequently by Mr. Balliet until his death. In 1837 Mr. Balliet built Penn furnace, near the forge. About 1858 this furnace was purchased by John Balliet, a son of Stephen Balliet, by whom it was owned and operated until 1886 when it was abandoned after the death of its owner in that year. It had long been called East Penn furnace. It was the last charcoal furnace in operation in the Lehigh valley.

In the collection of the foregoing details concerning the enterprises of the Heimbachs and Stephen Balliet and Samuel Helfrick we have had the assistance of Mr. Hungerford.

In 1836 a small rolling mill was built at South Easton, in Northampton county, by John Stewart and others. This was probably the first rolling mill in the Lehigh valley. John Stewart died at Easton on April 13, 1885, in his 89th year.

Two charcoal bloomaries were built in Carbon county after the beginning of the anthracite era—Anthony's, near Lehigh Gap, in 1843, and Pine Run, near Lehighton, in 1848. A bloomary forge called Analomink was built near Strouds-burg, in Monroe county, in 1829. In 1843 Day styled it a "large forge." All the forges and ore bloomaries in the Le-high valley have been abandoned. All the bloomaries, six in number, were supplied with ore from Northern New Jersey.

The Cheltenham rolling mill, on Tacony creek, in Mont-gomery county, one mile below Shoemakertown, was built in 1790, probably by James and Maxwell Rowland. In 1849 and subsequently it was operated by Rowland & Hunt, mak-ing boiler plates from blooms. It was abandoned in 1858. At first it was used to slit nail rods. The firm of Rowland & Hunt was composed of Mrs. Harriet M. Rowland, a widow, and Mr. Alfred Hunt, Mrs. Rowland owning the mill.

Alfred Hunt, who had been the president of the Bethle-hem Iron Company from its organization in 1860, died on March 27, 1888, at the residence of his brother, Mordecai Hunt, at Moorestown, New Jersey. Mr. Hunt was born of Quaker parentage, at Brownsville, Pa., on April 5, 1817. He was buried at Moorestown on March 31st.

In 1790 Benjamin Longstreth erected a rolling and slit-ting mill at Phœnixville in Chester county, where the found-ry now stands. This was the beginning of the present exten-sive works of the Phœnix Iron Company.

Clemens Rentgen, a native of the Palatinate, in Germany, emigrated in 1791 from the town of Zweibrücken, in Bava-ria, to Kimberton, in Chester county, about six miles from Phœnixville, where he purchased a forge on French creek. At Knauertown he unsuccessfully undertook to manufacture steel. His forge was continued, and to it he added a small rolling mill. His various enterprises were known as the Pikeland works, Pikeland being the name of the township in which they were situated.

On November 17, 1796, Mr. Rentgen obtained a patent for an invention for "forging bolts or round iron" by a machine which he described in the following words : "This machine consists of a strong platform, of a given size, in which are fixed two upright posts. In these posts is fixed an axle going through the handle of a concave hammer or sledge, at the extreme end of which is fixed a cog-wheel, whose cogs, operating on the lever or handle of the said concave hammer or sledge, cause it to operate upon a concave anvil upon which the iron to be wrought is placed. The concavity of this anvil is about one-eighth of the dimensions of that of the said hammer or sledge. This machine is set in motion by water or any other adequate power, by wheels operating upon the said cog-wheel."

On June 27, 1810, Mr. Rentgen obtained a patent for "rolling iron round, for ship bolts and other uses," by the following method: "This machine consists of two large iron rollers, fixed in a strong frame. Each roller has concavities turned in them, meeting each other to form perfect round holes, of from half inch to one and three-quarter inches or any other size in diameter, through which rollers the iron is drawn from the mouth of the furnace with great dispatch, and the iron is then manufactured better and more even than it is possible to forge it out. The force applied to the end of these rollers is like that applied to mills."

The original patents granted to Mr. Rentgen have been shown to us by his descendant, Mr. William H. Wahl, of Philadelphia. We learn from this gentleman that Mr. Rentgen made some use of his patent anvil and hammer, and that, before obtaining the patent in 1810 for his method of rolling round iron, he built an experimental set of rolls, which were replaced after the patent was granted by a permanent set, with which he rolled round iron as early as 1812 or 1813, some of which was for the Navy Department of the United States Government. We do not learn that he ever rolled bar iron, and it is not claimed that he used puddling furnaces. The fact that a patent was granted to him as late as June 27, 1810, for a machine to roll iron in round shapes would seem to furnish conclusive proof that Cort's rolls had not then been introduced into the United States.

In 1798 there were six furnaces and six forges in Berks county; in 1806 there were eight furnaces, twenty forges, and one slitting mill; and in 1830 there were eleven furnaces and twenty-four forges.

Schuylkill county has had many forges, the earliest of

which, near Port Clinton, appears to have been built in 1801. Before 1806 a small charcoal furnace was built by Reese & Thomas at Schuylkill Gap, near Pottsville. About that year it was purchased by John Pott, the founder of Pottsville, who tore it down and in 1807 erected Greenwood furnace and forge. In 1832 there were in operation in Schuylkill county Greenwood furnace and forge and Schuylkill, Brunswick, Pine Grove, Mahanoy, and Swatara forges. Swatara furnace, six miles from Pine Grove, and Stanhope furnace, still nearer to Pine Grove, were built between 1830 and 1840. About 1840 Jefferson furnace, at Schuylkill Haven, was built. All these early enterprises in Schuylkill county have been abandoned.

In 1805 there were seven forges and one slitting mill in Delaware county. Franklin rolling mill, at Chester, in this county, was built in 1808. In 1828 there were in Delaware county five rolling and slitting mills and several manufactories of finished iron products.

Federal slitting mill, on Buck run, about four miles south of Coatesville, in East Fallowfield township, Chester county, was built in 1795 by Isaac Pennock. The name of this mill was afterwards changed to Rokeby rolling mill. It was used to roll sheet iron and nail plates and to slit the latter into nail rods. It continued in operation until 1864, when it was burned down and abandoned. During the latter part of its history it rolled boiler plates. A paper mill now occupies its exact site. About 1810 Mr. Pennock built Brandywine rolling mill at Coatesville, which was purchased from him about 1816 by Dr. Charles Lukens, who had been employed at the Federal slitting mill. It is claimed that the first boiler plates made in the United States were rolled at this mill by Dr. Lukens. The puddling mill of the Lukens rolling mill at Coatesville now occupies the site of the Brandywine mill. In 1825, upon the death of Dr. Lukens, who had become the owner of the Brandywine mill, the management of the mill devolved upon his wife, Rebecca W. Lukens, by whom the business was greatly extended and profitably conducted for twenty years. After her death the name of the works was changed to Lukens rolling mill as a tribute to her memory.

Mount Hope furnace, located on Big Chiquisalunga creek, in Lancaster county, about ten miles south of Lebanon, was built in 1785 by Peter Grubb, Jr., and it is still owned by members of the Grubb family. Colebrook furnace, on the Conewago, in Lebanon county, seven miles southwest of Cornwall furnace, was built by Robert Coleman in 1791 and abandoned about 1860. Mount Vernon furnace, on the same stream, about twenty-three miles west of Lancaster, and in Lancaster county, was built in 1808 by Henry Bates Grubb. A second furnace of the same name was built near the first in 1831. Between the building of the first furnace and the second a forge was built. All have been abandoned. Conowingo furnace, on the creek of the same name, and about sixteen miles southeast of Lancaster, was built in 1809. About 1840 steam-power for driving the blast was successfully introduced by its owner, James M. Hopkins, the boilers being placed at the tunnel-head. Soon after the introduction of steam at Conowingo furnace it was successfully applied to Cornwall furnace by the manager, Samuel M. Reynolds.

In 1786 there were seventeen furnaces, forges, and slitting mills within a radius of thirty-nine miles of Lancaster. In 1838 there were 102 furnaces, forges, and rolling mills within a radius of fifty-two miles of Lancaster. At this time Lancaster was the great iron centre of Eastern Pennsylvania.

In 1805 there were two forges in York county, one of which was Spring forge and the other was Codorus forge. Castle Fin forge, at first called Palmyra forge, on Muddy creek, in York county, was built in 1810 by Joseph Webb and rebuilt in 1827 by Thomas Burd Coleman, who also added a blister steel furnace about 1832. Both have been abandoned. In its day Castle Fin forge was a very prominent enterprise. In 1850 there were five furnaces and three forges in this county. Since then its iron industry has sensibly declined.

Major Samuel M. Reynolds died in Philadelphia on May 29, 1888. He was born at Lancaster on April 17, 1814. His younger brothers were Admiral William Reynolds, of the United States navy; General John F. Reynolds, who fell at Gettysburg on July 1, 1863; and General James L. Reynolds, a lawyer of Lancaster. Samuel M. Reynolds was for many years manager of Castle Fin forge and farm, was also for several years manager of Cornwall furnace, and was at one time part owner of a charcoal furnace in Clarion county.

He was a paymaster in the United States army during the Rebellion. He was buried at Lancaster.

In 1826 Maria furnace was built in Hamiltonban township, Adams county, by James D. Paxton & Co., the firm consisting of James D. Paxton, Thaddeus Stevens, (the "great commoner,") John B. McPherson, and Thomas C. Miller. In 1828 the last two members of the firm retired. Hon. Edward McPherson, of Gettysburg, writes us as follows concerning this furnace, which continued to be operated by the remaining members of the original firm: "The Maria furnace was worked, in all, about twelve years—from 1826 to 1838. The first effort was to make stoves; but the ores produced plates which were so often brittle that the business proved precarious and unremunerative. The new owners, in an effort to make other use of the Maria furnace iron, bought in 1830 the Caledonia property near Fayetteville, and built a forge. They ran this till 1833, when it was burned on the night of the 'falling stars.' They promptly rebuilt the forge, and in 1837 built the furnace at Caledonia, in evident preparation for the abandonment of the original works in Adams county, which took place in 1838. This transfer was from an inferior ore bank to a very superior ore bank, but in neither place was money made in amounts worth considering." Chestnut Grove furnace, at Idaville, in Adams county, was built in 1830 and is still active.

The first furnace in Franklin county was Mount Pleasant, in Path valley, about three miles north of Loudon, which was built in 1783 by three brothers, William, Benjamin, and George Chambers. A forge was also erected by them about the same time. The furnace was abandoned in 1834 and the forge in 1843. A furnace called Richmond, built in 1865, now occupies the site of Mount Pleasant furnace. Soundwell forge, on Conodoguinet creek, at Roxbury, sixteen miles north of Chambersburg, was built in 1798 by Leephar, Crotzer & Co., and was active as late as 1857. Roxbury furnace, at or near the same place, was built in 1815 by Samuel Cole, and is now abandoned. Carrick forge, four miles from Fannettsburg, was built in 1800, and was in operation as late as 1856. Carrick furnace, which has been idle since 1884, was built in 1828 by General Samuel Dunn and Thomas G.

McCulloh. Loudon furnace and forge were built about 1790 by Colonel James Chambers and abandoned about 1840. Valley forge, near Loudon, in this county, was built in 1804. A furnace of the same name was built near the forge at a later day. Both have been abandoned. Mont Alto furnace, in the same county, was built in 1807 by Daniel and Samuel Hughes and is still active. Two forges of the same name, about four miles from the furnace, were built in 1809 and 1810, and were abandoned in 1866. A foundry was built in 1815, a rolling mill in 1832, and a nail factory in 1835. In 1850 the nail factory was burned down, and in 1867 the rolling mill was abandoned. The foundry and a new steam forge close to the furnace are still active.

Caledonia forge, in Franklin county, on Conococheague creek, ten miles southeast of Chambersburg, built in 1830 by Stevens & Paxton, and Caledonia furnace, at the same place, built in 1837 by the same firm, have already been noticed in connection with Adams county. For many years before 1863 this furnace and forge were owned by Thaddeus Stevens, in which year they were burned by the Confederates under General Lee when on their march to Gettysburg. Franklin furnace, in St. Thomas township, was built by Peter and George Housum in 1828, was still running with charcoal in 1882, and has since been idle. There were a few other pioneer charcoal furnaces and forges in this county. Early in the present century nails and edge tools were made in large quantities at several establishments at Chambersburg and in its vicinity. One of these, the Conococheague rolling mill and nail factory, was built by Brown & Watson in 1814. Two furnaces called Southampton, not far from Shippensburg, but in Franklin county, were built about 1830 and torn down in 1854. A forge near them was torn down in 1849.

Liberty forge, at Lisburn, on Yellow Breeches creek, in Cumberland county, was built in 1790 and abandoned in 1888. An older forge, long abandoned, is said to have been built at Lisburn in 1783. A few other forges in this county were built prior to 1800. Cumberland furnace, ten miles southwest of Carlisle, on Yellow Breeches creek, is said to have been built in 1794 by Michael Ege. It blew out permanently in 1854. Two furnaces, now abandoned, once stood near Shippensburg—Augusta, built in 1824, and Mary Ann, built in 1826. Big Pond furnace, built in 1836, between Augusta and Mary Ann furnaces, was burned down in 1880.

About 1806 Jacob M. Haldeman removed from Lancaster county to New Cumberland, at the mouth of Yellow Breeches creek, on the Susquehanna. He purchased a forge at this place and added a rolling and slitting mill, which were operated until about 1826, when they were abandoned. Fairview rolling mill, about a mile from the mouth of Conodoguinet creek, in Cumberland county, and two miles above Harrisburg, was built in 1833 by Gabriel Heister and Norman Callender, of Harrisburg, to roll bar iron. Jared Pratt, of Massachusetts, leased it in 1836 and added a nail factory.

The Haldeman family has been prominent in the manufacture of iron in Pennsylvania during the whole of the present century. A sketch of the family is herewith given.

Jacob Haldeman, the grandfather of Jacob M. Haldeman, was born October 7, 1722, in the canton of Neufchatel, Switzerland, and died December 31, 1784, in Rapho township, Lancaster county, Pennsylvania. He was a member of the Committee of Public Safety at the breaking out of the Revolution. John Haldeman, son of Jacob, was born in 1753, and married Maria Breneman, and they became the parents of Jacob M. Haldeman, who was born in Manheim township, Lancaster county, on March 4, 1781. John Haldeman was one of the boldest and most successful business men in the State. About 1806, assisted by his father to the extent of some $30,000, Jacob M. purchased the water power and forge at the mouth of Yellow Breeches creek, Cumberland county, and established himself in the iron business. In six years he had paid back the $30,000 borrowed from his father. In 1810 he married Elizabeth E. Jacobs, who was born at Mount Hope furnace, Lancaster county, on June 13, 1789. In 1830 he removed to Harrisburg, where he died on December 15, 1857, aged 76 years, 9 months, and 11 days. His wife died at the same place on March 18, 1884, aged 94 years, 9 months, and 5 days.

In 1836 Mr. Haldeman owned one-third of the Mary Ann and Augusta furnaces, near Carlisle, the Carlisle bank owning the other two-thirds. He was one of the incorporators of the Chestnut Hill Iron Ore Company, of Columbia, in 1851. Mr. Haldeman's son, Jacob S., was United States Minister to Sweden in 1862, and another son, Richard, who married a daughter of General Simon Cameron, was for several years a member of Congress.

Jacob M. Haldeman's younger brother, Henry, built in 1846, for his sons, the late Dr. E. Haldeman and Professor S. S. Haldeman, a blast furnace at Chickies, to use anthracite coal, now known as " Chickies No. 1," and operated by the Chickies Iron Company. But little of the original structure now remains. Paris Haldeman, president of the Chickies Iron Company, is the youngest son of Henry Haldeman.

Michael Ege, a brother of George Ege, already mentioned, was for many years the most prominent ironmaster in the
Cumberland valley, owning, a short time before his death,
Pine Grove furnace, the Carlisle iron works, Holly furnace,
and Cumberland furnace. He died on August 31, 1815.

In 1840 there were eight furnaces and eleven forges
and rolling mills in Franklin county, and six furnaces and
five forges and rolling mills in Cumberland county.

In 1785 Henry Fulton established a "nailery" in Dauphin county, probably at Harrisburg. It is said to have been
"only a little remote from a smithy." In 1805 there were two
furnaces and two forges in this county. Oakdale forge, at
Elizabethville, appears to have been built in 1830. Victoria
furnace, on Clark's creek, was probably built in that year. In
1832 there were three forges and two furnaces in the county.
Emeline furnace, at Dauphin, was built about 1835. The
first furnace at Middletown in this county was built in 1833,
and the second furnace was built in 1849—both charcoal furnaces. Manada furnace, at West Hanover, was built in 1837
by E. B. & C. B. Grubb. The first rolling mill in the county
was the Harrisburg rolling mill, at Harrisburg, built in 1836.
The Pennsylvania steel works were commenced in 1865.

The manufacture of iron had a very early beginning in
the Susquehanna valley north of Harrisburg. About 1778 a
bloomary forge was built on Nanticoke creek, near the lower end of Wyoming valley, in Luzerne county, by John and
Mason F. Alden. Another bloomary forge was built in 1789
on the Lackawanna river, about two miles above its mouth,
by Dr. William Hooker Smith and James Sutton. Still another bloomary forge was built in 1799 or 1800, on Roaring
brook, at Scranton, then known as Slocum's Hollow, by two
brothers, Ebenezer and Benjamin Slocum. All these bloomaries continued in operation until about 1828. Their products were taken down the Susquehanna in Durham boats.

Lackawanna county owes its present prominence in the
iron industry mainly to the courage, energy, and business
sagacity of two brothers, George W. and Selden T. Scranton,
and their cousin, Joseph H. Scranton, the two brothers commencing operations in 1840 at Scranton and their cousin
joining them soon afterwards, their various enterprises cul-

minating in the organization of the Lackawanna Iron and Coal Company. The Lackawanna steel works, at Scranton, were completed in 1875, and the Scranton steel works went into operation in 1883.

Esther furnace, about three miles south of Catawissa, on East Roaring creek, in Columbia county, was built in 1802 by Michael Bitter & Son, who " cast many stoves." In 1836 it was rebuilt by Trago & Thomas. In 1811 Francis McShane established a small cut-nail factory at Wilkesbarre " and used anthracite coal in smelting the iron." Catawissa furnace, near Mainville, in Columbia county, was built in 1815, and in 1824 a forge was built near the same place. The furnace has long been abandoned, and the forge, called Mainville forge, which has in late years been employed in producing blooms for boiler plates, has also been abandoned.

A furnace was built in Lycoming county in 1820, four miles from Jersey Shore, and named Pine Creek furnace. In 1832 it was owned by Kirk, Kelton & Co. A forge was added to this furnace in 1831. Heshbon forge, on Lycoming creek, five miles above its mouth, was built in 1828 and was soon followed by other iron enterprises on the same stream. Washington furnace, at Lamar, on Fishing creek, in Clinton county, was built in 1810 by John Dunlop, who added a forge in 1812. He was killed in a mine in 1815. In 1812 Nathan Harvey built a forge at Mill Hall, in Clinton county, to which a furnace was afterwards added. A furnace at Farrandsville, near the mouth of Lick run, in this county, which was built about 1834 to use coke, is said to have sunk, in connection with a nail mill, foundry, and other enterprises, over half a million dollars contributed by Boston capitalists. The furnace was abandoned a few years after its erection.

In 1814 Peter Karthaus, a native of Hamburg, in Germany, but afterwards a merchant of Baltimore, and Rev. Frederick W. Geissenhainer, a native of Mühlberg, in Saxony, built a blast furnace at the mouth of the Little Moshannon, or Mosquito creek, in the lower end of Clearfield county. The firm of Karthaus & Geissenhainer was dissolved on December 18, 1818. It had been organized in 1811 partly to mine and ship to eastern markets the bituminous coal of Clearfield county. The furnace was operated with partial success with charcoal for several years. We shall refer to Dr. Geissenhainer in a subsequent chapter.

The foregoing summary of early iron enterprises in the Susquehanna valley could be very much extended by including other charcoal furnaces and forges and several rolling mills which were erected about 1820 and subsequently in the counties of Lackawanna, Luzerne, Columbia, Montour, Northumberland, Union, Snyder, Lycoming, and Clinton, most of which have been abandoned, but this is not necessary. Our object in this chapter has been simply to preserve the names, location, and date of erection of the earliest charcoal iron enterprises which were established in Eastern and Central Pennsylvania outside of the Juniata valley after the Revolution. Juniata valley will occupy the next chapter.

We may properly close this chapter by giving some information concerning the primitive method of transporting iron and other articles by pack-horses from Cumberland and Franklin counties to the headwaters of the Ohio river at the close of the last century and after the beginning of the present century, when wagon roads were rare in Central and Western Pennsylvania. The following account is taken from I. D. Rupp's *History of Cumberland County*, published in 1848.

Sixty or seventy years ago 500 pack-horses had been at one time in Carlisle, going thence to Shippensburg, Fort Loudon, and further westward, loaded with merchandise, also salt, iron, etc. The pack-horses used to carry bars of iron on their backs, crooked over and around their bodies; barrels or kegs were hung on each side of these. Colonel Snyder, of Chambersburg, in a conversation with the writer in August, 1845, said that he cleared many a day from $6 to $8 in crooking or bending iron and shoeing horses for Western carriers at the time he was carrying on a blacksmith shop in the town of Chambersburg. The pack-horses were generally led in divisions of 12 or 15 horses, carrying about two hundred-weight each, all going single file and being managed by two men, one going before as the leader and the other at the tail to see after the safety of the packs. Where the bridle road passed along declivities or over hills the path was in some places washed out so deep that the packs or burdens came in contact with the ground or other impeding obstacles, and were frequently displaced. However, as the carriers usually traveled in companies, the packs were soon adjusted and no great delay occasioned. The pack-horses were generally furnished with bells, which were kept from ringing during the day drive, but were let loose at night when the horses were set free and permitted to feed and browse. The bells were intended as guides to direct their whereabouts in the morning. When wagons were first introduced the carriers considered that mode of transportation an invasion of their rights.

Day, in his *Historical Collections*, says that "Mercersburg, in Franklin county, was in early days an important point for trade with Indians and settlers on the Western frontier. It was no uncommon event to see there 50 or 100 pack-horses in a row, taking on their loads of salt, iron, and other commodities for the Monongahela country." In 1789 the crank for the first saw-mill built in Ohio was carried by pack-horses over the mountains to the Yoùghiogheny river, and thence sent by water to its destination on Wolf creek, sixteen miles from Marietta. It weighed 180 pounds, and was made in New Haven, Connecticut, for the New England Ohio Company.

CHAPTER XVIII.

THE MANUFACTURE OF CHARCOAL IRON IN THE JUNIATA VALLEY.

As EARLY as 1767 a company called The Juniata Iron Company was organized, doubtless by capitalists of Eastern Pennsylvania, to search for iron ore in the Juniata valley, and probably with the ulterior object of manufacturing iron. Joseph Jacobs was the promoter and head of the company. It was in existence from 1767 to 1771, during which time its agent, Benjamin Jacobs, made for it some surveys and explorations and dug a few tons of iron ore, but where these operations were conducted and who were the members of this pioneer company some future antiquarian must discover.

The first iron enterprise in the Juniata valley was Bedford furnace, on Black Log creek, below its junction with Shade creek, at Orbisonia, in Huntingdon county, which was soon followed by Bedford forge, on Little Aughwick creek, four miles southwest of the furnace. The furnace and forge derived their name from Bedford county, which then embraced Huntingdon county, the latter county not having been organized until 1787. George Ashman was the leading spirit in originating and promoting these enterprises. He was a large owner of land at Orbisonia in 1780, and at this time or soon afterwards he became interested in the iron-ore deposits which had been discovered on his property. On November 8 and 9, 1786, he entered into an agreement with Charles Ridgely, Thomas Cromwell, and Tempest Tucker, all apparently of Washington county, Maryland, for the sale to them of "three-fourths of two tracts of land, called Bedford and Black Log tracts," upon which a saw mill and grist mill had been built, retaining the other fourth himself, upon which tracts it was agreed that "an iron works" should be built. The erection of a furnace appears to have been immediately undertaken. Mr. Tucker died in 1788, and was the first man buried at Orbisonia. The company thereafter consisted of Edward Ridgely, (son of Charles Ridgely,) Thomas Cromwell, and George

Ashman. The furnace was probably completed in 1788. It was certainly in operation before 1790, as on the 2d day of March of that year Hugh Needy entered into an agreement with the company to deliver twenty-eight ten-gallon kettles and seven Dutch ovens, the whole weighing 12 cwt., 3 qrs., and 21 lbs., to Daniel Depue, " on or near the Monongahela river, near Devor's Ferry, in eight days ensuing the date hereof." These articles were carried on pack-horses. The forge appears to have been built in 1791, as is shown by an itemized statement of iron made by the company from " the time the forge started" in that year until October 12, 1796, the product in these six years being 497 tons, 8 cwt., 2 qrs., and 26 lbs.

For the foregoing details we are indebted to C. R. McCarthy, Esq., of Saltillo, Huntingdon county. The following additional details are gathered from other sources. The furnace was of small capacity and constructed partly of wood. When it was not engaged in producing castings it made from eight to ten tons of pig iron weekly. The forge made horseshoe iron, wagon tire, harrow teeth, etc. Stoves as well as other articles were cast at the furnace. At the Philadelphia Exhibition of 1876 a stove-plate cast at this furnace in 1792 was exhibited. Bar iron made at the forge was bent into the shape of the letter U, turned over the backs of horses, and in this manner taken by bridle-paths to Pittsburgh. Bar iron and castings from Bedford furnace and forge, and from later iron works in the Juniata valley, were also taken down the Juniata river in arks, many of which descended to Middletown on the Susquehanna, whence the iron was hauled to Philadelphia or sent in arks down the Susquehanna to Baltimore.

Bedford furnace and forge were abandoned early in the present century. Three other charcoal furnaces, all now abandoned, have since been built on or near its site. One of these was Rockhill furnace, on Black Log creek, three-quarters of a mile southeast of Orbisonia, built in 1830. It was in operation in 1872, but in the following year it gave place to two coke furnaces built by the Rockhill Iron and Coal Company.

Centre furnace, on Spring creek, in Centre county, was the

second furnace in the Juniata valley. It was built in the summer of 1791 by Colonel John Patton and Colonel Samuel Miles, both Revolutionary officers. The first forge in Centre county was Rock forge, on Spring creek, built in 1793 by General Philip Benner. A rolling and slitting mill, nail factory, another forge, etc., were soon added. General Benner had made iron at old Coventry forge after the Revolution. He died at Rock on July 27, 1832, aged 70 years. In 1852 the extensive works which he had established were abandoned. In 1795 Daniel Turner built Spring Creek forge, and Miles, Harris & Miles built Harmony forge, also on Spring creek. In 1798 John Dunlop built Bellefonte forge, which was recently operated by Valentines & Co., and in 1802 he built Logan furnace, three miles south of Bellefonte. In 1824 Valentines & Thomas added a rolling mill to the Bellefonte forge. Tussey furnace, in Ferguson township, was built in 1810 by General William Patton, son of Colonel Patton. In 1810 Roland Curtin, a native of Ireland, and father of Governor Andrew G. Curtin, in company with Moses Boggs erected Eagle forge, on Bald Eagle creek, about five miles from Bellefonte, Boggs remaining a partner only a short time. In 1818 he built Eagle furnace near Eagle forge. In 1830 a small rolling mill was added, for the manufacture of bar iron and nails, and about the same year he built Martha furnace, on Bald Eagle creek, which has long been abandoned. His other works are still in operation and are owned by his children and grandchildren. He died in 1850, aged 86 years. In 1817 Hardman Philips, an enterprising Englishman, erected a forge and screw factory at Philipsburg, the latter being one of the first of its kind in this country. Cold Stream forge, in Rush township ; Hecla furnace, near Hublersburg ; Hannah furnace, about ten miles northeast of Tyrone ; and Julian furnace, on Bald Eagle creek, all in Centre county, were built between 1825 and 1840. In 1829 and 1833 two furnaces were built at Howard by Harris, Thomas & Co., to which a rolling mill was added in 1840. These works have been owned and operated by Bernard Lauth, together with a forge which was built in 1879, but they are now operated by a new company. Both furnaces have been abandoned.

Barree forge, on the Juniata, in Huntingdon county, was

built about.1794 by Bartholomew & Dorsey, to convert the pig iron of Centre furnace into bar iron. Huntingdon furnace, on Warrior's Mark run, in Franklin township, was built in 1796, but after one or two blasts it was removed a mile lower down the stream. The furnace was built for Mordecai Massey and Judge John Gloninger by George Anshutz, who in 1808 became the owner of one-fourth of the property. At the same time George Shoenberger bought a one-fourth interest. Before 1808 Martin Dubbs had become a part owner. A forge called Massey, on Spruce creek, connected with Huntingdon furnace, was built about 1800. The furnace has been silent since 1870. Tyrone forges, on the Juniata, were built by the owners of Huntingdon furnace, the first of the forges in 1804. Gordon, in 1832, in his *Gazetteer of the State of Pennsylvania*, stated that these forges, with a rolling and slitting mill and nail factory attached, formed "a very extensive establishment," owned by Messrs. Gloninger, Anshutz & Co. "The mill rolls about 150 tons, 75 of which are cut into nails at the works, 50 tons are slit into rods and sent to the West, and about 25 tons are sold in the adjoining counties."

Juniata forge, at Petersburg, was built about 1804 by Samuel Fahnestock and George Shoenberger, the latter becoming sole owner in 1805. George Shoenberger was born in Lancaster county, and during the closing years of the last century settled on Shaver's creek, in Huntingdon county, as did also his brother Peter. The town of Petersburg was laid out in 1795 by Peter Shoenberger. In 1800 Peter sold to his brother George the Petersburg tract of land. George Shoenberger died in 1814 or 1815. His only son, Dr. Peter Shoenberger, succeeded to the ownership of his iron enterprises.

Coleraine forges, on Spruce creek, were built in 1805 and 1809 by Samuel Marshall. There have been many forges on this creek, none of which are now in operation. Union furnace, in Morris township, and Pennsylvania furnace, on the line dividing Huntingdon from Centre county, were built soon after 1810 ; the latter was in operation as late as 1888, using coke. About 1818 Reuben Trexler, of Berks county, built a bloomary called Mary Ann, in Trough Creek valley, and about 1821 he added Paradise furnace. In 1832 John

Savage, of Philadelphia, built a forge near Paradise furnace, which is said to have been the first forge in this country "that used the big hammer and iron helve on the English plan." There were many other early furnaces and forges in Huntingdon county, but the earliest have been mentioned.

Etna furnace and forge, on the Juniata, in Catharine township, Blair county, were built in 1805 by Canan, Stewart & Moore. The furnace was the first in Blair county. Cove forge, on the Frankstown branch of the Juniata, was built between 1808 and 1810 by John Royer, who died at Johnstown in 1850, aged about 71 years. Allegheny furnace was built in 1811 by Allison & Henderson, and was the second furnace in Blair county. In 1835 it was purchased by Elias Baker and Roland Diller, both of Lancaster county. The next furnace in Blair county was Springfield, built in 1815 by John Royer and his brother Daniel. Springfield furnace and Cove forge were for many years owned and operated by John Royer, son of Daniel, but are now idle, the furnace having been last in blast in 1885. John Royer was born in Franklin county, Pennsylvania, and died at Cove forge on November 21, 1885, aged 88 years. The next furnace in this county was Rebecca, built in 1817. It was the first furnace erected by Dr. Peter Shoenberger, who afterwards became the most prominent ironmaster in Pennsylvania. The doctor was born at Manheim, Lancaster county, in 1781; died at Marietta, Lancaster county, on June 18, 1854, aged 73 years; and was buried in Laurel Hill cemetery, Philadelphia.

Elizabeth furnace, near Antestown, in Blair county, is said to have been the first furnace in the country to use gas from the tunnel-head for the production of steam. The furnace was built in 1832, and the improvement was patented about 1840 by Martin Bell, the owner of the furnace.

A furnace and forge were built at Hopewell, in Bedford county, about the year 1800, by William Lane, of Lancaster county. On Yellow creek, two miles from Hopewell, he built Lemnos forge and slitting mill in 1806, which were in operation as late as 1833. In 1841 Loy & Patterson built Lemnos furnace, on the same creek, two miles west of Hopewell. Bedford forge, on Yellow creek, was built by Swope & King in 1812. Elizabeth furnace was built at Woodbury, in Bedford county, in 1827, by King, Swope & Co. In 1845 it was removed to Bloomfield, Blair county, but it is now abandoned. In 1840 Bedford county, which then embraced Fulton county and a part of Blair county, contained nine furnaces and two forges. Hanover furnace and forge, nine miles below McConnellsburg, in Fulton county, were known as the Hanover iron works. The forge was built in 1822 by John Doyle and the furnace in 1827 by John Irvine. Both were abandoned about 1850. There are now no iron·enterprises in Fulton county.

The account books of the Hanover iron works from 1831 to 1833 have recently been discovered. Among the frequent charges in them against the workmen is whisky, in quantities of from one to five gallons, at 33⅓ cents per gallon. Flour is charged at $3.50 per barrel, and boarding at $1.40 per week ; James Downs is charged with $6, "paid him to git married."

Many other charcoal furnaces and forges and a few rolling mills were built in the upper part of the Juniata valley before 1850. In 1832 there were in operation in Huntingdon county, which then embraced a part of Blair county, eight furnaces, ten forges, and one rolling and slitting mill. Each of the furnaces yielded from 1,200 to 1,600 tons of pig iron annually. In the same year an imperfect list enumerated eight furnaces and as many forges in Centre county. In 1850 there were in Huntingdon, Centre, Mifflin, and Blair counties (the last formed out of Huntingdon and Bedford in 1846) forty-eight furnaces, forty-two forges, and eight rolling mills, nearly all of which were in Huntingdon and Centre counties. Most of these enterprises have been abandoned.

Mr. Hungerford advises us that the earliest information obtainable of the erection of any iron works in Mifflin county is found in the court records of that county for August, 1795. At a court held in that month a petition was presented asking for a road "from Freedom forge, thence the nearest and best way to the river Juniata near to, or at, McClelland's landing." The forge stood on the present site of the Logan iron and steel works, at Logan, on Kishacoquillas creek. The landing mentioned was at the mouth of the creek, now within the limits of the borough of Lewistown.

The forge was erected by William Brown and William Maclay. It was sold in 1812 to Miller, Martin & Co., who began the erection of a furnace in that year. On November 12, 1812, they advertised in the *Juniata Gazette* for workmen, " as they are engaged in building a furnace at Freedom forge." This furnace stood where the present Emma furnace was built at Logan in 1867, and the power was obtained from Hungry run, which enters Kishacoquillas creek at that place. Miller, Martin & Co. had many successors. The forge built in 1795 was continued until 1878, when it was torn down by the Logan Iron and Steel Company. The first furnace was torn down about 1820, and upon its site was erected a new furnace, which was abandoned about 1830. In 1847 the forge property, consisting of 40,000 acres of land, was sold to the Freedom Iron Company. It is now owned by the Logan Iron and Steel Company. The Standard steel works are also located at this place. In 1832 there were three furnaces and one forge in Mifflin county, and in 1850 there were five furnaces and two forges.

In June, 1797, General William Lewis, of Berks county, began the purchase of lands on Brightsfield run and the Juniata river, in Mifflin county, intending to build a furnace. In a mortgage dated June 2, 1798, the furnace tract and ore-bank lot are mentioned. In the assessment of 1798 William Lewis is assessed on 430 acres of land and a furnace and as an ironmaster. The furnace was operated by James Blaine, of Cumberland county, a son-in-law, and was known as Hope furnace. In 1804 General Lewis built Mount Vernon forge on Cocalamus creek, below Millerstown, in Perry county, which was operated with the furnace. The forge appears to have been abandoned in 1817. In that year the furnace was operated by Blaine, Walker & Co., who continued in business for several years. It was subsequently operated by various owners until 1860, when it was abandoned.

There was a very early forge in Juniata county. It was built in 1791 on Licking creek, two miles west of Mifflintown, by Thomas Beale and William Sterrett. It had two hammers and was in operation about four years. The pig iron for this forge was obtained mainly from Centre furnace, but some was brought from Bedford furnace.

Juniata furnace, three miles from Newport, was built in 1808 by David Watts, of Carlisle. In 1832 it was owned by Captain William Power. A forge called Fio was built on Sherman's creek, about four miles from Duncannon, in 1829, by Lindley & Speek. A forge was also built at Duncannon in the same year by Stephen Duncan and John D. Mahon. Duncannon rolling mill was built in 1838 by Fisher, Morgan & Co. Montebello furnace, at Duncannon; Oak Grove, four miles from Landisburg; Caroline, at Baileysburg; and Perry, four miles from Bloomfield, all in Perry county, were built between 1830 and 1840. All of the charcoal iron enterprises in Perry county have been abandoned.

Steel (doubtless blister steel) was made at Caledonia, near Bedford, for several years before the beginning of this century by William McDermett, who was born near Glasgow, in Scotland, and came to this country at the close of the Revolutionary war. Mr. McDermett's works continued in successful operation for about ten years, when financial reverses caused their abandonment. A few years later he removed to Spruce creek, in Huntingdon county, and there ended his days about 1819. Josephine, one of his daughters, married in 1820 David R. Porter, then a young ironmaster on Spruce creek but afterwards Governor of Pennsylvania. About 1818 David R. Porter and Edward B. Patton built Sligo forge, on Spruce creek. After Mr. McDermett's removal to Spruce creek a forge and steel works, called Claubaugh, were built on the creek by his nephew, Thomas McDermett, at which steel was made by the method that had been in use at Caledonia. These works became the property of Lloyd, Steel & Co. about 1819, by whom they were abandoned in a few years.

Among the persons who have been prominent in the manufacture of iron in the Juniata valley special reference may be made, in addition to those already mentioned, to Henry S. Spang, John Lyon, Anthony Shorb, Andrew Gregg, George Schmucker, and General James Irvin.

Much of the iron made in the Juniata valley during the palmy days of its iron industry was sold at Pittsburgh, first in the form of castings, afterwards in both pigs and bars, and finally chiefly in the form of blooms. Before the completion of the Pennsylvania Canal and the Portage Railroad it was transported with great difficulty. Bar iron from Centre county was at first carried on the backs of horses to the Clarion river, and was then floated on boats and arks to Pittsburgh. Pig and bar iron from Huntingdon county were hauled over the Frankstown road to Johnstown, and thence floated to Pittsburgh by way of the Conemaugh river. Subsequently blooms were sent to Pittsburgh from Huntingdon county by wagon. "Juniata iron" was also largely sold in Eastern markets, the Juniata and Susquehanna rivers furnishing an outlet before the building of the Pennsylvania Canal. It was noted throughout the country for its excellence.

We are indebted to Isaac Craig, Esq., of Allegheny City, for a copy of the following advertisement, which appeared in a Pittsburgh newspaper in 1813. The advertiser was then operating the first rolling mill built at Pittsburgh.

WAGGONS WANTED.—The subscriber wishes to employ from 30 to 50 waggons, for three or four trips to the ironworks near Belfont, Centre county; and would be anxious to engage 20 or 30 out of the above number to haul by the year. A very considerable advance will be made on the former rate of carriage. This added to the low price of feed this season holds out greater inducements to embark in this business than at any former period. Applications to me here; on which I will give my orders, and will engage to pay for any delay which may arise to the waggoners at the different forges.   C. COWAN. September 9, 1813.

In 1828, before the Pennsylvania Canal was completed, the hauling of blooms by wagon was still an important business. In the Blairsville *Record* for January 31, 1828, Mulhollan & McAnulty advertise for teams to haul blooms from Sligo iron works, in Huntingdon county, to Blairsville, offering $15 per ton. After the canal was finished the shipment of Juniata blooms to Pittsburgh greatly increased.

SINCE the preceding chapters were printed we have obtained additional information from Mr. George R. Prowell concerning William Bennett's iron enterprise in Hellam township, York county, mentioned on page 184. Mr. Bennett built a furnace as well as a forge on Codorus creek about 1765. The furnace was in operation during the Revolution, as is proved by official documents which are still preserved at York. Iron ore was probably obtained on the opposite side of the Susquehanna river.

CHAPTER XIX.

THE EARLY MANUFACTURE OF IRON IN WESTERN PENNSYLVANIA.

THE earliest mention we have found of the existence of iron ore in Western Pennsylvania occurs in the careful investigations of Mr. Austin N. Hungerford into the early history of Fayette county. We quote from him the following interesting particulars. It will be seen that the facts cited antedate the final settlement, on September 23, 1780, of the boundary dispute between Pennsylvania and Virginia.

There is a tradition that the first discovery of iron ore west of the Allegheny mountains was made by John Hayden in the winter of 1789–90. This statement has been so often made in the writings of Judge Veech and others without contradiction that it has come to be almost universally regarded as entirely authentic. That such is not the case, however, and that iron ore was known to exist in the valley of the Youghiogheny at least nine years before the alleged first discovery by Hayden, is proved by an entry found in the First Survey Book of Yohogania county, Va., and made a century ago by Col. William Crawford, then surveyor of the said county. The following is a copy of the entry:

"July 11, 1780. No. 32.—State Warrant.—Benjamin Johnston produced a State Warrant from the Land Office for five hundred acres of land, dated the 12th day of May, 1780—No. 4926. Sixty acres thereof he locates on a big spring in the Allegany and Laurel Hills, on the waters of the Monongalia—and one hundred and fifty acres of s^d Warrant he locates on lands of s^d Hills, where an old deadening and Sugar Camp was made by Mr. Chr. Harrison, situate on the waters of Yohogania, to include a Bank of Iron Ore."

Yohogania county, as established by the Virginia Legislature in 1776, included all the northern and northeastern part of the present county of Fayette. The Survey Book referred to is still in existence in a good state of preservation, and in possession of Boyd Crumrine, Esq., of Washington, Pa.

The precise location of the tract referred to as including the ore bank is not known, nor is it material. The quotation is given above merely to disprove the long-accepted statement that the existence of iron ore west of the Alleghenies was unknown prior to 1789.

The Hon. James Veech, to whom reference is above made, published in the Pittsburgh *Commercial*, on March 29, 1871, an account of the discovery of "blue lump" iron ore by John Hayden, of Haydentown, in Fayette county, in 1790, from which he made in a smith's fire a piece of iron "about as big as a harrow-tooth." Taking the sample on horseback to Philadelphia he enlisted his relative, John Nicholson, of that city, then State Comptroller, in a scheme for building a furnace and forge at Haydentown, on George's creek, about seven miles south of Uniontown. Mr. Hungerford says that a bloomary was built by this firm in 1792 but that it never built a furnace. Before the bloomary was built William Turnbull and Peter Marmie, with Colonel John Holker as a silent partner, all of Philadelphia, built a furnace and a forge on Jacob's creek, a mile or two above its entrance into the Youghiogheny river. The court records of Fayette county mention " the furnace on Jacob's creek " in June, 1789, but it had not then been put in blast. It was first blown in on November 1, 1790, and the iron was tried the same day in the forge. The furnace and forge were on the Fayette county side of the creek, and were called the Alliance iron works. The furnace was fitfully operated until 1802, when it finally went out of blast. The stack is still standing but in ruins. This was the first furnace west of the Allegheny mountains. An extract from a letter written by Major Isaac Craig, deputy quartermaster-general and military storekeeper at Fort Pitt, to General Knox, dated January 12, 1792, says: "As there is no six-pound shot here I have taken the liberty to engage four hundred at Turnbull & Marmie's furnace, which is now in blast." This shot was required for General Wayne's expedition against the Indians in 1792.

Union furnace, on Dunbar creek, four miles south of Connellsville, was built by Isaac Meason in 1790 and was put in blast in March, 1791. It was succeeded in 1793 by a larger furnace of the same name, built near the same site by Isaac Meason, John Gibson, and Moses Dillon. An advertisement in the Pittsburgh *Gazette*, dated April 10, 1794, mentions that Meason, Dillon & Co. have for sale " a supply of well-assorted castings, which they will sell for cash at the reduced price of £35 per ton ($93.33)." There was a forge connected with this furnace, called Union forge. Afterwards another forge was built by Mr. Meason at the mouth of Dunbar creek. Another of Mr. Meason's enterprises was Mount Vernon furnace, on Mountz's creek, eight miles east of its mouth, built before July, 1800, and possibly as early as 1795.

It was rebuilt in 1801. It is still standing, but has long been abandoned. Dunbar furnace now stands near the site of the original Union furnace.

Spring Hill furnace, on Ruble's run, in Fayette county, within three miles of Cheat river, in West Virginia, and near its junction with the Monongahela, was built in 1794 by two Welshmen, Benjamin and Robert Jones. This furnace was in operation until 1881, but in 1883 it was dismantled. About 1797 Old Laurel furnace, on Laurel run, in Dunbar township, was built by Joshua Gibson and Samuel Paxson. This furnace passed into the possession of Reuben Mochabee and Samuel Wurtz before 1800, who added Hampton forge, located on Indian creek, half a mile from the Youghiogheny river. Both the furnace and forge were kept in operation for a number of years. Pine Grove forge, in George's township, was built a short time prior to 1798 by Thomas Lewis.

Prior to 1794 Jeremiah Pears built a forge at Plumsock, in Menallen township, which was the forerunner of a rolling and slitting mill built by Mr. Pears at the same place before 1804. In 1805 the rolling and slitting mill and the remainder of Mr. Pears's property were sold by the sheriff. This was probably the first rolling and slitting mill erected west of the Alleghenies. In 1815 the Plumsock property passed into the hands of Isaac Meason. In 1797 Mr. Pears built Old Redstone furnace, in South Union township, Fayette county. The dilapidated stack of this furnace is still standing.

In 1797 John Hayden built Fairfield furnace, on George's creek. John and Andrew Oliphant and Nathaniel Breading bought an interest in this furnace in 1798, and in a few years the Oliphants became its sole owners. Fairchance furnace, on George's creek, six miles south of Uniontown, was built in 1804 by John Hayden. J. & A. Oliphant bought it about 1805. It was rebuilt two or three times and kept in operation until 1887, when it was abandoned and torn down. A new Fairchance furnace was built near the site of the old one in 1887. The Oliphants built Sylvan forges, on George's creek, below Fairfield and Fairchance furnaces. It is said that while the Oliphants operated Fairfield furnace they cast a quantity of shot which was used by General Jackson's artillery in the battle of New Orleans. It was shipped down

the Monongahela, the Ohio, and the Mississippi rivers. The
furnace was operated by the Oliphants and others for many
years, but was abandoned before 1850.

In 1805 there were five furnaces and six forges in Fayette county. In 1805 a rolling and slitting mill was built
by John Gibson on the right bank of the Youghiogheny
river, below Connellsville. In 1811 the county had ten furnaces, one air furnace, eight forges, three rolling and slitting
mills, one steel furnace, and five trip-hammers. At a later
date there were twenty furnaces in this county. Fayette
county was a great iron centre at the close of the last century and far into the present century. For many years Pittsburgh and the Ohio and Mississippi valleys were almost
entirely supplied by it. with all kinds of castings and with
hammered bar iron. In 1804 a large order for sugar kettles,
to be used on the sugar plantations of Louisiana, was filled at
Union furnace. Long before 1850, however, the fires in most
of the furnaces and forges of Fayette county were suffered
to die out. In 1849 only four of its furnaces were in blast.
Other furnaces, to use coke, have since been built within its
boundaries, and in late years a large rolling mill and Bessemer steel works have been built at Uniontown, but its fame
as a centre of the iron industry has departed. In its stead
it now enjoys the reputation of being the centre of production of the famous Connellsville coke. Connellsville, on the
Youghiogheny, was a shipping point for Fayette county iron.

The steel furnace above referred to as existing in 1811 was
at Bridgeport, adjoining Brownsville, was owned by Truman
& Co., and made good steel. It was known as the Brownsville steel factory. In 1811 Truman & Co. advertised that
they had for sale "several tons of steel of their own converting, which they will sell at the factory for cash, at 12 dollars
per cwt., and 20 dollars per faggot for Crowley." The latter
was an English brand.

The first nail factory west of the Alleghenies was built
at Brownsville, about 1795, by Jacob Bowman, at which
wrought nails were made by hand in one shop and cut nails
were made by machines in another. These machines were
worked by the foot of the workman, while his hands guided
the flat and thin bar of iron from which the nails were cut.

The rolling and slitting mills which were in existence in Pennsylvania prior to 1816 neither puddled pig iron nor rolled bar iron, but, with the exception of Mr. Rentgen's enterprise, already noted, rolled only sheet iron and nail plates from blooms hammered under a tilt-hammer.

The first rolling mill erected in the United States to puddle iron and roll iron bars was built by Isaac Meason in 1816 and 1817 at Plumsock, on Redstone creek, about midway between Connellsville and Brownsville, in Fayette county, on the site of the rolling and slitting mill built by Jeremiah Pears before.1804. Thomas C. Lewis was the chief engineer in the erection of the new mill, and George Lewis, his brother, was the turner and roller. They were Welshmen. F. H. Oliphant told us in his lifetime that the new mill was built "for making bars of all sizes and hoops for cutting into nails." He further said that "the iron was refined by blast and then puddled." Samuel C. Lewis, son of the above Thomas C. Lewis, assisted as a boy in rolling the first bar of iron. He died at Pittsburgh on Friday, August 11, 1882, in the 80th year of his age. The mill contained two puddling furnaces, one refinery, one heating furnace, and one tilt-hammer. Raw coal was used in the puddling and heating furnaces and coke in the refinery. The rolls were cast at Dunbar furnace, and the lathe for turning the rolls was put up at the mill. The mill went into operation on September 15, 1817, and was kept in operation for several years, the latter part of the time by Arthur Palmer. A flood in the Redstone caused the partial destruction of the mill in 1831. The machinery was subsequently taken to Brownsville.

Isaac Meason, who did so much to develop the iron resources of Fayette county, was a native of Virginia. He died in 1819. Prior to his death his son, Colonel Isaac Meason, was associated with him in the management of his various iron enterprises, and after his death he succeeded to their entire management. Isaac Meason, Sr., was a member of the supreme executive council of Pennsylvania in 1783, and for many years prior to his death he was an associate judge of Fayette county.

A furnace named Mary Ann was erected at an early day

in Greene county. It was located on Ten-mile creek, opposite Clarksville, and about twenty miles from Uniontown. It was abandoned early in the present century. An advertisement for its sale, by "Samuel Harper, .agent for the proprietors," dated July 23, 1810, styles it "The Iron Works," late the property of Captain James Robinson.' It was probably built about 1800. Gordon, in his *Gazetteer*, (1832,) says that "there were formerly in operation on Ten-mile creek a forge and furnace, but they have been long idle and are falling to decay." This reference is to Robinson's works. Greene county has probably never had any other iron enterprises.

Westmoreland county speedily followed Fayette county in the manufacture of iron. Westmoreland furnace, on Four-mile run, near Laughlinstown, in Ligonier valley, was built about 1792 by John Probst, who also built a small forge about the same time. Neither the furnace nor the forge was long in operation, both probably ceasing to make iron before 1810. On the 1st of August, 1795, George Anshutz, manager of Westmoreland furnace, advertised stoves and castings for sale. General Arthur St. Clair built Hermitage furnace, on Mill creek, two miles northeast of Ligonier, about 1802. It was managed for its owner by James Hamilton, and made stoves and other castings. It was in blast in 1806. In 1810 it passed out of the hands of General St. Clair and was idle for some time. In 1816 it was started again by O'Hara & Scully, under the management of John Henry Hopkins, afterwards Protestant Episcopal bishop of Vermont. In October, 1817, Mr. Hopkins left the furnace, himself a bankrupt, and it has never since been in operation. The stack is yet standing. General St. Clair died a very poor man in 1818, aged 84 years, and was buried at Greensburg.

Mount Hope furnace, in Donegal township, was built in 1810 by Trevor & McClurg. Mount Pleasant furnace, on Jacob's creek, in Mount Pleasant township, was built about 1810 by Alexander McClurg, and went out of blast in 1820 while operated by Mr. Freeman. Mr. McClurg owned it in 1813. Washington furnace, near Laughlinstown, was built about 1809 by Johnston, McClurg & Co. It was abandoned in 1826, but rebuilt in 1848 by John Bell & Co. It was in blast as late as 1855. Jonathan Maybury & Co. owned Fountain furnace, on Camp run, in Donegal township, at the base of Laurel hill, before 1812. The firm was dissolved on August 19, 1812, when the furnace fell into the hands of Alexander McClurg, who operated it in 1813. Kingston forge, erected in 1811 on Loyalhanna creek, ten miles east of Greensburg, by A. Johnston & Co., went into operation early in 1812. Ross furnace, on Tub-mill creek, in Fairfield township, was built in 1814 by either Isaac Meason or his son, and abandoned about 1850. It made pig iron, stoves, kettles, pots, ovens, skillets, etc. Hannah furnace, on Tub-mill creek, in Fairfield township, a short distance below Ross furnace, was built about 1810 by John Beninger. He also built a small forge on the same stream, where the town of Bolivar now stands. The furnace and forge both ceased to make iron soon after they were built. Baldwin furnace, on Laurel run, near Ross furnace, is said to have been built by James Stewart about 1818. It ran but a short time.

In 1832 there were in operation in Westmoreland county only one furnace, (Ross,) operated by Colonel Mathiot, and one forge, (Kingston,) operated by Alexander Johnston. The latter gentleman, whose name appears above in connection with another iron enterprise, was the father of Governor William F. Johnston. He was born in Ireland in July, 1773, and died in July, 1872, aged 99 years.

Seven other charcoal furnaces were built in Westmoreland county between 1844 and 1855. All the charcoal furnaces in this county have been abandoned. The early furnaces in Westmoreland county, besides supplying local wants, shipped castings by boats or arks on the Youghiogheny, the Conemaugh, and the Allegheny rivers to Pittsburgh, some of which found their way down the Ohio river to Cincinnati and Louisville. Subsequently they shipped pig iron by canal to Pittsburgh rolling mills.

Shade furnace, on Shade creek, in Somerset county, was built in 1807 or 1808, and was the first iron enterprise in the county. It used bog ore, the discovery of which led to its erection, although the location was otherwise unfavorable. It was built by Gerehart & Reynolds upon lands leased from Thomas Vickroy. In November, 1813, Mr. Vickroy advertised Shade furnace for sale at "a great bargain." A sale was effected in 1819 to Mark Richards, Anthony S. Earl, and Benjamin Johns, of New Jersey, composing the firm of Richards, Earl & Co., which operated the furnace down to about 1830. In 1820 they built Shade forge, below the furnace, which was operated by William Earl for four or five years, and afterwards by John Hammer and others. About 1811 Joseph Vickroy and Conrad Piper built Mary Ann forge, on Stony creek, about five miles below Shade furnace and half a mile below the mouth of Shade creek. David Livingston was subsequently the owner of the forge, and operated it for several years. Richard Geary, the father of Governor John W. Geary, was the manager of the forge for about one year, and was supercargo of a load of bar iron which was shipped from the forge down the Stony creek, the Conemaugh, and other streams to Pittsburgh. Pig iron was sometimes packed on horseback to this forge from Bedford county, the horses taking bar iron from the forge and also salt from the Conemaugh salt works as a return load.

In the year 1809 or 1810 Peter Kimmell and Matthias Scott built a forge for the manufacture of bar iron on Laurel Hill creek, now in Jefferson township, in the western part of Somerset county. It ceased operations about 1815. Supplies of pig iron were obtained in Bedford and Fayette counties. About the year 1810 Robert Philson erected a forge and furnace on Casselman's river, in Turkeyfoot township. This enterprise was a failure. Four other charcoal furnaces were afterwards built in Somerset county. All the furnaces and forges in this county have long been abandoned.

The first iron enterprise in Cambria county was a forge at Johnstown, built on Stony creek, about 1809, probably by John Holliday, a resident of Hollidaysburg. John Buckwalter was the first manager. The dam of this forge was washed away about 1811, and subsequently the forge was removed to the Conemaugh river, below Johnstown, where the schoolhouse on Iron street now stands, in the Millville addition to Johnstown, and where it was operated down to about 1822, Rahm & Bean, of Pittsburgh, being the lessees at this time. It was used to hammer bar iron out of Juniata pig iron and blooms. In 1817 Thomas Burrell, the proprietor, offered wood-cutters " fifty cents per cord for chopping

two thousand cords of wood at Cambria forge, Johnstown."
About 200 pounds of nails, valued at $30, were made at
Johnstown by one establishment in the census year 1810.
About this time an enterprise was established at Johnstown
by Robert Pierson, by which nails were cut with a machine
worked by a treadle, but without heads, which were afterwards added by hand. Cambria county has been noted as
an iron centre since its first furnace, Cambria, was built by
George S. King, David Stewart, John K. Shryock, and William L. Shryock, in 1841, on Laurel run. It was followed in
the next six years by five other charcoal furnaces. All these
furnaces have been abandoned. The extensive works of
the Cambria Iron Company, at Johnstown, were commenced
in 1853 by a company of which Mr. King was the origina-
tor and Dr. Peter Shoenberger was a member. They were
built expressly to roll rails, the Pennsylvania Railroad, passing through Johnstown, having been completed from Philadelphia to Pittsburgh in the preceding year, and furnishing
a local incentive to their erection as well as a convenient
means of communication with other sections of the country
in need of rails. Dr. Shoenberger had previously become a
half owner of Cambria furnace and a part owner of several
other furnaces and of large tracts of land near Johnstown.
In 1832 Gordon referred to the prospect of making iron
from native ore in Cambria county as follows: "And there
is iron, as it is said by some, but denied by others." Mr.
King tested at Ross furnace in 1839 or 1840 the ore which
he had found in the hills near Laurel run.

The first iron-enterprise in Indiana county was Indiana
forge, on Finley's run, near the Conemaugh, built about 1837
by Henry and John Noble, who also built a small furnace
as early as 1840. The forge was operated by water-power
but the furnace by steam-power. Both enterprises were running in the last-named year. Pig iron for the forge was at
first obtained from Allegheny furnace, now in Blair county.
Some iron ore for the furnace was obtained from the Allegheny furnace mines. About 1837 John Noble owned a farm
of about 200 acres in the heart of the present city of Altoona, which he sold to David Robinson, of Pleasant valley, for
$4,500, taking in payment the contents of Mr. Robinson's

country store, which he removed to Finley's run and added
to the capital stock of the firm of Henry and John Noble.
The Altoona farm is now worth many millions of dollars.
About 1846 the Indiana property passed into the hands of
Elias Baker, who built a new furnace and forge. Three other
charcoal furnaces were built in Indiana county in 1846 and
1847. All its furnaces and its solitary forge have long been
abandoned.

A blast furnace was built at Beaver Falls, on the west
side of Beaver river, in Beaver county, in 1802, by Hoopes,
Townsend & Co., and blown in in 1804. A forge was connected with it from the beginning, and was in operation in
1806. The furnace and forge were both in operation in 1816.
The whole enterprise was abandoned about 1826. The ore
used was picked out of gravel banks in the neighborhood
in very small lumps. There was another early furnace in
Beaver county, named Bassenheim, built in 1814 by Detmar
Basse Müller, on Connoquenessing creek, about a mile west
of the Butler county line. In February, 1818, $12 per ton
were paid for hauling the pig iron made at this furnace to
Pittsburgh, thirty miles distant, over a bad road. The furnace was abandoned at an early day. John Henry Hopkins, previously mentioned in connection with General St.
Clair's furnace near Ligonier, was engaged about 1815 as a
clerk at Bassenheim furnace.

Prior to 1846 there were a few furnaces in the Shenango
valley, all charcoal, one of which was Springfield furnace,
half a mile from Leesburg and seven miles southeast of
Mercer, built in 1837 and active in 1849, while another was
Temperance furnace, about six miles east of Greenville, built
by J. Green Butler about 1840. Day, in 1843, says: "Two
furnaces were wrought formerly, but have since been abandoned." In 1806 the geographer Joseph Scott says that "a
forge and furnace are now nearly erected" at New Castle.
About 1810 there was a forge on Neshannock creek, "midway between Pearson's flour mill and Harvey's paper mill,"
for the manufacture of bar iron from the ore. The first
rolling mill in Lawrence county was built in 1839 at New
Castle by James D. White, of that place, with the assistance
of Shubal Wilder, of Massachusetts, Joseph H. Brown, and

other practical ironworkers. It made cut nails and bar iron. At first only Juniata blooms were used, as the mill did not contain any puddling furnaces. In 1841, after the death of Mr. White, Messrs. A. L. and J. M. Crawford and George K. Ritter, all of Montgomery county, Pennsylvania, bought the mill property, and, with the practical men above mentioned, organized the firm of J. M. Crawford & Co., which enlarged the mill and continued to make bar iron and nails. In 1850 the Cosalo Iron Company was organized, with A. L. Crawford as president and Mr. Wilder as superintendent. In 1853 a new and larger mill was built. In 1846 and afterwards several furnaces were built in this valley to use its block coal and also charcoal, and several rolling mills were also built.

Alexander L. Crawford died at New Castle on April 1, 1890, aged about 76 years. He was for fifty years one of the country's most prominent iron manufacturers. He was also prominent in the building of railroads and in the development of our coal mines, his various enterprises extending to many States. Shubal Wilder died suddenly at Middleboro, Massachusetts, in May, 1888, aged about 79 years.

The first furnace in the once important but now nearly neglected ironmaking district composed of Armstrong, Butler, Clarion, Venango, and other northwestern counties was Bear Creek, in Armstrong county, which was commenced in 1818 by William Stackpole and Ruggles Whiting, who then owned the Pittsburgh rolling mill. In 1819, owing to the failure of this firm, the furnace passed uncompleted into the hands of Baldwin, Robinson, McNickle & Beltzhoover, of Pittsburgh. It went into operation in that year. It was built to use coke, with steam-power, and its first blast was with this fuel, but the blast was too weak and the furnace chilled after two or three tons of iron had been made. Charcoal was then substituted. The furnace was abandoned long before 1850, but it was running in 1832, in which year Gordon says that it was owned by Henry Baldwin, Esq., and was reputed to be the largest furnace in the United States, having made forty tons of iron in a week. This furnace had a tram-road, with wooden rails, in 1818.

Slippery Rock furnace, in Butler county, and Clarion furnace, in Clarion county, were built in 1828, the latter by

Christian Myers, of Lancaster county, who built another furnace about 1844, which he called Polk. Allegheny furnace, at Kittanning, in Armstrong county, and Venango furnace, on Oil creek, in Venango county, were built in 1830. From 1830 to 1850 this section of the State produced large quanti-ties of charcoal pig iron. In 1850 there were eleven furnaces in Armstrong county, six in Butler, twenty-eight in Clarion, and eighteen in Venango : sixty-three in all. In 1858 there were eighteen in Armstrong, six in Butler, twenty-seven in Clarion, and twenty-four in Venango : seventy-five in all. All these were charcoal furnaces, except four coke furnaces at Brady's Bend. Many of these furnaces had, however, been abandoned at the latter date, and every one has since been abandoned. Most of these furnaces were built to supply the Pittsburgh rolling mills with pig iron.

The Great Western iron works at Brady's Bend, embrac-ing four furnaces to use coke and a rolling mill, were com-menced by Philander Raymond and others in 1840. The furnaces were finally blown out in 1873 and the rolling mill was abandoned in the same year. It was built in 1841 to roll bar iron, but it afterwards rolled iron rails, which were at first mere flat bars with holes for spikes countersunk in the upper surface. The mill continued to make rails until after the close of the civil war. In 1849 the original Great Western Iron Company failed, and upon its reorganization the name was changed to the Brady's Bend Iron Company. There was a large amount of Boston capital at one time in-vested in these works.

Erie charcoal furnace, at Erie, was built in 1842 and aban-doned in 1849. It used bog ore. It was owned by Charles M. Reed. Liberty furnace, on the north side of French creek, in Crawford county, was built in 1842 by Lowry & Co., of Meadville, and abandoned in 1849.

The iron manufactured in the Allegheny valley was tak-en down the Allegheny river to Pittsburgh on keel-boats and arks, the business of transporting it in this primitive man-ner being quite extensive down to about 1850.

CHAPTER XX.

EARLY IRON ENTERPRISES IN ALLEGHENY COUNTY, PENNSYLVANIA.

THE beginning of the iron industry at Pittsburgh was made at a comparatively recent period. George Anshutz, the pioneer in the manufacture of iron at Pittsburgh, was an Alsacian by birth, Alsace at the time being under the control of France. He was born near Strasburg, on November 28, 1753. In 1789 he emigrated to the United States, and soon afterwards located at a suburb of Pittsburgh now known as Shady Side, where he built a small furnace on Two-mile run, probably completing it in 1792. In 1794 it was abandoned for want of ore. It had been expected that ore could be obtained in the vicinity, but this expectation was not realized, and the expense entailed in bringing ore from other localities was too great. The enterprise seems to have been largely devoted to the casting of stoves and grates. The ruins of the furnace were visible until about 1850. After the abandonment of his furnace Mr. Anshutz accepted the management of John Probst's Westmoreland furnace, near Laughlinstown, and remained there about one year, whence he removed to Huntingdon county, where, in connection with Judge John Gloninger and Mordecai Massey, he built Huntingdon furnace in 1796, as has already been stated in a preceding chapter. He died at Pittsburgh on February 28, 1837, aged 83 years and 3 months. Many of his descendants reside in Pittsburgh and its vicinity.

We have received from Mr. George A. Berry, president of the Citizens' National Bank, of Pittsburgh, and a grandson of George Anshutz, the following interesting reminiscences of Mr. Anshutz's pioneer iron enterprise at Shady Side. His letter containing these reminiscences is dated at Pittsburgh, May 8, 1891. We give his statement in its entirety.

I am now on the verge of entering my 74th year, and I have a very clear recollection of things fifty and even sixty years ago. I often heard my grandfather speak of the furnace, as well as my uncles and aunts, all brothers and sisters of my mother, some of whom have lived to within the last fifteen years. Mrs. Rahm, my mother's oldest sister, who was born on February 17, 1788, and died on July 31, 1878, was four years old when the furnace was built. She had a very clear recollection of it and told me many circumstances connected with it. I have a family Bible which has been in our family for over seventy years and in which my mother's birth, on December 27, 1793, is recorded, and I had it from her as well as from all the family that she was born at the furnace referred to above.

In my younger days I heard many of the older residents of the east end of the city speak of seeing the old stack. Major William B. Negley, one of our oldest and best-known citizens, told me to-day that, when he first built on the site now occupied by the mansion of M. K. Moorhead, Esq., he took down part of the old stack, and going through the cinder pile found several relics of the business, such as a shovel, pick, etc. John A. Renshaw, Esq., who also built on part of the property, told me he could locate the spot occupied by the furnace as well as the tail-race which carried the water from the furnace. On several occasions I talked with the late William M. Lyon on this subject. He mentioned several things in connection with the furnace, among others that after my grandfather abandoned it it was used by Anthony Beelen as a foundry. The family of the late Jonas Roup had in use until a recent period pots, skillets, etc., made at the furnace.

The late Judge James Veech was considered authority on all matters of the olden time. He came here from Fayette county, and I think wrote a history of the county. In a long newspaper article now before me, in which he endeavors to establish the fact that the first blast furnace west of the Allegheny mountains was built in Fayette and not in Allegheny county, he says, speaking of my grandfather's furnace : "My researches on the subject put the abortive enterprise at least two years later." [That is, 1792 instead of 1790.] "The facts on this subject which I am about to state are made out mostly from records consulted and from original papers." He thus admits the existence of the furnace but is a little doubtful of dates. Of course if the furnace was built, of which there is no doubt, it was put in blast, but for how long I have no positive knowledge. However this may be I always heard that ore was not found in sufficient quantity in the neighborhood of the furnace, and that the supply for awhile was brought down the Allegheny river, but this being too expensive the enterprise was abandoned.

My grandfather next turns up at Westmoreland furnace, as will be seen from an advertisement in the Pittsburgh *Gazette*, as follows : "*Westmoreland Furnace.*—For sale at said furnace, about 3 miles from Fort Ligonier, near the State Road, stoves and a fine assortment of the best castings, at the most reasonable prices. GEO. ANSHUTZ, *Manager*. August 7th, 1795."

I think that the above information will satisfy you that George Anshutz built the first furnace that was built in Allegheny county, and that it was in operation about the years 1792 to 1794. GEO. ANSHUTZ BERRY.

The first iron foundry at Pittsburgh was established about 1805 by Joseph McClurg on the site of the present post-office and the city hall, on the northeast corner of Smithfield street and Fifth avenue. Rev. A. A. Lambing says that Joseph Smith and John Gormly were associated with Mr. McClurg in this enterprise. They retired, however, before 1807. Mr. McClurg subsequently took his son Alexander into partnership. The enterprise was styled the Pittsburgh foundry. Isaac Craig, Esq., informs us that on February 12, 1806, Joseph McClurg advertised in the *Commonwealth* that "the Pittsburgh Foundry is now complete." In 1812 it was converted by Mr. McClurg into a cannon foundry and supplied the General Government with cannon, howitzers, shells, and balls. Commodore Perry's fleet on Lake Erie and General Jackson's army at New Orleans received their supplies of these articles in part from this foundry.

According to Cramer's *Pittsburgh Almanack* there were three nail factories at Pittsburgh in 1807—Porter's, Sturgeon's, and Stewart's, " which make about 40 tons of nails yearly." In 1810 about 200 tons of cut and wrought nails were made at Pittsburgh. In 1813 there were two iron foundries in this city, McClurg's and Anthony Beelen's, and one steel furnace, owned by Tuper & McCowan. In the following year there were two additional foundries. Mr. Beelen's foundry was put in operation in November, 1810.

The condition of the iron industry at Pittsburgh in 1810 is thus summed up by a writer in *The Navigator* for 1811 : " The manufacture of ironmongery has increased in this place beyond all calculation. Cut and wrought nails of all sizes are made in vast quantities, about, we think, 200 tons per year. Fire shovels, tongs, drawing-knives, hatchets, two feet squares, augers, chissels, adzes, axes, claw hammers, door hinges, chains, hackles, locks, door handles, spinning-wheel irons, plough irons, flat-irons, &c·, tons of these, together with a number of other articles in the iron way, are exported annually. Abner Updegraff attempted the making of *files*, which he finds he can do to advantage. He also makes gimblets, and by way of experiment made a neat penknife, which he says could be made here as cheap as those imported." The making of screws for butt hinges is also noted.

A rolling mill was built at Pittsburgh in 1811 and 1812 by Christopher Cowan, a Scotch-Irishman, and called the Pittsburgh rolling mill. This mill had no puddling furnaces.

Cramer's *Pittsburgh Almanack* for 1813 says of this enterprise: " C. Cowan is erecting a most powerful steam engine to reduce iron to various purposes. It is calculated for a *seventy horse power*, which [will] put into complete operation a *Rolling-mill*, a *Slitting-mill*, and a *Tilt-hammer*, all under the same roof. With these Mr. Cowan will be enabled to furnish sheet-iron, nail and spike rods, shovels and tongs, spades, scythes, sickles, hoes, axes, frying-pans, cutting-knives. In addition to Mr. Cowan's already extensive nail business he makes a great supply of chains, plough irons, shingling hatchets, clew hammers, chissels, screw augers, spinning wheel irons, and smiths' vices of superior quality." This rolling mill stood at the intersection of Penn street and Cecil's alley, where the fourth ward school-house now stands. In 1816 it was owned by William Stackpole and Ruggles Whiting, of Boston, who failed in 1819, and who seem to have made nails chiefly by nail-cutting machines which both cut and headed the nails. In 1826 it was operated by R. Bowen.

In the *Pittsburgh Almanack* for 1819 the following account is given of an ambitious manufacturing establishment in Pittsburgh " within the year 1818 :" " Rolling and Slitting Mill.—A very extensive establishment under the superintendence of Joshua Malen, formerly of Valley Forge, and whose talents will be an important acquisition to this section of the Union, has been made by the 'Pittsburgh Steam Engine Co.' Wm. Robinson, jr. & Joshua Malen. At their rolling mill, which has two engines, each of 120 horse power, will be manufactured *Bar, Rolled, and Sheet Iron*." Our extracts from the *Almanack* are taken from its pages *verbatim*. We can not locate the above enterprise.

The Union rolling mill was the next mill built at Pittsburgh. It was located on the Monongahela river, was built in 1819, and was accidentally blown up and permanently dismantled in 1829, the machinery being taken to Covington, Kentucky. This mill had four puddling furnaces—the first in Pittsburgh. We think that it was also the first to roll bar iron. It was built by Baldwin, Robinson, McNickle & Beltzhoover. It is claimed that the first angle iron rolled in the United States was rolled at this mill by Samuel Leonard, who also rolled " L " iron for salt pans. On Pine creek, on the site of the present works of Spang, Chalfant & Co., at Etna, Belknap, Bean & Butler manufactured scythes and sickles as early as 1820, but in 1824 their works were enlarged and steam-power introduced for the purpose of rolling blooms. In 1826 the works were operated by M. B. Belknap. They afterwards passed into the hands of Cuddy & Ledlie, and were purchased by H. S. Spang in 1828 to roll bar iron from Juniata blooms. A rolling mill on Grant's Hill was built in 1821 by William B. Hays and David Adams. It stood near where the court-house now stands. Water for the generation of steam at this mill had to be hauled from the Monongahela river. The Juniata iron works were built in 1824 by Dr. Peter Shoenberger on the site which they now occupy. Sligo rolling mill was erected where it now stands by Robert T. Stewart and John Lyon in 1825, but it was partly burned down in that year. The Dowlais works, in Kensington, were built in 1825 by George Lewis and Reuben Leonard. In 1826 all these mills did not make bar iron; one or two rolled and hammered iron in other forms.

The condition of the iron industry at Pittsburgh at the close of the first quarter of the present century is thus summed up in Cramer's *Magazine Almanac* for 1826:

The manufactures of Pittsburgh, particularly in the article of iron, begin to assume a very interesting aspect. Not less than five rolling mills are now in operation, and a sixth will soon be ready, for the various manufactures of iron. Four of the mills are capable of making iron from the *pig*, besides rolling, slitting, and cutting into nails. The other (occupied by Mr. R. Bowen, formerly by the Messrs. Whitings, and owned and built by Mr. C. Cowan) is engaged only in rolling bar and boiler iron and cutting nails. The fuel to supply the engines—the metal and other materials required in conducting the operation of these works, and in their repairs, it is computed afford employment to upwards of fifteen hundred people, the value of whose labour may be estimated at fifteen hundred dollars each per annum, or two million two hundred and fifty thousand dollars, while the total product may be estimated at three million of dollars!! How important an addition to the national wealth in this section of the Union! Great credit is due to Messrs. Baldwin, Robinson & McNickle for their perseverance in establishing this important branch of business, and for bringing it to that perfection which it has attained. Great facilities are now afforded to mechanics in all the various branches of smith work and hardware by the preparation of iron into whatever shape (slit, rolled, square, or round) that may be required for any particular description of work. It is generally believed that no other place in the Union affords greater advantages for the extensive manufacture of anvils, vices, and all kinds of iron work. The competition which at present exists, and which is increasing by the erection of new works, will ensure a plentiful supply of iron and nails for the Western States, of an improving quality, on better terms than they can be procured from the seaboard.

The first rolling mill in Allegheny City was the Juniata rolling mill, built in 1827. It bore the same name as Dr. Shoenberger's mill previously erected in Pittsburgh in 1824, but it must not be confounded with it. The following circumstantial account of the Allegheny City enterprise we take from *Recollections of Seventy Years*, by Judge John E. Parke, who died in Allegheny City on April 22, 1885, aged 78 years.

The Juniata rolling mill was built on the lot extending from Robinson street along the west side of Darragh street to the Allegheny river, at the former outlet of the Pennsylvania Canal, by Sylvanus Lothrop, James Anderson, and Henry Blake, in the years 1826 and 1827. Mr. Blake sold his interest to Capt. William Stewart, and Messrs. Lothrop, Anderson, and Stewart sold out their interest in 1834 to John Bissell, William Morrison, and Edward W. Stephens. The mill, having been constructed for the exclusive use of Juniata blooms, was extended by the latter firm to the manufacture of iron by the puddling and boiling process, and was the first boiling furnace erected in Allegheny county. Here, too, was also erected the first coffee-mill squeezer, under the personal superintendence of the patentee, Mr. Burden, of New York. The manufacture of iron, nails, and steel of the lowest grade was successfully carried on by the latter firm and their successors until the year 1859, when it was deemed advisable to dismantle the works. The machinery was sold to Messrs. Reis, Brown, Berger, and James Ward, and was removed to Niles, Ohio.

In the United States a rolling mill is understood to mean an establishment for rolling iron or steel, and it may have one train of rolls or many trains.

In 1829 Allegheny county had eight rolling mills, using 6,000 tons of blooms and 1,500 tons of pig iron, all brought from other localities. In that year there were nine foundries, which consumed 3,500 tons of iron. In 1828 the iron rolled was 3,291 tons, in 1829 it was 6,217 tons, and in 1830 it was 9,282 tons. In 1831 there were two steel furnaces at Pittsburgh. Cast iron began to be used in this year for pillars, the caps and sills of windows, etc. In 1836 there were nine rolling mills in operation and eighteen foundries, engine-factories, and machine-shops. In 1856 there were at Pittsburgh and in Allegheny county twenty-five rolling mills. In 1890 there were sixty iron rolling mills and steel works in Allegheny county. The Pittsburgh rolling mills were largely supplied from the first with blooms from the Juniata valley and with pig iron from nearer localities, but large quantities of blooms were also brought to Pittsburgh from Ohio, Kentucky, and Tennessee. Allegheny county has long enjoyed the reputation of leading all other iron districts in the country in the production of rolled iron and the various kinds of steel. Of its enterprise in the manufacture of steel we will speak in subsequent chapters.

Clinton furnace, built in 1859 by Graff, Bennett & Co., and blown in on the last Monday of October in that year, was the first furnace built in Allegheny county after the abandonment in 1794 of George Anshutz's furnace at Shady Side, a surprisingly long interval if we consider the prominence of this great iron centre in the manufacture of rolled iron after its second large rolling mill, the Union, was built in 1819. This furnace was built to use coke made from coal from the Pittsburgh vein, but it did not prove to be a good furnace fuel, and coke from the Connellsville region was soon substituted with great success. This success led to the building of other coke furnaces at Pittsburgh and in Allegheny county. Their aggregate production of pig iron in 1883 was greater than that of any other district in the United States, not excepting the celebrated Lehigh valley district in Pennsylvania. This position of supremacy has since been maintained. The production of pig iron by Allegheny county in 1890 was greater than that of any State in the Union, Pennsylvania excepted. It amounted to 1,337,309 gross tons. Iron ore for the furnaces of this county is chiefly obtained from the Lake Superior region, but some other native ores are used and also considerable quantities of foreign ores. About twenty years ago Missouri ores were used in large quantities. There are now twenty-six coke furnaces in this county, and many of them are among the best in the country. The best blast-furnace record that has been made in this or any other country must be credited to the furnaces connected with the Edgar Thomson steel works at Braddock, Allegheny county. We will refer to this record hereafter.

In 1810 there were in Pennsylvania 44 blast furnaces, 78 forges, 4 bloomaries, 18 rolling and slitting mills, 6 air furnaces, 50 trip-hammers, 5 steel furnaces, and 175 naileries. The furnaces produced 26,878 gross tons of " cast iron," the product of the whole country, with 153 blast and air furnaces, being 53,908 tons. Of the 5 steel furnaces in Pennsylvania one was in Philadelphia city and one each in Philadelphia, Lancaster, Dauphin, and Fayette counties, and their product was 531 tons of steel, valued at $81,147. In 1840 there were 213 furnaces in Pennsylvania and 169 forges and rolling mills. In 1850 there were 298 furnaces, 121 forges, 6 bloomaries, and 79 rolling mills. Of the furnaces existing in 1850 nearly all were charcoal furnaces, only 57 being anthracite and 11 bituminous coal and coke furnaces. The production of the furnaces in 1849 was 253,035 tons; of the bloomaries, 335 tons; of the forges, 28,495 tons; and of the rolling mills, 108,358 tons.

The charcoal iron industry of Pennsylvania still exists, but its glory has departed. About 1840 a revolution was created in the iron industry of the country by the introduction of bituminous and anthracite coal in the blast furnace, and soon afterwards the manufacture of charcoal iron in Pennsylvania furnaces commenced to decline. About 1830 rolling mills in many parts of the State began to puddle iron extensively, and this innovation drove out of existence many charcoal forges which had been employed in producing blooms for rolling mills as well as to be reduced to bar iron under their own hammers. Most of the charcoal furnaces and forges and all of the primitive charcoal bloomaries have been abandoned.

Since about the middle of the last century Pennsylvania has been noted as the leading iron and steel making State in the Union. For many years it has produced one-half of all the pig iron, one-half of all the rolled iron, and more than one-half of all the steel made in the United States. In 1890 it made 48 per cent. of the large product of pig iron in that year ; 61 per cent. of the Bessemer steel ingots produced ; 70 per cent. of the Bessemer steel rails produced ; 81 per cent. of the open-hearth steel produced ; 75 per cent of the crucible steel produced ; 52 per cent. of the rolled iron produced ; and 54 per cent. of the product of rolled steel other than steel rails.

CHAPTER XXI.

THE EARLY MANUFACTURE OF IRON IN DELAWARE.

IN the *Colonial Records of Pennsylvania*, volume I., page 115, mention is made of one James Bowle, who was "living near iron hill about eight miles distance from New Castle," Delaware, in 1684. In Oldmixon's *British Empire in America*, edition of 1708, in referring to New Castle county, then in Pennsylvania but now in Delaware, it is said that there is a place in the county "called iron hill, from the iron ore found there," but the existence of an "iron mill" to use the ore is expressly denied. This iron hill is undoubtedly the one referred to in the *Colonial Records* as having been known as early as 1684. It may be that it was in the neighborhood of this deposit where Richard Frame's forty pounds of iron were made as early as 1692, and which he credits to Pennsylvania, and that it was the iron ore in this hill to which Gabriel Thomas referred in 1698 in his description of Pennsylvania, the territory now embraced in the State of Delaware forming an integral part of Penn's province down to a much later date than the one last mentioned.

Mr. Hungerford says that iron hill, in Pencader hundred, in New Castle county, Delaware, was called by that name as early as May, 1661, and that iron ore was discovered at that place by the Dutch soon after their occupancy of the territory in 1655, if not earlier by the Swedes. He further informs us that in April, 1661, four Englishmen were murdered by Indians while on their way from New Amstel (now New Castle) to the head of Chesapeake bay.· The affair caused a correspondence between Vice-Director William Beekman, of the Dutch West India colony, then at Fort Altena, (Wilmington,) and Vice-Director Alexander De Hinijossa, of the colony of the City of Amsterdam, at New Amstel, on one side, and the Director-General, Petrus Stuyvesant, upon the other. Beekman recites the fact in his letter dated May 27th, but does not locate the place. De Hinijossa, under date of May 15th, says it occurred at "Morettica, on iron hill."

Mrs. James says that on the 24th of September, 1717, Sir William Keith, Governor of Pennsylvania, " wrote to the Board of Trade in London that he had found great plenty of iron ore in Pennsylvania," and Bishop says that "Sir William Keith had iron works in New Castle county, Delaware, erected previous to 1730, and probably during his administration from 1717 to 1726." Emanuel Swedenborg, in his *De Ferro*, printed in 1734, gives some particulars of the early iron works in Delaware, which he derived from the Swedish settlers on the Delaware river. He mentions smelting works on the Christiana river, built by Sir William Keith during the latter part of his administration, which produced large quantities of iron in the first two years of their existence but were abandoned the next year owing to the difficulty of smelting the ore. He also mentions another enterprise, about a mile distant from the other works. Mr. Hungerford says that this last enterprise was on the south bank of Christiana creek, north of iron hill, and was called Abbington furnace. It was built by a company in 1726 or 1727. A forge was built near this furnace before 1734, when it and an eighth part of the furnace were owned by Samuel James. A bloomary, located near St. James's church, on the Huitleer river, (White Clay creek,) is mentioned by Swedenborg, the owner being John Ball, who was a blacksmith. We give herewith a translation of Swedenborg's whole reference to the early iron works in Delaware, reminding the reader that the volume from which it is taken was printed in 1734.

About nine years ago works for smelting iron were constructed by the Governor of the Province, Sir William Keith, on the banks of the river Christiana. For the first two years of their existence they produced a sufficient quantity of iron; but during the third year, because the ore failed, they were abandoned. It is asserted that the ore of this region contains much iron, but that it is refractory, and without limestone as a flux (of which there is little to be had) can not be smelted. At the distance of one mile from that place there is another smelting works erected, but it is said that, on account of the exceeding dryness of the ore and scarcity of limestone, smelting has not been undertaken there; but the ore is now reduced by itself in hearths, small bars, or reworked crude iron, being produced at pleasure. In the neighborhood, on the river Huitleer, are similar small works near the church of St. James, and owned by Mr. John Ball, where also from ore, or crude iron, bars for blacksmith's work, or forgings, are produced by successive reheatings, but these works have but one hearth.

Mr. Hungerford says that Sir William Keith commenced purchasing lands in Delaware in 1722 and made his last purchase in 1726, in which year seven tracts of land, embracing in all 1,260 acres, and lying in the hundreds of Pencader, White Clay, Mill Creek, and Christiana, were all sold by Sir William to John England, then manager of Principio furnace, in Maryland.

We have seen an autograph legal opinion of Andrew Hamilton, not published, dated Philadelphia, March 6, 1730, from which we learn that Sir William Keith agreed to convey to John England "sundry lands and tenements in New Castle county, on Dellaware, upon which lands there was a small iron forge and supposed to be a great quantity of iron ore." It was afterwards ascertained, however, that the ore referred to was on the land of John Evans and not on Sir William's lands, but the existence of a forge on the lands of the latter is not called in question by the author of the opinion. Undoubtedly Sir William owned a forge, as appears from the opinion, and it probably succeeded a furnace.

In a biographical and critical sketch of Sir William Keith, written by Charles P. Keith, and published in the *Pennsylvania Magazine of History and Biography* for 1888, we find the following reference to Sir William's iron enterprises in Delaware: "The *Just and Plain Vindication of Sir William Keith*, published about the middle of 1726, says that he had laid out not only two thousand pounds on a farm, but '4,000l. in another Place; where, by Erecting an Iron-Work, it is improved to near double the prime Cost, and this last Estate Sir William all along design'd as a Security to his Creditors, until they were fully satisfy'd and paid;' while the *More Just Vindication* answers that scarcely any one would take the works as a gift, if obliged to maintain them." Sir William's "iron work" was probably built between 1722 and 1726, as it was in the year first mentioned when he appears to have commenced to purchase lands in Delaware.

The exact location of Sir William Keith's iron enterprise, which was probably the first of its kind in Delaware, we have been unable to determine, but it is exceedingly probable that it was located near iron hill. That it was on the Christiana river is made certain by Swedenborg's exact statement. The

Christiana skirts the foot of iron hill. It will be remembered that, on the 24th of September, 1717, Sir William wrote to the Board of Trade in London that he had found "great plenty of iron ore" in Pennsylvania, the reference being most probably to New Castle county, Delaware, where Sir William afterwards engaged in the manufacture of iron. He did not engage in that manufacture at any other place in Pennsylvania or Delaware. There is not any "great plenty of iron ore" anywhere else in New Castle county than at iron hill.

There is a local tradition that there was a furnace at the foot of iron hill about 1730. In the gable of an old Baptist church near iron hill is a cast-iron plate, dated 1746, which was probably cast at Abbington furnace. In the edition of Oldmixon for 1741 the author says that "between Brandy-wine and Christiana is an iron mill." This reference must be to Abbington furnace. The original members of the company which built this furnace are given by Mr. Hungerford as follows from a deed dated October 27, 1727, at which time it is stated in the deed that the furnace had been completed: "Samuel James, of Penkadder hundred, in yᵉ county of New Castell, upon Deleware, millwright, of the first part; Reece Jones, of Penkadder hundred, tanner, of the second part; Samuel Nutt, of Chester county, Pennsylvania, ironmonger, of the third part; Evan Owen, of the city of Philadelphia, merchant, of the fourth part; William Branson, of Philadelphia, merchant, of the fifth part; Thomas Rutter, of the same city, smith, of the sixth part; John Rutter, of the same city, smith, of the seventh part; and Caspar Wistar, of Philadelphia brass-button maker, of the eighth part." No mention is made of Abbington furnace or the forge of Samuel James after 1768. Both furnace and forge are often referred to as the Abbington iron works. The furnace stood on the south bank of Christiana creek near the Anabaptist meeting-house, and the forge stood on land now owned by the Cooch brothers and above the Cooch mill. The furnace was situated on land now owned by William McConaughey.

Mr. Hungerford informs us that one John Ball owned a tract of land in Mill Creek hundred, containing 400 acres, called "New Design," which in a deed is described as lying on the west side of a branch of White Clay creek, called Mill creek, between Mill creek and William Ball's land, and he also owned 100 acres of land adjoining. St. James's church is on the east side of Mill creek, nearly opposite the tract "New Design," upon which the Balls lived. Iron hill was about six or seven miles distant. The ore for John Ball's bloomary was doubtless hauled from iron hill.

The iron hill to which reference has above been made is situated about three miles south of Newark, near the Maryland line and in sight of Christiana creek. Ore taken from this place has been used at Principio furnace, in Cecil county, Maryland, since 1847. This ore has also been used at some furnaces in Pennsylvania. Previous to 1847 the mines had been worked but little. Between 1832 and 1847 some ore was mined here and taken to a furnace in New Jersey.

Bishop says that in Sussex county, in the southern part of Delaware, "where bog ore in the shape of a very pure hydrate, yielding from 55 to 66 per cent. of iron, exists in large beds in the vicinity of Georgetown and on the branches of the Nanticoke and Indian rivers, the manufacture of iron and castings was carried on before the Revolution to a considerable extent. The compact hydrated peroxide of some of these beds has, since the early part of this century, been raised in quantities for exportation, and the local production of iron is consequently less than it might have been." Tench Coxe, in his report on *The Arts and Manufactures of the United States* in 1810, mentions five forges in Sussex county, which produced in that year 215 tons of iron, but he makes no reference to a blast furnace in the whole State. Bog ore from near Milton, in Sussex county, was at one time taken to Millville, New Jersey, to be smelted in a furnace at that place which was built in 1815. Sussex ore has also been shipped to other places.

In 1763 a company, under the leadership of Colonel Joseph Vaughan, built a furnace near Concord, in Sussex county, on Deep creek, a tributary of Nanticoke river, to which a forge on Nanticoke river was added in 1769. They were known as the Deep Creek iron works, the furnace being known as Deep Creek furnace and the forge as Nanticoke forge. The company had a stone wharf at the head of Nanticoke river, and shipped its iron direct to England.

The iron was called "Old Meadow." "The stone wharf is there yet," said Mr. Francis Vincent, of Wilmington, in a letter we received from him a few years ago. The Revolutionary war practically ended these enterprises. Colonel Vaughan commanded one of the Delaware regiments during the Revolution. Another furnace at Concord, also located on Deep creek, was built by a company in 1764, the furnace being known as Pine Grove. This furnace was abandoned soon after the close of the Revolution. Unity forge, on the main branch of Nanticoke river, was built as early as 1771 and continued in operation as late as 1816.

As late as 1850 there was a forge on Gravelly branch, in Nanticoke hundred, in Sussex county, known as Collins's forge, which made bar iron in large quantities from iron ore from lands farther east for the Baltimore and Philadelphia markets. It was built about 1808 by John Collins, who was afterwards Governor of Delaware. In 1808 Shadrach Elliot built a forge at the mouth of Gravelly branch and at the upper end of the Middleford pond. In a deed for part of the land, dated August 4, 1812, the forge is mentioned as "Gravelly Delight forge." It probably went out of operation between 1816 and 1820. In 1807 Josiah Polk was in possession of a forge which had been erected some time before on the south side of Broad creek, about a mile and a half east of Laurel, in Sussex county. It was operated by him until his death, which occurred about 1840, and was then abandoned.

We are indebted to Mr. Hungerford for exact information concerning all of the above-mentioned early Sussex county iron works, not one of which now remains.

About 1820, as we were informed in his lifetime by Hon. Caleb S. Layton, of Sussex county, a blast furnace was established at Millsborough, on Indian river, about eight miles south of Georgetown, by Colonel William D. Waples and others. In connection with this furnace was a foundry. An interest in the furnace was purchased in 1822 by Hon. Samuel G. Wright, of New Jersey, and in 1830 his son, Colonel Gardiner H. Wright, obtained an interest, and afterwards operated the furnace until 1836, when it went out of blast. The foundry continued in operation until 1879. In 1859 Lesley stated that "Millsborough charcoal furnace, owned by Gardiner H. Wright, of Millsborough, Sussex county, Delaware, is the only furnace in the State, and has not made iron for ten years. A cupola furnace is in activity beside it." Mr. Vincent informed us that the castings for the Eastern Penitentiary of Pennsylvania and for Moyamensing Prison, and the iron railing which once surrounded Independence Square, in Philadelphia, were cast at Millsborough furnace; we presume at the "cupola furnace." In 1828 and in the two succeeding years Millsborough furnace and foundry produced 450 tons of pig iron and 350 tons of castings.

A rolling mill near Wilmington, Delaware, existing and in operation in 1787 or 1788, has already been referred to in the chapter relating to New York. This mill then rolled Swedish and Russia iron for the use of a New York cut-nail factory. It occupied the site of the present Hagley powder works. It was built before 1783 and was abandoned about 1812.

Tench Coxe says that in 1810 there were three rolling and slitting mills in New Castle county. Lesley stated in 1859 that the Delaware iron works, located five miles northwest of Wilmington, then owned by Alan Wood, of Philadelphia, and built in 1812, "began to manufacture sheet iron thirty years ago in what had been a nail-plate works. At that time only Townsend in New Jersey made sheet iron." Marshall's rolling mill, on Red Clay creek, two miles west of Newport, was built in 1836 by Caleb and John Marshall, to roll sheet iron. The Wilmington rolling mill, near Wilmington, was built in 1845, and the Diamond State rolling mill, at Wilmington, was built in 1853. These were the only rolling mills existing in Delaware in 1859. Others have since been built. The business of iron shipbuilding has been added to the iron industry of Delaware within the last few years. There is now neither a blast furnace nor a forge nor a bloomary remaining in the State.

CHAPTER XXII.

EARLY IRON ENTERPRISES IN MARYLAND.

In his *Report on the Manufacture of Iron,* addressed to the Governor of Maryland in 1840, Alexander gives 1715 as the " epoch of *furnaces* in Maryland, Virginia, and Pennsylvania." This statement is not strictly accurate except in regard to Virginia. Pennsylvania's first furnace was not built until about 1720 ; certainly not before that year. Maryland had no iron enterprises but a bloomary or two until 1724, when its first furnace was built. Scrivenor says that in 1718 " Maryland and Virginia " exported to England 3 tons and 7 cwt. of bar iron, upon which the mother country collected a duty of £6 19s. 1d. This bar iron could only have been made in Maryland, as Virginia had no forges at this time.

In 1719 the general assembly of Maryland passed an act "authorizing 100 acres of land to be laid off to any who would set up furnaces and forges in the province." Other inducements were offered in 1721 and subsequently to those who would engage in the manufacture of iron. The preamble to the act of 1719 recites that " there are very great conveniences of carrying on iron works within this province, which have not hitherto been embraced for want of proper encouragement to *some first undertakers,*" which clearly implies that iron enterprises had already been undertaken in Maryland but were not then in operation. As a result of the encouragement given by the general assembly authentic reports show that in 1749 and again in 1756 there were eight furnaces and nine forges in Maryland, and that on the 21st of December, 1761, there were eight furnaces, making about 2,500 tons of pig iron annually, and ten forges, capable of making about 600 tons of bar iron annually. During the colonial period Maryland had no manufacturing industry worthy of the name except that of iron. Tobacco-growing and wheat-growing formed the principal employments of the people.

The first iron works in Maryland were probably erected

in Cecil county, at the head of Chesapeake bay. We suppose that a bloomary at North East, on North East river, erected previous to 1716, formed the pioneer iron enterprise. That iron works were built at North East prior to 1716 is proved by a deed dated in that year, in which Robert Dutton conveyed a flour mill near the "bottom of the main falls of North East," and also fifty acres of land, to Richard Bennett for £100 in silver money. In this deed "iron works" are mentioned as among the appurtenances which were conveyed by it. We quote from Johnston's *History of Cecil County*. These works could have embraced only a bloomary, as there was not at this time a blast furnace, to supply a forge with pig iron, in either Maryland or Pennsylvania, and the first blast furnace in Virginia had just been built. The works were probably not then active.

Johnston says that in 1722 Stephen Onion & Co. leased two tracts of land, called Vulcan's Rest and Vulcan's Trial, the first of which joined Dutton's mill-dam on the south, and also another tract in Susquehanna Manor called Diffidence, lying on the north side of the North East river.

About the time of the passage of the act of 1719, above alluded to, Joseph Farmer, an ironmaster, of England, came to Maryland in behalf of himself and other adventurers in the manufacture of iron. Whether he was interested in the works at North East or not can not now be learned. In 1722 Mr. Farmer and his associates, afterwards known as the Principio Company, commenced the erection of a furnace on Talbot's manor, in Cecil county, near the mouth of Principio creek, which empties into Chesapeake bay about six miles distant from the town of North East. Johnston says that Mr. Farmer's associates at this time embraced Stephen Onion, Joshua Gee, William Russell, and John Ruston. He thinks that the North East company, known as Stephen Onion & Co., was consolidated with the Principio Company. The latter company was at first styled Joseph Farmer & Co. After having made some progress in the erection of the furnace Farmer returned to England, probably early in 1722, leaving the enterprise in charge of Stephen Onion as general manager. A son of Joshua Gee and Thomas Russell, a son of William Russell, were at Principio at this time.

At the beginning of 1723 the Principio Company was composed of William Chetwynd, of Grindon, in Warwickshire, a gentleman of wealth and position; Joshua Gee, a merchant of London; William Russell, an ironmaster of Birmingham; John England, an ironmaster of Staffordshire; John Ruston, and Joseph Farmer. It is very clear that the company had been enlarged, as the result of glowing representations made by Farmer. Several of the members, including Joshua Gee and John England, were members of the Society of Friends. William Chetwynd was the leading capitalist of the company. Walter Chetwynd also became a member as early as 1725. In consequence of the mismanagement of Stephen Onion it was at this time decided to put John England, who resided at or near Tamworth, in immediate charge of the Principio enterprise, with entire control of the company's operations in America. Accordingly, in April, 1723, John England and his wife sailed from Bristol for Philadelphia, which place they reached after a passage of seven weeks and one day. A few days afterwards they arrived at Principio.

On June 25th of the same year Mr. England wrote to Mr. Farmer a long letter of complaint concerning the condition in which he found the affairs of the company at Principio. He says: " When I came I found I think everything contrary to my expectations on thy information; for as to ye furnace, which, according to thy information when at London, was very near ready to blow, is but 18 inches above ye second couplings, and ye inner wall is but 6 feet high. . . Neither did I think thee wouldest have been guilty of ordering a furnace to have been built until thee hadst been sure of mine, that which was good and enough of it for perpetuity; for I have been at Patapsco, Bush river, and North East, and seen all ye mine along shore in every place, and can not find any more than will serve for one blast, if that. . . And when I treated with thee I feared interest was in ye bottom, which now I find true. . . As to stock of both cole and mine, there may be about two months' stock in of both cole and mine, and when there will be a stock for a blast I can not tell, cole lying three miles from ye furnace and stone at such a distance. . . You may assure yourselves here hath been and is such ruin as I never saw." The letter dwelt at length upon the unhealthiness of Principio. It may here be stated that his wife died in this year and that he was himself seized with a severe illness. The letter further dwelt upon the inefficiency, drunkenness, and mutinous temper of the workmen, many of whom appear to have been convicts from England, while others were "redemptioners" from various European countries. After stating that his disgust was at first so great that he had thought of immediately returning to England he adds: "I concluded to stay and set up a little forge to try ye iron if ever ye furnace runs any mettle." This letter was intended to be seen by other members of the company, to some of whom similar letters were written on the same day.

Subsequent letters from John England to various members of the company are largely devoted to the narration of other difficulties with which he had to contend, chief of which was the financial and other demoralization produced by the mismanagement of the company's affairs by Stephen Onion. At the close of the year Onion, who had been retained as clerk, was dismissed, and after that event Mr. England appears to have had less trouble.

Stephen Onion had made false representations in 1722 of the progress that had been made in building the furnace. On the 11th of August of that year he wrote to the company as follows: "We hope we shall finish the stack of the furnace, casting-house, and bridge ditto in a month more. The collyers are at work, and hope to have in by Christmas 400 load of cole." Of the actual progress made in building the furnace down to John England's arrival in 1723 we have already been informed in that gentleman's letters. In 1724 Stephen Onion and Thomas Russell sailed from New Castle for Great Britain in the same ship with Benjamin Franklin, who says in his autobiography that they were "masters of an iron work in Maryland" and had engaged "the great cabin." Franklin would not, of course, receive from Mr. Onion a true account of the situation at Principio.

The hopeful temper and the wise determination of the Principio Company after the true situation of its affairs had been explained by Mr. England are seen in the following extracts from a letter to him from the company, dated at

Birmingham, September 25, 1723 : "We must tell you it is
greatly to our satisfaction that we have you upon the place,
in whom we can entirely depend that you will use your
utmost care in regulating these disorders and in bringing
those refractory workmen to better discipline. . . We hope
mine cannot be wanting in the several rivers. Joseph Farmer says that upon tryal of the gritty mine in several places
he found by the loadstone as much iron in it as there is
in most of the mines that are worked in England, and hope
you will experience it to be so, and y^t when it is mixed
with a tougher mine will make a good sort of piggs for the
English market. We are also pleased with your resolution
to build a small forge to try the piggs. Our resolution is
steady for carrying on our works, for we think it would be
too great a reflection upon our conduct to quit a business
of this nature till we have try'd fully what may be done.
. . We give you full power in everything that relates to
our concern under your care, to manage, direct, and put
them forward in such manner as you shall judge for the
interest of the company."

On September 12, 1723, John England wrote to Joshua
Gee as follows : "I have been at a bloomary with some of our
mine, and it maketh very good iron, and iron taketh a very
good price here, £40 per ton, and hath done for several years
past." Where this bloomary was located we can not discover,
nor by whom it was owned, but it can easily be conjectured
that it was at North East, where there were "iron works" as
early as 1716, as has already been stated.

On January 13, 1724, Mr. England wrote to Joshua Gee
that he was "going on with ye forge dam and race to bring
water to ye forge." In the same month he wrote to Joseph
Farmer concerning the bellows for the chafery and finery,
which he desired to have made in England. On the 2d of
April, 1724, he wrote to Joshua Gee that he had heard of
"mine" near Annapolis, which he was going to see. In the
same month he wrote to William Russell that "ye furnace
might have blowed some time since, but did not think it
proper so to do without a better stock of cole and mine upon
ye bank;" also that the company's sloop was then employed
"in fetching shells to burn for lime to build a great stone

wall for ye fore bay of ye forge," and that other preparations for building the forge and its accessories were then in active progress. In both letters the hope was expressed that there would soon be a sufficient supply of charcoal to keep the furnace in blast for some time, "if we can but get mine." Mr. England was continually apprehensive of a scarcity of iron ore of good quality, which he had not found in abundance in the neighborhood of the furnace, but for which he sought diligently in other places.

We do not again hear of the Principio works until September 15, 1725, when William and Walter Chetwynd, John Wightwick, William Russell, and Thomas Russell write to Mr. England from Grindon a long and a very important letter, conveying to him "full and absolute power over all persons employed in America in our service," and also "full power to act in all things with ye authority as we ourselves were we on ye spot." This fresh expression of confidence and fresh grant of authority had a special object in view, as we shall presently see, but we are now interested in learning from this letter that "our furnace and forge in Maryland" were finished when it was written. We presume that the furnace was put in blast in 1724 and that the forge was started in 1725. The letter says: "We hear you have a good stock of pigs on ye bank, therefore desire you not to fail sending us by ye first shipping what pigs you can spare over and above what can be worked up at ye forge till ye furnace goes again, which we hope may be between 3 and 400 tons; for tho ye forge should be worked double hand, which we intend it shall, it will hardly work up above 8 tons of pigs per week, and to have ye overplus of ye pigs lying dead will be great loss to ye company." This extract would seem to indicate that the furnace had finished its first blast and was then idle. It was certainly in blast as early as May 9, 1725, on which date Joseph Growdon, of Bensalem, on Neshaminy creek, in the extreme southern corner of Bucks county, Pennsylvania, ordered a "hammer, anvil, and other iron work necessary for one single bloomary" to be cast at the furnace, Mr. Growdon having found iron ore on his land. (We can not learn that Mr. Growdon's bloomary was ever built.) Reference is made in the letter from the company to "two finers and hammermen" who had been sent to work at the forge, and others were promised "in a short time." Mr. England is advised to "sell all ye iron you make at ye forge at Principio" in American markets instead of sending it to England to be sold. Stephen Onion appears to have had sufficient address to secure from the company his partial restoration to favor, as the letter advises Mr. England that he had been appointed clerk of the furnace and forge, but subject wholly to Mr. England's authority, who is expressly told that he can discharge him if he does not give satisfaction.

It will be observed from the names of the signers of the above letter that the *personnel* of the Principio Company had undergone some changes. In a letter from William Chetwynd to John England, dated September 19th, he refers to the signers of the above letter as "all ye company except Mr. Gee," who was not wanted but could not be shaken off. The names of John Ruston and Joseph Farmer do not appear, thus indicating that they were no longer members of the company. In subsequent years other names are added.

We now come to consider the particular object which the company had in view in writing the letter of the 15th of September to Mr. England. It appears that this gentleman in his search for iron ore had found valuable deposits on the land of Captain Augustine Washington, on the north side of the Rappahannock river, in Virginia. This Captain Washington was the father of George Washington. Mr. England had been so favorably impressed with the value of the ore on Captain Washington's land, and with the other advantages which the location offered for the manufacture of iron, that he had contracted with that gentleman in the name of the company to erect a furnace upon his land, Captain Washington to have an interest in its ownership. The company being informed of this new venture was so well satisfied that all its members except Joshua Gee united in writing to Mr. England the letter of September 15th already referred to. It began: "We that sign are met together at Grindon, and give you hereby full power to build iron works on Captain Washington's land on ye terms you have agreed with him, and to use your own judgment and discretion in all things relating thereto." They added that they thought the location of the proposed new iron works was "exceedingly well chosen," and further said: "You will try ye Captain's mine in ye furnace and forge as soon as you can." In this letter the company also approved of Mr. England's selection of Ralph Falkner "to be clerk of ye Virginia furnace," and authorized him to "buy what negroes you think fit and draw for ye money." The letter of the 15th of September made a division of the shares of ownership in the new venture.

Mr. England at once proceeded with the erection of a furnace on Captain Washington's land. This was Accokeek furnace, about which we shall have something further to say in a later chapter devoted to Virginia. It was long known as "England's iron works." The clerk at Accokeek furnace when it was built was Ralph Falkner, but as early as 1730 Nathaniel Chapman was the clerk. Johnston has fallen into an error in his *History of Cecil County* where he says: "At what time the Washingtons first became connected with the company is uncertain, but it was probably in 1733." It was as early as 1725. Accokeek furnace was probably put in blast in 1726.

On September 19, 1725, William Chetwynd wrote to Mr. England as follows: "We hope very soon to send you over workmen sufficient to work ye forge double hand and also a couple of castors. You have full power to buy at any time 40 or 50 blacks, or what number you think proper, and draw for ye money. I am of opinion it would be proper to secure more land near Captain Washington's mine, because if ye mine is so considerable a one as you mention it must answer very well to have two furnaces there."

In various letters from the company to Mr. England he is advised to send pig iron freely to England but to sell his bar iron in America.

In 1730 John England was still in charge of all the company's iron enterprises in this country, including an abandoned project on James river which had not been given tangible shape. Stephen Onion was still the clerk at Principio, but the company was annoyed at his failure to settle his accounts. The Principio furnace and forge and the Accokeek furnace were in operation in this year. At this time we hear nothing of a forge at North East.

Prior to 1730 Mr. England bought conditionally from Sir William Keith, as has been stated in the Delaware chapter, "sundry lands and tenements in New Castle county, on Delaware, upon which lands there was a small iron fforge and supposed to be a great quantity of iron ore." It was his intention to erect upon this land "works for carrying on the making of pigg and barr iron if a sufficient quantity of iron ore or mine could be found on yᵉ land." This project was abandoned, and we hear no more of his connection with the iron business in Delaware. In 1726 Mr. England had purchased for himself an estate on White Clay creek, in New Castle county. He passed the last years of his life on this estate and at Snowdens' iron works on the Patuxent river, in Maryland, in which he had an interest. He died in 1734.

John England wås one of the most intelligent, enterprising, and successful of early American ironmasters. He undoubtedly built the first furnace and the first forge in Maryland. The various works of the Principio Company, of which he was so efficient a manager, were in the front rank of our colonial iron enterprises for fifty years. They were foremost in the production of pig iron and possibly of bar iron.

For the facts contained in the foregoing very full and absolutely accurate history of the commencement of the Principio iron works we are wholly indebted to the courtesy of James B. England, Esq., of Philadelphia, a descendant of Joseph England, (a brother of John England,) who placed in our hands the original correspondence between John England and the Principio Company. This correspondence is now in the library of the Maryland Historical Society, at Baltimore.

We are unable to glean any further particulars about the first works at North East than have already been given, but in an inventory of the possessions of the Principio Company in May, 1723, there is an entry which probably refers to these works. This entry credits the company with the purchase, on July 9, 1722, of 383 acres of land "in Lord Baltimore's Mannor of North East, called Vulcan's Tryal, Vulcan's Enlargement, and Diffidence." This purchase may have embraced the North East "iron works," upon the site of which, at the "bottom of the main falls of North East," the company subsequently erected a new forge, probably about 1735. It was in operation and briskly employed in 1743. The first entry in the inventory mentions the purchase on October 14, 1721, of 8,110 acres of land called Gee Faruson, near North East. It is exceedingly probable that Joseph Farmer and his associates made investments at North East preliminary to the manufacture of iron at that place before they decided to build the furnace at Principio.

In Emanuel Swedenborg's *De Ferro*, published in 1734, we find at the beginning of an account of iron works "in Maryland and Pennsylvania in the West Indies" the following reference to the Principio works: "There are several furnaces for the smelting of iron ore, as well as works for the smelting of raw iron, not so very long since built. The principal work is called Principio, in the upper part of the province of Maryland, upon the river called Principio, from which it also derives its name; its water is said to fall from a height of 25 feet. At this iron work little two-oared boats and little ships land laden with iron ore, which is dug 50 miles from there. The ore is said to be of a white or gray color, not unlike the vases of Holland pottery, containing 50 per cent. of iron. The iron from this ore is said to carry off the palm from the rest."

Alexander says that a part of the hearth of the original Principio furnace was still standing in 1840, when his report was written. The same excellent authority says that on February 5, 1734, (old style,) in pursuance of the act of 1719, already referred to, a precept for 100 acres of land on North East river, forming part of North East manor, was issued to John Ruston, who had been one of the members of the Principio Company; and he further says that on August 31, 1736, this tract was assigned to William Chetwynd, of Beddington, in Surrey, England, who was probably William Chetwynd, of Grindon. It was about this time that the company built its forge at North East. Alexander says that this forge was in his day "commonly called Russell's forge," reference being made to the last Russell who was connected with it.

In 1744 William Black, secretary of the commissioners who were appointed by Governor Gooch, of Virginia, to unite with those from Pennsylvania and Maryland to treat with the

Iroquois, or Six Nations of Indians, in reference to the lands west of the Alleghenies, wrote in his journal, on May 25th, while at North East, in Maryland: "I must not forget that in the forenoone the Com'rs and their company went to the Principio iron works, in order to view the curiosities of that place. They are under the management of Mr. Baxter, a Virginian, and was at work forming barr-iron when we came there. For my part I was no judge of the workmanship, but I thought everything appeared to be in very good order, and they are allowed to be as compleat works as any on the continent by those who are judges." The furnace and forge at Principio were both in operation in that year, the manager of which at this time was William Baxter, but the visit of the commissioners may have been to the forge at North East.

We obtain additional information concerning the famous Principio Company from a valuable historical essay prepared a few years ago by Mr. Henry Whiteley, of Philadelphia.

Ore for Principio furnace was at first obtained in the immediate neighborhood, but as early as September 4, 1724, it was obtained from Gorsuch's Point, below Canton, on the eastern shore of the Patapsco, about opposite to Fort McHenry. In 1727 the Principio Company, through John England, purchased all the iron ore, "opened and discovered, or shut and not yet discovered," on Whetstone Point, at the extremity of which Fort McHenry now stands, for £300 sterling and £20 current money of Maryland. This was for many years one of its principal sources of ore supply. Iron ore has been taken from Whetstone Point in recent years.

Kingsbury furnace was the next furnace of the company after Accokeek. It was situated on Herring run, at the head of Back river, in Baltimore county. It was built in 1744 and went into blast in April, 1745, producing at the first blast, which lasted till December 18th of the same year, 480 tons of pig iron. The first four blasts embraced the period extending from April 1, 1745, to December 26, 1751, and produced 3,853 tons, or an average of 75 tons per working month. More than 3,300 tons of the iron were shipped to the company in England. In 1751 Lancashire furnace was purchased from Dr. Charles Carroll, of Annapolis. It was located near Kingsbury, on the west side of a branch of Back river, a few miles northeast of Baltimore. The deed embraced 8,200 acres of land, and was "signed" on behalf of the company by Lawrence Washington, who had succeeded to the interest of his father, Captain Washington. Lawrence was a half-brother of George Washington. Lancashire furnace was operated by the company from the time of its purchase until the Revolution. It was its last acquisition of property in America. At the time of its purchase the company outranked all competitors, being the sole proprietor of four furnaces and two forges, viz. : Principio furnace, Cecil county, Maryland, finished in 1724 ; Principio forge, at the same place ; North East forge, Cecil county, Maryland, built about 1735 ; Accokeek furnace, Virginia, built in 1726 ; Kingsbury furnace, Baltimore county, Maryland, built in 1744 ; Lancashire furnace, Baltimore county, Maryland, purchased in 1751. The company owned slaves and live stock in abundance, and its landed estates were of great extent, amounting to nearly thirty thousand acres, exclusive of the Accokeek lands in Virginia. One-half of the pig iron exported to Great Britain from this country before the Revolution is said by Mr. Whiteley to have come from the furnaces of this company.

After 1776 the company had no actual control over any of its American property. Thomas Russell, who had been the company's general manager, continued to operate the furnaces and forges, and supplied bar iron and cannon balls in large quantities to the Continental army. In the Lancashire furnace ledger is an "account of shott made at Lancashire furnace in the year 1776."

In 1780 the general assembly of Maryland passed an act to seize and confiscate all British property within the State, and this was the formal end of the Principio Company, after an existence of nearly sixty years. All the property of the company, with two exceptions, now passed under the auctioneer's hammer and into new hands. The works at North East were retained by Thomas Russell, one of the company and a son of the first Thomas Russell, who had cast his fortunes with the patriotic cause. "A certain Mr. Washington" owned a one-twelfth interest in the possessions of the company, and was also an adherent of the patriotic cause. This "Mr. Washington" was probably one of the brothers of George

Washington; he was certainly a relative. What action was taken by Virginia concerning the possessions of the company in that State we are not advised, but Mr. Washington's interest in them and in the company's Maryland possessions could not be confiscated.

Thomas Russell, at his death in 1786, left a son Thomas, the third of the name. On his arrival at the age of twenty-one, his mother having previously married Daniel Sheredine, he revived the iron industry at North East with the aid of Sheredine, and in 1802 built a furnace, which was in operation only four years. Not proving as profitable as had been anticipated it was blown out on the death of young Thomas Russell, which occurred in 1806. Thenceforward the various iron works at North East met with many vicissitudes until they fell into the hands of the present enterprising owners.

Iron works have been almost continuously in operation at Principio and North East since their first establishment, or for about one hundred and seventy years. At Principio Mr. George P. Whitaker and his associates have had a charcoal furnace in operation since 1837 near the site of the first Principio furnace; and at North East, on the very site of the forge built by the Principio Company about 1735, are the present extensive iron works of the McCullough Iron Company, including probably the largest forge in the United States for the production of blooms from pig iron.

Pig iron from early Virginia furnaces near tidewater was taken to Principio forge, and also to the forge at North East, to be refined into bar iron.

About forty years ago a whole pig of iron was found near the site of the first Principio furnace, which was plainly stamped "Principio, 1727." Over twenty years ago several pigs of iron, marked "Principio * 1751," were discovered in the bed of the Patapsco river. The relics of 1751 have been preserved by the Stickney Iron Company.

A furnace at the foot of Gwynn's falls, and a forge called Mount Royal, at Jones's falls, were built by the Baltimore Company soon after 1723 and before 1730—Messrs. Carroll, Tasker, and others forming the company. This was the second blast furnace in Maryland.

Stephen Onion severed his connection with the Principio

Company and built a furnace and two forges of his own at the head of Gunpowder river, about a mile from Joppa, then one of the principal towns of Maryland, but now wholly deserted. These works were advertised for sale in 1769, after Stephen Onion's death. The exact date of their erection has not been preserved.

Bush furnace, in Hartford county, and Northampton furnace, in Baltimore county, were built about 1760, the latter by members of the Ridgely family. The proprietors of this furnace owned a forge on the Great Gunpowder river, called Long Cam forge, which was probably older than the furnace. Bush furnace, located on Bush creek, was owned about 1767 by John Lee Webster. On the Patapsco, near Elkridge Landing, were Elkridge furnace and forge, owned by Edward Dorsey; at a locality not now known was York furnace; in Anne Arundel county were the Patuxent furnace and forge, owned by Thomas, Richard, and Edward Snowden. Richard Snowden was the proprietor of "iron works" on the eastern branch of the Patuxent as early as 1734. John England, who died in that year, had an interest in these works. There was an early furnace on Stemmer's run, about seven miles from Baltimore. There was also a furnace on Curtis creek, in Patapsco county, built by William Goodwin and Edward Dorsey, which remained in operation until 1851. Nottingham furnace, in Baltimore, was built before the Revolution.

In 1762 Robert Evans, Jonathan Morris, and Benjamin Jacobs built Unicorn forge at a place called Nasby, in Queen Anne county. The castings for the forge were procured at "Bush river furnace," which appears to have been then operated by Isaac Webster. The firm of Evans, Morris & Jacobs was not long in existence.

In Frederick county were several early iron enterprises, particulars of which have been preserved by Alexander. Old Hampton furnace, on Tom's creek, about two miles west of Emmetsburg, was built between 1760 and 1765 by persons whose names have not survived. Legh furnace was built about the same time by an Englishman named Legh Master, at the head of Little Pipe creek, two or three miles southwest of Westminster. Both of these furnaces were soon abandoned. Catoctin furnace, situated about twelve miles northwest of Frederick, was built in 1774 by James Johnson & Co. It was rebuilt in 1787 by the same company, "about three-fourths of a mile further up Little Hunting creek, and nearer the ore banks." It was again rebuilt about 1831. This furnace and two later furnaces of the same name were in blast in 1880. The original Catoctin furnace yielded at first from twelve to eighteen tons of pig iron weekly. Shortly after its erection the same owners erected on Bush creek, about two miles above its mouth, the Bush Creek forge, which was in operation until 1810, when it was abandoned. About the time when Catoctin furnace and Bush Creek forge were built the Johnsons built a rolling and slitting mill at a spot known in 1840 as Reel's mill. About 1787 they built Johnson furnace on a small stream one mile above the mouth of the Monocacy. In 1793 the various iron properties belonging to the Johnsons were divided, and Johnson furnace fell to Roger Johnson, who soon afterwards built a forge in connection with the furnace. It was situated on Big Bennett's creek, about five miles above its junction with the Monocacy, and was called Bloomsburg forge. Its weekly product was between four and five tons of finished iron. The furnace and forge were abandoned soon after 1800. Fielderea furnace, on the Harper's Ferry road, three miles south of Frederick, was built by Fielder Gantt soon after the Revolution, but after making one blast it was abandoned. This event occurred before 1791.

In Washington county there were many iron enterprises at an early day, most of which have been noted by Alexander. In 1770 James Johnson superintended the erection of Green Spring furnace, on Green Spring run, one mile above its entrance into the Potomac. It was owned by Mr. Jacques and Governor Johnson. The neighboring iron ore not being of good quality the furnace was abandoned in a few years. James Johnson also built Licking Creek forge, at the mouth of Licking creek, for the same firm. It was at first supplied with pig iron from Green Spring furnace, but was afterwards sold to "Mr. Chambers, of Chambersburg, who carried it on for several years with pig supplied from his furnace in Pennsylvania." Mount Etna furnace, on a branch of Antietam creek, five or six miles north of Hagerstown, was built by Samuel and Daniel Hughes about 1770 and was in successful operation for many years. During the Revolution it cast the first Maryland cannon. About a mile and a half from the furnace, and about four miles from Hagerstown, the same owners built Antietam forge, which was in operation after the furnace was abandoned. Bishop states that General Thomas Johnson and his brother were the owners in May, 1777, of a furnace at Frederick, but it was not then in blast. Between 1775 and 1780 Henderson & Ross built a furnace at the mouth of Antietam creek. A forge was built at the same place about the same time. There were at least three forges on Antietam creek during the last century. In 1845 a new furnace was built on the site of the original Antietam furnace, but it has recently been dismantled. A small rolling mill, with a nail factory attached, was built at the same place about 1831 and abandoned about 1853.

Bishop says that a slitting mill was established at or near Baltimore in 1778 by William Whetcroft, and that about the same time two nail factories were established in the city, one by George Matthews and the other by Richardson Stewart. At Elkridge Landing Dr. Howard owned a tilting forge in 1783. On Deer creek, in Harford county, a forge and slitting mill were built during the last century. During the Revolution there were seventeen or eighteen forges in operation in Maryland, in addition to furnaces and other iron enterprises.

After the Revolution the iron manufacture of Maryland experienced a healthy enlargement, which continued without serious interruption until in recent years. One of the most successful rolling mills in the State was the celebrated Avalon iron works, on the Baltimore and Ohio Railroad, half a mile from the Relay House, "built by the Dorseys" about 1795 and in use down to about 1860. It first made nails and bar iron, and in its latter days large quantities of both, but afterwards, as early as 1848, it also rolled rails. A rolling mill was built on the Big Elk river, five miles north of Elkton, in 1810, on the site of copper works which had existed before the Revolution. It was active until about 1860, making sheet iron chiefly. Octorara forge, and Octorara rolling mill, on Octorara creek, above its mouth and a few miles north of Port Deposit, were built many years ago. The rolling mill is still active. This mill and another Maryland rolling mill of modern origin are owned by the McCullough Iron Company. The once numerous forges of Maryland have gradually given place to rolling mills. In 1840 several forges were in operation; in 1856 two forges were active; and in 1891 there were again two forges active, at North East and Principio.

The development of the iron ores belonging to the coal measures of the extreme western part of Maryland appears to have been undertaken over fifty years ago. Near the village of Friendsville, on Bear creek, a branch of the Youghiogheny river, there were erected, in 1828 and 1829, the Yohogany iron works, consisting of a furnace and two forges, to use charcoal. These works were abandoned about 1834. In 1837 a furnace fifty feet high and fourteen and one-half feet wide at the boshes was built at Lonaconing, eight miles southwest of Frostburg, by the George's Creek Coal and Iron Company, to use coke. In June, 1839, it was making about seventy tons of good foundry iron per week with coke as fuel. Overman claims that this was the· first successful coke furnace in the United States. Two large blast furnaces were built in 1840 by the Mount Savage Iron Company, nine miles northwest of Cumberland, also to use coke. This enterprise was also successful. In 1845 the same company built an additional furnace, but it was never lined. The Mount Savage rolling mill was built in 1843, especially to roll iron rails, and in 1844 it rolled the first rails rolled in this country that were not strap rails. These rails were of the inverted U pattern and weighed forty-two pounds to the yard. Alleghany county, Maryland, is thus entitled to two of the highest honors in connection with the American iron trade. It built the first successful coke furnace and it rolled the first heavy iron rails. The furnaces and rolling mill of the Mount Savage Iron Company have long been abandoned.

In 1846 a furnace called Lena was built at Cumberland, which at first used charcoal and afterwards used coke. It was not long in operation.

Alexander mentions a furnace on the Eastern Shore of Maryland, built in 1830 by Mark Richards, about five miles from Snow Hill, to use bog ore yielding only 28 per cent. of iron. Its annual production about 1834 was 700 tons. In 1840 the furnace was owned by T. A. Spence. It was called

Naseongo, and it was the only furnace in the State which used bog ore exclusively. A bloomary which used bog ore once stood near Federalsburg, but it was abandoned long ago. The prominence of Maryland as an iron-producing State was relatively much greater in 1870 than in 1880. In the former year it was fifth in rank but in the latter year it was only twelfth in rank. In 1890 it was the eleventh in rank in the production of pig iron, but its rank as a producer of rolled iron was still lower. Its production of steel in 1890 was very small, but the completion in 1891 of the extensive Bessemer steel works of the Pennsylvania Steel Company at Sparrow's Point will soon place the State in the front rank of all the steel-producing States, and the recent completion of four large furnaces by the same company will soon advance its rank in the production of pig iron.

A FURNACE was built at Georgetown, in the District of Columbia, in 1849. It went out of blast finally about 1855. A second stack was built at the same place but was never lined, and consequently was never put in blast. Both of these were small furnaces. The furnace which was in operation used charcoal and was blown with steam-power. Both enterprises were owned by William A. Bradley, of Washington. Before 1812 the United States Government built an anchor forge at the navy yard at Washington, which was enlarged about 1830 and was afterwards used to produce anchors, shafts, chains, etc. About the time when this forge was established there was a cannon foundry "about a mile beyond Georgetown, on the Potomac river." "A cannon was cast at this foundry of 100 lbs. ball, to which was given the name of Columbiad." The District of Columbia had no other iron enterprises until 1878, when the Government established a small rolling mill at the navy yard, which was, however, abandoned in 1887. The forge is still in operation, and connected with it the Government now has also in operation an extensive gun factory, which has been recently fitted up with powerful machine tools, immense traveling cranes, and other mechanical appliances for manufacturing from forgings made elsewhere the heaviest as well as the lightest ordnance for the new American navy.

CHAPTER XXIII.

THE IRON INDUSTRY ESTABLISHED IN VIRGINIA.

AFTER the failure to make iron on Falling creek in 1622 no successful effort was made to revive the iron industry in Virginia until after the beginning of the succeeding century, a delay of almost a hundred years. As late as 1670 Sir William Berkley reported to the Lords Commissioners of Foreign Plantations that but little iron ore had been discovered in Virginia up to that time, and he does not mention any iron works as then existing in the colony. Additional evidence that there was no iron made in Virginia in the seventeenth century is given in a preceding chapter. To Colonel Alexander Spotswood, who was Governor of Virginia from 1710 to 1723, the honor of having established the iron industry of the colony on a firm and permanent basis is fairly due, although the exact date of the commencement of his various iron enterprises is lost. We are indebted to the researches of Mr. R. A. Brock, of Richmond, for the following information concerning the inception of Governor Spotswood's schemes to effect a revival of the iron industry in Virginia.

In the collections of the Virginia Historical Society are two MS. volumes of the letters of Governor Spotswood to the Lords Commissioners the Council of Trade at London, covering the period from 1710 to 1721. On October 24, 1710, the Governor writes: "There is a project to be handed to the next assembly for improvement of the iron mines, lately discovered in this country, the ores of which upon tryall have been found to be extraordinary rich and good. It is proposed that the work be carried on at publick charge." This scheme appears not to have been acted upon by the assembly. On December 15, 1710, the Governor writes: "I humbly propose to your lordships' consideration whether it might not turn to good account if Her Majesty would be pleased to take that work [the iron] in her own hands, sending over workmen and materials for carrying it on." He states that the "iron mines lie at the falls of James river." On January 27, 1714, he asks that the German Protestants settled at the head of the Rappahannock river, who came over with Baron de Graffenreidt "in hopes to find out mines," be exempted from the payment of levies for the support of the government.

In the latter part of 1716 elaborate charges of malfeasance in office were anonymously preferred against Governor Spotswood to the Council of Trade, the counts of which are numerous. In one of them Governor Spotswood is charged, under pretense of guarding the frontiers, with building, at the cost of the government, two forts, one at the head of James river and another at the head of Rappahannock river, only to support his two private interests, at least one of which, that on the Rappahannock, related to the manufacture of iron. Another account charges the maintenance at public cost at these forts of a corps of "rangers" for three years ending in December, 1716. The beginning of this period would be near that of the German settlement, the members of which became the workmen of Governor Spotswood. It may be assumed that one of his iron enterprises, the furnace built by the Germans, was in operation certainly in 1716 and most likely one year earlier.

But did Governor Spotswood or the Germans acting independently of him *set on foot* the first of these enterprises? This is not clear. In John Esten Cooke's *History of the People of Virginia* it is stated that these Germans, who were Palatinates, had been "sent over by Her Majesty Queen Anne to make wine and help in the iron business," and it will be remembered that the Governor in 1710 proposed that the Queen should send over workmen and materials for the express purpose of inaugurating the iron industry in the colony.

In 1727 the general assembly of Virginia passed "an act for encouraging adventurers in iron works," which begins as follows: "Whereas, divers persons have of late expended great sums of money in erecting furnaces and other works for the making of iron in several parts of the country, . . . and forasmuch as it is absolutely necessary for roads to be laid out and cleaned from all such iron works to convenient landings," therefore, etc., etc.

In *A Progress to the Mines*, in 1732, by Colonel William Byrd, of Westover, Virginia, the second of the name, there is given a very full account of the iron enterprises of Virginia at that time, embracing three blast furnaces and one air furnace, but no forge. One of the blast furnaces was at Fredericksville, a village which has entirely disappeared from the maps, but which, as will hereafter appear, was located about thirty miles southwest of Fredericksburg, in Spottsylvania county, and about one-half mile north of the North Anna river. Mr. Chiswell, the furnace manager, told Colonel Byrd that the pig iron produced at the furnace was carted in ox carts over an uneven road to the Rappahannock river, a mile below Fredericksburg. This furnace was built of brick, but it had been idle "ever since May, for want of corn to support the cattle." Colonel Byrd says: "The fire in the furnace is blown by two mighty pair of bellows, that cost £100 each, and these bellows are moved by a great wheel of twenty-six foot diameter." The owners of the furnace had invested about £12,000 in land, negroes, cattle, etc., and had made 1,200 tons of iron. "When the furnace blows it runs about twenty tons a week." Colonel Byrd says that the company was formed as follows: "Mr. Fitz Williams took up the mine tract, and had the address to draw in the Governor, [Spotswood,] Captain Pearse, Dr. Nicolas, and Mr. Chiswell to be jointly concerned with him, by which contrivance he first got a good price for the land, and then, when he had been very little out of pocket, sold his share to Mr. Nelson for £500, and of these gentlemen the company at present consists. And Mr. Chiswell is the only person amongst them that knows anything of the matter." One of the mines attached to the furnace was fifteen or twenty feet deep, and the ore was dislodged by blasting, after which it was carried away "in baskets up to the heap." It was calcined before being used, layers of charcoal and ore alternating. The limestone used at the furnace was brought from Bristol, in England, as ballast, and carted from the Rappahannock to the furnace by the ox teams which brought down the iron. Colonel Byrd recommended the substitution of oyster shells for limestone, but without effect. If this furnace had made only 1,200 tons of iron as late as 1732, when Colonel Byrd visited it, it is evident that it had not been built many years. We place the date of its erection at about 1727.

The next furnace visited by Colonel Byrd was directly controlled by Colonel Spotswood, and was situated in Spottsylvania county, about ten miles northwest of Fredericksburg and about ten miles east of the small town of Germanna. This last place was situated in Orange county, on the south side of the Rapidan, and about ten miles above its junction with the Rappahannock. It had been settled by Germans and afterwards abandoned for another location on "land of their own, ten miles higher, in the Fork of Rappahannock." This furnace, according to Colonel Spotswood, was the first in Virginia. It was built of rough stone, "having been the first of that kind erected in the country." The iron made at this furnace was carted fifteen miles to Massaponax, on the Rappahannock, five miles below Fredericksburg, where Colonel Spotswood had recently erected an air furnace, which he "had now brought to perfection, and should be thereby able to furnish the whole country with all sorts of cast iron, as cheap and as good as ever came from England." The blast furnace "had not blown for several moons, the Colonel having taken off great part of his people to carry on his air furnace at Massaponax." The ore at this furnace was also blasted with gunpowder. "Here the wheel that carried the bellows was no more than twenty feet diameter." "All the land hereabouts seems paved with iron ore, so that there seems to be enough to feed a furnace for many ages." Colonel Spotswood resided at Germanna at the time of Colonel Byrd's visit.

Colonel Byrd next mentions "England's iron mines, called so from the chief manager of them, tho' the land belongs to Mr. Washington." These mines, he states, were on the north side of the Rappahannock river, twelve miles distant from Fredericksburg. Two miles distant from the mines was a furnace. "Mr. Washington raises the ore and carts it thither for twenty shillings the ton of iron that it yields. The furnace is built on a run, which discharges its waters into Potomeck. And when the iron is cast they cart it about six miles to a landing on that river. Besides Mr. Washington and Mr. England there are several other persons in England concerned in these works. Matters are very well managed there, and no expense is spared to make them profitable, which is not the case in the works I have already mentioned." This was Accokeek furnace, already referred to in the Maryland chapter. It was situated in Stafford county. The "Mr. Washington" referred to was Augustine Washington, the father of George Washington.

Colonel Byrd did not visit Accokeek furnace. He visited Colonel Spotswood's air furnace at Massaponax, which he describes. It was a very ambitious and creditable enterprise, and it appears to have been successfully managed. Colonel Spotswood used it "to melt his sow iron, in order to cast it into sundry utensils, such as backs for chimneys, andirons, fenders, plates for hearths, pots, mortars, rollers for gardeners, skillets, boxes for cart wheels, and many other things. And, being cast from the sow iron, are much better than those which come from England, which are cast immediately from the ore for the most part." "Here are two of these air furnaces in one room, that so in case one want repair the other may work, they being exactly of the same structure." Colonel Spotswood informed Colonel Byrd that Robert Cary, of England, was a silent partner of his in all his iron enterprises. In Cooke's *History of the People of Virginia* it is stated that in 1760 about 600 tons of iron were smelted at "Spotswood's furnaces," most of which was sent to England.

Colonel Byrd was the owner of a princely estate, on the north bank of the James river, called Westover, where he died and was buried. He was born on March 28, 1674, and died on August 26, 1744. He was the founder of both Richmond and Petersburg. Colonel Spotswood died in 1740.

Mr. W. H. Adams, of Mineral City, Virginia, has recently undertaken an investigation of the exact location of Colonel Spotswood's various iron enterprises, and has placed in our hands the results of his labors. He locates the furnace built by the Germans, and which he calls Rappahannock furnace, on a small stream flowing into the Rappahannock river, about ten miles above Fredericksburg, and he locates the Fredericksville furnace in the southwestern part of Spottsylvania county. He says that few vestiges of the town of Germanna now exist. Its site was on the Rapidan river, in Orange county, about twenty miles west of Fredericksburg. The Massaponax air furnace he locates on the Rappahannock, on a neck of land at the outlet of the Massaponax river, on lands now owned by Dr. Morton, and about five miles below Fredericksburg. From his description of the location and remains of the Rappahannock and Fredericksville furnaces we condense the following interesting statement.

The Rappahannock furnace stood close to the fords of the Rappahannock river, and on the almost precipitous banks of a small stream which was relied on for the necessary power. Considerable grading was done to provide for the operation of the furnace, the storage of charcoal, limestone, ores, etc. Protected by its isolated position the structures remained in an excellent state of preservation. The furnace is almost intact, its cleanly cut stone work and auxiliary walls, race, and chambers being about as they were left by the last workmen one hundred and sixty years ago. A giant black-walnut tree is growing from the mouth of the furnace, binding with its roots the heavy walls in place, and closing every aperture against the ravages of time. The slag piles, fluxes, coal, and considerable amounts of pig iron, found in odd shapes in the cinder beds and the bed of the brook; the dam, of generous extent but faulty construction; the race-way, tail-race, etc., are interesting evidences of this early enterprise.

The location of the Fredericksville furnace is an isolated one, in the southwestern part of Spottsylvania county, off the main line of travel, about 30 miles southwest from Fredericksburg, 10 miles from the new town of Mineral City, and one-half mile from the North Anna river. The exact site of the furnace is just off the main county road from Fredericksburg to Mineral City. The furnace was placed on a small stream, which flowed into the North Anna river. The dam, which was established about 1,000 feet above the furnace; the race which brought the water down to the furnace; the walls of the flume which carried the water to the overshot wheel; and the space for the blowing apparatus are all to be seen. The ores, fluxes, charcoal, masonry, etc., are plentiful in the great quantity of *débris* scattered about. It is a matter of regret, however, that the furnace itself has been thought of so little account by the owners of the land during the past twenty years that no care has been taken of the materials used in its construction, and at least half its original height has been sacrificed to furnish foundations and chimneys for the cabins of the neighborhood. A few of the bricks, unique in their shape and weight, and evidently brought from some foreign land, are still in the ruins of the furnace. About 10 feet of the stack are yet standing.

The connection of the Washington family with the iron industry of Virginia and Maryland justifies further reference to the Accokeek furnace. Custis, in his *Recollections*, relates that Augustine Washington, after the burning of his house in Westmoreland, removed to a situation near Fredericksburg, on the Rappahannock, where he became connected with the Principio Company. Colonel Byrd has partly explained the nature of this connection, and in the Maryland chapter it is still further explained. In 1750 Accokeek furnace sent to England 410 tons of pig iron, which was about one-sixth of the quantity exported from Maryland and Virginia in that year. Augustine Washington, at his death in 1743, left the estate afterwards known as Mount Vernon and his interest in *all the possessions of the Principio Company* to his son Lawrence, an elder half-brother of George Washington. Lawrence died in 1752. Mr. Whiteley says that Augustine Washington's interest in the Principio Company at his death was one-twelfth. He had probably exchanged for this interest his shares in the Accokeek property, which will hereafter be explained.

We have examined the will of Lawrence Washington, of Fairfax county, Virginia, as it is recorded in Albert Welles's *History of the Washington Family*. It is dated June 20, 1752. We make the following literal extract: "I give and bequeath to my daughter Sarah, . . after my just debts are discharged, all my real and personal estate in Virginia and the Province of Maryland, not otherwise disposed of. But in case it should please God my said daughter should die without issue, it is then my will and desire that my estate, both real and personal, be disposed of in the following manner. First. I give and bequeath unto my loving brother Augustine Washington and his heirs forever all my stock, interest, and estate in the Principio, Accokeek, Kingsbury, Laconshire, & No. East iron works, in Virginia and Maryland, reserving one-third of the profits of the said works to be paid my wife as hereafter mentioned." George Washington was one of the executors of the will. Sarah did not long survive her father, and upon her death Augustine Washington succeeded to the ownership of his iron interests and George Washington succeeded to the ownership of Mount Vernon. Mr. Whiteley says that Accokeek furnace was abandoned soon after Lawrence Washington's death, owing to the failure of a supply of ore within a reasonable distance. In 1753 the slaves, horses, cattle, and wagons were sold, and affairs were gradually closed up until nothing but the real estate was left, of which Augustine Washington probably afterwards became sole owner. But he continued to retain an interest in the Principio Company's other iron enterprises until the Revolution, during which they passed into new hands. Mr. Whiteley also says that it was at the solicitation of Augustine Washington, "in behalf of himself and other adventurers in iron works," that in 1757 the Virginia Council remitted the port duties and fees on pig and bar iron imported into that province from Maryland.

Before parting with the Washington family we will here refer to a well-preserved deed which is now in the possession of the Maryland Historical Society. This deed, which was executed on March 2, 1729, recites that on July 24, 1726, Augustine Washington "did demise, grant, bargain, and sell unto" John England as trustee "the said Augustine Washington's plantation and lands situate, lying, and being at Accokeek run in Stafford county in Virginia, . . containing by estimation one thousand six hundred acres, or thereabouts, together with all the soil thereof, with all manner of iron mines and iron oar . . within the limits of the said plantation, together also with all and singular the woods, trees, rivers," etc. "And the said Augustine Washington did by the said verited lease grant unto the said John England the full right and authority to cutt and make any shafts, pitts, or devoids upon the said lands, to open or draw any of the mines, oars, and mineralls aforesaid," and "to refine, mill, and manufacture the oars and mineralls aforesaid, and to set up any furnaces, buildings, or engines upon the said land or any part thereof."

In consideration of these grants to John England, which were confirmed to the Principio Company by the deed from which we have above quoted, and which it was to hold for a thousand years, Augustine Washington was to receive "the yearly rent of one ear of corn if demanded" and a two-twelfths interest in the lands conveyed and in the furnace and other improvements which should be made upon them, the whole ownership to be divided as follows: Walter Chetwynd, two-twelfths; William Chetwynd, two-twelfths; Joshua Gee, one-twelfth; William Russell, one-twelfth; Thomas Russell, one-twelfth; John Wightwick, two-twelfths; Augustine Washington, two-twelfths; and John England, one-twelfth. The instrument from which we have quoted recites that "since the making of the said lease," on July 24, 1726, "the said John England hath on the said premises erected an iron furnace, dam, and other works and buildings for the rosting of iron." The instrument further recites that the lease of July 24, 1726, is recorded in folios 524 to 529 of Book No. 1 of the court of Stafford county, session of June 10, 1728. And it further says that "the said John England, for and on account of the said works, . . hath purchased and taken in fee, or for years, or some other estate, several other parcells of land in Virginia aforesaid, amounting in the whole to one thousand five hundred acres or thereabouts."

Mr. Brock writes us that, in *Hening's Statutes*, volume IX., there is "an act for the encouragement of iron works," passed in May, 1777, which recites that, "Whereas, the discovery and manufacturing of iron ore requisite for the fabricating the various implements of husbandry, small arms, intrenching tools, anchors, and other things necessary for the army and navy, is at this time essential to the welfare and existence of this State, as the usual supplies of pig and bar iron from foreign States is rendered difficult and uncertain, and James Hunter, near Fredericksburg, hath erected and is now carrying on, at considerable expense and labour, many extensive factories, slitting, plating, and wire mills, and is greatly retarded through the want of pig and bar iron; and whereas, there is a certain tract of land in the county of Stafford, called or known by the name of Accokeek furnace tract, on which a furnace for the making of pig iron was formerly erected and carried on, which has been since discontinued," etc., etc., James Hunter is therefore authorized to enter upon two hundred acres of the Accokeek tract, including the old furnace, if its owners or agents should fail in one month to begin and within six months to erect thereon a furnace equal to or larger than the former one, and prosecute the same for the making of pig iron and other castings. We think that this proposed new furnace was never built, as it is not referred to in Thomas Jefferson's *Notes on the State of Virginia*, to be quoted from hereafter, while "a forge of Mr. Hunter's, at Fredericksburg," is distinctly noted by Jefferson.

Mr. Chiswell told Colonel Byrd that "we had as yet no forge erected in Virginia, tho' we had four furnaces. But there was a very good one set up at the head of the bay in

Maryland, that made exceeding good work." The forge referred to was doubtless the one at Principio, the North East
forge not having been built until about 1735. Colonel Spotswood told Colonel Byrd that "he was not only the first in this
country, but the first in North America, who had erected a
regular furnace; that they ran altogether upon bloomerys in
New England and Pennsylvania till his example had made
them attempt greater works." This statement is correct only
so far as it relates to the manufacture of pig iron exclusively
and not castings. By the phrase, "a regular furnace," Colonel
Spotswood meant a furnace which was built expressly to
make pig iron. Colonel Byrd's statement, that the furnace
near Germanna was the first furnace in the country that was
"built of rough stone," is not correct.

In the Valley of Virginia many furnaces and forges were
built before the Revolution and others were built before the
close of the last century. Zane's furnace and forge, on Cedar
creek, in Frederick county, were "built before any iron works
in this region." Pine forge, in Shenandoah county, three and
a half miles north of New Market, was built at an early day.
Isabella furnace, on Hawksbill creek, near Luray, in Page
county, was built about 1760. About 1775 a furnace was built
on Mossy creek, Augusta county, by Henry Miller and Mark
Bird, of Berks county, Pennsylvania. Bird soon sold his interest to Miller. A forge was soon added to this furnace.

Union forge, near Waynesborough, in Augusta county,
was built about 1800. In Rockbridge county were two forges, built about 1800—Gibraltar forge, on North river, nine
miles north of Lexington, and Buffalo forge, on Buffalo creek,
the same distance south of Lexington. Moore's furnace, on
Steele's creek, in this county, and a furnace on Smith's creek,
in Rockingham county, were built before 1800.

A furnace was built in Loudon county before 1800, concerning which Bishop states that Mr. Clapham, its owner,
"cut a canal through the end of Cotocktin mountain, 500 feet
through solid rock and 60 feet beneath the surface, to obtain
water for his furnace and mill."

Iron works were erected in Craig, Grayson, Wythe, Washington, Carroll, and other southwestern counties before the
close of the last century. A forge on Chestnut creek, in Car-

roll county, was built about 1790, and another on Little Reed Island creek was built about the same time. Poplar Camp furnace, on Poplar Camp creek, in Wythe county, appears to have been built in 1778, as a stone bearing that date and identified with the furnace is still preserved. A few of the old charcoal furnaces that are still in existence in Southwestern Virginia retain all their primitive characteristics. They are blown by water-power with wooden "tubs," are placed against a bank of the same level as the tunnel-head, have a cold blast, and are operated by "the rule of thumb." The stacks are built of stone. But even in Southwestern Virginia modern methods are now obtaining full recognition.

Bishop says that an excellent "air furnace" was built at Westham, six miles above Richmond, on the north side of the James river, during the Revolution; there was also a cannon foundry here at the same period. The "air furnace" is said to have used bituminous coal, from the mines of Chesterfield county, in the manufacture of shot and shells for the Continental army. Benedict Arnold destroyed the works at Westham in 1781. A rolling and slitting mill was afterwards built at this place.

At Lynchburg and its vicinity, in the James River valley, several furnaces and forges were built in the last century, some of which are referred to in the following extract from Jefferson's *Notes on the State of Virginia*, written in 1781 and 1782 but not printed until 1788.

The mines of iron worked at present are Callaway's, Ross's, and Ballendine's on the south side of James river; Old's on the north side, in Albemarle; Millar's in Augusta; and Zane's in Frederick. These two last are in the valley between the Blue ridge and North mountain. Callaway's, Ross's, Millar's, and Zane's make about 150 tons of bar iron each in the year. Ross's makes also about 1,600 tons of pig iron annually; Ballendine's, 1,000; Callaway's, Millar's, and Zane's, about 600 each. Besides these, a forge of Mr. Hunter's, at Fredericksburg, makes about 300 tons a year of bar iron, from pigs imported from Maryland; and Taylor's forge, on Neapsco of Patowmac, works in the same way, but to what extent I am not informed. The indications of iron in other places are numerous, and dispersed through all the middle country. The toughness of the cast iron of Ross's and Zane's furnaces is very remarkable. Pots and other utensils cast thinner than usual, of this iron, may be safely thrown into or out of the wagons in which they are transported. Salt-pans made of the same, and no longer wanted for that purpose, cannot be broken up, in order to be melted again, unless previously drilled in many parts.

This account by Jefferson seems to establish the fact that
the iron industry of Virginia was not very extensive about
the close of the Revolution. Ross's works were on Beaver
creek, seven miles southeast of Lynchburg, and Thomas Callaway's were near Rocky Mount, or Franklin court-house.
Lesley mentions Saunders's furnace at the latter place as having been abandoned about 1800. Henry Miller's works were
near the northern boundary of Augusta county, "at the foot
of North mountain." In 1777 Old's furnace was referred to
in the Virginia legislature as an "old furnace" that was "yet
standing, tho' somewhat out of repair," but it was proposed
to put it in blast, to aid by its product in accomplishing the
independence of the colonies. This proposition took the form
of a resolution appropriating a loan of £2,000 to one of the
proprietors. The furnace was then said to have been owned
by Messrs. Old, Wilkinson & Trent, and Wilkinson was the
partner to be benefited by the loan from the Virginia treasury. The furnace appears to have been promptly put in blast,
as Jefferson says that the mines belonging to this furnace
were "worked" when his *Notes* were written. The furnace
was located about twelve miles from Charlottesville.

About 1790 the iron industry of Virginia took a fresh
start, as did many other industries of the State. No State in
the Union gave more attention to domestic manufactures after the close of the Revolution than Virginia. This activity
continued for many years, but it was partly checked in subsequent years by the greater attention given by the people
of Virginia to agricultural pursuits. Richmond, Lynchburg,
Staunton, Winchester, and some other places became noted
for the extent and variety of their manufactures. Household
manufactures were everywhere promoted. The manufacture
of nails was one of these household industries. Thomas Jefferson required about a dozen of the younger slaves owned
by him to make nails, and it is said that "they made about
a ton of nails a month at a considerable profit." The Government armory at Harper's Ferry was established in 1798.

Lesley enumerates no less than eighty-eight charcoal furnaces and fifty-nine forges and bloomaries as having been
built in Virginia prior to 1856; also twelve rolling mills.
Several of these enterprises were within the limits of the

present State of West Virginia. The furnaces were located in thirty-one counties and the forges in twenty-five counties. The first rolling mill of any kind west of the Allegheny mountains and outside of Pennsylvania of which we can obtain exact information was located in West Virginia, and is described in Cramer's *Pittsburgh Almanack* for 1813, issued in 1812, as follows: " Jackson & Updegraff, on Cheat river, have in operation a furnace, forge, rolling and slitting mill, and nail factory—nails handsome, iron tough." Like all the rolling and slitting mills of that day the Cheat river mill did not puddle iron nor roll bar iron, but rolled only sheet iron for salt pans, domestic utensils, and nail plates from blooms made in forges. Hon. James Veech informed us in his lifetime that the location of the Cheat river mill was on the road from Uniontown to Morgantown, about three miles south of the Pennsylvania State line and eight miles north of Morgantown. It was in Monongalia county.

In the old days before the civil war Wheeling was the centre of the rolling-mill industry of Virginia, having seven of the twelve rolling mills in the State. Of the remaining five mills four were in Richmond and one was on Reed creek, in Wythe county, twelve miles east of Wytheville. Since the war a few new rolling mills have been built in the old State of Virginia and new mills and steel works have been built at Wheeling. The first rolling mill at Wheeling was built in 1832 by Dr. Peter Shoenberger and David Agnew, both Pennsylvania ironmasters. This mill was called the Wheeling iron works, and the firm was styled Shoenberger & Agnew. The most prominent nail-manufacturing district in the United States at the present time is the Wheeling district, which includes the nail factories in West Virginia and in that part of Ohio which lies near Wheeling.

The works of the Tredegar Iron Company at Richmond, Virginia, are among the most notable of their kind in the United States. They were founded in 1836 by the late Francis B. Deane, and embrace a large rolling mill, an extensive foundry and machine shop, and a large car factory. During the civil war these works were a tower of strength to the Southern Confederacy, manufacturing cannon, cannon balls, and other munitions of war in large quantities down to the evacuation of Richmond in April, 1865. Prior to the war, however, they had achieved a national reputation. The United States steam frigates *Roanoke* and *Colorado* and the United States revenue cutter *James K. Polk* were furnished with engines, boilers, and guns from these works. Nearly all the machinery of the Tredegar works is driven by water-power from the James river.

A large number of the furnaces and forges of Virginia were abandoned before 1850. In 1856 there were thirty-nine charcoal furnaces and forty-three forges enumerated by Lesley as being then in operation or prepared to make iron. Since 1856 many of the charcoal furnaces and nearly all the forges that were then in existence have been abandoned. Insufficient transportation facilities, coupled with the failure of ore in certain localities, have had much to do with the abandonment of many charcoal furnaces in Virginia, while the disappearance of the forges is due to the competition of rolling mills. Of late years, however, the extension of railroads and the discovery of new and valuable ore deposits have given a fresh impetus to the manufacture of pig iron in Virginia and West Virginia, much of which is made with coke obtained in the now celebrated Pocahontas Flat Top coal region, which is found in both Virginia and West Virginia. The future of the iron industry of these two States is to-day very promising. The young State took higher rank in both 1870 and 1880 among iron-producing States than the old State. It ranked tenth in 1870 and seventh in 1880; whereas Virginia ranked thirteenth in 1870 and sixteenth in 1880. Since 1880, however, the old State has made remarkable progress in the erection of large blast furnaces to use coke as fuel. Some of the best furnaces in the country are now to be found in Virginia. Its total production of pig iron in 1880 was only 26,726 gross tons, but in 1883 it was 136,524 tons, and in 1890 it was 292,779 tons. In 1890 Virginia ranked sixth among the States in the production of pig iron. In the same year West Virginia ranked fourth in the production of steel but was twelfth in the production of pig iron.—The early iron history of West Virginia is so closely interwoven with that of Virginia that we could not devote to it a separate chapter.

CHAPTER XXIV.

THE MANUFACTURE OF IRON IN NORTH CAROLINA.

SCRIVENOR says that in 1728-29 there were imported into England from "Carolina" one ton and one cwt. of pig iron, and that in 1734 there were imported two qrs. and twelve lbs. of bar iron. Shipments of pig iron and bar iron from "Carolina" were made in subsequent years prior to the Revolution. We regret that we can not locate the first iron enterprises in this State. Some future antiquarian may be able to do this. They were probably situated near the coast, in the neighborhood of bog-ore deposits. It is a curious fact that hoes made in Virginia and "Carolina" were sold in New York long before the Revolution.

Bishop says that several iron works were in operation in North Carolina before the Revolution, some of which were put out of blast by that event. They were situated on tributaries of the Cape Fear, Yadkin, and Dan rivers. When the shadow of the approaching conflict with the mother country reached North Carolina her patriotic citizens, first in convention at New Berne and afterwards in the provincial legislature, encouraged by the offer of liberal premiums the manufacture of crude and finished iron and steel, as well as other manufactured products. "John Wilcox was the proprietor of a furnace and iron works on Deep run in the beginning of the war. There were also iron works in Guilford county, probably on the same stream. In April, 1776, the provincial congress sent commissioners to treat with Mr. Wilcox for the use of his furnace and works for two years, or to purchase and repair those in Guilford, for casting ordnance, shot, etc., and empowered them to draw on the treasury for £5,000 for that purpose." Troublesome forge, in Guilford county, was in operation during the Revolution. Buffalo Creek furnace and forge were also built before the Revolution on Buffalo creek, in Cleveland county, not far from King's mountain, on the southern border of the State.

Prior to 1800 there were in operation in Lincoln county

two bloomaries, four forges, and two furnaces. One of the furnaces, Vesuvius, on Anderson's creek, built in 1780, was in operation down to 1873. Of other iron enterprises established in North Carolina in the last century we gather from Lesley and Bishop, and from Dr. William Sharswood, a local historian, of Danbury, North Carolina, the following information : Union bloomary forge, on Snow creek, in Stokes county, six miles northeast of Danbury, was built in 1780 by Peter Perkins and James Martin. Other iron works were built on Snow creek, in the same county, and conducted with spirit before 1800. Dr. Sharswood mentions a furnace and forge on this creek which were built by Peter Perkins and James Taylor about 1795 : they were located about half a mile from the mouth of the creek. Davis's mill now stands on the site of the furnace. He also says that Matthew Moore built a forge on Big creek, where George's mill now stands, before 1800. Kiser's bloomary forge, on the headwaters of Town fork, in the same county, ten miles southwest of Danbury, was built in 1796 by George Hauser and Philip Kiser. Hill's bloomary forge, on Tom's creek, in Surry county, nineteen miles west of Danbury, was built in 1791. In the same county, near the Yadkin, iron works were erected a few years after the Revolution, probably by Moravians from Pennsylvania, who had settled in the county as early as 1753. In Wilkes county a forge was built about the same time. A furnace and forge were erected on Troublesome creek, in Rockingham county, at an early day. In Burke county, at the foot of the Blue ridge, two bloomaries and two forges were erected before the close of the last century.

After 1800 the iron industry of North Carolina was still further developed. This development was, however, mainly confined to the manufacture of bar iron in bloomaries, the magnetic and hematite ores of North Carolina being well adapted to this mode of treatment. In 1810, according to Tench Coxe, there were six bloomaries, two rolling and slitting mills, and two naileries in Lincoln county ; one bloomary in Iredell county ; six bloomaries and one trip-hammer in Burke county; and five bloomaries in Surry county—eighteen bloomaries in all. In 1856 Lesley enumerated about forty bloomaries and a few forges, most of which were then in operation. They were located in Stokes, Surry, Yadkin, Catawba, Lincoln, Gaston, Cleveland, Ashe, Watauga, Rutherford, and Cherokee counties. The *trompe* was in general use. He also described six furnaces : Vesuvius, already referred to; Madison, on Leiper's creek, in Lincoln county, built in 1810; Rehoboth, on the same creek and in the same county, built in 1810 ; Columbia, seven miles west of High Shoals, in Gaston county, then in ruins ; Tom's Creek, near Hill's forge, on Tom's creek, destroyed by a flood in 1850; Buffalo Creek, already referred to, and then in ruins. Vesuvius, Madison, and Rehoboth were blown with wooden "tubs." There was also active at this date a small rolling mill on Crowder's creek, in Gaston county, a mile and a quarter north of King's mountain, owned by Benjamin F. Briggs, of Yorkville, South Carolina, and built in 1853. At the same time another small rolling mill and forge, known as High Shoals iron works, and situated in Gaston county, were in ruins.

There have been other early iron works in North Carolina than those mentioned by Lesley or the other authorities from whom we have quoted. A furnace called Washington is said to have been built in Gaston county in 1788. Iron was made in a bloomary near the line of Nash and Wilson counties in the war of 1812, and during the civil war iron was made in a blast furnace in the same locality. About 1840 there was a furnace called Shuford in Catawba county, and at the same period there was a furnace called Beard's on the Catawba river, probably in Catawba county. Iron was also made about the same time on Gunpowder creek, in Caldwell county, probably in a bloomary.

In the census year 1840 there were eight furnaces in North Carolina, which produced in that year 968 gross tons of cast iron, including both pig iron and castings, and forty-three bloomaries, forges, and rolling mills, which produced 963 tons of bar iron.

In Mitchell county, in the northwestern part of the State, and within a few miles of the Tennessee line, there exists an extensive deposit of iron ore known as the Cranberry mines, the deposit taking its name from Cranberry creek, which flows at the foot of the steep mountain spurs in which the ore is found. This ore is a pure magnetite, and is practically free from sulphur and phosphorus. This valuable deposit has been in part developed by Northern capital. The Cranberry Iron Company has shipped some ore to distant furnaces, and it has also built at the mines a small charcoal furnace which was put in blast in the spring of 1884. Cranberry ore was long worked in bloomaries in the neighborhood.

At least three furnaces were built in North Carolina during the civil war, one in Chatham county, another in Lincoln county, and another, already referred to, on the line of Nash and Wilson counties. Two furnaces were built in Chatham county after the war, but of these five furnaces, and Vesuvius, Madison, and Rehoboth, all of which were lately standing, as may have been one or two other furnaces, not one made a pound of iron from 1877 until 1881. In that year Rehoboth furnace was in operation, and in 1882 it was still active, but in 1883 it was silent and it has since been idle. In 1890 it was reported as having been abandoned. The furnace built in Lincoln county during the war was named Stonewall.

Nearly all of the iron works that have been referred to have been built in the western part of North Carolina. Of the long list of bloomaries and forges which this State could once boast only two bloomaries in Mitchell and Surry counties have recently been active, and we are informed that neither of these is likely to be operated again. Of all the furnaces that North Carolina once possessed only Cranberry furnace has been active in late years, and it is a comparatively new furnace. There is not to-day a rolling mill or steel works in the State.

CHAPTER XXV.

THE MANUFACTURE OF IRON IN SOUTH CAROLINA.

IF the iron industry of North Carolina has rapidly declined in late years that of South Carolina has suffered even
a worse fate; it has been an extinct industry for many years.
Yet this State made some iron as early as the Revolutionary
period, and subsequently it made iron in considerable quantities. In the northwestern part of South Carolina, including
the counties of Union, Spartanburg, and York, are valuable
deposits of magnetic ores, and here, according to Dr. Ramsay,
the historian of South Carolina, the first iron works in the
State were erected by Mr. Buffington in 1773, but they were
destroyed by the Tories during the Revolution.

At the beginning of the Revolution South Carolina followed the example of many other colonies by offering liberal premiums to those who would establish iron works, but
we do not learn that the manufacture of iron was thereby
increased. Mr. Buffington's experience probably deterred others from embarking in the business.

Several furnaces and forges were erected in this State a
few years after the peace, the principal of which were the Era
and Etna furnaces and forges in York county. The Era was
built in 1787 and the Etna in 1788. These enterprises were
situated on a creek flowing into the Catawba river and about
two miles west of it. In 1795 the nearest landing to these
works was at Camden, seventy miles below. They were on
the road leading from Charlotte, in North Carolina, to Yorkville. Iron ore was abundant in the neighborhood, and was
easily smelted after having been roasted. "It was obtained,
massive, in such quantity above the surface that it was
thought there would be no occasion to resort to shafts or
levels for half a century." William Hill was one of the principal owners of the works. He is said to have devised "a
new blowing apparatus," by the aid of which he contrived to
blow "all the fires, both of the forges and furnaces, so as to
render unnecessary the use of wheels, cylinders, or any other

kind of bellows." This apparatus was doubtless the *trompe*, or water-blast, but Mr. Hill did not invent it, nor was he the first in this country to use it. The statement, which Bishop quotes from some unknown authority, is, however, valuable, as it contains one of the few references to the use of the *trompe* in this country in blowing a blast furnace that have come under our notice. Bishop says that other iron works soon followed those of Mr. Hill, and that "they were erected in different places, including several in the mountain district of Washington, where iron, the only article made for sale to any extent, was manufactured at the beginning of this century as cheap and good as the imported."

Tench Coxe enumerates two bloomaries in Spartanburg county in 1810, four in Pendleton county, two in Greenville county, and one in York county—nine in all. He also mentions one small nailery and one small steel furnace in the State. He makes no reference to blast furnaces, but his statistics were probably not complete.

Scrivenor mentions the following enterprises in South Carolina as existing apparently about 1815, but the source of his information we have been unable to discover. "On Allison's creek, in York district, there are a forge, a furnace, a rolling mill for making sheet iron, and a nail manufactory. On Middle Tiger river are iron works on a small scale; also on the Enoree river and Rudy river, on the north fork of Saluda river, on George's creek, and on Twenty-six mile creek. In 1802 an air furnace was erected on a neck of land between Cooper and Ashley rivers, where good castings are made." York district is the same as York county, the subdivisions of South Carolina having been known as districts down to 1868.

In the census year 1840 there were four furnaces in South Carolina, which produced in that year 1,250 gross tons of castings and pig iron, and nine bloomaries, forges, and rolling mills, which produced 1,165 tons of bar iron.

In 1856 South Carolina had eight furnaces—one in York, one in Union, and six in Spartanburg county. They are described by Lesley. Four of these furnaces were then in operation, producing in the year named 1,506 tons of charcoal iron, but three others had been "out of repair for twenty years," and the remaining furnace had been abandoned. In 1856 there were also three small rolling mills in the State— one on Pacolet river, in Spartanburg county; one on Broad river, in Union county; and one on the same river, in York county. At the first two of these mills dry wood was used in the puddling and heating furnaces. In 1856 the three mills made 1,210 tons of bar iron and nails. In the same year there were also in South Carolina two "bloomaries," one connected with the rolling mill in Union county and the other connected with the rolling mill in York county. Their joint product was 640 tons of blooms. Strictly speaking these "bloomaries" were forges, as they doubtless used pig iron.

But South Carolina no longer makes iron. Every iron-producing establishment in the State is to-day silent and has been silent for many years, and all are in a more or less dilapidated condition. South Carolina and Vermont furnish the only instances in the history of the country of States having wholly abandoned the manufacture of iron.

CHAPTER XXVI.

THE EARLY MANUFACTURE OF IRON IN GEORGIA.

GEORGIA is the last of the original thirteen colonies whose iron history remains to be noticed. Unlike its sister colonies, however, Georgia has no colonial iron history. It was the last of the thirteen to be settled, and it was not until within a few years of the commencement of the Revolutionary struggle that the few settlements on the coast began to experience even moderate prosperity. After the close of the Revolution the settlement of the interior was for many years retarded by difficulties with the Indians, and it was not until 1838 that the Cherokees were induced to surrender their claims to a portion of the territory of the State. It will be seen that, under the circumstances which have been mentioned, the manufacture of iron in Georgia was destined to be the result of comparatively modern enterprise.

In 1810 there was a bloomary in Warren county, a forge in Elbert county, and a nailery in Chatham county. Two of these enterprises were near the Atlantic coast, and were doubtless among the first of their kind in the State, dating probably from about 1790. The coast sections of Georgia did not possess ample resources for the manufacture of iron. No iron industry exists there to-day. Sequee bloomary forge, three miles south of Clarkesville, in Habersham county, was built about 1830 and abandoned about 1835. Hodge's forge, in the same county, was probably built at an earlier date. Lesley says of it: "Situation unknown; history unknown; abandoned very long ago."

Bloomary forges in Cass county, now Bartow county, were built as follows: Etowah, No. 1, in 1838; Etowah, No. 2, in 1841; Allatoona, about 1846. Ivy Log bloomary, in Union county, was built about 1839. Aliculsie bloomary, in Murray county, was built about 1843. A bloomary was built on Armuchy creek, in Walker county, about 1848. Lookout bloomary, in Dade county, was built at an earlier day. All these enterprises were abandoned before 1856, in which year, however, several other bloomaries of more recent origin were in operation. In 1880 only two bloomaries in the State were reported to be in use. One forge, at Allatoona, made blooms from scrap iron in that year. In 1890 there was neither a forge nor a bloomary in Georgia that was active.

The first furnace in Georgia of which we have any information was Sequee furnace, near Clarkesville, in Habersham county, built prior to 1832 and abandoned in 1837. Etowah furnace, on Stamp creek, in Cass county, now Bartow county, was built in 1837, abandoned in 1844, and torn down in 1850. A new furnace, built by its side in 1844, is now in ruins. Allatoona furnace, in Cass county, built in 1844; Union furnace, in the same county, built in 1852; Lewis furnace, in the same county, built about 1847; and Cartersville furnace, in the same county, built in 1852, have all been abandoned. Clear Creek furnace, in Walker county, built about 1852 and rebuilt in 1857, has also been abandoned. All these were charcoal furnaces. Of the furnaces existing in Georgia in 1880 Bartow county contained five charcoal furnaces and two coke furnaces—seven in all. Of these the two Bear Mountain charcoal furnaces, built in 1842, were the oldest. Four other furnaces in the State were situated in Polk, Floyd, and Dade counties—two in Polk and one in Floyd using charcoal and one in Dade using coke. Of the eleven furnaces in the State in 1880, some of which were not then active, several have since been torn down or abandoned. Two new charcoal furnaces have recently been built—one at Tallapoosa, blown in in 1890, and one at Rome, blown in in 1891. Rising Fawn furnace, in Dade county, is 65 feet high by 17 feet wide, and was the first furnace in the United States to use the Whitwell hot-blast stove, blowing in for the first time on June 18, 1875. In 1891 there were six furnaces in Georgia, two of which used coke as fuel, three used charcoal, and one was built to use either coke or charcoal.

Georgia had two rolling mills in 1859—Etowah, in Cass county, built about 1849, and Gate City, at Atlanta, built in 1858. It is a curious fact that this State had just two rolling mills twenty-one years later, in 1880—Atlanta, built in 1865, and Rome, built in 1869. The latter had been idle for several years prior to 1880 and has since been dismantled. The

Atlanta rolling mill was burned on September 21, 1881, and not rebuilt. There is now only one rolling mill in the State, a new mill at Rome, built in 1889 partly to roll cotton-ties.

In 1859 Lesley thus describes the Etowah rolling mill and its blast furnace and other connections, located on the Etowah river: "This property has been building up and developing for twelve years. On it there has been expended $250,000. It contains a rolling mill, nail and spike factory, and all necessary apparatus; a blast furnace and foundry, with full equipment; a wheat mill (150 to 250 bushels per day), warehouse, cooper-house, hotel, and operative houses, two corn grist mills, two saw mills, and a coal. mine; all using not one-tenth of the water-power on the premises. River 600 feet wide. Iron ore and wood are abundant. It is on the metamorphic rocks of the gold and copper belt, both minerals being found on it," etc. The Etowah Iron Company has recently purchased this property and is making preparations to develop its iron-ore deposits.

From the foregoing summary it will be seen that the iron industry of Georgia is not now so prominent as in former years. There does not seem to be any reason why it should not in the next ten or twenty years become much more active than it now is or ever has been.

CHAPTER XXVII.

THE EARLY MANUFACTURE OF IRON IN KENTUCKY.

THE first iron enterprise in Kentucky whose history has been preserved was Bourbon furnace, often called Slate furnace, which was built in 1791 on Slate creek, a branch of Licking river, in Bath county, then Bourbon, and about two miles southeast of Owingsville. This is also the only furnace in Kentucky which has a history that can be traced back to the last century. In his *Notes on the State of Virginia* Jefferson says that there were iron mines " on Kentucky, between the Cumberland and Barren rivers," and also " between Cumberland and Tanissee." This was written before the close of the Revolution. The whole of Jefferson's reference to western iron mines is as follows:

> In the western country we are told of iron mines between the Muskingum and Ohio; of others on Kentucky, between the Cumberland and Barren rivers, between Cumberland and Tanissee, on Reedy creek, near the Long island, and on Chestnut creek, a branch of the Great Kanhaway near where it crosses the Carolina line. What are called the iron-banks, on the Mississippi, are believed, by a good judge, to have no iron in them. In general, from what is hitherto known of that country, it seems to want iron.

Bourbon furnace was not within the limits of any of these boundaries, but was located not far from the Ohio river. Nor is it probable that there were any iron enterprises in the Kentucky portion of the regions mentioned by Jefferson prior to the building of Bourbon furnace. This furnace was the first *furnace* outside of the present limits of the original thirteen colonies of which we can obtain any information.

We have received from V. B. Young, Esq., of Owingsville, Kentucky, a very full historical account of Bourbon furnace, which we present as follows:

> In October, 1782, Jacob Myers came from Baltimore, Maryland, to the region now embraced in Bath county, Kentucky, but then in Bourbon county, and soon afterwards patented 5,434 acres of land on Slate creek. In March, 1791, he commenced the erection of a furnace on this land, and on the 24th of May following he sold to John Cockey Owings, of Baltimore, Christopher Greenup, of Mercer county, Kentucky, Walter Beall, of Nelson

county, Kentucky, and Willis Green, of Lincoln county, Kentucky, seven-eighths of his interest in the furnace and in the land, the consideration being £1,426 8s. 6d. On the same day all the persons mentioned formed themselves into a company and subscribed to an agreement which stipulated that "the furnace now building on Slate creek shall hereafter be styled, called, and known by the name of the Bourbon furnace, and the firm of the company shall be John Cockey Owings and Company, owners and proprietors of the Bourbon furnace." During the erection of the furnace, and afterwards while the hands employed by the company were digging ore, the workmen had to be guarded by men with guns against the Indians; hence it became necessary to build a strong block-house on the principal ore bank for the better security of the laborers. The first blast made by the furnace was in 1792.

On March 6, 1795, George Thompson, Colonel George Nicholas, John Breckinridge, and John Hollingsworth became members of the company, adding to its capital lands and other property equal in value to the original investment. On June 27, 1798, Christopher Greenup sold his interest to George Nicholas and Walter Beall. In July, 1799, George Nicholas died. On January 15, 1800, Walter Beall sold his interest to Colonel Thomas Dye Owings, a son of John Cockey Owings, who had inherited his father's interest. In 1806 Colonel Owings became the sole owner of Bourbon furnace. He operated it successfully until 1822, when he became involved in debt and was compelled to make an assignment. The furnace was then operated by trustees for several years, when it was sold for the benefit of the creditors, passing into the hands of Robert Wickliffe, of Lexington, Kentucky, who leased it to Major John C. Mason and Samuel Herndon, who operated it until August, 1839, when its last blast came to an end. The stack is still standing.

The owners of Bourbon furnace built Slate forge, on Slate creek, three miles above the furnace, in 1798, to convert its pig iron into bar iron. This forge was in operation until 1818. Maria forge, three miles above the mouth of Slate creek, was built for the same purpose in 1810 by Joseph and Carlisle Harrison. It was in operation until 1840.

Bourbon furnace used the Clinton ore from two banks two miles south of the furnace—one called the Howard hill bank and the other called the Block-house bank. The water-power furnished by Slate creek was often insufficient to keep the furnace working regularly. The production of the furnace was about three tons per day. The iron made at the furnace had a poor reputation for strength, but it was very hard, which was due to the large amount of phosphorus it contained.

Bourbon furnace supplied the early settlers of Kentucky with all the castings they needed, such as heating stoves, cooking utensils, flat-irons, etc. After Slate forge was built the blacksmiths of the State were supplied by it with bar iron. The castings and bar iron were hauled in wagons to all parts of the State, and distributed through the principal stores in the towns. There are many heating stoves and cooking utensils still in use in Kentucky that were made at this furnace. Products of the furnace and the forge were also hauled to Licking river, a distance of seven miles, and put into flat-boats and floated to Cincinnati and Louisville on the Ohio.

In 1810 Colonel Owings had a contract with the United States Government to furnish cannon balls, grape shot, etc., to the navy. He also furnished General Jackson with cannon balls, grape shot, chain shot, etc., to use against the British, and they were so used at the battle of New Orleans on the 8th of January, 1815. I have in my possession the original receipt of General Jackson's sergeant-major for the cannon balls, etc., and also the receipts of several naval officers.

The owners of Bourbon furnace carried on a large general store. They brought their goods from Philadelphia. The Kentucky merchant in those early days traveled all the way to Philadelphia on horseback, carrying in saddle-bags the silver to pay for his goods. They brought their goods in wagons to Pittsburgh, thence down the Ohio on flat-boats to the mouth of the Limestone, now Maysville, in Mason county, Kentucky, and thence hauled them to the furnace, a distance of forty-five miles. The company also built and carried on a grist mill, which had a widely extended custom.

The founders and early owners of Bourbon furnace were all remarkable men, and their names are among the most eminent in the history of Kentucky. Jacob Myers, the pioneer, was a German, and a man of very fine sense. Christopher Greenup was a Virginian by birth, a soldier in the Revolution, a member of Congress from Kentucky in 1792, and Governor of Kentucky from 1804 to 1808. Greenup county was named after him. He died in 1818 in his 69th year. George Nicholas was a Virginian by birth, and a great lawyer and a great statesman. He was a soldier in the Revolution, was a member of the convention to frame a Constitution for Kentucky, was the author of that instrument, and was the first Attorney-General of the State. John Breckinridge was a Virginian by birth, and was the author of the Kentucky Resolutions of 1798. He was a United States Senator from Kentucky in 1801, and was appointed Attorney-General of the United States in 1805. He was the grandfather of Vice-President John C. Breckinridge. Walter Beall and Willis Green were surveyors from Virginia, and the latter held various local offices in Kentucky. John Cockey Owings, was a large landholder in Maryland.

The original of the following memorandum was handed to the editor of the Portsmouth (Ohio) *Tribune* in 1880 by Mr. L. C. Robinson. It refers to Bourbon furnace.

KENTUCKY, ss.: Memorandum of an Agreement made and Concluded upon this day between John Cockey Owings & Co., in Iron Works at the *Bourbon* Furnace of the one part, and Robert Williams (potter) of the other part. Witnesseth that the aforesaid Company doth this day agree to give the said Williams five pounds p. month for three months' work and to find him provisions during the time he shall work until the three months are expired, and said Company doth further agree, in case the furnace is not ready to blow before or at the expiration of the three months, if the water will admit, or as soon as the water will admit after that time, to give him p. month as much as he can make in a month at the potting Business for such time as said Furnace may not be Ready to put in Blast—as witness our hands this second day of June, 1793.   JN. COCKEY OWINGS.
                                                              WALTER BEALL.
Test: JNO. MOCKBEE.   CHRIST GREENUP.

For a number of years after 1800 the iron industry of Kentucky made steady progress. Tench Coxe mentions four furnaces and three forges in 1810. One furnace was in Estill county, one in Wayne, and two were in Montgomery. One of the forges was in Estill county, one in Wayne, and one in Montgomery. His enumeration, however, is incomplete, no mention, for instance, being made of the iron enterprises in Bath county, which were in operation long after 1810. In the same year, or soon afterwards, there were four nail factories at Lexington, making seventy tons of nails annually.

About 1815 Richard Deering, a farmer of Greenup county, smelted in a cupola the first iron ore used in the Hanging Rock district of Kentucky. His experiment with the cupola proving to be successful he took into partnership David and John Trimble, and these three persons built in 1817 or 1818 one of the first furnaces in the district. It was called Argillite, and was located in Greenup county, about six miles southwest of Greenupsburg, upon the left bank of the Little Sandy river. The stack, which was 25 feet high and 6 feet wide at the boshes, was cut in a cliff of black slate—hence the name, Argillite. Lesley says: "It was not a structure, but an excavation in the solid slate rock of the cliff, the archway below being excavated to meet it." This furnace was operated only a few years, when it was abandoned. Its product was always small.

Another early furnace in this district was Pactolus, built by Ward & McMurtry soon after 1818 on the Little Sandy river, in Carter county, above Argillite furnace. It was soon abandoned. A forge was connected with this furnace. Another early enterprise in this district was Steam furnace, in Greenup county, situated about three miles from the Ohio river and five miles from Greenupsburg. It is said by Lesley to have been built in 1817 by Leven Shreeves & Brother. It was operated with steam. It was abandoned after 1860. Enterprise furnace, on Tygart's creek, in Greenup county, was built in 1826, but Richard Deering is said to have erected a forge of the same name on the same creek in·1824. Bellefonte furnace, on Hood's creek, two and a half miles southwest of Ashland, in Boyd county, was built in 1826 by A.

Paull, George Poague, and others, and was the first furnace in this county. It was in operation in 1890.

Between 1817 and 1834 at least thirteen furnaces were built in Greenup, Carter, and Boyd counties. One of the earliest of these was Camp Branch, or Farewell, situated on Little Sandy river, fourteen miles from Greenupsburg, near the Carter county line, built by David and John Trimble. Subsequent to 1834 about fifteen other charcoal furnaces were built in these three counties and in Lawrence county. Most of the charcoal furnaces of this district have been abandoned. A few excellent bituminous coal and coke furnaces have, however, been erected in late years. Notwithstanding these additions to its furnace capacity this district is not now so prominent in the manufacture of iron as it has been.

About 1830 there were a dozen forges in Greenup, Estill, Edmonson, and Crittenden counties, all of which, with one exception, were abandoned before 1850. Two forges were built below Eddyville, in Lyon county, about 1840. All the forges mentioned refined pig iron into blooms, many of which found a market at Pittsburgh, Cincinnati, and Kentucky rolling mills. A few years ago there was only one forge remaining in the State, Red River, in Estill county, but it has since been abandoned. If any bloomaries ever existed in Kentucky they were abandoned early in this century.

In addition to the iron enterprises in the Hanging Rock region of Kentucky furnaces were built before 1860 in several of the middle and western counties of the State—in Bath, Russell, Bullitt, Nelson, Muhlenburg, Lyon, Crittenden, Trigg, Calloway, and Livingston counties. Two of these furnaces, Caney and Clear Creek, were in Bath county. In this period eight rolling mills were also built in Kentucky. The period from about 1825 to 1860 witnessed great activity in the development of the iron industry of Kentucky. Since the close of the civil war this activity has not been maintained. It can not be said that the State has devoted that attention to the manufacture of iron which its position and resources most certainly invite.

Kentucky was seventh in the list of iron and steel producing States in 1870 and eleventh in 1880. In 1890 it was fourteenth in rank among the States producing pig iron and it occupied the same position among the States producing rolled iron. Of twenty-two furnaces in the State in 1880 eighteen used charcoal and four used bituminous coal. In the same year there were eight rolling mills—two at Covington, two at Newport, two at Louisville, one at Ashland, and one in Lyon county; there were also two steel works connected with the rolling mills at Covington and Newport. The first rolling mill in Kentucky appears to have been built at Covington in 1829, a portion of its machinery having been obtained from the dismantled Union rolling mill at Pittsburgh.

In 1890 there were five coke furnaces and one charcoal furnace in Kentucky and six rolling mills and one open-hearth steel plant, the last named being at Covington. A Bessemer steel plant was in course of erection at Ashland, in Boyd county. This place has in late years become prominent as an iron centre, having three active coke furnaces. At Middlesborough, in Bell county, an English company has recently undertaken the erection of iron and steel works on an extensive scale, embracing two coke furnaces and a basic open-hearth steel plant, none of which had been completed at the beginning of 1891. The South Boston Iron Works are to be removed to this place in 1891. There is also a charcoal furnace in course of erection at Cumberland Gap, and two charcoal furnaces are also in course of erection at Grand Rivers, in Livingston county.

It is a favorable sign that the coking coals of Kentucky are now in a fair way to be developed on an extensive scale.

CHAPTER XXVIII.

THE EARLY MANUFACTURE OF IRON IN TENNESSEE.

THE first settlers of Tennessee erected iron works within its limits soon after the close of the Revolution. Bishop says that a bloomary was built in 1790 at Embreeville, in Washington county. At Elizabethton, on Doe river, in Carter county, a bloomary was built about 1795. Wagner's bloomary, on Roane creek, in Johnson county, is said to have been built in this year. A bloomary was also erected on Camp creek, in Greene county, in 1797. Two bloomaries in Jefferson county —the Mossy Creek forge, ten miles north of Dandridge, and Dumpling forge, five miles west of Dandridge—were built in the same year. About the same time, if not earlier, David Ross, the proprietor of iron works in Campbell county, Virginia, erected a large furnace and forge at the junction of the two forks of the Holston river, in Sullivan county, near the Virginia line, on "the great road from Knoxville to Philadelphia." Bishop states an interesting fact in the following words : "Boats of twenty-five tons burden could ascend to Ross's iron works, nearly 1,000 miles above the mouth of the Tennessee, and about 280 above Nashville. At Long Island, a short distance above, on the Holston, where the first permanent settlement in Tennessee was made in 1775, boats were built to transport iron and castings made in considerable quantities at these works, with other produce, to the lower settlements and New Orleans." A bloomary was built about 1795 below the mouth of the Watauga, and another at the same time about twenty-five miles above the mouth of French Broad river and thirty miles above Knoxville.

All the above-mentioned enterprises were in East Tennessee. In West Tennessee iron was also made in the last decade of the last century. Nashville was founded in 1780, and a few years later iron ore was discovered about thirty miles west of the future city. In 1792 Cumberland furnace was erected on Iron fork of Barton's creek, in Dickson county, seven miles northwest of Charlotte, by James Robinson. This furnace was rebuilt in 1825, and was in operation in 1888. Dickson county and its neighbors, Stewart and Montgomery counties, afterwards became very prominent in the manufacture of charcoal pig iron. Other counties in the same section of the State have also, but in a less conspicuous degree, made iron in charcoal furnaces. The first furnace in Montgomery county was probably Yellow Creek, situated fourteen miles southwest of Clarksville, and built in 1802.

The iron industry of Tennessee made steady progress after the opening of the present century. Both furnaces and bloomaries multiplied rapidly. In 1856 Lesley enumerated over seventy-five forges and bloomaries, seventy-one furnaces, and four rolling mills in Tennessee, each of which had been in operation at some time after 1790. Of the furnaces twenty-nine were in East Tennessee and forty-two in Middle and West Tennessee. Fourteen of the latter were in Stewart county, twelve in Montgomery, seven in Dickson, two in Hickman, two in Perry, two in Decatur, two in Wayne, and one in Hardin county. There were at one time forty-one furnaces on the Cumberland river in Tennessee and Kentucky. The furnaces in East Tennessee were mainly in Sullivan and Carter counties, Sullivan having five and Carter seven; but Johnson, Washington, Greene, Cocke, Sevier, Monroe, Hamilton, Claiborne, Campbell, Grainger, and Union counties each had one or two furnaces, while Roane county had three. There was an early furnace in Polk county, which is not noted by Lesley but is mentioned by Bishop. The forges and bloomaries were mainly located in East Tennessee. Johnson county contained fifteen, Carter ten, Sullivan six, Washington three, Greene ten, Campbell seven, Blount four, Roane seven, Rhea three, and a few other counties one and two each. Nearly all of these were bloomaries. In West Tennessee there were less than a dozen refinery forges and one or two bloomaries. The forges of West Tennessee, like those of Kentucky, were largely employed from about 1825 to 1860 in the manufacture of blooms for rolling mills, many of which found a market in the Ohio valley. Most of the furnaces and all of the forges enumerated by Lesley have long been abandoned, and all of the bloomaries except two or three have also been abandoned. There are now in Tennessee ten charcoal furnaces.

In 1883 there were in this State eight coke furnaces, all of recent origin, four rolling mills, and two steel works. In 1890 there were ten completed coke furnaces and several building, four rolling mills, and three steel works, two of which were connected with the rolling mills. Cumberland rolling mill, on the left bank of the Cumberland river, in Stewart county, was built in 1829 and was probably the first rolling mill in the State. It was the only one in Tennessee as late as 1856.

Since the close of the civil war Chattanooga has become the most prominent iron centre in Tennessee, having several iron enterprises of its own and others in its vicinity. Prior to the war, in 1854, Bluff furnace had been built by Robert Cravens, James A. Whiteside, and James P. Boyce, to use charcoal. In 1857 Lesley said of this furnace: " The bituminous coal of the Raccoon mines, now leased and worked by the Etna Mining Company, can be brought to the furnace by railway; it is excellent for coke, and some thoughts are entertained of turning the present furnace into a coke furnace." In 1859 the limestone stack was torn down by the East Tennessee Iron Company, of which James Henderson, of New York, was the manager, and a new iron cupola stack, 11 feet wide at the boshes, was erected in its place, and Raccoon coke was thereafter used as fuel. The new furnace was blown in in May, 1860, but owing to a short supply of coke the blast lasted only long enough to permit the production of about 500 tons of pig iron. All the machinery and appointments of the furnace worked satisfactorily. The furnace was started on a second blast on the 6th of November, the day of the Presidential election, but political complications and the demoralized state of the furnace workmen were obstacles too great to be overcome, and the furnace soon chilled from the cause last mentioned, and in December Mr. Henderson abandoned the enterprise and returned to New York. In the summer of 1862, before the Union troops took possession of Chattanooga, the machinery of the furnace was removed to Alabama by Giles Edwards, who used it in the equipment of a small charcoal furnace near the site of the present town of Anniston. This furnace was active for about two years. The stack of the furnace at Chattanooga was used by the Union troops as a lime kiln, by whom it was subsequently torn down.

This was the first coke furnace in either of the States of Tennessee or Alabama, which are now the theatre of such great present and prospective activity in the manufacture of pig iron with this fuel.

The first coke furnace that was built in the South after the war was the first of the two Rockwood furnaces, at Rockwood, Roane county, Tennessee. This furnace was built in 1867 by the Roane Iron Company, of which General J. T. Wilder and Captain H. S. Chamberlain were the leading spirits. It was successful from the start and is still active.

At the beginning of the war, in 1861, S. B. Lowe commenced the erection of the Vulcan rolling mill at Chattanooga, to roll bar iron. This mill was not finished in 1863, when it was burned by the Union forces. Mr. Lowe rebuilt the mill in 1866. It was owned and operated by the South Tredegar Iron Company in 1890. In 1864 a rolling mill to re-roll rails was built by the United States Government, under the supervision of John Fritz, then superintendent of the Bethlehem iron works. It was afterwards owned and operated by the Roane Iron Company. The first open-hearth steel made in any Southern State was made by the Siemens-Martin process at Chattanooga by this company on the 6th day of June, 1878, and in December of the same year the first steel rails ever made in the South were rolled at its works. Subsequently Bessemer steel works were built by this company, its supply of pig iron coming from the Rockwood furnaces and the iron ore coming from the Cranberry mines. They made their first blow on May 7, 1887, and on that day the first Bessemer steel rail ever made in the South outside of Wheeling was successfully rolled at these works, but the rolling of steel rails by this company has not since been actively continued. The first basic open-hearth steel ever made in Tennessee was made at the works of this company by the Southern Iron Company on the 15th of September, 1890. Lookout rolling mill was built by the Tennessee Iron and Steel Company in 1876, and was started in October of that year. Lewis Scofield was at the time the president of the company.

S. B. Lowe died at Chattanooga on April 13, 1891, aged about 63 years.

The prominence of Chattanooga as an iron centre is in part due to the excellent bituminous coal which is found in the neighborhood and in part to its superior transportation facilities. Next to Chattanooga the most prominent iron centre in Tennessee is Knoxville, which has a varied and prosperous iron industry. The Knoxville Car ·Wheel Company many years ago established a high reputation for its car wheels, which were made from pig iron produced from limonite ores at Carter and other furnaces in East Tennessee. Nashville and South Pittsburg are also growing iron centres.

Carter furnace, on Stony creek, a branch of the Watauga, was abandoned a few years ago. It was one of the last furnaces in the country to obtain its blast from a pair of square wooden cylinders, or "tubs," driven by water-power. The pioneer Cumberland furnace, which was built in 1792, was blown by a *trompe*.

Tennessee is destined to become much more prominent in the manufacture of iron than it has ever been. It will owe this prominence partly to the abundance of good bituminous coal which it possesses, but partly also to the improvements in the manufacture of charcoal pig iron which have already been adopted in many instances in this State, and partly to the adaptability to the basic steel process of pig iron made from its ores. Of the good quality of Tennessee ores for general purposes nothing needs to be said.

CHAPTER XXIX.

THE MANUFACTURE OF IRON IN ALABAMA.

THE oldest furnace in Alabama mentioned by Lesley was built about 1818 a few miles west of Russellville, in Franklin county, and abandoned in 1827. This unsuccessful venture appears to have had a dispiriting effect on other schemes to build furnaces in Alabama, as we do not hear of the erection of any others for many years after it was abandoned. A furnace was built at Polksville, in Calhoun county, in 1843 ; one at Round Mountain, in Cherokee county, in 1853; and Shelby furnace, at Shelby, in Shelby county, in 1848. These were all charcoal furnaces, and were the only ones in Alabama enumerated by Lesley in 1856. The total product in that year of the three last-named furnaces was 1,495 gross tons of pig iron. Shelby furnace was built by Horace Ware, who many years afterwards added a small foundry and a small mill for rolling cotton-ties and bar iron. The furnace was burned in 1858, but was immediately rebuilt. The mill was commenced in 1859, and on the 11th of April, 1860, the first iron was rolled. It was burned in 1865 by General Wilson's command of Union cavalry and has not been rebuilt. Part of the machinery was, however, removed to Helena, in Shelby county, a few years afterwards, where a rolling mill was built in 1872 and is now in operation. In place of the original furnace at Shelby there are now two modern charcoal furnaces.

Alabama had a bloomary two and a half miles southwest of Montevallo, in Shelby county, in 1825; several bloomaries in Bibb county between 1830 and 1840; one in Talladega county in 1842; two in Calhoun county in 1843; and others in various counties at later periods. In 1856 Lesley mentioned seventeen forges and bloomaries, mostly the latter, as having been built at various periods prior to that year, about one-half of which were then in operation, producing 252 tons of blooms and bar iron. Since 1856 all these forges and bloomaries in Alabama have disappeared. Most of them were blown with the *trompe* and the remainder with wooden "tubs."

It will be noticed that as late as 1856 Alabama possessed a very small iron industry. During the civil war several new iron enterprises were undertaken. A furnace in Sanford county was built in 1861; Cornwall furnace, at Cedar Bluff, in Cherokee county, was built in 1862; a second Shelby furnace, in Shelby county, to take the place of the original stack, was built in 1863; Alabama furnace, in Talladega county, was built in 1863, burned by General Wilson in April, 1865, and rebuilt in 1873. Two furnaces and a small rolling mill were built at Brierfield, in Bibb county, in 1863 and 1864. All the furnaces were built to use charcoal. The Brierfield rolling mill was first used for rolling bar iron and rails. In 1863 or early in 1864 it was sold to the Confederate Government, by which it was operated until 1865, when it was burned by the Union troops under General Wilson. It was rebuilt after the war, and for some time was used to roll bar iron and cotton-ties, principally the latter. This mill was again rebuilt in 1882 and 1883.

The following interesting history of the Shelby furnace and rolling mill, and of the part taken by them in supplying the Southern Confederacy with iron for its military operations, was sent to us in 1888 by the assistant secretary of the Shelby Iron Company, Mr. E. T. Witherby.

The first blast furnace erected here went into blast in 1848. Horace Ware was its proprietor. In 1854 Mr. Robert Thomas made iron in a forge near here. This iron was sent to England and returned in razors and knives. In 1859 Mr. Ware began the erection of a rolling mill. It was completed and started in the spring of 1860. In 1862 Mr. Ware sold his property to the Shelby County Iron Manufacturing Company, which erected a new furnace, the one which we have recently torn down, and on whose site we are erecting a new stack. The rolling mill was enlarged in 1862 and was operated continuously until March 31, 1865, when it was destroyed by General Wilson of the Union army. It was in this mill, in 1864, that the plates were rolled for the armor of the ironclad ram *Tennessee*. Judge James W. Lapsley, one of the stockholders and directors of the present Shelby Iron Company, was made a prisoner by the Union forces in 1863 while in Kentucky looking for puddlers for this mill.

When I came here, nearly twenty years ago, we had plates, merchant bars, and strap rails on hand made entirely of Shelby iron and rolled in this mill. Some of the plates, known to us now as the "gunboat iron," are still in our store house, but they have been slowly disappearing under the demand of our blacksmiths for an "extra good piece of iron" for "this job" or "that particular place," etc. Some of these plates are 8 inches by

3 inches and others 11 inches by 5 inches, and of various lengths; originally they were, perhaps, 10 feet long.

Shelby pig iron was also shipped to the Confederate arsenal and foundry at Selma, Alabama, in 1864, where the *Tennessee* was constructed and fitted out. This iron doubtless went into guns and other castings for this vessel. Catesby ap Jones was superintendent of the arsenal, and with his senior in rank, Franklin Buchanan, both pupils of that sea-god, Matthew Calbraith Perry, wrought out the *Tennessee*. They were as full of progressive ideas regarding steam and armor as their master, and nothing but the scanty means at their disposal prevented a much more formidable ironclad than the *Tennessee* from being set afloat. Car-wheel makers are now the exclusive users of our iron.

The existence of bituminous coal in Alabama was first observed in 1834 by Dr. Alexander Jones, of Mobile, but little was done to develop the ample coal resources of the State until after the close of the civil war, when it was found that the coal in the neighborhood of Birmingham and at other places would produce excellent coke for blast furnaces, and that at least two coal fields—the Black Warrior and Coosa—were so extensive as to set at rest all apprehension concerning a constant supply of coal for a long period of time. These discoveries, joined to the possession of an abundant supply of good ores, at once gave Alabama prominence as a State which would in a few years boast a large iron industry, and this promise has been fulfilled. Birmingham is now the centre of the most extensive manufacture of coke pig iron in the Southern States. There are also at Birmingham and its vicinity several rolling mills, all built during the last few years. The first rolling mill at Birmingham was built in 1880. The rapid growth of this place as a centre of iron production is one of the marvels of our wonderful industrial development, both North and South, since the close of the war. But the manufacture of charcoal pig iron in Alabama has also grown rapidly since the close of the war, and the State can now boast more charcoal furnaces than ever before in its history.

Colonel J. W. Sloss was the pioneer in the coke pig-iron industry of Alabama. In 1876 he and his associates built the Eureka coke furnace at Oxmoor. Subsequently he was instrumental in developing the celebrated Pratt seam of coking coal. Colonel Sloss was born in Alabama in 1820 and died on May 4, 1890. The first furnace at Birmingham was Alice furnace, built by H. F. DeBardeleben in 1879 and 1880.

It was put in blast on November 23, 1880. It was followed
by the first of the Sloss furnaces, which was put in blast on
April 12, 1882.

As Alabama is the last of the Southern States which has
an iron industry worthy of special consideration we will here
present the record of the marvelous progress in the production of pig iron made by all the Southern ironmaking States
from 1880 to 1890. In this table, following the *ante bellum*
geographical divisions, we class Maryland among the Southern States.

STATES.	Net tons of 2,000 pounds.						
	1880.	1882.	1884.	1886.	1888.	1889.	1890.
Alabama	77,190	112,765	189,664	283,859	449,492	791,425	914,940
Tennessee	70,873	137,602	134,597	199,166	267,931	294,655	299,741
Virginia	29,984	87,731	157,483	156,250	197,396	251,356	327,912
West Virginia	70,338	73,220	55,231	98,618	95,259	117,900	144,970
Kentucky	57,708	66,522	45,052	54,844	56,790	42,518	58,604
Georgia	27,321	42,440	42,655	46,490	39,397	27,559	32,687
Maryland	61,437	54,524	27,842	30,502	17,606	33,847	165,559
Texas	2,500	1,321	5,140	3,250	6,587	4,544	10,865
North Carolina		1,150	435	2,200	2,400	2,898	3,181
Total	397,301	577,275	657,599	875,179	1,132,858	1,566,702	1,953,459

From 1880 to 1883 Alabama more than doubled its production of pig iron; from 1883 to 1888 it was again more
than doubled; and from 1888 to 1890 it was once more
doubled.

Late in 1890 there were thirty-seven completed coke furnaces in Alabama and two in course of erection, and fifteen
completed charcoal furnaces and others that were projected.
At the same time there were in Alabama eight completed
rolling mills and others in course of erection. There was
a small steel plant at Birmingham, and a larger plant was
in course of erection at Fort Payne and others were projected. It can not be said, however, that Alabama has yet made
any noteworthy progress in the establishment of a steel industry. Its strength has thus far been mainly devoted to the
manufacture of pig iron.

CHAPTER XXX.

PRIMITIVE CHARACTERISTICS OF THE SOUTHERN IRON INDUSTRY.

THE establishment at an early day of so many charcoal furnaces and bloomaries in Western North Carolina and East Tennessee, sections of our country remote from the sea-coast and from principal rivers, is an interesting fact in the iron history of the country. The people who built these furnaces and bloomaries were not only courageous and enterprising but they appear to have been born with a genius for making iron. With scarcely an exception they were Scotch-Irish emigrants from the North of Ireland or their descendants. Wherever they went they seem to have searched for iron ore, and having found it their small charcoal furnaces and bloomaries soon followed, the furnaces to produce simple castings and the bloomaries to make bar iron. No pioneers in any of the States of the Union have shown more intelligent appreciation of the value of an iron industry than the people of North Carolina and Tennessee, and none have been more prompt to establish it. In a less degree but upon precisely the same lines of activity the pioneers of Northern Georgia and Northern Alabama have shown praiseworthy enterprise. It is true that the aim of all these people until in very recent years has been mainly to supply their own wants, but this is a motive to be commended, and no community should be found fault with if a lack of capital and of means of transportation prevents it from cultivating a commercial spirit.

The enterprise of the early ironworkers of all the States and sections above mentioned assumes a picturesque aspect when viewed in connection with the primitive methods of manufacture which were employed by them and which have been continued in use until the present day, when they may be said to have at last yielded to modern methods. Their charcoal furnaces were blown through one tuyere with wooden " tubs " adjusted to attachments which were slow in motion and which did not make the best use of the water-power

298 THE MANUFACTURE OF

that was often insufficiently supplied by mountain streams of limited volume. A ton or two of iron a day, usually in the shape of castings, was a good yield. The bloomaries, with scarcely an exception, were furnished with the *trompe*, or water-blast, a small stream with a suitable fall supplying both the blast for the fires and the power which turned the wheel that moved the big hammer. Of cast-iron cylinders, steam-power, two and three tuyeres, the hot-blast, and other valuable improvements in the charcoal-iron industry these people knew but little, and that little was mainly hearsay. They were pioneers and frontiersmen in every sense; from the great world of invention and progress they were shut out by mountains and streams and hundreds of miles of unsubdued forest. Nor would other than primitive methods of manufacturing iron have been adapted to their wants and their isolated condition. It is to their credit that they diligently sought to utilize the resources which they found under their feet, and that they made good use of the only means for the accomplishment of this purpose of which they had any accurate knowledge.

It is a curious fact that the daring men who pushed their way into the wilds of Western North Carolina and East Tennessee in the last century, and who set up their small furnaces and bloomaries when forts yet took the place of hamlets, founded an iron industry which has only lately yielded the primitive features which so long characterized it. Less than ten years ago there were furnaces still in operation in these sections which used wooden "tubs," and there were in Tennessee about two dozen bloomaries and in North Carolina a dozen or more which were in all respects the counterparts in construction of those which the pioneers established. Nearly every one of these bloomaries was blown with the *trompe*, and in all other respects they were as barren of modern appliances as if the world's iron industry and the world itself had stood still for a hundred years. They were fitfully operated, as the wants of their owners or of the neighboring farmers and blacksmiths required, or as the supply of water for the *trompes* and hammers would permit. "Thundergust forges" is an irreverent term that was frequently applied to them. They furnished their respective neighborhoods with iron for horseshoes, wagon-tires, and harrow-teeth. Mr. J. B. Killebrew, of Nashville, informed us a few years ago that throughout the counties of Johnson and Carter in Tennessee, where many of these bloomaries were located, bar iron was still used as currency. He then said: " Iron is taken in exchange for shoes, coffee, sugar, calico, salt, and domestic and other articles used by the people of the country. It is considered a legal tender in the settlement of all dues and liabilities. This bar iron, after being collected by the merchants, is sent out and sold in Knoxville, Bristol, and other points affording ,a market." The same usage prevailed in some other Southern States not many years- ago, and it prevailed in many Northern States long after they began to make iron a century or two ago. In New England the salaries of some of the preachers were once paid in bar iron.

The explanation of the survival in this country and until a late day of primitive methods of making iron which had long been abandoned by progressive communities lies in the fact that the obstacles to free intercourse with other communities which hedged about the pioneers of whom we are writing have never been broken down and have only recently been modified. Few of the mountains and streams and forests of these sections had been tunneled, or bridged, or traversed by modern means of communication twenty years ago. The iron horse had made but slow progress in bringing this part of our country into association with other sections. There were no canals, and good roads were scarce. The pioneers were cut off by their isolated situation and their poverty from all intimate relations with the outside world.

Until a few years ago there were some bloomaries still left in Southwestern Virginia which were similar in all respects to those of Western North Carolina and East Tennessee, and which were used for precisely similar purposes. But the manufacture of iron in bloomaries was never so prominent a branch of the iron industry of Virginia as of the other two States mentioned. Virginia learned at an early day to convert the pig iron of its furnaces into bar iron in refinery forges. It was settled long before Western North Carolina, or Tennessee, or Georgia, or Alabama, and it had from the first an active commerce with Europe and with the other colonies along the Atlantic coast. Its environments were favorable to the acquisition of progressive ideas in the manufacture of iron.

But old things must pass away, even in the iron industry of the mountain regions of the Southern States. The transformation in Tennessee and Alabama has already taken place. North Carolina, with its magnificent iron and other resources, must soon feel the pulse of a new industrial life. Georgia has at least abandoned methods which are no longer profitable. Before another century is far advanced the sons of the people of whom we have been writing will wonder that the old ways of making iron stayed with their fathers as long as they did.

Nevertheless our sympathy goes out to these old and dying ways, which well served the people of this country in the early days. Among the treasures of our office is a piece of bar iron, made in a Catalan forge in Virginia, which has the ring of the best steel, and many of our readers know of pots and kettles, still perfect and in all respects of the neatest workmanship, which were cast at the old-fashioned furnaces and are now precious heir-looms, having faithfully ministered to the wants of generations that are now gone.

CHAPTER XXXI.

THE EARLY MANUFACTURE OF IRON IN OHIO.

THE beginning of the iron industry of Ohio is cotemporary with the admission of the State into the Union. It was admitted in 1802, and in 1803 its first furnace, Hopewell, was commenced by Daniel Eaton, and in 1804 it was finished. The furnace stood on the west side of Yellow creek, about one and a quarter miles from its junction with the Mahoning river, in the township of Poland, in Mahoning county. On the same stream, three-fourths of a mile from its mouth, and on the farm on which the furnace of the Struthers Furnace Company now stands, in the town of Struthers, another furnace was built in 1806 by Robert Montgomery and John Struthers. This furnace was called Montgomery. Thomas Struthers says: " These furnaces were of about equal capacity, and would yield about two and a half or three tons each per day. The metal was principally run into moulds for kettles, bake-ovens, flat-irons, stoves, andirons, and such other articles as the needs of a new settlement required, and any surplus into pigs and sent to the Pittsburgh market." The ore was obtained in the neighborhood. Hopewell furnace is said by Mr. Struthers to have had a rocky bluff for one of its sides. It was in operation in 1807, but it was soon afterwards blown out finally. Montgomery furnace was in operation until 1812, when, Mr. Struthers says, " the men were drafted into the war and it was never started again." This furnace stood " on the north side of Yellow creek, in a hollow in the bank." We are informed by Hon. John M. Edwards, of Youngstown, that about 1807 Hopewell furnace was sold by Eaton to Montgomery, Clendenin & Co., who were then the owners of Montgomery furnace, John Struthers having sold his interest in this furnace, or part of it, to David Clendenin in 1807 and Robert Alexander and James Mackey having about the same time become part owners.

The above-mentioned enterprises were the first furnaces in Ohio, and, as will be observed, they were both on the Western Reserve. There were other early iron enterprises on the Reserve. At Nilestown, now Niles, in Trumbull county, as we are informed by Colonel Charles Whittlesey, of Cleveland, James Heaton built a forge in 1809, for the manufacture of bar iron from "the pig of the Yellow Creek furnace," Montgomery furnace. "This forge produced the first hammered bars in the State." It continued in operation until 1838. About 1812 James Heaton built a furnace at Nilestown, near the mouth of Mosquito creek, where the Union school building now stands. It was called Mosquito Creek furnace. For many years it used bog ore, the product being stoves and other castings. It was in operation until 1856, when it was abandoned.

About 1816 Aaron Norton built a furnace at Middlebury, near Akron, in Summit county, and in 1819 Asaph Whittlesey built a forge on the Little Cuyahoga, near Middlebury. A furnace at Tallmadge, in the same county, was built about the same time. These two furnaces were in operation until about 1835. Bog ore was used.

The beginning of the iron industry in the counties on Lake Erie probably dates from 1825, when Arcole furnace was built in Madison township, in the present county of Lake, by Root & Wheeler. Concord furnace, in the same county, was built by Fields & Stickney about 1828. In 1830 John Wilkeson became the owner of Arcole furnace. Geauga furnace, one mile north of Painesville, in Lake county, and Railroad furnace, at Perry, in Geauga county, were built about 1828, the former by an incorporated company and the latter by Thorndike & Drury, of Boston. During the next ten or twelve years many other furnaces were built near Lake Erie, in Ashtabula, Cuyahoga, Erie, Huron, and Lorain counties. At a still later period other charcoal furnaces were built in the lake counties. All these lake furnaces, writes John Wilkeson in 1858, "were blown some eight months each year, and made about 30 tons per week of metal from the bog ore found in swales and swamps near and generally to the north of a ridge of land which was probably once the shore of Lake Erie, found extending, with now and then an interval, along from the west boundary of the State of New York to the Huron river in Ohio. The want of wood for charcoal, consequent upon the clearing up of the land, has occasioned the stoppage of most of these works. For a long time the settlers upon the shores of Lake Erie and in the State of Michigan were supplied with their stoves, potash kettles, and other castings by these works."

All of the above-mentioned iron enterprises were on the Western Reserve. Just outside of its limits Gideon Hughes built a furnace in 1807 or 1808, on the Middle fork of Little Beaver creek, one and a half miles northwest of New Lisbon, in Columbiana county. It was in operation in 1808 and 1809. It was first called Rebecca of New Lisbon, but was afterwards named Dale furnace. Attached to this furnace a few years after its erection was a forge, which was used for making bar iron. John Frost, of New Lisbon, to whom we are indebted for this information, also writes us that "some two or three miles up the same stream Mr. Hughes and Joshua Malin erected a rolling mill in 1822, to which a company of Englishmen, said to be from Pittsburgh, not long afterwards added nail-making machinery. In addition to manufacturing bar iron these works placed large quantities of nails in the market. This concern was more or less active till 1832, when the great flood of waters early in that year destroyed it, and it was never rebuilt." New Lisbon is located about twelve miles from the mouth of Little Beaver creek, which empties into the Ohio river.

Soon after the beginning of the iron industry on the Western Reserve the manufacture of iron was undertaken in some of the interior and southern counties of the State. Bishop says that Moses Dillon, who had been associated with Isaac Meason and John Gibson in the building of Union furnace in Fayette county, Pennsylvania, in 1793, "afterwards erected a forge on Licking river, near Zanesville, Ohio, possibly the first in the State." This enterprise was preceded or immediately followed by a furnace which is said to have been erected in 1808, but it may have been built a few years afterwards. It was located "at the Falls of Licking," four miles northwest of Zanesville, in Muskingum county, and its capacity was about one ton per day. It was used to produce castings, as well as pig iron for the forge. Lesley says that this furnace was not abandoned "until 1850 or later." The forge was also operated until about 1850. The furnace and forge were known as Dillon's, and were widely celebrated.

Mary Ann furnace, ten miles northeast of Newark, in Licking county, was built about 1816 by Dr. Brice and David Moore. It was burned down about 1850. In Tuscarawas county the Zoar Community owned two early charcoal furnaces. One of these, called Tuscarawas, was built about 1830 by Christmas, Hazlett & Co., and was afterwards sold to the Community; the other, called Zoar, was built about the same time by the Community. Both furnaces were finally blown out before 1850.

Three furnaces were built in Adams county between 1811 and 1816 to use the bog ores of the Brush creek valley. The first of these, Brush Creek, located twelve miles from the Ohio river, was built in 1811 and operated in 1813 by James Rodgers. It was probably built by Andrew Ellison, Thomas James, and Archibald Paull. It was in operation as late as 1837, when it produced 200 tons of iron in 119 days. On the same stream, twenty-two miles from the Ohio, was Marble furnace, built in 1816. Another furnace, known as Old Steam, was built in 1814. It is said to have been built by James Rodgers, Andrew Ellison, and the Pittsburgh Steam Engine Company. Thomas W. Means once informed us that "the first blast furnace run by steam in Southern Ohio, if not in the United States, was built by James Rodgers in Adams county about 1814." This reference is to Old Steam furnace. "Its product was less than two tons of iron a day. Brush Creek furnace, in the same county, and other furnaces of that period which were run by water hardly averaged one ton of iron a day." Marble and Old Steam furnaces were abandoned about 1826. Lesley mentions three forges in Adams county — Steam, at Old Steam furnace; Scioto, on the Little Scioto; and Brush Creek, probably connected with Brush Creek furnace. The date of the erection of these forges is not given, but they were doubtless built soon after the three Adams county furnaces. They were all abandoned many years ago. There is now no iron industry in Adams county.

In the chapter relating to Kentucky the beginning of the iron industry in the Hanging Rock region has been noted.

This celebrated iron district embraces Greenup, Boyd, Carter, and Lawrence counties in Kentucky, and Lawrence, Jackson, Gallia, Vinton, and Scioto counties in Ohio. Just north of the Ohio portion of this district is the newly-developed Hocking Valley iron district, embracing Hocking county and several other counties. The Hanging Rock district takes its name from a projecting cliff upon the north side of the Ohio river, situated back of the town of Hanging Rock, which is in Lawrence county, three miles below Ironton. The first furnace in the Ohio part of the Hanging Rock district was Union furnace, located a few miles northwest of Hanging Rock, built in 1826 and 1827 by John Means, John Sparks, and James Rodgers, the firm's name being James Rodgers & Co. Franklin furnace was the second on the Ohio side. It stood sixteen miles east of Portsmouth, in Scioto county, and half a mile from the Ohio river, and was built in 1827 by the Rev. Daniel Young and others. The next furnace was Pine Grove, on Sperry's fork of Pine creek, back of Hanging Rock, in Lawrence county, five miles from the Ohio river, built in 1828 by Robert Hamilton and Andrew Ellison. In the same year Scioto furnace, in Scioto county, fifteen miles north of Portsmouth, was built by William Salters. From this time forward furnaces increased rapidly on the Ohio side of the district, as well as on the Kentucky side. From 1826 to 1880 the whole number built on the Ohio side was about sixty and on the Kentucky side about thirty. All the early furnaces were built to use charcoal, but timber becoming scarce coke was substituted at some of them while others were abandoned. In late years a few furnaces have been built in the district expressly to use coke or raw coal. In 1880 there were on the Ohio side thirty-one charcoal furnaces and seventeen bituminous coal or coke furnaces, but in 1890 the number of charcoal furnaces had been reduced to eleven and the number of bituminous furnaces to fifteen.

At Vesuvius furnace, on Storm's creek, in Lawrence county, Ohio, six miles northeast of Ironton, the hot-blast was successfully applied in 1836 by John Campbell and others, William Firmstone putting up the apparatus. It was also at once applied at the La Grange and other Hanging Rock furnaces.

The Hanging Rock district, on both sides of the Ohio, has produced many eminent ironmasters, and its iron resources have been developed with great energy. John Campbell, of Ironton, and Thomas W. Means, of Hanging Rock, both prominent among its early ironmasters, have lived to a good old age. Mr. Campbell was born in 1808 in Brown county, Ohio, and was in good health in June, 1891. With the aid of others he has built eleven furnaces in the Hanging Rock district. He projected the town of Ironton and gave it its name, and also assisted in the founding of Ashland, Kentucky, and in building its railroad. Like many of the ironmasters of this district he is of Scotch-Irish extraction, his ancestors having removed in 1612 from Inverary, in Argyleshire, Scotland, to the neighborhood of Londonderry, in Ulster, Ireland. Their descendants removed in 1729 and 1739 to Augusta county, Virginia; thence, in 1790, to Bourbon county, Kentucky; and thence, in 1798, to that part of Adams county, Ohio, which is now embraced in Brown county. Mr. Means was born in Union district, South Carolina, in 1803, and was of English ancestry. He removed from Hanging Rock to Ashland, Kentucky, in 1881, and died at that place on June 8, 1890, aged about 87 years. Andrew Ellison, Robert Hamilton, James Rodgers, and Andrew Dempsey, all of whom are now dead, were enterprising and prominent iron manufacturers. In December, 1844, Mr. Hamilton successfully tried the experiment of ·stopping Pine Grove furnace, which he then owned, on Sunday, and his example has since been generally followed in the Hanging Rock region. This furnace is still active. John Campbell, Robert Hamilton, and Thomas W. Means were united in marriage with members of the Ellison family. The third generation of this family is now engaged in the iron industry of Southern Ohio.

John Means, a native of Exeter, in Devonshire, England, removed to Pennsylvania in 1735. His son, William Means, removed from Pennsylvania to South Carolina shortly before the Revolution, where he married Anna Newton, a relative of Sir Isaac Newton. Their son, John Means, removed to Adams county, Ohio, in 1819, taking with him his slaves, whom he liberated. He died on his farm near Manchester, in Adams county, on March 15, 1837, and was buried in the churchyard at Manchester. He was part owner of a furnace and a forge in Adams county in the early days. He was the father of Thomas W. Means.

In the first number of the *Journal of the United States Association of Charcoal Iron Workers* for 1891 Mr. John Birkinbine, the editor, describes Olive furnace, in Lawrence county, Ohio, in the Hanging Rock region, which, he says, "is the only active blast furnace in the United States the stack of which is largely hewn from the solid rock." It will be remembered that in our Kentucky chapter we mentioned Argillite furnace in that State as having been similarly constructed, but that furnace was long ago abandoned. It will also be remembered that in one of our earlier chapters we described two furnaces in Scotland, known as the Devon iron works, which were cut out of the solid rock. Mr. Birkinbine's description of Olive furnace is as follows.

The Olive furnace was constructed and first operated in the year 1846, and with the exception of one year it has been in blast every year since its completion. Originally the furnace was run with cold-blast, the pig iron being consumed principally by charcoal forges along the Ohio river for the production of blooms, to be used in the manufacture of boiler plates. After being operated in this way for ten years, during which time the output averaged about six to eight tons per day, a hot-blast of the ring pattern was added. Throughout the various changes the original stack, built in 1846, was retained, and beyond an addition of 4 feet to the top masonry, making the total height 40 feet, and widening one tuyere arch, the main structure is as it was first built.

The peculiarity of construction consists in the lower half of the blast-furnace stack being hewn from a ledge of solid rock, which is exposed for a height of over 20 feet. This rock ledge is a sandstone, which cuts easily when first hewn but hardens upon exposure. A suitable site having been selected the earth in front of the rock was removed, and the entire rock face thus exposed was dressed for a length of 60 feet, and from this space the blast-furnace stack was cut, the additional height of stack, 20 feet, being obtained by masonry built upon the rock.

In general appearance and outline the lower portion of the stack of the Olive furnace does not, except in a total absence of bracing, differ materially from the older stacks which were built of stone masonry; the stack is square in plan, with sloping sides, the bottom being 48 feet square and the top (20 feet above the bottom) 36 feet square. It stands at the sides and rear from 4 to 6 feet and at the top still further away from the mass of rock of which it originally formed a part. It is cored out to accommodate the lining of the furnace, and the sides are pierced for one fore arch and two tuyere arches, all cut in the solid rock.

Originally the inwall was laid with sandstone, and the hearth and bosh were constructed of the same material. In later years, however, fire-brick has been used for the inwall and lining; but hearth and bottoms are still cut from the sandstone, which occurs in great quantity and of excellent quality convenient to the Olive furnace.

The frequent changes of temperature have caused the mass of rock forming the lower portion of the stack to develop a number of cracks. At first these were small, but at each blast they have opened until they exhibit in a remarkable manner the marvelous power of expansion. This portion of the stack being without bands or buck-staves has an appearance of weakness, which, however, on closer examination, is removed, and it is probable that the old hewn stack is good for years of service.

The good quality of Hanging Rock charcoal pig iron and the conditions surrounding its production during the last sixty years are told with a pleasing touch of sentiment in the following anonymous newspaper paragraph, which appeared in the latter part of 1890.

The old charcoal furnace of the Hecla Iron and Mining Company, at Ironton, Ohio, which was succeeded by a new stack during the past summer, is one of the most celebrated in the Hanging Rock region, and will for a long time remain as a landmark in that locality. The furnace was built in 1833 and abandoned on April 15, 1890, and was a stone stack, 36 by 10½ feet, cold-blast, open top. The ores used were siderite and limonite, and for years the product held an enviable place in the estimation of consumers. The iron produced has commanded such customers as the United States Government during the civil war (one or two blasts being about all engaged) for ordnance, etc., cast at Pittsburgh. Its metal went into the guns mounted in the Swamp Angel battery which besieged the city of Charleston. The metal was also used in the armor plates of the gunboats which stormed Forts Donelson and Henry. For many years the Pennsylvania Railroad Company has taken about all the furnace would make of certain grades, for use in the best class of car wheels. Other customers used the metal for a fine quality of chilled rolls, etc., and the strongest parts of machinery. The iron was produced in the simplest manner, many of the employés having lived at the furnace all their lives, some 45, 55, and one 65 years. The charcoal used was from the company's lands, made in old style and hauled by ox teams, producing iron at large cost and selling at large prices, $80 and $90 during the war, $65 during the booms of 1873 and 1880, but since then at a minimum price, necessitating the abandonment for more modern and cheaper methods, though the old stack will be preserved. Scarred, rugged, moss-grown, picturesque, and unique, it will serve as a reminder of pioneer days, of war's fierce alarms, and that sentiment still lives amidst this latter-day strife in ironmaking.

In 1833 a forge was built at Hanging Rock, after which it was named, to manufacture blooms. It was owned by J. Riggs & Co., and was built under the superintendence of John Campbell and Joseph Riggs. A rolling mill was added before 1847. Both the forge and rolling mill have long been abandoned. A forge was built at Sample's Landing, fifteen miles below Gallipolis, soon after 1830, to make blooms for the Covington rolling mill. Bloom forge was built at Portsmouth, in Scioto county, in 1832, and in 1857 a rolling mill was added. A forge called Benner's, on Paint creek, near Chillicothe, in Ross county, once owned by James & Woodruff, was abandoned about 1850. There never were many forges in Ohio for refining iron, and there have been few, if any, for making bar iron directly from the ore. The first iron enterprises in the State preceded by only a few years the building of rolling mills at Pittsburgh.

The first rolling mill at Cincinnati was the Cincinnati rolling mill, built about 1830 by Shreeve, Paull & McCandless. The Globe rolling mill was built at Cincinnati in 1845. Joseph Kinsey writes us that " it was the first built in Cincinnati for the purpose of making general sizes of merchant iron, hoops, sheets, and plates. It was built by William Sellers and Josiah Lawrence, and was considered a great enterprise at that time. Soon afterwards a wire mill was added for the purpose of making the first wire used for the lines of telegraph extending through this country." There are now in Cincinnati and in its vicinity on the Ohio side of the Ohio river two rolling mills but no blast furnaces or steel works.

Ohio is entitled to the honor of having had established within its boundaries the first successful works in the United States for the manufacture of *crucible steel of the best quality.* The proof of this claim is ample, and it will be presented in a subsequent chapter when we come to speak of this branch of our steel industry. The works alluded to were located on the bank of the Miami Canal, in Cincinnati, and were built in 1832 by two brothers, Dr. William Garrard and John H. Garrard, who were natives of England but residents of the United States after 1822. After the works were built William T. Middleton and Charles Fox were successively partners with Dr. Garrard, his brother having retired. Dr. Garrard was the inspiration of the enterprise and its master spirit during the whole period of its existence. The firm failed in 1837, but the business was continued for some time afterwards. During the first five years the best crucible steel was made

at these works by Dr. Garrard, entirely with American materials. It was used for saws, springs, axes, reaper knives, files,
and tools generally.

The foregoing details relate to what may be termed the
charcoal era of the Ohio iron industry. The second stage
in the development of the iron industry of this State dates
from the introduction in its blast furnaces of the bituminous
coal of the Mahoning valley in its raw state. This coal is
known as splint coal, or block coal, or as Brier Hill coal, from
a locality of that name near Youngstown, where it is largely
mined. The first furnace in Ohio to use the new fuel was
built expressly for this purpose at Lowell, in Mahoning county, in 1845 and 1846, by Wilkeson, Wilkes & Co., and it was
successfully blown in on the 8th of August, 1846. The name
of this furnace was at first Anna and afterwards Mahoning.
A letter from John Wilkeson, of Buffalo, New York, informed us a few years ago that William McNair, a millwright, was
the foreman who had charge of its erection. It was blown
in by John Crowther, who had previously had charge of the
furnaces of the Brady's Bend Iron Company, at Brady's Bend,
Pennsylvania. Mr. Wilkeson and his brothers were for many
years prominent charcoal-iron manufacturers on the Western
Reserve. They were of Scotch-Irish extraction. Their father
was a native of Carlisle, Pennsylvania.

Immediately after the successful use of uncoked coal in
the furnace at Lowell many other furnaces were built in the
Mahoning valley to use the new fuel, and it was also substituted for charcoal in some old furnaces. At a later day the
use of this fuel in other parts of Ohio contributed to the further development of the manufacture of pig iron in this State,
and at a still later and very recent date the opening of the
extensive coal beds of the Hocking valley and the utilization
of its carbonate ores still further contributed to the same
development, the Hocking valley coal being used in its raw
state. At the present time, however, Connellsville coke has
almost entirely superseded the use of raw coal in the Mahoning valley, and in the Hocking valley coke is now largely
mixed with raw coal.

The proximity of the coal fields of Ohio to the rich iron
ores of Lake Superior has been, however, the most impor-

tant element in building up the blast-furnace industry of the
State. The use of these ores in Ohio soon followed the first
use in the blast furnace of the block coal of the Mahoning
valley. An increase in the rolling-mill capacity of Ohio was
naturally coincident with the impetus given to the production of pig iron by the use of this coal and Lake Superior
ores. David Tod, afterwards Governor of Ohio, bore a prominent part in the development of the coal and iron resources
of the Mahoning valley. In a sketch of *Youngstown, Past and
Present,* (1875,) we find the following notice of Mr. Tod's enterprise in developing the coal trade of the Mahoning valley.

In 1840 David Tod was operating a mine at Brier Hill, and upon the
completion of the Pennsylvania and Ohio Canal from Akron, Ohio, to Beaver, Pennsylvania, he shipped a couple of boat loads to Cleveland for the
purpose of introducing it as fuel on lake steamers, which was not easily
accomplished, there being considerable hostility manifested towards it by
engineers and firemen. Mr. Tod, however, was not to be discouraged by
these difficulties, and finally succeeded in making a successful experiment,
and in 1845 coal supplanted wood on the steamers on the lower lakes.
Large quantities were subsequently mined and shipped to Cleveland from
the Mahoning valley by Mr. Tod, and but a few years elapsed until the
mining and shipping of coal became a prominent industry; later the
opening of the Cleveland and Mahoning Railway from Cleveland to
Youngstown, traversing the heart of the coal region, gave fresh impetus
to the mining interests.

The beginning of the iron industry at Youngstown, which
now has within its own limits or in the immediate vicinity
fifteen furnaces and eleven rolling mills, dates from about
1835, when a charcoal furnace, called Mill Creek, was built
on a creek of the same name, a short distance southwest of
the city, by Isaac Heaton, a son of James Heaton. There was
no other furnace at Youngstown until after the discovery at
Lowell that the block coal of the Mahoning valley could be
successfully used in the smelting of iron ore. In a sketch
of the history of Youngstown Hon. John M. Edwards says:
"In 1846 William Philpot & Co. built in the northwestern
part of Youngstown, adjoining the present city, and near the
canal, the second furnace in the State for using raw mineral
coal as fuel. In the same year a rolling mill was built in the
southeastern part of the village, and adjoining the canal, by
the Youngstown Iron Company. This mill is now owned by
Brown, Bonnell & Co."

In *Youngstown, Past and Present*, a more detailed account is given of its first bituminous furnace. It was known as the Eagle furnace, and was "built in 1846 by William Philpot, David Morris, Jonathan Warner, and Harvey Sawyer, on land purchased of Dr. Henry Manning, lying between the present city limits and Brier Hill. The coal used was mined from land contiguous, leased from Dr. Manning." The second furnace at Youngstown to use raw coal was built in 1847 by Captain James Wood, of Pittsburgh. It was called Brier Hill furnace. There was a steam forge at Youngstown, called the Fairmount iron works, whose history antedates that of all the rolling mills of that place. We are indebted to Mr. J. G. Butler, Jr., of Youngstown, for the following circumstantial account of this almost forgotten enterprise.

The firm of Spencer & Co. operated a small steam forge about 1840 on or near the present site of Smith's brewery, on West Federal street, Youngstown. They used a small upright boiler, with a brick chimney. The forge, after being operated for a time, failed to be profitable and was sold under execution to Mr. Asahel Tyrrell, of Tyrrell Hill, Trumbull county, Ohio, now a station on the Lake Shore and Michigan Southern Railway. The forge was removed to Tyrrell Hill in the summer season, leaving the chimney standing. The succeeding winter, after snow had fallen, Mr. Tyrrell came to haul away the brick used in the construction of the chimney. To this Jonathan Edwards, (a lineal descendant of his great namesake,) who owned and leased the ground which Spencer & Co. occupied, objected, claiming that the chimney was fixed property, or a part of the realty. A law-suit grew out of the difference in opinion, and two young lawyers were pitted against each other, both of these lawyers subsequently becoming famous; one, the Hon. John Crowell, and the other, Judge Rufus P. Ranney. Mr. Tyrrell won his suit and the chimney was taken away. I get this information from old settlers and you may consider it reliable.

The iron industry of Cleveland has been built up during recent years, and this city is now one of the most prominent centres of iron and steel production in the country. Charles A. Otis, of Cleveland, writes us as follows concerning the first rolling mills in that city: "The first rolling mill at Cleveland was a plate mill, worked on a direct-ore process, which was a great failure. It went into operation in 1854 or 1855. The mill is now owned by the Britton Iron and Steel Company. The next mill was built in 1857 by A. J. Smith and others to re-roll rails. It was called Railroad rolling mill, and is now owned by the Cleveland Rolling Mill Company.

At the same time a man named Jones, with several associates, built a mill at Newburgh, six miles from Cleveland, also to re-roll rails. It was afterwards operated by Stone, Chisholm & Jones, and is now owned by the Cleveland Rolling Mill Company. In 1852 I erected a steam forge to make wrought-iron forgings, and in 1859 I added to it a rolling mill to manufacture merchant bar, etc. The Union rolling mills were built in 1861 and 1862 to roll merchant bar iron." The first furnace at Cleveland was the first of the Newburgh furnaces, built in 1864. The Bessemer steel plant of the Cleveland Rolling Mill Company was commenced in 1867. The open-hearth works of the Otis Steel Company Limited were built in 1873 and 1874. There are now in Cleveland nine rolling mills and steel works and five blast furnaces, as well as several iron and steel establishments of a reproductive character.

In the list of persons connected with the development of the iron and steel industries of Cleveland the name of Henry Chisholm is the most prominent. Mr. Chisholm was born at Lochgelly, in Fifeshire, Scotland, on April 27, 1822, and died at Cleveland on May 9, 1881, aged 59 years.

From 1846 to 1890 the iron industry of Ohio has made steady progress, and the State now ranks second among the iron-producing States of the Union. This was also its rank in 1870 and in 1880. In the production of steel it was third in the list in 1880, and this rank it has since maintained, Pennsylvania being first and Illinois second.

CHAPTER XXXII.

EARLY IRON ENTERPRISES IN INDIANA.

INDIANA possessed a small charcoal-iron industry before 1840, but at what period in the present century this industry had its beginning can not now be definitely determined. Tench Coxe makes no reference to it in 1810, but mentions one nailery in the Territory, which produced in that year 20,000 pounds of nails, valued at $4,000. He does not locate this enterprise. In 1840 the census mentions a furnace in Jefferson county, one in Parke, one in Vigo, one in Vermillion, and three in Wayne county, the total product being 810 tons of "cast iron." A forge in Fulton county, producing 20 tons of "bar iron," is also mentioned. The furnaces of 1840 were probably all used as foundries, producing hollow-ware and other castings from bog ores.

In a chapter on the geology of Monroe county, by George K. Greene, printed in 1881, it is stated that "nearly forty years ago an iron furnace was erected by Randall Ross, of Virginia, on the lands of George Adams, of Monroe county, on section 7, township 7, range 2 west. The investment soon proved a failure, and the furnace has long gone to decay. The ruins of the 'old iron furnace' are to-day the mournful monument of an early spirit of enterprise that deserved a better fate."

The Fulton-county forge was only a bloomary. It was located at Rochester, and was built about 1840. It used bog ore, which was converted into bar iron. Dr. Ryland T. Brown, of Indianapolis, told us in his lifetime that it had a hearth about four feet square, with a stack about ten feet high, much like the stack of an ordinary foundry. There was an opening on one side large enough to admit of the process of puddling, from which the bloom of iron was taken and placed under the trip-hammer. The blast was supplied by a pair of bellows like the ordinary bellows of the blacksmith but larger. The bellows and the hammer were driven by water-power. It was Dr. Brown's opinion that the Fulton-county forge possessed all the characteristics of a *stückofen*, but Mr. D. S. Ross, who was still living at Rochester in 1891, informs us that the forge was "an open-hearth charcoal fire." He also informs us that the water-power at Rochester being insufficient the forge was removed "after a couple of years" to the Tippecanoe river, "at the point where the railroad crosses the river, two and a half miles north of Rochester." It was abandoned in 1858. The last iron made by it was bought by a Pittsburgh firm to be converted into carpet tacks.

There was another early forge "in the Twin lakes country, in Marshall county," about 1845. It was built by Charles Crocker, afterwards the California millionaire, and a partner. The forge was located at Sligo. Mr. Crocker had previously worked at a forge at Mishawaka, in St. Joseph county, which was owned by a Mr. Wilson. The bar iron made at these forges was largely used for wagon tires. Bog ore was used, as at Rochester. There were probably a few other bog-ore bloomaries in Indiana at an early day like those at Rochester, Sligo, and Mishawaka.

In 1859 Lesley enumerated five charcoal furnaces in Indiana, as follows: Elkhart, in Elkhart county, date of erection unknown; Mishawaka, in St. Joseph county, built about 1833; Indiana, a few miles northwest of Terre Haute, in Vigo county, built in 1839; Richland, on Richland creek, in Greene county, built in 1844 by A. Downing; and La Porte, near the town of that name, in La Porte county, built in 1848. Mishawaka, Indiana, and Richland were in operation in 1857, but were abandoned about 1860. Elkhart and La Porte furnaces were idle in 1857, and probably had been abandoned at that time. Elkhart, La Porte, and Mishawaka used bog ore exclusively, and Richland used it in part; in 1857 Mishawaka was still using it. Indiana used brown hematite found in the neighborhood.

In 1860 there was only one furnace in blast in Indiana—Richland. It was probably abandoned in that year, and from this time until 1867 no pig iron was made in Indiana. In the latter year the manufacture of pig iron in this State was revived, the development of the block-coal district in the neighborhood of Brazil, in Clay county, having led to the belief that this fuel might be profitably used in blast furnaces. Planet furnace, at Harmony, in Clay county, built in the summer of 1867 and put in blast in November of that year, was the first of eight furnaces that were built in Indiana between 1867 and 1872 to use this coal, the ores for the furnaces being mainly obtained from Missouri and the Lake Superior district of Michigan. Five of these furnaces were in Clay county. Of the eight furnaces built six have been abandoned and torn down since 1872, and only two now remain—Brazil and Vigo. No furnaces have been built in Indiana since 1872.

The first rolling mill in Indiana was probably the Indianapolis mill, built by R. A. Douglas, which was completed in the autumn of 1857 and put in operation in November of the same year. In 1858 Lesley says: "The machinery and building were planned by Lewis Scofield, of Trenton, New Jersey, who also built the Wyandotte mill and is building the mill at Atlanta, Georgia." There were in 1883 eight rolling mills in Indiana—two at New Albany, two at Terre Haute, and one each at Indianapolis, Greencastle, Aurora, and Brazil. The State contained no works in that year for the manufacture of steel. Early in 1891 there were thirteen completed rolling mills in Indiana. Connected with some of these rolling mills were a few small steel plants. The discovery a few years ago of natural gas in Indiana gave a fresh start to its rolling-mill industry and partly created its steel industry. At the works of the Premier Steel Company in Indianapolis the Adams direct process was introduced about the beginning of 1890.

CHAPTER XXXIII.

EARLY IRON ENTERPRISES IN ILLINOIS.

In 1839 a small charcoal furnace was built four miles northwest of Elizabethtown, in Hardin county, in the extreme southeastern part of Illinois, by Leonard White, Calen Guard, & Co. It was called Illinois. This is the first furnace in the State of which there is any record, and it probably had no predecessor. In 1853 it was purchased by C. Wolfe & Co., of Cincinnati, who tore down the stack and built a larger one in 1856, with modern additions. In 1873 this furnace, after having been out of blast for several years, was repaired, but it was never again active. A charcoal furnace called Martha, also in Hardin county, was built in 1848 by Daniel McCook & Co. about two miles east of Illinois furnace. It was probably the second furnace in the State. Illinois and Martha furnaces were both in blast in 1850, but in 1860 Illinois only was in blast. Martha had not been in operation since 1856, and it probably never made any iron after that year. It has long been abandoned. These furnaces were supplied with hematite ore from the immediate neighborhood.

In the census of 1840 mention is made of a furnace in Cook county, one in Fulton, one in Hardin, and one in Wabash county. The furnaces in Fulton and Hardin counties were idle, the furnace in Wabash county produced eight tons of "cast iron," and the furnace in Cook county produced 150 tons. As the census of 1840 sometimes confounds blast furnaces with foundries full reliance can not be placed on the correctness of its statements concerning furnaces in Illinois. We have definitely ascertained that there was no furnace in Cook county in that year, and that the furnace with which it is credited in the census was Granger's foundry, the only one in Chicago at that time.

There appears to have been no furnace in operation in Illinois from 1860 to 1868. Soon after the close of the civil war the attention of iron manufacturers was attracted to the Big Muddy coal fields, in the southwestern part of Illinois, and to the proximity to these coal fields of the rich iron ores of Missouri. In 1868 the Grand Tower Mining, Manufacturing, and Transportation Company built two large furnaces at Grand Tower, in Jackson county, Illinois, to use the Big Muddy coal in connection with Missouri ores ; and in 1871 another large furnace, called Big Muddy, was built at Grand Tower by another company to use the same fuel and ores. The two Grand Tower furnaces have been out of blast for several years and are now abandoned, but the Big Muddy furnace was in blast in 1881, since which year it has been idle. At East St. Louis the Meier Iron Company built two large coke furnaces between 1873 and .1875. These furnaces were in .operation in 1882, their fuel being mainly Carbondale coke, from Jackson county, Illinois, but they were never afterwards in blast. In 1890 they were removed to Big Stone Gap, Virginia.

The iron industry at Chicago and its vicinity properly dates from 1857, when Captain E. B. Ward, of Detroit, built the Chicago rolling mill, on the right bank of the Chicago river, "just outside of the city." This mill was built to re-roll iron rails. It formed the nucleus of the extensive works afterwards built by the North Chicago Rolling Mill Company. There was no furnace at Chicago until 1868, when two furnaces were built by the Chicago Iron Company. They were afterwards owned by the Union Steel Company. One furnace was blown in early in 1869 and the other late in the same year. Two furnaces were built at Chicago in 1869 by the North Chicago Rolling Mill Company. No other furnaces were built at Chicago until 1880, when seven new furnaces were undertaken, three of which were finished in that year, two in 1881, and two in 1882. At Joliet, thirty-seven miles southwest of Chicago, the Joliet Iron and Steel Company built two furnaces in 1873. They are now owned by the Illinois Steel Company.

In 1883 there were seventeen rolling mills and steel works in Illinois, four of which were Bessemer steel works—three at Chicago and one at Joliet; two were open-hearth steel works —one at Springfield and one at Chicago ; and one was a crucible steel works at Chicago. At the beginning of 1884 there were seventeen blast furnaces in the State, including the pioneer furnace, Illinois, which has since been abandoned.

In 1890 there were fifteen completed furnaces in Illinois and five more were in course of erection. In the same year there were seven standard Bessemer steel works in the State, four of which were owned by the Illinois Steel Company, which had absorbed in 1889 the business of the North Chicago Rolling Mill Company, the Union Steel Company, and the Joliet Steel Company. There was also a Robert-Bessemer steel plant in Illinois in that year. There were four open-hearth steel plants and one crucible steel plant. The whole number of rolling mills in Illinois was twenty-one, and two others were projected.

In the aggregate production of iron. and steel in 1880 Illinois ranked fourth among the iron and steel producing States of the Union, making a great stride since 1870, when it was fifteenth in rank. The State has long been second in the production of Bessemer steel, and for a number of years it was third in the production of pig iron, but in 1889 it fell below Alabama as a producer of pig iron, Alabama taking the third place. This State draws its supply of iron ore from the Lake Superior region and its supply of coke almost wholly from the Connellsville district in Pennsylvania.

CHAPTER XXXIV.

EARLY IRON ENTERPRISES IN MICHIGAN.

IF we could credit the census of 1840 there were fifteen blast furnaces in Michigan in that year—one in each of the counties of Allegan, Branch, Cass, Kent, Monroe, and Oakland, two in Calhoun, two in Washtenaw, and five in Wayne county. Some of these furnaces were doubtless foundries, particularly in counties lying upon or near to Lake Erie, vessels upon which could bring pig iron for these foundries from the neighboring States. Others were undoubtedly true blast furnaces, producing household and other castings from bog ores. All of the fifteen enterprises mentioned were in the southern part of the State. Their total production in 1840 was only 601 tons of "cast iron." Neither forges nor bloomaries are mentioned in the census of 1840.

From 1840 to 1850 the iron industry of Michigan certainly made no progress, and possibly declined. From 1850 to 1860 a marked improvement took place. Three new furnaces were built in the southern part of the State to use bog ore, and in the northern peninsula and at Detroit and Wyandotte a commencement was made in smelting the rich ores which had been discovered in the now celebrated Lake Superior iron-ore region. In 1859 Lesley enumerated the following bog-ore furnaces in the southern part of the State: Kalamazoo, at the city of that name, in Kalamazoo county, built in 1857 to take the place of an earlier furnace; Quincy, three miles north of the town of that name, in Branch county, built in 1855; and Branch County, one mile from Quincy furnace, built in 1854. All of these bog-ore furnaces made pig iron in 1857. It is a curious fact that furnaces to use bog ore should have been built in this State after 1850.

The development of the Lake Superior iron-ore region marks an important era in the history of the American iron trade, and the incidents attending its commencement have fortunately been preserved.

We learn from A. P. Swineford's *History of the Lake Supe-*

rior Iron District that the existence of iron ore on the southern border of Lake Superior was known to white traders
with the Indians as early as 1830. The same writer further
informs us that the first discovery by white men of the iron
ore of this region was made on the 16th of September, 1844,
near the eastern end of Teal lake, by William A. Burt, a deputy surveyor of the General Government. In June, 1845, the
Jackson Mining Company was organized at Jackson, Michigan, for the purpose of exploring the mineral districts of the
southern shore of Lake Superior, and in the summer of the
same year this company, through the disclosures of a half-
breed Indian named Louis Nolan and the direct agency of
an old Indian chief named Man-je-ki-jik, secured possession
of the now celebrated Jackson iron mountain, near the scene
of Mr. Burt's discovery. It appears, however, that the representatives of the company had not heard of Mr. Burt's discovery until they met Nolan and the Indian chief. P. M.
Everett, the president of the company, was the leading spirit
of the exploring party which secured possession of this valuable property. The actual discovery of Jackson mountain
was made by S. T. Carr and E. S. Rockwell, members of
Mr. Everett's party, who were guided to the locality by the
Indian chief.

Referring to the iron ore of Jackson mountain in a letter
written at Jackson, Michigan, on the 10th of November, 1845,
Mr. Everett says that "since coming home we have had some
of it smelted, and find that it produces iron and something
resembling gold—some say it is gold and copper." This
smelting is not further described. In 1846 A. V. Berry, one
of the Jackson Mining Company, and others brought about
300 pounds of the ore to Jackson, and in August of that year,
writes Mr. Berry, "Mr. Olds, of Cucush Prairie, who owned a
forge, then undergoing repair, in which he was making iron
from bog ore, succeeded in making a fine bar of iron from our
ore in a blacksmith's fire, the first iron ever made from Lake
Superior ore." Mr. Swineford says that "one end of this bar
of iron Mr. Everett had drawn out into a knife-blade."

In 1847 the Jackson Mining Company commenced the
erection of a forge on Carp river, about ten miles from its
mouth and near Jackson mountain. It was finished early

in 1848, and on the 10th of February of that year the first iron made in the Lake Superior region was made here by Ariel N. Barney. Mr. Swineford says that the forge, which was named after Carp river, had " eight fires, from each of which a lump was taken every six hours, placed under the hammer, and forged into blooms four inches square and two feet long, the daily product being about three tons. The first lot of blooms made at this forge, the first iron made on Lake Superior, and the first from Lake Superior ores, except the small bar made by Mr. Olds, was sold to the late E. B. Ward, and from it was made the walking-beam of the side-wheel steamer *Ocean*." The forge was kept in operation until 1854, when it was abandoned, having in the meantime "made little iron and no money."

In 1849 the Marquette Iron Company, a Worcester (Massachusetts) organization, undertook the erection of a forge at Marquette, and in July, 1850, it was finished and put in operation. Mr. Swineford says that " it started with four fires, using ores from what are now the Cleveland and Lake Superior mines." It was operated irregularly until December, 1853, when it was burned down and was not rebuilt.

The Collins Iron Company was organized in 1853, with Edward K. Collins, of New York, at its head, and in 1854 it built a forge on Dead river, about three miles northwest of Marquette, and in the fall of 1855 the manufacture of blooms was commenced from ore obtained at the company's mines. This forge was in operation in 1858, after which time it seems to have been abandoned.

Another forge on Dead river was built in 1854 or 1855 by William G. McComber, Matthew McConnell, and J. G. Butler. The company failed in a few years, and in 1860 Stephen R. Gay erected Bancroft furnace on the site of the forge. Before 1860 every forge in Michigan appears to have been abandoned. (Mr. Butler was the father of J. G. Butler, Jr., of Youngstown, Ohio, the present general manager of the Brier Hill Iron and Coal Company.)

It will be observed that all of the pioneer iron enterprises in the Lake Superior region were bloomary forges, the intention evidently having been to build up an iron industry similar to that of the Lake Champlain district.

The first pig iron produced in the Lake Superior region was made in 1858 by Stephen R. Gay, who then leased the forge of the Collins Iron Company and converted it in two days, at an expense of $50, into a miniature blast furnace. In February, 1858, as we learn from the records of the American Iron and Steel Association, Mr. Gay wrote to C. A. Trowbridge that this furnace was "$2\frac{1}{2}$ feet across the bosh, 8 feet high, and 12 inches square at the top and 15 inches square in the hearth," and would hold eight bushels of coal. He gives the following details of its first and only blast: "Began on Monday, finished and fired on Wednesday, filled with coal Thursday noon, blast turned on Friday noon, and thenceforth charged regularly with 1 bushel coal, 20 pounds of ore, and 7 pounds of limestone. Cast at six o'clock 500 pounds, and again at eight o'clock Saturday morning, half a ton in all, 92 pounds of which were forged by Mr. Eddy into an 85-pound bloom. This little furnace was run two and a half days, made $2\frac{1}{2}$ tons, carrying the last eight hours 30 pounds of ore to a bushel of coal, equal to a ton of pig iron to 100 bushels of coal." These experiments were made in February.

The first regular blast furnace in the Lake Superior region was built by the Pioneer Iron Company in the present city of Negaunee, convenient to the Jackson mine. It was commenced in June, 1857, and in February, 1858, it was finished. Another stack was added in the same year. These furnaces took the name of the company. Pioneer No. 1 was put in blast in April, 1858, and Pioneer No. 2 on May 20, 1859. Both furnaces are now owned by the Iron Cliffs Company. They were burned and rebuilt in 1877. They were both in operation in 1883 and have since been active. The second regular blast furnace in this region was the Collins furnace, built in 1858 by Stephen R. Gay, near the site of the Collins forge. It made its first iron on December 13th of that year. It was abandoned in 1873, owing to the failure of a supply of charcoal. Other furnaces in the Lake Superior region soon followed the erection of the Pioneer and Collins furnaces. Mr. Swineford's history contains a record of these early enterprises.

While these early furnaces and the few forges that have been mentioned were being built on the shore of Lake Superior two furnaces were built at or near Detroit to smelt Lake Superior ores. These were the Eureka furnace, at Wyandotte, built in 1855 by the Eureka Iron Company, of which Captain E. B. Ward was president, and put in blast in 1856; and the Detroit furnace, at Detroit, built in 1856 by the Detroit and Lake Superior Iron Manufacturing Company, of which George B. Russell was president, and put in blast in January, 1857. These furnaces and the others that have been mentioned used charcoal as fuel.

The first shipment of iron ore from the Lake Superior region was made in 1850, according to Mr. Swineford, and consisted of about five tons, "which was taken away by Mr. A. L. Crawford, of New Castle, Pennsylvania." A part of this ore was reduced to blooms and rolled into bar iron. "The iron was found to be most excellent, and served to attract the attention of Pennsylvania ironmasters to this new field of supply for their furnaces and rolling mills." Mr. Crawford informed us in his lifetime that he received at New Castle in 1850 about ten tons of Jackson ore which had been hauled around the falls of Sault Ste. Marie on a strap railroad one and a quarter miles long. In 1853 a few tons of Jackson ore were shipped to the World's Fair at New York.

The first use of Lake Superior ore in a blast furnace occurred in Pennsylvania. This important event is described in a letter to us from the late David Agnew, of Sharpsville, Mercer county, Pennsylvania, from which we quote as follows.

The Sharon Iron Company, of Mercer county, Pennsylvania, about the year 1850 or 1851 purchased the Jackson mines, and, in expectation of the speedy completion of the Sault canal, commenced to open them, to construct a road to the lake, and to build docks at Marquette, expending a large sum of money in these operations. The opening of the canal was, however, unexpectedly delayed until June, 1855. Anxious to test the working qualities of this ore the Sharon Iron Company brought, at great expense, to Erie, in the year 1853, about 70 tons of it, which were shipped by canal to Sharpsville furnace, near Sharon, owned by David and John P. Agnew. The first boat-load of ore, on its receipt, was immediately used in the furnace, partly alone and partly in mixture with native ores, and the experiment was highly successful, the furnace working well and producing an increased yield of metal, which was taken to the Sharon iron works and there converted into bar iron, nails, etc., of very superior quality. The second boat-load of ore was also brought to Sharpsville, but, having been intended to be left at the Clay furnace, owned by the Sharon Iron Company, was returned and used at that establishment.

The historical interest which attaches to the first use of Lake Superior iron ore leads us to copy the following details concerning the Sharon Iron Company and its connection with the development of the Jackson iron mountain ore. Our authority is a pamphlet copy of the prospectus of the Sharon Iron Company, printed in 1852. We quote from the pamphlet, (which is signed by J. B. Curtis, president,) as follows.

The Sharon Iron Company was organized at Sharon, Mercer county, Pennsylvania, in 1850, with a capital of $70,000, under the general manufacturing law of the State of Pennsylvania, and possesses a charter from that State. The manufacture of iron and nails was commenced in December, 1850, and the mill is in successful operation at the present time. The company also own a blast furnace, with the necessary buildings, ore, and coal privileges—now making forty-five tons of pig iron weekly, at a cost of eighteen dollars per ton—situated one mile from the canal, and eight miles from the mill, which they purchased on very advantageous terms.

The president of the company having visited the iron region of Lake Superior in the fall of 1850 became so impressed with the boundless extent, unrivaled richness, and great facilities of obtaining the ore of that region, (and the specimens he procured having proved, on test, the superior quality and purity of the iron,) he recommended the company to purchase the Jackson mountain, as being the nearest, largest, and best location, a property owned by a corporate company, located in Jackson county, Michigan. This property consists of 640 acres of land, (the Iron mountain,) 200 acres lying between the mountain and lake, on which there is a good water power, a forge for making blooms in operation, and twenty dwelling-houses, and also 60 acres of land at the harbor, on Lake Superior, called Iron bay. After several attempts at negotiation the president of the Sharon Iron Company, with others in interest, succeeded, in September, 1851, in purchasing a controlling interest in said property, obtaining 1,507 shares out of 3,000 at $15 per share, amounting to $22,605.

The Sharon Iron Company have manufactured this season 150 tons blooms, made at the Jackson forge, into bar, boiler plate, nails, etc. They have readily sold the bar iron at $80 per ton, when common puddled iron goes begging at $50 per ton. It has been tested for steel wire and fine tacks, and proved equal to the best Swedes.

In 1854, 1855, and 1856 Clay furnace, which was located on Anderson's run, nine miles west of Mercer, continued the use of Lake Superior ore, most of it mixed with native ore, and used in all until August, 1856, about 400 tons. "Up to that date," as is stated by Mr. Frank Allen, its manager, "the working of it was not a success. In October, 1856, we gave the Clay furnace a general overhauling, put in a new lining and hearth, and made material changes in the construction of the same, put her in blast late in the fall, and in a few days were making a beautiful article of iron from Lake Superior ore alone." The fuel used at Sharpsville and Clay furnaces was the block coal of the Shenango valley. After 1856 other furnaces in Pennsylvania and in other States began the regular use of Lake Superior ore.

David Agnew was born at Frankstown, in Blair county, Pennsylvania, on September 25,1805, and died at Sharpsville, in Mercer county, on August 24, 1882, aged almost 77 years. His whole life was devoted to the manufacture of iron.

Until about 1877 the mining of iron ore in the Lake Superior region was confined to the territory in the immediate vicinity of Marquette. Since 1877, and particularly since 1879, a new iron-ore region has been developed in the northern part of Menominee county and the southern part of Marquette county, in Michigan, and in Florence county, Wisconsin. It is called the Menominee district. This region has proved to be very productive and the ore to be very pure.

In 1884 the Vermilion iron-ore district, in St. Louis county, Minnesota, on the northern shore of Lake Superior, became a competitor with the Marquette and Menominee districts in the production and shipment of iron ore, and in the same year the Gogebic district, which lies west of the Menominee district and is partly in Michigan and partly in Wisconsin, also became a competitor. The shipments from the Vermilion district in 1884 aggregated 62,124 gross tons, and the shipments from the Gogebic district in the same year aggregated 1,022 tons. The total shipments of iron ore from the Marquette, Menominee, Gogebic, and Vermilion districts from 1884 to 1890 have been as follows, in gross tons.

Districts.	1884.	1885.	1886.	1887.	1888.	1889.	1890.
Marquette......	1,558,083	1,430,422	1,627,383	1,851,717	1,926,954	2,634,817	2,997,927
Menominee.....	895,634	690,435	880,006	1,199,343	1,191,097	1,796,764	2,289,017
Gogebic..........	1,022	119,590	756,237	1,285,265	1,433,689	2,016,391	2,845,171
Vermilion.......	62,124	225,484	304,396	394,252	511,953	844,782	880,264
Total..........	2,516,818	2,465,931	3,568,022	4,730,577	5,063,693	7,292,754	9,012,379

In addition to the shipments above recorded there were also shipped in 1884 and 1885 a few tons of iron ore from a few small mines in Michigan which are not properly in any of the districts mentioned. These shipments amounted to 1,879 gross tons in 1884 and to 441 tons in 1885. Shipments from these mines do not appear to have been continued. From the Marquette *Mining Journal* we compile the following table of the aggregate shipments from *all* the Lake Superior iron-ore mines for each calendar year since the commencement of regular mining operations in the region.

Years.	Gross tons.	Years.	Gross tons.	Years.	Gross tons.
1854....................	3,000	1867....................	473,567	1880....................	1,908,745
1855....................	1,449	1868....................	491,449	1881....................	2,306,505
1856....................	36,343	1869....................	617,444	1882....................	2,965,412
1857....................	25,646	1870....................	830,940	1883....................	2,353,288
1858....................	15,876	1871....................	779,607	1884	2,518,692
1859....................	68,882	1872....................	900,901	1885....................	2,466,372
1860....................	114,401	1873....................	1,162,458	1886....................	3,568,022
1861....................	49,909	1874....................	919,557	1887....................	4,730,577
1862....................	124,169	1875....................	891,257	1888....................	5,063,693
1863....................	203,055	1876....................	992,764	1889....................	7,292,754
1864....................	243,127	1877....................	1,015,087	1890....................	9,012,379
1865....................	236,208	1878....................	1,111,110		
1866....................	278,796	1879....................	1,375,691	Total............	57,149,082

The iron ores of Lake Superior which are not used in Michigan are mainly shipped to Ohio, Pennsylvania, Illinois, and Wisconsin. They have been shipped as far east as the Hudson river valley in New York for blast-furnace use and as far south as Alabama for use in puddling furnaces. About one-half of all the pig iron that is now manufactured in the United States is made from these ores.

From the discovery of iron ore in the Lake Superior region until 1883 there had been built on the upper peninsula, in the vicinity of the mines, twenty-five furnaces, of which thirteen had been abandoned. There had also been built at other points in Michigan, to use Lake Superior ore, sixteen furnaces, of which none had been abandoned in 1883. All of these furnaces, with the exception of two at Marquette and one at Detroit, were built to use charcoal, and the abandonment of many of them is attributable to the scarcity of timber for fuel. Since 1883 there have been five furnaces built or restored in Michigan, while a few have been abandoned, the whole number of furnaces in the State at the beginning of 1891 being twenty-nine, all charcoal furnaces except one. Michigan has long been the first State in the Union in the manufacture of charcoal pig iron. Its largest production of pig iron, all made with charcoal, was in 1890, when 258,461 net tons were produced. The three bog-ore furnaces in Kalamazoo and Branch counties have long been abandoned.

In 1884 there were three active rolling mills in Michigan : the Eureka, formerly the Wyandotte, at Wyandotte, built in 1855; the rolling mill of the Baugh Steam Forge Company, at Detroit, built in 1877, the forge having been built in 1870; and the works of the Detroit Steel and Spring Company, at Detroit, which had recently commenced the manufacture of crucible steel. In 1891 the same rolling mills were still in operation, and a new one, built in 1890, was in operation at Muskegon. The Detroit Steel and Spring Company added a Robert-Bessemer steel plant to its works in 1889. In 1871 a rolling mill was built at Marquette which has since been abandoned. In 1872 a rolling mill was built at Jackson, in Jackson county, but it was torn down in 1879 and the machinery removed to the mill of the Springfield Iron Company, at Springfield, Illinois.

Captain Ward was the most prominent of all the pioneer iron manufacturers of Michigan, his enterprise in this respect extending to other States than his own.

In 1870 Michigan ranked eighth in the list of iron and steel producing States, and in 1880 its rank was the same. In 1890 it was the ninth in rank.

CHAPTER XXXV.

THE EARLY MANUFACTURE OF IRON IN WISCONSIN.

THE census of 1840 mentions a furnace in "Milwaukee town," which produced three tons of iron in that year. This was probably a small foundry. In 1859 Lesley mentions three charcoal furnaces in Wisconsin—Northwestern, or Mayville, at Mayville, in Dodge county, forty miles northwest of Milwaukee and five miles from the Iron ridge, built in 1848 by the owners of Mishawaka furnace in Indiana, and to which a foundry was added in 1858; Ironton, at Ironton, in Sauk county, built in 1857 by Jonas Tower; and Black River, built in 1857 by a German company on the east bank of Black river, near the falls, in Jackson county. Of these furnaces at least one, Ironton, was built to produce castings. A description of it in 1858 says: "It is a small blast furnace, capable of producing about three tons of iron per day, and intended for the manufacture of stoves, castings, etc." The Ironton furnace has recently produced castings as well as pig iron. The Mayville furnace is still in operation, having been rebuilt in 1872, but the Black River furnace has long been abandoned. In its stead there was erected in 1885 and 1886 a modern charcoal furnace, known as the Minneapolis furnace, owned by the York Iron Company. There appear to have been neither forges nor bloomaries in Wisconsin in the census years 1840, 1850, and 1860.

The furnaces which have been mentioned were all that Wisconsin could boast until 1865, when a charcoal furnace at Iron Ridge, in Dodge county, was built by the Wisconsin Iron Company. This was soon followed by several other furnaces, some of which were built to use native ores and some to use Michigan ores from Lake Superior. The Appleton Iron Company built two furnaces at Appleton, in Outagamie county, in 1871 and 1872; C. J. L. Meyer built a furnace at Fond du Lac in 1874, but it was not put in blast until the summer of 1883; the Fox River Iron Company built two furnaces at West De Pere, in Brown county, in 1869 and 1872; the Green

Bay Iron Company built a furnace at Green Bay, in the same county, in 1870 ; and the National Furnace Company built two furnaces at De Pere, in the same county, in 1869 and 1872. All of these furnaces were built to use charcoal. In 1870 and 1871 the Milwaukee Iron Company built two large furnaces at Bay View, near Milwaukee, and in 1873 the Minerva Iron Company built a furnace at Milwaukee. These three furnaces were built to use anthracite coal and bituminous coke and Lake Superior ores. A furnace called Richland was built in 1876 at Cazenovia, in Richland county, but was torn down in 1879. In 1883 there were fifteen furnaces in the State, twelve of which used charcoal and three used anthracite coal and coke. In 1890, however, the whole number of completed furnaces had been reduced to ten, of which six used charcoal and four used coke. A new coke furnace was in course of erection at West Superior, in Douglas county. In 1887 and 1888 there was built at Ashland, in Ashland county, a charcoal furnace, 60 feet high by 12 feet in width at the boshes, which has made the best record in production of any charcoal furnace in the United States. This furnace is called Hinkle. Nearly all the old charcoal furnaces of Wisconsin have been abandoned.

Wisconsin had no rolling mill until 1868, when its first and thus far its only active mill was built at Milwaukee by the Milwaukee Iron Company, of which Captain E. B. Ward was a leading member. This was from the first a large mill. It was built to re-roll iron rails, but soon commenced the manufacture of new rails. In 1874 a merchant bar mill was added, and in 1884 a nail mill was added. This mill and the two Bay View furnaces were operated in 1883 by the North Chicago Rolling Mill Company, but they are now owned by the Illinois Steel Company.

Within the last few years the mining of iron ore in Florence county, Wisconsin, forming the western continuation of the Menominee district in Michigan, has been prosecuted with much activity. In 1882 there were shipped from this county 276,017 tons of iron ore. But the greatest development of the iron-ore resources of Wisconsin has taken place since 1884 in the Gogebic district, situated in the counties of Ashland, in Wisconsin, and Ontonagon and Gogebic, in Michigan, the statistics of which district have already been given in the Michigan chapter. The early charcoal furnaces of Wisconsin used poor ores, which were not at all comparable with the rich ores now obtained in the Gogebic and other districts of the Lake Superior region.

Wisconsin advanced rapidly in the manufacture of iron in the decade between 1870 and 1880. In the latter year it ranked sixth among the iron and steel producing States of the Union. In 1870 it was twelfth in rank. In 1890 it had retrograded and was eighth in rank, being intermediate between its position in 1870 and 1880. It has not yet produced any kind of steel. In 1890 the building of a Bessemer steel plant was, however, undertaken at West Superior, in Wisconsin. Its completion in the latter part of 1891 is promised.

CHAPTER XXXVI.

EARLY IRON ENTERPRISES IN MISSOURI.

MISSOURI has an iron history which antedates its admission into the Union in 1821. The celebrated iron district in Iron and St. François counties, which embraces Iron Mountain and Pilot Knob, appears to have contained the first iron enterprise in this State.

Mr. William A. Fletcher, of Ironton, clerk of the court of Iron county, writes us as follows : " There was once an iron furnace in the northeast quarter of section 3, township 33, north of range 4 east, on Stout's creek, just two miles east of the Ironton court-house. Some of the débris remains to be seen to this day. I can recollect seeing some of the old castings, in the shape of wheels, scattered around when I was a small boy some forty years ago."

We are also in receipt of a letter from Mr. A. W. Holloman, of Arcadia, the county surveyor of Iron county for the last thirty-three years, who gives us the recollections of Mr. Leonard Sutton, an old settler, who distinctly remembers the iron enterprise on Stout's creek, which he styles Ashebran's furnace. Mr. Sutton says that the furnace was located on Stout's creek, about one and a half miles from the settlement of his father, who moved into the northeast corner of Iron county (then known as Upper Louisiana Territory) in 1817. He further says that the furnace was built by a person named Ashebran and others about 1815 or 1816, and that he has often seen "the old shaft," to haul which required the efforts of twelve oxen. Mr. Holloman says that he has himself often seen the site of the furnace, or, as he terms it, the forge. Mr. Sutton adds that the ore for the furnace was obtained on Shepherd mountain, which was about three miles northwest of the furnace. Mr. Holloman says that there can be no doubt of the existence of this pioneer enterprise as early as 1815 or 1816.

In a second letter from Mr. Holloman he says that Mr. Sutton tells him that "castings" were made on Stout's creek, "but mostly bar iron," and Mr. Holloman himself says that it is his own impression that "bar iron was what was mostly made by this infant enterprise." Mr. Sutton further says that "on one end of the big shaft was a water-wheel and on the other end was a wheel so arranged as to lift the hammer which beat out the bars of iron." He intimates that a water-blast was used. In a second communication Mr. Fletcher states that he often heard his father speak many years ago of the bar iron that was hammered at Ashebran's works, and of Ashebran himself as a hammerman. The evidence seems to be conclusive that both castings and bar iron were made by Ashebran. Either a furnace and a refinery forge were cotemporary enterprises or a furnace and a Catalan forge were built at different periods. The works were located on a stream which furnished excellent water-power.

Another early enterprise in Missouri of which we have obtained full information was a bloomary forge on Thicketty creek, a tributary of the Maramec river, in Crawford county, near the Washington county line, three miles south of the present town of Bourbon. Cresswell's mill was afterwards built about one hundred yards from the site of this early iron enterprise. The bloomary was variously styled Harrison's furnace, Harrison's forge, Harrison's bloomary, and the Harrison iron works. The works were of a primitive character, consisting of "a stone stack built into the hill so that it could be easily filled from the top. It was rudely constructed of logs and rock." They were built in 1819 or 1820 by William Harrison and Josiah Reeves, and were certainly in operation in 1820. Thomas Reeves was the forgeman. We are told that the bloomary "was built like a blacksmith's forge, only much larger, and was a water-blast. The ore was burnt, then crushed, and put into the forge with charcoal. The iron was made into long bars." It was used for wagon tires, mattocks, grubbing hoes, plowshares, horseshoes, etc. The bloom of iron was hammered under a spring-pole hammer on an anvil which rested upon "an anvil-block formed of a section of a tree four feet in diameter and buried mostly in the ground." The ore used was brown hematite mixed with blue ore; it was hauled in ox-carts from the adjacent hills by Battle Harrison, a son of William Harrison. The works continued in operation for several years. They have long been in ruins, as is also Cresswell's mill.

For the above circumstantial information concerning the Harrison bloomary we are indebted to the politeness of B. F. Russell, Esq., editor of the Crawford *Mirror*, at Steelville, Missouri. Judge Robinson, who was reared in the Iron Mountain country, and who has been consulted by Mr. Russell, says that there was " a log furnace " in Iron county which " was built about the time of the Harrison bloomary," thus confirming other information which we have given concerning that enterprise.

A few years after the establishment of the Harrison bloomary a blast furnace, called Springfield, was built in Washington county, about six miles south of Potosi. The geologist G. C. Swallow is quoted by Lesley on page 597 of *The Iron Manufacturer's Guide* as follows: " The earliest attempt in Missouri, and in all probability in any of the States west of the Ohio, to smelt iron ore was in 1823 or 1824, when a blast furnace was erected in Washington county by Eversol, Perry & Ruggles, between Potosi and Caledonia. This furnace was afterwards known as Perry's old iron furnace." The ore for this furnace was at first obtained from *Claer* creek, but afterwards "from near Absalom Eaton's place, and was mixed with ore brought from the Iron Mountain." Mr. Swallow continues: " In connection with this blast furnace were two forges. The first bar of iron made out of pig metal in Missouri, Colonel McIlvaine says, was made on Cedar creek in May, 1825, and the first blooms were made in 1832." The enterprise here referred to was Springfield furnace, but it was not the first furnace in Missouri, as has already been shown.

In the prospectus of the Missouri Iron Company, printed in 1837, we find it stated that Springfield furnace had been operated "for more than fifteen years " prior to that year. In that year the furnace was in operation, when it was called " a small furnace." A forge was then attached to it, and " a blooming forge" was promised " the ensuing year." The prospectus further states that " cannon balls, made from the Iron Mountain ore during the late war, after having been exposed for several years to the open atmosphere and rains, still maintained their original metallic lustre." The cannon balls referred to would probably be used in the Black Hawk war of 1832. Mr. Russell tells us that cannon balls were certainly made for the General Government at Springfield furnace in 1832, citing as his authority a history of Crawford and Franklin counties in his possession.

Maramec furnace, in Phelps county, about sixty miles west of Iron Mountain, was finished in January, 1829, and rebuilt many years afterwards. It was probably projected in 1826, as in that year the ore banks in the vicinity, about half a mile west of the Maramec river, were opened by Massey & James. The ore was tested at Harrison's bloomary before the furnace was built. This old furnace was still standing a few years ago, but it was not in operation and has now been abandoned. At an early day a forge was added to the furnace, to convert its pig iron into bar iron, and this forge, with eight fires, was also recently standing but abandoned, its product being charcoal blooms. In 1843 a rolling mill was added to the furnace and forge, but it was "abandoned after one year's trial, because of the sulphur in the stone coal obtained at a bank fourteen miles southeast." The Maramec furnace and forge were long called the Massey iron works.

In the census of 1840 Missouri is credited with two furnaces, one in Crawford county and one in Washington county. It is also credited with three forges in Crawford county and one in Washington county. The furnace in Crawford county was Maramec, Phelps county not having then been organized, and the forges in Crawford county were doubtless attached to Maramec furnace. The furnace in Washington county was Springfield, and the forge was doubtless the one which was attached to this furnace. We do not hear of Springfield furnace and forge after this time.

In 1836 the remarkable iron-ore mountains already mentioned—Iron Mountain and Pilot Knob—attracted the attention of some Missouri capitalists, and in the fall of that year the Missouri Iron Company, with a nominal capital of $5,000,-000, was formed to utilize their ores, the legislature chartering the company on December 31, 1836. In January, 1837, the company was fully organized under the presidency of Silas Drake, of St. Louis, who was soon succeeded by J. L. Van Doren, of Arcadia, but active work in the development of its property does not appear to have been undertaken until some years afterwards, when a few furnaces were erected at the foot of the mountains by other companies. In 1846 a furnace was built at the southwest base of Little Iron Mountain, which was followed in 1850 by another furnace at the same place, and in 1854 by still another. In 1849 a furnace was built on the north side of Pilot Knob, which was followed in 1855 by another at the same place. These were all charcoal furnaces, and were exceptionally well managed in 1857, when they were visited and described by Charles B. Forney, of Lebanon, Pennsylvania. At that time two of the Iron Mountain furnaces and one of the Pilot Knob furnaces used hot-blast. Of all these furnaces only one of the Pilot Knob furnaces is now left, and it was remodeled in 1879.

In 1846 Moselle furnace was built at Moselle, in Franklin county, and in 1859 a furnace was built at Irondale, in Washington county, both furnaces to use charcoal. These, with the furnaces previously mentioned, appear to have been all that were built in Missouri prior to 1860. Both the Moselle and the Irondale furnaces have been abandoned. Since 1860, and particularly since 1870, other charcoal furnaces have been built in Missouri, but most of these have been abandoned, only two of the new furnaces, Midland, in Crawford county, built in 1875, and Sligo, in Dent county, built in 1880, being now active.

The iron industry of St. Louis appears to have had its commencement in 1850, when the St. Louis, or Laclede, rolling mill was built. It was followed by the Missouri rolling mill, built in 1854; by the Allen rolling mill, built in 1855; by the Pacific rolling mill, built in 1856; and by Raynor's rolling mill, built in 1858.

In 1880 there were seven rolling mills in St. Louis, and there were then no others in Missouri. One of these, the Vulcan, built in 1872, was built to roll iron rails but afterwards rolled steel rails. Two other mills rolled light iron rails and bar iron. In 1882 there was one rolling mill less than in 1880, six in all, and there were seven in 1890, five in St. Louis. The Bessemer works of the Vulcan Steel Company were built in 1875 and 1876. They and the rolling mill connected with them are now idle. They are owned by the St. Louis Ore and Steel Company. Missouri had no other steel works in 1883. In 1887 Mr. J. H. Sternbergh, of Reading, Pennsylvania, commenced the erection of bolt and nut works, to which was attached a small rolling mill, near Kansas City, and in 1889 a rolling mill of considerable capacity was built at St. Joseph, to which was added in 1890 a Robert-Bessemer steel plant.

St. Louis had no blast furnaces until 1863, when the Pioneer furnace was built at Carondelet, to use coke. It was in blast in 1873, but in 1874 it was torn down and removed by the Pilot Knob Iron Company. In 1869 the Vulcan Iron Works, now the St. Louis Ore and Steel Company, built two furnaces, which were followed in 1872 by another furnace built by the same company. In 1870 and 1872 the South St. Louis Iron Company built two furnaces; in 1870 the Missouri Furnace Company built two; and in 1873 Jupiter furnace was built, but it was not put in blast until 1880. These eight furnaces were all built to use Illinois or Connellsville coke and Missouri ores. Of the whole number only five are now standing, and not all of these are active.

In 1871 a large forge, called the Germania iron works, was built at South St. Louis to make charcoal blooms from pig iron, but it has been abandoned for several years. In 1873 a forge was built at Kimmswick, in Jefferson county, which was enlarged and remodeled in 1877 by the Peckham Iron Company, its product after the enlargement being charcoal blooms made direct from the ore. It was in operation in 1886, but has since been abandoned and dismantled.

In 1883 there were nine charcoal furnaces and eight coke furnaces in Missouri, but in 1890 there were only three charcoal furnaces and five coke furnaces which could be regarded as active or likely to be active. From 1870 to 1880 the iron industry of Missouri was the prey of adverse circumstances, and in the latter year it lost the prominent rank it had held among iron-producing States. It ranked sixth in 1870, but in 1880 it had fallen to the tenth place. In 1890 it was thirteenth in rank. The shipments of iron ore from Missouri to other States for many years averaged over 100,000 tons annually, but they have now greatly declined, and are so small that they do not attract any attention.

CHAPTER XXXVII.

THE MANUFACTURE OF IRON IN TEXAS.

TEXAS had one blast furnace before the beginning of the civil war. It was located in the extreme northeastern part of Cass county, and had been in operation for several years prior to 1859. In that year Dr. B. F. Shumard, State geologist, said of this furnace that "it was erected several years since by Mr. Nash," whose full name was J. S. Nash. Dr. Shumard said that it had been "in nearly constant, and I believe profitable, operation up to the present time." This furnace continued in operation during the war.

In 1859 the erection of a furnace about one and a half miles southeast of Hughes Springs, in the southwestern part of Cass county, was commenced, but the furnace was not put in blast until 1861. "Mr. Hughes built the furnace but never operated it, as the Confederate Government took charge of it soon after its erection." In 1863 the Sulphur Fork Iron Company built a furnace "on Horton's headright, just west of Springdale," in Cass county. "The furnace was built of brick, and was 34 feet square and 36 feet high." During the war a furnace was built about eight miles from Jacksonville and three miles from the Neches river, in Cherokee county, which was known as Young's iron works, taking its name from Dr. Young, the president of the company which built it. This furnace was built of brown sandstone, and was 34 feet square at the base and the same number of feet high. About eight miles south of Rusk, in Cherokee county, were located Philleo's iron works, consisting of a blast furnace and foundry, which were also built during the war.

While these furnaces were in operation during the civil war, partly in aid of the Confederate Government, other iron enterprises were undertaken in Texas. All these enterprises were ore bloomaries. Near Nechesville, in Anderson county, a bloomary was erected in 1863 by Dr. Charles Bussey and Joseph P. Griggs, with whom was afterwards associated Dr. J. B. Bussey. This bloomary was operated with steam-power

IRON IN ALL AGES.

"and two tub bellows, or blowing cylinders." Good iron was made with ore from a neighboring mountain and pine charcoal. The works were burned before the war closed. A bloomary called Montalbo was built about 1863 on the southern bank of Mount Prairie creek, eight or nine miles north of Palestine, in Anderson county, and about ten miles south of the Nechesville bloomary, which was operated by the Confederate Government. "From the iron smelted there gun barrels and other munitions of war were manufactured." A short distance north of the Nechesville bloomary, in the vicinity of Kickapoo, the Confederate Government began the erection of Kickapoo bloomary, but, as far as can be ascertained, it was never completed. A bloomary, known as McLain, or Linn Flat, was built during the latter part of the war in the northern part of Nacogdoches county, about twelve miles from the town of Nacogdoches and six miles from Linn Flat. It was in operation eight months, and during that time made about 150,000 pounds of hammered iron bars. This bloomary, like the Nechesville bloomary, was burned. In addition to the bloomaries above mentioned another was undertaken by the Confederate Government a few miles east of Nechesville, in Cherokee county, but it was never finished.

Without an exception all the furnaces and bloomaries in Texas which have been mentioned were abandoned either during the civil war or soon after its close.

For the information contained in the foregoing summary of early iron enterprises in Texas we are indebted to a valuable paper contributed by E. T. Dumble and to be found in the second annual report of the Geological Survey of Texas, published by the State in 1891.

In 1869 a charcoal furnace was built five miles north of Jefferson, in Marion county, which went into blast in 1870 but was rebuilt in 1874. It was in operation in 1880, and was then the only active furnace in the State. It was called Kelly furnace, after Mr. G. A. Kelly, the president of the Jefferson Iron Company, by which it was built. In 1882 it was sold to the Marshall Car Wheel and Foundry Company, which changed its name to Lou-Ellen furnace and operated it until 1885, when it was finally blown out. It was torn down in 1888. It used brown hematite ore found in the neighborhood. In 1883 a furnace was built by the State of Texas at Rusk, in Cherokee county, and called Old Alcalde. It was put in blast in February, 1884, since which time it has been almost continually in operation. A pipe foundry is connected with the furnace, and melted iron is run directly into water pipe of all sizes. These works are owned and operated by the State of Texas in connection with the State penitentiary at Rusk. In 1890 the Lone Star Iron Company built a large furnace at Jefferson, in Marion county, which was blown in in the spring of 1891. The name of the furnace is Jefferson. In 1890 the New Birmingham Iron and Land Company built a large furnace called Tassie Belle at New Birmingham, in Cherokee county, which was put in blast in the latter part of that year. In 1890 the Cherokee Iron Manufacturing Company commenced the erection at New Birmingham of a large furnace, at first called La Mascotte and now known as Star and Crescent, which would probably be completed in 1891. All these are charcoal furnaces.

The first rolling mill in Texas was started at Houston in May, 1884. A small rolling mill at Fort Worth was built in 1890 and 1891 and put in operation in the latter year. The Houston and Fort Worth mills do not have puddling furnaces.

Texas is well supplied with iron ores, some of which are said to be of Bessemer quality, and for many years to come there will be no scarcity of timber for charcoal. Brown coal exists in many parts of the State, and good coking coal has been found in the southwestern portion. Much is expected from the promised development at an early day of the extensive iron-ore deposits of Llano and adjacent counties. From this time forth Texas is entitled to recognition as one of the promising iron-producing States of the Union.

CHAPTER XXXVIII.

THE MANUFACTURE OF IRON IN VARIOUS WESTERN STATES AND IN THE TERRITORIES.

In 1884 Minnesota had one charcoal furnace, situated at Duluth, which was commenced in 1872 and not finished until 1880. It was put in blast on July 12, 1880, and ran irregularly until 1883, after which year it was virtually abandoned. It is now wholly abandoned. Its projectors failed, and after passing through the hands of creditors it was purchased by the Duluth Iron Company. It obtained its supply of ore from the Lake Superior mines in Michigan. In 1889 the Duluth Iron and Steel Company commenced the erection at Duluth of a large coke furnace, 75 feet high by 16 feet wide, which has since been completed but had not been blown in early in 1891. In 1884 a small rolling mill was built and put in operation at Minneapolis by Strothman Brothers, but it was abandoned and dismantled in 1887. In 1885 and 1886 Morgan, Williams & Co. built a small rolling mill at St. Paul, which was afterwards known as the Capital iron works, but it was not long in operation and has been abandoned. In 1888 and 1889 a more ambitious rolling-mill enterprise was undertaken at Duluth by the Minnesota Iron Car Company, and in the latter year it was put in operation. It was in active operation in 1890. The valuable iron-ore deposits in the Vermilion district of Saint Louis county, Minnesota, have already been referred to in the Michigan chapter. The ore of this district possesses the same general characteristics as that of Northern Michigan. Iron ore has been found in other counties in Minnesota.

In 1857 a bloomary called Big Creek was built about six miles southwest of Smithville, in Lawrence county, Arkansas, by Alfred Bevens & Co. In 1858 Lesley describes it as "a bloomary with two fires and a hammer, making 250 pounds of swedged iron per day per fire, with a cold-blast in November, 1857, but has now a hot-blast, and is making perhaps 800 pounds, using 300 bushels of charcoal to the ton of finished bars, made out of brown hematite ore." The bloomary was driven by water-power. It is not mentioned in the census of 1860 or 1870, and has been abandoned. Mr. Clarke W. Harrington, of Berryville, Carroll county, writes us that in 1850 an Englishman named Abram Beach built a bloomary in this county, which was in operation for a few years, when it was swept away by a freshet. It was succeeded by the "Higgins grist mill." The hammer used at this bloomary may now be seen on its site. Mr. Harrington says that "Beach made a large number of plow coulters, many of which are still in use." From the same gentleman we learn that old residents of Carroll county have a tradition that iron was once made in that county in hollow stumps of trees, which is not improbable, the iron ore of this county being a soft hematite, which could easily be reduced. Iron ore of the quality mentioned is very abundant near Berryville. We have no knowledge that any other iron enterprises than those above mentioned have ever existed in this State.

Arkansas is, however, not lacking in the natural resources which are required for the production of iron. It has iron ore, coal, and limestone, and extensive forests of timber. In 1885 two companies commenced the development of the manganese deposits in the neighborhood of Batesville, in the northeastern part of this State, but their operations have not been very actively prosecuted. The total production of manganese in Arkansas in 1889 was 2,528 gross tons.

In a pamphlet, entitled the *Products and Resources of Arkansas*, compiled by D. McRae, and published by direction of the Governor of Arkansas in 1885, we find the following reference to a deposit of iron ore which is found in Southwestern Arkansas. "Altogether the most remarkable and interesting mineral of all this region is the white malleable iron, regarding the existence and malleability of which a great deal of skepticism is said to exist. It is found in the corner of Howard county adjoining the frontier of Montgomery, Polk, and Pike. During the war, it is stated on good authority, the inhabitants of the vicinity used to take the ore as it was picked up from the ground and in an ordinary blacksmith's forge hammer it into horseshoe nails. The outcrop of this ore, as far as it has been explored, runs for two miles west to east, showing a width of from 15 to 30 feet, with an unknown depth."

Kansas had two rolling mills in operation in 1880, both of which were built to re-roll rails. One of these, at Rosedale, in Wyandotte county, three miles from Kansas City, was then owned by the Kansas Rolling Mill Company. This mill was once in operation at Decatur, Illinois, where it was built in 1870, and whence it was removed to Rosedale in 1875. It is now owned by the Western Iron Company. It has been idle since 1882. The other mill was located at Topeka, and was built in 1874 by the Topeka Rolling Mill Company. This mill was burned in April, 1881, and was not rebuilt.

In 1885 the Iowa Rolling Mill Company built a rolling mill for the manufacture of bar iron at Burlington, Iowa, and in the same year it was put in operation. In 1887 it was enlarged and in 1889 it was still further enlarged. It was idle in 1890. This is the only iron enterprise in Iowa.

Nebraska had one iron enterprise in operation in 1880, a rolling mill and cut-nail factory at Omaha, owned by the Omaha Iron and Nail Company. These works were first built at Dunleith, Illinois, in 1875 and 1876, and were removed to Omaha in 1879 and considerably enlarged. They had an annual capacity of 65,000 kegs of nails.' These works have been abandoned. The machinery was removed to St. Joseph, Missouri, in 1888 and 1889.

The first iron enterprise in Colorado was a small charcoal furnace at Langford, in Boulder county, in the northern part of the State. Its erection was undertaken in 1862 by a company called Langford & Co., composed of A. G. Langford, J. M. Marshall, William L. Lee, and Milo Lee, and it was finished and put in blast in 1864. In 1865 it went out of blast and was soon afterwards abandoned. It is said that " in a two-months' run some 250 tons of pig iron " were produced. Iron ore was obtained in the neighborhood and charcoal was burned " in the foot-hills." Mr. Marshall was the manager. The furnace was abandoned because oxen furnished the only mode of transportation, which was too expensive. In 1861 the same company built a foundry at Denver, but during the next year it was removed to Blackhawk, in Gilpin county. The furnace at Langford was built to supply pig iron for foundry purposes. Bituminous coal is now mined at Langford, and extensive deposits of iron ore are near at hand.

In 1877 a rolling mill was removed by William Faux from Danville, Pennsylvania, to Pueblo, Colorado, and put in operation on March 1, 1878, the product being re-rolled rails. In the same year it was removed to Denver. In 1880 this mill was purchased from the Denver Rolling Mill Company by the Colorado Coal and Iron Company. It was at work in 1883, rolling bar iron as well as re-rolling rails. It was abandoned in 1889. In 1880 the Colorado Coal and Iron Company commenced the erection of a large coke furnace at Pueblo, Colorado, which was put in blast on September 7, 1881. In the former year it also commenced the construction of Bessemer steel works at the same place, which were finished in 1882. These enterprises formed the beginning of a very extensive and complete establishment, which now embraces two blast furnaces, Bessemer steel works, rolling mills for rolling steel rails, bar iron, etc., a pipe foundry, and a nail mill. The erection of a third blast furnace has been commenced. Extensive coke works have been built by the company at El Moro, Crested Butte, and elsewhere. At Gunnison the erection of two furnaces to use coke was undertaken by the Gunnison Coal and Steel Company in 1884, but the furnaces were never built. At Trinidad, in Los Animas county, a rolling mill was built in 1888 and 1889 and put in operation in April, 1889, to roll bar iron and light rails.

The Union Pacific Railroad Company built a rolling mill to re-roll rails at Laramie City, Wyoming, in 1874, and put it in operation in April, 1875. It has ever since been in operation, but its products are now bar iron, mine rails, nuts, bolts, spikes, and track fastenings.

In 1859 Lesley reported a forge in Utah Territory, "smelting iron ore found in the mountains east of Salt Lake City, but no reliable information could be obtained respecting it." It does not appear in the census of 1860. Dr. J. S. Newberry writes that in 1880 he "visited the deposit of crystalline iron ore of Iron county, in the southern part of the Territory. These ore beds have been long known, and were to some extent utilized by the Mormons in their first advent thirty years ago. The iron region referred to lies nearly 300 miles directly south of Salt Lake City." In 1873 and 1874 the Great Western Iron Company, of which John W. Young was president, built a charcoal furnace at Iron City, in Iron county. It was in blast in 1874 and the two following years, but was afterwards abandoned and has had no successor. It was a very small furnace, being only 19 feet high and 4 feet wide at the boshes, with a daily capacity of 5 tons. The erection of a much larger furnace, also to use charcoal, was commenced at Ogden City, Utah, in 1875, by the Ogden Iron Manufacturing Company, and was intended to use hematite and magnetic ores found in the neighborhood. The furnace was completed and put in blast in 1882, but was blown out after making a small quantity of pig iron, and has been abandoned. The same company commenced building a rolling mill at Ogden City in 1875, which was not completed until 1882. It appears to have never been put in operation. In 1884 the machinery was removed to Pueblo, Colorado, where it was added to the plant of the Colorado Coal and Iron Company. Utah not only contains extensive deposits of very pure iron ore in Iron county and elsewhere but it also contains plenty of coal in Iron and other counties, some of which is said to make good coke.

CHAPTER XXXIX.

THE IRON INDUSTRY ON THE PACIFIC COAST.

CALIFORNIA has had for many years a complete rolling mill at San Francisco, owned by the Pacific Rolling Mill Company. It was first put in operation on July 25, 1868. It rolls rails, bar iron, angle iron, shafting, etc. An open-hearth steel plant was added in 1884, and the first steel on the Pacific coast was made on July 15, 1884. These works were in operation in 1891, and have always been well employed. In 1881 the Central Pacific Railroad Company built a rolling mill at Sacramento to roll bar iron and shaped iron. In 1883 the Judson Manufacturing Company completed and put in operation a rolling mill at Oakland for the manufacture of bar and plate iron; and in the same year the Pacific Iron and Nail Company completed and put in operation at the same place a large rolling mill and nail factory, with an annual capacity of more than 100,000 kegs of nails. At San Francisco there is an extensive shipyard for building iron and steel vessels, known as the Union Iron Works, at which large war ships for the United States navy have recently been built.

The first vessel of iron or steel built on the Pacific coast was the *Arago*, a screw steamer of 828 gross tons. She was built by the Union Iron Works, of San Francisco, for the Newport Coal Company, of Coos bay, Oregon, and she was launched on April 2, 1885. This vessel was built entirely of steel, the steel shapes being rolled by the Pacific Rolling Mill Company, of San Francisco, and the steel plates by Carnegie, Phipps & Co., of Pittsburgh. Her compound engine is of 450 nominal horse-power. She has been steadily engaged in the coal trade between Coos bay and San Francisco.

California has been unfortunate with her only blast furnace. The California Iron and Steel Company commenced in 1880 the erection of a charcoal furnace at Clipper Gap, in Placer county, where iron ore had been discovered, and the furnace was put in blast in April, 1881, and the first cast was made on the 24th of that month. It was burned down in 1882 and rebuilt in 1883 and again put in operation, but it has been out of blast since 1886 and may be regarded as abandoned. Its fuel was charcoal. Unless good coking coal should be discovered in California it is not probable that this State will ever make much pig iron, although it possesses many deposits of good iron ore, some of which are of Bessemer quality. It is doubtful whether the Mexican inhabitants of California ever engaged in the manufacture of iron even in the most primitive manner. In Lower California, just over the California State line, extensive deposits of rich iron ore and anthracite coal have recently been discovered.

At Oswego, in Clackamas county, Oregon, nine miles from Portland, a furnace to use charcoal was built in 1866 and 1867 by the Oswego Iron Company and blown in on August 27, 1867. It was enlarged in 1879 by other proprietors. In 1883 it produced 7,000 net tons of pig iron. It was operated irregularly until 1886, when it was purchased by the Oregon Iron and Steel Company, which built a new furnace in 1888, abandoning the old one in the same year. The charcoal for both furnaces has been made exclusively from the fir tree.

A furnace at Irondale, near Port Townsend, in Jefferson county, Washington, was built in 1880 and put in blast on January 27, 1881. It was rebuilt in 1882 and 1883 and remodeled in 1884. It is still a small furnace. It was built to make charcoal pig iron from Puget sound bog ore mixed with Texada Island magnetic ore. It is owned by the Puget Sound Iron Company, of San Francisco. It has not recently been in blast. In 1891 plans were in progress for the erection of a furnace at Kirkland, near Seattle. This State contains extensive deposits of hard coal, some of which makes good coke, and as iron ores are to be found within its own borders and near at hand on British territory, some in Washington just discovered, it is expected that other iron enterprises will soon follow those which have been mentioned.

THE States and Territories which have not been referred to in these pages are believed to have never been engaged in the manufacture of iron, although iron ore has been found in Louisiana and in some of the States and Territories of the Rocky Mountain region which have not been mentioned.

CHAPTER XL.

THE FIRST IRON WORKS IN CANADA.

A NOTICE in these pages of the first iron works in Canada will be read with interest, especially as these works were recently in operation. They are known as the forges of St. Maurice, and are located near Three Rivers, in the province of Quebec. Mr. A. T. Freed, the editor-in-chief of the Hamilton (Ontario) *Spectator*, informs us that iron ore in the vicinity of Three Rivers was discovered as early as 1667. In 1672 the Count de Frontenac reported that he had commenced to mine the ore at Three Rivers. He strongly urged the establishment of forges and a foundry. In 1685 the Marquis de Denonville sent to France a sample of the ore at Three Rivers, which the French ironworkers found to be "of good quality and percentage." But no effort to establish iron works at this place appears to have been made until the next century, when the St. Maurice works were undertaken. Dr. T. Sterry Hunt, of Montreal, supplied us in 1880 with the following brief history of these works.

King Louis XV. gave a royal license in 1730 to a company to work the iron ores of St. Maurice and the vicinity, and advanced 10,000 livres for aid in erecting the furnace, etc. No work being done he took back the license, and in 1735 granted it to a new company, which received 100,000 livres in aid and in 1737 built a blast furnace. In 1743, however, the works reverted to the crown, and were worked for the king's profit. He then sent out from France skilled workmen, who rebuilt, in part at least, the blast furnace as it now stands, and erected a Walloon hearth, which is still in use, for refining. The works became the property of the British Crown at the conquest, and were at first rented to a company and afterwards sold. Smelting has been carried on at this place without interruption to the present time, the bog ores of the region being exclusively used. Three tons of ore make one ton of iron.

There seems to be no doubt that the stack is the one built in 1737, and it is still in blast. It is 30 feet high, and the internal diameter at the hearth is 2½ feet, at the boshes 7 feet, and at the throat 3½ feet. There are two tuyeres, and the blast is cold, with a pressure of one pound. The daily production of iron is four tons, and the consumption of charcoal is 180 bushels, (French,) of about 12 pounds each, per ton of iron. The metal was formerly used in the district for ordinary castings, but is now in great demand for car-wheels. A very little is, however, refined in the Walloon hearth, and is esteemed by the blacksmiths for local use. The analysis of a sample of the gray pig of St. Maurice made by me in 1868 gave: phosphorus, .450; silicon, .860; manganese, 1.240; graphite, 2.820; carbon combined, 1.100.

In addition to the above information we find some facts of interest concerning the St. Maurice iron works in Peter Kalm's *Travels into North America*, written in 1749.

The iron work, which is the only one in this country, lies three miles to the west of Trois Rivieres. Here are two great forges, besides two lesser ones to each of the great ones, and under the same roof with them. The bellows were made of wood, and everything else as it is in Swedish forges. The melting ovens stand close to the forges, and are the same as ours. The ore is got two French miles and a half from the iron works, and is carried thither on sledges. It is a kind of moor ore, which lies in veins, within six inches or a foot from the surface of the ground. Each vein is from six to eighteen inches deep, and below it is a white sand. The veins are surrounded with this sand on both sides, and covered at the top with a thin mould. The ore is pretty rich and lies in loose lumps in the veins, of the size of two fists, though there are a few which are eighteen inches thick. These lumps are full of holes, which are filled with ochre. The ore is so soft that it may be crushed betwixt the fingers. They make use of a grey limestone, which is broke in the neighborhood, for promoting the fusibility of the ore; to that purpose they likewise employ a clay marble, which is found near this place. Charcoals are to be had in great abundance here, because all the country round this place is covered with woods which have never been stirred. The charcoals from evergreen trees, that is from the fir kind, are best for the forge, but those of deciduous trees are best for the smelting oven. The iron which is here made was to me described as soft, pliable, and tough, and is said to have the quality of not being attacked by rust so easily as other iron; and in this point there appears a great difference between the Spanish iron and this in shipbuilding.

This iron work was first founded in 1737, by private persons, who afterwards ceded it to the king; they cast cannon and mortars here, of different sizes, iron stoves, which are in use all over Canada, kettles, etc., not to mention the bars which are made here. They have likewise tried to make steel here, but can not bring it to any great perfection because they are unacquainted with the manner of preparing it.

Mr. Freed says that the French company which established the St. Maurice iron works in 1737 was known as *Cugnet et Cie*. He also says that there was a French garrison at Three Rivers at the time, and that the soldiers were the principal workmen. He sends us a copy of a report made in 1752 to M. Bigot, Intendant of New France, residing at Quebec, by M. Franquet, who had been instructed to visit and examine the St. Maurice works. From this report the following liberal extract is taken.

On entering the smelting forge I was received with a customary ceremony; the workmen moulded a pig of iron about 15 feet long for my especial benefit. The process is very simple: it is done by plunging a large ladle into the liquid-boiling ore and emptying the material into a gutter made in the sand. After this ceremony I was shown the process of stove moulding, which is also a very simple but rather intricate operation. Each stove is in six pieces, which are separately moulded; they are fitted into each other and form a stove about three feet high. I then visited a shed where the workmen were moulding pots, kettles, and other hollow-ware. On leaving this part of the forge we were taken to the hammer forge, where bar iron of every kind is hammered out. In each department of the forges the workmen observed the old ceremony of brushing a stranger's boots, and in return they expect some money to buy liquor to drink the visitor's health. The establishment is very extensive, employing upward of 180 men. Nothing is consumed in the furnaces but charcoal, which is made in the immediate vicinity of the post. The ore is rich, good, and tolerably clean. Formerly it was found on the spot; now the director has to send some little distance for it. This iron is preferred to the Spanish iron, and is sold off in the king's stores in Quebec.

In 1760 Canada passed into the possession of the British Government, and with it the St. Maurice forges. For nearly a hundred years the Crown leased these works to various companies, by which they were operated with more or less success.

In 1815 the St. Maurice works were still in active operation, as we learn from Joseph Bouchette's *Lower Canada.* They are thus described: "The establishment is furnished with every convenience necessary to an extensive concern; the furnaces, the forges, the founderies, workshops, etc., with houses and other buildings, present the appearance of a tolerably sized village. The principal articles manufactured are stoves of all kinds used in the province, large potash kettles, machines for mills, and various kinds of cast and wrought iron; also a great quantity of pig and bar iron for exportation. The number of men employed is from 250 to 300."

The St. Maurice works remained in the ownership of the British Government until 1846, when they were sold to Henry Stuart. A report to the Dominion Parliament in 1879 says that they were then owned by F. McDougall & Son, of Three Rivers, and were using bog ore and making good iron with charcoal. "The first furnace was erected in 1737; still running; capacity four tons."

In a valuable paper on the manufacture of iron in Canada, read at the Halifax meeting of the American Institute of Mining Engineers in September, 1885, Mr. James Herbert Bartlett, of Montreal, recorded in the following words the end of the long career of the blast furnace of 1737 which was connected with the St. Maurice forges: "The property is now owned by George McDougall, of Three Rivers, the furnace having been in blast until the summer of 1883, when, owing to the ore and fuel becoming exhausted, it was finally closed."

At the time of its abandonment in 1883 the St. Maurice furnace was *the oldest active furnace on the American continent.* In that year there were still standing two very old furnaces in the United States—Oxford, in New Jersey, and Cornwall, in Pennsylvania, both built in 1742, but neither of these furnaces was in blast in 1883. They were last in blast in 1882. Since that year Oxford furnace has been abandoned, but Cornwall is still standing and in good repair.

Canada has had a few other iron enterprises and a few steel works, but it has never been prominent as a manufacturer of either iron or steel. Of late, however, much interest has been taken by Canadians in the development of the iron and steel resources of the Dominion, and in this movement the people of the United States will heartily sympathize.

IT would not be profitable to give such fragmentary information as is at our command concerning the very small iron industry of Mexico and Central and South America.

CHAPTER XLI.

THE MANUFACTURE OF IRON WITH ANTHRACITE COAL IN THE UNITED STATES.

THE details which have been given in preceding chapters of the early iron history of every part of the United States relate almost entirely to the manufacture of iron with charcoal as fuel, no other fuel having been used in American blast furnaces until about 1840, and but little use of any other fuel having been made before that time in any other branches of the American iron industry. The period of our iron history prior to 1840 may therefore very properly be styled the charcoal era. The later development of the iron and steel industries of the United States will be generally instead of provincially or geographically treated in the present chapter and in succeeding chapters.

The line which separates the charcoal era of our iron history from the era which succeeded it, and which may be said to still continue, is marked by the almost simultaneous introduction of anthracite and bituminous coal in the manufacture of pig iron. This innovation at once caused a revolution in the whole iron industry of the country. Facilities for the manufacture of iron were increased; districts which had been partly closed to this industry because of a scarcity of timber for the supply of charcoal were now fully opened to it; and the cheapening of prices, which was made possible by the increased production and the increased competition, served to stimulate consumption. A notable result of the introduction of mineral fuel was that, while it restricted the production of charcoal pig iron in the States which, like Pennsylvania, possessed the new fuel, it did not injuriously affect the production of charcoal pig iron in other States. Some of these States, notably Michigan, which scarcely possessed an iron industry of any kind in 1840, now manufacture large quantities of charcoal pig iron. The country at large now annually makes more charcoal pig iron than it did in 1840 or in any preceding year. Our production of charcoal pig iron in 1890 was the largest in our history. The introduction of mineral fuel did not, therefore, destroy our charcoal-iron industry, but simply added to our resources for the production of iron. This introduction, however, marked such radical changes in our iron industry, and so enlarged the theatre of this industry, that we are amply justified in referring to it as a revolution, and as one which ended the distinctive charcoal era.

Of the two forms of mineral fuel, anthracite and bituminous coal, anthracite was the first to be largely used in American blast furnaces, and for many years after its adaptability to the smelting of iron ore was established it was in greater demand for this purpose than bituminous coal, coked or uncoked. In recent years the relative popularity of these two fuels for blast-furnace use has been exactly reversed.

The natural difficulties in the way of the successful introduction of anthracite coal in our blast furnaces were increased by the fact that, up to the time when we commenced our experiments in its use, no other country had succeeded in using it as a furnace fuel. We had, therefore, no other guide in its use than our own unaided intelligence. The successive steps by which we were enabled to add the manufacture of anthracite pig iron to that of charcoal pig iron will be presented in chronological order.

In the suit of Farr & Kunzi against the Schuylkill Navigation Company in 1840 Jesse B. Quinby testified that in 1815 he used anthracite coal for a short time at Harford furnace, in Maryland, mixed with one-half charcoal. Between 1824 and 1828 Peter Ritner, whose brother, Joseph Ritner, was afterwards Governor of Pennsylvania, was successful for a short time in using anthracite coal mixed with charcoal in a charcoal furnace in Perry county, Pennsylvania. In 1826 the Lehigh Coal and Navigation Company erected at Mauch Chunk, in Pennsylvania, a small furnace intended to use anthracite coal in smelting iron ore. The enterprise was not successful. In 1827 unsuccessful experiments in smelting iron ore with anthracite coal from Rhode Island were made at one of the small blast furnaces at Kingston, in Plymouth county, Massachusetts. In 1827 and 1828 a similar failure in the use of anthracite coal took place at Vizille, in France. These experiments failed because the blast used was cold.

In 1828 James B. Neilson, of Scotland, obtained a patent for the use of hot air in the smelting of iron ore in blast furnaces, and in 1829 pig iron was made in several Scotch furnaces with the apparatus which he had invented. But the coal used was bituminous. It was not until 1837 that the smelting of iron ore with anthracite coal by means of the hot-blast invented by Neilson was undertaken in Great Britain. In the meantime the application of the hot-blast to anthracite coal in American furnaces was successfully experimented with by an enterprising American citizen, the Rev. Dr. Frederick W. Geissenhainer, a Lutheran clergyman of New York city. A copy in his own handwriting of a letter written by him in November, 1837, to the Commissioner of Patents gives some interesting and valuable details concerning his experiments. In this letter, which we have lying before us, he says: "I can prove that, in the month of December, 1830, and in the months of January, February, and March, 1831, I had already invented and made many successful experiments, as well with *hot air* as with an atmospheric air blast, to smelt iron ore with *anthracite coal* in my small experimenting furnace here in the city of New York."

On the 5th of September, 1831, Dr. Geissenhainer filed in the Patent Office at Washington an account of his invention, for which he claimed a patent. On the 19th of December, 1833, a patent was granted to him for "a new and useful improvement in the manufacture of iron and steel by the application of anthracite coal." From the long and remarkably clear and learned specification by the Doctor, which accompanied the patent, we learn that he discovered that iron ore could be smelted with anthracite coal by applying "a blast, or a column, or a stream, or current of air in or of such quantity, velocity, and density or compression as the compactness or density and the continuity of the anthracite coal requires. The blast may be of common atmospheric *or of heated air*. *Heated air* I should *prefer* in an economical point of view."

The Doctor distinctly disclaims in his specification "an exclusive right of the use of heated air for any kind of fuel," from which it is to be inferred that he had full knowledge of Neilson's experiments with hot air in Scotland. He specifically claimed as his invention the adaptability of anthracite coal to the manufacture of iron and steel, and he appears to have largely relied for success upon the effect of a strong blast.

The patent having been granted, Dr. Geissenhainer proceeded to build a furnace for the practical application of his invention. This was Valley furnace, located on Silver creek, in Schuylkill county, Pennsylvania, about ten miles northeast of Pottsville. In August and September, 1836, he was successful in making pig iron at this furnace exclusively with anthracite coal as fuel. His own testimony on this point is given in the letter from which we have already quoted. The blast used varied from $3\frac{1}{2}$ to $3\frac{1}{4}$, to 3, and to $2\frac{3}{4}$ pounds to the square inch. That the furnace did not continue to make iron after the autumn of 1836 is explained by Dr. Geissenhainer to have been due to an accident to its machinery. He adds: " My furnace would have been put in operation again long before this time with strong iron machinery, and *a hot-air apparatus*, had I not been prevented by the pressure of the times and by a protracted severe sickness from bestowing my attention to this matter. The drawings for the iron machinery and for the hot-air apparatus are already in the hands of Messrs. Haywood & Snyder, in Pottsville, who are to do the work." The blast used at Valley furnace was *heated*.

The quantity of pig iron made at Valley furnace is not stated by the Doctor. It probably did not exceed a few tons. Governor Ritner visited the furnace on July 30, 1836, while the Doctor's experiments were in progress. In the Pottsville *Miners' Journal* for August 6, 1836, it is stated that specimens of Dr. Geissenhainer's pig iron were then on exhibition at Pennsylvania Hall in Pottsville.

Before the Doctor's plans for improving his furnace were completed he was called to another world. He died at New York on the 27th of May, 1838, aged 66 years and 11 months. He was born at Muhlberg, in the Electorate of Saxony, in 1771, and came to this country when he was about 18 years old. His remains rest in the family burial vault in the Lutheran cemetery, in Queens county, New York.

Prior to the erection of Valley furnace Dr. Geissenhainer had been engaged in the development of the iron and coal resources of Pennsylvania. As early as 1811 he was associated with Peter Karthaus, of Baltimore, in the mining of bituminous coal in Clearfield county, and a few years later in the ownership of a charcoal furnace in that county. For two or three years prior to 1830 he owned and operated a small charcoal furnace in Schuylkill county, and it was near this furnace that he afterwards built Valley furnace. Attached to the charcoal furnace was a puddling furnace. He was the pioneer in the development of the Silver creek anthracite coal mines, the projector of the Schuylkill Valley Railroad, and the sole owner of the Silver Creek Railroad. Dr. Geissenhainer was, as has been seen, a man of great enterprise. His memory as the first manufacturer of pig iron with anthracite coal and the hot-blast, even if only in a small way, is entitled to greater honor than it has yet received.

On the 28th of September, 1836, when Dr. Geissenhainer's Valley furnace was successfully making pig iron, and almost three years after the Doctor had obtained a patent for his invention, George Crane, the owner of several furnaces at Yniscedwin, in South Wales, obtained a patent from the British Government for the application of the hot-blast to the smelting of iron ore with anthracite coal. On the 7th of February, 1837, he successfully commenced the use of anthracite with the hot-blast at one of his furnaces, obtaining 36 tons a week. In May of that year Solomon W. Roberts, of Philadelphia, visited his works and witnessed the complete success of the experiment, which was the first successful experiment with anthracite coal in a blast furnace in Europe. It was through Mr. Roberts's representations to his uncle, Josiah White, and to Erskine Hazard and others that the first successful anthracite furnace in the Lehigh valley was built at Catasauqua in 1839 and 1840 by the Lehigh Crane Iron Company.

Solomon White Roberts was born in Philadelphia on August 3, 1811, and died in the same city on March 22, 1882. He is buried in Woodlands cemetery, in West Philadelphia.

Mr. Crane endeavored to obtain a patent in this country for his application of the hot-blast to anthracite coal in the blast furnace, but was unsuccessful, Dr. Geissenhainer's patent covering the same principle. The Doctor's patent, which was only for the United States, was sold by his executors in 1838 to Mr. Crane, who in November of that year patented in this country some additions to it. The patents were not generally enforced here, but Mr. Crane compelled Welsh ironmasters to pay him for the use of his invention. Dr. Geissenhainer never attempted to enforce his patent. The consideration which his executors received from Mr. Crane was $1,000 and the privilege of erecting, free of royalty, fifteen furnaces for the use of anthracite coal with the hot-blast. The following advertisement by Mr. Crane's agents in this country we take from a Philadelphia newspaper published in December, 1839, over fifty years ago.

ANTHRACITE IRON.—The subscribers, agents of George Crane, Esq., are prepared to grant licenses for the manufacture of iron with anthracite coal, under the patent granted to Mr. Crane by the United States, for smelting iron with the above fuel, in addition to which Mr. Crane holds an assignment of so much of the patent granted to the late Reverend Dr. Geissenhainer as pertains to making iron with anthracite coal. The charge will be 25 cents per ton on all thus manufactured. It has been completely successful both in Wales and at Pottsville, one furnace at the latter place yielding an average product of 40 tons per week of excellent iron. All persons are cautioned against infringing upon either of the above patents. Any application of hot-blast in the smelting of iron ore with anthracite coal, without a license, will be an infringement, and will be treated accordingly.

Apply to	A. G. RALSTON & Co.,
dec 9—1m	4 South Front st.

We shall refer hereafter to the furnace at Pottsville which had made "40 tons per week" with anthracite coal.

George Crane was born about 1784 at Bromsgrove, in Worcestershire, England, whence he removed in 1824 to Wales. He died on the 10th of January, 1846, in the 62d year of his age. An obituary notice of Mr. Crane, written by Solomon W. Roberts, is printed in the *Journal of the Franklin Institute* for March, 1846.

Two interesting experiments in the use of anthracite coal in the blast furnace were made in this country about the time when Dr. Geissenhainer succeeded with his experiment at Valley furnace. In 1836 and 1837 John Pott experimented at Manheim furnace, at Cressona, in Schuylkill county, with anthracite coal as a fuel for smelting iron ore. He first used a mixture of anthracite coal and charcoal with cold-blast. The results accomplished were so encouraging that he added a hot-blast and gradually reduced the proportion of charcoal until only anthracite was used. This he used alone and successfully for a short time. But the blast was too weak, and the furnace was not long in operation. Before the necessary improvements could be made it was destroyed by a freshet. In 1837 Jarvis Van Buren, acting for a company, built a furnace at South Easton, in Northampton county, for the purpose of experimenting with anthracite coal. Early in 1838 he was successful in making 20 tons of pig iron, when further operations were stopped because the blast was too weak. We are not informed whether it was hot or cold.

It is claimed that a successful experiment in the manufacture of pig iron with anthracite coal was made in 1837 by a Mr. Bryant in a foundry cupola at Manayunk, near Philadelphia. The blast used was produced by " wooden bellows." A few tons of the iron made were used by Parke & Tiers, the owners of the foundry, " and proved to be of good gray quality and of uncommon strength." The experiment was conducted under the auspices of this firm and of Mr. Abraham Kunzi, of the firm of Farr & Kunzi, manufacturing chemists, of Philadelphia. The blast was cold.

The record which we shall now give of the successful use of anthracite coal in American furnaces, after Dr. Geissenhainer and George Crane had established the practicability of such use, will embrace only a few of the early anthracite furnaces, and this we condense from Walter R. Johnson's *Notes on the Use of Anthracite*, published in 1841, and from William Firmstone's " Sketch of Early Anthracite Furnaces," published in the third volume of the *Transactions of the American Institute of Mining Engineers*. In each of the instances to be referred to, all in Pennsylvania, the blast used was heated.

Late in 1837 Joseph Baughman, Julius Guiteau, and Henry High, of Reading, experimented in smelting iron ore with anthracite coal in the old furnace of the Lehigh Coal and Navigation Company at Mauch Chunk, using about 80 per cent. of anthracite. The results were so encouraging that they built a small water-power furnace near the weigh-lock at Mauch Chunk, which was completed in July, 1838. Blast was applied to this furnace on August 27th and discontinued on September 10th, the temperature being heated to about 200° Fahrenheit. The fuel used was mainly but not entirely anthracite. A new heating apparatus was procured, placed in a brick chamber at the tunnel-head, and heated by the flame therefrom. Blast was applied in November, 1838, the fuel used being anthracite exclusively, and "the furnace worked remarkably well for five weeks" to January 12, 1839, when it was blown out for want of ore. Some improvements were made, and on July 26, 1839, the furnace was again put in blast, and so continued until November 2, 1839. Francis C. Lowthorp, of Trenton, was one of the partners at this time. For "about three months" no other fuel than anthracite was used, the temperature of the blast being from 400° to 600°. About 100 tons of iron were made. Mr. Lowthorp died at Trenton on June 1, 1890, aged 81 years.

The next furnace to use anthracite was the Pioneer, built in 1838 and 1839 at Pottsville by William Lyman, of Boston, under the auspices of Burd Patterson, an enterprising citizen of Pottsville, who inaugurated the enterprise. Until 1844 Pioneer furnace was called Pottsville. Blast was unsuccessfully applied on July 10, 1839. Benjamin Perry then took charge of the furnace, and blew it in on October 19, 1839, with perfect success. This furnace was blown by steam-power. The blast was heated with anthracite, in ovens at the base of the furnace, to a temperature of 600°. The product was about 28 tons a week of good foundry iron. This furnace continued in blast for some time. A large premium was paid by Nicholas Biddle and others to Mr. Lyman as the first person in the United States who had made anthracite pig iron continuously for three months. On January 18th, 1840, a dinner was given to Mr. Lyman at Pottsville in honor of the important event, at which a notable address was delivered by Mr. Biddle. Pioneer furnace was practically rebuilt in 1853, torn down in 1866, and again rebuilt. In April, 1888, the hot-blast fell down, and the furnace was torn down in 1889 and a new furnace built in its stead. Other furnaces and a large rolling mill and steel works, owned by the Pottsville Iron and Steel Company, have been added to the original furnace and its successors.

We have before us the original agreement between Robert Ralston, attorney in fact for George Crane, and William Lyman, which conveyed to the latter a license to use Crane and Geissenhainer's patents for the use of anthracite coal in the manufacture of pig iron. It is dated at Philadelphia, on December 4, 1839, and the consideration named is twenty-five cents per ton of pig iron made.

Danville furnace, in Montour county, was successfully blown in with anthracite in April, 1840, producing 35 tons of pig iron weekly with steam-power. Roaring Creek furnace, in Montour county, was next blown in with anthracite on May 18, 1840, and produced 40 tons of pig iron weekly with water-power.

A charcoal furnace at Phœnixville, built in 1837 by Reeves, Buck & Co., was blown in with anthracite on June 17, 1840, by William Firmstone, and produced from 28 to 30 tons of pig iron weekly with water-power. The hot-blast stove, which was planned and erected by Julius Guiteau, of the Mauch Chunk furnace, was situated on one side of the tunnel-head and heated by the flame of the furnace. This furnace continued in blast until 1841.

Columbia furnace, at Danville, was blown in with anthracite by Mr. Perry on July 2, 1840, and made from 30 to 32 tons of pig iron weekly, using steam-power.

The next furnace to use anthracite, and the last one we shall mention, was built at Catasauqua, for the Lehigh Crane Iron Company, in 1839, by David Thomas, who had been associated with Mr. Crane in his experiments at Yniscedwin, and had there been successful in making anthracite pig iron. This furnace was blown in by Mr. Thomas on July 3, 1840, and its first cast was made on July 4th. From the first this furnace produced 50 tons a week of good foundry iron, water-power from the Lehigh being used. The furnace was in active use until 1879, when it was torn down. Mr. Firmstone says that "with the erection of this furnace commenced the era of higher and larger furnaces and better blast machinery, with consequent improvements in yield and quality of iron produced." Four other furnaces built by Mr. Thomas for the same company at Catasauqua soon followed the first furnace, one built in 1842, another in 1846, and two in 1850. In all Mr. Thomas built five furnaces for the Lehigh Crane Iron Company. The prefix "Lehigh" was dropped in 1872.

In a memoir of Josiah White, by his son-in-law, Richard Richardson, we find the following statement: "In 1838 Erskine Hazard went to Wales, and there made himself acquainted with the process and manner of making the anthracite iron, with the machinery and buildings needful for its manufacture. He ordered such machinery as was necessary to be made for the company, under the direction of George Crane, the inventor, and engaged David Thomas, who was familiar with the process, to take charge of the erection of the works and the manufacture of the iron. He arrived in the summer of 1839, and to his faithful and intelligent management much of the success of the enterprise is due." We do not hesitate to say that to Mr. Thomas's management was due the whole of the success of the anthracite furnaces built by the Lehigh Crane Iron Company.

David Thomas was born on November 3, 1794, at a place called, in English, Grey House, within two and a half miles of the town of Neath, in the county of Glamorgan, South Wales. He landed in the United States on June 5, 1839, and on July 9th of that year he commenced to build the furnace at Catasauqua. He died at Catasauqua on June 20, 1882, in his 88th year. At the time of his death he was the oldest ironmaster in the United States in length of service, and he was next to Peter Cooper the oldest in years. David Thomas's character and services to the American iron trade are held in high honor by all American iron and steel manufacturers. He is affectionately styled the Father of the American anthracite iron industry, because the furnace built under his directions at Catasauqua and blown in by him was the first of all the early anthracite furnaces that was completely successful, both from an engineering and a commercial standpoint, and also because he subsequently became identified with the manufacture of anthracite pig iron on a more extensive scale than any of his cotemporaries. He was the founder of the Thomas Iron Company, at Hokendauqua, which has long been at the head of the producers of anthracite pig iron. The first two furnaces of this company were built by Mr. Thomas in 1855. An obituary notice of Mr. Thomas will be found in *The Bulletin of The American Iron and Steel Association* for June 28, 1882. William Cullen Bryant and David Thomas were born on the same day.

Mr. Thomas's three sons, John, Samuel, and David, all became identified with their father's occupation and enterprises. John and Samuel have been and still are among the most prominent of our pig-iron manufacturers. David was killed while the Hokendauqua furnaces were under construction.

In 1835 the Franklin Institute, of Philadelphia, offered a premium of a gold medal "to the person who shall manufacture in the United States the greatest quantity of iron from the ore during the year, using no other fuel than anthracite coal, the quantity to be not less than twenty tons," but we can not learn that the medal was ever awarded to any of the persons who were instrumental in establishing the manufacture of anthracite pig iron in this country. The offer of the medal proves that down to 1835 all efforts to manufacture pig iron with anthracite coal had been unsuccessful.

The discovery that anthracite coal could be successfully used in the manufacture of pig iron gave a fresh impetus to the iron industry in New York, New Jersey, and Maryland, as well as in Pennsylvania. In 1840 there were only six furnaces in the United States which used anthracite coal, and they were all in Pennsylvania. The first anthracite furnace outside of Pennsylvania was built at Stanhope, New Jersey, in 1840 and 1841, by the Stanhope Iron Company, and it was successfully blown in on April 5, 1841. On the 1st of April, 1846, there were forty-two furnaces in Pennsylvania and New Jersey which used anthracite coal as fuel, their annual capacity being 122,720 tons. In 1856 there were 121 anthracite furnaces in the country which were either "running or in running order"—ninety-three in Pennsylvania, fourteen in New York, six in Maryland, four in New Jersey, three in Massachusetts, and one in Connecticut. These figures show rapid progress in building up in a brief period a new branch of the American iron industry. Soon after 1856 many other furnaces were built to use the new fuel.

Although the revolution to which we have referred properly dates from the first successful use of anthracite coal in the blast furnace the new fuel had previously been used in a small way in this country in other ironmaking operations. Its use in these operations became general about the time when pig iron was first made with it.

To encourage the use of anthracite coal the Lehigh Coal Mine Company executed, on the 18th of December, 1807, a lease for twenty-one years to James Butland and James Rowland of two hundred acres of its land in Northampton county, Pennsylvania, with the privilege of digging iron ore and coal free for the manufacture of iron. The enterprise was unfruitful and the lease was abandoned about 1814. No iron was made and we think that no coal was mined. The following extract from the proposition of Butland & Rowland, dated November 30, 1807, is worthy of preservation: "The subscribers, having obtained by patent from the United States an exclusive right of using a natural carbon or peculiar kind of coal, such as is found in the neighborhood of the Lehigh and Susquehanna rivers, and other parts of the United States, for the purpose of manufacturing pig, cast, and bar iron, propose commencing the operation in such a situation as may be deemed best adapted to the purpose."

The first use of anthracite coal in connection with the manufacture of iron in the United States dates from 1812, in which year Colonel George Shoemaker, of Pottsville, Pennsylvania, loaded nine wagons with coal from his mines at Centreville and hauled it to Philadelphia, where with great difficulty he sold two loads at the cost of transportation and gave the other seven loads away. He was by many regarded as an impostor for attempting to sell stone to the public as coal. Of the two loads sold one was purchased by White & Hazard, for use at their wire works at the Falls of Schuylkill, and the other was purchased by Malin & Bishop, for use at the Delaware County rolling mill. By the merest accident of closing the furnace doors Mr. White obtained a hot fire from the coal, and from this occurrence, happening in 1812, we may date the first successful use of anthracite coal in the manufacture of iron in this country and in the manufacture of other American products. At both the establishments mentioned it was used in heating furnaces. Previous to this time bituminous coal from Virginia and Great Britain had been relied upon for manufacturing purposes in the Atlantic States in all cases where wood was not used. The war of 1812 prevented the importation of British coal and interfered with the supply of Virginia coal, and there were as yet no means of communication with the bituminous coal fields of Western Pennsylvania or Western Maryland. The firm of White & Hazard was composed of Josiah White and Erskine Hazard.

In the latter part of 1823 the Boston Iron Company, owning the Boston iron works, obtained a full cargo of Lehigh anthracite coal for use in heating iron to be rolled in its mill and for smith-work. A short time previous to this transaction, but in the same year, Cyrus Alger, of South Boston, obtained a lot of about thirty tons of Lehigh coal, which he used in a cupola for melting iron for castings.

Anthracite coal for the generation of steam was first used in this country in January, 1825, under the boilers of the rolling mill at Phœnixville, of which Jonah and George Thompson, of Philadelphia, were the proprietors. It is also claimed that, two years later, in 1827, the first use of anthracite coal in the puddling furnace in this country was made at the same rolling mill, Jonah and George Thompson still being the proprietors. It is stated that anthracite coal was used in 1834 in puddling at a rolling mill at Pottsville, owned by Buckley & Swift. But the use of anthracite coal for puddling did not become general until about 1840. In 1839 it was used in puddling at the Boston iron works by Ralph Crooker, the superintendent. About 1836 Thomas and Peter Cooper, brothers, used anthracite in a heating furnace at their rolling mill on Thirty-third street, near Third avenue, New York, and about 1840 they began puddling with anthracite. In April, 1846, there were twenty-seven rolling mills in Pennsylvania and New Jersey which were using anthracite coal in puddling and heating furnaces as well as in producing steam.

The following notice of the success of the Messrs. Thompson in the use of anthracite coal for the production of steam appeared in 1825 in a newspaper published at West Chester, Pennsylvania: "We understand that the Messrs. Thompson, at the Phœnix nail works, on French creek, have fully succeeded in constructing a furnace for a steam engine calculated for the use of anthracite coal, and in discovering a mode by which this fuel may be most advantageously applied to that important purpose. We would heartily congratulate the eastern section of our State upon this valuable discovery. Nothing within our knowledge has occurred of recent date which can have a more auspicious influence upon our manufacturing interests."

We may properly close this chapter and introduce its successor by quoting the following extract from the letter of instructions addressed to its European agent, William Strickland, by the Acting Committee of the Pennsylvania Society for the Promotion of Internal Improvement. This letter is dated at Philadelphia, March 18, 1825. In speaking of the manufacture of iron in Pennsylvania, and the necessity of enlarging it by the adoption of European methods, the committee says:

"No improvements have been made here in it within the last thirty years, *and the use of bituminous and anthracite coal in our furnaces is absolutely and entirely unknown.* Attempts, and of the most costly kind, have been made to use the coal of the western part of our State in the production of iron. Furnaces have been constructed according to the plan *said* to be adopted in Wales and elsewhere; persons claiming experience in the business have been employed; but all has been unsuccessful."

CHAPTER XLII.

THE MANUFACTURE OF IRON WITH BITUMINOUS COAL IN THE UNITED STATES.

It is remarkable that the introduction of bituminous coal in the blast furnaces of this country should have taken place at so late a day in our history and within the memory of men who are not yet old. Bituminous coal had been discovered in the United States long before any attempt was made to use it in our furnaces, and Great Britain had taught us while we were still her colonies that it could be so used. In 1735 Abraham Darby, at his furnace at Coalbrookdale, in Shropshire, had successfully made pig iron with coke as fuel; in 1740 a coke furnace was built at Pontypool, in Monmouthshire; and in 1796 charcoal furnaces had been almost entirely abandoned in Great Britain. Our delay in following the example of the mother country may be variously explained. There was a lack of transportation facilities for bringing iron ore and coke together; not all of the bituminous coal that had been discovered was suitable for making coke; the manufacture of coke was not well understood; the country had an abundance of timber for the supply of charcoal; and, finally, a prejudice existed in favor of charcoal pig iron and of bar iron hammered in charcoal forges. It was not until about 1840 that successful efforts were made to introduce the use of bituminous coal in American blast furnaces, but its use made slow progress for many years, the principal reason being the poor quality of the coke that was made. Our best coking fields had not been developed. As late as 1849 Overman, in his *Manufacture of Iron*, in treating of coke furnaces in the United States, said: "As there is but little prospect of an addition to the number of coke furnaces which now exist we shall devote but a limited space to this subject."

The successful introduction of bituminous coal as a fuel in American blast furnaces was naturally preceded by many experiments in its use, which were attended with varied success, but none of them with complete success. It appears to

be mathematically certain that down to 1835 all of these experiments had been unsuccessful, as in that year the Franklin
Institute, of Philadelphia, offered a premium of a gold medal
" to the person who shall manufacture in the United States
the greatest quantity of iron from the ore during the year,
using no other fuel than bituminous coal or coke, the quantity to be not less than twenty tons." The Institute would
not have been likely to make this offer if even so small a
quantity as twenty tons of pig iron had been made in one
furnace with bituminous coal, either coked or uncoked.

The earliest experiment in the United States in the manufacture of pig iron with bituminous coal that appears to be
fully authenticated was made at Bear Creek furnace, in Armstrong county, Pennsylvania, in 1819. This furnace was built
to use coke, with steam-power, and in the year named it was
blown in with this fuel, but the blast was cold and too weak
and the furnace chilled after two or three tons of iron had
been made. Charcoal was then substituted.

In a report by a committee of the Senate of Pennsylvania,
of which Hon. S. J. Packer was chairman, read in the Senate
on March 4, 1834, it was stated that " the coking process is
now understood, and our bituminous coal is quite as susceptible of this operation, and produces as good coke, as that
of Great Britain. It is now used to a considerable extent by
our iron manufacturers in Centre county and elsewhere." It
is certain that, at the time this report was written, coke could
not have been used in blast furnaces in any other way than
as a mixture with charcoal, except experimentally. Its use
as a mixture with charcoal would naturally precede its sole
use as a blast-furnace fuel. Mr. Packer doubtless also had
in mind the use of coke in melting pig iron in " run-out "
or " finery " fires preparatory to converting it into blooms
or bars in charcoal forges. We have elsewhere referred to
the use of coke in a refinery at Plumsock, in Fayette county,
Pennsylvania, as early as 1817.

The offer of the gold medal by the Franklin Institute
doubtless assisted in stimulating action upon a subject which
had already attracted much attention. In the year in which
this offer was made, 1835, that accomplished furnace manager, William Firmstone, was successful in making good gray

forge iron for about one month at the end of a blast at Mary Ann furnace, in Huntingdon county, Pennsylvania, with coke made from Broad Top coal. This iron was taken to a forge three miles distant and made into blooms. The coke used at the furnace was not prepared to be so used, but had been made for use in the " run-out " fires at the forge connected with the furnace. Mr. Firmstone did not claim the medal. He may not have known that a premium had been offered for the achievement which he undoubtedly accomplished.

In a pamphlet published in April, 1836, Isaac Fisher, of Lewistown, Pennsylvania, stated that " successful experiments have lately been tried in Pennsylvania in making pig iron with coke." It is probable that Mr. Fisher had in mind Mr. Firmstone's experiment at Mary Ann furnace.

William Firmstone was born at Wellington, in Shropshire, England, on October 19, 1810. When quite a young man he was manager at the Lays works, near Dudley, which were then owned by his uncles, W. &. G. Firmstone. In the spring of 1835 he emigrated to the United States. After filling many responsible positions in connection with the manufacture of pig iron in his adopted country he died at his residence near Easton, Pennsylvania, on September 11, 1877, and is buried at that place. He was one of the first to introduce the hot-blast in the United States, having successfully added this improvement to Vesuvius furnace, in Lawrence county, Ohio, in 1836. In 1839 he added a hot-blast to Karthaus furnace, in Pennsylvania.

About 1837 F. H. Oliphant, a skillful ironmaster, made at his furnace called Fairchance, near Uniontown, in Fayette county, Pennsylvania, a quantity of coke pig iron exceeding twenty tons, and probably exceeding 100 tons. He did not, however, long continue to make coke iron, and resumed the manufacture of iron with charcoal. Mr. Oliphant had heard of the offer of the gold medal, and in a letter to the Institute, dated October 3, 1837, he modestly referred to his success in making pig iron with coke, and suggested that possibly he was entitled to the premium. Accompanying his letter was a box of pig iron and the raw materials of its manufacture. We can not learn that he ever received the medal, or that anybody received it.

Between 1836 and 1839 other attempts to use coke were made at several furnaces in Pennsylvania, but all the experiments were unsuccessful or unfortunate. The legislature of Pennsylvania passed an act on June 16, 1836, "to encourage the manufacture of iron with coke or mineral coal," which authorized the organization of companies for the manufacture, transportation, and sale of iron made with coke or coal. At Farrandsville, in Clinton county, six miles north of Lock Haven, half a million dollars were sunk by a Boston company in a disastrous attempt to smelt the neighboring ores with coke and to establish other iron and mining enterprises. This company had commenced operations in mining coal as early as 1833. The furnace was blown in in the summer of 1837 and ran probably until 1839. About 3,500 tons of iron were made, but at such great cost, owing to the impurity of the coal and the distance from the ore, that further efforts to make iron with coke were abandoned. At Karthaus, in Clearfield county, the Clearfield Coal and Iron Company, embracing Henry C. Carey, Burd Patterson, John White, and others, succeeded in 1839, under the management of William Firmstone, in making pig iron with coke in a furnace which was built in 1836 by Peter Ritner (brother of Governor Ritner) and John Say, but at the close of the year the whole enterprise was abandoned, owing to the lack of proper transportation facilities. A furnace at Frozen run, in Lycoming county, made some pig iron with coke in 1838, but in 1839 it was using charcoal. The furnaces at Farrandsville and Karthaus were both supplied with hot-blasts, the former in 1837 and the latter in 1839. The apparatus at Farrandsville was made at Glasgow and was the best then known.

Henry Charles Carey, the distinguished political economist and son of Mathew Carey, who was also similarly distinguished, was born in Philadelphia on the 15th of December, 1793, and died in the same city on the 13th of October, 1879, having nearly completed his 86th year. He was buried at Burlington, New Jersey, where his wife had previously been buried. It is not generally known that Henry C. Carey was ever interested pecuniarily in the manufacture of iron, as we have shown above.

The first notable success in the use of bituminous coal in

the blast furnace in this country was achieved at three furnaces in Western Maryland. Lonaconing furnace, at Lonaconing, in the Frostburg coal basin, on George's creek, about eight miles southwest of the National Road at Frostburg, in Alleghany county, was built in 1837 by the George's Creek Company to use coke, and in June, 1839, as is stated by Johnson, in his *Notes on the Use of Anthracite*, it was making about seventy tons per week of good foundry iron. Alexander says that this furnace was fifty feet high, and that "the air was heated by stoves placed near the tuyere arches, and attained a temperature of 700 degrees Fahrenheit." The furnace was blown by an engine of sixty horse-power. In the same coal basin, on the south branch of Jenning's run, nine miles northwest of Cumberland, two large blast furnaces were built in 1840 by the Mount Savage Iron Company to use the same fuel. These furnaces were for several years successfully operated with coke. It is worthy of notice that Alexander's report to the Governor of Maryland, made in 1840, and which was the first able and comprehensive contribution to the technical literature of the iron and steel industries of this country, was written partly to show to the people of Maryland the feasibility of substituting coke for charcoal in the manufacture of pig iron, the British blast-furnace practice at that time being largely drawn upon for illustrations of what had already been accomplished with the new fuel.

But the use of coke did not come rapidly into favor, and many experiments with it were attended with loss. It was not until after 1850 that its use began to exert an appreciable influence upon the manufacture of pig iron. In 1849 there was not one coke furnace in blast in Pennsylvania. Overman stated in that year in his book that he knew of no coke furnaces in this country which were then in operation. Thus far the use of coke had not contributed to the revolution to which we have referred in the preceding chapter. In 1856 there were twenty-one furnaces in Pennsylvania and three in Maryland which were using coke or were adapted to its use, and their total production in that year was 44,481 gross tons of pig iron. After 1856 the use of this fuel in the blast furnace increased in Pennsylvania and was extended to other States, but it was not until after 1865 that its use for this purpose increased rapidly. Not more than 100,000 gross tons of coke were consumed in the production of pig iron in this country in that year. A tremendous stride was taken in the next fifteen years, however, the quantity of coke consumed in the blast furnaces of the United States in the census year 1880 having been 2,128,255 net tons. In the census year 1890 the consumption was about 10,000,000 net tons.

The first furnaces south of the Potomac which used coke as fuel appear to have been Potomac furnace, on the Potomac river, in Loudoun county, Virginia, about three-quarters of a mile below Point of Rocks; Clinton furnace, nine miles south of Morgantown, in Monongalia county, West Virginia; and Vulcan furnace, in Hampshire county, Virginia, nine miles southeast of Cumberland. These furnaces were originally built to use charcoal; but they used small quantities of coke before the civil war. Potomac furnace is said by Lesley to have commenced to use coke in 1848, and Clinton furnace used the same fuel in 1856. About 1858 Vulcan furnace was blown in with coke. We presume that all these furnaces drew their supply of coke from the Frostburg region. We know of no other coke furnaces south of the Potomac and the Ohio rivers prior to 1860. Potomac furnace was owned in 1859 by John W. Geary, afterwards Governor of Pennsylvania. Anna furnace, on the right bank of Cheat river, in the village of Pridevale, in Monongalia county, West Virginia, made an unsuccessful experiment with coke in 1854, after having previously used charcoal.

In our Tennessee chapter we have given the history of the first coke furnace which was built south of the Potomac region. This was Bluff furnace, at Chattanooga, which was successfully blown in with coke in May, 1860, after having previously used charcoal.

The first coke furnace built in the South after the war was the first of the two Rockwood furnaces, at Rockwood, in Roane county, Tennessee. This furnace was built by the Roane Iron Company in 1867.

While the effort was being made in a few localities in Pennsylvania and Maryland to introduce the use of coke in the blast furnace attention was also directed to the possibility of using uncoked coal for the same purpose. Alexander says that the proprietors of Lonaconing furnace, in Western Maryland, used raw coal before the appearance of his report in 1840. He leaves the reader to infer that it was successfully used, but he probably wrote from imperfect information. Some unsuccessful experiments were made with raw coal in Clarion county, Pennsylvania, about 1840. In the sketch of Mercer county, Pennsylvania, in Day's *Historical Collections*, printed in 1843, it is stated that, "in the vicinity of Sharon, on the Pittsburgh and Erie canal, exists a most valuable bed of coal of peculiar quality, between anthracite and bituminous, without the least sulphur. It has been tried successfully for smelting iron in a common charcoal furnace." It is very probable that the furnace referred to was in Mercer county. The coal mentioned is now classed among bituminous varieties. At Arcole furnace, in Lake county, Ohio, operated by Wilkeson & Co., raw coal from Greenville, Mercer county, Pennsylvania, was experimented with about 1840. John Wilkeson, one of the owners of the furnace at that time, writes us that the experiment "met with a small measure of success." Doubtless the several experiments mentioned were not the only ones that were made with raw coal before success in its use was fully achieved; and doubtless, too, none of the experiments mentioned produced any more satisfactory results than the qualified success attained at Arcole furnace.

The first completely successful use of raw bituminous coal in the blast furnace occurred in the autumn of 1845. It is circumstantially described in the following extract from a pamphlet entitled *Youngstown, Past and Present*, published in 1875. "In July, 1845, Himrod & Vincent, of Mercer county, Pennsylvania, blew in the Clay furnace, not many miles from the Ohio line, on the waters of the Shenango. About three months afterwards, in consequence of a short supply of charcoal, as stated by Mr. Davis, their founder, a portion of coke was used to charge the furnace. Their coal belongs to seam No. 1, the seam which is now used at Sharon and Youngstown, in its raw state, variously known as 'free-burning splint,' or 'block coal,' and which never makes solid coke. A difficulty soon occurred with the cokers, and, as Mr. Himrod states, he conceived the plan of trying his coal without coking. The furnace continued to work well and to produce a fair quality of metal. It is admitted that Mr. David Himrod, late of Youngstown, produced the first metal with raw coal about the close of the year 1845."

The furnace here alluded to was situated on Anderson's run, in Mercer county, Pennsylvania, about two and one-half miles southeast of Clarksville, and was built in 1845. It has been abandoned for many years. In the chapter relating to Michigan we have mentioned the part taken by this furnace at a later day in smelting Lake Superior iron ores with the block coal of the Shenango valley.

In 1845 Messrs. Wilkeson, Wilkes & Co., of Lowell, in Poland township, Mahoning county, Ohio, commenced the erection of Mahoning furnace, as related in the chapter devoted to Ohio, expressly to use coal in its raw state from their mine near Lowell. The furnace was successfully blown in with this fuel by John Crowther on the 8th of August, 1846. It was while this furnace was in course of erection that the use of raw coal at Clay furnace was commenced. It may be added that Mr. Davis, the founder of Clay furnace, visited and inspected Mahoning furnace while work upon it was progressing, and that he had been an employé of the owners of Arcole furnace and was familiar with the experiments that had been made at it in the use of raw coal about 1840. The *Trumbull Democrat*, of Warren, Ohio, for August 15, 1846, in an account of the blowing in of Mahoning furnace, states that "to these gentlemen (Wilkeson, Wilkes & Co.) belongs the honor of being the first persons in the United States who have succeeded in putting a furnace in blast with raw bituminous coal."

John Crowther was an Englishman, born at Broseley, in Shropshire, on May 7, 1797. He emigrated to the United States in 1844, immediately prior to which time he had been the manager of seven blast furnaces in Staffordshire—five at Stowheath and two at Osier Bed. Prior to his connection with the Lowell furnace he had been employed as manager of the furnaces at Brady's Bend. He adapted many furnaces in the Mahoning and Shenango valleys to the use of block coal, and instructed three of his sons in their management, namely, Joshua, Joseph J., and Benjamin. He died on April 15, 1861, at Longton, in Staffordshire, England, where he is buried. Joshua Crowther died in this country in October, 1883, aged over 60 years.

After it had been demonstrated at Clay and Mahoning furnaces that the block coal of the Shenango and Mahoning valleys could be used in the manufacture of pig iron other furnaces in these two valleys were built to use this fuel, and some charcoal furnaces were altered to use it. In 1850 there were, however, only four furnaces in the Mahoning valley and only seven in the Shenango valley which used raw coal. After 1850, and especially after the introduction into these valleys of Lake Superior ores about 1856, the use of raw coal greatly increased. In 1856 six furnaces in Pennsylvania and thirteen in Ohio were using this fuel, their total production in that year being 25,073 gross tons. Some progress was afterwards made in its use in other States, particularly in Indiana, and also in the Hocking valley in Ohio, but down to 1880 its use had been mainly confined to the Shenango and Mahoning valleys. Since 1880 its use has gradually declined, coke having almost entirely taken its place, even in these two valleys.

Probably the first use of raw bituminous coal in a furnace south of the Ohio river was at "Alexander's steam, hot-blast, stone-coal furnace," afterwards called Airdrie furnace, located on the south bank of Green river, at Paradise, in Muhlenburg county, Kentucky. Lesley says that this furnace was built in 1857 "for bituminous coal from the Airdrie bed and black-band iron ore, both mined close by the furnace."

An air furnace was built at Westham, on the James river, six miles above Richmond, during the Revolution, which is said to have used bituminous coal from Chesterfield county, Virginia, in the manufacture of shot and shells for the Continental army until the furnace was destroyed by Benedict Arnold in 1781.

But a much earlier use of bituminous coal in connection with the manufacture of iron in this country was at Colonel Spotswood's air furnace at Massaponax, which is mentioned in our Virginia chapter. Colonel Byrd says that "sea coal," the old name for pit coal or bituminous coal, was used at this air furnace when he visited it in 1732. "Sea coal" was so named because it was originally taken to London from the north of England by sea. The phrase entered into common use, and was applied indiscriminately to all bituminous coal, even if it had not been near the sea. It may still be heard in New England. The "sea coal" used at Massaponax had undoubtedly come from England or Wales.

Bituminous coal was used at an early day in a raw state in the heating furnaces attached to American rolling and slitting mills, and in 1817, when a rolling mill was built at Plumsock, in Fayette county, Pennsylvania, it was so used in both heating and puddling furnaces. In the same year coke was used in a refinery at this mill. It was not, however, until about 1830, when rolling mills became numerous at Pittsburgh, that the use of bituminous coal in puddling and heating furnaces assumed noteworthy prominence.

BEFORE the close of the charcoal era in 1840 steam had been applied to the blowing of American furnaces, but water-power was still in general use. The necessity of increasing the blast and other considerations soon led to the more general use of steam blowing engines in connection with anthracite and bituminous furnaces. Another improvement in blast-furnace management also had its beginning about the close of the charcoal era, namely, the utilization of the combustible gases emitted from blast furnaces. These gases were first used to heat the boilers for the blowing engines and afterwards to heat the hot-blast stoves. This branch of our general subject will be referred to hereafter.

CHAPTER XLIII.

STATISTICS OF THE PRODUCTION OF PIG IRON IN THE UNITED STATES.

The following table, compiled from statistics obtained by the American Iron and Steel Association, exhibits the production of pig iron in the United States in each year from 1854 to 1890, classified according to the fuel used. In the bituminous column is included pig iron made with both raw coal and coke. Net tons of 2,000 pounds are used.

Years—Net tons.	Anthracite.	Charcoal.	Bituminous.	Total tons.
1854...	339,435	342,298	54,485	736,218
1855 (anthracite passes charcoal)......	381,866	339,922	62,390	784,178
1856..	443,113	370,470	69,554	883,137
1857..	390,385	330,321	77,451	798,157
1858..	361,430	285,313	58,351	705,094
1859..	471,745	284,041	84,841	840,627
1860..	519,211	278,331	122,228	919,770
1861..	409,229	195,278	127,037	731,544
1862..	470,315	186,660	130,687	787,662
1863..	577,638	212,005	157,961	947,604
1864..	684,018	241,853	210,125	1,135,996
1865..	479,558	262,342	189,682	931,582
1866..	749,367	332,580	268,396	1,350,343
1867..	798,638	344,341	318,647	1,461,626
1868..	893,000	370,000	340,000	1,603,000
1869 (bituminous passes charcoal)......	971,150	392,150	553,341	1,916,641
1870..	930,000	365,000	570,000	1,865,000
1871..	956,608	385,000	570,000	1,911,608
1872..	1,369,812	500,587	984,159	2,854,558
1873..	1,312,754	577,620	977,904	2,868,278
1874..	1,202,144	576,557	910,712	2,689,413
1875 (bituminous passes anthracite)..	908,046	410,990	947,545	2,266,581
1876..	794,578	308,649	990,009	2,093,236
1877..	934,797	317,843	1,061,945	2,314,585
1878..	1,092,870	293,399	1,191,092	2,577,361
1879..	1,273,024	358,873	1,438,978	3,070,875
1880..	1,807,651	537,558	1,950,205	4,295,414
1881..	1,734,462	638,838	2,268,264	4,641,564
1882..	2,042,138	697,906	2,438,078	5,178,122
1883..	1,885,596	571,726	2,689,650	5,146,972
1884..	1,586,453	458,418	2,544,742	4,589,613
1885..	1,454,390	399,844	2,675,635	4,529,869
1886..	2,099,597	459,557	3,806,174	6,365,328
1887..	2,338,389	578,182	4,270,635	7,187,206
1888..	1,925,729	598,789	4,743,989	7,268,507
1889..	1,920,354	644,300	5,951,425	8,516,079
1890..	2,448,781	703,522	7,154,725	10,307,028

This table shows the growth of the manufacture of pig iron with anthracite and bituminous coal since 1854, and also the periods at which the use of anthracite coal and bituminous coal respectively overtook that of charcoal in the blast furnace, and the period when the use of bituminous coal overtook that of anthracite coal.

Some of the pig iron classed above as having been produced with anthracite and bituminous coal, respectively, was produced with a mixture of these fuels, the quantity of pig iron so produced being mainly represented in the anthracite column. The mixed fuel referred to was not used to any noticeable extent until about 1875, and its use has increased in every succeeding year. The total quantity of pig iron made with mixed anthracite and bituminous fuel in the census year 1880 was 713,932 net tons. Of the production of 1,885,596 net tons of so-called anthracite pig iron in 1883 not less than 920,142 tons were produced with mixed fuel, or nearly one-half of the total quantity. Of the production of 2,448,781 net tons of anthracite and mixed anthracite and bituminous pig iron in 1890 only 279,184 net tons were made with anthracite alone. Very little of the pig iron in the bituminous column was made with mixed anthracite and bituminous fuel. In late years mixed fuel has only been used in the furnaces represented in the anthracite column.

Prior to the organization of the American Iron and Steel Association, at Philadelphia, on March 6, 1855, the statistics of our production of pig iron were not annually obtained. Such statistics as were obtained and have been preserved are herewith presented, in gross tons, by decades. For 1810 and 1840 they embrace castings from the furnace as well as pig iron. For 1810, 1840, and 1850 the figures given are census statistics; for 1820 and 1830 they are from estimates by reputable authorities.

Production of pig iron in the United States in 1810— 53,908 gross tons; in 1820—20,000 tons; in 1830—165,000 tons; in 1840—286,903 tons; in 1850—564,755 tons. We have no statistics for an earlier period than 1810.

For the first time in our history the production of pig iron in the United States in 1890 exceeded that of Great Britain in her year of greatest production.

CHAPTER XLIV.

THE MANUFACTURE OF BLISTER AND CRUCIBLE STEEL IN THE UNITED STATES.

STEEL was manufactured in a small way in several of the American colonies, either "in the German manner" or by the more clearly defined cementation process. We have in preceding chapters incidentally recorded some of the earliest attempts that were made to manufacture steel by these pioneer methods. In this chapter and in the next two chapters we will endeavor to present in sufficient detail the leading facts in the development of the present magnificent steel industry of our country. To do this we must first briefly notice the very insignificance of our small steel industry as it existed in colonial times and long after the close of the Revolutionary struggle.

Bishop states that the first suggestion of the manufacture of steel in the colonies was made in 1655, when John Tucker, of Southold, on Long Island, informed the general court of New Haven "of his abilitie and intendment to make steele there or in some other plantation in the jurisdiction, if he may have some things granted he therein propounds." In October, 1655, and May, 1656, special privileges were granted to the petitioner, but we are not told whether he ever made any steel or not. Bishop cites Hoadly's *New Haven Colonial Records* as his authority for these statements.

We will here copy from Colonel William Byrd's *Progress to the Mines*, in 1732, from which we have heretofore quoted, a part of his interview with Mr. Chiswell, the manager of a Virginia furnace: "He told me a strange thing about steel, that the making of the best remains at this day a profound secret in the breast of a very few, and therefore is in danger of being lost, as the art of staining of glass and many others have been. He could only tell me they used beech wood in the making of it in Europe, and burn it a considerable time in powder of charcoal; but the mystery lies in the liquor they quench it in." As Mr. Chiswell was himself a skilled metallurgist it may be assumed that he correctly expressed the sentiment of his day, that the manufacture of cemented steel, otherwise known as blister steel, was a great mystery. Crucible steel had not then been invented. It is not strange, however, that it should have been supposed as late as 1732 that the quality of steel should at all depend upon the "liquor" in which it was quenched, as the same antiquated notion still exists in Sheffield. It will be remembered by the reader that in the early chapters of this history we referred to the use by the ancient steelmakers of certain waters in Italy and Spain, as is recorded by Pliny and Livy.

In the chapter relating to the extension of the manufacture of iron in New England we have stated that in 1728 Samuel Higley, of Simsbury, and Joseph Dewey, of Hebron, in Connecticut, represented to the legislature that the first-named had "with great pains and cost found out and obtained a curious art, by which to convert, change, or transmute common iron into good steel, sufficient for any use, and was the very first that ever performed such an operation in America." They asked the exclusive right "of practicing the business or trade of steel-making" for twenty years. A patent was granted to them for ten years, provided that "the petitioners improve the art to any good and reasonable perfection within two years after the date of this act." They do not seem to have succeeded in placing their enterprise on a firm foundation. Mr. Charles J. Hoadly, the librarian of the Connecticut State Library, sends us a copy of the certificate of two smiths who certified to the excellence of Mr. Higley's steel.

This may certify all concerned that Samuel Higley of this town of Simsbury came to the shop of us the subscribers being blacksmiths, some time in June in the year one thousand seven hundred and twenty-five, and desired us to let him have a pound or two of iron made at the new works near Turkey Hills, which we according to his desire let him have, shapeing severall peices according to his order. He desired that we would take notice of them that we might know them again, for, said he, I am a going to make Steel of this Iron, and I shall in a few days bring them to you to try for steel. Accordingly he brought the same pieces which we let him have, and we proved them and found them good steel, which was the first steel that ever was made in this country that ever we saw or heard of. Since which he hath made farther experiment, taking from us Iron & returning it in good Steel. As witness óur hands this 7th day of May, 1728.

TIMO^{TH} PHELPS. JOHN DRAKE.

Mr. Hoadly informs us that the mother of Governor Jonathan Trumbull, of Connecticut, ("Brother Jonathan,") was a member of the Higley family, and that John Brown, of Ossawatomie, was descended from the same family.

In October, 1740, the Connecticut legislature granted to Messrs. Fitch, Walker, and Wyllys "the sole privilege of making steel for the term of fifteen years, upon this condition, that they should in the space of two years make half a ton of steel." It appears, however, that this condition was not complied with, and that the privilege was extended two years longer, or until 1744, before which time Aaron Eliot and Ichabod Miller certified that, "after many expensive and fruitless trials with which sundry of the owners were discouraged, the affair being still pursued by others of them, it has so far succeeded that there has been made more than half a ton of steel at the furnace in Symsbury which was erected for that purpose by the gentlemen to whom the aforesaid grant was made." Fitch, Walker, and Wyllys were not mechanics, the first two being lawyers and the last-named being the secretary of the colony. These facts we learn from Mr. Hoadly.

Some time previous to 1750 Aaron Eliot owned a steel furnace at Killingworth, in Middlesex county, Connecticut, and in this furnace he succeeded in 1761 in converting into good steel a bar of iron made in a common bloomary from magnetic sand by his father, the Rev. Jared Eliot, who received a gold medal from the London Society of Arts "for producing malleable iron from the American black sand." It was sent through "the care of our friend, Ben Franklin."

In May, 1772, the following petition was presented to the legislature of Connecticut by Aaron Eliot, for a copy of which document we are indebted to the politeness of Mr. Hoadly.

To the Honl General Assembly now sitting in Hartford. The memorial of Aaron Eliot of Killingworth humbly sheweth,

That your memorialist has for a number of years carried on the Steel Manufacture in this Colony and has made very large quantities, sufficient to supply all the necessary demands of that article in this Colony as well as to export large quantities for supplying the neighbouring governments; that the fortune of your memorialist has not been large enough to supply himself with a sufficient stock to carry on his business, & has therefore hitherto been obliged to procure his stock of iron at New York on cred and pay for the same in his steel when made at the moderate price of £56 per ton, [$186.66⅔, the £ being equal to $3.33⅓,] from whence it has been again purchased in this Colony at the price of £75 and £80 per ton, and for several years past almost the whole supply of steel in this Colony has been from New York of the manufacture of your memorialist at the afores⁴ enormous advance, and your memorialist humbly conceives that the interest of the Colony is to incourage necessary and advantageous manufactories within the Colony, not only for the necessary consumption of the Colony but for export, which. your memorialist will be able to effect in the afores⁴ article of steel with some small assistance from your Honᵐ to procure him a sufficient stock and thereby save larger sums of money within this Colony which is annually paid to New York for the steel manufactured in this Colony : Wherefore your memorialist humbly prays your Honours to loan to him £500 out of the publick treasury for three years without interest, whereby he will be enabled to carry on the afores business to considerable publick advantage, and he as in duty bound shall ever pray.

AARON ELIOT.

Mr. Eliot's petition was granted in 1772, and in 1775 the loan was continued for two additional years.

In 1750 Massachusetts had one steel furnace. In the New England chapter already referred to we have stated that steel was made by Eliphalet Leonard at Easton, in Massachusetts, about 1775 or 1776, and that in 1787 his son, Jonathan Leonard, increased the facilities for its manufacture at the same place. It is stated that "the article was made in considerable amount, and cheaper than imported steel," but it was inferior to foreign steel for edge tools and cutlery. This was cemented steel. By reference to the same chapter it will be seen that during the Revolution steel was made at Cumberland, in Rhode Island, by a German, "from the pig after the mode of his country," and that about 1799 steel was made at Canton, in Massachusetts, "from crude iron by the German process." Other early steel enterprises in Massachusetts are recorded in the same chapter.

Peter Townsend, who became the proprietor of the Sterling iron works in New York before the Revolution, produced in 1776 the first steel made in that province. It was made "at first from pig and afterwards from bar iron, in the German manner." Blister steel was made in 1810 by Peter Townsend, Jr., which is said to have been of as good quality for the manufacture of edge tools as steel made from Dannemora iron. At Amenia, in Dutchess county, New York, steel was made for the use of the Continental army.

New Jersey had one steel furnace in 1750. Steel was made

at Trenton during the Revolution, "but the business afterwards declined."

Pennsylvania had a steel furnace in Chester county, called Vincent's, about 1750, and in that year it had two other steel furnaces at Philadelphia. Of one of the last named, William Branson's, Richard Hockley writes to Thomas Penn on June 3, 1750 : "As to steel, Mr. Branson says the sort he made, which was blistered steel, 10 tons would be ten years in selling." The other furnace, Stephen Paschal's, which was built in 1747, was owned in 1787 by Nancarrow & Matlock, when it was visited by General Washington, and is said to have been "the largest and best in America." In 1770 Whitehead Humphreys was the proprietor of a steel furnace on Seventh street, in Philadelphia. During the Revolution he made steel for the Continental army from Andover iron. In 1786 the legislature of Pennsylvania loaned £300 to Mr. Humphreys for five years to aid him in making steel from bar iron "as good as in England."

During the Revolution Henry Hollingsworth, at Elkton, in Cecil county, Maryland, manufactured muskets for the Continental army. Some of his bayonets were complained of as being too soft, "which he ascribed to the bad quality of the American steel with which they were pointed." Bishop does not mention any steel furnace in Maryland, and we are therefore unable to conjecture where Mr. Hollingsworth obtained his poor steel. We are also without positive information concerning the colonial or Revolutionary steel industry of Virginia and other southern colonies. In most of these colonies bounties were offered at the beginning of the Revolution for the establishment of steel furnaces as well as other manufacturing enterprises.

In the celebrated report of Alexander Hamilton, dated December 5, 1791, it is stated that "steel is a branch which has already made a considerable progress, and it is ascertained that some new enterprises on a more extensive scale have been lately set on foot." In the same year, 1791, in a reply to Lord Sheffield's *Observations on the Commerce of the United States*, Tench Coxe stated that "about one-half of the steel consumed in the United States is home-made, and new furnaces are building at this moment. The works being few, and the importations ascertained, this fact is known to be accurate." The works here referred to were all doubtless cementation furnaces, which produced blister steel.

In 1805 there were two steel furnaces in Pennsylvania, which produced annually 150 tons of steel. One of these was in Philadelphia county. In 1810 there were produced in the whole country 917 tons of steel, of which Pennsylvania produced 531 tons in five furnaces, one at Philadelphia, and one each in Philadelphia, Lancaster, Dauphin, and Fayette counties. The remainder was produced in Massachusetts, Rhode Island, New Jersey, Virginia, and South Carolina, each State having one furnace. In 1813 there was a steel furnace at Pittsburgh, owned by Tuper & McKowan, which was the first in that city. Tench Coxe declared in this year that the manufacture of "common steel, iron wire, and edge tools" had been greatly advanced since 1810.

In 1818 John and Jacob Rodgers, Isaac Smedley, and James Wood were engaged in the manufacture of saws at Valley Forge, Pennsylvania, on the Montgomery county side of Valley creek. Mr. Wood was the manager of the works. The company built a furnace in that year for the manufacture of crucible steel for saw plates, John Parkins and his son, John Parkins, Jr., both from England, being employed as practical steelmakers. These persons are said to have made an unsuccessful attempt to make cast steel at New York city in 1812. The company at Valley Forge is said by Mr. Wood's son, Mr. John Wood, of Conshohocken, who is now living, to have made some excellent steel, but the project was soon abandoned. Clay for crucibles was brought from Perth Amboy, and some plumbago crucibles were imported from England. This is the first important crucible-steel enterprise in our history that has been brought to our notice.

In 1831 a convention of the friends of American industry assembled at New York, at which were submitted many able reports upon the iron and steel industries of this country as they existed at that time. From one of these reports, prepared by Mr. John R. Coates, of Philadelphia, we learn that there were then in the United States fourteen blister-steel furnaces, distributed as follows: two at Pittsburgh, one at Baltimore, three at Philadelphia, three at New York, one in

York county, Pennsylvania, one at Troy, New York, two in New Jersey, and one at Boston. The report mentioned that "these furnaces are known to be now in operation, and of a capacity sufficient to supply more than 1,600 tons of steel annually, an amount equal to the whole importation of steel of every kind." The report continued: "But it should be observed that steel for common agricultural purposes is not the best, although it is most used; and that American is quite equal to English steel used for such purposes in England. American competition has excluded the British common blister steel altogether. The only steel now imported from Great Britain is of a different and better quality than that just mentioned." The common blister steel of American manufacture which is above referred to was used for plowshares, shovels, scythes, and cross-cut and mill saws.

The better qualities of steel which were not made in this country in 1831, but were imported from Europe, almost entirely from England, were known as (1) best blister steel, made from iron from the Dannemora mines in Sweden; (2) shear steel, of the same origin; and (3) cast steel, made in crucibles. Concerning blister steel of the best quality the report from which we have quoted says that "steel is now made at Pittsburgh, and may be made in New York and Connecticut, bearing a fair comparison with the best hoop L or Dannemora steel. No difference is observed where trials have been made without disclosing to the judges the origin of either." The report adds that iron equal to Swedish for the manufacture of steel had been recently manufactured "by improved processes from the ore of Juniata, and both sides of the line between New York and Connecticut." Shear steel was the best blister steel of the cementation furnace reworked under a hammer into bars suitable for the manufacture of coarse cutlery and edge tools. The manufacture of this steel was then about being introduced into this country. The report says: "England has hitherto monopolized this branch also, from being in possession of the only European steel that would bear the expense of preparation, and from the perfection of her machinery. She has now the honor of transferring a portion of her experience and skill to the United States."

Cast steel, which was then made only from the best blister steel, was not made in the United States. Several attempts to make it with profit had been unfortunate in their results. "The causes of failure," says the report, "were, first, the want of the best quality of blister steel at a reasonable price, and, second, the want, or expense, of crucibles of proper quality, wherein the blister steel is to be melted and smelted. Black lead and a variety of clays have been tried, but the weakness of these materials has heretofore caused a loss to the manufacturer." The English Stourbridge clay was the only clay which in 1831 was known to possess the qualities required for crucibles. The report says that "the explorations of the present year have disclosed the existence of clay analogous to that of Stourbridge," the discoveries being made in Centre, Clearfield, and Lycoming counties in Pennsylvania and in the vicinity of Baltimore. The expectations created by these discoveries were never realized.

From 1831, the date of the report from which we have just quoted, to 1860 very little progress was made in developing the manufacture of the finer qualities of steel in the United States. In the first edition of Appletons' *Cyclopædia*, printed in 1860, it was stated that "American cast steel is hardly known in the markets." During this period of thirty years, however, indeed just after its commencement, there was one notable and successful attempt to make steel of the best quality, the detailed history of which we shall now give.

In August, 1832, William Garrard and John Hill Garrard, brothers, commenced the manufacture of crucible steel on the Miami Canal, at Cincinnati, in works which had been previously erected by them, and which were projected in the autumn of 1831. Both were comparatively young men, natives of England, but residents of the United States for ten years previous to the year mentioned. The style of the firm was Garrard Brothers, but William, the elder brother, was the projector and practical manager of the enterprise. To him and to his friend, Mr. James E. Emerson, of Beaver Falls, Pennsylvania, we are indebted for the very full details we are enabled to present of the first successful works in the United States for the manufacture of crucible steel of the best quality. Mr. Emerson has also sent us an illustration of the works, printed from a wood-cut made in 1833. They were called the Cincinnati steel works.

The works were located on Canal street, extending back to Providence street, and were built upon a portion of the ground now occupied by the Lion brewery. They embraced a furnace for converting bar iron into blister steel; two pot-holes, each accommodating two pots, or crucibles; and the necessary machinery for manufacturing saws and files. In August, 1832, the first cast steel was made, and in November, 1832, the first mill and cross-cut saws were made. Dr. Garrard wrote us in 1884 as follows concerning his enterprise.

I made my own blister steel. You will see in the picture of my works a large round stack that contained my converting furnace. It was built for two ten-ton converting furnaces. The first crucibles I experimented with were German plumbago pots, but they were a failure, as they spoiled the steel by giving out too much gross carbon. I then went to Western Virginia, near New Cumberland, and found a clay that very much resembled English Stourbridge clay, and by putting in the pots made of it about the same proportion of burnt material they stood about as well as the Stourbridge pots, and answered my purpose very well. In respect to the building of my works, I was my own architect, drew a plan for my works on paper, and superintended the brick-laying myself; in fact, the building and machinery were all made from my own drawings and under my own superintendence. I sold my steel and manufactured articles principally to manufacturers. There were some wholesale houses that bought of me, but they were importing houses, and when the Sheffield manufacturers found that I was making as good steel and manufactured saws and files as good as they did they gave our merchants such an extended time of credit that they bought as little as possible from us.

Mr. Emerson furnished us in 1883 with the following additional information concerning the Cincinnati steel works.

The Doctor still has his old moulds in which he formed his crucibles, in the regular English way. For best cast steel he first used Swedes' iron. For steel used for saws, springs, etc., he used Tennessee charcoal iron. For best cast steel he also used considerable Missouri charcoal iron. In addition to saws and springs he made steel for chopping axes, files, and tools in general. The material used was all very high-priced, so that the owners were obliged to sell their spring steel at from 10 to 15 cents per pound, and best cast steel at from 18 to 25 cents. The very crude machinery and manner in which all of the work had to be done added also to the cost.

The enterprise was started during Jackson's first term of office, and about the time that the law was passed for a gradual reduction of duties on all imports for a decade, and with this gradual reduction of duties foreign importation increased, to pay for which the country was drained of money. Manufactures were closed, culminating in the great panic of 1837, at which time the enterprise of our venerable friend went down in the general wreck that engulfed the infant manufactures in their cradles all over the country.

After Garrard Brothers had commenced the manufacture of steel W. T. Middleton became a partner in the enterprise, taking the place of Dr. Garrard's brother. Subsequently Charles Fox, a lawyer, became a partner. After the failure in 1837 the business was continued in a restricted way until 1844 by Dr. Garrard and Mr. Fox, the principal product of the works being blister steel.

In the Cincinnati Directory for 1834, published by E. Deming, at No. 5 Johnston's Row, there will be found the following announcement on page 233 : " Steel, Saw, and File Factory, on Plumb Street, near the corporation line, owned by Middleton, Garrard & Co., manufacturers of all kinds of Cast Steel, by steam-power. Attached to this establishment is a Saw and File Factory, in which these articles are made equal in quality to those imported."

Mr. Emerson has sent us a file made in 1833 from the crucible steel of these works, and a turning-tool made from some of the very first steel made by them in 1832, and used in the works for turning their chilled rolls for sheet steel. He has also sent us other interesting relics of these works, which he thus describes in a letter written in 1884.

At the first available opportunity, after receiving your letter of the 26th of December, I visited the home of Dr. Garrard and secured an old turning tool and an old punch used as a die for cutting teeth in saws, the steel of which the Doctor informed me was made in 1832. I have forged quite a ghastly-looking knife-blade off the end of the old turning tool, and a smaller blade off the end of the saw-tooth punch, and have hardened, tempered, and finished them. I have been working steel for about forty years. At Trenton, New Jersey, during the civil war, I manufactured over 75,000 cavalry sabres and over 100,000 officers' swords for the United States Government, and I think that I know something about steel and about tools. I am willing to submit these tools to any expert and risk my reputation that in quality they are fully equal to the best steel made in this country to-day, and also equal to the best imported English steel. Here is an affidavit from the Doctor:

Personally appeared Dr. William Garrard, of Fallston, Beaver county, Pennsylvania, and being duly sworn deposes and says : That the two pieces of steel from which these two knives were forged, tempered, and finished by Messrs. Emerson, Smith & Co., of Beaver Falls, Pennsylvania, were made by him at Cincinnati, Ohio, in 1832, by first converting Missouri charcoal iron into blister steel by the usual cementation process, then by melting in pots made by himself, pouring into ingots, then forging or tilting in the usual manner. The large piece was used as a lathe turning tool, and the small one as a punch for toothing saws. Furthermore the said William Garrard sayeth not.

Sworn and subscribed before me this 28th day of }
January, A. D. 1884. WINFIELD S. MOORE,   } WILLIAM GARRARD.
[SEAL]   *Notary Public.* }

The Doctor has placed in my hands numerous testimonials from manufacturers who used his steel for different purposes—for chopping axes, files, springs, saws, etc.

All of the articles mentioned above are now in our possession and we prize them highly. An examination of them by experts will fully sustain the claim that they are made *of the best crucible tool steel.*

At our request Mr. J. Blodget Britton, the eminent metallurgical chemist, has made an analysis of liberal borings from the end of the turning tool from which Mr. Emerson has forged the "ghastly-looking knife-blade," the remaining part forming the handle of the knife. The analysis is as follows. It will possess great interest for all our readers who would know the chemical elements of the first tool steel of best quality that this country has produced.

Pure iron	98.770	Manganese	.019
Carbon	1.048	Sulphur	doubtful traces
Silicon	.102		
Silicates	.020	Total	99.974
Phosphorus	.015		

Dr. Garrard was born in Laxfield parish, Suffolk county, England, on the 21st of October, 1803. He removed with his father's family to the United States in 1822, the whole family finding a home near Pittsburgh. The Doctor says: "It was during the last two years that I was with my father that I built a small converter and experimented on the various kinds of bar iron, converting them into blister steel, and through a careful test of the same I became convinced that I could make steel equal to the English." He was not a trained steelmaker, nor even an ironmaker. His trade was that of a bricklayer, but he had a liking for chemistry, and his attention being turned to the manufacture of steel this taste was utilized. The rest of his story we have told.

John Hill Garrard died at Pittsburgh in 1883, aged 78 years, and Dr. Garrard died at Fallston, in Beaver county, Pennsylvania, on March 18, 1889, aged over 85 years.

The following is a list of all the works in Pennsylvania that were engaged in the conversion of steel in 1850, with their product: James Rowland & Co., Kensington, (Philadelphia,) 600 tons; J. Robbins, Kensington, 500 tons; Earp & Brink, Kensington, 100 tons; Robert S. Johnson, Kensington, 400 tons; W. & H. Rowland, Oxford, (Philadelphia,) 700 tons; R. & G. D. Coleman, Martic, Lancaster county, 400 tons; R. H. & W. Coleman, Castle Fin, York county, 100 tons; Singer, Hartman & Co., Pittsburgh, 700 tons; Coleman, Hailman & Co., Pittsburgh, 800 tons; Jones & Quigg, Pittsburgh, 1,200 tons; Spang & Ço., Pittsburgh, 200 tons; G. & J. H. Shoenberger, Pittsburgh, 200 tons; S. McKelvy, Pittsburgh, 178 tons; total, thirteen works, with a product of 6,078 tons. Of this quantity only 44 tons were cast steel. The foregoing information is not found in the census of 1850, but was obtained by an association of Pennsylvania ironmasters. The census of that year greatly understates the extent of our steel industry, and erroneously makes no mention of the manufacture of steel in any other State than Pennsylvania.

From about 1830 to 1860 many attempts were made at Pittsburgh to produce blister and crucible steel. Between 1828 and 1830 Simeon Broadmeadow, an Englishman, and his son made blister steel, and about 1831 they made some cast steel in pots of their own manufacture. The attempt to manufacture cast steel was a failure. Josiah Ankrim & Son, file-makers, are said to have succeeded in making their own steel after 1830, but by what process is not stated. In 1831 Wetmore & Havens successfully produced blister steel. In 1833 the firm of G. & J. H. Shoenberger commenced to manufacture blister steel, and in 1841 Patrick and James Dunn attempted the manufacture of crucible cast steel for this firm. This last enterprise was abandoned in a year or two. "The crucibles employed were made of American clay, and, as may be supposed, were ill-suited to the purpose required." The firm continued to make blister steel until 1862, when its further manufacture was abandoned. It used Juniata blooms exclusively. About 1840 the firm of Isaac Jones & William Coleman was formed to manufacture blister steel, which business was successfully prosecuted until 1845, when the firm was dissolved, Mr. Jones retiring. In the same year Jones &

Quigg built the Pittsburgh steel works, also to manufacture blister steel. Mr. Coleman continued alone the manufacture of blister steel until 1846, when a partnership was formed under the name of Coleman, Hailman & Co. Both of these new firms were successful in making blister steel of good quality. They were also successful in manufacturing some cast steel of a low grade. The first slab of cast plow steel ever rolled in the United States was rolled by William Woods at the steel works of Jones & Quigg, in 1846, and shipped to John Deere, of Moline, Illinois. About 1846 the firm of Tingle & Sugden, file-makers, made its own steel. This is said to have been cast steel. The firm is also reported to have made some cast steel for sale. Juniata iron was used by nearly all of these manufacturers.

In 1852 McKelvy & Blair, of Pittsburgh, who had commenced the manufacture of files in 1850, made cast steel of good quality, but not always of the best quality. It was, however, of a quality so creditable, and so uniformly superior to any that had previously been made at Pittsburgh, that the firm may be regarded as the pioneer in the production of cast steel in large quantities in that city. In 1853 the firm of Singer, Nimick & Co., of Pittsburgh, which had been organized in 1848 for the manufacture of blister steel, and in 1855 Isaac·Jones, then doing business in his own name, were successful in producing the usual grades of cast steel for saw, machinery, and agricultural purposes, but they did not make tool steel of the best quality as a regular product. That honor was reserved for the firm of Hussey, Wells & Co., which began business in 1859 and in the following year was successful in making crucible cast steel of the best quality as a regular product. This was done with American iron. In 1862 the firm of Park, Brother & Co., also of Pittsburgh, accomplished the same achievement, also with American iron. These were the first firms in this country to meet with complete financial as well as mechanical success in this difficult department of American manufacturing enterprise. Both of the works referred to are still in operation.

For many of the foregoing details concerning the manufacture of steel at Pittsburgh we are indebted to an anonymous publication, entitled *Pittsburgh, its Industry and Com-*

merce, published in 1870, and to George H. Thurston's *Pittsburgh and Allegheny in the Centennial Year.*

While these experiments in the manufacture of the best quality of steel were being made at Pittsburgh other localities were engaged in making similar experiments. By far the most important of these were made by the Adirondack Iron and Steel Company, whose works were at Jersey City, New Jersey. They were built in 1848 to make blister steel from charcoal pig iron made at Adirondack, in Essex county, New York, and also to make cast steel. The pig iron was puddled with wood at Adirondack, and then formed into bars under a hammer, which were sent to Jersey City, where they were converted into blister steel. An attempt to make cast steel by melting the blister steel in clay crucibles was a failure, but subsequently cast steel of good quality was made in black-lead crucibles. This result was reached as early as February, 1849, and possibly a few months earlier. Of the excellent quality of the cast steel manufactured at this time at these works there is abundant evidence in the testimony of government experts and also of many consumers, all of which is now before us. It was used for chisels, turning and engravers' tools, drills, hammers, shears, razors, carpenters' tools, etc. Its manufacture was continued with encouraging results until 1853, when the business was abandoned by the company. It had not proved to be profitable, partly because of the prejudice existing against American cast steel. The works were then leased for ten years, during which time they were operated with varying success. James R. Thompson was the manager from 1848 to 1857. In 1863 they were purchased by Dudley S. Gregory, one of the original stockholders, and were from that time managed with uniform success for the owner by H. J. Hopper. In 1874 Mr. Gregory died, and the works descended to his sons. They were afterwards owned by Andrew Williams. In 1885 they were abandoned and dismantled. At the time of their abandonment they were the oldest active cast-steel works in the United States, having been continually employed in the production of this kind of steel since 1849.

It is proper to add that, while good cast steel was made after 1849 at the works of the Adirondack Iron and Steel

Company, the product was not for many years of uniform excellence. Much of it was good tool steel, but much of it was also irregular in temper. The exact truth appears to be that the cast steel produced by this company during the early years of trial, or from 1849 to 1853, was more uniformly excellent than that which had been produced by earlier or by cotemporary American steel works, the Cincinnati steel works of Garrard Brothers alone excepted. This excellence was due to the superiority of Adirondack iron. Since 1852 the Adirondack works have had many rivals in the production of crucible cast steel, the earliest of which have already been described.

James R. Thompson died on Monday, April 18th, 1887, at his home, No. 128 Fifth avenue, New York. He was born at Broadalbin, in Fulton county, New York, about 1822.

Mr. Thomas S. Blair, of Pittsburgh, has kindly furnished us with the following reminiscences of the American steel industry as it existed at Pittsburgh about 1850.

The blister steel made at Pittsburgh was sent all over the West, and was used by the country blacksmiths for the pointing of picks, mattocks, etc., and for plating out into rough hoes, etc. It was usually made from Juniata blooms, especially in the period anterior to 1850. After that date Champlain ore blooms were used to a considerable extent. German steel was simply blister steel rolled down. The two leading applications of German steel were springs and plow-shares. The business was very large at one time. G. & J. H. Shoenberger pushed this brand vigorously from about 1840 to 1860. Meanwhile quite a number of other concerns entered into the competition at various times.

The Shoenberger experiment in the manufacture of crucible steel failed on account of the inferior quality of the product. The firm were so confident that no iron could be found in this country that could in any respect excel the Juniata iron that, when that article failed to produce steel equal to that of Sheffield, they gave up the manufacture of crucible steel. In the light of the experience gained under the scientific methods which the Bessemer process has made a necessity we now understand that the Shoenbergers could not make good crucible steel out of iron containing two-tenths of one per cent. of phosphorus.

McKelvy & Blair at first made their pots out of Darby and Stannington clay, imported from England. The brilliant success of Joseph Dixon, of Jersey City, New Jersey, in perfecting the manufacture of plumbago crucibles, for which the crucible steel interest in the United States owes him a monument, gave to that firm and to the Jersey City steel works a very valuable lift. With these crucibles and with Adirondack blooms Mr. Thompson made some excellent steel. Along in 1853 and 1854 McKelvy & Blair made steel from the Adirondack blooms which was used in the nail factory of G. & J. H. Shoenberger. It may be added, also, that the knives and dies of nail-cutting machines afford an admirable test of endurance in tool steel. The American steel made from American iron was fully up to the English steel in every particular.

It was not possible for McKelvy & Blair to obtain the Adirondack blooms in any quantity, and they had no other resource than the Champlain and Missouri blooms, all of which produced red-short steel. This, notwithstanding that drawback, found a market so extensive that the firm sent to Sheffield and brought out several skilled workmen, and the business of manufacturing handsomely finished bars, plates, and sheets was fairly inaugurated. The drawbacks, however, of pioneer operations, chief among which was the abominable English system, imported with the skilled labor, of "working to fool the master," were too much for the financial strength of the firm, and in 1854 they were forced to drop the enterprise.

The manufacture in this country of crucible cast steel of the best grades may be said to have been established on a firm basis after Hussey, Wells & Co., Park, Brother & Co., and Gregory & Co., in the years 1860, 1862, and 1863, respectively, succeeded in making it of uniform quality as a regular product. The event was one of great importance, as it marked the establishment in this country of a new industry which was destined to assume large proportions and to be of very great value. It met a want that had long been felt, and dissipated the long-standing belief that this country possessed neither the iron nor the skill required to make good cast steel. The establishment of this new industry, following closely in the wake of our successful application of anthracite and bituminous coal in the manufacture of pig iron, assisted greatly to advance our metallurgical reputation and to create confidence in our future metallurgical possibilities. But none of the three firms named could have succeeded in giving to this country a crucible-steel industry worthy of the name if the Morrill tariff of 1861 and its supplements had not encouraged our manufacturers by imposing for the first time in our history really protective duties on steel of foreign manufacture. Our whole steel industry of every description is indeed in an eminent degree the child of protective legislation.

Sixty years ago, when the convention of the friends of home industry met at New York, we were struggling with the difficulties which then prevented the manufacture of blister steel of best quality; now we have not only solved that problem but thirty years ago we solved the greater problem of the manufacture of crucible steel, and a few years later we achieved the still greater triumph of firmly planting upon American soil the Bessemer steel industry. To this marvelous industry we have added the manufacture of steel by the open-hearth, or Siemens-Martin, process—a method of producing steel second only to the Bessemer process in cheapness and productiveness.

Yet we might have had and should have had a crucible-steel industry at a much earlier day. The success of Garrard Brothers in manufacturing the best quality of tool steel at Cincinnati from 1832 to 1837, and of the Adirondack Iron and Steel Company in accomplishing the same result at Jersey City in 1848 and for several years afterwards, in both instances from raw materials of domestic production, proves that this country was long prevented from having a creditable crucible-steel industry because the injurious effects of foreign competition were not sufficiently guarded against in the framing of tariff legislation. The compromise tariff of 1833 closed the Cincinnati steel works. The tariffs of 1846 and 1857 gave no encouragement to our people to engage in the manufacture of crucible steel. Even the manufacture of blister steel in this country was almost destroyed by foreign competition prior to 1860. With the establishment after that year of our crucible-steel industry upon a firm basis, through protective legislation, there was no need to revive on a large scale the manufacture of the inferior product, except as an adjunct of the manufacture of crucible steel.

The production of crucible steel in the United States amounted to 89,762 net tons in 1881, which is the highest annual product yet attained. As late as 1877 the production was only 40,430 tons, which had not previously been exceeded in any year. The production of crucible steel in this country has been practically stationary for many years, the failure of this branch of our steel industry to advance being chiefly due to the competition of open-hearth steel. Bessemer steel is also a sharp competitor. The crucible-steel industry of Great Britain and the Continent of Europe has also made no progress for a number of years and for the same reasons.

Dr. C. G. Hussey was born near York, Pennsylvania, in August, 1802, and was in good health in August, 1891.

CHAPTER XLV.

THE INVENTION OF THE BESSEMER PROCESS.

The Bessemer process for the manufacture of steel consists in forcing streams of cold air, usually under a high pressure, into a pear-shaped vessel called a converter, which has been partly filled with melted cast iron, by which operation the oxygen of the air combines with and eliminates the carbon and silicon in the iron, the product being decarburized and desiliconized iron.   But, as some carbon is always required to produce steel, a definite quantity of manganiferous pig iron (spiegeleisen) or ferro-manganese is added to the contents of the converter while they are still in a state of fusion, by which addition the requisite amount of carbon is obtained, while the manganese combines with and liberates the oxygen that has united with the iron during the blast.   The product is Bessemer steel, of a quality or temper corresponding to the character and proportions of the materials used. A distinguishing feature of the Bessemer process consists in the entire absence of any fuel whatever in converting the already melted cast iron into steel, the carbon and silicon in the iron combining with the oxygen of the atmospheric blast to produce an intensely high temperature.   The Bessemer converter holds from five to twenty tons.   The charge of cast iron which it receives preliminary to a conversion, or blow, may be supplied directly from a blast furnace or from a cupola in which pig iron has been melted.   The latter method is generally employed in both Europe and the United States, although the direct method is employed at some of the large Bessemer works in our own country.

Sir Henry Bessemer, of London, the generally accredited inventor of the process which bears his name, commenced in 1854 to experiment in the manufacture of iron for an improved gun. " In the course of his experiments," says Mr. J. S. Jeans, in his comprehensive work on *Steel*, " it dawned upon him that cast iron might be rendered malleable by the introduction of atmospheric air into the fluid metal." In 1855

and 1856 patents were granted to Mr. Bessemer for this discovery, but it was not until 1858 that complete success was
achieved by him in the conversion of cast iron into cast steel.
Nor was this success achieved without the assistance of others, Robert Forester Mushet, of Cheltenham, England, and
Goran Fredrik Goransson, of Sandviken, Sweden, contributing
greatly to this result. Without the assistance rendered by Mr.
Mushet, of which we shall speak hereafter, Mr. Bessemer's invention would not have been of much value. It may also
be added that many and valuable improvements have been
made in the application of the Bessemer process since its
introduction in Europe and America. These improvements,
however, detract nothing from the honor that is due to Sir
Henry Bessemer, since it is true of all valuable inventions
that their value is increased by the ingenuity and skill of
those who use them. In addition to discovering that melted cast iron could be decarburized and desiliconized and rendered malleable by blowing cold air through it at a high
pressure, Sir Henry is entitled to the whole credit of inventing the wonderful machinery by which this discovery has
been applied to the rapid production of large quantities of
Bessemer steel. The purely engineering feats accomplished
by him in the development of his invention were essential
to its success, and they amaze us by their novelty and magnitude. Those who have never seen this machinery in operation can form but a faint idea of its exquisite adaptation
to the purposes to be accomplished. A Bessemer converter,
weighing with its contents from twenty to forty tons, is moved
at will on its axis by machinery controlled by the touch of
a man or boy, and receives, in response to the same touch,
a blast so powerful that every particle of its many tons of
metallic contents is heated to the highest temperature ever
known in the mechanic arts. The honor of inventing this
machinery is all claimed for Sir Henry Bessemer.

In 1856 Mr. Bessemer obtained in this country two patents for his invention, but was immediately confronted by a
claim of priority of invention preferred by William Kelly,
an ironmaster of Eddyville, Kentucky, but a native of Pittsburgh, Pennsylvania. This claim was heard by the Commissioner of Patents and its justice was conceded, the Commis-

sioner granting to Mr. Kelly a patent which at once operated as an impediment to the use of the patents granted to Mr. Bessemer. The effect of this action by the Commissioner was to prevent for several years any serious effort from being made to introduce the Bessemer process into this country. As a matter of interest and of history we here give, before proceeding further, a complete account of Mr. Kelly's invention, prepared for these pages by Mr. Kelly himself.

In 1846 I purchased, in connection with my brother, John F. Kelly, a large iron property in Lyon county, Kentucky, known as the Eddyville iron works; and the beginning of 1847 found the firm of Kelly & Co. fairly under way, making pig metal and charcoal blooms. Our forge contained ten forge fires and two large finery, or run-out, fires.

To the processes of manufacture I gave my first and most serious attention; and, after close observation and study, I conceived the idea that, after the metal was melted, the use of fuel would be unnecessary—that the heat generated by the union of the oxygen of the air with the carbon of the metal would be sufficient to accomplish the refining and decarbonizing of the iron. I devised several plans for testing this idea of forcing into the fluid metal powerful blasts of air; and, after making drawings of the same, showed them to my forgemen, not one of whom could agree with me, all believing that I would chill the metal, and that my experiment would end in failure. I finally fixed on a plan of furnace which I thought would answer my purpose. This consisted of a small blast furnace, about 12 feet high, having a hearth and bosh like a common blast furnace. In this I expected to produce decarbonized metal from the iron ore; but, if I failed in this, I could resort to pig metal and thereby have good fluid metal to blow into. The novelty of this furnace was that it had two tuyeres, one above the other. The upper tuyere was to melt the stock; the lower one was fixed in the hearth near the bottom, and intended to conduct the air-blast into the metal. That portion of the hearth in which the lower tuyere was placed was so arranged as to part from the upper portion, and consisted of a heavy cast-iron draw, lined inside with fire-brick, so that, when the iron was blown to nature by the lower tuyere, the draw could be run from under the hearth, and the iron taken out, carried to the hammer, and forged.

I began my experiments with this furnace in October, 1847, but found it impossible to give it sufficient attention, as I had then commenced to build a new blast furnace, the Suwannee, on our property. This occupied so much of my time that I had but little left in which to attend to my new process. In the year 1851, having finished our new blast furnace, I found myself more at leisure, and again directed my attention to my experiments; and, on looking for the cause of failure in my experimental furnace, found that my chief trouble lay in the melting department, not in the more important matter of blowing into the iron, so that the question presented itself to my mind, Why complicate my experiments by trying to make pig metal in a furnace not at all suited to the business? Why not abandon altogether the melting department and try my experiments at our new blast furnace, where I could have the metal already melted and in good condition for blowing into? I fully believed that I could make malleable iron by this process. In my first efforts with this object in view I built a furnace consisting of a square brick abutment, having a circular chamber inside, the bottom of which was concave like a moulder's ladle. In the bottom was fixed a circular tile of fire-clay, perforated for tuyeres. Under this tile was an air-chamber, connected by pipes with the blowing engine. This is substantially the plan now used in the Bessemer converter.

The first trial of this furnace was very satisfactory. The iron was well refined and decarbonized—at least as well as by the finery fire. This fact was admitted by all the forgemen who examined it. The blowing was usually continued from five to ten minutes, whereas the finery fire required over an hour. Here was a great saving of time and fuel, as well as great encouragement to work the process out to perfection. I was not satisfied with making refined or run-out metal; my object was to make malleable iron. In attempting this I made, in the course of the following eighteen months, a variety of experiments. I built a suitable hot-blast oven; but, after a few trials, abandoned it, finding the cold-blast preferable, for many reasons. After numerous trials of this furnace I found that I could make refined metal, suitable for the charcoal forge fire, without any difficulty, and, when the blast was continued for a longer period, the iron would occasionally be somewhat malleable. At one time, on trying the iron, to my great surprise, I found the iron would forge well, and it was pronounced as good as any charcoal forge iron. I had a piece of this iron forged into a bar four feet long and three-eighths of an inch square. I kept this bar for exhibition, and was frequently asked for a small piece, which I readily gave until it was reduced to a length of a few inches. This piece I have still in my possession. It is the first piece of malleable iron or steel ever made by the pneumatic process. The variability of results in the working of my experimental furnace was then a mystery which is now explained. An analysis having since been made of all the ore deposits of Suwannee furnace they were found to embrace cold-short, red-short, and neutral ores. Some of the deposits showed a large percentage of manganese.

I now decided that, if I could not succeed in making malleable iron, I could turn my invention to practical account by putting up a furnace of sufficient capacity to supply our forge with refined or run-out metal, and at the same time continue my experiments as before. The difficulty here was in my blast. The furnace engine, though large and powerful, would not give over 5 pounds' pressure to the square inch. To overcome this difficulty I built a converting vessel and placed it in the pig-bed convenient to the tapping-hole of the hearth. This furnace was circular, built of boiler-plate iron, was about 5 feet high and 18 inches inside diameter; and, instead of blowing up through the bottom, the blast was applied to the sides, above the bottom, through four three-quarter-inch tuyeres. Experience soon proved that a single tuyere, an inch in diameter, answered my purpose best. In this vessel I could refine fifteen hundredweight of metal in from five to ten minutes. Should the blast prove weak, as was often the case, the tuyeres could be snuffed in the same way as in a finery fire. In this way a heavy charge could be worked with a weak blast. This furnace had an opening in the side, about nine inches square, three feet from the bottom, to run in the metal; also a tap-hole to let out the metal into a set of iron moulds such as are used about finery fires. This furnace was found to answer a valuable purpose, supplying a cheap method of making run-out metal, and, after trying it a few days, we entirely dispensed with the old and troublesome run-out fires.

Our blooms were in high repute, and were almost entirely used for making boiler plates, so that many steamboats on the Ohio and Mississippi rivers were using boilers made of iron treated by this process some years before it was brought out in England. My process was known to every iron-maker in the Cumberland river iron district as Kelly's air-boiling process. The reason why I did not apply for a patent for it sooner than I did was that I flattered myself I would soon make it the successful process I at first endeavored to achieve, namely, a process for making malleable iron and steel. In 1857 I applied for a patent, as soon as I heard that other men were following the same line of experiments in England; and, although Mr. Bessemer was a few days before me in obtaining a patent, I was granted an interference, and the case was heard by the Commissioner of Patents, who decided that I was the first inventor of this process, now known as the Bessemer process, and a patent was granted me over Mr. Bessemer.

It will be seen that Mr. Kelly claims for himself the discovery of the pneumatic principle of the Bessemer process several years before it dawned upon the mind of Mr. Bessemer. The validity of this claim can not be impeached. But it must also be said that Mr. Bessemer, with the aid of Mr. Mushet, successfully employed this principle in the production of steel and that Mr. Kelly did not. The Kelly process produced refined iron of good quality. Furthermore, the machinery with which Mr. Kelly operated his process was not calculated to produce rapidly or at all large masses of even refined iron; whereas Mr. Bessemer's machinery was successful after it was perfected in producing steel in large quantities and with great rapidity.

Mr. Kelly claimed that his process, if successful in connection with the limited operations of the refinery forge attached to his blast furnace at Eddyville, would be applicable also to the refining of iron for rolling mills, and would take the place of puddling. Some experiments with this end in view were made at the Cambria iron works, at Johnstown, Pennsylvania, in 1857 and 1858, in a converting vessel similar to that now used in the Bessemer process. They were so far successful that Mr. Kelly wrote from Johnstown on the 29th of June, 1858, that he had not "the slightest difficulty in converting crude pig iron into refined plate metal by blowing into it for about fifteen to twenty-five minutes." These experiments were not, however, continued. Mr. Robert W. Hunt, in his *History of the Bessemer Manufacture in America*, read before the American Institute of Mining Engineers in 1876, says that at Johnstown Mr. Kelly "met with the usual number of encouraging failures." The converting vessel used by Mr. Kelly at Johnstown was built by himself. Mr. Hunt says that it was "the first Bessemer converter ever erected in America." We give this honor to the Eddyville converter.

Mr. Bessemer's process having failed in 1855 and 1856 to produce any successful result in the manufacture of steel, Robert F. Mushet, then of the Forest steel works, and late of Cheltenham, England, on the 22d of September, 1856, took out a patent for his process of adding to melted cast iron, which had been decarburized and desiliconized by a pneumatic blast, a melted triple compound of iron, carbon, and manganese, of which compound spiegeleisen was the cheapest and most convenient form. The addition of from one to five per cent. of this compound to the cast iron mentioned at once overcame the obstacle which had been fatal to the success of Mr. Bessemer's invention. Mr. Bessemer had decarburized and desiliconized melted cast iron, but he had not been able to retain or restore the small quantity of carbon that was necessary to produce steel, and in the oxygen of his powerful blast he had given to the contents of his converter an element which prevented the production of even good iron. Mr. Mushet's invention regulated the supply of carbon and eliminated the oxygen. It must be added that, even with the assistance of Mr. Mushet's invention, only pig iron which is practically free from phosphorus was found to be adapted to the Bessemer process as it was originally employed. The basic modification of the Bessemer process, an invention of later years, permits the use of pig iron that is high in phosphorus.

Early in 1857, pending the publication of Mr. Mushet's patent, and during the erection for him of a blowing apparatus and small converter, provided by the late Samuel Holden Blackwell, of Dudley, Mr. Mushet obtained from the Ebbw Vale Iron Company a supply of Bessemerized hematite cast iron. This he melted in crucible-steel melting pots, adding to the forty-four pounds' charge of each pot, when melted, two pounds of melted spiegeleisen. From this mixture ingots of from 500 to 800 pounds were cast, and one of these ingots was rolled at the Ebbw Vale works into a double-headed rail, which was sent to Derby railway station, on the Midland Railroad, to be laid down there at a place where iron rails had sometimes to be renewed within three months. This was early in 1857. Sixteen years afterwards, in June, 1873, the rail referred to was taken out. *This was the first Bessemer steel rail ever laid down.* During its lifetime about 1,250,000 trains and a like number of detached engines and tenders passed over it.

Having obtained the blowing apparatus and converter already mentioned Mr. Mushet was enabled in 1857 to cast small ingots of tool steel by the direct Bessemer process with the addition of spiegeleisen by his own process. The first charge of Bessemer steel ever made with the addition of spiegeleisen was tapped from the small converter at Mr. Mushet's Forest steel works by a young workman, William Phelps. Soon afterwards Bessemer steel was produced in England in commercial quantities by Mr. Bessemer and his business associates.

At the international meeting of the Iron and Steel Institute of Great Britain, the *Verein deutscher Eisenhüttenleute,* and the American Institute of Mining Engineers, held in the hall of the Carnegie Library in Allegheny City, Pennsylvania, in October, 1890, Sir James Kitson, president of the British Institute, delivered the opening address. In his remarks Sir James said that Sir Henry Bessemer had prepared, at his request, an account of his discovery of the process of manufacturing Bessemer steel. A letter in Sir Henry Bessemer's own handwriting was then read. The letter is dated at Denmark Hill, September 10, 1890, and is addressed to Sir James Kitson. As a history of the successive steps by which Sir Henry's great invention was developed and perfected it is very disappointing. We look in vain, for instance, in its elaborate and detailed statements for any recognition whatever of Mr. Mushet's invaluable aid in perfecting the Bessemer process; even Mr. Mushet's name is not mentioned.

Mr. Bessemer's first public account of his invention was read by him at the annual meeting of the British Association for the Advancement of Science, held at Cheltenham, in August, 1856. It was entitled: "On the Manufacture of Malleable Iron and Steel without Fuel." His first English patent in connection with his great invention was granted on October 17, 1855. The paper read at Cheltenham in 1856 is clear and satisfactory.

Mr. Mushet's English patent for the use of spiegeleisen as a recarburizer was permitted to lapse because of his poverty and other causes which he could not control and before he had received any pecuniary benefit from his invention. Mr. Mushet says of this turning point in his life: "So my process became public property, and Mr. Bessemer had a perfect right to make use of it, and his prosperity dated from that period." Mr. Bessemer afterwards recognized his indebtedness to Mr. Mushet's invention by allowing him an annuity of £300, and the Iron and Steel Institute of Great Britain in 1876 awarded to him the Bessemer gold medal for that year in recognition of the great value of his invention. Mr. Bessemer's profits from his own invention have been enormous. In 1879 Mr. Jeans said that "from first to last Bessemer's patents have brought him royalties to the value of over £1,057,000." Mr. Jeans also gives some interesting particulars concerning the profits of the first company that was organized in England to work the Bessemer process. Mr. Bessemer was the projector of this company and a member of it, his associates being his earlier partner, Mr. Robert Longsdon, his brother-in-law, Mr. Allén, and William and John Galloway of Manchester. The works were located at Sheffield. Mr. Jeans' statement is as follows. It is confirmed in the letter of Sir Henry Bessemer, dated September 10, 1890.

On the expiration of the fourteen years' term of partnership of this firm, the works, which had been greatly increased from time to time, entirely out of revenues, were sold by private contract for exactly twenty-four times the amount of the whole subscribed capital, notwithstanding that the firm had divided in profits during the partnership a sum equal to fifty-seven times the gross capital, so that by the mere commercial working of the process, apart from the patent, each of the five partners retired, after fourteen years, from the Sheffield works with eighty-one times the amount of his subscribed capital, or an average of nearly cent. per cent every two months—a result probably unprecedented in the annals of commerce.

With the exception of the annuity and the gold medal mentioned above Mr. Mushet's profits and honors from his great invention have been inconsiderable. He lived and died a poor man. In a monograph which he printed in 1883 in advocacy of his own claims to recognition as an inventor of the process which should rightly be called the Bessemer-Mushet process he makes the following pathetic complaint of the ingratitude of his countrymen.

My invention and Sir Henry Bessemer's have made a great mark in the world, a very great mark indeed; so great that I have sometimes thought that the Iron and Steel Institute might have made me an honorary member and the Royal Society an F. R. S., or that Her Gracious Majesty might have revived my ancestors' title of knights banneret, which was forfeited during the rebellion of Montrose. At all events the vast industry of steel makers, including his Grace the Duke of Devonshire, who gets £12,000 per annum out of my little process, might at least accord me a vote of thanks for the wealth my invention has brought to them. I should value any of these honors very much, as I have valued the gold medal so kindly presented to me by the Iron and Steel Institute and Sir Henry Bessemer in 1876.

In looking back twenty-six years, to the time when Mr. Bessemer's process and mine were made the subject of patents, I may observe that the loss of my patent, through the inconceivable neglect of the trustees in whose hands it was placed, left me without any share in the enormous royalties reaped from the success of our joint processes. In consequence of this the world, true to itself, has done its best to ignore me and my process. The world shuns the man who does not get the money.

Like the majority of inventors, I have benefited others but not myself, and I have been very hardly dealt with, as much so, perhaps, as any inventor has ever yet been; but I have accepted it all cheerfully and without repining, though I have often felt sorry for those who, in their dealings with me, forsook the paths of honor and integrity and took an unworthy advantage of me.

Mr. C. I. Valentine, of the Moss Bay Iron Company, is the only member of the iron trade from whom since the loss of my patent I ever received either kindness or sympathy; and Mr. Samuel Osborn, of the Clyde Steel Works, is the only steel manufacturer who has dealt honorably and kindly with me: and to both these gentlemen, and their respective firms, I tender thus publicly my sincere thanks. I do not, of course, class Sir Henry Bessemer as a steel manufacturer, but as an inventor, who has called into successful activity a great many steel manufacturers. For what he has kindly done for me I thank him also very much.

The British Government has conferred upon Mr. Bessemer the honor of knighthood in recognition of the value of his invention of an official stamp, and he is now Sir Henry Bessemer by virtue of that honor.

In 1858 Mr. Goran Fredrik Goransson, a Swedish iron-master, was enabled by using pure manganesic Swedish pig iron to produce Bessemer steel of excellent quality *without adding spiegeleisen*, the iron used being practically free from phosphorus and sulphur but having the requisite percentage of manganese. Except in rare instances, when pure manganesic pig iron can be obtained, Mr. Mushet's process still continues to be absolutely essential to the manufacture of Bessemer steel. We give below Mr. Goransson's own account of the important part taken by him in the development of the Bessemer process, which account, in his own handwriting, is now in our possession. This account was given to Professor Richard Åkerman, of Stockholm, who had at our request in 1879 addressed a letter to Mr. Goransson requesting a statement of the facts which are of such great historical value.

PROFESSOR RICHARD ÅKERMAN, *Stockholm.*

DEAR SIR: In conformity to your friendly letter of the 2d instant I will try to give you in English a short sketch of the difficulties I had in commencing with the Bessemer method and how I at last overcame them.

My full name is Goran Fredrik Goransson. I bought part of the Swedish Bessemer patent in June, 1857, after a conversation with, then, Mr. Henry Bessemer, and on his promise that he would arrange the necessary plant and send over an engineer for starting the manufacture in accordance with his patents.

In the autumn he sent over his plant, namely, a converter of his construction and a steam blast engine constructed by Messrs. Galloway & Co., of Manchester, accompanied by an engineer for conducting the manufacture. We started in November, but we soon found that the converter was impracticable, difficult to handle, and giving no good result. We then constructed a fixed converter on the same principle as the small fixed vessel which Mr. Bessemer used for his first experiments at Baxter House, in London, but, according to Mr. Bessemer's advice, with two rows of tuyeres, six in each row, the lower row at the bottom of the converter and the other some inches above; but the result was not good. Mr. Bessemer then advised us to augment the pressure of the blast, and to effect this we took away the upper tuyeres and used only the six below, each about five-eighths of an inch in diameter, and we then sometimes succeeded, particularly during the cold, dry, winter days, in getting malleable ingots, but very irregular and generally full of slag. The engineer, not knowing anything more than myself, then left the works.

We tried every possible means of augmenting the pressure of the blast by reducing the diameter of the tuyeres and using smaller charges, as we had reached the limit of the pressure which could be produced by the blast engine, but all with less and less success, and, on the point of giving up the experiments, I resolved, in spite of all advisers, to diminish the pressure and instead use a larger quantity of air. For this purpose we put all the twelve tuyeres in one line at the bottom of the converter, and augmented the diameter of them to seven-eighths of an inch, to see what change they would produce. The result was astonishing. The temperature of the fluid steel was very much raised, the slag came up on the top beautifully, the ingots turned out perfectly even in temper, free from slag, and extremely malleable, more so than any iron made on the old process. The first charge with the converter so arranged was made on the 18th of July, 1858, and from that date the Bessemer method can be regarded as started.

I sent fifteen tons of ingots to a firm in Sheffield and fifteen tons to Messrs. Henry Bessemer & Co.'s works at the same place, and went over to England in September to have them tried. I found then that Mr. Bessemer had not succeeded, but had to granulate in water the steel he got from the converter and afterwards remelt it in crucibles. As such a process could not give any profit the friends who assisted him were losing all hope of success, but they all came down to Sheffield to see my ingots tried before they finally gave up this business. The Sheffield firm, thinking it their interest not to forward the Bessemer method, got the whole lot burnt at the washwelding, but the fifteen tons hammered and tilted at Messrs. Henry Bessemer & Co.'s works turned out to full satisfaction after having been tried for knives, scissors, razors, other tools, and plates.

The result of these trials has led to the further improvement and to the present extension of the Bessemer process, for which Mr. Bessemer and others have done much, but Professor Viktor Eggertz's practical invention to find out the percentage of carbon in the steel has overcome the greatest difficulty then remaining. Faithfully Yours,   G. F. GORANSSON.

SANDVIKENS JERNVERKS, AKTIE BOLAG, SANDVIKEN, November 6, 1879.

An important improvement upon the Bessemer process is the work of two English chemists, Sidney Gilchrist Thomas and Percy C. Gilchrist, both of London. It renders possible the use in the converter of cast iron which contains a large percentage of phosphorus, no method of eliminating from it this hostile element having previously been in use. The first patent of Mr. Thomas, the principal inventor of this successful method of dephosphorizing iron, is dated November 22, 1877, and relates to the application of a lime lining to the Bessemer converter and to the use of lime in combination with its melted contents. The Thomas-Gilchrist process is now employed with success in the manufacture of Bessemer steel in Great Britain, France, Germany, Austria, Belgium, and Russia, but it has met with the greatest favor in Germany. It has been introduced in this country in connection with the Bessemer process, but only in a small way.

Mr. George J. Snelus, of England, claims to have solved the problem of dephosphorization in the same way that Thomas and Gilchrist solved it, and some time before their attention was turned to the subject. His invention was patented in 1872. A consolidation of his interests with those of Thomas and Gilchrist was effected without difficulty. Mr. Jacob Reese, of Pittsburgh, Pennsylvania, also claims priority over Messrs. Thomas and Gilchrist in the invention of the basic process, and this claim was long a subject of controversy in the United States. It rests upon patents which were granted to Mr. Reese in this country in 1866. These patents and the Thomas-Gilchrist patents were purchased in 1879 for this country by the Bessemer Steel Company Limited, but controversy concerning the exact scope and significance of Mr. Reese's patents did not end until 1888, when the ownership of all the patents for the United States was finally vested in the company mentioned.

Mr. James Henderson, of New York city, made many interesting experiments in the use of lime as a dephosphorizer before Mr. Snelus had conceived that it could accomplish this result. Mr. Henderson took out a patent in England for his invention in 1870, and his process was used with satisfactory results at Du Motay's experimental works in Belgium in the summer of 1872. The pig iron which was dephosphorized and converted was obtained at the Bowling works, in England.

Colonel J. B. Kunkel, of Frederick county, Maryland, took out letters-patent in the United States in 1876 for the elimination of phosphorus from pig iron by the use of magnesian limestone in the blast furnace. He also claimed that by the use of this agent pig iron could be freed from phosphorus while being refined into iron or steel. No notable results appear to have attended the granting of this patent.

The Clapp-Griffiths and Robert-Bessemer processes for the manufacture of Bessemer steel are recent modifications of the standard Bessemer process which need not be described in these pages. They are in limited use in Europe and the United States. Both are slow processes, and they are used to secure special products. As in the standard process the pneumatic principle is an essential adjunct of both these minor processes. Neither process appears to be growing in favor either in this country or in Europe. Nor have we deemed it necessary to devote any part of our space to a consideration of the experiments about 1855 of Joseph Gilbert Martien, of Newark, New Jersey, in refining melted cast iron by the use of a blast of cold air. They were not successful in producing any practical results. They are interesting simply because they show that Martien, as well as Kelly, undertook to refine melted cast iron with a cold blast before Bessemer set out to accomplish the same result. The following letter from Mr. Martien to Messrs. Munn & Co., of New York, the well-known patent agents, written in 1857, is of interest in this connection.

MESSRS. MUNN & Co., *New York.*

GENTLEMEN : Relative to the claims of William Kelly, of Lyon county, Kentucky, and myself to certain improvements in the manufacture of iron without the use of fuel, I take this occasion of informing you and the public generally that agreeably to appointment for the examination of various witnesses in the above case for priority of invention between myself and Mr. Kelly I have found and have been made perfectly satisfied from the ample testimony laid before me in the case that Mr. Kelly is honestly the first and original inventor of the said process of manufacturing iron without fuel. I find, moreover, that he has quietly been and is making improvements and advancing with his invention in a very praiseworthy manner, and of which the public will be put in possession in a short time. I have therefore deemed it a duty that I owe to myself and the original inventor to come out and publicly state the above facts and thereby give publicity to the same, trusting he may receive the due honour therefor and be richly rewarded for his genius.

Respectfully,   J. G. MARTIEN.

NEWARK, NEW JERSEY, May 29, 1857.

The establishment of the Bessemer steel industry in many countries is justly regarded as constituting a much more important revolution in the production and use of iron and steel than had been created by any preceding influence or combination of influences in any age of the world's history. And yet this great industry did not for many years after it was established in Europe attract the attention either on that continent or on this which its importance deserved. In his report on the Paris Exposition of 1867 the Hon. Abram S. Hewitt said: "In view of the small amount of Bessemer steel as yet produced in the United States we are struck in Europe with surprise at the enormous provision made for its supply; and it is quite evident that the business is overdone, and, contrary to all past experience, the inventor and the public at large seem to have profited by its introduction at the expense of the manufacturer." Since Mr. Hewitt's admirable report was written how great has been the development in Europe of an industry which was then "overdone," and how great have been the profits of the European manufacturer of Bessemer steel! And for how many years after the appearance of Mr. Hewitt's report did the new industry literally languish in this country!

Although Bessemer steel is adapted to all purposes for which other steel is used, except perhaps the manufacture of fine cutlery, its use in Europe has been mainly confined to the production of railway bars, and its use in this country has been even more narrowly limited to the same product. For many years after the introduction of the Bessemer process in the United States it was used to produce nothing but rails. In both geographical divisions it is now widely used for other purposes.

Robert Forester Mushet, without whose triple compound of iron, carbon, and manganese the Bessemer process for making steel could not have been successful, died at Cheltenham, England, on January 29, 1891, in his 80th year. He was the youngest son of the celebrated steelmaker, David Mushet, and was born at Coleford, in the Forest of Dean, in 1811. To his birth in the Forest Mr. Mushet owed his middle name of Forester.

Sidney Gilchrist Thomas, to whom the chief credit is undoubtedly due for the invention of the basic process by which phosphorus is eliminated from pig iron, was born in England in April, 1850, and died on February 1, 1885, in his 35th year. In a biographical sketch of Mr. Thomas Mr. George W. Maynard truly says: "It has rarely fallen to the lot of one so young to add so much to the world's knowledge and wealth as did Sidney Gilchrist Thomas."

CHAPTER XLVI.

THE BESSEMER PROCESS IN THE UNITED STATES.

As EARLY as 1861 Captain E. B. Ward, of Detroit, and Z. S. Durfee, of New Bedford, obtained control of the patents of William Kelly, and in that year Mr. Durfee went to Europe to study the Bessemer process. During his absence Captain Ward invited Mr. William F. Durfee, also of New Bedford, and a cousin of Z. S. Durfee, to erect an experimental plant at Wyandotte, Michigan, for the manufacture of pneumatic steel, and this work was undertaken in the latter half of 1862. In May, 1863, Daniel J. Morrell, of Johnstown, and William M. Lyon and James Park, Jr., of Pittsburgh, having become partners of Captain Ward and Z. S. Durfee in the control of the patents of Mr. Kelly, the Kelly Pneumatic Process Company was organized, Mr. Kelly retaining an interest in any profits which might accrue to the company. It was resolved to complete the experimental works already undertaken, and also to acquire the patent in this country of Mr. Mushet for the use of spiegeleisen as a recarburizing agent. The patent was granted in England in 1856 and in this country in 1857. Mr. Z. S. Durfee accordingly went to England to procure an assignment of Mr. Mushet's patent. The latter purpose was effected on the 24th of October, 1864, upon terms which admitted Mr. Mushet, Thomas D. Clare, and John N. Brown, of England, to membership in the Kelly Process Company. On the 5th of September, 1865, the company was further enlarged by the admission to membership of Charles P. Chouteau, James Harrison, and Felix Vallé, all of St. Louis. In September, 1864, William F. Durfee succeeded in making Bessemer steel at the experimental works at Wyandotte. *This was the first Bessemer steel made in the United States.* A part of the machinery used at the Wyandotte works was an infringement upon Mr. Bessemer's American patents.

The control in this country of Mr. Bessemer's patents was obtained in 1864 by John F. Winslow, John A. Griswold, and Alexander L. Holley, all of Troy, New York, Mr. Holley visiting England in 1863 in the interest of himself and his associates. In February, 1865, Mr. Holley was successful at Troy in producing Bessemer steel at experimental works which he had constructed for his company at that place in 1864. Mr. Mushet's method of recarburizing melted iron in the converter was used at Troy, and this was an infringement upon his patent in this country.

As the Kelly Process Company could not achieve success without Mr. Bessemer's machinery, and as the owners of the right to use this machinery could not make steel without Mr. Mushet's improvement, an arrangement was made by which all of the American patents were consolidated early in 1866. Under this arrangement the titles to the Kelly, Bessemer, and Mushet patents were vested in Messrs. Winslow, Griswold, and Morrell, the first two being owners of seven-tenths of the property and Mr. Morrell holding the other three-tenths in trust for the Kelly Process Company. This arrangement continued until the formation of the Pneumatic Steel Association, a joint-stock company organized under the laws of New York, in which the ownership of the consolidated patents was vested. Z. S. Durfee acted as the secretary and treasurer of the company. The ownership of the patents was afterwards vested in the Bessemer Steel Company Limited, an association organized in 1877 under the laws of Pennsylvania. This association has been succeeded by the Steel Patents Company, organized in 1890. All the original English and American patents have expired. The Steel Patents Company, however, owns other patents relating to the manufacture of Bessemer steel which have not expired.

Mr. Wm. F. Durfee has described in the following words the quality of the Bessemer steel first made at Wyandotte.

Various experiments were tried to test the ductility and working qualities of the steel produced at Wyandotte. Some of the early product was sent to Bridgewater, Massachusetts, and there rolled into tack plate and cut into tacks which were pronounced to be very much superior to any previously made of iron. In order to test the welding qualities of the steel John Bishop, the blacksmith of the works, made a tobacco-pipe the size of an ordinary clay pipe, the bowl and stem of which were welded up of Wyandotte steel, and when perfectly polished there was no visible evidence of a weld. I have now two jackknives and a razor made from' this steel; the knives are rather soft, but the razor was used regularly by my father for fifteen years to his entire satisfaction.

The consolidation in 1866 of the various interests above mentioned was followed by a large reduction in fees and royalties, and thenceforward the business of making Bessemer steel was rapidly extended in this country. The order in which the pioneer Bessemer steel works of the United States were established down to 1876 is presented below. From 1876 to 1881 no Bessemer steel works were established in this country. Beginning with 1881 many new Bessemer works have been built in the United States, but a list of these works in these pages would occupy too much space.

1. Kelly Pneumatic Process Company, Wyandotte, Wayne county, Michigan. One 2½-ton experimental converter. Made its first blow in September, 1864. Bought by Captain E. B. Ward in 1865 and abandoned in 1869. These experimental works were connected with an iron rolling mill.

2. Albany and Rensselaer Iron and Steel Company, Troy, New York. Experimental Bessemer plant established by Winslow, Griswold & Holley. One 2½-ton converter. Made its first blow February 15, 1865. Now two 10-ton converters. Added to an iron rail mill.

3. Pennsylvania Steel Works, Pennsylvania Steel Company, Steelton, Dauphin county, Pennsylvania. Two 7-ton converters. Made its first blow in June, 1867. An entirely new works. Three 8-ton converters added in 1881.

4. Freedom Iron and Steel Works, Lewistown, Mifflin county, Pennsylvania. Two 5-ton converters. Made their first blow May 1, 1868. Added to the works of the Freedom Iron Company. Failed in 1869 and Bessemer works dismantled; most of the machinery was taken to Joliet, Illinois.

5. Cleveland Rolling Mill Company, Cleveland, Ohio. Two 6½-ton converters. Made its first blow October 15, 1868. Now two 10-ton converters. Added to an iron rail mill.

6. Cambria Iron and Steel Works, Cambria Iron Company, Johnstown, Pennsylvania. Two 6-ton converters. Made its first blow July 10, 1871. Added to an iron rail mill. Now two 11½-ton converters.

7. Union Steel Company, Chicago, Illinois. Two 6-ton converters. Made its first blow July 26, 1871. Added to an iron rail mill. Now two 10-ton converters.

8. North Chicago Rolling Mill Company, Chicago, Illinois. Two 6-ton converters. Made its first blow April 10, 1872. Added to an iron rail mill.

9. Joliet Steel Works, Joliet Steel Company, Joliet, Illinois. Two 8-ton converters. Made its first blow January 26, 1873, and its first steel rail March 15, 1873. An entirely new works.

10. Bethlehem Iron Company, Bethlehem, Pennsylvania. Two 7-ton converters. Made its first blow October 4, 1873, and its first steel rail October 18, 1873. Now four 7-ton converters. Added to an iron rail mill.

11. Edgar Thomson Steel Works, Carnegie Brothers & Co. Limited, Bessemer station, Allegheny county, Pennsylvania. Two 7-ton converters. Made their first blow August 25, 1875, and their first steel rail September 1, 1875. An entirely new works. Now four 15-ton converters.

12. Lackawanna Iron and Steel Works, Lackawanna Iron and Coal Company, Scranton, Lackawanna county, Pennsylvania. Two 5-ton converters. Made its first blow October 23, 1875, and its first steel rail December 29, 1875. Added to an iron rail mill. Now three 7-ton converters.

13. St. Louis Ore and Steel Company, St. Louis, Missouri. Two 7-ton converters. Made its first blow September 1, 1876. Added to an iron rail mill. These works have long been idle.

Mr. Robert W. Hunt informs us that the first conversion made at Troy was from Crown Point charcoal pig iron, melted in a reverberatory furnace, and Mr. William F. Durfee informs us that the first steel made at Wyandotte was converted from Lake Superior charcoal pig iron, also melted in a reverberatory furnace, although on a number of subsequent occasions the metal for conversion was taken directly to the converter from the Eureka charcoal blast furnace.

It is supposed that the first attempt made in the world to melt pig iron in a cupola for conversion into steel by the Bessemer process was made by Mr. Z. S. Durfee at the works at Wyandotte during the spring of 1865. This attempt failed of success, owing to the small size of the cupola and the length of time required to accumulate enough iron in the traveling ladle for use in the converter; but the present general employment of the cupola whenever pig iron is used for conversion into Bessemer steel is sufficient evidence that the thought which prompted this first experiment had a substantial and practical foundation. Mr. Hunt states that on July 20, 1865, Mr. Holley successfully used the cupola at Troy in connection with the Bessemer process. The English practice at this time was to use the reverberatory furnace.

The first Bessemer steel rails ever made in this country were rolled at the North Chicago rolling mill on the 24th of May, 1865, from ingots made at the experimental steel works at Wyandotte under the supervision of William F. Durfee, superintendent. The rolls with which the steel rails were rolled at the North Chicago rolling mill had been in use for rolling iron rails. The steel rails came out sound and well-shaped. Several of these rails were laid in the track of one of the railroads running out of Chicago and were still in use in 1875. The American Iron and Steel Association was in session at Chicago at the time, and several of its members witnessed the rolling of the rails.

The following letter from Mr. O. W. Potter, of Chicago, long president of the North Chicago Rolling Mill Company, written to Mr. William F. Durfee in 1865, two days after the rolling of the first American steel rails in that city, is of historical value and worthy of preservation.

MY DEAR DURFEE: The meeting of the iron and steel men adjourned yesterday to meet in Cleveland the fourth Wednesday in August. I regret very much you could not have been here, particularly to see how well your steel behaved, and you must allow me to congratulate you upon its entire success, and I assure you I was but too proud for your sake that everything we had to do with it proved so very successful. The hammer was altogether too light of course and it took more time than it otherwise would to draw the ingot down, yet all the pieces worked beautifully, and we have made six good rails from the ingots sent over, and not one bad one in any respect. The piece you sent over forged is now lying *in state* at the Tremont House, and is really a beautiful rail, and has been presented to the Sanitary Fair by Captain Ward. We rolled three rails on Wednesday and three on Thursday. At the first rolling only your cousin and George Fritz were present; at the rolling yesterday were Senator Howe, of Wisconsin; B. F. Jones, of Pittsburgh; R. H. Lamborn, of Philadelphia; Mr. Phillips, of Cincinnati; Mr. Swift, of Cincinnati; Mr. Kennedy, of Cincinnati; Mr. May, of Milwaukee, and three ladies; Mr. Scofield, of Milwaukee; Mr. Fritz, of Johnstown; and Mr. Thomas, of Indianapolis, with four strangers. Everything went so well I really wanted you to see some of the good of your labors for so long a time and under such trying circumstances. You have done what you set out to do, and done it well, and I am glad to congratulate you and rejoice with you, for I can appreciate some of your difficulties, and wanted you to hear some of the praises bestowed upon your labors as you richly deserve. I know this would make no sort of difference to you, yet we all have vanity enough (especially in such cases as this) to feel gratified at any little compliments we know we are entitled to, but I will not tire you with any more, as your cousin [the late Z. S. Durfee] can tell you all and more than I can write, but with kindest regards allow me to remain

Yours Most Obt.,   O. W. POTTER.

OFFICE OF THE CHICAGO ROLLING MILL, CHICAGO, May 26, 1865.

The first steel rails ever rolled in the United States upon order, in the way of regular business, were rolled by the Cambria Iron Company, at Johnstown, Pennsylvania, in August, 1867, from ingots made at the works of the Pennsylvania Steel Company near Harrisburg, Pennsylvania; and by the Spuyten Duyvil Rolling Mill Company, at Spuyten Duyvil, New York, early in September of that year, from ingots made at the Bessemer steel works at Troy, New York, then owned by Winslow & Griswold.

Important improvements upon Mr. Bessemer's machinery

have been invented and patented by A. L. Holley, George Fritz, Robert W. Hunt, William R. Jones, and other American engineers. Of these improvements the most notable is the Fritz blooming mill, which is in general use in this ,country and in Europe. The largest number of improvements were made by Mr. Holley. The inventive genius and rare mechanical skill of Mr. John Fritz, of the Bethlehem Iron Company, have also produced many valuable improvements which were clearly patentable but have not been patented.

In the early stages of the Bessemer steel industry in this country great difficulty was experienced in obtaining suitable pig iron and also materials for the lining of the converters. Large quantities of Bessemer pig iron were annually imported. Our manufacturers were uncertain whether American ores would make good Bessemer pig iron, and many failures occurred in using domestic pig iron that was unsuited for conversion into steel. The lack of skilled workmen was also severely felt. All difficulties, however, have long been overcome. It is now universally admitted that in the United States this industry has been brought to a higher state of perfection than it'has attained in any other country. The American Bessemer steel works have been constructed after plans which are in the main greatly superior to those of European works. The United States is now not only independent of óther countries for its supply of Bessemer pig iron but it is also the largest producer of Bessemer pig iron in the world.

Since 1867 the American Iron and Steel Association has annually ascertained the production of Bessemer steel ingots in the United States. It has been as follows, in net tons.

Years.	Net tons.	Years.	Net tons.	Years.	Net tons.
1867	3,000	1875	375,517	1883	1,654,627
1868	8,500	1876	525,996	1884	1,540,595
1869	12,000	1877	560,587	1885	1,701,762
1870	42,000	1878	732,226	1886	2,541,498
1871	45,000	1879	928,972	1887	3,288,357
1872	120,108	1880	1,203,173	1888	2,812,500
1873	170,652	1881	1,539,157	1889	3,281,829
1874	191,933	1882	1,696,450	1890	4,131,535

The Association has also ascertained as follows the production of Bessemer steel rails in the United States in net tons since the commencement of their manufacture in this country as a commercial product in 1867. The total production of rails from 1867 to 1890 was 19,483,930 net tons.

Years.	Net tons.	Years.	Net tons.	Years.	Net tons.
1867	2,550	1875	290,863	1883	1,286,554
1868	7,225	1876	412,461	1884	1,116,621
1869	9,650	1877	432,169	1885	1,074,607
1870	34,000	1878	550,398	1886	1,763,667
1871	38,250	1879	683,964	1887	2,354,132
1872	94,070	1880	954,460	1888	1,552,631
1873	129,015	1881	1,330,302	1889	1,691,264
1874	144,944	1882	1,438,155	1890	2,091,978

A comparison of the production of ingots and rails will show approximately the quantity of Bessemer steel that has annually been used in miscellaneous forms. Virtually all of the Bessemer steel that has been produced in this country has been used at home; only a small quantity has been exported.

The following table shows in gross tons the production of Bessemer steel ingots and Bessemer steel rails in the United States and in Great Britain from 1877 to 1890.

Years.	United States—Gross tons.		Great Britain—Gross tons.	
	Ingots.	Rails.	Ingots.	Rails.
1877	500,524	385,865	750,000	508,400
1878	653,773	491,427	807,527	622,390
1879	829,439	610,682	834,511	520,231
1880	1,074,262	852,196	1,044,382	732,910
1881	1,374,247	1,187,770	1,441,719	1,023,740
1882	1,514,687	1,284,067	1,673,649	1,235,785
1883	1,477,345	1,148,709	1,553,380	1,097,174
1884	1,375,531	996,983	1,299,676	784,968
1885	1,519,430	959,471	1,304,127	706,583
1886	2,269,190	1,574,703	1,570,520	730,343
1887	2,936,033	2,101,904	2,089,403	1,021,847
1888	2,511,161	1,386,277	2,032,794	979,083
1889	2,930,204	1,510,057	2,140,791	943,048
1890	3,688,871	1,867,837	2,014,843	1,019,606

The benefits which this country has derived from home-made steel rails, which have long been cheaper than iron rails were ever sold, are so numerous and enter so largely into the daily life of all our people that they have ceased to excite comment, like the natural blessings of light, air, and water. The wearing qualities of a steel rail being much superior to those of an iron rail it is capable of supporting a much heavier weight of cars, locomotives, freight, and passengers, and it permits trains to be moved at a much greater rate of speed; hence the carrying capacity of our railroads has been greatly increased and the cost of operating them has been greatly decreased. The life of a steel rail being much longer than that of an iron rail the cost to our railroad companies for renewals of track is many times less than if iron rails were still used. The immense agricultural crops of the country in the last twenty years never could have been moved to either home or foreign markets if iron rails had been continued in use; the attempt to transport them upon iron rails would have so worn out the rails that the tracks would constantly have been torn up for repairs, and this would have resulted in a continual interruption to all traffic. If our dependence for steel rails had been on foreign sources of supply the cost of transportation resulting from the high prices of foreign rails would have been so great that it would not have been profitable to grow these immense crops; indeed the prices of foreign rails would have been so high that few railroads would have been built in the Western States and Territories, and the marvelous development of that section could not have taken place. Finally it may be said that, but for our cheap home-made steel rails, flour and meat, lumber and coal, and other heavy products could not have been cheaply distributed to consumers; the necessaries of life would have been largely enhanced in price through the high cost of transportation; and the whole country would have had a much less rapid growth than it has experienced.

The following persons who were prominently identified with the introduction of the Bessemer steel industry into this country have passed to the other world.

John A. Griswold was born at Nassau, Rensselaer county, New York, on November 14, 1818, and died at Troy, New York, on October 31, 1872, aged almost 54 years.

George Fritz was born in Londonderry township, Chester county, Pennsylvania, on December 15, 1828, and died at Johnstown, Pennsylvania, on August 5, 1873, aged almost 45 years. For many years he was the chief engineer of the Cambria iron works.

Captain E. B. Ward was born in Canada, of Vermont parents, on December 25, 1811, and died suddenly at Detroit, Michigan, on January 2, 1875, aged over 63 years.

Z. S. Durfee was born at Fall River, Massachusetts, on April 22, 1831, and died at Providence, Rhode Island, on June 8, 1880, aged over 49 years.

Alexander L. Holley was born at Lakeville, Connecticut, on July 20, 1832, and died at Brooklyn, New York, on January 29, 1882, aged nearly 50 years.

James Park, Jr., was born at Pittsburgh, Pennsylvania, on January 11, 1820, and died at Allegheny City, Pennsylvania, on April 21, 1883, aged over 63 years.

Daniel J. Morrell was born in North Berwick, York county, Maine, on August 8, 1821, and died at Johnstown, Pennsylvania, on August 20, 1885, aged over 64 years. At the time of his death Mr. Morrell was the president of the American Iron and Steel Association.

Thomas M. Carnegie, one of the founders of the Edgar Thomson steel works, was born at Dunfermline, Scotland, on October 2, 1844, and died at Homewood, near Pittsburgh, on October 19, 1886, aged over 42 years.

William Kelly, the American inventor of the pneumatic process for making steel, was born at Pittsburgh on August 21, 1811, of Irish parentage, and died at Louisville, Kentucky, on February 11, 1888, in his 77th year.

Samuel M. Felton, president of the Pennsylvania Steel Company, and one of its founders, was born at West Newbury, Massachusetts, on July 17, 1809, and died at Philadelphia on January 24, 1889, in his 80th year.

William M. Lyon was born at Harrisburg, Pennsylvania, on April 29, 1809, and died at Pittsburgh on July 3, 1889, aged over 80 years.

Captain William R. Jones, general superintendent of the Edgar Thomson steel works, was born at Hyde Park, (Scranton,) Luzerne county, Pennsylvania, on February 23, 1839, and died at Braddock on September 28, 1889, in his 51st year. He was fatally burned by the bursting of Furnace C.

The deaths of Henry Chisholm and Alfred Hunt, which properly should be recorded in this connection, have already been noticed in the Ohio and Pennsylvania chapters.

CHAPTER XLVII.

THE MANUFACTURE OF OPEN-HEARTH STEEL.

THE open-hearth process for the manufacture of steel, of which the Siemens-Martin furnace is the most popular type, consists in melting pig iron in a large dish-shaped vessel, or reverberatory furnace, and afterwards decarburizing it by adding wrought iron, steel scrap, or iron ore, a deficiency of carbon being supplied, as in the Bessemer process, by the application of spiegeleisen or ferro-manganese. The product is steel, containing any percentage of carbon that may be desired. The materials used are melted by the union in the furnace of atmospheric air and combustible gases, affording an intense heat. All of the heat employed is obtained by the use of a regenerative gas furnace. The melted pig iron, previous to receiving the decarburizing ingredients, is termed a bath. The quantity of steel which may be made at one operation, or heat, ranges from five to thirty-five tons, according to the size of the furnace.

The open-hearth process, although capable of producing as large masses of steel as the Bessemer process, is much slower in its operation, but it possesses the advantage over its rival that the melted mixture may be indefinitely kept in a state of fusion until experiments with small portions determine the exact conditions necessary to produce a required quality of steel. Another important distinction may be noticed. While the cardinal features of both the Bessemer and the open-hearth processes embrace strictly chemical operations on a large scale, no direct manipulation of the contents of the Bessemer converter or the open-hearth furnace being necessary, there is this mechanical difference, that the success of the former mainly rests upon the wonderful power and perfection of the machinery by which it is operated, while the success of the latter mainly rests upon the appliances for producing and storing up the gases used in creating combustion.

Both processes may be combined with already-existing

iron rolling mills or crucible steel works, but the open-hearth process can be most economically added to such establishments, and this is one cause of its increasing popularity, although, as already intimated, its productive capabilities are much less than those of the Bessemer process. The open-hearth process is also especially adapted to the utilization of the scrap steel and rail ends which accumulate at Bessemer steel works, and very naturally, therefore, many open-hearth furnaces have been built in connection with these works, both in Europe and in the United States. Another advantage of this process is its ready adaptation to the remelting of worn-out steel rails for the production of steel in other forms. A popular use of the open-hearth process in both Europe and America is the production of steel plates for boilers and fire-boxes. On both continents open-hearth steel is also largely used as a substitute for iron in shipbuilding and bridge-building. It is also rapidly coming into use in all countries in the manufacture of all kinds of tools, and generally as a competitor of wrought iron and other kinds of steel.

The importance of the two processes which have been mentioned, and the extent of the revolution they have effected, may be inferred from the fact that they have unitedly increased the world's production of steel at least one hundred fold in the last thirty-five years.

Previous to 1856, the same year in which Mr. Bessemer obtained his most important patent, (February 12, 1856,) Dr. Charles William Siemens, in conjunction with his brother, Frederick Siemens, both of whom were natives of Hanover, in Germany, but at the time were citizens of England and residents of London, devoted his inventive genius to the construction of a gas furnace for the manufacture of iron, steel, glass, and other products which require a high and uniform heat. These gentlemen were in that year successful in perfecting the Siemens regenerative gas furnace, which has since been widely introduced in Europe and in this country, and without which no open-hearth steel can be made. The first patent in connection with this invention was granted in 1856 to Frederick Siemens alone.

As early as 1861 Dr. Siemens experimented with the regenerative furnace in the production of cast steel in a reverberatory furnace, or open-hearth, for which application of the regenerative furnace he obtained a patent. He subsequently encountered great practical difficulties in establishing his process of making steel, efforts to accomplish this result being made in 1862 at Tow Law and in 1863 and 1864 at Barrow and Fourchambault, the first two places being in England and the last place being in France.

In 1864 Messrs. Emile and Pierre Martin, of the Sireuil works, in France, erected with the assistance of Dr. Siemens one of the Siemens regenerative gas furnaces to melt steel in an open-hearth, or reverberatory furnace, of their own construction. In this furnace they produced cast steel of good quality and various tempers, and at the Paris Exposition of 1867 their product secured for them a gold medal. Previous to this time and subsequently the Messrs. Martin obtained patents for various inventions which were applicable to the manufacture of steel by the Siemens regenerative furnace. Their principal patent, describing the combined process of decarburization and recarburization, was obtained in France in 1865.

Dr. Siemens claims, in a letter which is now before us, that both at Tow Law and Fourchambault cast steel had been produced from pig iron, spiegeleisen, and scrap iron upon an open-hearth which had been especially constructed by himself for that purpose *previous* to the Messrs. Martin's connection with the process. The furnace at Tow Law was a small one, and several such furnaces were at work there a few years ago in the manner originally designed by Dr. Siemens. In 1865 Dr. Siemens commenced the erection at Birmingham, in England, of steel works of his own, in which the regenerative furnace should be used in producing steel. These works, which were completed in 1867, have produced satisfactory results.

The Messrs. Martin devoted their efforts to the production of steel by the use of wrought iron and steel scrap and also iron ore as decarburizers in a bath of pig iron, while the efforts of Dr. Siemens were more especially directed to the production of steel by the use of iron ore alone as a decarburizer in a bath of pig iron, the ore being either in the raw state or in a more or less reduced condition. Until recently the "pig and ore" method was generally employed in Great Britain. The "pig and scrap" method is chiefly used on the Continent and in this country. In Great Britain a combination of both methods is to-day in use. Under an agreement between the Messrs. Martin and Dr. Siemens the open-hearth process as developed by them was called the Martin-Siemens process on the Continent and the Siemens-Martin process in Great Britain. In this country this process is uniformly styled the Siemens-Martin process. The credit of introducing the "pig and scrap" method into this country is due to the Hon. Abram S. Hewitt, of New York, who was favorably impressed with it when visiting the Paris Exposition in 1867 as a commissioner of the United States. At his request Mr. Frederick J. Slade, his assistant, went to Sireuil to study the process that it might be put into practice in this country.

Dr. Siemens and the Messrs. Martin obtained patents in this country for the use of their respective processes for manufacturing steel, and Dr. Siemens also obtained American patents for the Siemens gas furnace. The validity of the Martin patents in this country was never sustained by the courts.

The open-hearth process in the manufacture of steel did not originate with either Dr. Siemens or the Martins, having been proposed and experimented with by various other inventors prior to their connection with it, among whom Josiah Marshall Heath was most prominent as early as 1845, but it is entirely just to add that it was not made a success until the great heat supplied by the Siemens regenerative gas furnace was applied to it.

In the conversion into steel of the raw materials used in the open-hearth process the invention of Mr. Mushet, described in the preceding chapter, is indispensable. The dephosphorizing process of Messrs. Thomas and Gilchrist is also applicable to the manufacture of steel in the open-hearth when the materials to be used contain a large percentage of phosphorus.

On the 1st of December, 1862, Park, McCurdy & Co., of Pittsburgh, sent Lewis Powe, the manager of their copper works, to England to study the manufacture of tinplates. While there he visited Birmingham and saw a Siemens gas furnace and procured one of the Siemens pamphlets containing a full description of it. On his return home he called the attention of Mr. James Park, Jr., to the merits of the furnace. Immediately after July 4, 1863, the erection of a Siemens gas furnace was commenced at the copper works. This furnace was erected for the purpose of melting and refining copper, and was completed on the 14th of August, 1863. It was constructed after the drawings contained in the Siemens pamphlet and worked well. In the fall of 1863 Mr. Powe revisited England, and while there had an interview with Dr. Siemens. Soon afterwards the firm of Park, Brother & Co. built a Siemens furnace to heat steel, but it was not a success. In 1864 James B. Lyon & Co., of Pittsburgh, built a Siemens gas furnace for making glass. The enterprise, however, although mechanically successful, met with an accident which suddenly brought it to an end. This furnace was also constructed after published designs. The introduction into this country of the Siemens furnace by each of the above-named firms was accomplished in an irregular manner, without first obtaining licenses from Dr. Siemens.

The first Siemens gas furnace that was regularly introduced into this country for any purpose was built by John A. Griswold & Co., at Troy, New York, and used as a heating furnace in their rolling mill, the license having been granted on the 18th of September, 1867. The next gas furnace that was regularly introduced was used as a heating furnace by the Nashua Iron and Steel Company, of New Hampshire, the license for which was granted on the 26th of September, 1867. The next furnace that was regularly introduced was built by Anderson & Woods, of Pittsburgh, for melting steel in pots, the license for which was dated in November, 1867. About 1869 the owners of the Lenox plate-glass works, in Massachusetts, also built a Siemens gas furnace. All of these furnaces gave satisfaction.

The first open-hearth furnace introduced into this country for the manufacture of steel by the Siemens-Martin process was built in 1868 by Frederick J. Slade for Cooper, Hewitt & Co., owners of the works of the New Jersey Steel and Iron Company, at Trenton, New Jersey. The building of this furnace was commenced in the spring of 1868, and in December of the same year it was successfully put in operation.

The Pernot furnace is a modification of the open-hearth process which has been introduced into the United States from France, but, while producing good steel, it is not likely to grow in favor because of the great trouble and expense which are necessary to keep it in working order. The Ponsard furnace is another modification, but it has not been experimented with in this country and is not likely to be.

The first successful application in this country of the Siemens regenerative gas furnace to the puddling of iron was made under the direction of William F. Durfee at the rolling mill of the American Silver Steel Company, at Bridgeport, Connecticut, in 1869. Prior to this event an unsuccessful attempt was made to accomplish the same result at the Eagle rolling mill of James Wood & Co., on Saw Mill run, near Pittsburgh.

Experimental works were erected at Pittsburgh in 1877 by Park, Brother & Co., in conjunction with Miller, Metcalf & Parkin, for the manufacture of refined iron directly from the ore by a process invented by Dr. Siemens and successfully tested by him at his experimental works at Towcester, England. The process embodies the application of the Siemens gas furnace. The experiment was abandoned in 1879, the results not being satisfactory. The same process was subsequently applied at Tyrone Forges, in Pennsylvania, by Anderson & Co., of Pittsburgh. In 1881 Robert J. Anderson and his associates, under the name of the Siemens-Anderson Steel Company, built extensive works of the same character at Pittsburgh. Neither the enterprise at Tyrone Forges nor the last-mentioned enterprise at Pittsburgh was long in operation. Other processes for the manufacture of iron or steel directly from the ore have been tried in this country and have commended themselves more or less to popular favor, all being used in connection with the open-hearth furnace. The Adams direct process has been in use at Indianapolis, Indiana, and at Pittsburgh. Some preparations have been made to introduce it at other places. The Carbon Iron Company has in successful operation at Pittsburgh another direct process; and at Brewster, in Putnam county, New York, the Conley-Lancaster direct process has attracted some attention.

In an official report by Dr. Wm. M. Sweet, special agent

for the collection of the statistics of iron and steel in the census year 1890, dated on October 31, 1890, we find the following statement concerning the manufacture of basic open-hearth steel in the United States.

The first basic steel made in the United States was produced experimentally at Steelton, Pennsylvania, by the Pennsylvania Steel Company, on May 24, 1884, in a Bessemer converter. The beginning of the manufacture of basic steel in this country as a commercial product, however, dates from 1888, on the 28th of March of which year the first basic open-hearth steel was produced at the Homestead steel works of Carnegie, Phipps & Company Limited, at Homestead, near Pittsburgh, Pennsylvania. Since that date the manufacture of basic open-hearth steel has been continued at these works, and during 1890 this firm commenced the erection of eight additional open-hearth furnaces for the, manufacture of basic steel, of which number four are now in operation and the remaining four furnaces are expected to be ready for working in a short time. When completed these works will contain 16 open-hearth furnaces prepared to manufacture basic steel. The manufacture of basic steel is now also regularly carried on at the Steelton works of the Pennsylvania Steel Company, where a combination of the Bessemer and open-hearth processes is used. During 1890 the Henderson Steel and Manufacturing Company, at Birmingham, Alabama, produced steel experimentally by the basic process. Since the close of the census year the Southern Iron Company has successfully commenced the manufacture of basic open-hearth steel at its works at Chattanooga, Tennessee, [the exact date of this event being September 15, 1890.] The Pottstown Iron Company, at Pottstown, Pennsylvania, has also produced steel by the basic process.

The total production of basic steel in the United States during the census year 1890 [ending on June 30, 1890,] amounted to 62,173 tons of 2,000 pounds, nearly all of which was made by the basic open-hearth method, a small part being produced by the duplex process, a combination of the Bessemer and open-hearth methods.

The production of basic steel by the open-hearth and duplex processes in the calendar year 1890 probably amounted to about 90,000 net tons, or over one-seventh of the open-hearth production of the year. On August 24, 1891, basic steel was successfully produced in the Bessemer converter of the Southern Iron Company, at Chattanooga, Tennessee. This was the first basic Bessemer steel produced in the South.

The production of open-hearth steel in the United States in 1870 was only 1,500 net tons, and in 1873 it was only 3,500 tons. The production in the census year 1880 was 84,302 net tons. Only 9,105 tons of rails were made. At the close of the census year 1880 there were 37 completed open-hearth furnaces in the United States. Since 1884 the production of open-hearth steel has steadily increased, amounting in 1890 to 574,820 net tons. Only 4,018 tons of rails were made, nearly all in California. The total number of completed open-hearth steel works in the United States at the close of 1890 was 62.

Our open-hearth steel industry is already an important factor in supplying the domestic demand for steel for all purposes for which Bessemer steel and the ordinary qualities of crucible steel may be used. This industry is destined to be still further developed in the immediate future.

The following table shows in net tons the production of open-hearth steel in the United States from 1870 to 1890.

Years.	Net tons.	Years.	Net tons.	Years.	Net tons.
1870	1,500	1877	25,081	1884	131,617
1871	2,000	1878	36,126	1885	149,381
1872	3,000	1879	56,290	1886	245,250
1873	3,500	1880	112,953	1887	360,717
1874	7,000	1881	146,946	1888	352,036
1875	9,050	1882	160,542	1889	419,488
1876	21,490	1883	133,679	1890	574,820

Great Britain is the largest producer of open-hearth steel in the world, and in this branch of the steel industry the United States is still a long distance behind its great iron and steel rival. Only a small part of Great Britain's annual production is made by the basic process. The following table gives in gross tons the production of open-hearth steel in Great Britain from 1879 to 1890.

Years.	Gross tons.	Years.	Gross tons.	Years.	Gross tons.
1879	175,000	1883	455,500	1887	981,104
1880	251,000	1884	475,250	1888	1,292,742
1881	338,000	1885	583,918	1889	1,429,169
1882	436,000	1886	694,150	1890	1,564,200

The distinguished scientist, Dr. Charles William Siemens, died suddenly at London, on November 20, 1883, of rupture of the heart, produced by a fall in Park Lane. He was born at Lenthe, in Hanover, on the 4th of April, 1823, and was consequently in his 61st year at the time of his death. In April of the year in which he died the honor of knighthood was conferred upon him for his distinguished services as a scientist. He was thereafter known as Sir William Siemens.

CHAPTER XLVIII.

THE EARLY HISTORY OF IRON RAILS IN THE UNITED STATES.

THE influence of railroads upon the development of the iron and steel industries of the United States has been so great that we may appropriately present in this chapter the leading facts connected with the laying of the first rails upon American railroads and with the manufacture of the first American rails.

The first railroads in the United States were built to haul gravel, stone, mineral coal, and other heavy materials, and were all short, the longest not exceeding a few miles in length. Strictly speaking they were tramroads and not railroads. One of these was built on Beacon Hill, in Boston, by Silas Whitney, in 1807; another by Thomas Leiper, in Delaware county, Pennsylvania, in 1809; and another at Bear Creek furnace, in Armstrong county, Pennsylvania, in 1818. The tracks of these roads were composed of wooden rails. Other short tramroads were built at various places early in this century and were similarly constructed. In George W. Smith's notes on Wood's *Treatise on Railroads* (1832) it is stated that in 1816 the first railroad in the United States on which self-acting inclined planes were used was "built by Mr. Boggs," on the Kiskiminetas river, in Western Pennsylvania. This road was used to convey bituminous coal to Andrew Boggs's salt works below Saltsburg.

Prior to 1809 Oliver Evans, of Philadelphia, to whom as much as to any other person the honor of inventing the locomotive is due, urged in repeated addresses to the public the construction of a passenger railroad from Philadelphia to New York, and in that year he unsuccessfully attempted to form a company for this purpose. In 1812 Colonel John Stevens, of Hoboken, New Jersey, published a pamphlet recommending the building of a passenger railroad from Albany to Lake Erie, but his suggestions were not heeded. In the *History of Morris County*, New Jersey, Mr. Halsey says : " As

early as 1815 a railroad, either of wood or iron, was chartered from the Delaware river near Trenton to the Raritan
near New Brunswick. This was the first railroad chartered
in America. It was never built."

On April 7, 1823, the New York legislature chartered the
Delaware and Hudson Canal Company to construct a canal
and railroad from the coal fields of Pennsylvania to the
Hudson river at Rondout, in New York. The canal was
completed in 1828, but the railroad was not completed until
1829. The latter was 16 miles long, and extended from
Honesdale to Carbondale. It was built to carry coal.

In 1826 the Quincy Railroad, in Massachusetts, 4 miles
long, including branches, was built by Gridley Bryant and
Colonel T. H. Perkins to haul granite blocks from the Quincy
quarries to the port of Neponset. The rails of this road were
made of wood, but strapped with iron plates 3 inches wide
and ¼ of an inch thick. In 1827 the Mauch Chunk Railroad,
in Carbon county, Pennsylvania, 9 miles long, with 4 miles of
sidings, was built to connect the coal mines of the Lehigh
Coal and Navigation Company with the Lehigh river. Its
rails were made of wood and strapped with iron. Gordon,
in his *Gazetteer of the State of Pennsylvania*, says of this road :
" The railway is of timber, about 20 feet long, 4 inches by 5,
and set in cross-pieces made of cloven trees placed 3½ feet
from each other and secured by wedges. The rail is shod on
the upper and inner edge with a flat bar of iron 2¼ inches
wide and ⅜ of an inch thick." In the Philadelphia *Railway World* for May 8, 1875, Mr. Solomon W. Roberts says of
the Mauch Chunk road : " It was laid mostly on the turnpike,
and was a wooden track, with a gauge of 3 feet 7 inches, and
the wooden rails were strapped with common merchant bar
iron, the flat bars being about 1½ inches wide and ⅜ of an
inch thick. The holes for the spikes were drilled by hand.
Although a great deal of bar iron of somewhat varying sizes
was bought for the purpose the supply fell short, and to
prevent delay in opening the road strips of hard wood were
spiked down in place of iron on about a mile and a half or
two miles of the road, as a temporary expedient."

Mr. Roberts relates that the Lehigh Coal and Navigation
Company made a short section of experimental railroad at its

Mauch Chunk foundry in the summer of 1826. "The idea then was to make a road with rails and chairs of cast iron, like those in use at the coal mines in the North of England. After casting a good many rails, each about four feet long, the plan was given up on account of its being too expensive."

In 1826 the New York legislature granted a charter for the construction of the Mohawk and Hudson Railroad, for the carriage of freight and passengers from Albany to Schenectady, a distance of 17 miles. Work on this road, however, was not commenced until August, 1830. It was opened for travel on September 12, 1831.

On February 28, 1827, the Maryland legislature granted a charter for the construction of the Baltimore and Ohio Railroad, which was the first railroad in the United States that was opened for the conveyance of passengers. Its construction was commenced on July 4, 1828, the venerable Charles Carroll, of Carrollton, laying the corner-stone. In 1829 the track was finished to Vinegar Hill, a distance of about 7 miles, and "cars were put upon it for the accommodation of the officers and to gratify the curious by a ride." Mr. Poor, in his *Manual of the Railroads of the United States*, says that the road was opened for travel from Baltimore to Ellicott's Mills, a distance of 13 miles, on May 24, 1830. The Washington branch was opened from Relay to Bladensburg on July 20, 1834, and to Washington City on August 25, 1834.

The next passenger railroad that was undertaken in the United States was the Charleston and Hamburg Railroad, in South Carolina, which was chartered on December 19, 1827. Six miles of the road were completed in 1829, but they were not opened to the public until December 6, 1830, when a locomotive was placed on the track. The road was completed in September, 1833, a distance of 135 miles. At that time it was the longest continuous line of railroad in the world. The Columbia branch was opened on November 1, 1840, and the Camden branch on June 26, 1848. We need not further note the beginning of early American railroads.

The rails used on the Charleston and Hamburg and the Mohawk and Hudson railroads were made of wood, with flat bar iron nailed on their upper surface. A writer in Brown's *History of the First Locomotives in America* says that the track of the Baltimore and Ohio Railroad consisted of cedar cross-pieces and of string-pieces of yellow pine "from 12 to 24 feet long and 6 inches square, and slightly beveled on the top of the upper side for the flange of the wheels, which was at that time on the outside. On these string-pieces iron rails were placed and securely nailed down with wrought-iron nails, 4 inches long. After several miles of this description of road had been made long granite slabs were substituted for the cedar cross-pieces and the yellow-pine stringers. Beyond Vinegar Hill these huge blocks of this solid material could be seen deposited along the track, and gangs of workmen engaged in the various operations of dressing, drilling, laying, and affixing the iron." Brown says that "iron strips were laid, for miles and miles, on stone curbs on the Baltimore and Ohio Railroad." Appletons' *American Cyclopædia* says that the iron used was ½ and ⅝ of an inch thick, and from 2½ to 4½ inches wide, and that the heads of the spikes which fastened it were countersunk in the iron.

Before the Baltimore and Ohio Railroad had been built to Point of Rocks in 1832 "wrought-iron rails of the English mode," says Brown, had been laid down on a part of the line. It had been found in practice that the strap rail would become loosened from the wooden or stone stringer, and that the ends of it, called "snakes' heads," were liable to be forced by the wheels through the bottom of the cars, to the jeopardy of the passengers. The English rails obviated this inconvenience and risk. Some account of these rails is here given.

About the time when the Baltimore and Ohio Railroad was finished to Point of Rocks various patterns of heavy rolled iron rails were in use in England. The first of these to be used was the fish-bellied rail, which was invented by John Birkinshaw, of the Bedlington iron works, and patented in October, 1820, and which fitted into a cast-iron chair. A thin wedge, or key, of wrought iron was driven between the inside of the chair and the rail, to keep the latter firmly in its place, and the operation of "driving keys" had to be repeated almost every day.

The Birkinshaw rail was used on the Stockton and Darlington Railroad in England, which was opened in September, 1825, and was the first railroad in the world that was opened for general freight traffic and passenger travel. The greater part of the Stockton and Darlington road, which was 37 miles long, was laid with rolled rails of this pattern, weighing 28 pounds to the yard; a small part of the line was laid with fish-bellied cast-iron rails. The Liverpool and Manchester Railroad, which was opened in September, 1830, and which was the second railroad built in England for general business in the transportation of freight and passengers, used rails which were also of the Birkinshaw pattern. "The rails used were made of forged iron, in lengths of 15 feet each, and weighed 175 pounds each. At the distance of every 3 feet the rail rests on blocks of stone. Into each block two holes, 6 inches deep and 1 inch in diameter, are drilled; into these are driven oak plugs, and the cast-iron chairs into which the rails are fitted are spiked down to the plugs, forming a structure of great solidity." This road was about 31 miles long.

The Clarence rail was an English improvement on the Birkinshaw rail; it also rested in a chair, but it did not have the fish-belly, its upper and lower surfaces being parallel to each other. Rails of the Clarence pattern were used on the Allegheny Portage Railroad in Pennsylvania, which was finished in 1833, and many of the stone blocks on which they were laid can yet be seen in its abandoned bed. The Columbia and Philadelphia Railroad was opened on the 16th of April, 1834. On a small part of this road flat rails were laid, either directly on granite blocks or on wooden string-pieces, but on the greater part of it Clarence rails were laid on stone blocks. On the Boston and Lowell Railroad, which was chartered in June, 1830, and completed in 1835, stone cross-ties were at first laid, some of which were in use as late as 1852. On one track of this road the fish-bellied Birkinshaw rail was used and on the other the H rail was laid. This rail, which rested in a chair, had a web, or flange, similar to that of the modern T rail. The H rail was laid on the Washington branch of the Baltimore and Ohio Railroad. It was 15 feet in length, weighed 40 pounds to the yard, and was laid on string-pieces of wood. Wooden cross-ties have been substituted for stone blocks on all American railroads.

The flat rail which was first used on American railroads continued in use for many years, notwithstanding the diffi-

culty experienced in keeping it in its place. At first the holes
for the spikes were drilled by hand. The flat rails that were
afterwards made were indented, or countersunk, at regular
distances in their passage through the rolls. The centre of
the countersunk surface was then punched through for the
admission of the spike. As late as 1837, when the Erie and
Kalamazoo Railroad was in course of construction from Toledo to Adrian, it was proposed to put down wooden rails of
oak studding 4 inches square, and to draw the cars by horses.
But wiser counsels prevailed, and by great exertions sufficient
funds were obtained to enable the management to iron the
road with flat rails $\frac{5}{8}$ of an inch thick. In 1839 the first
railroad in Illinois, known as the Northern Cross, which now
forms a part of the Wabash system, was completed. The road
extended from Jacksonville to Meredosia, a distance of 24
miles; it was built by the State and laid with flat iron. Mr.
Poor says: "It was not until 1850 that the longitudinal sill
and the flat rail were entirely removed from the Utica and
Schenectady Railroad, the most important link in the New
York Central line." Flat rails were in use on many other
railroads in this country after 1850, and may yet be seen on
some Southern railroads. They are also in use on street railroads and on some mine roads.

The following extract from a New York newspaper, dated
May 30, 1844, shows the risk to which travelers were subjected who journeyed on railroads the tracks of which were laid
with flat rails.

RAILROAD CASUALTY.—The cars on the railroad a short distance east of
Rome, New York, came in contact with a "snake head" on Saturday morning which threw several of the passenger cars and the mail car off the
track. The crush was tremendous, and the cars were torn to splinters,
though happily no lives were lost. Mr. Peter Van Wie was badly bruised
and some others slightly injured.

Cast-iron rails were made in this country in small quantities during the early years of our railroad history, notwithstanding the unfavorable experiment in their use at Mauch
Chunk which is noted by Mr. Roberts. Johnson, in his *Notes
on the Use of Anthracite*, published in 1841, records a series of
tests made in that year with rails for mine roads which were
cast in a foundry from pig iron made at the Pottsville fur-

nace of William Lyman. These rails were 6 feet long and were of various weights. It is particularly stated of one rail which was tested that it was "intended to sustain locomotives." The rails were bulbous at both the top and bottom, like the double-headed, or H, rail now used in England, but at each end, for about 3 inches along the base, they had flanges for securing them to the cross-ties, which caused an end view of them to resemble that of a modern T rail.

Many years elapsed after the first railroad was built in this country before any other than flat iron rails were made in American rolling mills. Among the proposals to furnish heavy rails for the Columbia and Philadelphia Railroad, received in May, 1831, there were none for American rails, and the whole quantity was purchased in England. It is necessary to explain here that previous to the passage of the tariff act of September 11, 1841, rails were admitted into the United States free of duty when proof was furnished that they had actually been laid on railroads and inclined planes. On the passage of that act and the more comprehensive tariff act of 1842 American capitalists began to prepare for the manufacture of heavy rails.

Early in 1844 there were still no facilities in this country for the manufacture of heavy iron rails to supply the wants of the 4,185 miles of American railroad which existed at the beginning of that year, and of a few hundred additional miles which were then projected. In a memorial which was laid before Congress in that year the Hon. John Tucker, the president of the Philadelphia and Reading Railroad Company, and afterwards Assistant Secretary of War, made the following declaration under date of May 4, 1844.

Immediately on the line of the road are rich mines of iron ore. Last fall and winter it was generally known in that section of the State through which the road passes, as well as on other portions of it, that this company intended to lay a second track, and that about 8,300 tons of railroad iron was wanted. Public proposals were issued for all the materials required, except the iron. The iron was not included in these proposals for the simple reason that I knew that it could not be furnished in this country but I had interviews with several of the largest ironmasters, and freely expressed my desire to contract for American railroad iron, provided it could be furnished at the time it was wanted. I received no proposition to deliver the rolled bars. I inclose a copy of a letter from one of the largest ironmongers in the State, offering cast-iron rails, which, I presume you are aware, have not answered any good purpose. I also inclose a copy of my answer, to which I have not received a reply. I unhesitatingly express my conviction that the railroad iron needed by this company could not have been obtained in this country, at the time they required it, at any price; and I am equally confident that there are no parties ready to contract to deliver such iron for a long time to come. This company was therefore compelled to import their iron.

The following is the correspondence referred to above concerning the proposition to make cast-iron rails for the Philadelphia and Reading Railroad Company.

PHILADELPHIA, November 7, 1843.

MR. TUCKER. DEAR SIR: Since my conversation with you, in relation to substituting cast-iron rails for your new track of rails which you contemplate laying soon, I have concluded to propose to you that I should cast eighteen bar-rails 15 feet long from the model in the Franklin Institute, as a sample of the strength and durability of rails made from cast iron. The price to be $30 per ton cash upon delivering at Broad street.

With respect, yours,   CLEMENT B. GRUBB.
Direct Lancaster, Pennsylvania.

———

OFFICE OF THE PHILADELPHIA AND READING RAILROAD COMPANY, }
PHILADELPHIA, November —, 1843. }

CLEMENT B. GRUBB, ESQ., *Lancaster.* DEAR SIR: I duly received your communication of the 7th instant. This company is not disposed to make any experiment with the cast-iron rails on their own account. But if you choose to send the eighteen bars they shall be laid on the road; and if, after a trial of six months, they are found to answer a good purpose the company will pay you $30 per ton for the rails. If they are not suitable for the road they will then be delivered to you, the company merely incurring the expense of laying down and taking up the rails.

Your obedient servant,   JOHN TUCKER, *President.*

No reply to this letter was received. The 8,300 tons of rails which were wanted by Mr. Tucker, and which he was compelled to buy in England, were of the H pattern, then very popular. The rails weighed 60 pounds to the yard and cost £5 10s. per ton in England.

In a letter dated May 22, 1844, which formed part of the above-mentioned memorial to Congress, Joseph E. Bloomfield made the following statement.

There is no doubt of the fact that there are no establishments for the manufacture of railroad iron in Pennsylvania prepared to produce a moiety of the iron required for the railways actually commenced. Mr. Oakley, of Brooklyn, made a statement, that at the time was combated and denied, that he could furnish from one set of works 10,000 tons of railroad iron per annum. This is so palpably incorrect that it needs no refutation. There is no iron establishment of this kind in this country.

On the 24th of April, 1844, the Hon. Edward Joy Morris, a member of Congress from Pennsylvania, declared that " not a ton of T rail had yet been made in this country." The manufacture of heavy iron rails in this country was commenced early in 1844 at the Mount Savage rolling mill, in Alleghany county, Maryland, which was built in 1843 by the Maryland and New York Iron and Coal Company especially to roll these rails. The first rail rolled at this rolling mill, and in honor of which the Franklin Institute of Philadelphia awarded a silver medal in October, 1844, (now in the museum at Ince Blundell, Lancashire, England,) was an inverted U rail, known in Wales as the Evans patent, of the Dowlais iron works, at Merthyr Tydvil. It was intended to be laid on a wooden longitudinal sill and to be fastened to it by an iron wedge, keying under the sill, thus dispensing with outside fastenings. This rail weighed 42 pounds to the yard. About 500 tons of rails of this pattern were rolled early in 1844 and laid in that year on a part of the road then being built between Mount Savage and Cumberland, a distance of nine miles. In that year rails weighing 50 pounds to the yard were also rolled at the Mount Savage rolling mill for the road leading from Fall River to Boston. These last rails were T rails, and were ordered by Colonel Borden, of Fall River. The foregoing information we have obtained from Mr. Henry Thomas Weld, of Mount Savage. Mr. Stephen S. Lee, of the old firm of Manning & Lee, of Baltimore, says that in 1845 and 1846 the firm sold to Boston purchasers T rails which were made at Mount Savage. The Mount Savage rolling mill was still rolling rails as late as 1856, but was dismantled in 1875, after having been abandoned for many years. Mr. Weld tells us that U rails were in use in the sidings of the Cumberland and Pennsylvania Railroad as late as 1869. We have a piece of an inverted U rail in our office.

The Montour rolling mill, at Danville, Pennsylvania, was built in 1845 expressly to roll rails, and it is claimed that here were rolled in October of that year the first T rails made in the United States. The facts above presented give this honor to the Mount Savage rolling mill. T-rail rolls were made for the Montour rolling mill by Haywood & Snyder, proprietors of the Colliery iron works at Pottsville, the work being done at their branch establishment at Danville. The Boston iron works were started in January, 1824, to manufacture cut nails, hoops, and tack plates, but they subsequently rolled rails, and on the 6th of May, 1846, they rolled the first T rails in Massachusetts, Ralph Crooker being superintendent. In 1845 the rolling mill of Cooper & Hewitt was built at Trenton, New Jersey, to roll heavy rails, and on the 19th of June, 1846, their first T rail was rolled. About the 1st of September, 1846, the New England Iron Company, at Providence, Rhode Island, commenced to roll T rails. The first lot of these rails rolled by the company was delivered to the Providence and Worcester Railroad on September 11, 1846. T rails were rolled in November, 1846, at Phœnixville, Pennsylvania; in the fall of the same year at the Great Western iron works at Brady's Bend, Pennsylvania, and at the Lackawanna iron works at Scranton, Pennsylvania; early in 1847 at the Bay State rolling mill, in Boston, then owned by the Massachusetts Iron Company; in January, 1848, at the Rough-and-Ready rolling mill at Danville, Pennsylvania; and in the same year at Safe Harbor, Pennsylvania. On May 10, 1848, Manning & Lee, the agents of the Avalon iron works, near Baltimore, Maryland, contracted to obtain at these works for the Baltimore and Ohio Railroad Company 400 tons of U rails, to weigh 51 pounds to the yard and to be from 19 to 21 feet in length, the price to be $65 per gross ton, delivered at Baltimore. These rails were made in 1848. All of the T rails made at the mills above mentioned were rolled with a base or flange similar to that of the present T rail. Some of them did not differ greatly from the H rail, and when laid rested, like it, in a chair. Indeed the H rail was sometimes called the T rail. A few other mills rolled heavy rails before 1850, but at the beginning of that year, owing to the severity of foreign competition under the tariff of 1846, only two out of fifteen rail mills in this country were in operation.

In a letter dated December 26, 1849, the Hon. Abram S. Hewitt described the state of our iron-rail industry at that time in the following language: "Of fifteen rail mills only two are in operation, doing partial work, and that only because their inland position secured them against foreign competition for the limited orders of neighboring railroads, and when these are executed not a single rail mill will be at work in the land."

From *A History of the Growth of the Steam Engine*, by Robert H. Thurston, we learn that the T rail which is now in general use is an American invention. Professor Thurston says: "Robert L. Stevens, the president and engineer of the Camden and Amboy Railroad, and a distinguished son of Colonel John Stevens, of Hoboken, was engaged, at the time of the opening of the Liverpool and Manchester Railroad, in the construction of the Camden and Amboy Railroad. It was here that the first of the now standard form of T rail was laid down. It was of malleable iron. It was designed by Mr. Stevens, and is known in the United States as the 'Stevens' rail. In Europe, where it was introduced some years afterwards, it is sometimes called the 'Vignoles' rail." This name is derived from Charles B. Vignoles, an English railroad engineer, who visited the United States in 1817 and remained here several years in the practice of his profession. The first Vignoles rail appears to have had a wider base and a shorter stem than the Stevens rail. (See *Life of Charles Blacker Vignoles*, by his son, 1889, page 224.) Professor Thurston adds that a part of the track of the Camden and Amboy Railroad at Bordentown was laid down and opened for business in 1831. T rails were laid on the whole line, which crossed the State of New Jersey.

Through the courtesy of Professor Thurston we have been furnished with a *fac-simile* of the circular issued by Mr. Stevens in 1830, inviting proposals from British manufacturers for supplying the Camden and Amboy Railroad with T rails. It will be found in our report on iron and steel forming a part of the tenth census (1880) of the United States. In this circular Mr. Stevens specified that the rail which he desired to have rolled should have a base, stem, and head like the T rail of the present day, the rail to be 12 or 16 feet long, and to be laid on cross-ties, but that it should have "projections on the lower flange at every two feet," where it would rest on the ties.

The sides of the rails rolled for Mr. Stevens were made straight, and without "the projections on the lower flange at every two feet" which were specified in his circular. These projections were intended to serve the purposes of the chairs then in use, by giving a broad base to the rail at its connection with the cross-ties. They were, of course, not necessary, but that the rails were rolled without them was clearly not in accordance with Mr. Stevens's original design. However, he may truthfully be said to have invented the T rail. It was the first heavy rail made which dispensed with chairs. Mr. Francis B. Stevens, of Hoboken, New Jersey, a nephew of Robert L. Stevens, has supplied us in the following letter with much valuable additional information concerning the history of the T rail.

HOBOKEN, NEW JERSEY, May 31, 1881.

DEAR SIR: In answer to your letter of the 27th instant I will say that I have always believed that Robert L. Stevens was the inventor of what is called the T rail, and also of the method of fastening it by spikes, and I have never known his right to the invention questioned.

The rail of the Liverpool and Manchester Railroad, on its opening, in September, 1830, was of wrought iron, divided into fish-bellied sections, each section being supported by a cast-iron chair, to which it was secured by a wooden wedge. This form was derived from the old cast-iron fish-bellied tram rail, cast in single sections, each about 36 inches long. This wrought-iron rail was afterwards improved by making its bottom straight uniformly throughout its length.

Mr. Stevens's invention consisted in adding the broad flange on the bottom, with a base sufficient to carry the load, and shaped so that it could be secured to the wood below it by spikes with hooked heads; thus dispensing with the cast-iron chair, and making the rail and its fastening such as it now is in common use. In the year 1836 and frequently afterwards he spoke to me about his invention of this rail, and told me that in London, after unsuccessful applications elsewhere in England, shortly after the opening of the Liverpool and Manchester Railroad, he had applied to Mr. Guest, a member of Parliament, who had large rolling mills in Wales, to take a contract to make his rail for the Camden and Amboy Railroad, of which he was the chief engineer; that Mr. Guest wished to take the contract, but considered that it would be impracticable to roll the rail straight; that, finally, Mr. Guest agreed to go to Wales with him and make a trial; that great difficulty was at first experienced, as the rails coming from the rolls curled like snakes, and distorted in every imaginable way; that, by perseverance, the rail was finally successfully rolled; and that Mr. Guest took the contract. The Camden and Amboy Railroad, laid with this rail, was opened October 9, 1832, two years after the opening of the Liverpool and Manchester Railroad. Of this I was a witness.

This rail, long known as the old Camden and Amboy rail, differed but little, either in shape or proportions, from the T rail now in common use, but weighed only 36 pounds to the yard. For the next six or eight years after the opening of the Camden and Amboy Railroad this rail was but little used here or abroad, nearly all the roads built in the United States using the flat iron bar, about $2\frac{1}{2}$ inches by $\frac{3}{4}$ inch, nailed to wooden rails, and the English continuing to use the chair and wedge.

My uncle always regretted that he had not patented his invention. He mentioned to me, upwards of forty years ago, that when advised by his friend, Mr. F. B. Ogden, the American consul at Liverpool, who was familiar with the circumstances of his invention, to patent it, he found that it was too late, and that his invention had become public property.

Yours Truly,   Francis B. Stevens.

Smith, in his notes on Wood's *Treatise on Railroads*, thus describes the T rail which was laid on the Camden and Amboy Railroad : " The rails are of rolled iron, 16 feet long, $2\frac{1}{8}$ inches wide on the top, $3\frac{1}{4}$ inches at the bottom, and $3\frac{1}{2}$ deep ; the neck half inch thick ; the weight is 209 pounds $= 39\frac{3}{16}$ pounds per yard ; they are secured by clamps of iron, riveted at the extremity of each bar. The rails are attached to the stone blocks and sleepers by means of nails or pins, at the sides, driven into wooden plugs ; chairs are dispensed with."

The first 30-foot rails rolled in this country are claimed to have been rolled at the Cambria iron works, at Johnstown, in 1855. These rails were perfectly made, but there being no demand for them they were used in the tracks of the Cambria Iron Company. It is claimed that the first 30-foot rails rolled in the country on order were rolled at the Montour rolling mill, at Danville, in January, 1859, for the Sunbury and Erie Railroad Company. The first 60-foot, or double-length, rails rolled in this country were rolled by the Edgar Thomson Steel Company, at Bessemer station, near Pittsburgh, in the fall of 1875, and were of steel. In 1877 the Lackawanna Iron and Coal Company, at Scranton, commenced to roll 60-foot steel rails. At the Centennial Exhibition at Philadelphia, in 1876, the Edgar Thomson Steel Company exhibited a steel rail which at that time was the longest steel rail that had ever been rolled. It was 120 feet long and weighed 62 pounds to the yard.

As late as 1880 the T rail was not much used in Great Britain. The pattern most in use in that country was the double-headed, or H, rail, which is set in a cast-iron chair. The bridge, or U, rail was in use on the Great Western Railway and on some other British railroads. The Clarence rail was used on the Great Eastern Railway, and perhaps on some other British railroads. In the United States the T rail is now almost exclusively used, and its weight per yard is heavier than formerly. It seems strange that this rail should not have become generally popular in this country until after 1845, having been used as early as 1831. We may here mention that the various patterns of rails which superseded the flat rail were long known as edge rails.

The first locomotive to run upon an American railroad was the *Stourbridge Lion*. It was first used at Honesdale, in Wayne county, Pennsylvania, on Saturday, August 8, 1829, on the coal, railroad of the Delaware and Hudson Canal Company. The *Stourbridge Lion* was built in England and weighed about six tons. Its use was not long continued because it was too heavy for the superstructure of a large part of the road. The first locomotive built in the United States and used on a railroad was the *Tom Thumb*, which was built by Peter Cooper at Baltimore and successfully experimented with on the Baltimore and Ohio Railroad in August, 1830. The fuel used for this pioneer American locomotive was anthracite coal. The boiler was tubular, and for want of specially-constructed tubes Mr. Cooper used gun barrels. The locomotive, which was also its own tender, did not weigh a ton ; the boiler was about as large as a flour barrel. Strictly speaking it was a working model, but it worked well and led the way to the construction of more powerful locomotives. Mr. Cooper was his own engineer. The first American locomotive that was built for actual service was the *Best Friend of Charleston*, which was built at the West Point foundry, in New York city, for the Charleston and Hamburg Railroad, and was successfully put in use on that road in December, 1830. On the Mohawk and Hudson Railroad, the Allegheny Portage Railroad, the Columbia and Philadelphia Railroad, and a few other railroads horse-power was exclusively used for some time after they were opened in the decade between 1830 and 1840.

Mr. Brown informs us that "the first charter for what are termed city passenger or horse railroads was obtained in the city of New York and known as the New York and Harlem, and this was the first road of the kind ever constructed, and was opened in 1832. No other road of the kind was completed till 1852, when the Sixth Avenue was opened to the public."

The first elevated city passenger railroad ever built was the Greenwich street railroad in New York, which was commenced in 1866 and has been in successful operation since 1872. It is now known as the Ninth Avenue Elevated Railway. The next project of this character was the Gilbert elevated railroad, in New York, for the construction of which a charter was granted in 1872. New York city has now several elevated local passenger railroads. As late as 1883 only one American city, Brooklyn, had copied the example of New York in building railroads of this class, but in 1891 Chicago also had an elevated railroad.

The first elevated railroad constructed in this country in connection with a regular freight and passenger railroad was undertaken by the Pennsylvania Railroad Company in 1880 and finished in 1881. It constitutes an extension of the main line of the Pennsylvania Railroad to the heart of the city of Philadelphia, and is over a mile long.

The production of iron rails in the United States has been as follows in net tons from 1849 to 1890. Since the beginning of 1883 the manufacture of iron rails has been almost entirely superseded by the manufacture of steel rails. Such iron rails as have since been made have been chiefly street rails and light rails for mines and tramways.

Years.	Net tons.	Years.	Net tons.	Years.	Net tons.
1849	24,318	1863	275,768	1877	332,540
1850	44,083	1864	335,369	1878	322,890
1851	50,603	1865	356,292	1879	420,160
1852	62,478	1866	430,778	1880	493,762
1853	87,864	1867	459,558	1881	488,581
1854	108,016	1868	499,489	1882	227,874
1855	138,674	1869	583,936	1883	64,954
1856	180,018	1870	586,000	1884	25,560
1857	161,918	1871	737,483	1885	14,815
1858	163,712	1872	905,930	1886	23.679
1859	195,454	1873	761,062	1887	23,062
1860	205,038	1874	584,469	1888	14,252
1861	189,818	1875	501,649	1889	10,258
1862	213,912	1876	467,168	1890	15,548

The excellent wearing qualities of American iron rails were well illustrated at the Philadelphia Exhibition in 1876, when the Cambria Iron Company exhibited an iron rail which had been in use nineteen years, three rails which had been in use eleven years, and five rails which had been in use ten years, all under severe wear. The same company also exhibited two iron rails which bridged a gap 12 feet wide and 12 feet deep that had been washed out under the track of a western railroad, and which carried safely over the gap an engine weighing 57,400 pounds and a train of seven cars.

In 1879 the American Iron and Steel Association collected a mass of statistics from American railroad companies relative to the wear of domestic and foreign steel rails, and the general conclusion was derived that American steel rails were superior to English steel rails, while the testimony of the Pennsylvania Railroad Company demonstrated that the American steel rails which had been laid in its tracks were wearing almost twice as well as the foreign steel rails it was also using.

In Poor's *Manual* for 1891 there appears the following table showing the extent to which steel rails had superseded iron rails in the United States down to 1890, double and side tracks being included in the figures given.

Years.	Miles of steel rails.	Miles of iron rails.	Total miles.	Per cent. steel of total.
1880	33,680	81,967	115,647	29.1
1881	49,063	81,473	130,536	37.5
1882	66,691	74,269	140,960	47.3
1883	78,491	70,692	149,183	52.7
1884	90,243	66,254	156,497	57.6
1885	98,102	62,495	160,597	61.0
1886	105,724	62,324	168,048	62.9
1887	125,459	59,588	185,047	67.7
1888	138,516	52,981	191,497	72.3
1889	151,723	50,513	202,236	75.0
1890	167,606	40,697	208,303	80.4

It will be noticed that, in the decade covered by the table, while the iron-rail mileage has decreased one-half the steel-rail mileage has increased fivefold, until at the present time 80 per cent. of our railroad tracks are laid with steel rails.

Henry Thomas Weld was in 1844 the managing agent and director for the English stockholders in the Mount Savage company. He was born at London on January 31, 1816, and was living at Mount Savage in September, 1891.

CHAPTER XLIX.

IRON SHIPBUILDING IN THE UNITED STATES.

In his admirable paper on the shipbuilding industry of the United States, to be found in the 8th volume of the reports of the census of 1880, Henry Hall says that in 1825 a small iron steamer, named the *Codorus*, was launched in Pennsylvania for service on the Susquehanna river, but he adds that this vessel may have been "one of several which were exported from England in pieces to America and put together here during that early period." Ten years later, in 1835, Mr. Hall says that "there were five iron steamers already on the Savannah river, which appear to have been built in the North." He also says that in 1836 an iron steam vessel was built at New York which engaged in the mail service to New Orleans. The iron vessels mentioned by Mr. Hall are the first in this country of which any record appears to have been preserved, and unfortunately the information which has been accessible to him is not complete.

In 1839 the first iron steamboat built for service on our western rivers was built at Pittsburgh and called the *Valley Forge*. She was launched on September 9, 1839. It was said when the *Valley Forge* was built that she was the first iron vessel "of any considerable size" that had been built in the country. The dimensions of the *Valley Forge* were as follows : Length on deck, 160 feet ; length of keel, 140 feet ; breadth of beam, 25 feet 4 inches ; depth of hold, 6 feet. For general navigation purposes the *Valley Forge* was completely successful. Other iron vessels were afterwards built at Pittsburgh which fully realized the hopes of their builders, among them an iron schooner for ocean service and an iron steamer, the *Michigan*, for service on the lakes—both built by order of the General Government about 1842. The *Michigan* was very recently in active service on the lakes as a revenue cutter. She was taken to Erie in sections on boats that were towed from the Ohio river through the Beaver Canal, and was put together at Erie. She was built of Sligo iron.

Mr. Hall says that in 1841 Jabez Coney built for the Government an iron revenue cutter, the *Saranac*, at Boston. Another authority says that Mr. Coney built the revenue cutter *McLaine* at Boston about 1842. Mr. Hall also says that "as early as 1842 Philadelphia had produced a line of small iron steamboats to trade to Hartford, Connecticut."

In 1842 Captain John Ericsson, of New York, furnished designs for four freight propeller iron steamers which were built for the Delaware and Raritan Canal, each 96 feet long, 24 feet beam, and 7 feet deep. In 1843 there was also built after his designs the propeller iron steamer *Legaré*, for the Government revenue service, 150 feet long, 26 feet beam, and 10 feet deep, and four iron propeller boats for the Erie Canal, each 80 feet long, 14 feet beam, and 6 feet deep. In the same year Captain Ericsson built two steam passenger boats of iron to run on the James River Canal, in Virginia, and about the same time other small iron vessels were built after his designs. In 1846 an iron passenger steamer, the *Iron Witch*, 220 feet long, 27 feet beam, and 13 feet deep, was built at New York, after designs furnished by Captain Ericsson, to run on the Hudson river to Albany. In 1845 R. B. Forbes, of Boston, built a powerful iron wrecking vessel of 300 tons' burden, which was named after himself. Other iron vessels were subsequently built at Boston and elsewhere. The building of iron vessels in this country made but slow progress, however, until after 1860, when the civil war created a demand for iron and ironclad war vessels, one of the first to be built being the celebrated *Monitor*.

Until recently the business of iron shipbuilding has not flourished in this country like other leading branches of American industry, but it has in the last few years attained to very respectable proportions, the building of a new American navy having given it a great impetus. In 1868 only five iron steamships were built for ocean service. Since that year over 600 iron and steel vessels have been built, chiefly at shipyards on the Delaware, not including naval vessels.

The first Transatlantic iron steamships to attract attention which were built in this country were the four vessels of the American Steamship Company's line, the *Pennsylvania*, *Ohio*, *Indiana*, and *Illinois*, built of Pennsylvania iron at Philadelphia in 1871, 1872, and 1873 by W. Cramp & Sons, and still running regularly between that port and European ports. Their tonnage capacity was originally 3,100 tons each. Most of the European visitors to the Centennial Exhibition came to Philadelphia and returned to their homes in the vessels of this line. In 1874 John Roach & Son built at Chester, Pennsylvania, for the Pacific Mail Steamship Company, two iron steamships of large size and superior equipment, which fully equaled in all respects the best British-built iron steamers. These were the *City of Peking* and the *City of Tokio*, twin vessels in every respect. Their registered tonnage was 5,000 tons each.

From a paper by Rev. Dr. Francis B. Wheeler, in which he acknowledges his indebtedness for valuable information to a paper by E. P. Dorr, which was read before the Buffalo Historical Society on the 3d of January, 1874, and from a statement prepared by Captain Ericsson we compile the following account of the building of the famous *Monitor*. This account we have submitted to the Hon. John F. Winslow, of Poughkeepsie, New York, one of the builders of the vessel, who pronounces it to be correct in every particular.

The *invention* of the *Monitor* belongs to Captain John Ericsson, of New York city, but its *creation* is due to two distinguished ironmasters of the State of New York, namely, the Hon. John F. Winslow and his partner in business, the Hon. John A. Griswold. They were not shipbuilders, had no special facilities for constructing vessels, and knew nothing by experience of the business, and there had never been any iron war ships built in this country ; hence for them to attempt to put afloat any kind of a war vessel was a hazardous experiment. The *Monitor* in all its parts was designed by Mr. Ericsson—hull, turret, steam machinery, anchor-hoister, gun-carriages, etc. ; all were built from working drawings made by his own hands, furnishing the rare instance of such a structure in all its details emanating from a single person. But the *Monitor* would not have been built if Messrs. Winslow & Griswold, who were iron manufacturers and men of the highest patriotism, had not pressed upon the Government the adoption of the inventor's daring scheme and afterwards furnished the means to secure the construction of the vessel.

Mr. Winslow carefully examined the plans prepared by Captain Ericsson for the construction of the *Monitor*—plans which had found no favor with the special naval board appointed in 1861, in accordance with an act of Congress, to examine and report upon the subject of iron-clad shipbuilding. Mr. Winslow became satisfied that Captain Ericsson's plans were both feasible and desirable. After conferring with his partner, Mr. Griswold, it was determined to lay the whole matter before President Lincoln. This was done in October, 1861. The earnestness with which Mr. Winslow and Mr. Griswold pressed the subject upon the attention of the President secured from him the promise that he would meet them on the next day at the office of Commodore Smith, a member of the board already referred to, and talk the subject over. The meeting took place. There were present Mr. Lincoln, the Secretary of the Navy, (Mr. Welles,) Commodore Smith, and other officials of the Navy Department. Mr. Winslow again presented the merits of Captain Ericsson's plans for the construction of the *Monitor*. The President expressed his wish that the subject should be still further investigated by Commodore Smith, and then withdrew. The interview resulted in a contract with Captain Ericsson and Messrs. Winslow & Griswold for the construction of the *Monitor*, the vessel to be placed in the hands of the Government within 100 days, at a cost of $275,000. Mr. C. S. Bushnell, the business associate of Captain Ericsson, also signed the contract. The contract was burdened with many exacting conditions and restrictions, which amounted to almost a prohibition of the enterprise. The contractors, however, at once entered upon their important undertaking. *Winslow & Griswold took all the risks of loss if the enterprise should prove to be a failure.* The hull of the vessel was built by Thomas F. Rowland, agent of the Continental iron works, at Green Point, Long Island, the plates, bars, and rivets being largely supplied to him by the Albany iron works of Winslow & Griswold. The Delamater iron works, of New York, were commissioned to manufacture the steam machinery, propellers, and internal apparatus of the turret. The Novelty iron works, of New York, built the turret, and the turret-plating and a part of the armor-plating, composed of a series of plates one inch thick, were rolled by H. Abbott & Son, of Baltimore. The port stoppers were assigned to Charles D. DeLancy, of Buffalo. The work was pushed with all diligence until the 30th of January, 1862, when the ship was launched at Green Point, 101 days from the execution of the contract. During its construction Captain Ericsson gave his personal attention to all the details, and the launching of the vessel in the remarkably brief period of 101 days from the signing of the contract was in large part the result of his untiring energy and devotion.

The first trial trip of the *Monitor* was on February 19, 1862, and on that day she was delivered to the navy yard for her armament and stores. She made two trial trips afterwards. The first and second trips were not satisfactory, the first because the cut-off valve had been improperly set and would not admit the steam properly to the cylinders; the second from some slight defect in the steering apparatus, which was speedily corrected.

On January 13, 1862, Lieutenant Worden, afterwards rear-admiral, was ordered to the command of the *Monitor*, then on the stocks. On the 20th of February, 1862, he received sailing-orders from the Secretary of the Navy to proceed to Hampton Roads, Virginia, and there report to the Navy Department. On the afternoon of the 6th of March, 1862, the *Monitor*, with a picked crew from the war ships *North Carolina* and *Sabine*, fifty-eight officers and men all told, left the lower bay of New York, with a moderate wind and smooth sea, in tow of a small tug, the *Seth Low*, and accompanied by the United States steamers *Currituck* and *Sachem*. After encountering a severe storm the *Monitor* passed Cape Henry light-house at four o'clock on the afternoon of March 8th. At this point heavy firing in the direction of Fortress Monroe indicated an engagement, and very soon Lieutenant Worden learned from a pilot of the advent of the *Merrimac* and the disaster to the ships *Cumberland* and *Congress*. On the information received from the pilot Lieutenant Worden ordered the *Monitor* to be prepared for action, and at nine o'clock that evening anchored at Hampton Roads near the frigate *Roanoke*, to the commander of which Lieutenant Worden reported.

The next morning, March 9, 1862, the *Merrimac* was observed under way, steaming slowly from Sewell's Point, where she had anchored during the night, to accomplish more perfectly her work of the day before. The *Monitor* immediately stood for her with crew at quarters, and the fierce and remarkable fight began, continuing from eight o'clock A. M. to one and a half o'clock P. M., and resulting in the discomfiture of the *Merrimac* and the full proof of all that had been claimed for the *Monitor*.

Orders for more monitors were at once given, and Captain Ericsson and the firm of Winslow & Griswold had the confidence and gratitude of the whole American people. The great regret was everywhere expressed that the *Monitor* was not at Hampton Roads one day sooner to save the *Cumberland* and the *Congress* with the brave men who went down with them.

The life of the *Monitor* was as short as it was eventful. From the 10th of March until the destruction of the *Merrimac* on the 11th of May, 1862, she lay in Hampton Roads as a guard for the vast interests centred there. On the 12th of May she led the vessels which went to Norfolk on the evacuation of that city by the Confederates, and subsequently performed other services on the James river. In September she was at the Washington navy yard for repairs, sailing again for Hampton Roads in November. On the 29th of December, 1862, she sailed for Beaufort, North Carolina, in company with the steamer *Rhode Island*, her convoy, and on the night of the 30th she foundered near Cape Hatteras, carrying down about one-half of her officers and crew.

The revolving turret of the *Monitor* and its successors of the same type was not the invention of Captain Ericsson but of Theodore R. Timby, who explains its history as follows in published letters dated March 7, 1888.

The first sight of the circular form of " Castle William," on Governor's Island, in the harbor of New York, suggested to me the idea of a revolving plan for defensive works, and in April, 1841, (when I was but nineteen years of age,) I came to Washington and exhibited a model and plans of a revolving battery, to be made of iron, to the then chief of engineers and the chief of ordnance, U. S. Army. I also submitted this model and these plans to the Hon. John C. Calhoun and many of his distinguished friends. In January, 1843, I made a model of a marine turret, which model is now in my possession. At this date I made my first record in the United States Patent Office, and from January, 1841, to 1861 I continued to urge the importance of my plans upon the proper authorities at Washington and elsewhere. In 1856 I exhibited the plans to the Emperor Napoleon III., and received some encouragement, but without practical results. In 1862 I entered into a written agreement with the contractors and builders of the original *Monitor*, (John F. Winslow and John A. Griswold, of

Troy, New York, C. S. Bushnell, of New Haven, Connecticut, and their associates,) for the use of my patents covering the revolving turret, by which they agreed to pay me, and did pay me, $5,000 as a royalty on each turret constructed by them. . . . .

It is in no degree probable that the *Monitor* or anything like it would ever have been built had it not been for the *liberality*, *patriotism*, and *persistence* of Hon. John F. Winslow and John A. Griswold.

The following table gives the number and gross tonnage of all iron and steel vessels, except those for the navy, which have been built in the United States in the fiscal years from 1868 to 1891. Nearly all were steam vessels. Since 1883 we have built many vessels of steel, and the tendency now is to use steel in constantly increasing quantities in the construction of both merchant and naval vessels. This table has been compiled from the reports of the Bureau of Navigation of the Treasury Department.

Years.	No.	Tons.	Years.	No.	Tons.	Years.	No.	Tons.
1868....	......	2,801	1876....	25	21,346	1884....	34	85,631
1869....	......	4,584	1877....	7	5,927	1885....	48	44,028
1870....	......	8,281	1878....	32	26,960	1886....	26	14,908
1871....	......	15,479	1879....	24	22,008	1887....	29	34,354
1872....	20	12,766	1880....	31	25,582	1888....	43	36,719
1873....	26	26,548	1881....	42	28,392	1889....	48	53,513
1874....	23	33,097	1882....	43	40,097	1890....	63	80,378
1875....	20	21,632	1883....	35	39,646	1891....	76	105,618

John Ericsson, distinguished on two continents as an engineer, was born in the province of Wermland, Sweden, on July 31, 1803, and died in New York city on March 8, 1889, aged over 85 years. In 1890 his remains were taken to Sweden in a United States naval vessel.

Mr. Winslow is now living in retirement at Poughkeepsie, New York, and was in good health late in 1891. He was born at Bennington, Vermont, on November 5, 1810.

CHAPTER L.

THE HISTORY OF CUT AND WIRE NAILS.

In one of our chapters devoted to the early iron history of New England and in our New York chapter we have referred to the invention in the closing years of the last century of machines for cutting nails and have claimed for this invention an American origin. We now supplement these statements with some additional information concerning the manufacture of both steel and iron cut nails and also concerning the manufacture of wire nails.

Knight, in his *Mechanical Dictionary*, thus briefly summarizes the leading facts connected with the invention of cut nails, some of which, derived from other sources, we have already presented in preceding chapters.

Cut nails were first made in this country. About 1775 Jeremiah Wilkinson, of Cumberland, Rhode Island, cut tacks from plates of sheet metal, and afterward made nails and spikes in a similar manner, forming the heads in a vise. Ezekiel Reed, of Bridgewater, Massachusetts, in 1786 invented a machine for cutting nails from the plate, and in 1798 obtained a patent for cutting and heading them at one operation. Benjamin Cochran had also constructed a machine of this kind; and Josiah Pierson, of New York, in 1794 patented a machine for cutting nails from the sheet. Perkins's machine, invented in 1790 and patented in 1795, is said to have been capable of making 200,000 nails per day. These and Odiorne's, which embraced some improvements upon them, attracted great attention in England, where they soon came into extensive use. At the close of the century twenty-three patents had been granted for improvements in nail machines.

In 1879 Mr. Shubal Wilder, of New Castle, Pennsylvania, then an old man, who had been employed as a nail-cutter from his boyhood, first at Wareham, Massachusetts, in 1826, and afterwards in Pennsylvania, published the following opinion of several nail-cutting and nail-heading machines which had been in use during his day.

From 1825 to 1835 there was a great increase in the number of nail machines and factories in New England, New York, and through New Jersey and Eastern Pennsylvania; consequently there was a great demand for men to run nail machines. Almost all the time men kept coming to Massachusetts from New Jersey and Pennsylvania on the hunt for nailers,

and this is the reason why so many New England people or their descendants are found in nearly every town where there are iron works and nail
factories. The Reed nail machine, now in use, is the only one among the
many that have been patented that has succeeded. The Perkins machine,
invented by Jacob Perkins, of Massachusetts, made a very good nail, but it
was very expensive to keep in order. The Odiorne machine also made
a good nail, but was attended with the same difficulty as the Perkins.
There were several other side shear machines built, but they never came
into use. The improvements made by Melville Otis on the Reed machine
have brought it to a high state of perfection : the only thing now remaining to be done is the introduction of a reliable self-feeder, which if not
already invented will be an accomplishment of the near future.

Since Mr. Wilder wrote these words the wire nail has
largely supplanted the cut nail, and his own town of New
Castle has become very prominent in its manufacture.
The primitive nail-cutting machines which were used
about the beginning of the present century and for some
years afterwards are doubtless correctly described in the
following extract from the *History of Indiana County*, Pennsylvania, reference being made to a machine used in 1818
by a blacksmith in the town of Indiana, who is said to have
manufactured all the cut nails that were used in Indiana
county and adjoining counties.

The machine used was propelled by one person using the right hand
on one lever and the right foot on another lever. The left hand was occupied in manipulating the iron from which the nails were cut. The iron was
called " nail iron," and was of different widths, according to the requisite
sizes desired, such as shingle, clapboard, brads, lathing, etc. Two-inch
shingle nails were sold for 37½ cents per pound ; clapboard do., 25 cents ;
brads, 18 cents ; lathing, 31 cents, etc. Before cutting, the iron was brought
to a red heat in the common blacksmith fire. After the nails were cooled
they were taken to a place to be headed. This was done with a spring vice,
which was closed by the pressure of the right foot. Only one nail was inserted at a time. One stroke of the hammer on the nail made a brad ; two
more made a clapboard or weather-boarding nail. The iron was procured
at the different rolling mills in Huntingdon county, and hauled in wagons
to Indiana county.

These nails were cut from plate iron, which was rolled in
the small rolling mills of the day and before the time when
bar iron was rolled. To these small rolling mills were sometimes added slitters for slitting the flat strips of iron into
nail-rods, which were converted into so-called wrought nails
exclusively by hand, as has been elsewhere explained. The
iron to be used in the early nail-cutting machines was first

hammered to the thickness of about half an inch and then rolled to the width and thickness required by the sizes of the nails to be cut.

In Knight's *Mechanical Dictionary*, published as late as 1877, the wire nail is thus referred to : " Chests and boxes from the Continent of Europe and from Asia are found to be fastened with nails of this character." Knight neither gives the origin of the wire nail nor describes any of the machines by which it is made. Since the publication of his *Dictionary* the wire nail has become a leading product of American skill.

The first wire nails manufactured in the United States were made in 1851 or 1852 at New York by William Hassall. Six of the machines at first used by Mr. Hassall are still in use in the wire-nail factory of his son, John Hassall, in Brooklyn. Previous to the introduction of wire made of Bessemer steel all the wire nails made by William Hassall were made from iron or brass wire. The wire nails made by William Hassall were of small sizes, escutcheon and up- holsterer's nails being specialties. William Hassall was born at Birmingham, England, in 1817, emigrated to New York city in 1850, and died there in 1888, aged 71 years.

The wire nail as a substitute for the cut nail did not, however, come into notice in this country until a very few years ago, in 1883 or 1884. Mr. E. J. Buffington, treasurer of the American Wire Nail Company, whose works are now located at Anderson, Indiana, sends us the following interest- ing account of the organization of his company, which was the first company to give the wire nail a start in American markets as a competitor of the cut nail.

The origin of the present American Wire Nail Company dates back as far as 1871, when a few German residents of Covington, Kentucky, contrib- uted to a fund for importing three German machines. These three ma- chines made nothing larger than a 3d fine nail, and were kept busy prin- cipally on cigar-box nails and small wire brads. For several years the pro- moters of this new industry met with no success. However they were not discouraged from adding to their then surplus capacity. The American Wire and Screw Nail Company, which was the predecessor of our present company, was organized in 1875, and its management passed into the hands of men with enthusiastic views as to the future of wire nails in this country. The trade in cigar-box nails had grown to be of considerable importance to them, and the plant was increased to twenty machines. Very great difficul- ty was experienced in inducing the hardware trade to recognize the wire brad and wire nail as a salable commodity. From 1878 to 1880 the growth of the wire nail was very slow and was attended with many difficulties. Deep-rooted prejudices of all kinds had to be overcome. It was not until the year 1883 or 1884 that the wire nail came into the market prominently as a competitor of the cut nail, and it was at this time that the standard wire nail was instituted. Each successive year after this the demand for wire nails increased phenomenally, and, in fact, passed beyond the wildest hopes of the most sanguine.

Down to 1883 all the cut nails manufactured in this country in commercial quantities were made of iron, but in that year cut nails made of Bessemer steel and others made of combined iron and steel were sold in American markets.

The production of iron and steel cut nails in the United States, not including wire nails, has been as follows from 1873 to 1890, in kegs of 100 pounds.

Years.	Kegs.	Years.	Kegs.	Years.	Kegs.
1873	4,024,704	1879	5,011,021	1885	6,696,815
1874	4,912,180	1880	5,370,512	1886	8,160,973
1875	4,726,881	1881	5,794,206	1887	6,908,870
1876	4,157,814	1882	6,147,097	1888	6,493,591
1877	4,828,918	1883	7,762,737	1889	5,810,758
1878	4,396,130	1884	7,581,379	1890	5,640,946

In 1884 the production of steel cut nails in the United States, including 500 kegs of combined iron and steel nails, was 393,482 kegs, or 5 per cent. of the total cut-nail production. Down to and including 1890 the maximum total production of cut nails was reached in 1886, with 8,160,973 kegs, and the maximum production of steel cut nails alone was reached in 1888, with 4,323,484 kegs. In 1889 and 1890 over two-thirds of the total production of cut nails was made of steel. The quantity of combined iron and steel nails made in 1890 was about 111,000 kegs.

In 1886 the production of wire nails was estimated to have amounted to 600,000 kegs of 100 pounds, made by 27 wire nail works; in 1887 the production was estimated to have been 1,250,000 kegs, made by 47 works; in 1888 it was estimated to have been 1,500,000 kegs; in 1889 it was estimated to have been 2,435,000 kegs. The actual production in 1890 was 3,135,911 kegs, nearly all the nails being made of steel. The wire nails made in 1890 were produced by 47 works.

CHAPTER LI.

IMPROVEMENTS IN AMERICAN BLAST FURNACE PRACTICE.

In our Maryland and Virginia chapters extracts are given from letters written by members of the Principio Company, which built Principio furnace and forge in Maryland, and afterwards, in connection with Augustine Washington, built Accokeek furnace in Virginia. We now make some additional extracts from one of these letters, written by John Wightwick to John England, and dated at London on. October 2, 1730, which we give to show the technical ideas which prevailed in those days in England and America concerning the manufacture of pig iron. Referring to letters from Nathaniel Chapman, the clerk at Accokeek furnace, Mr. Wightwick says:

He says he thinks it will be cheaper to send hearths from England than to bring the stones 20 miles land carriage from a quarry (where he says there are good ones) at that distance from the works, but I hope you will consider that point thoroughly, because sending hearths from hence is very chargable in freight, as well as troublesome to get them and put them on board. Bellows leather I suppose you must always have from hence. The price of piggs is very low at present; we hope in a short time it will be better. The Potomack piggs will not reach 5*l.* 15*s.*, they being cheap piggs are fittest for founderys, and I don't doubt but we might sell a large quantity yearly in London for that use. We have sold some of these last arrived, but the dealers complain they are too white; if they were grey they would go off much better.

The way to distinguish grey piggs from white is this: taber upon them with a hammer, and if they have a deadish leaden sound they are grey; they will also be pretty level in the belly of the pigg, & the edges of them will be blunt. If they are white by hammering on them they will ring much more, the under sides of them will be hollow, & the edges much more sharp, and if you strike the white ones at the end they will break short. This information I had from a Founder whom we sold a parcel to; and this difference is not so much owing to the ore as the fluxing, for we have pretty near an equal quantity of grey piggs mixed with the white, which inclines me to think this must be some mismanagement of the Founder that they are not all grey. I therefore hope you will consider and give directions to the Founder accordingly; and let the hearths at both works be always set burrow and not transheer, for white piggs will do us great prejudice in the sales.

Since the introduction into this country of the hot-blast in connection with the manufacture of pig iron, which occurred in the decade between 1830 and 1840, many methods of heating the blast have been in use. The first practical application of the hot-blast in this country was made at Oxford furnace, in New Jersey, in 1834, by William Henry, the manager. The waste heat at the tymp passed over the surface of a nest of small cast-iron pipes, through which the blast was conveyed to the furnace. The temperature was raised to 250° Fahrenheit, and the product of the furnace was increased about 10 per cent. In 1835 a hot-blast oven, containing cast-iron arched pipes, was placed on the top of the stack by Mr. Henry and heated by the flame from the tunnel-head. By this means the temperature of the blast was raised to 500°. This innovation in American blast-furnace practice increased the product of Oxford furnace about 40 per cent., with a saving of about the same percentage of fuel. No better device for heating the blast was in use in this country until about 1840. Hot-blast ovens, supplied with cast-iron arched pipes, of various patterns, were in general use in subsequent years down to about 1861, when an improvement in the construction of the oven, but embodying no essential modification of the system, was introduced by Samuel Thomas and adopted at many furnaces. In 1867 or 1868 John Player, of England, introduced his iron hot-blast stove into the United States, which soon became popular, owing to the facilities which it afforded for increasing the heat of the blast. Mr. Player personally superintended the erection of the first of his stoves in this country at the anthracite furnace of J. B. Moorhead & Co., at West Conshohocken, in Montgomery county, Pennsylvania. A few years ago it was still in use. Down to the introduction of the Player hot-blast the ovens, or stoves, were generally placed at the tunnel-head; Mr. Player placed his stove on the ground.

It is due to the memory of John Player that the fact should here be plainly stated that the introduction of his stove was instrumental in .greatly increasing the yield of American furnaces and decreasing the quantity of fuel used to the ton of pig iron. After its introduction the temperature of the blast was generally raised, even where the Thom-

as and other ovens were used, and before long powerful blowing engines were more generally used and higher furnaces
were built. Connellsville coke was found to work admirably
as a fuel for blast furnaces in connection with a powerful
blast and high temperature. Since 1868 cast-iron stoves of
various patterns have been increased in size, and in this
and other improvements their efficiency in raising the temperature of the blast has been greatly promoted.

The Whitwell fire-brick hot-blast stove, also an English
invention, was first used in this country at Rising Fawn
furnace, in Dade county, Georgia, on June 18, 1875. Its
next application was at Cedar Point furnace, at Port Henry, in Essex county, New York, on August 12, 1875. The
stoves at Cedar Point furnace were, however, built before
those at Rising Fawn furnace. The first application of this
stove in Pennsylvania was made as late as February, 1877,
at Dunbar furnace, in Fayette county. The Rising Fawn
and Dunbar furnaces used coke as fuel, while Cedar Point
furnace used anthracite. The first set of Siemens-Cowper-
Cochrane fire-brick hot-blast stoves erected in this country
was erected at one of the Crown Point furnaces, in Essex
county, New York, in 1877; but the first set of these stoves
in any part of America was erected at Londonderry, in Nova
Scotia, by the Steel Company of Canada Limited, in 1876.
The Siemens-Cowper-Cochrane stove is also an English invention. Both it and the Whitwell stove embody the regenerative principle in storing heat. Other stoves built upon the
same principle have been introduced in European and American blast-furnace practice in late years. The introduction of
all these stoves has greatly promoted the economic management of American blast furnaces and increased their yield,
supplementing and in all respects adding to the good work
inaugurated when the Player stove was introduced.

In the twenty years between 1840 and 1860 the plan of
conveying the escaping gases from the top of the blast furnace to the boilers and hot-blast ovens, or stoves, gradually
came into general use as a substitute for independent fires
or for the use of the flame at the tunnel-head. Its introduction was greatly promoted between 1844 and 1850 by the
efforts of C. E. Detmold, a German engineer, then residing

at New York, who had taken out a patent in this country as the assignee of Achilles Christian Wilhelm von Faber du Faur, the superintendent of the government iron works at Wasseralfingen, in Wurtemberg, Germany, who had invented a method of using furnace gases in heating the blast. The first practical experiments with this invention in utilizing furnace gases in the production of heat were made in 1836 and 1837 at Wasseralfingen.

David Thomas, of Catasauqua, Pennsylvania, was the first person in this country to fully realize the value of powerful blowing engines in the working of blast furnaces. About 1852 he introduced engines at his furnaces at Catasauqua which increased the pressure to double that which was then customary in England. The results were surprising. But many years elapsed before Mr. Thomas's example was generally followed in this country. Within the past few years, however, our superior blast-furnace practice has been mainly due to the use of blowing engines of great power. English ironmasters have only in late years commenced to imitate the best American practice in this respect.

Mr. Joseph C. Kent, superintendent of the blast furnaces of the Andover Iron Company, at Phillipsburg, New Jersey, writes us concerning two noteworthy achievements at one of these furnaces many years ago. These furnaces were then known as the Cooper furnaces. In one week in 1850 there were produced by No. 1 furnace 251½ tons of pig iron, and in one week in 1858 there were produced by the same furnace 319 tons of pig iron. The fuel used in both instances was anthracite coal; the engines used were not large, being capable of blowing only from 7,000 to 8,000 cubic feet of air per minute, under a pressure of from 3 to 3½ pounds per square inch. The blast was heated in ordinary syphon pipe ovens to 500° Fahrenheit. The size of this furnace was 20 feet by 55 feet. The above products were respectively the largest that had been anywhere produced down to the dates mentioned, but to-day we have furnaces which make as much pig iron in a day as they made in a week.

Isabella furnace No. 1, located at Etna, near Pittsburgh, closed early in 1884 a three-years' blast which produced results which were at that time justly regarded as remarkable and were certainly unexampled. Its product was as follows, in tons of 2,268 pounds. Pig iron made in 1881, 324 days, 37,437½ tons; in 1882, 365 days, 59,032 tons; in 1883, 365 days, 66,408½ tons; in 1884, 19 days, 3,927 tons: total in three years, less 22 days, 166,805 tons, or an average of 1,090 tons per week. The unexampled good work of this furnace was obtained notwithstanding a serious interruption caused by a freshet in the Allegheny river, and notwithstanding other drawbacks. The furnace was 75 feet high, 20 feet in diameter at the bosh, and 11 feet in diameter at the hearth, contained a 14-foot stock line, and had seven 7-inch tuyeres. It was equipped with three Whitwell stoves of the largest size and three engines having 7-foot blowing cylinders with a 4-foot stroke.

By far the best work ever done by a coke furnace was accomplished in 1889 and 1890 by one of the furnaces connected with the Edgar Thomson steel works at Braddock, Pennsylvania, known as furnace F, owned by Carnegie Brothers & Co. Limited. For the following account of the great record made by this furnace in the years mentioned, as well as of the good work which it had previously done, we are indebted to a paper by Mr. James Gayley, superintendent of the Edgar Thomson furnaces, which he read at the meeting of the Iron and Steel Institute at New York in October, 1890.

This furnace was built in 1885-6. The total height is 80 feet; the diameter of hearth, 11 feet; the diameter of bosh, 23 feet. The bell is 12 feet in diameter and the stock line 16 feet. The cubical capacity is 19,800 feet. There are 7 tuyeres, each 6 inches in diameter. The furnace was started in October, 1886. The record for the next three months is as follows.

Months.	Gross tons.	Pounds of coke per ton of iron.
November, 1886.....................................	6,785	2,128
December..	7,494	2,105
January, 1887..	8,398	1,935

From January to May, inclusive, the average monthly output was 8,150 tons on a coke consumption of 1,980 pounds. The volume of air blown was 27,000 cubic feet per minute, which was heated to an average temperature of 1,200 degrees. The pressure at the tuyeres varied from 9 to 10 pounds, and was generally the latter figure when the outputs were largest. In June the furnace was banked for eight days on account of a scarcity of coke. The monthly output from this time up to January, 1888, was 7,400 gross tons, when a second stoppage on account of labor troubles occurred. The length of this stop was sixty-seven days. A portion of the upper lining giving way in August, 1889, the furnace was blown out. The furnace was in blast (exclusive of the two stoppages I have mentioned) two years, seven months, and ten days, and made in that time 224,795 tons of iron on an average coke consumption of 2,317 pounds. The output for the first twelve full months was 88,940 tons on 2,150 pounds of coke. The furnace was relined without delay, and after a two weeks' drying out was put in blast on September 25, 1889, just seven weeks from the time of blowing out. The construction was the same in every particular except that the diameter of the bosh was reduced to 22 feet and the stock line to 15 feet 6 inches. This change reduced the cubical capacity to 18,200 feet. The same number and size of tuyeres were used. The volume of air blown was 25,000 cubic feet per minute, a reduction of 2,000 cubic feet from that used in the previous blast. Beginning with October the record of monthly outputs and coke consumption to June, 1890, was as follows.

Months.	Gross tons.	Pounds of coke per ton of iron.
October, 1889	6,521	2,450
November	9,097	1,897
December	10,603	1,756
January, 1890	10,536	1,737
February	8,954	1,859
March	9,941	1,845
April	10,075	1,847
May	10,085	1,884

The best output for any one week was 2,462 tons. The best output for a single day was 502 tons and 240 pounds, made on September 3, 1890. The temperature of the blast averaged 1,100 degrees, and the pressure 9½ pounds. The temperature of the escaping gases was 340 degrees.

Counting the time the furnace was running in the first blast, and up to the end of May, 1890, in the second blast, including also the time spent in relining, the period covered is three years and five months, and in that time this furnace made an output of 301,205 tons, a record which is unparalleled. In the month of May this furnace, together with a companion furnace of precisely the same dimensions, made an output of 20,192 tons on an average coke consumption of 1,882 pounds per ton of iron. The ores used were from the Lake Superior region, and yielded through the furnace 62 per cent. of iron. The proportion of limestone carried was 28 per cent. of the ore burden. The silicon in the iron averaged 1.60 per cent., the iron being run into ladles and sent to the converting mill direct. I shall not undertake to say what these furnaces will accomplish on an uninterrupted blast, but I believe the day is not far distant when we shall be able to show a record of 300,000 tons from a furnace in three years, and on a single lining. [The product for the first two years is 208,050 gross tons, showing that this prediction will probably be fulfilled.]

In the period covered by the last decade there are three steps in the development of American blast-furnace practice that might be mentioned. First, in 1880, the introduction of rapid driving, with its large outputs and high fuel consumption; second, in 1885, the production of an equally large amount of iron with a low fuel consumption by slow driving; and, third, in 1890, the production of nearly double that quantity of iron on a low fuel consumption through rapid driving.

The best record ever made by a charcoal furnace in this country or any other country was made in 1890 by a new furnace in Wisconsin. Mr. M. R. Hunt, the manager of the Hinkle charcoal furnace, at Ashland, Wisconsin, owned by the Ashland Iron and Steel Company, reports that in the seven days which ended on October 4th the furnace produced 1,009 gross tons of pig iron. The best day's run yielded 150 tons and the worst yielded 141 tons. The stack of this furnace is 60 feet high, and the diameter of the bosh is 12 feet. Neither scrap nor mill cinder was used. The ores came from the Gogebic range. The average consumption of ore per ton was 4,021 pounds; of charcoal, a little over 82 bushels of 22 pounds to the bushel; of limestone, 174 pounds.

Mr. J. King McLanahan informs us that in 1853 Frankstown charcoal furnace, in Blair county, Pennsylvania, was changed to a coke furnace, the first in that county, and made No. 1 foundry pig iron from Frankstown block fossil ore. The furnace buildings were burned down in 1855, and Mr. McLanahan, the manager, "banked up on a full burden." After a delay of exactly fourteen days the blast was again turned on, and in twelve hours the furnace was working as well as before the accident occurred. Mr. McLanahan says that this was the first attempt that was made in this country to "bank up" a coke furnace for so long a time.

Achilles Christian Wilhelm von Faber du Faur was born on December 2, 1786. He studied at Freiberg in 1808; was first assistant superintendent of the government iron works at Kœnigsbronn in 1810, and afterwards was superintendent for thirty-two years of the government iron works at Wasseralfingen. He died on March 22, 1855.

Christian Edward Detmold was born in Hanover, Germany, on February 2, 1810, and died at New York on July 2, 1887, aged over 77 years. He was a civil engineer, in which profession he became very prominent. He was also engaged in the manufacture of pig iron in Maryland, the mining of coal in Pennsylvania, and the manufacture of spiegeleisen from zinc residuum in New Jersey.

CHAPTER LII.

THE MANUFACTURE OF TINPLATES IN THE UNITED STATES.

THE manufacture of tinplates in the United States was undertaken in 1873 at Wellsville, Ohio, and at Leechburg, Pennsylvania. In 1875 it was also undertaken at Demmler, near Pittsburgh. Owing, however, to the low duty which was imposed on foreign tinplates domestic tinplates ceased in 1878 to be made at the three places mentioned, and no further attempts to establish the tinplate industry in our country were made until about the time of the passage of the tariff act of October 1, 1890, in which the previously existing duty on tinplates was more than doubled. Since that date several works for the manufacture of tinplates have been established in the United States, while the building of others has been commenced, and the prospects for the complete success of this new industry are now most favorable.

The following table, compiled from the publications of the Bureau of Statistics of the Treasury Department, shows the quantities of tinplates imported into the United States in each year from 1871 to 1890, with their foreign values.

Years.	Gross tons.	Values.	Years.	Gross tons.	Values.
1871	82,969	$9,946,373	1881	183,005	$14,886,907
1872	85,629	13,893,450	1882	213,987	17,975,161
1873	97,177	14,240,868	1883	221,233	18,156,773
1874	79,778	13,057,658	1884	216,181	16,858,650
1875	91,054	12,098,885	1885	228,596	15,991,152
1876	89,946	9,416,816	1886	257,822	17,504,976
1877	112,479	10,679,028	1887	283,836	18,699,145
1878	107,864	9,069,967	1888	298,288	19,762,961
1879	154,250	13,227,659	1889	331,311	21,726,707
1880	158,049	16,478,110	1890	329,346	23,670,158

The total quantity of tinplates imported into this country in these twenty years was 3,622,750 gross tons, and the total foreign value of these importations was $307,341,404. In addition to this sum American consumers paid freights and duties and importers' profits.

CHAPTER LIII.

MISCELLANEOUS FACTS RELATING TO THE AMERI-
CAN IRON AND STEEL INDUSTRIES.

It would far transcend the limits assigned to this work if all the modern inventions connected with the manufacture of iron and steel in this country were to be made the subject of historical and statistical inquiry. The most important of these inventions, and the history of their introduction in our country, have been referred to in preceding chapters. Several subjects of less prominence, but all of them relating to the mechanical development of our iron and steel industries, will now be noticed, with which notice this branch of our general subject will be dismissed.

At the Siberian rolling mill of Rogers & Burchfield, at Leechburg, in Armstrong county, Pennsylvania, natural gas, taken from a well 1,200 feet deep, was first used as a fuel in the manufacture of iron. In the fall of 1874 it was stated that during the preceding six months the gas had furnished all the fuel required for puddling, heating, and making steam, not one bushel of coal having been used. Between 1874 and 1881 natural gas for puddling was successfully used at the same rolling mill at Leechburg; at the works of Spang, Chalfant & Co. and Graff, Bennett & Co., in Allegheny county, Pennsylvania; and at the rolling mill of the Kittanning Iron Company, at Kittanning, Pennsylvania. In each instance the gas used at these works was obtained from wells that were sunk for oil but were found to produce only gas. Since 1881 natural gas has been introduced into many iron and steel works in Pennsylvania, Ohio, Indiana, and West Virginia. In 1884, however, there were still only six rolling mills and steel works in the United States which used natural gas as fuel. In 1886 there were 68; in November, 1887, there were 96; and in November, 1889, there were 104. Since the last date the use of natural gas in our iron and steel works has greatly declined, owing to a failure of the supply in many places. The method employed in using natural gas at Kittanning in the summer of 1881 is here preserved as a matter of historical interest.

The gas is brought from a well some three miles distant, in four-inch casing, and at the mill is distributed amongst eighteen boiling furnaces. The furnaces are the same as those in which coal is used. The gas enters the rear of the furnace in three small pipes, shaped at the end like a nozzle. There being quite a pressure the gas enters with considerable force, and by means of dampers to regulate the draft an intense and uniform heat is obtained. After a heat the furnace is cooled and prepared for the next heat in the same manner as with coal. When the metal is in place the gas is turned on, and the operation of puddling is the same, with the exception that it is somewhat slower. Only one-half of the well's production of gas is in fact consumed by the eighteen furnaces here described. The puddlers like the gas very much, as it reduces their labor to some extent, and they say they can make better weight than with coal. The furnaces being free from sulphur a better quality of iron is produced, and it brings a slightly advanced price in the market. These furnaces have been running all the time for some months past, and have used nothing but gas for fuel, which has proved satisfactory in every respect, and is found to be much cheaper than coal.

We have previously recorded the erection in 1817, at Plumsock, in Fayette county, Pennsylvania, of the first rolling mill in the United States for the production of bar iron. The first puddling in this country was also done at this rolling mill in the same year. It may seem strange to many of the present generation, who witness the number and magnitude of our iron and steel establishments, that such important processes as the puddling of pig iron and the rolling of bar iron should not have been introduced into the United States until 1817, but after careful inquiry we have been unable to place their introduction at an earlier period. Ralph Crooker, recently of the Bay State iron works, at Boston, the oldest rolling-mill superintendent in the United States, writes us that the first bar iron rolled in New England was rolled at the Boston iron works, on the mill-dam in Boston, in 1825, and that the first puddling done in New England was at Boston, on the mill-dam, by Lyman, Ralston & Co., in 1835.

Before the use of bituminous and anthracite coal became general in this country wood as it comes from the forest was sometimes used to puddle pig iron, as it is now used at some places in Sweden, and it was also used in the heating furnaces of rolling mills. From 1821 to 1825 the Fall River rolling mill, in Massachusetts, used wood in heating iron for nail plates. In 1848 pig iron was puddled with wood at Adirondack, in Essex county, New York. Prior to 1850 puddling with wood was done at Horatio Ames's works at Falls Village, in Connecticut. In 1858 the Hurricane rolling mill and nail works, on Pacolet river, 43 miles west of Yorkville, in South Carolina, used dry pine wood in its puddling and heating furnaces; and in the preceding year the Cherokee Ford rolling mill,.on Broad river, in Union county, in the same State, used " splint " wood for the same purpose.

The Phœnix wrought-iron column, or wrought-steel column, which is now in general use in this country and in Europe in the construction of bridges, viaducts, depots, warehouses, and other structures, is the invention of the late Samuel J. Reeves, of Philadelphia, a member of the Phœnix Iron Company, of Phœnixville, Pennsylvania. The invention was patented on June 17, 1862.

Down to 1846, when John Griffen built a rolling mill at Norristown, Pennsylvania, for Moore & Hooven, steam boilers had never been put over puddling and heating furnaces in any country. In this mill all the steam that was needed for driving the mill was generated in boilers over the puddling and heating furnaces, no auxiliary boilers being used, thus greatly economizing fuel. Mr. Griffen met with much opposition from observers while engaged in constructing the mill upon this plan, and many predictions were made that the new arrangement would be a failure. It was a great innovation on the practice then prevailing, but it was· a complete success, and its general adoption has effected a saving in fuel to the iron manufacturers in this country of many millions of dollars.

In 1856 two shafts were made for the steamship *Adriatic* at the Reading steam forge, at Reading, Pennsylvania. Each shaft when finished was 35½ feet in length, 27½ inches in diameter, and weighed 78,500 pounds, or 35 tons. Two cranks of 12-foot stroke were made at the same time, each weighing when finished 18,800 pounds, or 8.39 tons. The forge was then the largest and most complete in this country. It contained four hammers, of ½, ¾, 1½, and 7 tons' weight respectively. An account of the forging of the shafts says: "The shafts of the *Adriatic* were forged in twelve working days each. They were commenced on what is called a porter bar, forming a tapering handle, to which are attached levers, or cranks, to turn the shaft in its slings while under the hammer. The porter bar was first heated, and then flattened at its thick end to receive a pile of bloom bars each about 250 pounds' weight, all of which were welded solid with each other and the bar, thus forming the commencement of the shaft itself. The end of the shaft thus commenced was again heated to receive another pile of bars as already described, and the same process thus repeated until the shaft was made the length required. When the shaft becomes sufficiently long the porter bar is cut off and the turning cranks attached to the shaft itself."

On the 6th of September, 1881, Park, Brother & Co., of Pittsburgh, put in operation for the first time their 17-ton steam hammer, which was for many years the largest in the United States. It will work steel ingots two feet square. The hammer itself was built by William B. Bement & Son, of Philadelphia. The anvil, which was the heaviest iron casting then made in this country, weighing 160 tons, was cast a few feet from its place with five cupolas, under the direction of Park, Brother & Co., on October 5, 1880. It is 11 feet high, and measures 8 by 10 feet at the base and 4 by 6 feet at the top. The hammer and its fittings occupy a ground space 26 feet long by 13 feet wide. Its height from the ground is 32 feet. The framing is of wrought-iron plates from $\frac{7}{8}$ of an inch to $1\frac{1}{4}$ inches thick, bolted and riveted and strengthened with angle irons. The weight of the cast-iron cylinder is about 11 tons, the bore is 40 inches, and the stroke 9 feet. The piston, rod, ram, and die weigh about 17 tons. When the steam is admitted on top of the piston it will produce an additional force or weight of about 50 tons, making 67 tons' pressure in all when the ram or hammer is stationary. The whole cost of the hammer, anvil, and fittings, ready for operation, is estimated at $52,000. In August, 1883, Park, Brother & Co forged with this hammer a steel steamboat shaft $32\frac{1}{4}$ feet long and weighing 30,240 pounds, or $13\frac{1}{2}$ tons. The ingots used, which were of open-hearth steel, weighed 32,000 pounds. The shaft was hexagonal in the centre, tapering at each end to a circular shape.

Since the completion of the 17-ton hammer above described two other hammers of still larger proportions have been erected in this country, namely, the 20-ton hammer of the Latrobe steel works, at Latrobe, Pennsylvania, and the larger hammer of the Midvale steel works, at Philadelphia, both employing steam pressure to increase their forging power. But it has been left for the Bethlehem Iron Company to erect the largest and most efficient hammer in the world—a single-acting hammer of 125 tons. We are indebted to Lieutenant W. H. Jaques, ordnance engineer of the Bethlehem Iron Company, for the following description of this hammer.

The building in which this hammer has been erected is 500 feet long, and is located on ground that was partly an island and partly the bed of the southern channel of the Lehigh river, turned from its course to provide the hammer site. A pit 60 feet square was excavated below the water level, and piles were thickly driven both for the anvil foundation and hammer frames. The stone walls for supporting the latter have a depth of 30 feet, separated from the anvil foundation lest any sinking of this latter should affect the framework of the structure itself.

The hammer was designed by Mr. John Fritz, chief engineer and superintendent of the company; all of its parts were manufactured at the works; and, although the officers of the Bethlehem Iron Company had free consultation with the owners of the Creusot works in France, the hammer differs radically in many points from the celebrated Creusot hammer. It rises to a height of 90 feet from the floor line. The housings proper are each composed of two parts, the lower ones weighing 71 tons each, the upper ones 48 tons each. These are bolted together and surmounted by an entablature of 61 tons, carrying a 76-inch cylinder 24 feet high. The housings are clamped to base plates, each 10 feet by 8 feet, and weighing 56 tons, giving a 42-foot longitudinal width of frame and a working floor width inside of housings of 22 feet.

A 16-inch steel piston rod, 40 feet long, operates the enormous tup, which is composed of three parts, two forming the ram and a third the die. The hammer is single-acting, (steam-lifting only,) the total weight of falling parts, length of stroke, and gravity governing the work done.

The anvil foundation consists of piles driven to bed-rock or gravel, with timber frames, steel slabs and 22 iron blocks carefully machined and fitted forming a metal mass of 1,800 tons arranged in the form of a pyramid. To secure an even floor for working the spaces between the frame and anvil foundations are closed with cribbing, leaving exposed only the anvil block. The special valve gears designed at Bethlehem have worked most satisfactorily, one man easily controlling the motions with one hand.

The hammer is served by four heating furnaces, conveniently placed, and by four gigantic cranes, each of 300 tons' capacity, having longitudinal, transverse, vertical, and turning motions, by which every required position and movement of the forgings can be easily controlled.

In describing this hammer as one of 125 tons it is meant that the weight of the tup, (including die,) piston, and rod is 125 tons, which, falling a distance of 16½ feet, (full stroke,) *without* top steam, produces the full power of the hammer. *As such* the following hammers have comparative weights: Sir William G. Armstrong, Mitchell & Co. Limited, Elswick, England, 35 tons; Woolwich, England, 35 tons; Perm, Russia, 50 tons; Aboukoff Steel Works, Russia, 50 tons; Krupp, Essen, Germany, 50 tons; St. Chamond, France, 80 tons; Schneider & Co., Creusot, France, 100 tons; Marrel Brothers, Rive de Gier, France, 100 tons; and the Terni Steel Works, Italy, 100 tons. All these hammers are single-acting except those at Elswick, Woolwich, and Aboukoff.

Begun in 1889 the Bethlehem hammer was successfully put in operation on June 30, 1891, since which time many huge forgings for armor plates and other war and structural material have been shaped under it.

In 1884 there were still in existence in this country several old-fashioned slitting mills, which were used spasmodically in the conversion of iron into nail rods. There was a slitting mill at the Cambridge rolling mills near Boston; at the Norway steel and iron works at South Boston; at the Eagle iron works at Roland, Centre county, Pennsylvania; and at the Oxford iron and steel works at Frankford, in Philadelphia. The demand for slit nail rods grows less, however, every year, and it is probable that even the occasional use of the slitting mills above mentioned will soon be a thing of the past.

In his *History of Philadelphia* (1884) Thompson Westcott says that the first wire suspension bridge in the United States, if not in the world, was thrown across the Schuylkill river, near the Falls of Schuylkill, in Philadelphia, in 1816. Its history is as follows: In 1809 Robert Kennedy and Conrad Carpenter built a chain bridge at the Falls of Schuylkill which broke down in 1811. Josiah White and Erskine Hazard, afterwards prominent as the pioneers in the anthracite coal trade of Pennsylvania, had erected a rolling mill and a wire factory in the neighborhood, and after the bridge fell they formed a new company and another chain bridge was constructed in April, 1811, but this new bridge in turn gave way in 1816. White & Hazard then swung a wire suspension bridge across the river from an upper window of their factory to some large trees on the west bank, steps leading from the trees to the ground. This primitive bridge structure was intended for foot passengers only, and but eight persons were allowed to go upon the footway at one time.

The bridge is said to have cost $125. We find the essential parts of this statement accepted and presented in detail in a lecture delivered before the Engineers' Club of Philadelphia, in 1884, by Professor L. M. Haupt.

Wire fences are not a new thing under the sun. As far back as 1816 they were in limited use in the neighborhood of Philadelphia. The wire was manufactured by White & Hazard at their wire works at the Falls of Schuylkill. In a communication from this firm to Richard Peters, "President of the Agricultural Society," dated January 2, 1816, the use of wire fences was recommended, and an elaborate calculation was given to show the economy there would be in using them. In speaking of the strength of a wire fence they said: "We have given it a fair trial at the Falls, with the most breachy cows of the neighborhood, and it is remarkable that even dogs avoid passing over it." It was recommended that "living trees" be used as a substitute for posts, and that the wire used be protected by a coating of linseed oil or paint. The fence at the Falls was without barbs, which are a modern invention.

Samuel J. Reeves was born at Bridgeton, New Jersey, on March 4, 1818, and died at Phœnixville on December 15, 1878, aged over 60 years. For many years prior to his death he had been President of the American Iron and Steel Association and the head of the Phœnix Iron Company.

John Griffen was born at Mamaroneck, in Westchester county, New York, on February 16, 1812, and died at Phœnixville, Pennsylvania, on January 14, 1884, aged nearly 72 years. He was the inventor of the Griffen gun, and was for many years the general superintendent of the Phœnix iron works, at Phœnixville.

Ralph Crooker, the oldest rolling-mill superintendent in the United States at the time of his death, was born in the town of Bridgewater, Massachusetts, on May 28, 1801, and died at Roxbury, Massachusetts, on March 2, 1886, aged almost 85 years.

CHAPTER LIV.

EARLY DISCOVERIES OF COAL IN THE UNITED STATES.

THE abundance and wide distribution of mineral fuel in the United States have greatly assisted in the development of our iron and steel industries. A notice of the early discoveries of coal in our country therefore properly finds a place in these pages.

In the *Statistics of Coal*, by Richard Cowling Taylor, published in 1848, it is stated that the earliest historic mention of coal in this country is by the French Jesuit missionary, Father Hennepin, who saw traces of bituminous coal on the Illinois river in 1679. In his journal he marks the site of a "cole mine" above Fort Crevecœur, near the present town of Ottawa, in Illinois.

We find the next historic reference to coal in this country in a letter written by William Byrd, of Virginia, the first of the name, on May 10th and 11th, 1701, in part as follows: "The 10th of May, last, I with Coll. Randolph, Capt. Epes, Capt. Webb, &c., went up to the new settlements of ye ffrench Refugees at ye Manakan Town. . . . Wee went up to ye Cole, w'ch is not above a mile and a half from their settlement on the great upper Creeke, w'ch, riseing very high in great Raines hath washed away the Banke that the Coal lyes bare, otherwise it's very deep in the Earth, the land being very high, and near the surface is plenty of Slate." The discovery of coal had been made by a Huguenot settler. The Indian town referred to was situated about twenty miles above Richmond, on the south side of the James river, now in Powhatan county. For the above information we are indebted to the courtesy of Mr. R. A. Brock, of Richmond.

In his account of *A Progress to the Mines* of Virginia in 1732, from which we have quoted in our Virginia chapter, Colonel Wm. Byrd, in describing the air furnace at Massaponax, gives us the earliest mention of the *use* of coal in this country that we have found. He says: "There is an opening about a foot square for the fresh air to pass through from without. This leads up to an iron grate that holds about half a bushel of sea coal." This "sea coal" was probably brought from over the sea.

In the map of the middle colonies, published by Lewis Evans in 1755, we find mention of coal in Ohio, but no mention of coal is made anywhere within the limits of Pennsylvania. In Nicholas Scull's map of Pennsylvania, published in 1759, coal is not marked. But Mr. Hungerford calls our attention to the fact that coal in Western Pennsylvania is mentioned in 1759 in the journal of Colonel James Burd, written in that year. Colonel Burd was in command of a detachment of 200 of the king's troops, who were opening a road from Braddock's old road at Gist's plantation (now Mount Braddock) to the Monongahela river at the mouth of Dunlap's creek. Mr. Hungerford says that, having proceeded from Gist's toward the Monongahela to a point about four and a half miles from the river, Colonel Burd encamped there on the evening of the 21st of September, and on the following day moved on westward and made in his journal this entry namely: "Saturday, Sept. 22, 1759. The camp moved two miles to Coal Run. This run is entirely paved in the bottom with fine stone coal, and the hill on the south of it is a rock of the finest coal I ever saw. I burned about a bushel of it on my fire."

A coal seam near Pittsburgh took fire in 1765 and is said to have burned steadily for sixteen years. In William Scull's map of Pennsylvania, published in 1770, coal is marked in Berks county and at Pittsburgh. In George Washington's journal of a tour to the Ohio river in 1770 he says, under date of October 14th of that year: "At Captain Crawford's all day. We went to see a coal mine not far from his house, on the banks of the river. The coal seemed to be of the very best kind, burning freely, and abundance of it." The Captain Crawford referred to was the celebrated and unfortunate William Crawford, and his residence at the time of Washington's visit was at Stuart's Crossing, on the Youghiogheny river, where New Haven now stands, opposite Connellsville.

In 1763 Colonel Croghan, a British officer, noticed on the south side of the Wabash river "a high bank in which are several fine coal mines," which is the earliest reference, says Taylor, to coal in that region. In the map of Captain Hutchins, published at London in 1777, coal deposits are marked at various places in the basin of the Ohio river.

In a paper read before the Historical Society of Pennsylvania on the 4th day of January, 1875, Mr. William J. Buck quotes from the Penn manuscripts to show that the Penns were fully aware as early as 1769 of the existence of coal at Pittsburgh. Thomas Penn, in a letter of instructions dated at London, January 31, 1769, to his nephew, Lieutenant Governor John Penn, says: "We desire you will order 5,000 acres of land to be laid out about Pittsburgh, including the town, which may now be laid out, and I think from its situation will become considerable in time; and that the land may be laid out to Colonel Francis and his associates, and other gentlemen of whom I wrote, as contiguous as it may be, and in regular right-angled tracts, if possible." On the following 12th of May he writes to Mr. Tilghman respecting this survey, and says: "I would not engross all the coal-hills, but rather leave the greater part to others who may work them." The difficulties between the mother country and her colonies prevented these instructions from being carried out.

In 1784, however, the Penns, who retained their proprietary interest in large tracts of Pennsylvania after the close of the Revolution, including the manor of Pittsburgh, surveyed into building lots the town of Pittsburgh, and in the same year the privilege of mining coal in the " great seam " opposite the town was sold at the rate of £30 for each mining lot, extending back to the centre of the hill. This event may be regarded as forming the beginning of the coal trade of Pittsburgh.

On the 1st of November, 1785, Samuel Boyd patented a tract of bituminous coal land near Oldtown, in Clearfield county, Pennsylvania, but no coal from this tract was sent east of the Alleghenies until 1804. In that year William Boyd shipped the first ark-load of Clearfield county coal down the Susquehanna to Columbia, in Lancaster county, a distance of 260 miles. The new fuel, we are told, "was a matter of great surprise " to the good people of that county. Other ark-loads followed the first venture, and all the towns along the Susquehanna were soon familiar with bituminous coal. In 1828 the first cargo of Pennsylvania bituminous coal reached Philadelphia from Karthaus, in Clearfield county. This coal was shipped by the Allegheny Coal Company, under the superintendence of Dr. Frederick W. Geissenhainer. The coal was taken down the Susquehanna to Port Deposit, at the head of Chesapeake bay, and thence by vessel to Philadelphia. About the same time coal was sent to Baltimore from the same place. The distance from market was too great, however, and the means of transportation too imperfect to permit the building up of a large trade in bituminous coal between the Alleghenies and the seaboard, and the situation was not materially changed for many years after the completion in 1834 of the Pennsylvania system of internal improvements. The competition of domestic anthracite and of foreign and domestic bituminous coal, the last mentioned from Virginia and Maryland, was too great to be easily overcome, and in the case of anthracite it has never yet been overcome, although the shipments of Western Pennsylvania coal and coke to the seaboard are steadily increasing.

The Virginia coal mines were most likely the first that were worked in America. Bituminous mines were opened and operated on the James river, in Chesterfield county, probably about 1750. In July, 1766, in the *Virginia Gazette*, Samuel Duval advertises coal for sale at Rockett's, a lower landing of Richmond, at 12d. per bushel, "equal to Newcastle coal." Virginia coal was extensively used during the Revolution. An air furnace was built at Westham, on the James river, above Richmond, which used coal in the manufacture of shot and shell for the Revolutionary army. Virginia coal was exported to various cities on the Atlantic coast before the Revolution. On the 31st of August, 1776, Thomas Wharton, Jr., and Owen Biddle, of Philadelphia, were authorized to employ proper persons to bring coal from Virginia which had been contracted for by the Committee of Safety. In 1789 Virginia coal sold in Philadelphia at 1s. 6d. a bushel. In 1846 the price at the same city was 20 to 22 cents a bushel, which was two or three cents per bushel higher than Allegheny bituminous coal. It was the scarcity of Virginia coal in the Philadelphia market, especially during the war with Great Britain from 1812 to 1815, which largely contributed in the early part of the present century to the development of the vast anthracite coal deposits of Pennsylvania. The exportation of Virginia coal amounted to 42,-000 tons in 1822, and it reached its culmination in 1833, when 142,000 tons were shipped to neighboring States. In 1842 the shipments had fallen to 65,000 tons. Up to about that year it was a leading source of the domestic supply of mineral fuel in this country, and down to about 1850 it contributed the principal supply to the gas works of Philadelphia and other American cities, for which use it was well adapted. For about twenty years after 1833 the importation of bituminous coal from Great Britain and the British provinces into Philadelphia, principally for the gas works, steadily increased, owing to the growing scarcity of Virginia coal. About 1845 coal from the Pittsburgh seam began to be used in Philadelphia, transportation being by the Pennsylvania Canal, and about 1855 the gas coal of Western Pennsylvania, on the line of the Pennsylvania Railroad, was introduced into Philadelphia.

Coal is improbably said to have been discovered six miles northeast of Baltimore by Benjamin Henfrey in 1801. The Western Maryland coal basin was soon afterwards opened, and in 1820 the first shipment of coal from Alleghany county, Maryland, seems to have been made, when a few thousand tons were sent down the Potomac in boats. In 1832 the annual shipment of Cumberland coal down the Potomac had increased to about 300,000 bushels, most of which was not sent below Harper's Ferry. The price of Cumberland coal at tidewater at Georgetown in the District of Columbia in 1838 was 20 cents a bushel. In 1842 the shipment of Cumberland coal to Baltimore by the Baltimore and Ohio Railroad was commenced, with a total tonnage of 1,708 tons.

In 1804 the first discovery of coal west of the Mississippi was made by the exploring expedition under the leadership of Lewis and Clarke, who traced brown coal or lignite from about twenty miles above the Mandan villages, on the Missouri, nearly to the base of the Rocky mountains, and also upon the Yellowstone and other streams. In one of the exploring expeditions through Louisiana Territory which was

led by Captain Z. M. Pike "fine seams of coal" were discovered "far up the Osage river" in 1806.

Anthracite coal was discovered in the Wyoming valley as
early as 1766, as appears from Mr. Buck's paper. He says
that James Tilghman, of Philadelphia, addressed a letter to
the Proprietaries, Thomas and Richard Penn, at Spring Gar-
den, London, on the 14th day of August, 1766, in which he
stated that his brother-in-law, Colonel Francis, had gone "up
the N. E. Branch as far as Wyoming, where he says there is
a considerable body of good land and a very great fund of
coal in the hills, which surround a very fine and extensive
bottom there. This coal is thought to be very fine. With his
compliments he sends you a piece of the coal. This bed of
coal, situate as it is on the side of the river, may some time
or other be a thing of great value." By way of postscript he
adds: "The coal is in a small package of the Governor's."
In a reply from Thomas Penn to Mr. Tilghman, dated at
London on the following 7th of November, he says, in ac-
knowledgment: "I desire you will return my thanks to Colonel Francis for his good services in removing the intruders
that were settled on the Indians' land, and for the piece of
coal, which we shall have examined by some persons skillful
in that article and send their observations on it." It is further stated by Mr. Buck that the next mention of coal in this
section is in a draft by Charles Stewart from a survey made
in 1768 of a large tract of land on the west side of the
Susquehanna, opposite to the present city of Wilkesbarre,
which has "stone coal" marked thereon. The German traveler, Dr. Schoepf, tells us that in 1783 he found specimens
of coal in the Swatara creek, in Lebanon county, and learned
of its existence up the west branch of the Susquehanna.

The Wyoming valley was partly settled by a colony of
Connecticut people in 1762, representing "The Susquehanna
Company." In the same year the Indians murdered about
twenty of the colony and the remainder of the settlers were
driven away. Gradually the survivors and others associated
with them returned to the valley, and in 1768-9 it is claimed
that two of the settlers, being two brothers named Gore, from
Connecticut, who were blacksmiths, were the first persons in
this country to use anthracite coal, using it in a forge fire.

In 1776 and throughout the Revolutionary war anthracite coal was taken in arks from the Wyoming mines above Wilkesbarre down the Susquehanna to the United States armory at Carlisle. Mr. Buck says that the first shipment of about twenty tons of this coal "was obtained from a bed belonging to Judge Hollenback, one mile above Wilkesbarre, near the mouth of Mill creek." S. H. Daddow says in the *American Cyclopædia* that some of it also came from the old Smith mine in the vicinity of Plymouth.

At Carbondale, in the northeastern section of the Wyoming coal field, anthracite coal was discovered in 1804 by a surveyor named Samuel Preston, and in 1814 William and Maurice Wurtz commenced to make arrangements for its development. In 1815, after many discouraging attempts, they succeeded in sending one ark-load of coal to Philadelphia through the Lackawaxen and Delaware rivers, but the experiment was not repeated until 1823, after which shipments to Philadelphia were successfully made.

Anthracite coal appears to have been known to the settlers within the limits of the Schuylkill coal field as early as 1770. In William Scull's map of Pennsylvania, published in that year, " coal " is marked about the head waters of Schuylkill creek, thence stretching westward to those of the Swatara and to "the wilderness of St. Anthony." This " wilderness," we may mention, extended from Peters's mountain, in Dauphin county, westward to the Kittatinny or Blue mountains.

The act of the Pennsylvania legislature of March 15, 1784, for the improvement of the navigation of the Schuylkill, mentions "the coal mines at Basler's saw-mill " in Schuylkill county. A hunter named Nicholas Allen is said to have discovered coal in 1790 at the foot of Broad mountain, in the same county. No attempt to mine the coal discovered by Nicholas Allen seems to have been made. Reading Howell, in his map of Pennsylvania, published in 1792, marks the existence of " coal " near the source of Panther creek, about five miles east of the present town of Tamaqua, and on the border of Carbon county. In 1795 a blacksmith named Whetstone used anthracite coal near Pottsville, while others attempted to use it and abandoned it in disgust.

About 1800 William Morris took a wagon-load of anthracite coal from near Port Carbon to Philadelphia, but nobody wanted it, and Mr. Morris made no further efforts to mine or sell coal. About 1806 coal was found at Valley Forge, on the Schuylkill river, and a blacksmith named David Berlin and others successfully used it. In 1812 Col. George Shoemaker, of Pottsville, loaded nine wagons with coal from his mines at Centreville and hauled it to Philadelphia, where with great difficulty he sold two loads at the cost of transportation and gave the other seven loads away. He was by many regarded as an impostor for attempting to sell stone as coal.

The first discovery of anthracite coal in the Lehigh region is said to have been made in the Mauch Chunk mountain, about nine miles west of Mauch Chunk, where the town of Summit Hill is now located, by a poor hunter named Philip Ginter, in 1791. Pieces of the coal discovered by Ginter were taken to Colonel Jacob Weiss, at Fort Allen, who opened a "quarry" in the coal mountain that year. The discovery of coal on the Lehigh was announced as follows in the *New York Magazine* for February, 1792, in a communication dated Philadelphia, January 31st: "A coal mine has been discovered on the Lehigh, in the county of Northampton. The coal yet found is small, but there is every reason to believe that by searching deeper it will be found larger. The quality is good. If this natural advantage is improved it will be a prodigious resource to the city and cheapen the article of fuel, which now, from the labor of transportation, bears a high price."

In 1793 Colonel Weiss, John Nicholson, Michael Hillegas, Charles Cist, Robert Morris, (of Revolutionary fame,) J. Anthony Morris, and others organized the Lehigh Coal Mine Company, which obtained control of about six thousand acres of coal land, and several tons of coal were soon "dug up." But there was no market nearer than Philadelphia, and there were poor means of communication with that city. It was not until 1803 that the company succeeded in floating two arks to Philadelphia, through the Lehigh and Delaware rivers, laden with two hundred tons of coal. Five arks were started, but three of these were wrecked. The coal, however, could not be made to burn, probably because large lumps were used, and it was thrown away as useless for any purpose except to "gravel footwalks." In 1806 William Turnbull, of Philadelphia, floated three hundred bushels of coal from this region to Philadelphia in an ark he had constructed at Lausanne. The coal was sold to the officers of the Central Square water works, but it proved to be unmanageable, and Mr. Turnbull's experiment was not repeated.

In 1814 two ark-loads of Lehigh coal reached Philadelphia from the mines of the Lehigh Coal Mine Company, then leased by the Hon. Charles Miner and Jacob Cist, a son of Charles Cist, and this time the coal was sold at $21 a ton and successfully used by the purchasers, Josiah White and Erskine Hazard, who were then manufacturing wire at the Falls of Schuylkill. After this venture Miner and Cist abandoned the mining of anthracite coal. They had lost money.

In 1817 White & Hazard and George F. A. Hauto became interested in the improvement of the navigation of the Lehigh river for the purpose of aiding in the development of the Lehigh coal mines, and on the 20th of March, 1818, an act of the Pennsylvania legislature was passed authorizing the incorporation of the Lehigh Coal and Navigation Company. This company obtained a lease for twenty years of the Lehigh Coal Mine Company's lands, then amounting to ten thousand acres, for one ear of corn a year, if demanded; with the proviso that, from and after three years, the latter company should send, on its own account, at least 40,000 bushels of coal, or about 1,500 tons, per annum to Philadelphia. The new company commenced work immediately. In 1820 it sent 365 tons of anthracite coal to market; in 1821, 1,073 tons; in 1822, 2,240 tons; in 1823, 5,823 tons; and in 1826 its trade increased to 31,280 tons. During the next year, 1827, the Mauch Chunk Railroad was finished and the improvement of the ascending navigation was put under contract, soon after which shipments steadily increased.

The Middle coal region, occupying a wild and broken section of country between the Wyoming and Schuylkill regions, and extending on the east to the Lehigh region, was the last of the four great anthracite coal fields of Pennsylvania to be developed. The Mahanoy and Shamokin basins compose its principal divisions. Coal pits or mines are marked in the neighborhood of Mahanoy creek, above Crab run, in William Scull's map of Pennsylvania in 1770. But little mining was done in the region until 1834, owing mainly to its inaccessibility. In that year 500 tons were mined and hauled in wagons to neighboring districts.

Down to 1808 the anthracite coal of the Wyoming valley was used only in smiths' forges, but in that year Judge Jesse Fell, of Wilkesbarre, was successful in using it in a grate, as clearly appears from a memorandum signed with his name and dated February 11, 1808. This may have been the first successful attempt that had been made to use the new fuel for domestic purposes in a grate either in this country or in any other country. (Anthracite coal was not used in Wales until 1813, nor in France until 1814.) Its use in grates soon became general wherever it was mined or could be transported. "In the year 1788," says Judge Fell, " I used it in a nailery, and found it to be profitable in that business. The nails made with it would neat the weight of the rods, and frequently a balance over." It is claimed by Dr. T. C. James, of Philadelphia, in a paper read before the Historical Society of Pennsylvania on April 19th, 1826, that he successfully used anthracite coal in his house in 1804 and thenceforward. Unfortunately Dr. James does not say whether he used the coal in a stove or a grate.

The well-known Blossburg semi-bituminous coal region of Pennsylvania was not brought into public notice until after 1832, in which year it was geologically surveyed by Richard Cowling Taylor. In 1840 its development began by the building of a railroad to reach northern markets. In that year 4,235 tons were sent to market, followed by 25,-966 tons in 1841. The Broad Top semi-bituminous coal region of Pennsylvania was but very slightly developed until 1856, when the Huntingdon and Broad Top Railroad was completed and the first coal was sent eastward to market.

Anthracite coal of inferior quality was discovered in Rhode Island and Massachusetts about 1760. It has also been discovered in Virginia, Colorado, and New Mexico.

The existence of coal in Alabama was first noticed in 1834, by Dr. Alexander Jones, of Mobile.

The beginning of the regular manufacture of Connellsville coke, which is widely celebrated for its excellence as a

fuel for blast furnaces, dates from the summer of 1841, when
Provance McCormick and James Campbell made an agreement with John Taylor by which he was to erect two ovens
for making coke on his farm lying on the Youghiogheny
river, near Sedgwick station, a few miles below Connellsville,
Pennsylvania. The ovens were built of the bee-hive pattern.
After repeated failures a fair quality of coke was produced
in the winter of 1841–2. By the spring of 1842 enough
coke had been made to load two boats, each of which was 90
feet long. These boats were built by McCormick and Campbell, who were carpenters. Both boats were taken by William
Turner, pilot, down the Youghiogheny, the Monongahela, and
the Ohio to Cincinnati, where purchasers were obtained for
the coke after much difficulty. Others embarked in 1842 in
the manufacture of coke, and were more successful.

About 1844 improved ovens were introduced in the Connellsville district by Colonel A. M. Hill, whose energy and
success gave much impetus to the business of making coke.
In 1855 there were only 26 coke ovens at work in the district "above Pittsburgh," and in all Western Pennsylvania
there were probably less than a hundred; now the number
of ovens in the Connellsville district alone may be counted
by thousands, most of them built after improved models.
To-day Connellsville coke is extensively used in the blast
furnaces of many States, its use for this purpose extending
to the Mississippi valley, while it is used as far west as
Utah and California for other purposes. Over one-third of
the annual production of pig iron in this country is now
made with this fuel. Its use as a furnace fuel properly
dates from 1860, when it was first used at Pittsburgh in a
furnace owned by Graff, Bennett & Co., and known as Clinton .furnace. This was the first continuous and successful
use of Connellsville coke in a blast furnace. This coke is
free from sulphur, but contains more ash than the celebrated Durham coke of England. One hundred pounds of Connellsville coal will make 62½ pounds of coke.

The shipments of Connellsville coke in 1890 amounted
to 6,221,518 net tons. The shipments of Pocahontas Flat
Top coke, from Virginia and West Virginia, amounted in the
same year to 433,319 net tons.

We give below the official statistics of the production of coal in the United States in the census years 1870 and 1880, ending on the 31st day of May of each year, and in the census year 1889, ending on the 31st day of December.

Years—Gross tons.	Bituminous coal.	Anthracite coal.	Total.
Census year 1870	15,356,621	13,985,960	29,342,581
Census year 1880	38,242,641	25,580,189	63,822,830
Census year 1889	85,383,059	40,714,720	126,097,779

*The production of bituminous coal in the nine years and seven months ending with December 31, 1889, increased 123 per cent., while the production of anthracite coal increased 59 per cent. The total production in the same period increased about 98 per cent.

The following table gives in tons of 2,000 pounds the production of bituminous and anthracite coal in the United States in the census year 1889, by States and Territories.

States and Territories.	Production in 1889—Net tons.	States and Territories.	Production in 1889—Net tons.
Bituminous.		Ohio	9,976,787
Alabama	3,572,983	Pennsylvania	36,174,089
Arkansas	279,584	Tennessee	1,925,689
California and Oregon	184,179	Texas	128,216
Colorado	2,544,144	Utah	236,651
Illinois	12,104,272	Virginia	865,786
Indiana	2,845,057	Washington	1,030,578
Indian Territory	752,832	West Virginia	6,231,880
Iowa	4,095,358	Wyoming	1,388,947
Kansas and Nebraska	2,222,443	Total bituminous	95,629,026
Kentucky	2,399,755		
Maryland	2,939,715	*Anthracite.*	
Michigan	67,431	Pennsylvania	45,544,970
Missouri	2,557,823	Colorado, New Mexico, and	
Montana	363,301	Rhode Island	55,517
New Mexico	486,463	Total anthracite	45,600,487
North Carolina and Georgia	226,156		
North Dakota	28,907	Grand total	141,229,513

For the facts contained in this chapter we are indebted to many sources of information, but we have been most assisted by the patient researches of William J. Buck, by the exhaustive work of Samuel Harries Daddow and Benjamin Bannan on *Coal, Iron, and Oil*, published in 1866, and by the valuable *Introduction* to the report on manufactures accompanying the census of 1860. The census statistics for 1889 were compiled by Mr. John H. Jones, special agent.

CHAPTER LV.

BRITISH EFFORTS TO PREVENT THE DEVELOPMENT OF THE AMERICAN IRON INDUSTRY.

MANY of the difficulties encountered in the early development of all our industries were inseparable from the conditions which attend the settlement of a new country, but others were of a political character, and grew out of the dependent relation of the colonies to Great Britain. The first Lord Sheffield declared that "the only use and advantage of American colonies or West India islands is the monopoly of their consumption and the carriage of their produce." McCulloch, in his *Commercial Dictionary*, admits that it was "a leading principle in the system of colonial policy, adopted as well by England as by the other European nations, to discourage all attempts to manufacture such articles in the colonies as could be provided for them by the mother country." Dr. William Elder, in his *Questions of the Day*, says : "The colonies were held under restraint so absolute that, beyond the common domestic industries and the most ordinary mechanical employments, no kind of manufactures was permitted." Bancroft, in his *History of the United States of America*, says that "England, in its relations with other States, sought a convenient tariff ; in the colonies it prohibited industry." He further says: "The British nation took no part in the strifes between the governors and the colonies; but they were jealously alive to the interests of their own commerce and manufactures. That the British creditor might be secure lands in the plantations were, by act of Parliament, made liable for debts. Every branch of consumption was, as far as practicable, secured to English manufacturers ; every form of competition in industry, in the heart of the plantations, was discouraged or forbidden." In 1750 appeared the celebrated deliverance of a prominent Englishman, Joshua Gee, in which he boldly declared that the British people "ought always to keep a watchful eye over our colonies, to restrain them from setting up any of the manufactures which are carried on in

Great Britain, and any such attempts should be crushed in the beginning, for if they are suffered to grow up to maturity it will be difficult to suppress them." He especially recommended that "all slitting mills, and engines for drawing wire or weaving stockings, *be put down*." Mathew Carey, in his *Essays on Political Economy*, says: "The great Chatham, the least hostile to British America of British ministers, in his speech in the House of Lords, on the address to the throne, in 1770, expressed his utmost alarm at the first efforts at manufactures in America." Henry C. Carey informs us, in his *Principles of Social Science*, that even the distinguished Lord Chatham " declared that he would not allow the colonists to make even a hobnail for themselves."

A law of Virginia, to encourage textile manufactures in that province, passed in 1684, was annulled in England. In 1699 the exportation, by land or water, of wool and woolen manufactures from one colony to another was prohibited. This was done that English woolen manufacturers might have a monopoly in supplying the colonists with woolen goods. From 1719 to 1732 British merchants " complained in memorials to the government that the people of Massachusetts, New York, Connecticut, Rhode Island, and Maryland were setting up manufactures of woolen and linen for the use of their own families, and of flax and hemp for coarse bags and halters." Bancroft says: " In the land of furs it was found that hats were well made : the London company of hatters remonstrated, and their craft was protected by an act forbidding hats to be transported from one plantation to another." " In 1732," says Henry C. Carey, in his great work above mentioned, " the exportation of hats from province to province was prohibited, and the number of hatters' apprentices was limited by law." In 1750 a hatter-shop in Massachusetts was declared by the British Parliament to be a nuisance.

Concerning the attitude of Great Britain toward the woolen manufactures of the colonies at as late a period as the beginning of the Revolution we quote from Adam Smith, in his *Wealth of Nations*, published in 1776 : " She prohibits the exportation from one province to another by water, and even the carriage by land upon horseback or in a cart, of hats, of wools and woolen goods, of the produce of America; a regulation which effectually prevents the establishment of any manufacture of such commodities for distant sale, and confines the industry of her colonists in this way to such coarse and household manufactures as a private family commonly makes for its own use, or for that of some of its neighbors in the same province."

In the seventeenth century the colonial iron industry was so slowly developed that it attracted but little attention in Great Britain; but at the beginning of the eighteenth century, when Pennsylvania, Maryland, and Virginia began to manufacture iron and to export it to England, the possibilities of its development in competition with the English iron industry became a source of uneasiness to English ironmasters. In the following passage Bancroft details the results of this apprehension.

The proprietors of English iron works were jealous of American industry. In 1719 news came that, in some parts of Massachusetts, "the inhabitants worked up their wool and flax, and made a coarse sort for their own use; that they manufactured great part of their leather, that there were also hatters in the maritime towns; and that six furnaces and nineteen forges were set up for making iron." These six furnaces and nineteen forges were a terror to England, and their spectres haunted the public imagination for a quarter of a century. The House of Commons readily resolved that "the erecting manufactories in the colonies tended to lessen their dependence;" and, under pretense of encouraging the importation of American lumber, they passed a bill having the clause, "that none in the plantations should manufacture iron wares of any kind out of any sows, pigs, or bars whatsoever." The House of Lords added, "that no forge, going by water, or other works should be erected in any of the said plantations, for the making, working, or converting of any sows, pigs, or cast-iron into bar or rod iron." The opposition of the northern colonies defeated the bill; England would not yet forbid the colonists to manufacture a bolt or a nail; but the purpose was never abandoned.

The distinguished American historian records in the following language the culmination of the repressive policy of the mother country toward the iron industry of the colonies. "America abounded in iron ore; its unwrought iron was excluded by a duty from the English market; and its people were rapidly gaining skill at the furnace and the forge. In February, 1750, the subject engaged the attention of the House of Commons. To check the danger of American rivalry Charles Townshend was placed at the head of a committee.

After a few days' deliberation he brought in a bill which permitted American iron in its rudest forms to be imported duty free; but, now that the nailers in the colonies could afford spikes and large nails cheaper than the English, it forbade the smiths of America to erect any mill for slitting or rolling iron, or any plating-forge to work with a tilt-hammer, or any furnace for making steel. . . . The house divided on the proposal that every slitting mill in America should be abolished. The clause failed only by a majority of twenty-two ; but an immediate return was required of every mill already existing, and the number was never to be increased." The act of Parliament to which Bancroft here alludes contained many provisions, but its principal provisions were as follows.

WHEREAS, The importation of bar iron from His Majesty's colonies in America into the port of London, and the importation of pig iron from the said colonies into any port of Great Britain, and the manufacture of such bar and pig iron in Great Britain, will be a great advantage, not only to the said colonies, but also to this kingdom, by furnishing the manufacturers of iron with a supply of that useful and necessary commodity, and by means thereof large sums of money, now annually paid for iron to foreigners, will be saved to this kingdom, and *a greater quantity of the woolen, and other manufactures of Great Britain, will be exported to America, in exchange for such iron so imported;* be it therefore enacted by the King's most excellent majesty, by and with the advice and consent of the Lords, spiritual and temporal, and Commons, in this present Parliament assembled, and by the authority of the same, that from and after the twenty-fourth day of June, one thousand seven hundred and fifty, the several and respective subsidies, customs, impositions, rates, and duties, now payable on pig iron, made in and imported from His Majesty's colonies in America into any port of Great Britain, shall cease, determine, and be no longer paid ; and that from and after the said twenty-fourth day of June no subsidy, custom, imposition, rate, or duty whatever shall be payable upon bar iron made in and imported from the said colonies into the port of London; any law, statute, or usage to the contrary thereof in any wise notwithstanding.

And, that pig and bar iron made in His Majesty's colonies in America *may be further manufactured in this kingdom,* be it further enacted by the authority aforesaid, that from and after the twenty-fourth day of June, one thousand seven hundred and fifty, no mill or other engine for slitting or rolling of iron, or any plateing forge to work with a tilt hammer, or any furnace for making steel, shall be erected, or after such erection continued in any of His Majesty's colonies in America; and if any person or persons shall erect, or cause to be erected, or after such erection continue, or cause to be continued, in any of the said colonies, any such mill, engine, forge, or furnace, every person or persons so offending shall, for every such mill, engine, forge, or furnace, forfeit the sum of two hundred pounds of lawful money of Great Britain.

And it is hereby further enacted by the authority aforesaid, that every such mill, engine, forge, or furnace, so erected or continued, contrary to the directions of this act, *shall be deemed a common nuisance*, and that every governor, lieutenant-governor, or commander-in-chief of any of His Majesty's colonies in America, where any such mill, engine, forge, or furnace shall be erected or continued, shall, upon information to him made and given, upon the oath of any two or more credible witnesses, that any such mill, engine, forge, or furnace hath been so erected or continued, (which oath such governor, lieutenant-governor, or commander-in-chief, is hereby authorized and required to administer,) order and cause every such mill, engine, forge, or furnace to be abated within the space of thirty days next after such information given and made as aforesaid.

The provision in the above act which repealed the duties on colonial pig iron and bar iron imported into Great Britain was wholly based on the necessities of the mother country, and was not in the least due to a desire to build up a colonial iron industry for the benefit of the colonies themselves. There was in 1750 a scarcity of wood in England for the supply of charcoal, which was then the principal fuel used in the smelting and refining of iron, but forests everywhere abounded in the colonies and iron ore had been found in many places. The manufacture of pig iron and bar iron in the colonies, and their exportation to England, to meet a scarcity of the domestic supply of these raw products, and to be exchanged for British woolen and other manufactures, was therefore encouraged. The provision relating to articles made *from* pig iron and bar iron was intended to be prohibitory of their manufacture in the colonies. Adam Smith thus described in 1776 the character of this legislation, which had not been repealed nor altered down to that period, the beginning of the Revolution: " While Great Britain encourages in America the manufactures of pig and bar iron, by exempting them from duties to which the like commodities are subject when imported from any other country, she imposes an absolute prohibition upon the erection of steel furnaces and slit-mills in any of her American plantations. She will not suffer her colonists to work in those more refined manufactures even for their own consumption, but insists upon their purchasing of her merchants and manufacturers all goods of this kind which they have occasion for."

Bancroft comments as follows upon the reception which was given in England to the new law.

While England applauded the restriction, its owners of iron mines grudged to America a share of the market for the rough material; the tanners, from the threatened inaction of the English furnaces, feared a diminished supply of bark; the clergy and gentry foreboded injury to the price of woodlands. The importation of bar iron from the colonies was therefore *limited to the port of London, which already had its supply from abroad.* The ironmongers and smiths of Birmingham thought well of importing bars of iron free; but, from "compassion" to the "many thousand families in the kingdom" who otherwise "must be ruined," they prayed that "the American people" might be subject not to the proposed restrictions only, but to such others "as may secure for ever the trade to this country." Some would have admitted the raw material from no colony where its minute manufacture was carried on.

The act of 1750 was generally enforced in the colonies, and the further erection of slitting and rolling mills, plating forges, and steel furnaces was prevented. Works of the character described which had been erected previous to the passage of the act could not, however, be legally prevented from continuing in operation. The governors of the several colonies issued proclamations commanding obedience to the requirements of the new law. The proclamation of lieutenant-governor James Hamilton, of Pennsylvania, was printed by Benjamin Franklin. An original copy may be seen in the library of the Pennsylvania Historical Society in Philadelphia. It reads as follows.

By the Honourable JAMES HAMILTON, Esq., Lieutenant-Governor and Commander-in-Chief of the Province of Pennsylvania and Counties of New Castle, Kent, and Sussex, on Delaware.

A PROCLAMATION.

WHEREAS, By an act of Parliament passed in the twenty-third year of His Majesty's reign, entituled "An act to encourage the importation of pig and bar iron from His Majesty's colonies in America, and to prevent the erection of any mill, or other engine, for slitting or rolling of iron, or any plating-forge to work with a tilt-hammer, or any furnace for making steel in any of the said colonies," it is enacted —"That from and after the twenty-fourth day of June, in the year of our Lord one thousand seven hundred and fifty, every governor, lieutenant-governor, and commander-in-chief of any of His Majesty's colonies in America shall forthwith transmit to the commissioners for trade and plantations a certificate, under his hand and seal of office, containing a particular account of every mill or engine for slitting and rolling of iron, and every plating-forge to work with a tilt-hammer, and every furnace for making steel, at the time of the commencement of this act, erected in his colony; expressing, also, in the said certificate, such of them as are used, and the name or names of the proprietor or proprietors of each such mill, engine, forge, and furnace, and the place where each such mill, engine, forge, and furnace is erected, and the number of engines, forges, and furnaces in the said colony." To the end therefore that I may be the better enabled to obey the directions of the said act, I have thought fit, with the advice of the council, to issue this proclamation, hereby enjoining and requiring the proprietor or proprietors, or in case of their absence, the occupiers of any of the above-mentioned mills, engines, forges, and furnaces, erected within this province, to appear before me, at the city of Philadelphia, on or before the twenty-first day of September next, with proper and ample testimonials of the rights of such proprietor, proprietors, and occupiers therein, and sufficient proofs whether the said mills, engines, forges, and furnaces respectively were used on the said twenty-fourth day of June or not: And I do further hereby require and command the sheriff of every county in this province respectively, on or before the said twenty-first day of September, to appear before me, at the city of Philadelphia aforesaid, and then and there by writings, under their hands and seals, to certify and make known to me every mill or engine for slitting and rolling of iron, every plating-forge to work with a tilt-hammer, and every furnace for making steel, which were erected within their several and respective counties on the said twenty-fourth day of June, and the place and places where the same were erected, with the names of their reputed proprietor or proprietors, and the occupiers of them, and every of them; and whether they or any of them were used on the said twenty-fourth day of June or not, as they and each of them will answer the contrary at their peril.

Given under my hand and the great seal of the province of Pennsylvania, at Philadelphia, this sixteenth day of August, in the twenty-fourth year of the reign of our Sovereign Lord, GEORGE the Second, King of Great Britain, France, and Ireland, etc., and in the year of our Lord 1750.

By His Honour's command. JAMES HAMILTON.
RICHARD PETERS, *Secretary.*
GOD Save the KING.

PHILADELPHIA: Printed by B. FRANKLIN, Printer to the Province, MDCCL.

As may easily be imagined the passage of this act aroused anew the feeling of discontent in the colonies which had been created and kept alive by many repressive measures of the mother country directed against our colonial manufactures. These measures of repression formed a large part of that "long train of abuses and usurpations" which led to the war of independence.

From the passage of the act of 1750 down to the Revolution our iron industry was mainly confined to the production of pig iron and bar iron and castings from the blast furnace. The effect of this act was to repress the development of our steel industry and of the finished branches of our iron industry. During this period we made pig iron and bar iron in sufficient quantities for our own use and the surplus was sent to the mother country.

But the colonies suffered also from the general restrictive policy of Great Britain affecting the manufactures of all foreign countries, particularly from its numerous acts of Parliament prohibiting the exportation of skilled artisans and improved machinery. Adam Smith gives us these facts.

By the 7th and 8th of William III. [1696 and 1697], chapter 20, section 8, the exportation of frames or engines for knitting gloves or stockings is prohibited under the penalty not only of the forfeiture of such frames or engines so exported, or attempted to be exported, but of forty pounds— one-half to the king, the other to the person who shall inform or sue for the same.

By the 5th George I. [1718], chapter 27, the person who shall be convicted of enticing any artificer of, or in any of the manufactures of, Great Britain, to go into any foreign parts in order to practice or teach his trade, is liable, for the first offense, to be fined in any sum not exceeding one hundred pounds, and to three months' imprisonment, and until the fine shall be paid; and, for the second offense, to be fined in any sum at the discretion of the court, and to imprisonment for twelve months, and until the fine shall be paid. By the 23d George II. [1749], chapter 13, this penalty is increased, for the first offense, to five hundred pounds for every artificer so enticed, and to twelve months' imprisonment, and until the fine shall be paid; and, for the second offense, to one thousand pounds, and to two years' imprisonment, and until the fine shall be paid.

By the former of these two statutes, upon proof that any person has been enticing any artificer, or that any artificer has promised or contracted to go into foreign parts for the purposes aforesaid, such artificer may be obliged to give security at the discretion of the court that he shall not go beyond the seas, and may be committed to prison until he give such security.

If any artificer has gone beyond the seas, and is exercising or teaching his trade in any foreign country, upon warning being given to him by any of his majesty's ministers or consuls abroad, or by one of his majesty's secretaries of state for the time being, if he does not within six months after such warning return to this realm, and from thenceforth abide and inhabit continually within the same, he is from thenceforth declared incapable of taking any legacy devised to him within this kingdom, or of being executor or administrator to any person, or of taking any lands within this kingdom by descent, devise, or purchase. He likewise forfeits to the king all his lands, goods, and chattels, is declared an alien in every respect, and is put out of the king's protection.

Sir William Blackstone, in the chapter on offenses against public trade, in his *Commentaries on the Laws of England*, recites some of the details above given by Adam Smith, and adds important testimony to the character of the restrictive legislation adopted by Great Britain in 1774, during the long reign of George the Third. He says:

To prevent the destruction of our home manufactures by transporting and seducing our artists to settle abroad, it is provided, by statute 5 George I., c. 27, that such as so entice or seduce them shall be fined £100 and be imprisoned three months; and for the second offense shall be fined at discretion, and be imprisoned a year; and the artificers so going into foreign countries, and not returning within six months after warning given them by the British ambassador where they reside, shall be deemed aliens, and forfeit all their land and goods, and shall be incapable of any legacy or gift. By statute 23 George II., c. 13, the seducers incur, for the first offense, a forfeiture of £500 for each artificer contracted with to be sent abroad, and imprisonment for twelve months; and for the second, £1000, and are liable to two years' imprisonment; and, by the same statute, connected with 14 George III., c. 71, if any person exports any tools or utensils used in the silk, linen, cotton, or woolen manufactures (excepting wool cards to North America), he forfeits the same and £200, and the captain of the ship (having knowledge thereof) £100; and if any captain of a king's ship, or officer of the customs, knowingly suffers such exportation he forfeits £100 and his employment, and is forever made incapable of bearing any public office; and every person collecting such tools or utensils in order to export the same shall, on conviction at the assizes, forfeit such tools and also £200.

The policy which is epitomized above by the great English political economist and the great English commentator was continued throughout the Revolution and long after the colonies secured their independence. The details of British legislation at this period are worthy of preservation. The following summary of the provisions of various restrictive acts of Parliament enacted in 1781, 1782, 1785, and 1795 is derived from Pope's *Laws of the Customs and Excise.*

(1781.) It was enacted (21 Geo. III., c. 37) that any person who packed or put on board, or caused to be brought to any place in order to be put on board any vessel, with a view to exportation, "any machine, engine, tool, press, paper, utensil, or implement, or any part thereof, which now is or hereafter may be used in the woolen, cotton, linen, or silk manufacture of this kingdom, or goods wherein wool, cotton, linen, or silk are used, or any model or plan thereof," etc., should forfeit every such machine and the goods packed therewith and £200, and suffer imprisonment for twelve months. The like penalties attached to having in custody or power, or collecting, making, applying for, or causing to be made, any such machinery, and the forfeitures were to go to the use of the informer after the expenses of prosecution were paid. The exportation, and the attempt to put on board for that purpose, of "any blocks, plates, engines, tools, or utensils used in, or which are proper for the preparing or finishing of, the calico, cotton, muslin, or linen printing manufactures, or any part thereof," were the next year (1782) prohibited under penalty of £500. The same act interdicted the transportation of tools used in the iron and steel manufactures.

(1785.) The great improvements which had been made in England in

all branches of the iron manufacture, and the competition springing up in
Europe and America in the production of raw iron, doubtless prompted the
act of 1785 (25 Geo. III., c. 67) to prevent, under severe penalties, the enticing of artificers or workmen in the iron and steel manufactures out of
the kingdom, and the exportation of any tools used in these branches to
any place beyond the seas.

(1795.) The act of Parliament of 1785, prohibiting the exportation of
tools and machinery used in the iron and steel manufactures, was made
perpetual by the statute 35 Geo. III., c. 38. It recapitulates the several descriptions of machines, engines, implements, utensils, and models, or parts
thereof, employed in rolling, slitting, pressing, casting, boring, stamping,
piercing, scoring, shading, or chasing and die-sinking iron and other metals.
It included machines used in the button, glass, pottery, saddle and harness,
and other manufactures, wire moulds for paper, etc.

We copy below the leading provisions of the act of the
British Parliament, (chapter 37,) adopted in 1781, the twenty-
first year of the reign of George the Third, which prohibited
the exportation from Great Britain of machinery used in the
manufacture of cotton, linen, woolen, and silk goods.

An act to explain and amend an act made in the fourteenth year of
the reign of his present Majesty, intituled, An Act to prevent the exportation to foreign parts of utensils made use of in the cotton, linen, woollen,
and silk manufactures of this kingdom, . . . That if, at any time after the
twenty-fourth day of June, one thousand seven hundred and eighty-one,
any person or persons in Great Britain or Ireland shall . . . put on board
of any ship or vessel, which shall not be bound directly to some port or
place in Great Britain or Ireland, . . . any machine, engine, tool, press,
paper, utensil, or implement whatsoever, which now is, or at any time or
times hereafter shall or may be used in, or proper for the preparing, working, pressing, finishing, or completing, of the woollen, cotton, linen, or
silk manufactures of this kingdom . . . ; or any model or plan, or
models or plans, of any such machine, engine, tool, press, paper, utensil,
or implement, or any part or parts thereof, . . . the person or persons
so offending shall, for every such offence, not only forfeit all such machines, engines, tools, press, paper, utensils, or implements, models or
plans, or parts thereof respectively, together with the packages, and all
other goods packed therewith, if any such there be, but also the sum of
two hundred pounds of lawful money of Great Britain; and shall also suffer imprisonment . . . for the space of twelve months, without bail or
mainprize, and until such forfeiture shall be paid.

The act of 1785, in the twenty-fifth year of the reign of
George the Third, a little over one hundred years ago, was
undisguisedly passed to cripple if possible the iron industries
of foreign countries. Its principal provisions were as follows.

An act to prohibit the exportation to foreign parts of tools and utensils
made use of in the iron and steel manufactures of this kingdom ; and to

prevent the seducing of artificers or workmen, employed in those manufactures, to go into parts beyond the seas.

Whereas, the exportation of the several tools and utensils made use of
in preparing, working up, and finishing the iron and steel manufactures of
this kingdom, or either of them, will enable foreigners to work up such
manufactures, and thereby greatly diminish the exportation of the same
from this kingdom; therefore, for the preserving, as much as possible, to
His Majesty's subjects the benefits arising from those great and valuable
branches of trade and commerce, be it enacted, that if, at any time, after
the first day of August, one thousand seven hundred and eighty-five, any
person or persons in Great Britain shall, upon any pretence whatsoever, export, load, or put on board, or pack, or cause or procure to be loaden, put on
board, or packed, in order to be loaded or put on board of any ship or vessel which shall be bound to some port or place in parts beyond the seas
(except to Ireland), or shall lade, or cause or procure to be laden, on board
any boat or other vessel, or shall bring, or cause to be brought, to any quay,
wharf, or other place, in order to be so laden or put on board any such ship
or vessel, any tool or utensil hereafter mentioned; that is to say, hand
stamps, dog head stamps, pulley stamps, stamps of all sorts, hammers and
anvils for stamps, screws for stamps, iron rods for stamps, presses of all
sorts, in iron, steel, or other metal, which are used for giving impressions
to metal, or any parts of these several articles; presses of all sorts called
cutting-out presses, beds and punches to be used therewith; piercing presses
of all sorts, beds and punches to be used therewith, either in parts or pieces,
or fitted together; iron or steel dies to be used in stamps or presses either
with or without impressions on them; *rollers of cast iron, wrought iron, or
steel, for rolling of metal, and frames for the same;* flasks or casting moulds,
and boards used therewith; lathes of all sorts for turning, burnishing, polishing, either the whole together, or separate parts thereof; lathe strings,
polishing brushes, scoring or shading engines, presses for horn buttons, dies
for horn buttons, sheers for cutting of metal, rolled steel, rolled metal, with
silver thereon, parts of buttons not fitted up into buttons, or in an unfinish-
ed state; engines for chafing, stocks for casting buckles, buttons, and rings;
*cast-iron anvils and hammers for forging mills for iron and copper; roles, slit-
ters, beds, pillars, and frames for slitting mills;* die-sinking tools of all sorts,
engines for making button shanks, laps of all sorts, drilling engines, tools
for pinching of glass, engines for covering of whips, polishing brushes, bars
of metal covered with gold or silver, *iron or steel screw plates, pins, and stocks
for making screws,* or any other tool or utensil whatsoever, which now is, are,
or at any time or times hereafter shall or may be used in, or proper for the
preparing, working, finishing, or completing of the iron or steel manufactures of this kingdom, or either of them, by what name or names soever
the same shall be called or known, *or any model or plan,* or models or plans,
of any such tool, utensil, or implement, or any part or parts thereof; the
person or persons so offending shall for every such offence not only forfeit
and lose all such tools or utensils, or parts or parcels thereof, together with
the packages, and all other goods packed therewith, if any such there be,
. . . the person or persons so offending shall, for every such offence, forfeit the sum of two hundred pounds of lawful money of Great Britain, and
shall also suffer imprisonment, in the common gaol, prison, or house of cor-

rection, . . . for the space of twelve months, without bail or mainprize, and until such forfeiture shall be paid.

And whereas, *for the encouragement of such manufactories in this kingdom, it is necessary that provision should be made to prevent artificers, and others employed therein, from departing, or from being seduced to depart out of this kingdom;* be it therefore enacted by the authority aforesaid, that from and after the said first day of August, one thousand seven hundred and eighty-five, if any person or persons shall contract with, entice, persuade, or endeavor to seduce or encourage any artificer or workman concerned or employed, or who shall have worked at, or been employed in, the iron or steel manufactures in this kingdom, or in making or preparing any tools or utensils for such manufactory, to go out of Great Britain to any parts beyond the seas (except to Ireland), and shall be convicted thereof . . . shall, for every artificer so contracted with, enticed, persuaded, encouraged, or seduced, or attempted so to be, forfeit and pay the sum of five hundred pounds of lawful money of Great Britain, and shall be committed to the common gaol, . . . there to remain without bail or mainprize for the space of twelve calendar months, and until such forfeiture shall be paid; and in case of a subsequent offence of the same kind the person or persons so again offending shall, upon the like conviction, forfeit and pay, for every person so contracted with, enticed, persuaded, encouraged, or seduced, or attempted so to be, the sum of one thousand pounds, . . . and shall be committed to the common gaol as aforesaid, there to remain, without bail or mainprize, for and during the term of two years, and until such forfeitures shall be paid.

In 1786 some trifling changes were made in the list of articles the exportation of which was prohibited, but the principal tools used in the manufacture of iron and steel were carefully preserved in this list. At the same time tools for making paper, for making and working glass, and for making pottery and harness were added to the list. In 1795, as already stated, the act of 1785 was made perpetual. In 1799 an act was passed providing that, "Whereas, there have of late been many attempts to seduce colliers out of Scotland into foreign countries, be it therefore further enacted that all persons seducing, or attempting to seduce, colliers . . . from the kingdom of Great Britain shall be punished in the same manner as persons seducing, or attempting to seduce, manufacturers or other artisans are punishable by law." This last act would have a tendency to prevent the mining of coal in the United States, which had scarcely been commenced at the time of its passage.

The prohibition of the exportation of machinery for the manufacture of iron and steel and of other machinery continued until long after the beginning of the present century.

In 1825 and again in 1833 the exportation of machinery for the manufacture of cotton, woolen, linen, and silk goods was again *prohibited*. It was not permitted to be exported until 1845. In the London *Times* for October 30, 1811, will be found a detailed account of the arrest of Hugh Wagstaff for placing on board the American ship *Mount Vernon*, bound to New York, twenty-three boxes containing spindles used in the spinning of cotton. Wagstaff was committed to Lancaster Castle for trial under the act of 21 Geo. III., chapter 37, and the boxes were seized. The Hon. John L. Hayes, of Boston, the highest authority in the United States upon the literature of our textile industries, informs us that "the patriotic Tench Coxe, the able coadjutor of Alexander Hamilton in the Treasury, entered into a bond with a person in London who engaged to send him complete models of Arkwright's patents. The models were completed and packed, but were detected and forfeited." In 1832 the model of a roller for calico printing, to be used at Lowell, in Massachusetts, could be obtained from England only by concealing it in the trunk of a lady who was returning to this country. From a letter in the possession of Dr. Hayes it appears that when, in 1839, Messrs. Sharp & Roberts, of Manchester, England, desired to introduce their self-acting mule into this country, after obtaining a patent for it here, their American partner, Mr. Bradford Durfee, of Fall River, was compelled to smuggle through France the patterns for the castings. The statutes interfering with the emigration of artificers were not wholly repealed until 1825.

During the long period in the history of the mother country in which she endeavored by the legislation above recited to repress the development of our manufacturing industries she vigorously protected her own industries by customs duties from foreign competition. The protection which she gave to her iron industry after Cort had perfected for her the puddling furnace and the rolling mill, and the owners of her blast furnaces had generally introduced steam-power and the use of mineral fuel, is especially noticeable. Prior to this time Great Britain had not made enough iron to supply her own wants; now she could do this. We quote as follows from Scrivenor's *History of the Iron Trade.*

From 1782 till 1795 the duty on foreign bars was £2 16s. 2d. per ton. It rose to £3 4s. 7d. in 1797; from 1798 to 1802 it was £3 15s. 5d.; in two years it had got to £4 17s. 1d.; from 1806 to 1808 it stood at £5 7s. 5¾d.; in the three years between 1809 and 1812 it was £5 9s. 10d.; and in the five years ending with 1818 it had been £6 9s. 10d. At this date a distinction was made in the interest of British shipping; for whilst thenceforward, till the close of 1825, the duty on foreign bars was £6 10s. if imported in British ships, it was £7 18s. 6d. if imported in foreign. Nor was this all; iron slit, or hammered into rods, and iron drawn down, or hammered, less than three-quarters of an inch square, was made to pay a duty at the rate of £20 per ton; wrought iron, not otherwise enumerated, was taxed with a payment of £50 for every £100 worth imported; and steel, or manufactures of steel, were similarly loaded with a fifty per cent. duty.

It does not fall within the scope of this work to discuss the revenue policy of the British Government at any period of the history of our own country further than to show its effects in retarding the development of our iron and steel industries. This has been done. As germane, however, to what has already been presented the following additional testimony concerning the hostile policy of the British Government and people toward American manufacturing industries in the present century is of historical value.

In 1816 Lord Brougham, in a speech in Parliament advocating the increased exportation of British goods to the United States, declared that "it was well worth while to incur a loss upon the first exportation, in order by the glut to stifle in the cradle those rising manufactures in the United States which the war has forced into existence contrary to the natural course of things." Mr. Robertson, a member of Parliament, said in a memorable speech quoted by Henry Clay in 1832: "It was idle for us to endeavor to persuade other nations to join with us in adopting the principles of what was called free trade. Other nations knew, as well as the noble lord opposite and those who acted with him, what we meant by free trade was nothing more nor less than, by means of the great advantages we enjoyed, to get a monopoly of all their markets for our manufactures, and to prevent them, one and all, from ever becoming manufacturing nations." In 1843 the London *Spectator* said : " More general considerations tend to show that the trade between the two countries, most beneficial to both, must be what is commonly called a colonial trade; the new-settled country importing the manufactures of the old in exchange for its own raw produce. In all economical relations the United States still stand to England in the relation of colony to mother country." William Huskisson, the pioneer in the British free trade movement and long a prominent member of the British Parliament, declared in a speech in 1825 that, " to enable capital to obtain a fair remuneration, *the price of labor must be kept down.*" In 1854 a British Parliamentary commission declared : " The laboring classes generally in the manufacturing districts of this country, and especially in the iron and coal districts, are very little aware of the extent to which they are often indebted for their being employed at all to the immense losses which their employers voluntarily incur in bad times in order to destroy foreign competition and to gain and keep possession of foreign markets. . . . The large capitals of this country are the great instruments of warfare against the competing capital of foreign countries."

CHAPTER LVI.

THE AMERICAN IRON INDUSTRY LONG DEPRESSED BY FOREIGN COMPETITION.

DURING the Revolution and immediately after its close the iron industry of Great Britain was greatly stimulated by the general substitution of bituminous coal for charcoal, by the application of the steam engine to the blowing of blast furnaces, and by the introduction of the puddling furnace and of 'grooved rolls in refining and finishing iron. These improvements greatly increased and cheapened the products of British iron works, so that, instead of being dependent upon the United States for a supply of pig iron and bar iron, British iron manufacturers were enabled to send these and other iron products to the former colonies of Great Britain in successful competition with their own manufactures. The effect of these changes was to greatly retard the extension of our iron industry after the Revolution. The competition which produced this result might have been averted if the emancipated colonies had followed the example of the mother country and imposed duties upon foreign iron and steel which would have fully protected the domestic manufacture of these products. But they did not do this, although the desire for industrial independence was one of the leading causes of the Revolution, and although the fact was fully recognized after our political independence was secured that domestic manufactures were greatly in need of the protection against foreign competition which only high duties could give to them. Under the Articles of Confederation, and for many years after the establishment of our "more perfect union," duties upon foreign imports of every description were so low that they afforded no adequate protection to American manufactures. From 1789 to 1812 the duties on pig iron and bar iron ranged from only 5 per cent. to 19¼ per cent. of their value. In the same years the duty on steel ranged from 50 cents to $1.10 per cwt. These were but little else than revenue duties. During all of this period our manufactures of iron and steel did not flourish ; nor did any other American manufacturing industry.

The following petition, presented to the General Assembly of Pennsylvania on November 30, 1785, two years before the framing of the Federal Constitution, shows the effect at that time of foreign competition, principally from Great Britain, upon the manufacture of bar iron in Pennsylvania. It will be remembered that under the Articles of Confederation each State reserved to itself the control of all duties upon imported foreign commodities, a reservation which worked so badly in many ways that the creation of our present form of government soon became a necessity from this cause alone. Pennsylvania had, however, been slow to assert the need of protection for some of her infant manufactures, as the disastrous fate of the petition referred to will testify.

To the Honorable the Representatives of the Freemen of the Commonwealth of Pennsylvania in General Assembly met.

The petition of the subscribers, manufacturers of bar iron within the Commonwealth aforesaid, respectfully sheweth.

That, by an act passed during the last session of the late Assembly, additional duties are laid on the importation of divers manufactures of Europe and other foreign parts, for the purpose of protecting and encouraging the manufactures of this State, wherein your petitioners find the article of bar iron has been omitted.

That the manufacturing of bar iron within this State has not only been found very useful and important during the late war, but has always been considered as a source of public wealth and benefit; as great sums of money were thereby kept within the country ; which circulating through the hands of several thousand persons, employed in the manufacture of bar iron and furnishing the requisite materials, enabled them to maintain themselves and their families and contribute to the support of government by payment of taxes ; and an influx of specie and other considerable advantages were also derived to the trade of this State by the exportation of great quantities of bar iron to other parts of the continent.

That, although most of the iron manufactured within this State is confessedly superior in quality to the iron imported from foreign parts, yet, because iron can not be manufactured at so low a price here as in countries where the laborers are but little removed above the condition of slaves, the sale of divers large quantities of foreign iron lately imported into this State, notwithstanding its inferior quality, operates so much to the prejudice of all persons concerned in the manufacture of bar iron here that there is great reason to apprehend, unless the legislature shall extend their aid, further importations of foreign iron will in a short time occasion a total stoppage and destruction of that very useful and beneficial manufacture amongst us.

Your petitioners trust that, on full consideration of the premises, the

manufacture of bar iron within this State will appear to your Honorable
House essentially entitled to public protection and encouragement, and
therefore pray your Honorable House may be pleased to grant relief in the
premises by laying such additional duties on foreign bar iron as will prevent further importations thereof becoming destructive or oppressive to the
manufacture of bar iron within this State.   And your petitioners as in duty
bound shall ever pray, &c.

JACOB MORGAN, JR.	JOHN PATTON.	JAMES OLD.
DAVID POTTS.	GEORGE EGE.	JNO. EDWARDS.
JAMES HARTLEY.	JACOB WINEY.	WILLIAM BIRD.
ANDW. PETTITT.	VALENTINE ECKERT.	JACOB LESHET.
JESSE GRUNFIELD.	PETER GRUBB, JR.	MICHL. EGE.
THOS. HUMPHREYS.	CURTIS GRUBB.	JN. HELLINGS.
THOS. RUTTER.	PETER GRUBB, SR.	ABRM. SHARPLES.
THOS. MAYBURRY.	ROBT. COLEMAN.	HILARY BAKER.
SAML. POTTS.	MATTHIAS HOUGH.	C. DOUGLASS.
J. HOCKLEY.	WILLIAM OLDE.	RICHD. BACKHOUSE.
WM. HAYES.	DAVID JENKINS.	

This petition was referred on the day of its presentation
to a committee composed of Mr. Fitzimmons, Mr. Clymer,
and Mr. Whitehill, who submitted an adverse report on the
7th of December, as follows : " That with respect to bar iron
it appears that a sufficient quantity may be made in the
State, not only for its particular use, but a large overplus for
exportation, but that, by the large importations lately made,
the price is so much reduced as to disable the owners of forges to go on with their business.   Your committee, however,
viewing bar iron as necessary to the agriculture and manufactures of the State, are doubtful of the propriety of imposing a tax upon the importation thereof at this time."   The
committee, however, recommended the imposition of an additional duty of one penny per pound on all nails or spikes
imported into the State.   The report of the committee was
adopted.

Further evidence of the injurious effects of foreign competition upon our domestic iron industry immediately after
the peace is furnished in the following extract from the account of Dr. John D. Schoepf's travels in the United States,
published at Erlangen in 1788.

America is richly supplied with iron, especially in the mountainous districts, and the ore is moreover easily obtained; nevertheless, and in spite of
the abundance of wood, at present European iron can be brought to America
cheaper than the founders and forgers of that place are able to produce it, by
reason of the high wages of the workmen.   The owners of the iron works

in the different provinces, particularly in Pennsylvania and Jersey, tried in vain to induce their governments to prohibit the importation of foreign iron, or to clog it with high duties. As this proposition conflicted directly with the interests of the members of the assembly, as well as with those of their fellow countrymen, it certainly could not be expected that they should decide to pay dearer for their native iron and iron implements, when foreigners could supply them cheaper. Formerly the Americans were able to send their pig and bar iron to England with advantage, for they were relieved of the heavy tax which Russian and Swedish iron paid there. This was the case principally from the middle colonies, and in the years 1768–70 the exports to England amounted to about 2,592 tons of bar iron and 4,624 tons of pig iron, with which they paid for a part at least of their return cargoes in England. In return they took back axes, hoes, shovels, nails, and other manufactured iron implements, for, although some of these articles were occasionally manufactured in America just as good as in Europe, yet it could not be done under at least three times the cost. Therefore, up to this time, the manufacture of cast iron alone has been found to be particularly advantageous.

It was not until our second war with Great Britain that duties were so increased as to be really protective of domestic industries against foreign competition. But these duties were subsequently reduced, and again all our industries languished. The tariffs of 1824 and 1828 again revived them, but subsequent tariff legislation was for many years so fitful and in the main so unfriendly that no American industry can truthfully be said to have been placed upon a substantial basis of prosperity until after the adoption of the Morrill tariff at the beginning of the civil war, in 1861. The protective policy which was then reaffirmed has since continued in force without material modification, and the marvelous progress of the country in the years that have since elapsed is mainly the result of its beneficent operations.

The Morrill tariff act, as might be erroneously inferred from its date, was not a war measure, but a measure rendered absolutely necessary by the depressed condition of our manufacturing industries and by the low condition of the national finances before the war-cloud arose. The bill was reported to the House of Representatives on March 12, 1860, by Mr. Morrill, of Vermont, from the Committee on Ways and Means, and it passed that body on May 10th. It passed the Senate on February 20, 1861, and was approved by President Buchanan on March 2d, taking effect on April 1, 1861. Our present tariff, known as the McKinley bill, became a law on October 1, 1890, and it took effect on October 6, 1890.

CHAPTER LVII.

IMPEDIMENTS TO THE CHEAP PRODUCTION OF IRON AND STEEL IN THE UNITED STATES.

THE iron and steel industries of the United States are subject to permanent disadvantages from which the same industries of other countries are in a great measure relieved. It is true that it can not now be said, as was once said, that they lack the skill, or the capital, or the extensive and complete establishments of other countries. With the exception of our tinplate industry they are no longer infant industries in any sense. Nor can it be said that the natural resources of our country for the manufacture of iron and steel are not abundant and varied. But our iron and steel industries are at a disadvantage in two important particulars when compared with those of other countries. The wages of labor are much higher in this country than in any other ironmaking country in the world, while the raw materials of production, rich and abundant as they are, are in the main so remote from each other that a heavy cost for their transportation is incurred to which no other ironmaking country is subjected.

With reference to wages a single illustration will show the disparity which exists in the iron and steel industries of this country and Europe. At Pittsburgh the price of puddling, or boiling, iron was fixed for one year on the 30th of May, 1881, in an agreement between the employers and their workmen, at a minimum of $5.50 per ton, the price to be advanced if the price of bar iron should go above 2½ cents per pound. Of the $5.50 the puddler's helper received about one-third. These rates of wages still continue, with the exception that the base price of bar iron is now 2 cents. At Philadelphia, in an agreement between the employers and their workmen on the 24th of July, 1880, the price of puddling was fixed for an indefinite period, which still continues, at $4 per ton when bar iron should bring 2 cents per pound, of which sum the helper receives about one-third. When the price of bar iron is 2½ cents per pound the price of puddling is to be $4.50 per ton, the helper to receive about one-third. If the price of bar iron advances beyond 2½ cents per pound the price of puddling is to be still further advanced. The Pittsburgh schedule of wages for puddling prevails in the western parts of the United States, and the Philadelphia schedule is fairly representative of the wages paid in eastern rolling mills.

Now let these rates of wages be compared with the corresponding rates which prevail in England, in which country the wages of iron and steel workers are usually higher than in any other part of Europe. The North of England is the principal seat of the iron industry of that country. A board of arbitration and conciliation for the manufactured iron trade of the North of England adjusts the wages of all rolling-mill workmen in the district every three months upon the basis of the average net selling price of rolled iron during the three months preceding the month in which the board meets. The average net selling price of rolled iron for the three months which ended on the 30th of June, 1881, (a period of prosperity and good prices,) was £6 2s. 2d., and the wages of puddlers for the three months beginning on the 1st of August was officially declared to be 7s. per ton, or about $1.75, of which sum the puddler's helper, in accordance with the general custom, received about one-third. The official announcement of the adjustment of wages, dated July 29th, is as follows : " In accordance with the sliding-scale arrangement and the resolution of the employers' meeting of February 24th the above-named figure of £6 2s. 2d. gives 7s. per ton .as the rate for puddling over the three months commencing on the 1st of August, and a reduction of other forge and mill wages of 2½ per cent. upon last quarter." The same system of adjusting wages prevails in the North of England to-day, and wages are no higher now than in 1881. The difference in puddlers' wages in the North of England and in this country in the same periods of time is thus seen to be very great.

With regard to the cost of transporting raw materials in this country and in Europe the testimony of a distinguished English ironmaster will be sufficient to show the great disparity which exists in the distances over which they must be transported. Sir Lowthian Bell, a commissioner from Great Britain to the Philadelphia Exhibition of 1876, says in his official report: " The vast extent of the territory of the United States renders that possible which in Great Britain is physically impossible; thus it may and it does happen that in the former distances of nearly 1,000 miles may intervene between the ore and the coal, whereas with ourselves it is difficult to find a situation in which the two are separated by even 100 miles." From the iron-ore mines of Michigan and Minnesota to the coal of Pennsylvania is 1,000 miles. Connellsville coke is taken 600 miles to the blast furnaces of Chicago and 750 miles to the blast furnaces of St. Louis. The average distance over which all the domestic iron ore which is consumed in the blast furnaces of the United States is transported is not less than 400 miles, and the average distance over which the fuel which is used to smelt it is transported is not less than 200 miles. Great Britain is our principal competitor in the production of iron and steel. In France, Germany, Belgium, Sweden, and other European ironmaking countries the raw materials of production may not be found in such close proximity as in Great Britain, but they lie much nearer to each other than is usual in the United States. Even when it is necessary to transport raw materials from one European country to another, as in taking the iron ores of Spain to England or Germany, the cost of removal is usually an unimportant consideration because of the short distances they are carried and the facilities which in most cases exist for carrying them by water.

But it is not only on the raw materials that the cost of transportation operates as an impediment to European prices for iron and steel products in this country. The manufactured products themselves must frequently be transported long distances to find consumers. The conditions favorable to the production of iron and steel are not equal in many sections of the Union, and in some sections do not exist at all; iron and steel can not, therefore, be extensively or profitably manufactured in all sections. The country, too, is of vast extent, while its railroad and other enterprises which consume iron and steel are found in every part of it. It is noticeable, also, that railroads form the principal means of communication between the producers and consumers of iron and steel in this country, and that railroad transportation is more expensive than transportation by natural water routes. Heavy products of iron and steel, for instance, can be carried much more cheaply from Liverpool to the gulf ports of the United States than from our own rolling mills and blast furnaces which are not situated on the sea-coast or on the Mississippi river, and very few of them are so situated. Steel rails for railroads on the Pacific coast can be transported more cheaply from Liverpool to San Francisco than from Pittsburgh or Chicago. Even to ports on the Atlantic coast it can truthfully be said that, taking them as a whole, British iron and steel products can be carried more cheaply than from our own iron and steel works which are located only a short distance in the interior. No freight is better adapted to the ballasting of ships which come to this country for grain and cotton than heavy products of iron and steel, and these products are therefore usually carried at very low rates. Ocean freight charges afford no protection to our iron and steel manufacturers.

So much are high wages and the high cost of transportation hindrances to the cheap production of iron and steel in this country that English newspapers frequently boast of the superior facilities possessed by British manufacturers in these respects. The London *Colliery Guardian* for January 25, 1884, remarks upon this subject as follows : " The very smallness of Great Britain tells in its favor as a manufacturing country. Raw materials have to be carried comparatively limited distances, and coal, iron, and labor are collected and brought together with extreme ease, while the manufactured article, when ready for exportation, has to be carried only a few miles to some convenient port. All these elements of industrial success are more or less lacking in the United States. Labor is still comparatively scarce there and has to be remunerated at higher rates, while coal and iron have to be hauled great distances before they become available for use. When manufactured goods are turned out they have also in many cases to be carried heavy distances before they can be put on board ship."

CHAPTER LVIII.

WASHINGTON AND LINCOLN THE DESCENDANTS OF COLONIAL IRONMASTERS.

THE completeness of the narrative which will be presented in this chapter requires that we reproduce a few facts which have already been stated.

In our researches into the history of the manufacture of iron and steel in the United States we have been impressed by the fact that many of the men who have been prominent in shaping the destinies of the country, either as soldiers or statesmen, or whose descendants have been thus distinguished, have also been prominent as manufacturers of iron and sometimes also of steel. Among the ironmasters and ironworkers in colonial times we find the names of Mordecai Lincoln, the progenitor of Abraham Lincoln; Sir William Keith, Governor of Pennsylvania; Colonel Alexander Spotswood, Governor of Virginia; Captain Augustine Washington, the father of George Washington and his two elder half-brothers, Lawrence and Augustine Washington; Colonel Ethan Allen, General Daniel Morgan, and General Nathanael Greene, of the Revolutionary army; and Stephen Hopkins, George Taylor, George Ross, and James Smith, signers of the Declaration. Benjamin Franklin was the inventor of the Franklin stove. Since the Revolution we find that a still larger number of our public men have been identified with our iron and steel industries, many of whom have been members of Congress and Governors of States. Henry Baldwin, one of the Justices of the United States Supreme Court; John Henry Hopkins, Episcopal Bishop of Vermont; and General Arthur St. Clair were Pennsylvania ironmasters early in the present century. At a later day Thaddeus Stevens was a Pennsylvania ironmaster.

The close connection of the Washington family with our colonial iron history is a fact of special interest to all who care anything about the early history of our iron and steel industries. Captain Augustine Washington was engaged in making pig iron at Accokeek furnace, in Stafford county, Virginia, about fifteen miles from Fredericksburg, when his son George Washington was born. This furnace had been built by the Principio Company, composed of English capitalists, as early as 1726 on land owned by Augustine Washington, aggregating about 1,600 acres and containing iron ore, Captain Washington becoming the owner of one-sixth of the furnace property in consideration of the transfer of his land to the company. In Maryland the Principio Company had other iron enterprises. Captain Washington appears to have visited England in 1729 and 1730 in relation to the management of Accoceek furnace. During his absence his wife died, but this event excites no sympathy in a letter from John Wightwick, one of the English stockholders in the Principio Company, written at London on October 2, 1730, and addressed to John England, the company's general agent in Maryland and Virginia. From this letter we quote literally as follows.

You remember what steps we made with Captn Washington in order to his management at Accokeek, which we did suppose when he arrived there, & after he had agreed with the founder as to the quality of the pig metall, he would have given orders to his agent here to have exchanged the articles with us (which he left ready executed for that purpose) and on your arrival in Virginia to see the stock valued and to have the proper securities given for his returning it to us at the end of his term, he would have entered immediately on that work according to our agreement in the said articles, but we have Ltres. from him of the 10th of July in which he says that on his arrival, to his great grief, he found his wife was dead ; that he had been at the furnace, and that we might depend of his using as much prudence and caution 'till your arrival as if it was for himself, but says not one word whether he would take to his bargain with us or not, having had sufficient time to consider of it between the 26th May the time of his arrival & the 10th July the date of his letter. I think this is treating us neither kindly nor Honorably to leave us in so great a state of uncertainty. As to Mr. Gee he says he is on this account very unwilling to have anything to do with him. As to Mrs [Messrs.] Chetwynds and myself, & I believe Mr. Russell, we shall submit to what you shall advise us in case when you come to talk with him you find him inclined to pursue his bargain. If you find he does not pursue his bargain, I don't doubt but you will settle our affairs there on as good a foot as the nature thereof will allow, and I hope by the help of N. Chapman and your directions that work will be as well managed as if Captn W. undertook it.

Nathaniel Chapman was the clerk at Accokeek furnace.

Gee, Russell, and the Chetwynds were English stockholders. We have been unable to discover whether Captain Washington kept his " bargain " to manage the furnace or not, but in Colonel William Byrd's *Progress to the Mines*, written in 1732, he mentions " England's iron mines, called so from the chief manager of them, tho' the land belongs to Mr. Washington." Two miles distant from the mines was the furnace. Colonel Byrd says : " Mr. Washington raises the ore and carts it thither for twenty shillings the ton of iron that it yields. Besides Mr. Washington and Mr. England there are several other persons in England concerned in these works."

In 1731 Captain Augustine Washington married for his second wife Mary Ball, a daughter of Joseph Ball, who resided in Lancaster county, Virginia, forming a part of " The Neck." It was in this county that Mary Ball was born. Captain Washington's home was in Westmoreland county, and it was here that Mary Washington's first child, George Washington, was born, as all the world knows, on February 11, 1731–2, old style.

When Augustine Washington died in 1743 he owned an interest in all the property of the Principio Company, which he bequeathed to his son Lawrence, who died in 1752, bequeathing to his daughter Sarah his interest " in the Principio, Accokeek, Kingsbury, Laconshire, and North East iron works in Virginia and Maryland." George Washington was one of the executors of this will. Sarah dying soon afterwards her iron interests were conveyed, by the terms of her father's will, to her uncle, Augustine Washington. At the breaking out of the Revolution " a certain Mr. Washington " owned a one-twelfth interest in the possessions of the Principio Company. He was probably a son of George Washington's half-brother, Augustine Washington. We have in our possession a pig of iron which was made at Principio furnace in 1751, when Lawrence Washington was one of its owners. The facts which we have presented show that the Father of his Country was the son of a Virginia ironmaster, and that both his half-brothers and other relatives were also ironmasters.

Abraham Lincoln's paternal ancestry was also identified with the manufacture of iron. It is not so generally known as it should be that his ancestors on his father's side were natives of Massachusetts and were among its pioneer iron-masters. In *Johnson's Cyclopædia* there is preserved a biographical sketch of Abraham Lincoln, written in 1859 with his own hand, in which occurs the following reference to his father's family.

"My paternal grandfather, Abraham Lincoln, emigrated from Rockbridge county, Virginia, to Kentucky about 1781 or 1782, where a year or two later he was killed by Indians—not in battle, but by stealth, when he was laboring to open a farm in the forest. His ancestors, who were Quakers, went to Virginia from Berks county, Pennsylvania. An effort to identify them with the New England family of the same name ended in nothing more definite than a similarity of Christian names in both families, such as Enoch, Levi, Mordecai, Solomon, Abraham, and the like." Mr. Lincoln probably meant Rockingham county and not Rockbridge county.

Researches which have been made since Abraham Lincoln became President clearly establish the fact that the head of the American branch of his father's family, Samuel Lincoln, emigrated from Norwich, England, to Massachusetts, whence two brothers, his grandsons, emigrated to Pennsylvania, one of whom was the President's great-great-grandfather.

A communication to the Hingham *Journal* of October 10, 1879, says that among the early settlers of Hingham, Massachusetts, which was settled in 1635, were seven persons named Lincoln who became the heads of families. Four of these were named Thomas. Samuel Lincoln, who came to Hingham in 1637, had four sons, Samuel, Daniel, Mordecai, and Thomas. Mordecai Lincoln, born at Hingham on June 14, 1657, followed the trade of a blacksmith at Hull, from which he removed to Scituate, where "he built a spacious house and was a large contributor toward the erection of the iron works at Bound Brook" in 1703. These Bound Brook iron works comprised nothing more ambitious than a Catalan forge, which made wrought iron from the ore.

Mr. George Lincoln, of Hingham, informed us in a letter dated on October 28, 1879, that the Bound Brook iron works were located near the line dividing Scituate from Cohasset, at a place called Conahasset, and that Mordecai and Daniel

Lincoln were owners of the works. Cohasset until 1770 was the easterly precinct of Hingham, and Scituate was also near the Hingham boundary line. Mr. Lincoln also furnished us with abstracts of some deeds recorded in Plymouth and Suffolk counties proving the connection of Mordecai and Daniel Lincoln with the Bound Brook iron works, which are styled "a forge or iron works." From one of these abstracts we take the following circumstantial statement : " Dec. 21, 1713. George Jackson, of Marblehead, sells to Mordecai Lincoln, of Scituate, ' blacksmith,' two parcels of salt-meadow land lying and being in Cohasset within the township of Hingham," one of which is bounded " east by a brook or river called Bound Brook," etc. Other abstracts show that Mordecai Lincoln was a prime mover in the erection of the Bound Brook iron works, and that it was from him that Daniel Lincoln obtained a one-eighth interest in the works.

Mordecai Lincoln's first wife was Sarah Jones, the daughter of Abraham and Sarah Jones, of Hull. Their sons were Mordecai, Jr., born April 24, 1686 ; Abraham, born January 13, 1688–9 ; and Isaac, born October 24, 1691. The Hingham *Journal* says that Mordecai, Jr., and his brother Abraham removed from Scituate " it is supposed " to Pennsylvania, for their names afterwards appear among a list of taxables in Exeter township, Berks county, Pennsylvania. But first at least one of the brothers emigrated to New Jersey. Nicolay and Hay state in their life of Lincoln that Mordecai Lincoln removed from Massachusetts to Monmouth, New Jersey, and thence to Amity township, Berks county, Pennsylvania. He died there in 1736. His brother Abraham finally settled in Springfield township, Chester county, Pennsylvania, as early as 1729. Like his father he was a blacksmith. He died in 1745. The townships of Oley, Amity, and Exeter, in Berks county, are contiguous, and in their early records the name of Lincoln often appears.

Monmouth county, New Jersey, was settled in part by a colony of Massachusetts people, who erected iron works at Tintern Falls in the township of Shrewsbury about 1676. It is probable that the Lincoln brothers emigrated to this county because Massachusetts people were there already and because they were themselves ironworkers.

Mordecai Lincoln, who emigrated to Berks county, Pennsylvania, and died there in 1736, and who was a Quaker, left three sons, John, Mordecai, and Thomas, and probably, as a communication in the Philadelphia *American* says, a posthumous son named Abraham. A posthumous child was provided for in Mordecai Lincoln's will. John emigrated to Rockingham county, Virginia, about 1750. He had a son Abraham, who emigrated to Kentucky and was killed by the Indians, as the President states. This Abraham was the grandfather of the President, his father being Thomas Lincoln. It will be remembered that there were many Thomas Lincolns at Hingham, and that the father-in-law of Mordecai Lincoln of Scituate was Abraham Jones. The frequent appearance of the names Mordecai, Abraham, and Thomas at various periods in the history of the Massachusetts Lincolns and their descendants will be noticed by the reader.

An Abraham Lincoln of Berks county, who was either the posthumous son of Mordecai Lincoln or a grandson, was long prominent as a politician. He was one of the county commissioners of Berks county from 1773 to 1779, and from 1782 to 1786 he was a member of the General Assembly of Pennsylvania. A letter from Reading, published in the Philadelphia *Press*, says that after his service in the Assembly Abraham Lincoln was a justice of the peace and ex-officio one of the justices of the quarter sessions. "His signature, which can be found attached to various ancient documents in the commissioners' office, indicates that he was a man of affairs, and it is not unlike that of his illustrious namesake which is attached to the proclamation of emancipation." He was a member of the State Convention of 1787 which ratified the Federal Constitution of that year, and which he voted against, and he was an influential member of the State Constitutional Convention of 1790. He died in 1806 in his 70th year, having been born in 1736.

The connection of the Lincoln family with the manufacture of iron does not entirely end with Mordecai and Abraham who emigrated from Massachusetts to Pennsylvania. About 1775 a furnace was built on Mossy creek, Augusta county, Virginia, by Henry Miller and Mark Bird, of Berks county, Pennsylvania, Bird soon selling his interest to Miller.

The furnace was called Miller's furnace. Jefferson mentions it in his *Notes on the State of Virginia*. J. Marshall McCue, Esq., of Fishersville, Augusta county, Virginia, writes us an interesting letter concerning the early history of this furnace. He says : " Miller married Hannah, the oldest of seven children of William Winter and Annie Boone, the latter a cousin of Daniel Boone. Nancy, the second, married George Crawford, of this county, and Elizabeth, the fourth, married Abraham Lincoln, the grandfather of President Lincoln. Miller carried on the furnace successfully until some time in March or April, 1796, when he died. He left four sons and four daughters. The oldest son, Captain Samuel Miller, carried on the furnace energetically up to his death, which occurred in 1830. He built a forge, called Mt. Vernon, on South river, near Weyer's Cave, and two miles from Port Republic, in 1810." It will be seen from this letter that the grandmother of President Lincoln on his father's side was Elizabeth Winter, the sister-in-law of Henry Miller, and that Captain Samuel Miller was a cousin of President Lincoln's father. The Boones were Quaker neighbors of the Lincolns, residing in Berks county, Pennsylvania. The communication in the Philadelphia *American* from which we have already quoted says that George Boone was one of the trustees named in Mordecai Lincoln's will and was the uncle of Daniel Boone.

A communication in a recent issue of the Philadelphia *Ledger* says that there is an Abraham Lincoln still living in Pennsylvania. He lives in Caernarvon township, Lancaster county, about fourteen miles from Reading, and is about 80 years old. " He lives on a large and productive farm, has a family, never had any ambition for office, and in general appearance he is not unlike President Lincoln, having the same large, erect, gaunt form, and retaining to a remarkable degree some of the general characteristics of his famous relative and namesake." Other Lincolns are still living in Berks county.

It may not be inappropriate to mention, as an additional historical link, that Nancy Hanks, the mother of President Lincoln, was also descended from a Berks county family which emigrated first to Virginia and afterwards to Kentucky.

CHAPTER LIX.

PRODUCTION AND PRICES OF IRON AND STEEL IN THE UNITED STATES.

No TABULATED statistics of the production of iron in our colonial history are extant, and the materials for such a compilation appear to be entirely wanting; nor do the census statistics of the United States contain any reference to the industries of the country until 1810.

In 1814 there was published *A Statement of the Arts and Manufactures of the United States of America* as they existed in 1810, prepared by Tench Coxe, under the authority of Albert Gallatin, Secretary of the Treasury. From this report we obtain the following information concerning the condition of our iron industry in 1810. The tons are gross tons.

Establishments and products.	United States.	Pennsylvania.
Number of blast furnaces...⎫	153	44
Number of air furnaces...⎭		6
Tons of cast iron made...	53,908	26,878
Value of cast iron made...	$2,981,277	$1,301,343
Number of bloomaries...	135	4
Tons of iron made...	2,564	....
Value of iron made...	$226,034	$16,000
Number of forges...	330	78
Tons of bar iron, etc., made...	24,541	10,969
Value of bar iron, etc., made...	$2,874,063	$1,156,405
Number of trip hammers...	316	50
Product of trip hammers in tons...	600	....
Value of product of trip hammers...	$327,898	$73,496
Rolling and slitting mills...	34	18
Tons of rolled iron made...⎫	9,280	4,502
Product of slit iron in tons...⎭		98
Value of rolled and slit iron...	$1,215,946	$606,426
Number of naileries...	410	175
Pounds of nails made...	15,727,914	7,270,825
Value of nails made...	$2,478,139	$760,862

In the totals for the United States above given we believe the values to be correct, as they include returns from every State, but some of the quantities given are not strictly accurate, because some of the States did not report quantities although they reported values.

The product of the steel furnaces in Massachusetts, Rhode

Island, New Jersey, Pennsylvania, Virginia, and South Carolina in 1810 was 917 tons, valued at $144,736. Of the whole number of steel furnaces Pennsylvania contained 5, of which Philadelphia city and Philadelphia, Lancaster, Dauphin, and Fayette counties each contained one. The product of Pennsylvania was 531 gross tons, valued at $81,147.

In the census year 1820 the value of all the manufactures of pig iron and castings in the United States was $2,230,275, of which Pennsylvania's share was $563,810. In the same year the United States produced manufactures of wrought iron of the value of $4,640,669, of which Pennsylvania's share was $1,156,266. Quantities were not given.

In the census year 1830 the value of the pig iron and castings manufactured in the United States was $4,757,403, of which the share of Pennsylvania was $1,643,702. In the same year the country's production of manufactures of wrought iron amounted in value to $16,737,251, of which Pennsylvania's share was $3,762,847. Quantities were not given.

In the census year 1840 there were in the United States 804 furnaces, which produced in that year 286,903 gross tons of "cast iron." Pennsylvania had 213 furnaces, and it produced 98,395 tons of "cast iron." In the same year there were 795 bloomaries, forges, and rolling mills in the United States, of which Pennsylvania had 169. The number of gross tons of bar iron produced in that year was 197,233, of which Pennsylvania produced 87,244 tons.

In the census year 1850 there were produced in the United States 563,755 gross tons of pig iron by 377 establishments, of which Pennsylvania produced 285,702 tons in 180 establishments. In the same year the United States produced wrought iron manufactures of the value of $22,629,271 in 552 establishments, Pennsylvania contributing $9,224,256 in value in 162 establishments.

In the census year 1860 the United States, in 97 establishments, produced 51,290 gross tons of blooms, valued at $2,623,178; Pennsylvania, in 57 establishments, produced 24,700 tons of blooms, valued at $1,467,450. In the same year the United States, in 286 establishments, produced 987,559 tons of pig iron, worth $20,870,120; Pennsylvania, in 125 establishments, produced 580,049 tons of pig iron, worth $11,-262,974. In 256 establishments the United States produced 513,213 tons of rolled iron, worth $31,888,705; Pennsylvania, in 87 establishments, produced 266,253 tons of rolled iron, worth $15,122,842. In 13 establishments the United States produced 11,838 tons of steel, worth $1,778,240; Pennsylvania, in 9 establishments, produced 9,890 tons of steel, worth $1,338,200.

As has been stated the ton used in the census statistics of 1810, 1840, 1850, and 1860 was the gross ton of 2,240 pounds, but in the census statistics of 1870, 1880, and 1890 the net ton of 2,000 pounds was used. We do not give the census statistics for the last three decades because they are largely superseded by the statistics for the last thirty years which have already been presented in these pages or will yet be presented in this chapter, and which have been compiled by the American Iron and Steel Association from returns received annually from the manufacturers.

In preceding chapters we have given in their proper connection the statistics of the production of pig iron, iron rails, Bessemer steel ingots, Bessemer steel rails, and open-hearth steel in the United States for a long series of years. We now present some additional statistics of production in the United States down to the close of 1890.

The production of all kinds of crude steel in the United States in 1863 was 9,044 net tons; in 1864, 10,369 tons; in 1865, 15,262 tons; in 1866, 18,973 tons; and in 1867, 22,-000 tons, including 3,000 tons of Bessemer steel ingots. Our production of crude steel since that year has been as follows, the figures embracing Bessemer, open-hearth, and crucible steel; also a few thousand tons annually of blister and other kinds of steel.

Years.	Net tons.	Years.	Net tons.	Years.	Net tons.
1868	30,000	1876	597,174	1884	1,736,985
1869	85,000	1877	637,972	1885	1,917,350
1870	77,000	1878	819,814	1886	2,870,003
1871	82,000	1879	1,047,506	1887	3,739,760
1872	160,108	1880	1,397,015	1888	3,247,373
1873	222,652	1881	1,778,912	1889	3,792,020
1874	241,614	1882	1,945,095	1890	4,790,319
1875	436,575	1883	1,874,359		

The following table gives the production of all rolled iron in the United States, except iron rails, which have already been given, but including nail plate, from 1865 to 1890, covering the period since the close of our civil war.

Years.	Net tons.	Years.	Net tons.	Years.	Net tons.
1865......	500,048	1874......	1,110,147	1883......	2,283,920
1866......	595,311	1875......	1,097,867	1884......	1,931,747
1867......	579,838	1876......	1,042,101	1885......	1,789,711
1868......	598,286	1877......	1,144,219	1886......	2,259,943
1869......	642,420	1878......	1,232,686	1887......	2,565,438
1870......	705,000	1879......	1,627,324	1888......	2,397,402
1871......	710,000	1880......	1,838,906	1889......	2,576,127
1872......	941,992	1881......	2,155,346	1890......	2,804,829
1873......	1,076,368	1882......	2,265,957		

The following table shows the production of spiegeleisen and ferro-manganese in the United States from 1875 to 1890. This production is included in that of pig iron already given.

Years.	Net tons.	Years.	Net tons.	Years.	Net tons.
1875......	7,882	1881......	21,086	1887......	47,598
1876......	6,616	1882......	21,963	1888......	54,769
1877......	8,845	1883......	24,574	1889......	85,823
1878......	10,674	1884......	33,893	1890......	149,162
1879......	13,931	1885......	34,671		
1880......	19,603	1886......	47,982		

The geographical centre of total production of the iron and steel industries of the United States is the point at which equilibrium would be established were the country taken as a plane surface, itself without weight but capable of sustaining weight, and loaded with its production of iron and steel, each ton exerting pressure on the pivotal point directly proportioned to its distance therefrom. The centre of production of iron and steel in the United States in the census year 1880 was found to be at 40° 43′ north latitude and 79° 20′ longitude west from Greenwich. This point is in Pennsylvania, on the boundary line between Armstrong and Indiana counties, and about 12 miles northeast of Apollo and 12 miles west of Indiana, Laufman & Co's rolling mill at Apollo being the nearest iron works. At the centre of production thus ascertained iron has never been manufactured in any form. It will be interesting to note the equilibrium point of production as it will be established by the census of 1890, which is not yet completed.

The thoughtful reader will look for statistics of production to be accompanied by a record of the prices paid by our people for leading iron and steel products. This record is presented in the following tables. It goes back to the closing years of the last century and comes down to the end of 1890. It is as complete as it has been possible to make it, and no pains have been spared to make it accurate. We have not attempted a compilation of colonial prices, but the curious reader will find occasional references to them in preceding pages.

The first table contains the average prices of charcoal pig iron at Philadelphia from 1799 to 1849, when anthracite pig iron became the standard of comparison. Until 1827 the prices are for the best pig iron; from 1827 to 1833 they are for an average of all grades; from 1833 to 1840 they are for gray iron; and from 1840 to the close of the table they are for No. 1 foundry. The same table also gives the average prices of hammered bar iron at Philadelphia from 1794 to 1844, although its manufacture and sale, which had been declining prior to 1844, continued for several years afterwards.

In the second table the average prices of No. 1 anthracite foundry pig iron at Philadelphia are given from 1842, in which year quotations first appear, to 1890. In the same table the average prices of best refined rolled bar iron at Philadelphia are given from 1844 to 1890, and the average prices of iron rails delivered at Philadelphia are given from 1847 to 1882. In 1883 the manufacture in this country of iron rails of standard sections virtually came to an end, although a few light iron rails are still manufactured. A few standard iron rails, as well as light rails, were made ·in that year, but at higher prices than steel rails commanded. The column devoted to steel rails in the second table gives the average prices at works in Pennsylvania from 1867, when they were first made in commercial quantities, to 1890. The same table also gives the average wholesale prices of cut nails in eastern markets, in kegs of 100 pounds, from 1835 to 1890. The tons used in the tables are tons of 2,240 pounds.

TABLE 1. Years.	Charcoal pig iron.	Hammered bar iron.
1794	....	$77.50
1795	....	82.50
1796	....	106.50
1797	....	101.50
1798	....	97.50
1799	$36.25	98.50
1800	35.75	100.50
1801	32.75	117.50
1802	30.75	99.00
1803	29.25	97.50
1804	29.75	98.50
1805	30.75	101.00
1806	35.75	108.50
1807	38.75	110.50
1808	40.00	104.00
1809	40.00	107.50
1810	38.00	108.00
1811	44.00	105.00
1812	47.50	106.00
1813	47.25	106.00
1814	46.00	133.00
1815	53.75	144.50
1816	50.25	127.00
1817	47.00	114.00
1818	42.25	110.00
1819	36.50	110.00
1820	35.00	103.50
1821	35.00	90.50
1822	35.00	94.50
1823	35.25	90.00
1824	40.00	82.50
1825	46.75	97.50
1826	46.50	101.50
1827	39.25	100.00
1828	35.00	100.00
1829	35.00	97.00
1830	35.00	87.50
1831	35.00	85.00
1832	35.00	85.00
1833	38.25	82.50
1834	30.25	82.50
1835	30.25	81.50
1836	41.50	100.00
1837	41.25	111.00
1838	32.25	96.50
1839	30.00	96.50
1840	32.75	90.00
1841	28.50	85.00
1842	28.00	83.50
1843	26.75	77.50
1844	28.25	75.00
1845	32.25	....
1846	31.25	....
1847	31.50	....
1848	28.50	....
1849	24.50	....

TABLE 2. Years.	No. 1 anthracite foundry pig iron.	Best refined rolled bar iron.	Iron rails.	Steel rails.	Cut nails, per keg of 100 pounds.
1835					$6.00
1836					6.00
1837					6.00
1838					6.00
1839					6.12
1840					5.50
1841					5.25
1842	$25.60				4.75
1843					4.25
1844	25.75	$85.62			4.50.
1845	29.25	93.75			4.75
1846	27.88	91.66			4.50
1847	30.25	86.04	$69.00		4.50
1848	26.50	79.33	62.25		4.25
1849	22.75	67.50	53.88		4.00
1850	20.88	59.54	47.88		3.71
1851	21.38	54.66	45.63		3.28
1852	22.63	58.79	48.88		3.13
1853	36.12	83.50	77.25		4.85
1854	36.88	91.33	80.13		4.76
1855	27.75	74.58	62.88		4.10
1856	27.12	73.75	64.38		3.92
1857	26.38	71.04	64.25		3.72
1858	22.25	62.29	50.00		3.53
1859	23.38	60.00	49.38		3.86
1860	22.75	58.75	48.00		3.13
1861	20.25	60.83	42.38		2.75
1862	23.88	70.42	41.75		3.47
1863	35.25	91.04	76.88		5.13
1864	59.25	146.46	126.00		7.85
1865	46.12	106.38	98.63		7.08
1866	46.88	98.13	86.75		6.97
1867	44.12	87.08	83.13	$166.00	5.92
1868	39.25	85.63	78.88	158.50	5.17
1869	40.63	81.66	77.25	132.25	4.87
1870	33.25	78.96	72.25	106.75	4.40
1871	35.12	78.54	70.38	102.50	4.52
1872	48.88	97.63	85.13	112.00	5.46
1873	42.75	86.43	76.67	120.50	4.90
1874	30.25	67.95	58.75	94.25	3.99
1875	25.50	60.85	47.75	68.75	3.42
1876	22.25	52.08	41.25	59.25	2.98
1877	18.88	45.55	35.25	45.50	2.57
1878	17.63	44.24	33.75	42.25	2.31
1879	21.50	51.85	41.25	48.25	2.69
1880	28.50	60.38	49.25	67.50	3.68
1881	25.12	58.05	47.13	61.13	3.09
1882	25.75	61.41	45.50	48.50	3.47
1883	22.38	50.80		37.75	3.06
1884	19.88	44.05	....	30.75	2.39
1885	18.00	40.32	....	28.50	2.33
1886	18.71	43.12	....	34.50	2.27
1887	20.92	49.37	....	37.08	2.30
1888	18.88	44.99	....	29.83	2.03
1889	17.75	43.40	....	29.25	2.00
1890	18.40	45.92	....	31.75	2.00

A study of the foregoing tables reveals many and wide fluctuations in prices. The greatest uniformity will be noticed during the charcoal era, ending about 1844, allowance being made for the disturbing effects of the second war with Great Britain. The greatest fluctuations will be found since the close of that era, not counting the great enhancement in values during the civil war. In other words, before we began to produce iron largely, and especially while we held to the old ways of manufacturing it, the market for its sale was least excited and least depressed. The new methods reduced prices to lower figures than they had ever touched during the charcoal era, and the rebound has frequently been proportionately greater than at any time during that era. Until we began to manufacture pig iron with anthracite coal its yearly price after 1798 never fell below $29 per ton, but in 1878 the average price for the year of No. 1 anthracite foundry pig iron was $17.63. Until we began to roll the most of our bar iron, instead of hammering it, its yearly price after 1794 did not fall below $77.50 per ton, but in 1885 the average price for the year was $40.32, or much less than two cents per pound. The greatest fall in prices has been in steel rails, which have been sold at less than one-sixth the price charged for them when we began their manufacture in 1867. The lowest average annual price at which Bessemer steel rails have been sold in this country was reached in 1885, namely, $28.50 per ton, but sales were made at still lower figures in 1884, 1885, 1888, and 1889—as low as $26 and $27. Wholesale prices of cut nails have fallen from $6 per keg in 1835 to an average of $2 per keg in 1889 and 1890, sales having been made in eastern markets in the last years mentioned at $1.90 per keg.

The production of iron ore in the United States in the calendar year 1889 has been ascertained and published by the Census Office, the statistics having been gathered by Mr. John Birkinbine, special agent. The quantity of iron ore produced in the United States during the year 1889 was 14,-518,041 gross tons, valued at $33,351,978, an average of $2.30 per ton. The total production in the census year 1880 was 7,120,362 tons, valued at $23,156,957, an average of $3.25 per ton. The increase in production in 1889 over the census year 1880 was 103.89 per cent. Of the twenty-six States and two Territories producing iron ore in 1889 the four leading States were as follows: Michigan, 5,856,169 tons; Alabama, 1,570,319 tons; Pennsylvania, 1,560,234 tons; and New York, 1,247,537 tons: these four States producing 10,234,259 tons, or 70.49 per cent. of the total production. The details of the production of iron ore by all the iron-ore producing States and Territories in 1889 are as follows.

States and Territories.	Production in 1889—Gross tons.	States and Territories.	Production in 1889—Gross tons.
Alabama........................	1,570,319	New Mexico and Utah.......	36,050
Colorado........................	109,136	New York....................	1,247,537
Connecticut, Maine, and		Ohio........................	254,294
Massachusetts................	88,251	Oregon and Washington.....	26,283
Delaware and Maryland...	29,380	Pennsylvania................	1,560,234
Georgia and N. Carolina...	258,145	Tennessee...................	473,294
Idaho and Montana.........	24,072	Texas.......................	13,000
Kentucky......................	77,487	Virginia and West Virginia.	511,255
Michigan.......................	5,856,169	Wisconsin...................	837,399
Minnesota......................	864,508		
Missouri........................	265,718	Total.................	14,518,041
New Jersey.....................	415,510		

Mr. Birkinbine shows that 62.38 per cent. of the iron ore produced in the United States in 1889 was red hematite; that 17.38 per cent. was brown hematite; that 17.26 per cent. was magnetite; and that 2.98 per cent. was carbonate.

Mr. Birkinbine also shows that the total cost of the iron ore mined in the United States in 1889 aggregated $24,781,-658, equivalent to an average cost of $1.71 per ton, against $2.21 in the census year 1880, a decrease of 50 cents per ton, or 22.62 per cent. In the same year, 1889, the average earnings of iron-ore miners and other iron-ore producers, including foremen, in the United States amounted to $409.95, against an average of $308.94 in the census year 1880, an increase of 32.70 per cent.

It will be observed that the statistics of our iron-ore industry which are above presented show an increase in production in 1889 over the census year 1880 of over 100 per cent., an average decrease in the cost of mining of 50 cents per ton, an average decrease in value at the mines of 95 cents per ton, and an average increase in earnings per man of more than $100 per annum.

CHAPTER LX.

IMPORTS AND EXPORTS OF IRON AND STEEL BY THE UNITED STATES.

THE exportation of bar iron from the American colonies began in 1717, when 2 tons of bars were sent to England from the British West India islands of Nevis and St. Christopher, but which had evidently been taken there from one of the Atlantic coast colonies. We present below a table, compiled from Scrivenor's *History of the Iron Trade*, showing the quantity of colonial iron exported to England from 1718 to 1776, inclusive. The colonies which made the shipments were New England, New York, Pennsylvania, Maryland, Virginia, and the Carolinas. They were not permitted to export their iron to any country but Great Britain or one of its colonies, and not to Ireland until 1765.

Years.	Pig iron.				Bar iron.				Years.	Pig iron.				Bar iron.			
	Tons.	cwt.	qr.	lbs.	Tons.	cwt.	qr.	lbs.		Tons.	cwt.	qr.	lbs.	Tons.	cwt.	qr.	lbs.
1718......	....	...	...	...	3	7	0	0	1751....	3,210	11	1	0	5	4	2	9
1728-9...	1,132	2	3	4	......	...	..	...	1752....	2,980	1	3	2	81	7	0	26
1730......	1,725	14	3	7	......	...	..	..	1753....	2,737	19	3	27	247	19	3	11
1730-1...	2,250	5	3	14	......	...	..	...	1754....	3,244	17	1	23	270	15	1	4
1731-2...	2,332	14	3	15	......	...	..	...	1755....	3,441	2	3	8	389	18	3	20
1732-3...	2,404	17	1	12	......	...	..	...	1761....	2,766	2	3	12	39	1	0	0
1733......	....	...	...	...	0	11	3	0	1762....	1,766	16	0	2	122	12	2	14
1733-4...	2,197	10	1	14	......	...	..	...	1763....	2,566	8	0	25	310	19	3	2
1734......	....	...	..	...	0	0	2	12	1764....	2,554	8	3	21	1,059	18	0	10
1734-5...	2,561	14	3	11	......	...	..	...	1765....	3,264	8	1	22	1,078	15	0	16
1735......	. .....	...	...	...	55	6	3	21	1766....	2,887	5	1	15	1,257	14	3	9
1739......	2,417	16	2	4	......	...	..	...	1767....	3,313	2	1	19	1,325	19	0	18
1740......	2,275	7	1	0	5	4	1	21	1768....	2,953	0	2	14	1,989	11	0	6
1741......	3,457	9	0	18	5	0	0	0	1769....	3,401	12	2	2	1,779	13	1	23
1742......	2,075	0	0	23	......	...	..	...	1770....	4,232	18	1	18	1,716	8	0	21
1743......	2,985	9	2	8	......	...	...	...	1771....	5,303	6	3	13	2,222	4	3	24
1744......	1,861	16	1	22	57	0	0	0	1772....	3,724	19	2	25	965	15	0	23
1745......	2,274	5	1	17	4	5	2	14	1773....	2,937	13	0	2	837	15	0	6
1746	1,861	2	3	13	196	18	0	12	1774....	3,451	12	2	19	639	0	0	23
1747......	2,156	15	3	16	82	11	2	11	1775....	2,996	0	2	24	916	5	2	11
1748......	2,155	15	2	23	4	0	0	0	1776....	316	1	2	8	28	0	0	0
1750......	2,924	0	0	20	5	17	3	0									

In addition to the foregoing there were exported to Scotland 264 tons of pig iron and 11 tons of bar iron in the ten years from 1739 to 1749, and 229 tons of pig iron in the six years from 1750 to 1756. In 1770, as we learn from Timothy Pitkin's *Statistical View of the Commerce of the United States*, the following quantities of iron were exported to all countries, including England, which is given above separately: Pig iron, 6,017 tons, valued at $145,628; bar iron, 2,463 tons, valued at $178,891; castings, 2 tons, valued at $158; and wrought iron, 8 tons, valued at $810. These are all the particulars of our colonial iron exports that are obtainable.

From 1776 to 1791 there is no record of any shipments abroad of American iron, although some iron may have been shipped in each year immediately after the peace. Since 1791 our exports of iron and steel, except in the form of machinery and other manufactured products, have not constituted any considerable part of our foreign trade. Until 1840 our annual exports of iron and steel and manufactures thereof never amounted in value to one million dollars. In 1865 they first amounted to ten million dollars.

The foreign value of the imports into the United States from all countries of iron and steel and manufactures thereof, including tinplates, in the twenty calendar years from 1871 to 1890 is given in the following table, together with the value of the exports from the United States to all countries of domestic iron and steel and manufactures thereof in the same calendar years, agricultural implements not included.

Years.	Imports.	Exports.	Years.	Imports.	Exports.
1871	$57,866,299	$14,185,359	1881	$61,555,077	$18,216,121
1872	75,617,677	12,595,539	1882	67,075,125	22,348,834
1873	60,005,538	14,173,772	1883	47,506,306	22,716,040
1874	37,652,192	17,312,239	1884	37,078,122	19,290,895
1875	27,363,101	17,976,833	1885	31,144,552	16,622,511
1876	20,016,603	13,641,724	1886	41,630,779	14,865,087
1877	19,874,399	18,549,922	1887	56,420,607	16,235,922
1878	18,013,010	15,101,899	1888	42,311,689	19,578,489
1879	33,331,569	14,223,646	1889	42,027,742	23,712,814
1880	80,443,362	15,156,703	1890	44,540,084	27,000,134

Our exports of iron and steel in 1890 were the largest in our history. As in other years they consisted chiefly of machinery, hardware, sewing machines, saws and tools, locomotives, fire-arms, scales and balances, nails and wire, carwheels and miscellaneous castings, and engines and boilers. Our exports of pig iron and steel rails are increasing.

CHAPTER LXI.

MISCELLANEOUS STATISTICS OF IRON, STEEL, IRON ORE, AND COAL.

THE year 1890 is notable in the history of the iron and steel industries of the United States as the year in which our production of pig iron exceeded for the first time that of Great Britain, not only in 1890 but in 1882, the year of her greatest production. This achievement by American pig-iron manufacturers justifies of itself the presentation in these pages of complete statistics of Great Britain's production of pig iron for a long series of years.

In 1740, exactly 151 years ago, the production of pig iron in Great Britain was only 17,350 tons, the denudation of her forests having almost destroyed her pig-iron industry by decreasing the supply of charcoal, and mineral coal not yet having come into general use.

In 1788 there were only 77 active blast furnaces in England and Wales and 8 active furnaces in Scotland, and their production was 68,300 gross tons of pig iron. Of the whole number of furnaces 26 used charcoal and 59 used coke. The imports of pig iron by Great Britain in that year amounted to about 15,000 tons, and the imports of bar iron amounted to 51,469 tons. In 1796 there were 104 furnaces in blast in England and Wales, producing 108,993 tons of pig iron, and in Scotland there were 17 furnaces in blast, producing 16,086 tons. In 1806 there were 233 furnaces in all Great Britain, of which 173 were in blast, producing 243,851 tons.

The following table shows the growth of the pig-iron industry of Great Britain from 1788 to 1890. For this valuable and accurate table we are indebted to the courtesy of Mr. Richard Meade, of the Mineral Statistics Branch of the Home Department of Her Majesty's Government. The table is compiled from the official records of the Department. It begins with the revival of the British iron industry which followed the general introduction of coke in the blast furnace and of the puddling furnace and grooved rolls in finishing iron.

Years.	Gross tons.	Years.	Gross tons.	Years.	Gross tons.
1788............	68,300	1852..........	2,701,000	1872.........	6,741,929
1796............	125,079	1854..........	3,069,838	1873.........	6,566,451
1806............	243,851	1855..........	3,218,154	1874.........	5,991,408
1818............	325,000	1856..........	3,586,877	1875.........	6,365,462
1820............	400,000	1857..........	3,659,447	1876.........	6,555,997
1823............	455,166	1858..........	3,456,064	1877.........	6,608,664
1825............	581,367	1859..........	3,712,904	1878.........	6,381,051
1827............	690,000	1860..........	3,826,752	1879.........	5,995,337
1828	703,184	1861..........	3,712,390	1880.........	7,749,233
1830............	677,417	1862..........	3,943,469	1881.........	8,144,449
1833............	700,000	1863..........	4,510,040	1882.........	8,586,680
1836............	1,000,000	1864..........	4,767,951	1883.........	8,529,300
1839............	1,248,781	1865..........	4,825,254	1884..........	7,811,727
1840............	1,396,400	1866..........	4,523,897	1885.........	7,415,469
1842............	1,099,138	1867..........	4,761,023	1886.........	7,009,754
1843............	1,215,350	1868..........	4,970,206	1887.........	7,559,518
1844............	1,999,608	1869..........	5,445,757	1888.........	7,998,969
1845............	1,512,500	1870..........	5,963,515	1889.........	8,322,824
1847............	1,999,508	1871..........	6,627,179	1890.........	7,904,214

The production of pig iron in the United States in 1890 was 9,202,703 gross tons, which was 1,298,489 gross tons more than that of Great Britain in the same year.

Great Britain has been a large importer of iron ore in recent years from Spain, Italy, and other countries, but chiefly from Spain. In 1887 the quantity imported amounted to 3,765,788 tons, in 1888 to 3,562,071 tons, in 1889 to 4,031,-265 tons, and in 1890 to 4,471,790 tons. The total quantity of iron ore mined in Great Britain in 1887 amounted to 13,098,041 tons, in 1888 to 14,590,713 tons, in 1889 to 14,-546,105 tons, and in 1890 to 13,780,767 tons. Great Britain, therefore, now imports nearly one-fourth of her annual supply of iron ore. The sources of her supply of foreign ore in 1889 and 1890 and the quantities and values of the imports in these two years were as follows.

Countries from which imported.	1889.		1890.	
	Gross tons.	Values.	Gross tons.	Values.
Australasia....................................	1,858	£8,026	3,475	£15,266
Greece...	79,007	79,314	112,764	101,662
Algeria..	205,670	153,836	237,609	190,940
Italy..	79,312	68,542	46,517	43,411
Spain...	3,627,646	2,608,856	4,028,672	3,129,656
Turkey..	19,588	88,131	18,968	90,036
Other countries...............................	18,184	17,900	23,785	25,085
Total......................................	4,031,265	£3,024,605	4,471,790	£3,596,056

Great Britain also annually imports large quantities of cupreous iron pyrites, from which she obtains purple ore as a residuum for use in her blast furnaces. She obtained 447,580 tons of purple ore from this source in 1887, 464,-207 tons in 1888, 483,257 tons in 1889, and 492,669 tons in 1890.

Great Britain's exports of iron ore are usually only nominal, but in 1886 and 1887 they attained respectable proportions. In 1886 they amounted to 70,527 tons, of which 69,639 tons were sent to the United States. In 1887 they amounted to 56,394 tons, of which 53,817 tons were sent to the United States. They have since greatly declined.

As the prosperity of the British iron trade rests so completely upon the abundant home supply of bituminous coal the statistics of its production also properly find a place in these pages. The following table shows the annual production of coal in Great Britain from 1855 to 1890. This table has been carefully revised for these pages by Mr. Meade.

Years.	Gross tons.	Years.	Gross tons.	Years.	Gross tons.
1855...............	64,453,079	1867...............	104,500,480	1879.........	133,720,393
1856...............	66,645,450	1868...............	103,141,157	1880.........	146,969,409
1857...............	65,394,707	1869...............	107,427,557	1881.........	154,184,300
1858...............	65,008,649	1870...............	110,431,192	1882.........	156,499,977
1859...............	71,979,765	1871...............	117,352,028	1883.........	163,737,327
1860...............	80,042,698	1872...............	123,497,316	1884.........	160,757,779
1861...............	84,013,941	1873...............	128,680,131	1885.........	159,351,418
1862...............	81,638,338	1874...............	126,590,108	1886.........	157,518,482
1863...............	86,292,215	1875...............	133,306,485	1887.........	162,119,812
1864...............	92,787,873	1876...............	134,125,166	1888.........	169,935,219
1865...............	98,150,587	1877...............	134,179,968	1889.........	176,916,724
1866...............	101,630,544	1878...............	132,612,063	1890.........	181,614,288

A steady decline in the production of coal in Great Britain from 1883 to 1886 will be noticed, but in 1887 the production increased, in 1888 and 1889 it still further increased, and in 1890 it reached the astonishing total of 181,614,288 tons.

Germany has for a long time been third in the list of iron and steel producing countries, the United States and Great Britain being first and second. The growth of Germany's iron and steel industries in recent years has been rapid. The following table, which has been carefully revised for these pages by Dr. Hermann Wedding, of Berlin, shows the production of pig iron in Germany and the Grand Duchy of Luxemburg, included in the Zollverein, from 1844 to 1890.

Years.	Metric tons.	Years.	Metric tons.	Years.	Metric tons.
1844............	171,000	1869.........	1,413,029	1880.........	2,729,038
1854............	369,000	1870.........	1,391,124	1881.........	2,914,009
1860	529,087	1871.........	1,563,682	1882.........	3,380,806
1861....	591,593	1872.........	1,988,394	1883.........	3,469,719
1862............	696,350	1873.........	2,240,575	1884.........	3,600,612
1863............	812,555	1874.........	1,906,263	1885.........	3,687,433
1864............	904,658	1875.........	2,029,389	1886.........	3,528,658
1865............	988,191	1876.........	1,846,345	1887.........	4,023,953
1866............	1,046,954	1877.........	1,934,726	1888.........	4,337,421
1867............	1,113,606	1878.........	2,147,641	1889.........	4,524,558
1868............	1,264,347	1879	2,226,587	1890.........	4,637,239

In 1834, ten years earlier than the year first named in the table, the production of pig iron in Germany and Luxemburg was only 110,000 metric tons.

As the iron and steel industries of Germany owe their present prominence in large part to the possession by Germany of an abundant local supply of mineral fuel we give below a table, also verified for these pages by Dr. Wedding, showing the aggregate production of both coal and lignite in Germany from 1853 to 1890.

Years.	Metric tons.	Years.	Metric tons.	Years.	Metric tons.
1853............	10,714,556	1869.........	34,343,918	1880.........	59,118,035
1857............	14,867,121	1870.........	34,003,004	1881.........	61,540,485
1860............	16,730,492	1871.........	37,856,110	1882.........	65,378,211
1861............	18,755,361	1872.........	42,324,467	1883.........	70,442,648
1862............	20,660,677	1873.........	46,145,194	1884.........	72,113,820
1863............	22,366,203	1874.........	46,658,145	1885.........	73,675,515
1864............	25,612,899	1875.........	47,804,054	1886.........	73,682,584
1865............	28,552,762	1876.........	49,550,461	1887.........	76,232,618
1866............	28,162,805	1877..	48,229,882	1888.........	81,960,083
1867............	30,802,889	1878.........	50,519,899	1889.........	84,788,609
1868..,.........	32,879,123	1879.........	53,470,716	1890.........	89,051,527

In 1848 the total production of coal and lignite in Germany was only 5,800,985 tons.

Germany and Luxemburg produced 10,664,307 tons of iron ore in 1888, 11,002,187 tons in 1889, and 11,409,625 tons in 1890. The imports of iron ore into Germany and Luxemburg, chiefly from Spain, amounted to 1,163,373 tons in 1888, 1,234,789 tons in 1889, and 1,522,181 tons in 1890 ; and the exports, chiefly from Lothringen, amounted to 2,211,820 tons in 1888, 2,179,836 tons in 1889, and 2,208,120 tons in 1890.

In the following table we give the statistics of the production of basic steel by countries in the last four years.

Countries—Gross tons.	1887.	1888.	1889.	1890.
England..	864,526	408,594	493,919	503,400
Germany, Luxemburg, and Austria............	1,102,496	1,276,070	1,481,642	1,695,472
France..	176,500	222,333	222,392	240,638
Belgium, Russia, and the United States......	60,959	46,237	76,599	163,573
Total..	1,704,481	1,953,234	2,274,552	2,603,083

The increased production of basic steel in 1890 over 1889 was 328,531 gross tons. The total production of basic steel since the invention of the basic process down to the close of 1890 is reported to have been 13,448,000 gross tons.

Of the total production of basic steel in 1890 there were made by the basic Bessemer process 2,232,639 tons and by the basic open-hearth process 370,444 tons. Of the basic Bessemer production 1,593,148 tons contained under 17 per cent. of carbon, and of the basic open-hearth production 298,867 tons contained under .17 per cent. of carbon.

In the production of 2,603,083 tons of basic steel in 1890 there were also produced 623,000 tons of slag, containing about 36 per cent. of phosphate of lime, nearly the whole of which was used as a fertilizer.

The position of the United States among iron and steel producing countries at the present time is correctly indicated in the following table of the world's production of pig iron and steel of all kinds, which we have compiled from the latest and most 'reliable statistics that are accessible. Most of the details are derived from official sources, while only those relating to "other countries" have been estimated. This table places the world's production of pig iron in 1890 at 26,968,468 tons, and the world's production of steel in that year at 12,151,255 tons. The percentage of pig iron produced by the United States was 34.1, and its percentage of steel was 35.2. Tons of 2,240 pounds are used in. giving the statistics of Great Britain, the United States, Canada, and "other countries," and metric tons of 2,204 pounds for all the Continental countries of Europe. As the difference between the gross ton and the metric ton is so trifling it is not necessary to change official figures.

Countries.	Pig iron.		Steel.	
	Years.	Tons.	Years.	Tons.
United States...................................	1890............	9,202,703	1890............	4,277,071
Great Britain...................	1890............	7,904,214	1890............	3,679,043
Germany and Luxemburg...............	1890............	4,637,239	1890............	2,161,821
France.................................	1890............	1,970,160	1890............	704,013
Belgium.................................	1890............	781,958	1890............	239,266
Austria and Hungary.................	1890............	925,308	1890............	440,605
Russia (including Siberia)...............	1889............	745,872	1889............	263,719
Sweden	1890............	456,102	1890............	169,286
Spain.................................	1888............	232,000	1888............	28,645
Italy	1889............	13,473	1889............	157,899
Canada....	1890............	19,439	1889............	24,887
Other countries.....	1890............	80,000	1890............	5,000
Total.......................	....	26,968,468	....	12,151,255
Percentage of the United States.....	....	34.1	....	35.2

In the following table we also give the latest accessible information concerning the production of coal and iron ore throughout the world. The percentage of production of coal by the United States is seen by this table to have been 25.7 and its percentage of production of iron ore is seen to have been 31.4.

Countries.	Iron ore.		Coal.	
	Years.	Tons.	Years.	Tons.
United States.................................	1890............	18,000,000	1889............	126,097,779
Great Britain............................	1890............	13,780,767	1890............	181,614,288
Germany and Luxemburg...............	1890............	11,409,625	1890............	89,051,527
France........................	1887............	2,579,465	1890............	25,836,953
Belgium........................	1889............	202,431	1890............	20,343,495
Austria and Hungary......................	1890..	2,200,000	1889............	25,326,417
Russia (including Siberia)...............	1888............	1,433,513	1889............	6,228,000
Sweden................................	1890............	941,241	1890............	258,000
Spain....	1888............	4,500,000	1888............	1,203,119
Italy....	1889.....	173,489	1889............	390,320
Canada....	1890............	68,313	1890............	2,783,626
Other countries (including Cuba)....	1890............	2,000,000	1890............	11,200,000
Total........................	....	57,288,844	....	490,333,524
Percentage of the United States.....	....	31.4	....	25.7

It is not pretended that all of the details in the above tables are absolutely accurate; at the present stage of statistical inquiry even in highly civilized countries this would be impossible. But they are substantially accurate.

CHAPTER LXII.

SOME OF THE IMPORTANT USES OF IRON AND STEEL IN THE UNITED STATES.

In Ure's *Dictionary of Arts, Manufactures, and Mines* we find this comprehensive and eloquent description of iron: "Every person knows the manifold uses of this truly precious metal. It is capable of being cast in moulds of any form; of being drawn out into wires of any desired strength or fineness; of being extended into plates or sheets; of being bent in every direction; of being sharpened, hardened, and softened at pleasure. Iron accommodates itself to all our wants, our desires, and even our caprices; it is equally serviceable to the arts, the sciences, to agriculture, and war; the same ore furnishes the sword, the ploughshare, the scythe, the pruning-hook, the needle, the graver, the spring of a watch or of a carriage, the chisel, the chain, the anchor, the compass, the cannon, and the bomb. It is a medicine of much virtue, and the only metal friendly to the human frame."

The people of the United States are the largest *per capita* consumers of iron and steel in the world, and of all nations they are also the largest aggregate consumers of these products. Our annual consumption of iron and steel has for several years averaged over 300 pounds for every man, woman, and child in the United States. Great Britain makes about as much iron and steel as we do, but she exports about one-half of all the iron and steel that she makes, much of it in the form of iron and steel ships, machinery, cutlery, etc. We estimate Great Britain's annual *home* consumption of iron and steel in recent years to be less than 275 pounds *per cap-. ita*. No other European country equals Great Britain in the *per capita* consumption of iron and steel.

A simple enumeration of some of the more important uses to which iron and steel are applied by our people will show how prominent is the part these metals play in the development of American civilization and in the advancement of our greatness and power as a nation.

We have built more miles of railroad than the whole of Europe, and have used in their construction as many rails, and now use in their equipment fully as many railroad cars and locomotives. At the close of 1889 this country had 161,319 miles of railroad, Europe had 136,859 miles, and all the rest of the world had 71,965 miles. The United States had 25 miles of railroad to every 10,000 of population, while Europe had a little more than 4 miles to the same population. Railroads, it is well known, annually consume in rails, bridges, cars, and locomotives about one-half of the world's total production of iron and steel. The street railway is an American invention, and we are far in advance of every other nation in its use. We were also the first nation in the world to introduce elevated railways especially to facilitate travel in large cities. Beauty of design, fitness of parts, and strength of materials have been so perfectly combined in the construction of our elevated railways as to excite the admiration of all who behold them. We are the foremost of all nations in the use of iron and steel in bridge-building for railroads and ordinary highways, and the lightness and gracefulness of our bridges are nowhere equaled, while their strength and adaptability to the uses for which they are required are nowhere surpassed. The steel wire in the Brooklyn bridge, which is in many respects the most notable bridge in the world, is all of American manufacture.

In the use of iron for water, sewage, and illuminating gas pipes we are far in advance of every other nation, because our small cities and country towns now quickly adopt all the improvements of large cities.

We make more iron stoves for heating halls and dwellings and for the purposes of the kitchen than all the rest of the world, and in the use of kitchen ranges we are in advance of every other nation. Our household stoves, both for heating and cooking, are works of real art as well as of utility. They are ornaments of American homes instead of being conveniences simply. Our heating stoves are especially handsome, bright, cheerful, clean, and conducive to health. The heating of public and private buildings with hot-air heaters has long been more popular in our country than in any other country, but in late years steam and hot-water pipes are rapidly coming into use as rivals of hot-air flues. Cooking and other domestic utensils of iron have always, even in colonial days, been freely used in American households.

We make liberal use of both cast and wrought iron and steel in the construction of public and private buildings. Our use of iron and steel for these purposes has rapidly increased in late years, and in much of our work of this character we have given truly artistic effects to these metals. We probably excel all nations in the use of iron and steel for ornamental purposes in connection with masonry, brick-work, and wood-work. Fine illustrations of the artistic combination of iron with other materials ten years ago may be seen in the interior of the new State Department building at Washington and in the interior of the passenger station of the Pennsylvania Railroad at Philadelphia, while upon every hand are seen later illustrations of our artistic uses of iron and steel.

We consume large quantities of wire rope in our extended and varied mining operations, and we lead the world in the use of Bessemer steel wire for fencing purposes. We have more miles of telegraph wire in use than any other country. The electric telegraph and telephone are American inventions; barbed wire fencing is also an American invention. Large quantities of iron and steel are now required annually for the electrical machinery which is in general use in this country in the production of light and power.

We have made rapid progress in late years in the construction of iron and steel ships and lake and river steamers, and we would have made much greater progress if the same encouragement that has been given by other nations to their shipping interests had been given to ours. Our new navy is being built almost wholly of steel.

We use immense quantities of plate iron and steel in the storage, transportation, and refining of petroleum, in the production of which nature has given us a great advantage. The oil wells themselves yearly require thousands of tons of iron and steel pipes for tubing. Our natural gas wells also create a large demand for iron and steel pipes. We make liberal use of plate and sheet iron and steel in the construction of the chimneys of steamboats on our lakes and rivers, and in the construction of factory and rolling-mill chimneys and the stacks of blast furnaces. The jackets of hot-blast stoves also require large quantities of plate iron and steel in their construction. American planished sheet iron has almost entirely superseded Russia sheet iron in our markets. We use it for locomotive jackets, in the manufact-ure of stoves and stove-pipe, and for many other purposes. We are the largest consumers of tinplates in the world, Great Britain, their principal manufacturer, sending us annually more than three-fourths of her total exports ; indeed we con-sume more tinplates than all the rest of the world. We are also large consumers of galvanized sheet iron and steel for spouting, coal-buckets, portable heaters, and other purposes.

Our portable and stationary steam engines create a con-stant demand for large quantities of iron and steel. Porta-ble engines are widely used in the lumber districts of this country and in threshing grain upon American farms. Our extensive mining operations require the most powerful en-gines, while our manufacturing enterprises and the steam vessels on our lakes and rivers and on the ocean require both large and small engines. Steam cranes and elevators, steam dredges, steam hammers, and steam and hydraulic pumps create a market for large quantities of iron and steel. Our beautiful steam fire-engines are the product of American taste and skill, if they are not strictly an American inven-tion, and we annually make large numbers for home use and for exportation. Anchors and chains, cotton-presses and cotton-ties, sugar-pans and salt-pans, and general foundry and machine work require large quantities annually of both iron and steel. We make our own cotton and woolen manu-facturing machinery, and nearly all the other machinery that we use. The manufacture of the printing presses of the country consumes immense quantities of iron and steel. No other country makes such free use of the printing press as this country. We are the leading agricultural country of the world, and hence are the largest consumers of agri-cultural implements ; but we are also in advance of every other country in the use of agricultural machinery, the best of which we have invented.

We lead all nations in the manufacture of cut nails, wire

nails, and spikes. Having a larger and more rapidly-increasing population than any other country that is noted for its consumption of iron and steel we are consequently the largest consumers of nails and spikes in the construction of dwellings and public buildings, stores, warehouses, and like structures. The nail-cutting machine is an American invention. Our manufactures of scales and balances, letter-presses, burglar-proof and fire-proof safes, sewing-machines, and wagons and carriages consume iron and steel in large quantities. Sewing-machines are an American invention. We use more pleasure carriages in proportion to population than Great Britain, France, Germany, or any other country, and we also use many bicycles. Large quantities of iron and steel are used for fire-arms, sewer and other gratings, street-crossings, iron pavements, lamp-posts, posts and frames for awnings, posts for electric lights, fire-plugs, fire-escape ladders, builders' hardware and all sorts of small hardware, horseshoes and horseshoe nails, wire rope for miscellaneous purposes, barrel and baling hoops, cots and bedsteads, burial caskets, chairs and settees, woven-wire mattresses, screens, wire netting, wire mats, wire belting, railings, and street letter-boxes. In the manufacture of machine and hand tools and general cutlery we are excelled by no other country, and in the use of machine tools we are in advance of every other country. No other country makes such free use of labor-saving inventions of all kinds as this country, most of which require iron and steel in their manufacture. Our saws and axes especially enjoy a world-wide reputation, and so also do American shovels. Not the least important use to which iron and steel are put in this country is in the extension of the iron industry itself, every blast furnace, rolling mill, and steel works that is erected first consuming large quantities of these products before contributing to their general supply.

In the substitution of steel for iron this country has made rapid progress, especially in the construction and equipment of its railroads. During the past ten years virtually all the rails that have been laid on American railroads have been made of Bessemer steel. The manufacture of iron rails in this country is practically ended, steel rails now costing much less than iron rails. On most American railroads the boilers of all new locomotives are now required to be made of steel, and the tendency is toward the exclusive use of steel for locomotive boilers and its general use for stationary and marine boilers. The tires of American locomotives are now made exclusively of steel, and the fire-boxes of our locomotives are generally made of steel. The steel used in the construction of American locomotives is now chiefly produced by the open-hearth process. We have built many steel bridges, and there is a marked tendency to substitute steel for iron in bridge-building. In shipbuilding we commenced the use of steel as a substitute for iron several years ago. The use of rolled steel for building purposes in this country is making rapid headway. Steel is now largely used in the manufacture of wire for miscellaneous purposes, and for car and carriage axles, carriage tires, screws, bolts, rivets, and many other articles for which iron was formerly used. All of our barbed wire fencing is made of steel. Until recently steel had not been much used in this country for any kind of nails, but it is now in general use in their manufacture.

Mention has been made of the artistic finish of some of our iron and steel work, but the subject seems worthy of further notice. It is not only in stove-founding, in the graceful designs of bridges and elevated railways, and in the delicate combination of iron and steel with other materials in the construction and ornamentation of buildings that American ironworkers have displayed both taste and skill. The fine arts themselves are being enriched by our ironworking countrymen. An iron foundry at Chelsea, in Massachusetts, has reproduced in iron castings various works of art with all the fidelity and delicacy of Italian iron founders. The most delicate antique patterns have been successfully copied. Shields representing mythological groups and classic events, medallions containing copies of celebrated portraits, panels containing flowers and animals, an imitation of a Japanese lacquer tray one-sixteenth of an inch thick, and a triumphal procession represented on a large salver comprise some of the work of the Chelsea foundry. Some of the castings have been colored to represent bronze and others to represent steel, while others again preserve the natural color of the iron. The bronzed castings resemble beaten work in copper. American pig iron has been chiefly used. Other foundries have produced similar castings.

Until recently we conspicuously fell behind European countries in the use of iron and steel for military purposes. We maintain only a small standing army, and hence still have but little use for iron and steel for the supply of this branch of the public service. But we are now building a large navy, which will soon compare favorably in the number and size of its vessels and in their equipment with the navies of Europe. We are behind other countries in the use of iron and steel sleepers for railroad tracks. We yet have an abundance of timber for railroad cross-ties, and hence do not need to substitute either iron or steel cross-ties. Except as an experiment there is not an iron or steel cross-tie in use in this country. We have long used coal cars made of plate iron, but recently we have commenced the building of iron and steel cars for the transportation of ordinary freight. We still import many blacksmiths' anvils, their manufacture being a branch of the iron industry to which we have not yet given adequate attention. Anvils of the best quality are, however, made in this country. A far more serious hiatus in our iron and steel industries existed until recently in the total absence of the manufacture of tinplates, which are almost entirely composed of sheet iron or steel. As we can import the crude tin as easily as we import other commodities our failure to manufacture tinplates must be ascribed to the only true cause, our inability to manufacture sheet iron and steel and coat them with tin as cheaply as this is done by British manufacturers. Tin ore has been discovered in this country in several places and is now being smelted, and it is not improbable that block tin may yet be produced at home in sufficiently large quantities to supply any domestic demand for it that may be created. The passage of the McKinley tariff act in 1890 has led to the establishment of many tinplate enterprises in our country in 1891.

Other uses of iron and steel in the United States might be discovered upon further reflection and investigation, but enough particulars have been recited to show to how many uses these metals are applied and how large is their part in meeting the numerous wants of our American civilization.

CHAPTER LXIII.

CONCLUSION.

IN reviewing the preceding pages the most striking fact which presents itself for our consideration is the great stride made by the world's iron and steel industries in the last hundred years. In 1788 there were only 85 active furnaces in Great Britain, and their total production was only 68,300 gross tons of pig iron. In 1882 Great Britain had 929 furnaces, many of which were idle, and their production was 8,586,680 tons, which has not since been exceeded. In 1810 the production of pig iron in the United States was 53,908 gross tons, and in 1890 the production was 9,202,703 tons. A hundred years ago there were no railroads in the world for the transportation of freight and passengers. Iron ships were unknown; there were no steamships; and all the iron bridges in the world could be counted on the fingers of one hand. Without railroads and their cars and locomotives, and without iron ships and iron bridges, the world needed but little iron. Steel was still less a necessity, and such small quantities of it as were made were mainly used in the manufacture of swords and tools with cutting edges. It was at the beginning of the railroad era, at the close of the first quarter of the present century, that the first marked increase in the use of iron and steel in modern times took place. This was in 1825, just sixty-six years ago, when the Stockton and Darlington Railroad in England was opened. The invention of the steam engine in the latter half of the preceding century made the railroad era possible.

The great progress made by the world's iron and steel industries in the last hundred years is as plainly marked in the improvement of the processes of manufacture as in the increased demand for iron and steel products. A little over a hundred years ago all bar iron was laboriously shaped under the tilt-hammer and the trip-hammer; none of it was rolled. Nor was iron of any kind refined at that time in the puddling furnace; it was all refined in forges, and much of it was made in primitive bloomary forges directly from the ore. Cort had just perfected the rolling mill and the puddling furnace. Only a few years ago a prejudice still existed in favor of hammered bar iron. Nearly all the blast furnaces of a hundred years ago were blown with leather or wooden bellows by water-power, and the fuel used in them was chiefly charcoal. Steam-power, cast-iron blowing cylinders, and mineral fuel had just been introduced in Europe, but not in this country. Sixty-five years ago heated air had not anywhere been used in the blowing of blast furnaces, and fifty-six years ago anthracite coal had not been used in them, except experimentally. Forty years ago the Bessemer process for the manufacture of steel had not been heard of, and the open-hearth process for the manufacture of steel had not been made a practical success. Thirty-five years ago the regenerative gas furnace had just been invented. The nineteenth century has been the most prolific of all the centuries in inventions which have improved the methods of manufacturing iron and steel and which have facilitated their production in large quantities.

The next most important fact that is presented in the preceding chapters is the astonishing progress which the iron and steel industries of the United States have made within the last thirty years. During this period we have not only utilized all cotemporaneous improvements in the manufacture of iron and steel, but we have shown a special aptitude, or genius, for the use of such improvements as render possible the production of iron and steel in large quantities. Enterprising and progressive as the people of this country have always been in the manufacture of iron and steel they have shown in the last thirty years that they have in all respects been fully alive to the iron and steel requirements of our surprising national development. If we had not applied immense blowing engines and the best hot-blast stoves to our blast furnaces our present large production of pig iron would have been impossible. If we had not built numerous large rolling mills and steel works we could not have had a sufficient supply of plate iron and steel for locomotive and other boilers, and for the hulls and frames of ships, nor for oil tanks, nails and spikes, and other important uses ; nor of sheet iron and steel for stoves, the coverings for locomotives, and for domestic utensils; nor of beams, tees, angles, and channel iron for bridge-building and general construction purposes; nor of iron rails for our railroads; nor of bar iron and rod iron for a thousand uses. If we had not promptly introduced the Bessemer process the railroads of the country could not have been cheaply supplied with steel rails, and without the eighteen million tons of American steel rails which have been laid in American railroad tracks in the past twenty-four years our leading railroads could not have carried their vast tonnage of agricultural and other products, for iron rails could not have endured the wear of this tonnage. If we had not established the manufacture of crucible steel and introduced the open-hearth process there would have been a scarcity of steel in this country for the manufacture of agricultural implements, springs for railroad passenger cars, and springs and tires for locomotives. Foreign countries could not in late years have supplied our extraordinary wants for pig iron, rolled iron, iron and steel rails, and crucible and open-hearth steel; for, if there were no other reasons, the naturally conservative character of their people would have prevented them from realizing the magnitude of those wants. If our iron and steel industries had not been so largely developed in the past thirty years it is clear that our railroad system could not have been so wonderfully extended and strengthened as it has been; and without this extension of our railroads we could not have produced our large annual surplus of agricultural products for exportation, nor kept the price of these products to our own people within reasonable limits; nor could our population have been so largely increased by immigration as it has been.

We can not fully comprehend the marvelous nature of the changes which have taken place in the iron and steel industries of this country in recent years unless we compare the early history of those industries with their present development.

In Alexander Hamilton's celebrated *Report on the Subject of Manufactures*, presented to Congress on the 5th of December, 1791, just one hundred years ago, it was stated with evident satisfaction that "the United States already in a great

measure supply themselves with nails and spikes," so undeveloped and primitive was our iron industry at that time.
In the same report it was stated that in the fiscal year which
ended on the 30th of September, 1790, our imports of nails
amounted to 1,800,000 pounds. In 1790 Morse's *Geography*
claimed, in a description of New Jersey, that " in the whole
State it is supposed there is yearly made about 1,200 tons of
bar iron, 1,200 ditto of pigs, and 80 of nail rods," and in
1802 it was boastingly declared in a memorial to Congress
that there were then 150 forges in New Jersey, "which at
a moderate calculation would produce twenty tons of bar iron
each annually, amounting to 3,000 tons." In 1891 there were
several rolling mills in New Jersey and over one hundred in
the United States each of which could produce much more
bar iron in three months than all of the 150 forges of New
Jersey could produce in a year.

Sixty years ago the American blast furnace which would
make four tons of pig iron in a day, or 28 tons in a week,
was doing good work. We had virtually made no progress
in our blast-furnace practice since colonial days. In 1831
it was publicly proclaimed with some exultation that "one
furnace erected in Pennsylvania in 1830 will in 1831 make
1,100 tons of pig iron." But, as George Asmus has pleasantly said, "a time came when men were no longer satisfied
with these little smelting pots, into which a gentle stream of
air was blown through one nozzle, which received its scanty
supply from a leather bag, squeezed by some tired water-
wheel." After 1840 our blast-furnace practice gradually improved, but it was not until about 1850 that any furnace in
the country could produce 150 tons of pig iron in a week,
and not until 1865 that this product had ceased to excite surprise. Ten years later, in 1875, we had several furnaces each
of which could make 700 tons of pig iron in a week; in
1880 we had several each of which could make 1,000 tons in
a week; in 1881 we boasted of having one furnace which
had made 224 tons in a day, 1,357 tons in a week, and 5,598
tons in a month; but in 1890 we had one furnace which
had made 502 gross tons in a day, 2,462 tons in a week, and
10,603 tons in a month.

In 1810 we produced 53,908 gross tons of pig iron and

THE MANUFACTURE OF

cast iron; in 1840 we produced 286,903 tons of pig iron; in 1860 we produced 821,223 tons; in 1880 we produced 3,835,-191 tons; and in 1890 we produced 9,202,703 tons.

In his *Twenty Years of Congress* Mr. Blaine says that in the First Congress, in 1789, Mr. Clymer, of Pennsylvania, asked for a protective duty on steel, stating that a furnace in Philadelphia " had produced 300 tons in two years, and with a little encouragement would supply enough for the consumption of the whole Union." In 1810, eighty-one years ago, we produced only 917 tons of steel, none of which was crucible steel. In 1831, twenty-one years later, we produced only 2,000 tons of steel, certainly not one pound of which was crucible steel, all being blister steel. So humble were our attainments as steelmakers in 1831 that we considered it a cause of congratulation that " American competition had excluded the British common blister steel altogether." In 1849 Frederick Overman declared that " the United States are at present, and will be for some time to come, dependent upon other countries for steel." He added that " in Pittsburgh attempts have been made to manufacture steel, but we doubt whether an article of good quality can ever be produced in that region." In 1882 we had virtually ceased to make even the best blister steel, better American steel having taken its place, and in that year we produced 1,736,692 gross tons of steel of all kinds, 75,972 tons of which were crucible steel. In 1880 our production of Bessemer steel and Bessemer steel rails was larger than that of Great Britain, and in nearly every subsequent year our production of Bessemer steel ingots has continued to be larger, while our production of Bessemer steel rails has invariably been larger. In 1890 we produced a grand total of 4,277,071 gross tons of steel, which was far more than Great Britain had ever produced in one year.

It was not until 1844 that we commenced to roll any other kind of rails than strap rails for our railroads. In that year we rolled our first ton of T rails. In 1847 we rolled 40,966 gross tons of rails; in 1849 the production fell to 21,-712 tons; in 1854 it increased to 96,443 tons; and in 1855 it was hoped by the officers of the American Iron Association that it would amount to 135,000 tons, but this hope was not quite realized. In 1880 we produced 1,305,212 gross tons of rails, nearly two-thirds of which were steel rails. In 1881 we increased our production of rails to 1,646,518 gross tons, nearly three-fourths of which were steel rails. In 1882 and 1883 the proportion of steel rails to iron rails produced was much larger. In recent years we have rolled steel rails almost exclusively, and in 1887 our total production of rails of all kinds amounted to 2,139,640 gross tons, which has not since been exceeded owing to the decline in the building of new railroads.

Although this country can not produce iron and steel as cheaply as European countries which possess the advantages of cheap labor and proximity of raw materials it is not excelled by any other country in the skill which it displays or the mechanical and scientific economies which it practices in any branch of their manufacture, while in certain leading branches it has displayed superior skill and shown superior aptitude for economical improvements. Our blast-furnace practice is the best in the world, and it is so chiefly because we use powerful blowing engines and the best hot-blast stoves, possess good fuel, and carefully select our ores. The excellent quality of our pig iron is universally conceded. Our Bessemer-steel practice is also the best in the world. We produce much more Bessemer steel and roll more Bessemer-steel rails in a given time with a given amount of machinery, technically termed a plant, than any of our European rivals. No controversy concerning the relative wearing qualities of European and American steel rails now exists, and no controversy concerning the quality of American Bessemer ores ever has existed. We experience no difficulty in the manufacture of open-hearth steel in the Siemens-Martin or Pernot furnace, and our steel which is thus produced is in general use side by side with crucible steel. In the manufacture of crucible steel our achievements are in the highest degree creditable. In only one respect can it be said that in its manufacture we fall behind any other country; we have not paid that attention to the production of fine cutlery steel which Great Britain has done. This is, however, wholly due to commercial and not to mechanical reasons. American crucible steel is now used without prejudice in the manufacture of all kinds of surgical instruments and dental tools, and in the manufacture of many other articles for which the best kinds of steel are required.

In the quantity of open-hearth and crucible steel produced in a given time by a given plant we are certainly abreast of all rivals. Our rolling-mill practice is fully equal to the best in Europe. The quality of our rolled iron and steel is generally superior to and is always equal to that of foreign rolled iron and steel. In the rolling of heavy armor plates we have recently made great progress. In the production of heavy forgings and castings, as well as of all lighter products of the foundry and machine-shop, this country has shown all the skill of the most advanced ironmaking countries in Europe. At the works of the Bethlehem Iron Company we have the largest steam hammer in the world, and at the same works there are hydraulic forging presses which will favorably compare with any in Europe. In the production of steel castings we have also shown great skill and much enterprise.

All our leading iron and steel works and very many of our small works are now supplied with systematic chemical investigations by their own chemists, who are often men of eminence in their profession. The managers of our blast furnaces, rolling mills, and steel works are themselves frequently well-educated chemists, metallurgists, geologists, or mechanical engineers, and sometimes all of these combined. Our rapid progress in increasing our production of iron and steel is not merely the result of good fortune, or favorable legislation, or the possession of unlimited natural resources, but is largely due to the possession of accurate technical knowledge by our manufacturers and by those who are in charge of their works, combined with the characteristic American energy which all the world has learned to respect. The "rule of thumb" has long ceased to govern the operations of the iron and steel works of this country.

What wonderful changes have taken place since those "good old colony times" and the early days of the new republic, when our fathers needed only a little iron and what little they required was made by slow and simple methods!

A feature of our iron and steel industries which has attended their marvelous productiveness in late years is the aggregation of a number of large producing establishments in districts, or "centres," in lieu of the earlier practice of erecting small furnaces and forges wherever sufficient water-power, iron ore, and charcoal could be obtained. This tendency to concentration is, it is true, not confined to our iron and steel industries, but it is to-day one of the most powerful elements which influence their development. It had its beginning with the commencement of our distinctive rolling-mill era, about 1830, but it received a powerful impetus with the establishment of our Bessemer-steel industry within the last twenty years. Pittsburgh is to-day the most productive steel centre in the world.

How great has been the change! In colonial days and long after the Revolution our ironmaking establishments belonged to the class of manufacturing enterprises described by Zachariah Allen, in his *Science of Mechanics*, in 1829. "The manufacturing operations in the United States are all carried on in little hamlets, which often appear to spring up in the bosom of some forest, gathered around the waterfall that serves to turn the mill-wheel. These villages are scattered over a vast extent of country, from Indiana to the Atlantic, and from Maine to North Carolina, instead of being collected together, as they are in England, in great manufacturing districts." While these primitive and picturesque but unproductive methods could not forever continue it is greatly to be regretted that our manufactures of iron and steel and other staple products could not have grown to their present useful and necessary proportions unattended by the evils which usually accompany the collection of large manufacturing populations in small areas.

But the progressive spirit of this wonderfully creative age not only tends steadily toward still further concentration of our manufacturing industries in districts or centres but it also invites and in many instances even compels the consolidation under one management of large amounts of manufacturing capital and of separate manufacturing resources. The iron and steel industries of this country furnish in late years a notable illustration of this latter tendency. At Pittsburgh Mr. Andrew Carnegie and his associates, at Chicago the Illinois Steel Company, and at Steelton and Sparrow's

Point the Pennsylvania Steel Company respectively control plants for the manufacture of pig iron and steel which separately have greater producing capacity in each of these specialties than the plants of any European company, while the works of the Lackawanna Iron and Steel Company at Scranton can produce more steel alone than any European plant. Is it any wonder that in 1890 this country produced over 34 per cent. of the world's production of pig iron and over 35 per cent. of its production of steel!

Upon the future prospects of the iron and steel industries of this country it is not necessary for us to dwell. Our resources for the increased production of iron and steel for an indefinite period are ample, and all other essential conditions of continued growth are within our grasp. We are to-day the first ironmaking and steelmaking country in the world. We surpass even Great Britain in the production of pig iron and in the aggregate production of steel. We consume much more iron and steel than any other country. These conditions and results are certainly gratifying to our national pride. They mark wonderful industrial achievements by a young nation in a space of time so brief that we may almost say it dates from yesterday. They are also prophetic of other and still greater achievements. If it be true, as it is recorded in the second chapter of Daniel, that "iron breaketh in pieces and subdueth all things," then the country which produces and consumes the most iron and steel must take the first rank in extending and influencing the world's civilization.

Meanwhile the fact is worthy of notice that the saying of Bishop Berkeley, "westward the course of empire takes its way," has already received a new interpretation, for the iron industry, the source and sign of material power, which had its beginning in Asia and afterwards passed successively to the countries upon the Mediterranean, along the Rhine, and in the north and west of Europe, and thence crossed the Atlantic ocean, now finds a home in the shadows of the Rocky mountains and by the Golden Gate of the Pacific ocean. It has made the circuit of the world.

PERSONAL INDEX.

This index includes the names of only a few writers who have been quoted, and does not include the names of persons of antiquity, scriptural names, nor the names of emperors, kings, and other potentates. In the preparation of this index the main object has been to record the names of pioneer iron and steel manufacturers. Names of manufacturing companies and of iron and steel works are omitted.

A.

	Page
Abbott, Dr. Henry	2
Abbott, H., & Son	445
Acrelius, Israel	154, 155, 156, 171, 173, 174
	177, 182, 184, 186, 187, 188
Adam, John	117
Adams, David	229
Adams, George	314
Adams, John and John Quincy	113
Adams, W. H.	262
Agnew, David	270, 324, 326
Agnew, David and John P.	324
Agricola, Georgius	82, 83, 95
Åkerman, Professor Richard	93, 94, 404
Albright, Joseph J.	192
Alden, John and Mason F.	200
Alexander, J. H.	27, 28, 39, 240, 249, 253
	256, 370, 372
Alexander, Robert	301
Alexander, William (Lord Stirling)	152
Alexander's furnace	374
Alger, Cyrus	364
Allaire, James P.	158
Allison & Henderson	208
Allen, Mr. (Bessemer's brother-in-law)	402
Allen, Colonel Ethan	128, 129, 502
Allen, Frank	325
Allen, Job	148
Allen, John	157
Allen, Nicholas	473
Allen & Turner	156
Allen, William (chief justice)	155, 156
	159, 168
Allen, Zachariah	539
Ames, Fisher	133
Ames, Horatio	462
Anderson, James	230
Anderson, Robert J.	423
Anderson & Co.	423
Anderson and Cooper	151
Anderson & Woods	422
Ankrim, Josiah, & Son	389
Anshutz, George	207, 218, 225, 226, 231
Archibald, C. D.	44
Armstrong, John	185

	Page
Arnold, Benedict	268
Arnold (historian)	134
Ashbridge, George	158
Ashebran, Mr.	332, 333
Ashman, George	204, 205
Asmus, George	535

B.

	Page
Backhouse, Richard	496
Backus, Rev. Isaac	124
Baker, Elias	208, 222
Baker, Hilary	496
Baldwin, Judge Henry	223, 502
Baldwin, Robinson, McNickle & Beltzhoover	223, 228, 229
Ball, Daniel	129
Ball, John	234, 236, 237
Ball, Joseph	504
Ball, Mary, (mother of Washington)	504
Ball, William	237
Ballendine, Mr.	268
Balliet, James	192
Balliet, Stephen	192
Bancroft, George	479, 480, 482, 483
Bannan, Benjamin	478
Barkers, (Massachusetts iron workers)	120
Barney, Ariel N.	322
Barnum, Milo	130
Barnum, Hon. William H.	130, 135
Bartholomew & Dorsey	207
Bartlett, James Herbert	351
Baude, Peter	47
Bauerman, H.	75
Baughman, Joseph	358
Baxter, William	250
Beach, Abram	342
Beale, Thomas	210
Beall, Walter	282, 283, 284
Beekman, William	233
Beelen, Anthony	226, 227
Belcher, Governor of New Jersey	159
Belknap, M. B.	229
Belknap, Bean & Butler	229
Bell, Herbert C.	169

Page

Bell, Dr. John................................... 32, 68
Bell, John, & Co............................... 218
Bell, Sir Lowthian............................ 500
Bell, Martin..................................... 208
Bell, William................................... 91
Belzoni, Giovanni Battista................ 3
Bement, William B., & Son.............. 463
Benezet, Daniel................................ 179
Beninger, John.................................. 219
Benner, General Philip...................... 206
Benner's forge.................................. 309
Bennet, Nehemiah............................. 133
Bennett, Richard............................... 241
Bennett, William........................ 184, 212
Berkeley, Bishop................................ 540
Berkley, John............................... 104, 105
Berkley, Maurice............................... 104
Berkley, Sir William.......................... 258
Berlin, David.................................... 474
Berry, A. V....................................... 321
Berry, George A.......................... 225, 226
Bessemer, Sir Henry..... 63, 395, 396, 397, 399
  400, 401, 402, 403, 404, 405, 407, 409, 410, 419
Bessemer, Henry, & Co...................... 405
Bevens, Alfred, & Co......................... 341
Beverley, Robert.......... 103, 104, 105, 106
Biddle, Nicholas............................... 359
Biddle, Owen 470
Bigot, M... 349
Birch, George H................................ 44
Bird, Mark................... 175, 176, 184, 267, 507
Bird, William................................... 175
Bird, William (another)..................... 496
Birkinbine, John..................... 307, 515, 516
Birkinshaw, John........................ 429, 430
Bishop, John..................................... 410
Bissell, John.................................... 230
Bissell, Samuel................................ 127
Bitter, Michael, & Son...................... 201
Black, William.................................. 249
Blackstone, Sir William.................... 486
Blaine, James (ironmaster)................ 210
Blaine, Hon. James G........................ 536
Blaine, Walker & Co.......................... 210
Blair, Thomas S............................... 392
Blake, Henry.................................... 230
Blockley, Thomas.............................. 91
Bloomfield, Joseph E........................ 433
Board, Cornelius 149
Board, Joseph................................... 149
Bochs, Godfrey................................. 48
Boggs, Andrew.................................. 426
Boggs, Moses.................................... 206
Boone, Annie.................................... 508
Boone, Daniel................................... 508
Boone, George................................... 508
Borden, Colonel................................ 434
Borden, Joseph................................. 157
Bouchette, Joseph (historian)............ 350
Bowen, R.................................... 228, 229
Bowle, James................................... 233

Page

Bowman, Jacob................................. 216
Boyce, James P................................ 290
Boyd, Samuel................................... 469
Boyd, William.................................. 469
Bradford, William............................. 164
Bradley, William A............................ 257
Branson, William.....171, 173, 174, 178, 236, 382
Breading, Nathaniel.......................... 215
Breckinridge, John...................... 283, 284
Breckinridge, John C......................... 284
Brewster, Samuel.............................. 139
Brice, Dr... 304
Brick, Joseph W................................ 158
Bridges, Robert................................ 108
Briggs, Benjamin F............................ 274
Brinkerhoff, John........................ 143, 144
Britton, J. Blodget............................ 388
Broadmeadow, Simeon....................... 389
Brock, R. A.................... 106, 258, 266, 467
Brougham, Lord................................ 492
Brown, John..................................... 128
Brown, John, of Ossawatomie............. 380
Brown, John N.................................. 409
Brown, Joseph H............................... 222
Brown, Nicholas and Moses............... 127
Brown, Dr. Ryland T.......................... 314
Brown, William................................. 210
Brown, Bonnell & Co......................... 311
Brown & Watson............................... 198
Brown's History of Locomotives..428, 429, 439
Bruce, Mr................................... 72, 73
Bryant, Mr....................................... 358
Bryant, Gridley 427
Bryant, William Cullen...................... 361
Buchanan, Franklin 295
Buchanan, James.............................. 497
Buck, William J.............. 469, 472, 473, 478
Buckley & Swift................................ 364
Buckwalter, John.............................. 220
Budd, Eli and Wesley......................... 158
Budd, Thomas................................... 147
Buffington, Mr.................................. 276
Buffington, E. J................................ 450
Burd, Colonel James.......................... 468
Burden, Henry.............................. 145, 230
Burr, John....................................... 155
Burrell, Thomas................................ 220
Burrell, Walter, Esq........................... 86
Burrows, William.............................. 161
Burt, William A................................ 321
Bushnell, C. S............................. 445, 447
Bussey, Dr. Charles........................... 338
Bussey, Dr. J. B................................ 338
Butland, James................................. 363
Butland & Rowland........................... 363
Butler, J. Green............................... 222
Butler, J. G., Sr............................... 322
Butler, J. G., Jr........................... 312, 322
Byrd, Col. William, 1st................. 106, 467
Byrd, Colonel William, 2d...259, 260, 261, 262
  .... 263, 266, 267, 374, 378, 467, 504

C.

	Page
Caldwell, Charles and George	129
Calhoun, Hon. John C.	446
Callaway, Thomas	268, 269
Callender, Norman	199
Campbell, James	477
Campbell, John	305, 306, 308
Canan, Stewart & Moore	208
Canfield, Israel	160
Carey, Henry C.	369, 480
Carey, Mathew	369, 480
Carnegie, Andrew	539
Carnegie, Thomas M	417
Carnegie Brothers & Co. Limited	411, 456
Carnegie, Phipps & Co. Limited	424
Carpenter, Conrad	465
Carr, S. T.	321
Carroll, Charles (of Carrollton)	428
Carroll, Dr. Charles	250
Carroll, Tasker, and others	252
Cary, Colonel Archibald	106, 107
Cary, Robert	262
Chamberlain, Captain H. S.	291
Chambers, Colonel James	198, 254
Chambers, William, Benjamin, and George	197
Chapman, Nathaniel	247, 452, 503
Chatham, Lord	480
Chaucer, Godfrey	43
Chetwynd, Walter	242, 245, 265, 503, 504
Chetwynd, William	242, 245, 246, 247, 249
	265, 503, 504
Child, Robert	113
Chisholm, Henry	313, 417
Chiswell, Mr.	260, 266, 378
Chouteau, Charles P.	409
Chrisman family	167
Christmas, Hazlett & Co.	304
Cist, Charles	474, 475
Cist, Jacob	475
Clapham, Mr.	267
Clare, Thomas D.	409
Clarke, Captain Thomas	118
Clay, Henry	492
Clendenin, David	301
Clendenin & Co.	301
Clinton, Governor of New York	137
Clymer, Mr. (member of First Congress)	536
Coates, John R.	383
Cobb, Andrew B.	162
Cochran, Benjamin	448
Cockerill, John	54, 88
Cole, Samuel	197
Coleman, Hon. G. Dawson	180
Coleman, Robert	179, 180, 181, 183, 196, 496
Coleman, R. & G. D.	389
Coleman, R. H. & W.	389
Coleman, Thomas Burd	196
Coleman, William	389, 390
Coleman, Hailman & Co.	389, 390
Collins, Edward K.	322
Collins, John, Governor of Delaware	238
Colt, Samuel and John	160

	Page
Coney, Jabez	443
Conyngham, Redmond	168
Cooke, John Esten (historian)	259, 262
Cooper, Benjamin	151
Cooper, Peter	161, 361, 364, 439
Cooper, Thomas	364
Cooper & Hewitt	169, 435
Cooper, Hewitt & Co.	422
Cope, Gilbert	171
Corning, Erastus	144
Cort, Henry	53, 54, 56, 63, 90, 94, 98, 491, 533
Cosby, Governor of New York	136
Cowan, Christopher	212, 227, 228, 229
Cowan, Dr. Frank	9
Coxe, Colonel Daniel	157
Coxe, Tench	237, 239, 273, 277, 285, 314, 382
	383, 491, 509
Craig, Isaac, Esq.	212, 227
Craig, Major Isaac	214
Cramer's "Almanack"	227, 228, 229, 270
Cramp, W., & Sons	444
Crane, George	56, 63, 356, 357, 358, 359
	360, 361
Cravens, Robert	290
Crawford, Alexander L.	223, 324
Crawford, George	508
Crawford, A. L. and J. M.	223
Crawford, J. M., & Co.	223
Crawford, Colonel William	213, 468
Crawley, Ambrose	163
Creve-Cœur, Marquis de	140
Crocker, Charles	315
Croghan, Colonel	468
Cromwell, Thomas	204
Crooker, Ralph	364, 435, 461, 466
Crosby, John	177
Crowell, Hon. John	312
Crowther, John	310, 373
Crowther, Joshua, Joseph J., and Benjamin	374
Crumrine, Boyd	213
Cuddy & Ledlie	229
Cunningham, Messrs	139
Curtin, Andrew G., Governor of Penna.	206
Curtin, Roland	206
Curtis, J. B.	325
Custis's "Recollections"	263

D.

	Page
Daddow, S. H.	473, 478
Dankers, Jasper	163
Darby, Abraham	52, 53, 63, 366
Davenporte, John	118
Davies, Gabriel	181
Davies, Margaretta	181
Davies & Potts	183
Davis, Mr. (founder)	372, 373
Day, St. John V.	4, 8, 9, 66, 68, 79, 95
Day, Sherman	168, 193, 203, 222, 372
Dean, Theodore	115
Deane, Francis B.	270

544

Page

Deane, William Read.................... 115, 146
DeBardeleben, H. F............................ 295
Déby, M. Julian................................ 25
Deere, John.................................... 390
Deering, Richard.............................. 285
DeLancy, Charles D............................ 445
Delaplaine, Nicholas.......................... 160
Deming, E.................................... 387
Dempsey, Andrew............................... 306
Denonville, Marquis de........................ 348
Depue, Daniel................................. 205
Despard, Lambert and Mark.................... 120
Detmold, C. E........................... 454, 458
Devonshire, Duke of.......................... 408
Dewees, Colonel William 174
Dewey, Joseph.............................131, 379
Dexter, Thomas............................... 108
Dickerson, Hon. Mahlon........................ 147
Dickinson, Jonathan.......................164, 166
Dicks, Peter............................ 177, 184, 186
Diller, Roland................................ 208
Dillon, Moses.......................... 214, 303, 304
Dixon, Joseph................................. 392
Doddridge, Rev. Dr. Joseph.................... 101
Dorr, E. P.................................... 444
Dorsey family................................. 255
Dorsey, Edward................................ 253
Douglas, R. A................................. 316
Douglass (historian)..................... 121, 137
Douglass, C................................... 496
Downing, A.................................... 315
Downing, Samuel............................... 125
Doyle, John................................... 209
Drake, John................................... 379
Drake, Silas.................................. 335
Dredge James............................... 26, 76
Dubbs, Rev. Joseph Henry..................... 179
Dubbs, Martin................................. 207
Du Chaillu, Paul B............................ 30
Dudley, Dud............... 46, 51, 52, 53, 97
Dumble, E. T.................................. 339
Du Motay...................................... 406
Dunbar & Leonard............................. 126
Duncan, Stephen............................... 211
Dunlap's "Pennsylvania Packet" 178
Dunlop, John...............................201, 206
Dunn, Patrick and James...................... 389
Dunn, General Samuel......................... 197
Durfee, Bradford.............................. 491
Durfee, William F....... 409, 410, 412, 413, 423
Durfee, Z. S............. 409, 410, 412, 413, 417
Dutton, Robert................................ 241
Duval, Samuel................................. 470

E.

Eager (historian)....................... 137, 138
Earl, Anthony S............................... 220
Earl, William................................. 220
Earp & Brink.................................. 389
Eaton, Absalom................................ 334
Eaton, Daniel................................. 301

Page

Eckert, Valentine............................. 496
Eddy, Mr...................................... 323
Edwards, Giles................................ 290
Edwards, John................................. 496
Edwards, Hon. John M................... 301, 311
Edwards, Jonathan............................. 312
Ege, George...................... 176, 200, 496
Ege, Michael............... 185, 198, 200, 496
Eggertz, Professor Viktor..................... 405
Egle, Dr. William H..................... 166, 168
Egleston, Professor Thomas.................... 142
Eichelberger, Frederick....................... 184
Elder, Dr. William............................ 479
Eliot, Aaron................... 131, 132, 380, 381
Eliot, Rev. Jared....................... 131, 380
Eliot, John................................... 131
Elliot, Shadrach.............................. 238
Elliott, Charles G............................ 131
Ellison, Andrew................... 304, 305, 306
Emerson, James E........... 385, 386, 387, 388
Emerson, Smith & Co........................... 387
Endicott, Mr., of Salem....................... 108
England, James B., Esq........................ 248
England, John...... 235, 242, 243, 244, 245, 246
   247, 248, 250, 253, 261, 265, 266, 452, 503, 504
England, Joseph............................... 248
Ericsson, Captain John...443, 444, 445, 446, 447
Erskine, Rev. Ralph........................... 151
Erskine, Robert.......................... 150, 151
Erwin, Walter................................. 149
Estell, John.................................. 157
Evans, John................................... 235
Evans, Lewis.................................. 468
Evans, Oliver................................. 426
Evans, Robert................................. 253
Evans, Stephen................................ 174
Everett, P. M................................. 321
Eversol, Perry & Ruggles...................... 334

F.

Fackenthal, B. F., Jr......................... 169
Faesch, John Jacob.............. 150, 151, 152
Fahnestock, Samuel............................ 207
Fairbairn, William........................ 36, 73
Falkner, Ralph................................ 247
Fare, Thomas.................................. 165
Farmer, Joseph...........241, 242, 244, 246, 249
Farmer, Joseph, & Co.......................... 241
Farnsworth, Daniel............................ 157
Farr & Kunzi............................. 353, 358
Faur, Achilles Christian Wilhelm Von
   Faber du....................... 455, 458
Faux, William................................. 344
Fegar, Colonel J. M........................... 172
Fell, Judge Jesse............................. 476
Felton, Samuel M.............................. 417
Fields & Stickney............................. 302
Firmstone, William...305, 358, 360, 367, 368, 369
Firmstone, W. & G............................. 368
Fisher, Isaac................................. 368
Fisher, Thomas................................ 131

Page

Fisher, Morgan & Co.............................. 211
Fitch, Walker, and Wyllys.................... 380
Fitz Williams, Mr..................................... 260
Fletcher, H. A.. 39
Fletcher, William A..................... 332, 338
Flower, Philip William........... 49, 82, 90, 91
Flower, Samuel.. 173
Fobes, Rev. Dr.......................... 112, 115
Foley, Richard.. 48
Forbes, David, F. R. S............................ 71
Forbes, R. B... 443
Forbes, Samuel....................................... 128
Ford, Colonel Jacob, Sr......................... 153
Ford, Colonel Jacob, Jr......................... 153
Ford, Samuel... 151
Forney, Charles B................................... 336
Foster, John Wells.................................. 101
Foster, William E................................... 127
Fox, Charles, Esq........................... 309, 387
Frame, Richard.............................. 164, 233
Francis, Colonel............................. 469, 472
Franklin, Benjamin....... 131, 172, 243, 380, 484
.... 485, 502
Franklin, William, Governor of N. J...... 160
Franquet, M... 349
Franquoy, or François, M. Jules......... 25, 75
Frazer, Colonel Persifor......................... 178
Frazer, Mrs. Persifor............................. 178
Freed, A. T..................................... 348, 349
Freeman, Mr.. 218
Fritz, George.............................. 413, 414, 416
Fritz, John.................................. 291, 414, 464
Frost, John.. 303
Fulton, Henry.. 200
Fulton, James................................. 183, 189

G.

Gallatin, Albert....................................... 509
Galloway, William and John.................. 402
Galloway & Co... 404
Gantt, Fielder... 254
Garrard Brothers.............. 385, 387, 392, 394
Garrard, John H................. 309, 385, 387, 388
Garrard, Dr. William... 309, 310, 385, 386, 387
.... 388
Garret & Co. (Gurrit & Co.).................... 183
Gates, Sir Thomas......................, 103, 107
Gay, Stephen R............................. 322, 323
Gayley, James....................................... 456
Geary, John W., Governor of Penna... 220, 371
Geary, Richard.. 220
Gee, Joshua... 241, 242, 244, 246, 265, 479, 503
.... 504
Geissenhainer, Rev. Frederick W..... 201, 202
.... 354, 355, 356, 357, 358, 360, 470
Gerehart & Reynolds.............................. 219
Gibson (historian).................................. 184
Gibson, John................................. 214, 216, 303
Gibson, Joshua....................................... 215
Gifford, John... 113
Gilchrist, Percy C............... 405, 406, 421

Giles, Nathan.. 185
Ginter, Philip.. 474
Gladstone, Right Hon. William E........... 12
Gloninger, Judge John................... 207, 225
Gloninger, Anshutz & Co...................... 207
Gooch, Governor of Virginia.................. 249
Goodwin, William................................... 253
Göransson, Göran F........... 63, 396, 404, 405
Gordon's "Gazetteer"... 207, 218, 221, 223, 427
Gore Brothers.. 472
Gormly, John.. 227
Gorringe, Commander H. H................... 3
Grace, Robert.. 172
Graff, Bennett & Co.............. 281, 460, 477
Graffenreidt, Baron de.......................... 259
Green (historian).................................... 38
Green, Willis................................. 283, 284
Greene, George K................................... 314
Greene, Jabez.. 127
Greene, Nathanael................................. 127
Greene, Major General Nathanael.... 127, 502
Greenup, Christopher.............. 282, 283, 284
Gregg, Andrew....................................... 211
Gregory, Dudley S................................. 391
Gregory & Co... 393
Griffen, John.................................. 462, 466
Griffith, William.................................... 158
Griggs, Joseph P................................... 338
Griswold, Hon. John A...... 409, 416, 444, 445
....446, 447
Griswold, John A., & Co......................... 422
Grover, James.. 146
Growdon, Joseph................................... 245
Grubb family............................ 168, 183, 196
Grubb, Clement B................................... 433
Grubb, Curtis................................. 182, 496
Grubb, E. B. & C. B............................... 200
Grubb, Henry.................................. 184, 185
Grubb, Henry Bates............................... 196
Grubb, John.. 182
Grubb, Peter.................................. 182, 184
Grubb, Colonel Peter.................... 182, 496
Grubb, Peter, Jr............................ 196, 496
Grüner, Professor................................... 97
Grunfield, Jesse.................................... 496
Guard, Calen, & Co............................... 317
Guest, Mr. (member of Parliament)........ 437
Guiteau, Julius.............................. 358, 360

H.

Haldeman, Dr. E.................................... 199
Haldeman, Henry................................... 199
Haldeman, Jacob.................................... 199
Haldeman, Jacob M................................ 199
Haldeman, Jacob S................................. 199
Haldeman, John...................................... 199
Haldeman, Paris..................................... 199
Haldeman, Richard................................. 199
Haldeman, Professor S. S...................... 199
Hall, George.. 114
Hall, Henry.................................... 442, 443

	Page
Hall, John (of Philadelphia county, Pa.)	178
Hall, John (of Taunton)	114
Hall, Captain J. W. D.	114, 116, 117
Halsey, Hon. Edmund D...	148, 149, 151, 152
	155, 160, 426
Hamilton, Alexander	382, 491, 534
Hamilton, Andrew	235
Hamilton, James	218
Hamilton, Lieut. Governor James...	484, 485
Hamilton, Robert	305, 306
Hammer, John	220
Hanbury, Capel	56
Hanbury, Major John	53, 63, 90, 91, 94
Hanks, Nancy	508
Hanssien, a Voigtlander	27
Hariot, or Heriot, Thomas (historian)	102
Harper, Samuel	218
Harriman, John	153
Harrington, Clarke W.	342
Harris, Thomas & Co.	206
Harrison, Battle	333
Harrison, Chr.	213
Harrison, James	409
Harrison, Joseph and Carlisle	283
Harrison, William	333
Harrison, William Henry	121
Hartland, Mr. (Egyptian explorer)	4
Hartley, James	496
Harvey, Nathan	201
Haseltine, John	128
Hasenclever, Peter	149, 150
Hassall, John	450
Hassall, William	450
Hatherly, Timothy	120
Hathorne, Captain William	121
Haupt, Professor L. M.	466
Hauser, George	273
Hauto, George F. A.	475
Hawes, John	54
Hawkes, Adam	111
Hawkes, Nathan M.	110, 112
Hawkhurst, William	137
Hay, Sir George	59
Hayden, John	213, 215
Hayes, Hon. John L.	132, 491
Hayes, William	496
Hays, William B.	229
Haywood & Snyder	355, 434
Hazard, Erskine	356, 361, 364, 465, 475
Heath, Josiah Marshall	421
Heaton, Isaac	311
Heaton, James	302, 311
Heimbach, David, Sr.	191, 192
Heimbach, David, Jr.	191, 192
Heister, Gabriel	199
Helfrick, Samuel	192
Hellings, John	496
Henao, Father Gabriel de	23
Henderson, James	290, 406
Henderson & Ross	255
Henfrey, Benjamin	471
	Page
Hennepin, Father	467
Henry, Matthew S.	191
Henry, William (of Nazareth, Pa.)	191
Henry, William (of Oxford furnace)	453
Herndon, Samuel	283
Hewitt, Hon. Abram S.	150, 161, 407, 408
	421, 485
High, Henry	358
Highly, Levi	142
Higley family	380
Higley, Samuel	181, 379
Hill, Colonel A. M.	477
Hill, William	276, 277
Hill's bloomary	273, 274
Hillegas, Michael	474
Himrod, David	373
Himrod & Vincent	372
Hinijossa, Alexander De	233
Hoadly, Charles J.	378, 379, 380
Hockley, J.	496
Hockley, Richard	178, 382
Hodge's forge	279
Hoff, Charles	152
Hoff, Joseph	151, 152
Hogge, Ralph	47
Holker, Colonel John	214
Hollenback, Judge	478
Holley, A. H., Governor of Connecticut	130
Holley, A. L.	77, 130, 409, 410, 412, 414, 417
Holley & Coffing	129
Holliday, John	220
Hollingsworth, Henry	382
Hollingsworth, John	283
Holloman, A. W.	332, 333
Hoopes, Townsend & Co.	222
Hopkins, James M.	196
Hopkins, John Henry (bishop)	218, 222, 502
Hopkins, Stephen	127, 502
Hopper, H. J.	391
Horner, Isaac	157
Hough, Matthias	496
Houghton, John	88, 91, 92, 94
Housum, Peter and George	198
Howard, Dr.	255
Howe, Senator Timothy O.	413
Howell, Reading	473
Hubbard, Rev. William	110, 116
Huber, John	179
Hudson, Thomas	111
Hughes, Mr.	338
Hughes, Daniel and Samuel	198
Hughes, Gideon	303
Hughes, Samuel and Daniel	254
Humphreys, A. W.	138
Humphreys, Thomas	496
Humphreys, Whitehead	153, 178, 382
Hungerford, Austin N.	155, 157, 158, 192
	209, 213, 214, 233, 234, 235, 236, 238, 468
Hunt, Alfred	193, 417
Hunt, Mordecai	193
Hunt, M. R.	458

Page

Hunt, Robert.............................. 34, 53, 55
Hunt, Robert W........................ 400, 412, 414
Hunt, Dr. T. Sterry.............................. 348
Hunter, James...................... 266, 268
Huntsman, Benjamin.... 54, 55, 63, 67, 95, 96
.... 98, 99
Hurd, Jacob............... 148
Hurst, Rev. Joseph.................... 77
Huskisson, William (member of Parliament)...................................... 493
Hussey, Dr. C. G....................... 394
Hussey, Wells & Co........................ 390, 393
Hutchins, Captain...................... 469
Hutton (historian)............................. 49

I.

Illing, C. (German traveler)..................... 69
Irvin, General James............................... 211
Irvine, John........................ 209

J.

Jackson, General Andrew.. 215, 227, 284, 386
Jackson, George............................. 506
Jackson, John......................... 148
Jackson, Col. Joseph and William... 160, 161
Jackson & Updegraff......................... 270
Jacobs, Benjamin.................. 204, 253
Jacobs, Cyrus............... 182
Jacobs, Elizabeth E............... 199
Jacobs, Joseph....................... 204
Jacques, Mr. (Maryland pioneer)............. 254
James, Mrs. (historian)........ 164, 165, 166, 167
.... 168, 171, 172, 174, 234
James, Samuel................. 234, 236
James, Dr. T. C....................... 476
James, Thomas....................... 304
James & Woodruff..................... 309
Jaques, Lieutenant W. H..................... 464
Jeans, J. S..................... 395, 402
Jefferson, Thomas........ 266, 268, 269, 282, 508
Jenkins, David................ 173, 496
Jenkins, John..................... 173
Jenkins, Robert................ 173, 174
Jenks, Joseph.................. 111, 112, 119
Jenks, Joseph, Governor of Rhode Island. 119
Jenks, Joseph, Jr..................... 119
Johns, Benjamin................... 220
Johnson, Governor of Maryland............. 254
Johnson, Edward................... 110
Johnson, James................ 254
Johnson, James, & Co................ 254
Johnson, John and Thomas.................. 47
Johnson, Robert S................. 389
Johnson, Roger................... 254
Johnson, Dr. Samuel................. 90
Johnson, General Thomas 255
Johnson, Walter R.......... 358, 370, 431
Johnston (historian)................ 241, 247
Johnston, Alexander................ 219
Johnston, A., & Co................... 219
Johnston, Benjamin................ 213

Page

Johnston, John................... 153
Johnston, William F., Governor of Pa..... 219
Johnston, McClurg & Co..................... 218
Jones, Abraham..................... 506, 507
Jones, Dr. Alexander..................... 295, 476
Jones, Hon. B. F..................... 413
Jones, Benjamin and Robert................ 215
Jones, Catesby ap..................... 295
Jones, David................. 188
Jones, Isaac..................... 389, 390
Jones, John H..................... 478
Jones, Reece................... 236
Jones, Sarah (mother and daughter)...... 506
Jones, Captain William R............... 414, 417
Jones & Quigg................... 389, 390

K.

Kalm, Peter..................... 137, 177, 349
Kane, Charles................. 142
Karsten, Karl Johann Bernhard.... 25, 82, 83
Karthaus, Peter................. 201, 356
Karthaus & Geissenhainer..................... 201
Keith, Charles P................. 156, 235
Keith, Sir William....... 234, 235, 236, 248, 502
Kelly, G. A..................... 339
Kelly, John F................. 397
Kelly, William...... 396, 397, 399, 400, 407, 409
.... 410, 417
Kelsey, John..................... 129
Kennedy, Mr. (of Cincinnati)............... 413
Kennedy, Robert................. 465
Kent, Joseph C..................... 455
Kerpely, Professor Anton................... 18, 28
Killebrew, J. B..................... 299
Kimmell, Peter..................... 220
King, George S..................... 221
King, John................. 117
King, Seth..................... 129
King, Swope & Co................. 209
Kinsey, Joseph................... 309
Kinsley, Adam................. 126
Kirk, Kelton & Co..................... 201
Kirkbride, Joseph..................... 148
Kiser, Philip................. 273
Kitson, Sir James..................... 401
Knight, Edward H.................. 82, 448, 450
Knox, General Henry..................... 152, 214
Krupp, Alfred..................... 27
Krupp, Friedrich..................... 27
Krupp, Friedrich Alfred..................... 27
Krupp, Therese..................... 27
Kunkel, Colonel J. B..................... 406
Kunzi, Abraham..................... 358
Kurtz (Amish Mennonite)..................... 168

L.

Lamb, Thomas..................... 128
Lambing, Rev. A. A..................... 227
Lamborn, Robert H..................... 413
Landrin, M. H. C., Jr................. 45, 97
Lane, Ralph..................... 102

Page

Lane, William.. 208
Langford, A. G.................................... 343
Langford & Co...................................... 843
Lapsley, Judge James W.................... 294
Lardner, Lynford................................. 173
Latham, Joseph.................................... 148
Laubach, Charles.................................. 169
Laufman & Co...................................... 512
Lauth, Bernard.................................... 206
Laveleye, M. Ed. de...................... 80, 88
Lawrence, Josiah................................. 309
Layard, Austin Henry....................... 4, 5
Layton, Hon. Caleb S........................ 238
Leach, General..................................... 126
Leacock, John....................................... 165
Leader, Richard........... .... 109, 112, 113, 121
Lee, Anthony.. 165
Lee, Milo... 343
Lee, General Robert E........................ 198
Lee, Stephen S..................................... 434
Lee, William L..................................... 343
Leephar, Crotzer & Co........................ 197
Leiper, Thomas.................................... 426
Leonard, Eliphalet...................... 125, 381
Leonard, Elisha Clarke....................... 114
Leonard, George.................................. 116
Leonard, Henry.......... 112, 113, 114, 115, 146
Leonard, James.............. 110, 112, 113, 114
Leonard, James, 2d............................. 116
Leonard, Jonathan.................. 125, 126, 381
Leonard, Joseph, Benjamin, and Uriah.. 116
Leonard, Nathaniel, Samuel, and Thomas 115
.... 146
Leonard, Reuben.................................. 229
Leonard, Samuel (of Taunton)............. 117
Leonard, Samuel (of Pittsburgh).......... 228
Leonard, Thomas................................. 116
Leonard, Captain Thomas.................... 114
Leonard, Captain Zephaniah................ 117
Leonard & Kinsley.............................. 126
Lesher, John.. 171
Leshet, Jacob...................................... 496
Lewis, Mr. (of Philadelphia)................. 157
Lewis, Alonzo....... 108, 109, 110, 111, 112, 113
.... 114, 115
Lewis, George............................... 217, 229
Lewis, James................................ 165, 167
Lewis, James F.................................... 141
Lewis, Llewellyn and Arthur............... 112
Lewis, Samuel C.................................. 217
Lewis, Thomas.................................... 215
Lewis, Thomas C................................. 217
Lewis, General William........................ 210
Lewis and Clarke................................ 471
Lincoln, Abraham (President)... 444, 445, 502
.... 504, 505, 506, 507, 508
Lincoln, Abraham (of Berks county, Pa.). 507
Lincoln, Abraham (of Lancaster county,
Pa.)... 508
Lincoln, Abraham (of Scituate)............. 506
Lincoln, Abraham (of Virginia). 505, 507, 508

Page

Lincoln, Daniel (of Hingham)... 120, 505, 506
Lincoln, George (of Hingham).......... 505, 506
Lincoln, Isaac (of Scituate).................... 506
Lincoln, John (of Berks county, Pa.)...... 507
Lincoln, Mordecai (of Berks county, Pa.). 507
Lincoln, Mordecai (of Scituate).. 120, 502, 505
.... 506, 507
Lincoln, Mordecai, Jr. (of Scituate).. 506, 507
.... 508
Lincoln, Samuel (of Hingham).............. 505
Lincoln, Samuel (of Norwich, England). 505
Lincoln, Thomas (of Hingham).............. 505
Lincoln, Thomas (of Berks county, Pa.). 507
Lincoln, Thomas (of Kentucky)............. 507
Lindley & Speek................................... 211
Livingston, David................................. 220
Livingston, Philip........................... 136, 153
Livingston, Philip (signer of the Decla-
ration of Independence)............... 136, 153
Lloyd, Steel & Co................................. 211
Lobsinger, Hans............................... 27, 89
Logan, James.................. 163, 168, 169, 170
Longsdon, Robert................................ 402
Longstreth, Benjamin........................... 198
Losey, Jacob.. 160
Lossing, Benson J......................... 139, 140
Lothrop, Sylvanus................................ 230
Lowe, S. B... 291
Lower, M. A................. 35, 44, 46, 47, 51
Lowry & Co.. 224
Lowthorp, Francis C............................. 359
Loy & Patterson................................... 208
Lukens, Dr. Charles............................. 195
Lukens, Edmund T............................... 154
Lukens, Mrs. Rebecca W...................... 195
Luther, Martin....................................... 7
Lyman, William............................. 359, 432
Lyman, Ralston & Co........................... 461
Lyon, James B., & Co........................... 422
Lyon, John.................................... 211, 229
Lyon, William M.................. 226, 409, 417

M.

Macadam, W. Ivison.................. 58, 59, 78
McCaa, James...................................... 173
McCall, George.................................... 170
McCarthy, C. R., Esq........................... 205
McClurg, Alexander.............. 218, 219, 227
McClurg, Joseph............................ 226, 227
McComber, William G.......................... 322
McConaughey, William......................... 236
McConnell, Matthew............................ 322
McCook, Daniel, & Co.......................... 317
McCormick, Provance........................... 477
McCue, J. Marshall, Esq....................... 508
McCulloch's Commercial Dictionary....... 479
McCulloh, Thomas G............................ 198
McDermett, Josephine.......................... 211
McDermett, Thomas............................. 211
McDermett, William............................. 211
McDougall, F., & Son........................... 350

Page

McDougall, George.................................. 351
McKelvy, S... 389
McKelvy & Blair................... 390, 392, 393
McKinley, Hon. William, Jr............ 497, 531
McLanahan, J. King.............................. 458
McNair, William................................... 310
McPherson, Hon. Edward..................... 197
McPherson, John B............................... 197
McRae, D... 342
McShane, Francis.................................. 201
Machin, Captain Thomas....................... 139
Mackey, James..................................... 301
Maclay, William................................... 210
Mahon, John D..................................... 211
Malen, Joshua (or Malin)............... 228, 303
Malin & Bishop.................................... 363
Manning, Dr. Henry.............................. 312
Manning & Lee............................. 434, 435
Marmie, Peter...................................... 214
Marshall, Caleb and John...................... 239
Marshall, J. M..................................... 343
Marshall, O. H..................................... 140
Marshall, Samuel................................. 207
Martien, Joseph Gilbert........................ 407
Martin, Emile and Pierre................. 420, 421
Martin, James...................................... 278
Mason, Major John C............................ 283
Massey, Mordecai.......................... 207, 225
Massey & James................................... 335
Master, Legh....................................... 253
Mather, Cotton.................................... 101
Mathiot, Colonel.................................. 219
Matthews, George.:.............................. 255
Maw and Dredge (William H. Maw and
    James Dredge)............................ 26, 76
May, Mr. (of Milwaukee)...................... 413
Mayberry, Thomas............................... 155
Mayburry, Thomas.......................... 170, 496
Maybury, Jonathan, & Co..................... 218
Maynard, George W.............................. 408
Meade, Richard............ 60, 61, 78, 519, 521
Means, John, 1st.................................. 306
Means, John, 2d............................. 305, 306
Means, Thomas W................. 304, 306, 307
Means, William.................................... 306
Meason, Isaac............ 214, 215, 217, 219, 303
Meason, Colonel Isaac..................... 217, 219
Meason, Dillon & Co............................ 214
Medine, Don Pedro de............................ 22
Megee, George..................................... 170
Meyer, C. J. L..................................... 329
Middleton, William T..................... 309, 387
Middleton, Garrard & Co....................... 387
Mifflin, George.................................... 165
Mighill, Rev. Thomas........................... 120
Miles, Colonel Samuel.......................... 206
Miles, Harris & Miles............................ 206
Miller, Henry............ 267, 268, 269, 507, 508
Miller, Ichabod.................................... 380
Miller, Hon. Jacob W............................ 153
Miller, Michael.................................... 176

Page

Miller, Captain Samuel......................... 508
Miller, Thomas C................................. 197
Miller, William.................................... 192
Miller, Martin & Co.............................. 210
Miller, Metcalf & Parkin....................... 423
Miner, Hon. Charles.............................. 475
Mochabee, Reuben................................ 215
Mockbee, John..................................... 284
Montgomery, Morton L.................... 171, 176
Montgomery, Robert.............................. 301
Moore, David....................................... 304
Moore, Matthew.................................... 273
Moore's furnace................................... 267
Moore & Hooven................................... 462
Moorhead, J. B., & Co........................... 453
Moorhead, M. K................................... 226
Morgan, General Daniel.................. 169, 502
Morgan, Jacob, Jr................................. 496
Morgan, James..................................... 169
Morgan, Williams & Co......................... 341
Morosini, G. P...................................... 14
Morrell, Hon. Daniel J............ 409, 410, 417
Morrill, Hon. Justin S..................... 393, 497
Morris, Anthony................... 167, 168, 170
Morris, David...................................... 312
Morris, Hon. Edward Joy....................... 434
Morris, Mrs. Henry............................... 181
Morris, J. Anthony............................... 474
Morris, Jonathan.................................. 253
Morris, Joseph, John, and Samuel......... 185
Morris, Colonel Lewis..................... 146, 147
Morris, Robert..................................... 474
Morris, William................................... 474
Morrison, William................................ 230
Morse, Dr. Jedidiah............ 123, 161, 535
Mulhollan & McAnulty.......................... 212
Müller, Detmar Basse........................... 222
Munn & Co... 407
Mushet, David.................... 28, 46, 408
Mushet, Robert F........ 63, 396, 400, 401, 402
.... 403, 404, 408, 409, 410, 421
Myers, Christian.................................. 224
Myers, Jacob................................. 282, 284

N.

Nancarro, John.................................... 178
Nancarrow & Matlock........................... 382
Napoleon III., Emperor......................... 446
Nash, J. S... 338
Nasmyth, James.................................... 63
Needy, Hugh.. 205
Negley, Major William B....................... 226
Neill (History of the Virginia Company) 103
Neilson, James Beaumont......... 53, 63, 354
Nelson, Mr. (Virginia pioneer)............... 260
Nelson, William.................. 148, 150, 160
Newberry, Dr. J. S............................... 344
Newhall (historian)......... 108, 110, 113, 115
Newport, Captain Christopher............... 103
Nevin, Mrs. Martha J........................... 174
Nicholas, Colonel George............... 283, 284

Page

Nicholls (historian)............................ 38, 84
Nicholson, John............................ 214, 474
Nicolai, Friedrich............................... 27
Nicolai & Krupp................................. 27
Nicolas, Dr. (Virginia pioneer)............... 260
Nicolay and Hay................................ 506
Nikoll, John George........................... 176
Noble, Abel.................................... 137
Noble, Henry and John............... 221, 222
Nolan, Louis................................... 321
Norden, John................................... 46
Norton, Aaron.................................. 302
Nutt, Samuel........ 166, 171, 172, 173, 174, 236
Nutt, Samuel, Jr............................... 172

O.

Oakley, Mr. (of Brooklyn)..................... 433
Odiorne (inventor)...................... 448, 449
Ogden, F. B................................... 438
Ogden, Samuel................................. 160
Ogden's furnace............................... 155
Ogdens, the............................. 149, 155
O'Hara & Scully............................... 218
Old, Ann...................................... 181
Old, Davies.............................. 180, 182
Old, James.................... 180, 181, 182, 496
Old, Margaretta............................... 182
Old, William (son of James)................... 181
Old, William (brother of James)............... 181
Old, Wilkinson & Trent........................ 269
Old's furnace................................. 269
Olde, William................................. 496
Oldmixon (historian).......... 130, 147, 233, 236
Olds, Mr................................. 321, 322
Oliphant, F. H.......................... 217, 368
Oliphant, John and Andrew............. 215, 216
Oliver, Judge Peter........................... 121
Onion, Stephen..241, 242, 243, 246, 247, 252, 253
Onion, Stephen, & Co.......................... 241
Orban, Michael................................ 88
Orr, Hugh..................................... 120
Osborn, Jonathan.............................. 153
Osborn, Samuel................................ 403
Osborne, William.............................. 113
Otis, Charles A............................... 312
Otis, Melville................................ 449
Overman, Frederick....... 30, 81, 256, 366, 536
Owen, Evan.................................... 236
Owings, John Cockey............... 282, 283, 284
Owings, Colonel Thomas Dye.................... 283

P.

Packer, Hon. S. J............................. 367
Palmer, Arthur................................ 217
Pannebecker, Henry............................ 165
Park, James, Jr.................... 409, 417, 422
Park, Brother & Co..... 390, 393, 422, 423, 463
Park, McCurdy & Co............................ 421
Parke, Judge John E........................... 230
Parke & Tiers................................. 358
Parker (historian)............................ 41

Page

Parkins, John and John Jr..................... 383
Parsons, Dr................................ 85, 88
Paschall, Stephen...................... 178, 382
Patterson, Burd........................ 359, 369
Patton, Mrs. Bridget................... 175, 176
Patton, Edward B.............................. 211
Patton, John........................... 175, 496
Patton, Colonel John.......................... 206
Patton, General William....................... 206
Paul, John and Joseph M....................... 158
Paull, Archibald....................... 286, 304
Paxson, Samuel................................ 215
Paxton, James D............................... 197
Paxton, James D., & Co........................ 197
Payne, John..................53, 63, 90, 91, 94
Pears, Jeremiah........................ 215, 217
Pearse, Captain............................... 260
Pechar, Joh................................31, 78
Penn, Lieutenant Governor John................ 469
Penn, Richard................................. 472
Penn, Thomas.............. 178, 382, 469, 472
Penn, William.......... 153, 163, 164, 166, 174
Pennock, Isaac................................ 195
Pennypacker, Hon. Samuel W......... 165, 174
Percy, Dr. John.... 1, 27, 30, 37, 48, 55, 75, 80
.... 81, 82, 83, 90, 95, 97
Perkins, Jacob................... 183, 448, 449
Perkins, Peter................................ 273
Perkins, Colonel T. H......................... 427
Perry, Benjamin....................... 359, 360
Perry, Matthew Calbraith...................... 295
Perry, Commodore O. A......................... 227
Peters, Richard............................... 466
Peters, Richard (secretary)................... 485
Pettitt, Andrew............................... 496
Petty, Sir William............................ 57
Pettybone, Daniel............................. 126
Phelps, Timothy............................... 379
Phelps, William............................... 401
Philip, King (Indian chief)................... 114
Philips, Hardman.............................. 206
Phillips, Mr. (of Cincinnati)................. 413
Phillips, Wendell............................. 8
Philpot, William.............................. 312
Philpot, William, & Co........................ 311
Philson, Robert............................... 220
Pickering, Colonel Timothy.................... 189
Picton (English writer)....................... 43
Pierson, Isaac................................ 155
Pierson, Josiah G...................... 144, 448
Pierson, Robert............................... 221
Pike, Captain Z. M............................ 472
Piper, Conrad................................. 220
Pitkin, Timothy....................... 136, 518
Player, John.................................. 453
Poague, George................................ 286
Polhem, Christopher...................... 93, 94
Polhem, Gabriel............................... 94
Polk, Josiah.................................. 238
Poor, Henry V................... 428, 431, 441
Pope's Customs Laws........................... 487

Page

Porter, David R., Governor of Penna...... 211
Pott, John.. 195, 357
Potter, O. W.. 413
Potts, David... 496
Potts, Isaac and David 175
Potts, John........................ 167, 171, 172, 174
Potts, Joseph.. 174
Potts, Robert S...................................... 183
Potts, Samuel.. 496
Potts, Thomas.................... 157, 165, 167, 168
Potts, Thomas, Jr..................... 164, 167, 171
Pourcel, M. Alexandre............ 22, 23, 75, 76
Powe, Lewis.................................... 421, 422
Power, Captain William.......................... 211
Pratt, Jared 199
Prescott, William H............................... 101
Preston, Samuel..................................... 473
Probst, John.................................... 218, 225
Prowell, George R......................... 184, 212
Pullman, J. Wesley 172
Putnam, Professor F. W.......................... 101

Q.

Quinby, Jesse B..................................... 353

R.

Rahm, Mrs... 226
Rahm & Bean... 220
Raleigh, Sir Walter................................ 102
Ralston, A. G., & Co.............................. 357
Ralston, Robert...................................... 359
Ramsay, Dr. (historian).......................... 276
Randolph, John C. F.............................. 9
Ranney, Judge Rufus P.......................... 312
Ravenzon (early English ironmaster)...... 53
Rawle, Francis....................................... 165
Ray, John.. 86
Raymond, Philander............................... 224
Read, Hon. Charles.............. 156, 157, 158
Reading, John.. 148
Réaumur (French chemist)................. 96, 97
Reed, Charles M..................................... 224
Reed, Ezekiel................................... 448, 449
Reese, Jacob.. 406
Reese & Thomas 195
Reeves, Benjamin and David.................. 160
Reeves, Josiah 333
Reeves, Samuel J.......................... 462, 466
Reeves, Thomas..................................... 333
Reeves, Buck & Co................................. 360
Reis, Brown, Berger, and James Ward... 230
Renshaw, John A.................................... 226
Rentgen, Clemens................... 193, 194, 217
Reynolds, General James L..................... 196
Reynolds, General John F....................... 196
Reynolds, Major Samuel M..................... 196
Reynolds, Admiral William..................... 196
Rhodes, Barnabas................................... 165
Rice, Jacob.. 192
Richards, Mrs. Augustus H..................... 157
Richards, Jesse..................................... 158, 159

Page

Richards, Louis, Esq............................... 159
Richards, Mark..................... 159, 220, 256
Richards, Samuel 159
Richards, William................................... 159
Richards, Earl & Co............................... 220
Richardson, Richard............................... 361
Ridgely family.. 253
Ridgely, Charles 204
Ridgely, Edward..................................... 204
Rigby, John.. 185
Riggs, Joseph... 308
Riggs, J., & Co. 308
Ritner, Joseph, Governor of Pa... 353, 355, 369
Ritner, Peter 353, 369
Ritter, George K..................................... 223
Roach, John, & Son................................ 444
Robbins, J... 389
Robbins, Samuel S.................................. 129
Roberts, Solomon W.......... 356, 357, 427, 431
Robertson, Mr. (member of Parliament). 492
Robeson, Hon. George M........................ 154
Robeson, Jonathan................................. 154
Robinson, David..................................... 221
Robinson, James..................................... 288
Robinson, Captain James........................ 218
Robinson, Judge..................................... 334
Robinson, L. C....................................... 284
Robinson, Morris.................................... 158
Robinson, William, Jr............................. 228
Rock, James 85
Rockwell, E. S....................................... 321
Rodgers, James.................... 304, 305, 306
Rodgers, James, & Co............................ 305
Rodgers, John and Jacob........................ 383
Roebuck, Dr... 53
Rogers, Professor James E. Thorold.... 39, 41
.... 42, 55
Rogers & Burchfield.............................. 460
Root & Wheeler...................................... 302
Ross, D. S... 315
Ross, David....................... 268, 269, 288
Ross, George................................... 184, 502
Ross, George, & Co................................ 184
Ross, John... 171
Ross, Randall... 314
Roup, Jonas.. 226
Rowland, Mrs. Harriet M........................ 193
Rowland, James..................................... 363
Rowland, James and Maxwell................. 193
Rowland, James, & Co............................ 389
Rowland, Thomas F................................ 445
Rowland, W. & H.................................... 389
Rowland & Hunt.................................... 193
Royer, Daniel.. 208
Royer, John... 208
Royer, John (son of Daniel)..................... 208
Ruck, John 115
Ruggles, George..................................... 113
Rupp, Isaac D.................................. 180, 202
Rush, Dr. Benjamin................................ 166
Russell, B. F., Esq......................... 334, 335

Page
Russell, George B................................ 324
Russell, Ralph........................ 113, 114
Russell, Thomas... 241, 243, 245, 249, 251, 265
Russell, Thomas, 2d....................... 251, 252
Russell, Thomas, 3d............................ 252
Russell, William... 241, 242, 244, 245, 265, 503
.... 504
Ruston, John..................... 241, 242, 246, 249
Rutter, John.. 236
Rutter, Thomas.... 165, 166, 167, 170, 172, 175
.... 236
Rutter, Thomas (1785)........................... 496

S.

St. Clair, General Arthur.......... 218, 222, 502
Salters, William...............: 305
Sandys, George..................... 105
Saunders's furnace............................. 269
Savage, John........................... 208
Sawyer, Harvey................................ 312
Say, John 369
Schliemann, Dr. Heinrich.................. 12, 14
Schmucker, George............................ 211
Schoepf, Dr. John D.............. 187, 472, 496
Schwartz, Berthold............................ 44
Scofield, Lewis 291, 316
Scofield, Mr. (of Milwaukee).................. 413
Scott, Joseph........................... 222
Scott, Matthias............................. 220
Scott, Sir Walter........................ 22, 40, 58
Scranton, George W. and Selden T........ 200
Scranton, Joseph H........................... 200
Scrawley, Lawrence......................... 137
Scull, Nicholas.................. 168, 169, 173, 468
Scull, William... 166, 169, 173, 176, 468, 473, 476
Sellers, William............................. 309
Shakespeare, William........................... 22
Sharp & Roberts................................ 491
Sharples, Abraham............................. 496
Sharswood, Dr. William..................... 273
Shaw, Abraham............................... 108
Sheffield, Lord...................... 382, 479
Sheredine, Daniel............................. 252
Shippen & McMurtrie................... 158
Shoemaker, B................................ 178
Shoemaker, Charles...................... 158
Shoemaker, Colonel George.............. 363, 474
Shoenberger, George...................... 207
Shoenberger, G. & J. H............ 389, 392, 393
Shoenberger, Peter......................... 207
Shoenberger, Dr. Peter..207, 208, 221, 229, 230
.... 270
Shoenberger & Agnew...................... 270
Shorb, Anthony............................. 211
Shreeve, Paull & McCandless.............. 309
Shreeves, Leven, & Brother 285
Shryock, John K............................ 221
Shryock, William L.......................... 221
Shumard, Dr. B. F............................. 338
Siemens, Dr. Charles William..... 63, 419, 420
.... 421, 422, 423, 425

Page
Siemens, Frederick...................... 63, 419
Sinclair, Sir John.......................... 60
Singer, Hartman & Co..................... 389
Singer, Nimick & Co...................... 390
Slade, Frederick J.............. 161, 421, 422
Slocum, Ebenezer and Benjamin.......... 200
Sloss, Colonel J. W...................... 295
Sluyter, Peter 163
Smeaton, John 53, 63
Smedley, Isaac.............................. 383
Smiles, Samuel (historian)....... 37, 39, 40, 41
.... 43, 46, 47, 164
Smith, A. J................................. 312
Smith, Adam............... 480, 483, 486
Smith, Commodore...................... 445
Smith, Edward............................ 158
Smith, George W.................... 426, 438
Smith (historian of New Jersey)............ 146
Smith, James..................... 185, 502
Smith, Joseph............................ 227
Smith, Richard............................ 129
Smith, Thomas.................... 183, 189
Smith, Dr. William Hooker.................. 200
Snelus, George J.................... 405, 406
Snowden, Thomas, Richard, and Edward 253
Snyder, Benjamin......................... 158
Snyder, Colonel.......................... 202
Spang, Henry S.................... 211, 229
Spang & Co............................... 389
Spang, Chalfant & Co................. 229, 460
Sparks, John 305
Spence, T. A............................. 256
Spencer & Co............................. 312
Spotswood, Colonel Alexander... 258, 259, 260
.... 261, 262, 267, 374, 502
Stackpole, William.................. 223, 228
Stacy, Mahlon............................. 155
Stedman, Charles and Alexander 180
Stephens, Edward W...................... 230
Stephens, Richard......................... 117
Stephenson, George......................... 63
Sternbergh, J. H......................... 337
Sterrett, William......................... 210
Stevens, Francis B.................. 437, 438
Stevens, Colonel John.............. 426, 436
Stevens, Robert L.................. 436, 437
Stevens, Thaddeus........ 197, 198, 502
Stevens & Paxton......................... 198
Stevenson, Mr............................ 185
Stewart, Charles......................... 472
Stewart, David............................ 221
Stewart, James............................ 219
Stewart, John............................ 192
Stewart, Richardson........................ 255
Stewart, Robert T......................... 229
Stewart, Captain William................. 230
Stiegel, Elizabeth......................... 181
Stiegel, Henry William...... 176, 179, 180, 181
Stirling, Lord (William Alexander).. 138, 149
.... 151, 152
Stone, Chisholm & Jones................. 313

Page

Strickland, William.................................. 365
Strothman Brothers............................... 341
Struthers, John....................................... 301
Struthers, Thomas................................. 301
Stuart, Henry.. 350
Sturtevant, Simon............................. 46, 58
Stuttle, Amos.. 185
Sutton, James.. 200
Sutton, Leonard............................... 332, 338
Stuyvesant, Petrus................................. 233
Swallow, G. C.. 334
Swedenborg, Emanuel......... 93, 234, 235, 249
Sweet, Dr. William M............................. 428
Swift, Mr. (of Cincinnati)...................... 413
Swinburne, Sir John............................... 71
Swineford, A. P........... 320, 321, 322, 323, 324
Swope & King.. 208

T.

Taylor, George.................................. 170, 502
Taylor, Jacob.. 177
Taylor, James.. 273
Taylor, John (of Sarum iron works). 177, 178
Taylor, John (son of John Taylor)........ 178
Taylor, John (of Fayette county, Pa.).... 477
Taylor, Richard Cowling.......... 467, 469, 476
Taylor, W. & B. F.................................... 176
Taylor's forge.. 268
Templeton, Samuel P.............................. 192
Thacher, Dr. James.......... 120, 123, 124, 140
Thomas, Mr. (of Indianapolis)............... 413
Thomas, David,................. 360, 361, 362, 455
Thomas, David, Jr.................................. 362
Thomas, Gabriel............................. 164, 233
Thomas, John.. 362
Thomas, Robert....................................... 294
Thomas, Samuel.............................. 362, 453
Thomas, Sidney Gilchrist... 405, 406, 408, 421
Thompson, George.................................. 8
Thompson, George (another).................. 283
Thompson, James R..................... 391, 392
Thompson, Jonah and George................ 364
Thornburg, Robert, & Co........................ 185
Thornburg & Arthur............................... 185
Thorndike & Drury................................. 302
Throop, George....................................... 142
Thurston, George H................................ 391
Thurston, Robert H................................. 436
Tilghman, James.............................. 469, 472
Timby, Theodore R.................................. 446
Tingle & Sugden...................................... 390
Tod, David, Governor of Ohio................ 311
Torrey, James.. 120
Tower, Jonas... 329
Townsend, Peter......... 138, 139, 140, 141, 381
Townsend, Peter, Jr....................... 138, 381
Townsend, Peter, 3d............................... 141
Townsend, Captain Solomon............ 138, 142
Townshend, Charles (member of Parliament).. 481
Tracy, C. M........................ 111, 116, 119, 121

Page

Trago & Thomas..................................... 201
Trevor & McClurg.................................. 218
Trexler, Reuben...................................... 207
Trimble, David and John............... 285, 286
Trowbridge, C. A.................................... 323
Truman & Co.. 216
Trumbull, Jonathan, Governor of Conn... 380
Tucker, John... 378
Tucker, Hon. John.......................... 432, 433
Tucker, Tempest..................................... 204
Tunner, Professor Peter Ritter von......... 95
Tuper & McCowan........................... 227, 383
Turnbull, William........................... 214, 475
Turnbull & Marmie................................ 214
Turner, Daniel.. 206
Turner, Rev. Edward.............................. 35
Turner, Joseph............. 155, 156, 159, 168
Turner, Thomas............................... 96, 97
Turner, William...................................... 477
Tuttle, Rev. Dr. Joseph F... 147, 148, 149, 150
.... 151, 152
Tyrrell, Asahel....................................... 312

U.

Updegraff, Abner................................... 227
Ure, Dr. Andrew.............................90, 525

V.

Valentine, C. I....................................... 403
Valentines & Co..................................... 206
Valentines & Thomas............................. 206
Vallé, Felix... 409
Van Buren, Jarvis.................................. 358
Van Cullen, Peter (Van Collet)............. 47
Van Doren, J. L...................................... 335
Van Wie, Peter....................................... 431
Vaughan, Colonel Joseph................ 237, 238
Veech, Judge James................. 213, 226, 270
Verlit, M... 28
Vickroy, Joseph...................................... 220
Vickroy, Thomas.................................... 219
Vignoles, Charles B............................... 436
Vincent, Francis............................. 238, 239
Vincent steel works.................. 173, 178, 382

W.

Wagstaff, Hugh...................................... 491
Wahl, Dr. William H.............................. 194
Waldo, Samuel.. 127
Walker, Daniel....................................... 174
Walker, Lewis M.................................... 158
Wallace, James............................... 183, 189
Waples, Colonel William D.................... 238
Ward, Captain E. B.... 318, 322, 324, 328, 330
.... 409, 411, 413, 417
Ward, James... 230
Ward, Timothy....................................... 149
Ward & Colton.. 137
Ward & McMurtry.................................. 285
Ware, Horace................................... 293, 294
Warner, Jonathan.................................. 312

Page

Washington, "a certain Mr."... 251, 252, 504
Washington, Captain Augustine...... 246, 247
251, 261, 262, 263, 264, 265, 452, 503, 504
Washington, Augustine, 2d.. 264, 265, 502, 504
Washington, George..... 152, 175, 246, 251, 252
...................262, 264, 382, 468, 502, 503, 504
Washington, Lawrence 251, 264, 502, 504
Washington, Sarah........................... 264, 504
Watson's Annals................................ 178
Watt, James 53, 63
Watts, David.................................... 211
Wayne, General Anthony....................... 214
Webb, James..... 189
Webb, Joseph................................... 196
Webster, Isaac................................ 253
Webster, John Lee.'............................. 253
Wedding, Dr. Hermann............. 78, 521, 522
Weiss, Colonel Jacob.......................... 474
Welcker, Dietrich.............................. 176
Weld, Henry Thomas....................... 434, 441
Welles, Albert (Washington genealogist).. 264
Welles, Gideon (Secretary of the Navy).. 445
Wendel, Dr. August............................. 77
Westcott, Thompson............................. 465
Wetmore & Havens.............................. 389
Wharton, Thomas, Jr........................... 470
Wheeler, Rev. Dr. Francis B................. 444
Whetcroft, William 255
Whetstone (blacksmith).......................... 473
Whitaker, George P............................. 252
White, James D........................... 222, 223
White, John.................................... 369
White, Josiah........ 356, 360, 363, 364, 465, 475
White, Leonard.................................. 317
White & Hazard.......... 363, 364, 465, 466, 475
Whiteley, Henry................. 250, 251, 264, 265
Whiteside, James A............................. 290
Whiting, Ruggles........................ 223, 228
Whitings, Messrs............................... 229
Whitney, Silas 426
Whittlesey, Asaph............................. 302
Whittlesey, Colonel Charles.................... 302
Wickliffe, Robert............................... 283
Wightwick, John.............. 245, 265, 452, 503
Wilcox, John 272
Wilder, General J. T........................... 291
Wilder, Shubal................. 222, 223, 448, 449
Wilkeson, John.................. 302, 310, 372
Wilkeson & Co.................................. 372
Wilkeson, Wilkes & Co................... 310, 373
Wilkins, Bishop................................ 47
Wilkinson, Israel............................ 127

Page

Wilkinson, Jeremiah.................... 134, 448
Wilkinson, Sir John Gardner................. 66
Williams, Andrew............................... 391
Williams, Jonas................................ 139, 140
Williams, Joseph............................... 174
Williams, Robert............................... 284
Wilson, General................................ 293, 294
Wilson, Mr. (Indiana pioneer)................ 315
Winey, Jacob................................... 496
Winslow, Hon. John F... 409, 444, 445, 446, 447
Winslow & Griswold............. 413, 444, 445, 446
Winslow, Griswold & Holley................... 411
Winslow, Griswold & Morrell................. 410
Winter, Elizabeth.............................. 508
Winter, Hannah................................. 508
Winter, Nancy.................................. 508
Winter, William................................ 508
Winthrop, John, Governor of Mass.. 108, 109
Winthrop, John, Jr............ 108, 109, 113, 118
Wisselman and Cobelly......................... 191
Wistar, Caspar................................. 236
Witherby, E. T................................ 294
Wolfe, C., & Co............................... 317
Wood, Alan..................................... 239
Wood, Captain James.......................... 312
Wood, James.................................... 383
Wood, James, & Co............................ 423
Wood, John..................................... 383
Wood's Treatise on Railroads.......... 426, 438
Woodin, Abner or Peter....................... 129
Woods, William................................ 390
Woolman, Uriah................................ 178
Worden, Lieutenant (U. S. N.)........... 445, 446
Wright, Colonel Gardiner H............ 238, 239
Wright, Hon. Samuel G................ 158, 238
Wright, Thomas................................. 72
Wurtz, Samuel.................................. 215
Wurtz, William and Maurice................. 473

Y.

Yard, Benjamin................................ 159, 160
Yarranton, Andrew............................. 36, 49
Yoder, John.................................... 171
Young, Rev. Daniel............................ 305
Young, Dr...................................... 338
Young, Dr. Edward............................. 49
Young, John W.................................. 345
Young, V. B., Esq.............................. 282

Z.

Zane's furnace............................. 267, 268
Zimmerman, Captain Jacob.................. 180

Printed in the United States
By Bookmasters